Perryville

PERRYVILLE

THIS GRAND HAVOC OF BATTLE

KENNETH W. NOE

THE UNIVERSITY PRESS OF KENTUCKY

Publication of this volume was made possible in part by a grant
from the National Endowment for the Humanities.

Editorial and Sales Offices: The University Press of Kentucky
663 South Limestone Street, Lexington, Kentucky 40508-4008
www.kentuckypress.com

05 06 07 08 09   7 6 5 4 3

Library of Congress Cataloging-in-Publication Data
Noe, Kenneth W., 1957-
Perryville : this grand havoc of battle / Kenneth W. Noe.
p. cm.
Includes bibliographical references and index.
ISBN 0-8131-2209-0 (alk. paper)
1. Perryville (Ky.), Battle of, 1862. I. Title.
E474.39 .N64 2000
973.7'33—dc21   00-012285
ISBN 978-0-8131-2209-0

This book is printed on acid-free recycled paper meeting
the requirements of the American National Standard
for Permanence in Paper for Printed Library Materials.

Manufactured in the United States of America.

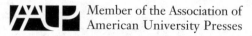 Member of the Association of
American University Presses

FOR NANCY

Contents

ILLUSTRATIONS

x   Illustrations

MAPS

PREFACE

On October 8, 1862, a hot and exceedingly dry day, Union and Confederate forces clashed in the Chaplin Hills just west of Perryville, Kentucky, a small market town located southwest of Lexington in the commonwealth's central bluegrass. The climax of a hard, six-week campaign that reversed dwindling Confederate fortunes in the western theater and shifted the focus of the western war from northern Mississippi toward the Ohio River, the battle ended inconclusively. Although a Confederate tactical victory, Gen. Braxton Bragg abandoned the hard-won field to his numerically stronger foe and commenced a retreat that eventually led back to Middle Tennessee and the Battle of Murfreesboro. Although the South's dream of adding Kentucky to the Confederacy did not die, the last realistic hopes of accomplishing it faded with Bragg's retreat.

In the memories of the men who fought there that day, two attributes would at least to a degree forever distinguish Perryville from other battles. Sheer confusion at all levels was one. Erroneously convinced that most of Maj. Gen. Don Carlos Buell's Army of the Ohio lay elsewhere, Bragg hastily and unwisely committed his army to battle without accurate intelligence of enemy strength. His lieutenants improvised thereafter, with varying results. In the end, Bragg certainly was lucky to escape with his outgunned army. Across the lines, Buell awoke that morning with a better grasp of the overall tactical situation, but because of a variety of factors—most notably an unusual atmospheric phenomenon called "acoustic shadow"—he did not learn of the battle until it was over. As a result, more than half of his force stood by idly while the rest fought for its life. The coming of night and sheer dogged courage more than any obvious leadership saved the Federal army at Perryville. Not surprisingly, a chorus of condemnation for both generals followed the fight for their perceived mismanagement and dereliction, and harsh words pursued the two commanding generals to their dying days. According to one embittered Perryville combatant, "Perryville was simply a useless slaughter, without special result to either combatant."[1]

With little good to remember about the disgraced higher-ups, many Perryville veterans claimed the lion's share of the glory for themselves. "Much credit is due to all the officers and soldiers of the regiment for their courage and coolness under a terrible fire of musketry and artillery;" reported Col. Alfred R. Chapin of the 10th Wisconsin Infantry, "but to the soldiers in the ranks is the most credit due, as the nature of the fight was such as to require no military science, but simply brave men."[2] But if Perryville was confusing, a "soldier's battle" remarkable for its relative lack of direction and result, it also was singular for its sheer savagery. Chapin was right; there was nothing scientific about the fighting at Perryville, which at moments erupted in blood splattered hand-to-hand melees of clubbed muskets and bayonets. Veterans of the bloodbath at Shiloh routinely described Perryville as the more ferocious fight. Indeed, some considered it the most violent clash of the entire war. The ubiquitous Confederate infantryman Sam Watkins remembered Perryville, where he fought hand-to-hand for control of a Federal battery, as "this grand havoc of battle" and swore that he never experienced anything else like it. "I was in every battle, skirmish and match that was made by the First Tennessee regiment during the war," he recorded in his memoir, "and I do not remember a harder contest and more evenly fought battle than that of Perryville. . . . Both sides claimed victory—both whipped. . . . Such obstinate fighting I never had seen before or since."[3]

Like Watkins, the other men who fought at Perryville could not forget it. Other Americans, however, displayed more selective memory in the years that followed. A Federal trooper who fought at Perryville, Capt. Marshall Thatcher of the 2nd Michigan Cavalry, could complain a mere twenty years later that the American public had shamefully forgotten the sacrifices made there, if they ever paid much attention in the first place. "The battle of Perryville has never been fully understood by the general public," he lamented. "It has been treated by newspaper historians as a mere skirmish. How many are there that ever knew that nearly 10,000 men were either killed or wounded, and that the struggle was almost continuous either on the right or left, and often at both wings, from sunrise until long after dark? Fourteen hours of fire and smoke, with lead and iron hail, deserves more than a contemptuous notice."[4]

Yet that is exactly what the Battle of Perryville continued to receive. How the public could treat Perryville as an affair of lesser importance so soon after its bloody occurrence says much about how the nation chose to remember the war. During the conflict itself, the eastern theater, eventually dominated by Robert E Lee's quest to protect the Confederate capital at Richmond, seemed to many to be the arena of greatest import. The major population centers of both the Union and the Confederacy lay closer to the fields fought over by the Army of Northern Virginia and the Army of the Potomac. Politicians played a role, as the Jefferson Davis administration, not surprisingly consumed by pressing events close at hand, seemed to forget about the western armies, eventually to their great detriment. Likewise, the Abraham Lincoln government in Washington placed a priority on winning the war fought at its front door. Timing also played a role. When news arrived on their doorsteps about a battle at Perryville, eastern readers were still digesting Lee's retreat from Antietam and the preliminary Emancipation Proclamation. George B. McClellan's ouster from command of the Army of the Potomac and the Federal debacle at Fredericksburg loomed on the horizon. Even the Union's more clear-cut western victories at Iuka and Corinth received more space in eastern newspapers in the fall of 1862.

Little changed after the war, when veterans of Lee's army, working through groups like the Southern Historical Society, succeeded in enshrining the campaigns of "Marse Robert" as the most important of the conflict. In so doing, they inaugurated what historian Thomas Connelly called a century later the "Lee tradition," a habit of exalting the eastern war at the expense of the west. Especially for Southerners, it was an unfair competition for memory. In contrast to Virginia, the western theater contained few glamorous generals, no Lees or Jacksons, but instead men such as Bragg. To a defeated South, the war in the east meant glorious victories aplenty, while in great part the campaigns and generals of the west could be remembered only for loss and retreat. Northerners more or less followed suit. In the decades that followed, historians simply maintained the historiographic status quo created by the Civil War generation. The war in the west never found its Douglas Southall Freeman, who more than anyone in the twentieth century set the Lee tradition in stone. Despite the eminent scholars who plowed the western furrow, the Civil War in popular culture more or less remained something that happened in or near Virginia.[5]

The tide did not turn conclusively until the Civil War centennial years of the 1960s, when a host of scholars began reasserting the importance of and, indeed in some cases, even proclaimed the primacy of the western campaigns. By the end of the twentieth century, so much had been said and published about the war in the west that scholars of Lee's army occasionally found themselves in the curious position of reminding readers that his campaigns really were important after all.[6] Despite the onslaught of western theater studies, however, Perryville somehow continued to slip through the scholarly cracks. While historians produced a host of detailed studies that took readers from Fort Donelson and Shiloh on to Franklin, Nashville, and Bentonville, Perryville remained curiously neglected. Nestled in the western war's chronology between larger battles at Shiloh and Stones River no less than between Antietam and Fredericksburg, Perryville somehow seemed less important, a curious sideshow marked largely by questionable leadership and an odd acoustic phenomenon. Were he alive, Marshall Thatcher probably would complain that little had changed in a hundred years.

It would be an overstatement, of course, to maintain that Civil War historians have ignored Perryville entirely. The battle, and indeed Bragg's entire Kentucky campaign, figure prominently in biographies of major figures who fought there, as well as in several scholarly studies of the force eventually renamed the Confederate Army of Tennessee.[7] Historian James

Lee McDonough, who as much as anyone else put the western battles back on the map, made the campaign in its entirety the subject of a justifiably well-received book published in 1994. Concerned with the campaign as a whole, however, McDonough devoted less than a third of his narrative to the battle itself. Much the same can be said of Earl Hess's recent study, which considers Perryville only within the context of the entire sweep of western arms from the aftermath of Shiloh to Stones River. Drawing largely from secondary sources, Hess dispenses with the battle in one chapter. In the end, the twentieth century as a whole saw only one lengthy narrative of the battle produced, Kenneth Hafendorfer's *Perryville*, originally published by the author in 1981 and revised ten years later.[8]

When that bibliography is contrasted with the dozens of good books written about, for example, Gettysburg, it seems fair to say that the Perryville theme cannot be exhausted. Indeed, there is much new that can be said about the battle. Unlike the better-chronicled fights, historians immersed in Perryville continue to grapple with issues long since settled elsewhere, including facts as fundamental as what units fought where and when. Several new interpretations appear here, based upon dozens of pertinent archival sources that have never been used to understand the battle. In many ways, we have only scratched the surface.

Moreover, Perryville offers the historian a fresh opportunity to explore new ways of understanding and interpreting Civil War battles. A decade has passed since Maris Vinovskis asked scholars if American social historians had "lost the Civil War?"[9] His now familiar query referred to the fact that Civil War historians and the rest of the scholarly community seemed to have gone down separate paths since the 1960s, each group increasingly regarding the other with disdain.[10] Volumes of Civil War history still weigh down shelves, as any stroll through a bookstore or library will attest, but according to James McPherson, surely the leading Civil War scholar of our time, much of it lacks the context of larger issues, the causes and results of the war that motivated Civil War soldiers in the first place and gave their sacrifices real meaning. "Just as the popular constituency of Civil War 'buffs' seems indifferent to the huge and crucial social, cultural, economic, and political dimensions of the war," he maintains, "so the academics fail to recognize that all of these dimensions were inextricably bound up with events on the battlefield."[11]

McPherson, however, wrote in a changing climate. In the 1980s, a new generation of historians attempted to bridge the two historiographical paths, creating something called the "new Civil War history." One obvious result has been an explosion of home front and community studies, the most obvious intersection of the war and American society. Women and African Americans are gaining their rightful places in the story of the war. In regard to the soldiers, historians have borrowed the techniques of social history to examine their motivations and activities in innovative ways. Regiments or armies, in the end, were societies with their own set or rules and expectations, as well as extensions of larger communities back home. Social historians and military historians finally realized that they each had something to offer, and both have been enriched.[12]

Battle history has proven the genre most resistant to new trends, but now even it begins to bear the marks of the new Civil War history, as a fine recent study of the Battle of Wilson's Creek attests.[13] What follows here is, in most cases, a rather traditional and, I hope, accessible battle narrative. However, it also exhibits my interest in the new Civil War history. Readers of this book, for example, will note my concern for those civilians caught in the wake of the armies, and not only those who stood in harm's way, but also friends and relatives back home whose lives also changed course that October day. Toward that end, the last chapter carries the narrative far beyond 1862, and back to the soldiers' hometowns and families. I place the battle within the wider political and social context of Civil War Kentucky, and I consider the way Americans, especially Kentuckians, remembered and commemorated Perryville in the years following the battle.

In an attempt to understand the experience of battle, I also let the soldiers speak for themselves when possible—even when their spelling, grammar, and prose deviate from modern usage. One need not embrace poststructuralist theory to recognize that the conventions of language, the rhetorical style of Victorian America, and expectations honed reading schoolboy histories often constrained combatants as much as it helped them express what they had seen and heard. Faced with a public that could never understand what truly happened on a battlefield without firsthand experience, soldiers either attempted in their letters and diaries to force narrative structure and prose conventions onto chaos, or else gave up and refused to try. The passing years only made it more difficult, as veterans began to follow new postwar conventions in memoirs and regimental histories.[14]

It is more difficult still for writers of another time. In his foreword to Wiley Sword's fine study of Shiloh, noted military historian S. L. A. Marshall perhaps best described the dilemma. "Battle," he wrote, "is more like a schoolyard in a rough neighborhood at recess time than a clash between football giants at the Rose Bowl. The extreme in chaos and disorder, it is messy, inorganic and little coordinated. It is only much later, after the clerks have tidied up their reports and the commanders, in retrospect, have made their estimates of the situation *ex post facto*, that the historian, with his orderly mind, professes to discern a moving hand and sensible pattern in what was at the time a frenzied and fear-filled scrambling, a desperate groping in the dark."[15]

In attempting to create order where there had been none, to shine light on the groping darkness, Perryville's survivors understandably applied a somewhat artificial and "tidy" narrative framework. There are other difficulties for the historian who approaches their descriptions and recollections. Participants' accounts usually disagree on details. Adrenalin distorts the measurement of time and space, while getting shot at usually precludes careful and systematic observation. Men sometimes had axes to grind. Old age further distorted reality. At the very least, the soldiers often do not tell the historian what he wants to know. Nonetheless, I have tried to give them their say, even if at times that has meant quoting them at more length than modern convention allows. Perryville was their battle, and they deserve to be heard, at least if we are to comprehend not just what happened there that hot October day, but also what it was like to be there.[16]

During the war, Federal nurse Walt Whitman despaired that those who had not personally experienced the Civil War would never truly understand it. In a now overused phrase familiar to even the casual student of the conflict, Whitman proclaimed: "the real war will never get into the books." Whitman said more than that, of course. He also worried that an exclusive focus on generals and strategy would dishonor the Americans most involved, the common soldiers he saw suffering and dying in his wards every day. He asked: "of scenes like these, I say, who writes—whoe'er can write the story? Of many a score—aye, thousands, north and south, of unwrit heroes, unknown heroisms, incredible, impromptu, first-class desperations—who tells? No history ever—no poem sings, no music sounds, those bravest men of all—those deeds. No formal general's reports, nor book in the library, nor column in the paper, embalms the bravest, north or south, east or west. Unnamed, unknown, remain, and still remain, the bravest soldiers."[17] Those soldiers, their families, their leaders, and their battle all deserve our consideration. I have tried to write their story fully and honestly, and so to make them truly named and known.

In the late summer of 1982, while a graduate student at the University of Kentucky, a young woman I met in class learned of my interest in the Civil War and volunteered to drive me to Perryville to see the battlefield. As a Virginian born and raised, the war's western theater seldom had interested me, and what happened at Perryville remained only a hazy memory derived from Bruce Catton's works. Unfortunately, my first Perryville trip did little to enlighten me further. With the visitor's center closed, we could only examine the extant markers and climb the old fire tower on what had been the Federal left. I drove away from Perryville that day with more questions than answers.

In the years that followed, as I embarked on doctoral studies and delved into other topics, Perryville remained in the back of my mind. Still, I only began to consider it seriously after a conversation with Nancy Grayson at the Louisville meeting of the Southern Historical Association in 1994. Not long after that, as I developed a proposal for a book-length study of the campaign, Kent Masterson Brown contacted me. A son of Kentucky, nationally prominent attorney, and fine Civil War historian in his own right, Kent at the time was deeply involved in preserving and expanding the Perryville battlefield. I well remember our first telephone conversation, for his exuberance and deep knowledge of the battle electrified me. By all rights he clearly was the person to write this book, yet he welcomed me into the Perryville fold without hesitation, walked with me all over the field, and finally forced me to put my thoughts in order by asking me to give a talk on the battle at the American Civil War Institute's week-long conference on Civil War Kentucky, headquartered at Campbellsville University in 1997. For all that, and for reading the entire manuscript as well, I am tremendously indebted.

While at Campbellsville that summer, I was able to bounce my ideas off some of the best scholars in the field, people like Anne Bailey, William C. "Jack" Davis, Lowell Harrison, Richard McMurry, Alan Nolan, Charles Roland, and Wiley Sword. Wiley particularly helped me shape my thoughts on the Bottom House fighting as we relaxed in front of that structure after a battlefield tour. This book is immeasurably better for all their insights and their friendly support of a younger scholar.

In 1995 I headed back to Perryville to gain a better appreciation of the field. Again with an introduction from Kent Brown, Mary Breeding and Stuart Sanders gave me the run of their offices at the Perryville Enhancement Project on Merchant's Row. Stuart has continued to offer help and much needed criticism ever since. Then, knocking at the door of battlefield park manager Kurt Holman, I innocently asked if he had any sources on the battle. Waving toward a four-drawer filing cabinet, he replied, "there you go. Where do you want to start?" Standing over the photocopier in his cramped office over the next two days, I soon realized that Kurt Holman was the other person who should have been writing about Perryville. In the years since that visit, Kurt's encyclopedic knowledge of the campaign, minute command of the field, sense of history, dedication to solid research, and ready wit have rescued me on more than one occasion. Kurt led me over every inch of the field and read every word of this book, usually managing to challenge my interpretations without any classic Holmanesque sarcasm (the "cannot ball" incident to the contrary). For all of that, he has asked only one thing of me in return: "Get it right." He is a model park historian, one of Kentucky's real treasures, and his input and dedication to my getting it right were vital to the completion of this work.

Kurt also introduced me to a small regiment of unselfish Perryville enthusiasts, all of whom provided vital information. Roger Adams gladly gave me his extensive Perryville bibliography, made suggestions for research, and provided curious comments about lancers from Nevada. Chuck Kays gladly gave me access to his research on the Russell House. Archeologists Richard Stallings and Nancy Ross-Stallings graciously shared their findings. Landowners such as Melvin and Gladys Bottom, Jimmy Crain, Ren Hankla, and Alan Hoeweler repeatedly allowed me to hike over their property. Darrell Young's contributions, especially concerning troop movements, artillery at Perryville, and local archeology, proved extraordinary. A lifelong resident, surely no one alive knows the field at Perryville better than Darrell, or shares his knowledge more gladly. John Walsh meanwhile surely is the world's leading expert on Austin's Sharpshooters. His knowledge, good sense in regard to movements on the Confederate left, and willingness to add to his phone bill straightened out more than one tangle I inadvertently created. He also provided several photographs, and is responsible for the excellent maps in this volume. Kurt, Darrell, and John all reviewed the manuscript and saved me from several egregious and embarrassing gaffes. Any remaining errors, whether due to omission or stubbornness, are my responsibility alone.

No work of this kind can be written without the assistance of dedicated archivists and librarians. I wish to thank Rickie Brunner and Ken Tilley of the Alabama Department of Archives and History; John L. Ferguson of the Arkansas Historical Commission; Stephen M. Chante at Bowling Green State University; Peter J. Bahra of the Cincinnati Historical Society; Rusty Koonts, Janie C. Morris, and Jason Tomberlin at Duke University; Jim Holmberg and Trace Kirkwood of the Filson Historical Society; James Cusick and Carla Summers at the University of Florida; David J. Coles and Joanna Norman at the Florida State Archives; Burt Altman at Florida State University; Kimberly Ball, Susan E. Dick, and Todd Groce of the Georgia Historical Society; Cheryl Schnirring at the Illinois State Historical Library; Carolyn Autry of the Indiana Historical Society; Steven Towne at the Indiana State Archives; Cynthia Faunce and John Selch at the Indiana State Library; Cinda May at Indiana University; Tom Fugate and Brandon Slone of the Kentucky Department of Military Affairs; James C. Klotter of the Kentucky Historical Society; Claire McCann at the Special Collections and Archives of the University of Kentucky; Judy Bolton and Glenn McMullen at Louisiana State University; Kimberlee J. Mayer at the Bentley Historical Library, University of Michigan; Ann Lipscomb at the Mississippi Department of Archives and History; Laurel Boeckman, Chuck Hill, and Dennis Northcott of the Missouri Historical Society; Randy Roberts of the Western Historical Manuscript Collection at the University of Missouri; James W. Martin and Michael Musick at the National Archives and Records Administration; Steven Niven, Richard Shrader, Jill Snider, and John White with the Southern Historical Collection at the University of North Carolina at Chapel Hill; Gary Arnold and Duryea Kemp of the Ohio Historical Society; Bobs M. Tusa at the University of Southern Mississippi; Dee A. Grimsrud of the State Historical Society of Wisconsin; Ann Alley at the Tennessee State Library and Archives; William Richter of the Center for American History at the University of Texas at Austin; Leon Miller at Tulane University; Alicia Maudlin and Deborah McKeon-Pogue at the U.S. Military Academy Library; Pamela Cheney, Randy W. Hackenbury, David Keough, Richard Sommers, and Michael Winey at the U.S. Army Military History Institute; Lynne Wolfe at the Wisconsin Veterans Museum; and Joshua P. Ranger at the University of Wisconsin-Oshkosh.

I also wish to thank several people at the State University of West Georgia, my academic home during nearly all of the period I completed this work. History department colleagues Cita Cook, Elmira Eidson, John Ferling, Jim Gay, and Mel Steely all offered support and sound advice. Rich Chapman did, too, although I am sure he still thinks I am too hard on "Pap" Thomas. Department Chair Steve Taylor and Dean Richard Miller provided much needed reassigned time. Upstairs in the Psychology department, Tobin Hart cheerfully tolerated my amateur psychoanalysis of Braxton Bragg and then supplied real professional input of immeasurable value. At Ingram Library, Joanne Artz, Nancy Farmer, Myron House, John McPhearson, and Gail Smith all assisted me in various ways. I also was lucky to have the assistance of four excellent graduate students: Lee Dorsett, Scott Ragsdale, Mark Smith, and Phil Wood.

Many others have helped in different ways, including David Coles, Mark Franklin, Steve Fratt, John Hoffmann, Nat Hughes, Perry Jamieson, Kirk Jenkins, Brian Pohanka, Lee White, and an unidentified reader recruited by the press. Richard Sauers kindly shared his manuscript index to the *National Tribune*, a vital source for Civil War historians. In Indianapolis, Michael Burlingame took time from his Lincoln research to have lunch with the guy at the other table and to stress the value of soldiers' letters found in period newspapers. Stephen Engle kindly gave me an advance look at the bibliography from his excellent Buell biography. Frank and Susan Quinn, and Shannon and Janie Wilson provided a lonely traveler with room, board, and friendship. Willie Don Cole loaned me his house and a copy of *Cold Mountain*. Ken Bindas, Tim Thornton, and the good folks at TechSideLine.com kept me sane.

As usual, my family has been more supportive than I ever have a right to ask them to be. All of them deserve praise, but special thanks are due to Ray and Carole Wahlbrink, who kindly fed me and gave me a place to sleep whenever I was in Kentucky—which turned out to be more frequently than I suspect they ever imagined. Tyler Kolb's penetrating observations about Louisville golfers gave me a much-needed break from thinking about the Civil War. Back home in Virginia, Ken and Marie Noe fueled me for my Washington research with some truly huge breakfasts and even more for dinner. My father also reads everything I write, which surely is more than a son can hope for. My brother Keith does, too. My son Jesse has asked me to acknowledge that no one is happier that this book is done than he. He is not kidding.

Writing about soldiers and their families often reminded me of my own forebears who endured their country's wars, all the way back to four gray-clad horse soldiers who rode to Gettysburg with the 16th Virginia Cavalry. In addition to my father, who celebrated my birth along the border of North and South Korea, I often thought of two veterans of World War II, William Jesse Noe of the USS *Satyr*, and Bennie Noe of the 173rd Field

Artillery, Fifth Army, and the girls they left behind: Betty, Thelma, and Emma. They are more part of this book than they can know.

Finally, and most importantly of all, I want to thank that young woman who drove me to Perryville one weekend, and in so doing unwittingly set the stage for this book, my career as a historian, and most of the happiness in my life. Almost two decades later, for reasons I cannot fathom, my wife Nancy still goes strange places with me. This book is all hers, even the endnotes.

ABBREVIATIONS

ADAH	Alabama Department of Archives and History, Montgomery
ArHC	Arkansas Historical Commission, Little Rock
B&L	Robert Underwood Johnson and Clarence Clough Buel, *Battles and Leaders of the Civil War.* 4 vols. New York: Century, 1887–88; reprint ed., New York: Thomas Yoseloff, 1956.
CHS	Chicago Historical Society
Duke	Rare Book, Manuscript, and Special Collections Library, Duke University, Durham, N.C.
EU	Emory Univ., Special Collections, Robert W. Woodruff Library, Decatur, Ga.
FHS	Florida Historical Society, Tebeau-Field Library, Cocoa
Filson	Filson Club Historical Society, Louisville
FSA	Florida State Archives, Tallahassee
FSU	Florida State University, Robert Manning Strozier Library, Tallahassee
GDAH	Georgia Department of Archives and History, Atlanta
IlSHL	Illinois State Historical Library, Springfield
InHS	Indiana Historical Society, Indianapolis
InSA	Indiana State Archives, Indianapolis
InSL	Indiana State Library, Indianapolis
Iowa	University of Iowa Libraries, Iowa City
KDMA	Kentucky Department of Military Affairs, Military Records and Research Branch, Frankfort
KHS	Kentucky Historical Society, Special Collections and Archives, Frankfort
LC	Library of Congress, Washington, D.C.
LSU	Louisiana and Lower Mississippi Valley Collections, Louisiana State Univ. Libraries, Baton Rouge

MHS   Missouri Historical Society, St. Louis
MOLLUS   Military Order of the Loyal Legion of the United States
NARA   National Archives and Records Administration, Washington, D.C.
OHS   Ohio Historical Society, Columbus
OR   U.S. War Department. *The War of the Rebellion: A Compilation of the Official Records of the Union and Confederate Armies.* 129 vols. Washington, D.C.: 1880–1901.
OR—Supp   Janet B. Hewett et al., eds. *Supplement to the Official Records of the Union and Confederate Armies.* 95 vols. Wilmington, N.C.: Broadfoot, 1994–   .
PEP   Perryville Enhancement Project, Perryville, Ky.
PSHS   Perryville State Historic Site, Perryville, Ky.
SHC-UNC   Southern Historical Collection, Wilson Library, Univ. of North Carolina, Chapel Hill
SHSW   State Historical Society of Wisconsin, Madison
TU   Louisiana Historical Collection, Tulane Univ., New Orleans
UF   Univ. of Florida, P. K. Yonge Library of Florida History, Gainesville
UMBHL   Univ. of Michigan, Bentley Historical Library, Ann Arbor
UMWHMC   Univ. of Missouri-Columbia, Western Historical Manuscript Collection, Columbia
USM   Univ. of Southern Mississippi, William D. McCain Library and Archives, Hattiesburg
USAMHI   U.S. Army Military History Institute Archives, Carlisle Barracks, Pa.
WKUL   Western Kentucky University Library, Bowling Green, Ky.
WRHS   Western Reserve Historical Society, Cleveland, Ohio
WVM   Wisconsin Veterans Museum, Madison

1

DIVIDED WE FALL

ON A GRAY, RAINY DAY IN JANUARY 1862, ONE OF MANY THAT DREARY winter, English novelist Anthony Trollope crossed the rising Ohio River from Cincinnati into the Commonwealth of Kentucky. He was in the midst of his second tour of North America, compiling information for a projected travel narrative to be written more or less in the manner of his celebrated and controversial mother, Frances. Kentucky was as far south as Trollope traveled that war-torn season, yet what he observed there immediately elicited the sympathy of an already pro-Confederate Briton. "Less inclined to rebellion, more desirous of standing by the North, than any other of the slave States" except Delaware, he explained to his readers, Kentucky nonetheless opposed abolition and Northern coercion as strongly as did the seceded states. Pulled in a tug-of-war between North and South after the American Civil War finally began, Kentucky struggled gamely to remain neutral and "put off the evil day of so evil a choice" as long as it could. Ultimately, it was all in vain. When neutrality failed and that evil day came, the state legislature held Kentucky in the Union. Kentuckians who disagreed quickly cast their lot with the new Confederacy.[1] "Men . . . became unionists or secessionists," Trollope contended, "not by their own conviction, but through the necessity of their positions; and Kentucky, through the necessity of her position, became one of the scenes of Civil War."[2]

Everywhere Trollope looked during his visit, he saw the shadow of the unwanted, tragic war lengthening across the commonwealth's precarious place on the sectional front line. Just before he entered the state, Federal and Confederate forces had clashed in south-central Kentucky at Logan's Cross Roads, the biggest fight in the state thus far, in a battle subsequently called a half-dozen names but most often Mill Springs. Federal troops there under the command of Brig. Gen. George H. Thomas, a son of seceded Virginia but also a committed loyalist, won the day. The resulting cheers of joyful Unionists still echoed as Trollope arrived in Louisville, the state's largest city. Despite the jarring Unionist clamor, he liked Louisville nonetheless, finding it "a well-built, handsome city," although admittedly rather provincial when compared to modern American cities such as Cincinnati or St. Louis.

In contrast to Louisville, Frankfort, the little state capital to the east, struck him "as quietly dull a little town as I ever entered. . . . The legislature of the State was not sitting when I was there, and the grass was growing in the streets." Not so farther east in Lexington, the commonwealth's other major city, for there he found commotion everywhere. Trollope memorably encountered six dozen army teamsters "hanging about" his hotel, "a dirty, rough, quaint set of men, clothed in a wonderful variety of garbs, but not disorderly or loud." The owner apologized profusely to the proper Englishman, explaining that there was nowhere else in the crowded town to quarter the soldiers. Trollope did not object to them, however, preferring to savor the local color the teamsters provided. Outside of Lexington, Trollope spent a day with someone of quite a different stripe, the well-heeled owner of a large estate, a celebrated horse breeder and an unapologetic slave owner. He gave the Englishman a tour of his slave quarters, impressing upon him both the necessity of slavery and the kindness of the state's slave owners, sentiments Trollope ached to believe.[3]

Trollope left for St. Louis after a few days, but he was not finished with Kentucky, and he returned a few weeks later. This time he journeyed farther south, to the Green River, where Brig. Gen. Don Carlos Buell's Federal Army of the Ohio confronted the Confederates occupying Bowling Green. Welcomed and feted by the staff of rotund Brig. Gen. Alexander McDowell McCook, one of Buell's division commanders, Trollope spent two reasonably pleasant days with the army despite the continuing cold, rainy weather that still marked the winter. Rations were surprisingly plentiful, he observed, and the soldiers appeared healthy, "light-spirited and happy." The men in blue also were less muddy than Army of the Potomac Federals he had seen back East—a decided plus in the mind of the prim Englishman. Clean men were better men. What fascinated him most, however, was their bitterness regarding secession, a sentiment he acknowledged but through the Old World lenses of the American Revolution barely comprehended.[4] "It is singular that such a people," Trollope observed, " a people that has founded itself on rebellion, should have such a horror of rebellion; but, as far as my observation may have enabled me to read their feelings rightly, I do believe that it has been as sincere as it is irrational." Kentucky, Anthony Trollope concluded, was most confusing.[5]

Despite only a brief sojourn, Trollope innately grasped the gist of Kentucky's dilemma. Although the state motto warned "United We Stand, Divided We Fall," Kentucky's divided house had collapsed nonetheless in 1861. Dire portents preceded that climax, of course. At least as far back as the late 1840s, when the Union's foundations began to shake noticeably after the Mexican War, Kentuckians realized that their state rested squarely on an ever widening national fault line. Bordered on the north by the Ohio River and beyond it the free states of Illinois, Indiana, and Ohio, the commonwealth otherwise was surrounded by three sister slave states: Missouri, Tennessee, and Virginia. In any conflict between North and South, the border slave states seemed all but foreordained to form a frontier between one warring section and the other. Kentucky, ominously, stood as the crucial keystone in the border arch.

Moreover, as Trollope quickly ascertained, divisions regarding the sectional issues of the day extended deeply into nearly every family and community within the state. Southern by virtue of tradition and settlement—most Kentuckians black and white traced their family roots back to Virginia, North Carolina, or Tennessee—Kentucky remained one of the nation's leading slave states throughout the antebellum period. Almost 20 percent of the state's population, 225,483 souls, still toiled in chattel bondage in 1860, and although the percentage of slaves to total population had declined, only Virginia and Georgia contained more slave owners that year.[6] However, slavery hardly brought statewide unity. Many white Kentuckians expressed discomfort regarding the institution despite its prevalence, and some were downright opposed to it. While a minority of delegates to the state constitutional convention of 1849 tried but failed to limit slavery in Kentucky, others took more direct action on the Underground Railroad. Kentucky also was the home of the South's most visible abolitionists, men like Newport publisher William Shreve Bailey, as well as the German emigres who issued the notoriously antislavery Louisville Platform of 1854. There also was a small but significant cell in Berea, south of Lexington, led by the Kentucky-born minister John G. Fee and supported by brawling, two-fisted Whig politician Cassius M. Clay. From 1854 until the end of 1859, when their Madison County neighbors finally drove them from the state after Fee publicly praised John Brown, the Bereans not only attacked slavery but also offered tangible evidence of Kentucky's divided mind.[7]

Fee made few converts, but quieter economic and social trends proved more successful at turning many Kentuckians' gazes northward. Kentucky's familial and commercial ties to the South, for example, increasingly found themselves matched by newer ones with the Northern states. Thousands of Kentuckians such as Thomas Lincoln and Jesse Grant, fathers of soon-to-be-famous sons, migrated from Kentucky into the Old Northwest to find better lives and, in some cases, territory free of slavery. Many of those former Kentuckians maintained their relationships with families and friends south of the Ohio River. Communication and trade between Kentucky and the Old Northwest resulted as the latter section grew, and business increased dramatically after 1830. The coming of the railroads further strenghtened the bond between Kentucky and the Midwest while simultaneously lessening to at least some extent the supremacy of the older, southbound Ohio-Mississippi River trade.

Kentucky politics into the late 1840s further reflected the state's Janus-faced stance between North and South. Politically, the state was best known as the home of the great Whig nationalist Henry Clay, author of three sectional compromises crafted to prevent secession and civil war. Like many Kentuckians, the slaveholder Clay subordinated his support of the peculiar institution to the preservation of the Union, and the increasing cries for "Southern Rights" emanating from South Carolina and elsewhere in the Deep South elicited little support in Clay's Kentucky during previous decades. Instead, a majority of Kentuckians endorsed Clay's "American System," his vision of an integrated, indivisible American economy fostered by a vibrant federal government that built roads, established banks, and levied tariffs on imported goods—just the sort of big national government state's rightists most feared.[8]

Kentucky, in short, could hardly be described as either "Northern" or "Southern" by 1860. Rather, it had become an idiosyncratic amalgam of both, independent and fiercely proud of its uniqueness. It remained solidly a slave state on the eve of war. Even many of the most prominent Unionists continued to be fervidly committed to slavery's survival. On the other hand, much of the rest of the state's Southern character found itself checked by newer Yankee notions. The end result was confusion and anxiety.

The unsettled election year of 1860 finally crystallized the state's muddled identity and its deepening dread. John C. Breckinridge, the sitting vice president of the United States and presidential candidate of the more radical Southern Democrats in 1860, was the favorite son. Breckinridge was a well-liked Kentucky moderate who, unlike many of his adherents, opposed immediate secession. However, because he was identified with the fire-eating extremists who had wrecked the Democratic Party and given him their nomination, he won only 37 percent of his state's votes. The majority went to a former Whig and Clay ally, Constitutional Unionist John Bell of Tennessee, who promised to preserve the national compact just as it was. Northern Democrat Stephen A. Douglas also fared surprisingly well in Kentucky. Together, Bell and Douglas—and moderate Unionism—won almost two-thirds of Kentucky's presidential votes. Significantly, only a few Kentuckians cast their ballot for the other, largely unacknowledged native son, Hardin County's Abraham Lincoln, whose "House Divided" speech with its dire prediction of the nation becoming all free or all slave terrified a majority of Kentuckians. Rejecting militancy at both ends of the political spectrum in 1860, the state's electorate sent a clear message calling for compromise and the preservation of the nation.[9]

It was an example rejected. The secession winter of 1860–61 that ended with the creation of the Confederacy in February, the firing on Fort Sumter the following April, and President Lincoln's subsequent, reactive call for seventy-five thousand volunteers to suppress the Southern rebellion anguished Kentuckians. Not only was it all but certain that a civil war between North and South would be fought, in part perhaps on the states' soil, there was also

the very real possibility of an internal war pitting Kentuckian against Kentuckian. The state government offered little direction or even hope during
the crisis, for it, too, was of two minds, with pro-Southern governor Beriah
Magoffin squared off against a pro-Union legislature. No fire-eater but a
fervent Democrat nonetheless, Magoffin championed the right of states to
secede. In April 1861 he ominously warned the Lincoln administration that
"Kentucky will furnish no troops for the wicked purpose of subduing her
sister Southern States."[10]

More dangerous still, Kentucky in the spring of 1861 contained within
in its borders two growing and competing state armies. Created in March
1860, the largely pro-Southern State Guard was created and led by Simon
Bolivar Buckner, a capable, stern-eyed veteran of army service in Mexico and
on the frontier. It soon confronted a rival in the newer, pro-Union Home
Guard. Just after the firing on Fort Sumter the legislature created the latter
force, ignoring the distrusted Magoffin and deliberately placing it in the
control of a five-member military board dominated by Unionists. As Unionists flocked to the Home Guard, many exuberant State Guardsmen slipped
across the Tennessee border with their weapons and went to the Confederate Camps Boone and Trousdale, near Clarksville. Some equally animated
Home Guardsmen crossed the Ohio River to join Federal units being formed
in Indiana and Ohio. However, enough of both remained at home to cause
trouble. Most were reasonably well armed, but the Unionists held an advantage thanks to five thousand "Lincoln guns" smuggled to them through Ohio
in May by the administration.[11] The threat of violence loomed constantly,
for the two groups rubbed elbows continually in the contest for Kentucky's
allegiance. "It was no uncommon sight in Louisville," a Unionist remembered, "to see a squad of recruits for the Union service marching up one side
of a street while a squad destined for the Confederacy was moving down the
other."[12]

As the nation continued to divide and the long-feared war finally began, Kentucky desperately grasped hold of the political fence like a man
caught in a whirlwind, casting about for any convention or compromise plan
that might avert bloodshed within the state—if not in the nation at large.
Characteristically, the most viable if ill-fated national compromise plan presented in Washington came from the pen of a Kentuckian, John J. Crittenden,
who had followed Henry Clay into the Senate. Crittenden had much to lose,
for even his own sons were divided on secession. His compromise plan ultimately failed. More importantly, at least in the short run, the state legislature
took the unusual and desperate step of declaring an armed neutrality. By a
vote of sixty-six to twenty-nine, the Kentucky House of Representatives announced on May 16 that "this state . . . shall take no part in the Civil War
now being waged, except as mediators and friends to the belligerent parties;
and that Kentucky should, during the contest, occupy the position of strict
neutrality."[13] After the state senate passed a similar resolution, Magoffin of-

ficially declared Kentucky's neutrality on May 20. To those who threatened to force the commonwealth to choose sides, the state government declared that Kentucky would resist invasion by either belligerent. As historian Lowell Harrison cogently has written, "A bewildered observer from abroad might well have concluded that the United States had become three countries: the Union, the Confederacy, and Kentucky."[14]

Few Kentuckians that May expected or even wanted neutrality to last very long. Proponents on both sides of the debate, but especially among the Unionists during the initial weeks, supported it only as a way to buy time for their respective causes. "The secessionists believed that neutrality . . . would educate the people to the idea of a separation of the Union and result in an alliance with the new Confederacy;" explained one Unionist, while "the Union men expected to gain time to organize their forces, elect a new legislature in sympathy with their views, and put the State decisively on the side of the Government."[15]

Even President Lincoln was willing to accept Kentucky's neutrality as long as necessary in order to hold the border states in the Union, although he reserved his right to alter his course if circumstances demanded. Contrary to legend, Lincoln probably did not say "I hope to have God on my side, but I must have Kentucky,"[16] but such sentiments at least characterized his thinking. In September, he did write: "I think to lose Kentucky is nearly to lose the whole game. Kentucky gone, we can not hold Missouri, nor, as I think, Maryland. These all against us, and the job on our hands is too large for us. We would as well consent to separation at once, including the surrender of this capitol."[17]

Lincoln almost certainly was correct. As historian James McDonough has noted, losing control of the Ohio River not only could have brought war into the Midwest, it also would have cost the Union control of that river's tributaries as well as perhaps the Mississippi—waterways that eventually formed the centerpiece of Federal western strategy. Moreover, several soon-to-be-crucial railroads, most notably the Louisville and Nashville line, emanated from port cities on those same rivers. As if that were not enough, losing the border states would have cost the Union many of the tools of war. Civil War scholar James McPherson has pointed out that control of Kentucky, Maryland, and Missouri together would have added 45 percent to the Confederacy's potential manpower, 80 percent to its manufacturing base, and almost 40 percent to its supply of horses and mules. Both sides desperately needed those states and their resources. Victory likely would go to the belligerent that occupied the border states, and securing that vital region meant holding Kentucky at all costs.[18]

By the time Lincoln wrote about losing "the whole game," however, he was doing little more than nervously hedging his figurative bets, for, bluffing aside, he held a strong hand. His ace in the hole was the simple fact that the tide of public opinion in the commonwealth had steadily shifted in his favor, and there frankly was little likelihood by the beginning of autumn that Kentucky would ever secede. During the summer of 1861, the state's traditional conservatism and Clayite Unionism recovered as the secession excitement subsided. Unionist leaders such as John Marshall Harlan started stirring up some enthusiasm of their own, using staged flag raisings and brass bands to attract crowds to their street corner speeches in Louisville. The city quickly earned the sobriquet "City of Flags" because of the frequency of such events. Other Kentuckians worried more and more about their state becoming a battleground. Many slave owners fretted that Kentucky's economy would suffer if the Confederates reopened the African slave trade, as some Deep Southerners wanted, and spurned Kentucky's surplus slave population. Lincoln's respect of neutrality gained him supporters as well. Thus, in June, with many pro-Confederates boycotting the election, Unionists won nine of ten of Kentucky's congressional seats. The following August, avowed pro-Union candidates achieved a three-to-one majority in the General Assembly, giving them the power to override any Magoffin veto.

After the election of the new legislature, Federal naval lieutenant William Nelson—a tall, burly, three-hundred-pound native Kentuckian with a bad temper and a booming voice laced with a sailor's profanity that all together had earned him the nickname "Bull"—opened a Federal recruiting station at Camp Dick Robinson in Garrard County, thirty miles south of Lexington. The camp's purpose was ostensibly to assist East Tennesseans in rallying to the Stars and Stripes, and thus technically, according to Unionists, it did not violate Kentucky's neutrality. When Governor Magoffin protested nonetheless, Lincoln defended his old friend Nelson with skillful legalisms, and the camp remained open despite its debatable legitimacy. About the same time, Lincoln instituted a land blockade against goods entering the Confederacy through Kentucky, a practice he had permitted for months. As a result of these Federal activities, as Magoffin's protest suggests, neutrality metamorphosed from a Unionist shield into an increasingly weak buckler of secessionists who realized that, at least in the short run, it was their only chance of blocking Kentucky's full allegiance to the Union.[19]

Neutrality could not have lasted much longer in any event, but it took a far-reaching political blunder to hasten its demise, wrecking Confederate hopes in the state and prematurely opening the western Confederacy to Federal invasion. After Tennessee seceded, the Confederates established a defensive line along the state's border with Kentucky west to the Mississippi River and Missouri, concentrating particularly on that nexus where the Cumberland, Mississippi, and Tennessee rivers drew close together. Those rivers perilously divided the Confederate defenders from one another and required close monitoring. The Federals responded by massing troops and supplies at Cairo, Illinois, at the extreme southern tip of the state. Only a thin strip of western Kentucky separated the opposing forces. In retrospect, it was only a matter of time before one side or the other blundered across

Kentucky's border and violated its neutrality. The two opposing commanders facing off just across the Mississippi River in Missouri, the Confederacy's
Brig. Gen. Gideon Pillow and the Union's Maj. Gen. John C. Frémont, constantly and foolishly fantasized about staging a glorious preemptive strike
into Kentucky. They clearly were the wrong men in the wrong place at the
wrong time, having all but defined military incompetence since their dubious Mexican War service.

In the end, the political general Pillow stole a march on the slower but
equally hapless "Pathfinder." He campaigned for weeks for permission to
cross the Mississippi and seize the town of Columbus, Kentucky. Columbus
was the railhead of the Mobile and Ohio Railroad and, with its high river
bluffs, offered a promising site for blocking the Mississippi. He finally persuaded the popular but inexperienced former Episcopal bishop Leonidas Polk,
momentarily commanding the Confederacy's "Western" Department No. 2,
to allow him to occupy Columbus on September 4. Egotistical and used to
having his own way, Polk stubbornly stood by his decision once he made it,
claiming that the incursion was vital if he was to control the bluffs above
Columbus and thus secure his position. From Cairo, Ulysses S. Grant
promptly seized Paducah for the Union. Seemingly acting in response to the
Southern incursion, Grant in fact had been preparing to violate Kentucky's
border himself under orders from Frémont. Polk and Pillow in the end only
beat Frémont to the punch, but the damage to the Confederate cause was
done.

The Pillow-Polk incursion made some sense militarily, although control of Columbus was useless without Paducah as well. Politically it was a
disaster. The Confederate government in Richmond angrily debated Polk's
incursion, most cabinet members advocating a complete disavowal in hopes
of preserving Kentucky's neutrality. In the end the bishop's old friend from
West Point, President Davis, backed him fully, probably for personal as well
as strategic reasons. Davis rationalized Polk's activities by maintaining that
Federal activities in Kentucky, especially at Camp Dick Robinson, already
had made the state's neutrality a dead letter. The Unionist state legislature
disagreed. Freed from the necessity of hewing to the neutrality proclamation, it voted on September 18 to end neutrality and align Kentucky with the
Union. The legislature curtly ordered all Confederates out of the state and
gave command of Kentucky's volunteers to a native son, Brig. Gen. Robert
Anderson, the Federal hero of Fort Sumter, who at that moment commanded
the Department of the Cumberland from his headquarters in Cincinnati.[20]

Federal forces moved quickly to solidify their position after Polk's invasion and the end of neutrality. Soldiers in blue poured across the Ohio,
particularly into Louisville and Covington, the latter just across the river
from Cincinnati. Anderson promptly moved his headquarters to Louisville,
and soon troops spread out across the state to arrest the disaffected and shut
down pro-Southern newspapers. The state government meanwhile called

for forty thousand loyal volunteers. Men enlisted slowly but steadily, and more than twenty-nine thousand had joined Federal companies by the end of the year. Thereafter, white Kentuckians in blue would always outnumber those in gray by at least three-to-one, with emancipation in 1863 further increasing the ratio of Federals to Confederates through the induction of African Americans. Such numbers were the most visible evidence of the commonwealth's prevailing Unionism. The legislature also reorganized the Military Board, established earlier in the year, so as to completely bypass the distrusted Magoffin. The legislators eventually forced him to resign the following year.[21]

The Confederate government also acted decisively once the decision was made to hold Kentucky territory. In East Tennessee, Brig. Gen. Felix Zollicoffer, a popular prewar Tennessee politician and newspaper editor, received orders to move onto the Cumberland Plateau in eastern Kentucky. Hoping to forestall the Federal capture of Cumberland Gap, Zollicoffer advanced until halted late in October in a skirmish known as the Battle of Rockcastle Hills. Concurrently, Brig. Gen. Simon B. Buckner, having turned down an offer from Lincoln to serve the Union, occupied Bowling Green and seized control of the Louisville and Nashville Railroad on September 18. He quickly opened several recruiting stations in the vicinity. Brigadier General William J. Hardee's rough-and-ready brigade of Arkansans subsequently reinforced Buckner from Missouri in October.

Also arriving in Bowling Green in mid-October was the newly appointed department commander, Gen. Albert Sidney Johnston. The Kentucky-born Johnston was a well-regarded veteran of the old army who, since their cadet days together, had been the unsurpassed idol of President Davis. At first commanding from Columbus, Johnston later shifted his headquarters to Bowling Green, taking command of what was by then being called the Central Army of Kentucky. By the end of October, an imperfect Confederate line centered on Bowling Green ran from Columbus, on the Mississippi River, through southern Kentucky, to Zollicoffer's position in the Appalachian Mountains. Undermanned everywhere, as Johnston had only forty-eight thousand men to cover a front almost four hundred miles wide, its weakest spots were those points where the Cumberland and Tennessee Rivers flowed into Tennessee. There, the Confederates had constructed two inadequate forts, Henry and Donelson, to control access to the rivers. Built in Tennessee before neutrality ended in Kentucky, they created a dangerous salient in Johnston's defensive line. Although well aware of the problem, Johnston passively did little to beef up the defenses there, trusting the task to subordinates. He had convinced himself that any Federal advance would approach Bowling Green.[22]

Behind Johnston's thin gray line, Kentucky secessionists went through the motions of joining the Confederacy. In Russellville, a self-appointed rump convention passed a secession ordinance and created the provisional government of Kentucky, with Bowling Green as the temporary state capital. Planter George W. Johnson, a reluctant secessionist at best, took office as governor. Commissioners then headed to Richmond, where they secured Davis's critical backing. The Confederate Congress admitted Kentucky to the Confederacy in December, and soon Kentuckians sat in that body, as symbolized by a new star in the Confederate flag.[23]

North of Johnston's line, the situation in Federal territory remained in flux. At first, Confederate weakness went unappreciated. Indeed, many anxious Unionists expected rebel hordes to descend on Louisville and sweep across the Ohio. Brigadier General William Tecumseh Sherman, who replaced a sickly and overwhelmed Anderson as the Union commanding general in the department in October, worried the most. Habitually nervous, the chain-smoking Sherman, convinced that he was vastly outnumbered and ripe for the picking, dispatched repeated pleas for as many as two hundred thousand men—all of whom, he insisted, were necessary to hold the state. Sherman, suffering from depression and perhaps even a mental breakdown, was pilloried in the press as being "insane." In November, he, too, had to go.[24]

The next man to occupy the hot seat in Union Kentucky was Sherman's old friend Don Carlos Buell, whose newly created Department of the Ohio covered Kentucky and Tennessee east of the Cumberland River and Indiana, Michigan, and Ohio. Under the coolly professional if uninspiring and distant Buell, sanity finally began to prevail in Federally occupied Kentucky. Known for his stolid competence, immaculate if perpetually scowling appearance, high personal standards of morality and professionalism, and great physical strength—a favorite stunt was to pick up his wife by the waist and place her on the mantle—the compact, barrel-chested Ohioan was forty-four years old when he took command. Orphaned at age five by a beloved father, raised by various relatives, young Carlos Buell grew into a shy and serious loner with few friends. The pattern continued at West Point. There, he impressed very few except as a compiler of demerits, his friend Sherman being a notable exception. Buell gained further notoriety after his 1841 graduation when he was court-martialed for repeatedly striking a defiant private with the flat of his sword. The Buell case blew up into a cause célèbre for congressmen hoping to embarrass and ultimately dismantle the "aristocratic" academy. It took Pres. John Tyler's intervention to rescue the beleaguered lieutenant and his alma mater. Although acquitted, Buell had earned a reputation for being a martinet. Having already served in Florida against the Seminoles, he rebuilt his career in Mexico, where he fought in most of that war's major battles and was brevetted a major for gallantry. Wounded in the initial fighting along the Rio Grande as well as that outside Mexico City, Buell emerged from the conflict as a rising star. After the war he made a significant mark in the Adjutant General's Department, where superiors

Figure 1.1. Maj. Gen. Don Carlos Buell. Photograph courtesy Library of Congress, LC-USZ62-9979.

praised his self-discipline, talent for organization, and meticulous attention to detail and organization. Increasingly valued in Washington, he eventually held down a desk there from 1859 into 1861 as an assistant to the controversial secretary of war, Virginian John B. Floyd. Following Fort Sumter, Buell was appointed brigadier general of volunteers. Sponsored by West Point instructor Dennis Hart Mahan and another old friend, George B. McClellan, Buell fought in Virginia. Then, again with "Little Mac's" support, he assumed his new post in Kentucky, much to the relief of the country.[25]

Upon taking command, Buell discovered that he had at his disposal only about twenty-three thousand poorly trained men to guard a department that stretched three hundred miles westward across Kentucky to the Cumberland River. While lacking the sort of McClelleanesque flair that inspired men, his experience as an army bureaucrat provided most of the qualities necessary to accomplish the immediate task at hand: building a viable fighting force. Buell immediately instituted stringent discipline and ordered his volunteers to drill incessantly. He himself worked late into the night endeavoring to arm and equip the men he had as well as those he hoped to recruit. No detail escaped him; today he would be known as a micromanager. None of his exacting, bureaucratic ways or sheaves of regulations disseminated from his headquarters endeared him to his men, who found him cold, aloof, and vaguely threatening. Nevertheless, like his friend and sponsor

McClellan, Buell proved that he excelled at building an army. By the end of 1861 he had forty thousand combat-ready men prepared to defend the state.

Unfortunately, also like McClellan, Buell the commander displayed a remarkable talent for annoying superiors with stubborn arrogance and political naiveté. Like many West Pointers, Buell scorned the rough-and-tumble of mid-nineteenth-century American politics and particularly abhorred politicians who interfered in military affairs. Those views put him on a collision course with powerful Midwestern governors Oliver Morton of Indiana, Davis Tod of Ohio, and Richard Yates of Illinois over control of the regiments from their states. He ultimately mixed regiments from different states when creating brigades solely to foil the governors' considerable meddling in his army. His personal views further alienated him from the politicians. A Douglas Democrat whose family had once owned slaves, and who had married the daughter of a wealthy Alabama slaveholder as well, Buell had owned eight slaves through marriage. Still a slaveholder in 1861 (he sold all but one after Fort Sumter), he not surprisingly despised abolitionists and, once in the field, consistently turned away runaway slaves seeking sanctuary behind his lines. His strongly conciliatory views toward Southern civilians, ostensibly intended to win back the hearts and minds of reluctant secessionists, also rankled the three governors as well as Tennessee Unionist leader Andrew Johnson. Many of the more radical soldiers under Buell's command, as well as an increasingly suspicious press corps, invariably suspected that their distant slaveholder-general secretly harbored Southern sympathies, and little that subsequently occurred would dissuade them.

Buell also frustrated his president, inflexibly resisting constant pressure from Lincoln, and ultimately even his ally McClellan, to move quickly into largely Unionist East Tennessee in order to liberate it from Confederate control. East Tennessee by then had become the president's pet project, but Buell exhibited little patience with his meddling. To Buell, war was a science. A disciple of West Point's Mahan, Swiss military theorist Baron Henri de Jomini, and France's Maurice Comte de Saxe, as well as a halting perfectionist by nature, the conservative Buell had fully absorbed his role models' beliefs in thorough organization and groundwork before undertaking an offensive. He was convinced that a commander should fight only when he held a carefully prepared tactical advantage on the field. Service in Mexico not only had taught him the importance of logistics, but also aroused in him a suspicion of volunteers, who he was convinced needed careful training and preparation for combat. Thus, while he had supported a quick strike into East Tennessee while in Washington, he balked after arriving in Kentucky. His army, he maintained, was nowhere near ready to go on the offensive. Bad roads, meager supplies, and the lack of transportation would make movement into East Tennessee all but impossible even for a veteran army.

Nor was he convinced that East Tennessee was the right target. The loyalty of Lincoln's much-beloved East Tennessee Unionists undoubtedly would survive as it had so far. They could wait until Federal soldiers arrived, Buell sniffed, if they truly were as noble as Lincoln believed. Just as Albert Sidney Johnston suspected, Bowling Green and Nashville instead quickly became the centerpieces of Buell's strategic thinking. Buell asserted that it would be better to strike south along the Louisville and Nashville Railroad, toward Bowling Green and then on to Nashville. Opened in 1859, the railroad functioned as the spine of the Southern railroad network, in many ways superseding the Tennessee-Cumberland River system as the western Confederacy's "strategic axis." Possession of it was vital to hold any gains made south of the Ohio. Buell's march along the Louisville and Nashville in theory would be coupled with a column into eastern Kentucky, a demonstration against Columbus, and a strike via the Cumberland and Tennessee Rivers on Forts Henry and Donelson. The last offensive would require the cooperation of his bitter rival, Maj. Gen. Henry W. Halleck, the new commander of the Department of the Missouri. Such a campaign would drive the Confederates from Kentucky and all of Tennessee, including the eastern counties, he argued. Sound militarily, Buell's insistence on occupying Middle Tennessee rather than the eastern section of the state nonetheless ignored the political realities of a popular civil war. The great result of his foot-dragging was that Buell steadily lost the confidence of his commander in chief, who grew to believe that, like his friend and fellow Democrat McClellan, Buell had a case of the "slows."[26]

Not surprisingly, Lincoln's repeated calls to action and his refusal to see things Buell's way increasingly upset the general. In time, Buell would come to blame Lincoln and the men around the president not only for the failure of his career, but for the war as a whole. Buell was no closet secessionist as many feared, but in truth there was an iota of substance to allegations that he had unusual sympathies for the enemy. Coupled with his fading prospects, those views would become public knowledge in 1864, when a remarkable private letter appeared against his wishes in the *New York Times*. In it, he declared that Southern secession largely was the result of "an *honest conviction in the minds of those who engaged in it;* that the control of the Government had passed permanently into the hands of a sectional party which would soon trample on the political rights of the South." Had the Lincoln administration adopted and stuck to a just, conciliatory policy, Buell bitterly maintained, a majority of such people would have abandoned such fears and again embraced the Union. Instead, "injudicious or unfaithful" Republicans, motivated by sectional hatred, proved the secessionists right, and in so doing prolonged the war. Buell did not attack Lincoln directly, but the implication was clear. Few Confederate generals could have mounted a defense of the creation and continued struggle of the Confederacy as well as Buell did.[27]

In 1861, however, Buell remained only annoyed with Washington, his real views only suspected. While the politicians badgered him, he doggedly refined his army and stonewalled on East Tennessee. At least he was an im-

provement on Sherman, for he expressed certainty that he was in no danger
of attack, doubting that Sidney Johnston ever could or would seize the initiative. Buell knew Johnston, having briefly served in Texas as his assistant adjutant general during the mid-1850s. He thus assured McClellan that "as for
his attacking . . . I should almost as soon expect to see the Army of the Potomac
marching up the road as Johnston."[28] Not for the last time, Buell displayed
what later would be unmasked as a dangerously unhealthy characteristic: the
utter confidence that an enemy would sit patiently and wait for him to unfold his carefully laid plans. This time he was right, but one day it would cost
him his command.

Buell in fact read Johnston perfectly. The Confederates remained ensconced
behind their thin line through the miserable, rainy winter, too weak and
poorly supplied to mount any offensive beyond bluff. Early in the new year,
having built up their manpower and resources, the western Federals finally
struck, piercing and rolling back Johnston's defensive line as if it were the lid
of a tin can. In southeastern Kentucky, near the Virginia line, a brigade under the command of Col. James A. Garfield scored victories over the portly
Kentucky Whig politician Humphrey Marshall at Middle Creek in January
and Pound Gap in March. After Pound Gap, where sick and hungry Confederates threw down their arms and ran, Marshall surrendered eastern Kentucky and retreated deep into southwestern Virginia. More importantly, as
noted by Anthony Trollope, in January forces under George Thomas advanced into the Kentucky mountains on the road to East Tennessee and defeated a poorly armed and outnumbered Confederate force during a bitter
downpour at Mill Springs. Forcing the Rebels back into Tennessee, Thomas
achieved one of the first significant Union victories of the war. Ominously
for the South, Zollicoffer fell, and his just-appointed superior officer, John J.
Crittenden's alcoholic son George, found himself in disgrace after a drunken
flight from the field. Their army, all but destroyed, limped back into Tennessee, minus numerous deserters. Defeat at Mill Springs completely uncovered Johnston's right and, as Trollope found in Louisville, emboldened
Kentucky Unionists. Thomas no doubt could have continued advancing into
East Tennessee as he, McClellan, and Lincoln had wanted for months, but
Buell reined his eager subordinate in and ordered him back to Lebanon,
where he could support Buell's main projected movement toward Nashville.
In the coming months their tendency of working at cross-purposes would
not improve.

Meanwhile, a jealous and ambitious Halleck, worried that the victory
at Mill Springs would dim the prospects of his obtaining the overall western
command he craved, unleashed Grant on Fort Henry. Grant, acting on his
own initiative, captured Fort Donelson as well. The loss of the river forts
dangerously threatened Confederate communications and opened up both
the Cumberland and Tennessee rivers to Federal gunboats. The end result

was the bitter abandonment of Columbus and Bowling Green and, ultimately, Nashville itself. Within only a few weeks, Buell's and Halleck's forces, united in cause and effect if divided by the egos of the two sparring commanders, drove the Confederate army completely from Kentucky. Buell, moving cautiously down the Louisville and Nashville line, at last occupied the coveted Tennessee capital in mid-February.[29]

A cold and demoralized Confederate Central Army of Kentucky staggered out of its namesake state along frozen roads, and the surrender of Nashville led to further demoralization in the ranks. Nashville was the second largest city in the Confederacy west of the Appalachians, a major industrial center and military storehouse of vast proportions. The loss of the city, its hinterlands in the Middle Tennessee "heartland," and its railroad connections proved a major blow to the Confederacy. Beset by freezing rain and sleet, Johnston's retreating army first fell back to Murfreesboro, where it was joined by the more committed survivors of Mill Springs, and then retreated to Decatur, Alabama. There it turned west. The ultimate destination was the vital railroad center at Corinth, Mississippi, the center of a new, hastily created Confederate line that ran from Chattanooga through Florence, Alabama, and Corinth, to Fort Pillow on the Mississippi. At Corinth, the western Confederacy concentrated the bulk of its forces for a counterattack. Manassas hero P. G. T. Beauregard, who had been transferred to the west by an antagonistic Davis to serve as Johnston's second in command, already had begun to assemble a force there to await Johnston's column. In addition to asking for state levies, Beauregard ordered Leonidas Polk to abandon Columbus and fall back toward Corinth. More importantly, Corinth was reinforced from the Gulf Coast at the beginning of March with a contingent of well-drilled and disciplined troops under the command of Maj. Gen. Braxton Bragg.[30]

Generations of Civil War historians have succeeded in making Braxton Bragg's name synonymous with pettiness, bitterness, incompetence, and in some cases even paranoia and insanity. In early 1862, however, no one foresaw the bitter failures on his horizon, nor the vicious backbiting and headquarters politics that one day would eat away at his command like a cancer. Rather, when he came to Corinth in the spring of 1862, Bragg was one of the best-regarded officers in the Confederate army, and in truth he had done much to earn his positive reputation.

Bragg was born to a humble North Carolina family, according to tradition in jail while his mother awaited trial on murder charges. Pushed by an ambitious father, Bragg graduated high in the West Point class of 1837 and served for the next several years on the Florida frontier. His rising status within the military, sadly, failed to improve his degenerating disposition. Increasingly plagued with chronic illnesses, some almost certainly psychosomatic, the young officer's ill-humor, contentiousness, sarcasm, and tactlessness constantly threatened to ruin his career, especially after he was court-martialed

Figure 1.2. Gen. Braxton Bragg. Photograph courtesy Library of Congress, LC-USZ262-4888.

for blasting army chief Winfield Scott in a national magazine. A second court-martial later cemented Bragg's negative reputation as the most quarrelsome soldier in the army, a man who, according to army wags, would argue with himself through official memoranda if no one else was around to badger. Bragg's career, and indeed his life, began spiraling out of control by the mid-1840s.

As in the case of Buell, the Mexican War providentially saved Bragg from himself. Assigned to Zachary Taylor's army along the Texas-Mexico border, the young artilleryman distinguished himself at Monterrey and most notably at Buena Vista, the same battle that cemented the reputation of former Taylor son-in-law Jefferson Davis. For his part, Bragg respected Taylor like few other men and learned much from him. As historian Grady McWhiney sagely pointed out, that was not necessarily a good thing, as Taylor was an indifferent tactician and logistician whose answer to every situation was to attack. Just as importantly, Taylor placed Bragg among the pantheon of the war's heroes when he allegedly turned to the young officer at the critical moment at Buena Vista and ordered "a little more grape, Captain Bragg!" Taylor of course said no such thing—Bragg remembered his commander bellowing less pithily, "Give 'em hell!" But the legend of "a little more grape" transformed the troublesome young officer into an overnight celebrity. Lost in the hoopla was the lesser known fact that America's new young hero had proven so unpopular with his men that two of them had tried to kill him by blowing up his tent as he slept.

Bragg emerged from the war with a promotion, enjoyed honors across the nation, and used his newfound reputation to court and win a wealthy Natchez belle. He had come a long way from his jailhouse cradle. Reassigned to the western frontier, however, Bragg soon was up to his old disputatious tricks. He finally resigned from the army in 1855 after quarreling with Secretary of War Jefferson Davis, and used his wife's fortune to buy a Louisiana sugar plantation. Bragg could not distance himself totally from the military, however. He played a major role in establishing the state's military school and securing as its first president a down-on-his-luck army friend, Tecumseh Sherman.

As war clouds gathered, Bragg hoped that Northern Democrats would find a way to rein in their Republican neighbors and prevent disunion. When they failed and Louisiana seceded in 1861, Bragg followed, but without any notable enthusiasm. Briefly suggested for the office of Confederate secretary of war, he instead took command of the state army, accepted Confederate rank, and went to Pensacola, Florida, to confront the Federal Fort Pickens and secure the Gulf Coast. Bragg drove his men hard, but with a genuine concern for their welfare. Soon he had built a well-trained and disciplined force that, although smaller, mirrored in many ways Buell's Federal Army of the Ohio. Later, Bragg's Pensacola men would remain his most loyal supporters. His growing reputation for steady competence led to his promotion to major general and command of the Department of Alabama and West Florida, headquartered in Mobile. In early March 1862 he brought much of his force from Mobile to Corinth, a concentration that he had urged as far back as February. Noting his graying hair, bushy brow, sickly appearance, and sour scowl, many observers on first sight concluded that he had to be older than his stated forty-five years.[31]

In Bragg's case, the metaphorical book cover seems to suggest a deeper story. Civil War historians over the years have referred routinely to Braxton Bragg's negative personality, and many have suggested some sort of mental instability. Yet, despite its obvious relevance in understanding his actions during the Civil War, most have been content to dismiss him as a bad leader and an obnoxious personality who eventually began to act "insane." As a group, historians largely avoid psychoanalyzing historic figures, while modern psychiatrists and psychologists routinely disagree over the symptoms, causes, and cures of mental illness, even in regard to living patients able to offer information and feedback. Reading modern psychology into the mute pages of the past threatens a host of wider pitfalls, especially when undertaken by nonspecialists, and threatens at worst to descend into spurious diagnosis and psychobabble. Still, considering its impact on his career and indeed the war, one cannot help but wonder if Braxton Bragg's behavior suggests symptoms of a deeper and specific problem, and if so, what problem? Biographer Judith Lee Hallock, for example, suggested that his sour personality might have derived from his chronic ailments, and worsened with self-medicated doses of mercury-based calomel and perhaps opiates as well. Heavy use of such drugs would have left Bragg both confused and paranoid.[32]

Another hypothesis involves manic-depression, sometimes called bipolar affective disorder. The negative and well-chronicled manifestations of Bragg's health and personality already apparent by the spring of 1862—digestive problems, hypochondria, irritability, anxiety, and self-destructive behavior coupled with delusions of grandeur (as a young officer lecturing Winfield Scott on how to run the army, for example)—comprise a catalogue of the lesser known early symptoms of manic-depression. Most often characterized by violent mood springs between mania—exemplified by frenetic overactivity, exultation, overconfidence, increased cognition, irritability, and paranoia—and the corresponding hopelessness and inactivity of depression, bipolar disorders of varying degree affect many. Insofar as Bragg is concerned, there is little evidence that he veered noticeably from mania to depression before 1862. Yet that would not be uncommon, for manic-depression can appear full-blown after age forty, although onset usually occurs in one's mid-twenties. Critically, Bragg exhibited dramatic mood swings in Kentucky later in 1862. The causes of bipolar disorders remain debated, with psychologists and psychiatrists alternately suggesting environmental, biological, or genetic factors. One would love to know, for example, more about Bragg's mother and what behaviors landed her in jail on the eve of childbirth.[33]

A more likely possibility, one that would lead to similar symptoms, is what psychologists term narcissistic personality disorder. Narcissistic individuals typically grow up in households where parents place great demands on children to live up to their grand, predetermined expectations, as Bragg's ambitious father did. Denied the chance to be himself, shamed or humiliated as a child for any self-expression that runs counter to his parents' demands and needs, the adult narcissist usually projects a competent and idealized "false self" to the world but secretly doubts himself, worried that others will find out his perceived secret failings. In terms of behavior, the narcissist, much like the manic-depressive, swerves from active periods of real achievement, characterized by competence, pride, perfectionism, a desire for power and greatness, and a lack of concern for others, to deep depressions notable for feelings of shame and self-doubt, psychosomatic illnesses, anxiety, panic, inertia, and isolation. Unable to accept their real selves, dependent on others' perceptions for validation and self-worth, narcissists routinely blame others when things go wrong.[34]

More than a century after his death, it is impossible to determine which disorder, if any, truly affected Braxton Bragg. One at least can say, however, that he exhibited the symptoms of narcissistic personality disorder. More importantly, those behaviors would come to play a crucial role in the army he now joined and soon would lead.

Albert Sidney Johnston's Central Army of Kentucky, beset with more immediate problems than one general's questionable psyche, started drifting into
Corinth on March 20. Soon Johnston combined it with Beauregard's gathered units into the restyled Army of the Mississippi. Johnston took command with Beauregard officially serving as second in command. The latter,
however, called most of the shots for the weak-willed, indecisive, and depressed
Johnston, all but paralyzed by the winter's reverses. Bragg also helped to prop
up Johnston by serving both as a corps commander and as chief of staff.

The major dilemma facing the new army was an impending concentration of superior Federal force in its front. After Fort Donelson, Buell and
Halleck bickered for weeks over whose strategy to follow. While their armies
sat idly, Johnston escaped to Corinth. Finally, without Buell's cooperation,
Halleck dispatched Grant's army south, up the flooded Tennessee River toward Corinth. At the same time Halleck's open campaigning for overall command in the west reached fruition on March 9. Lincoln's War Order No. 3
not only relieved McClellan as commander in chief but also placed Halleck
in command of the newly created Department of the Mississippi, combining
Buell's Ohio Department with Halleck's old command. Denied McClellan's
protection even if promoted to major general, Buell suddenly found himself
subordinate to Halleck, whose first orders were to march from Nashville
toward Savannah, Tennessee. There, Buell would link up with Grant so that
together they could drive on Corinth. Buell obeyed his orders, but without
haste. Halleck after all had implied that all was well on the Tennessee, and at
any rate Buell was in no hurry to give up independent command. As a result,
his army moved at a snail's pace, notably spending ten days outside Columbia, Tennessee, methodically attempting to build a permanent bridge across
the flooded Duck River before Bull Nelson impatiently demonstrated that
the falling waterway could be forded.[35]

Meanwhile, Grant's confident, unsuspecting army waited for Buell's and
drilled at Pittsburg Landing, a riverboat landing nine miles from Savannah
and twenty-three miles from Corinth. Hesitant for days, Johnston at last
concluded that he had to attack Grant before Buell arrived. On April 6, despite a mismanaged and unlucky march from Corinth, his army surprised the
Federals at Pittsburg Landing. Vicious, confused fighting swirled all day
around little Shiloh Church as the Confederates drove their foes backward a
mile toward the river. Johnston fell mortally wounded, and Beauregard called
a halt to the fighting at dusk, unaware that advance units of Buell's army, led
by Nelson's command, already were arriving at the landing. The following
morning, the reinforced Federals did all the attacking, retaking all their lost
ground and forcing the Confederates to fall back to Corinth. Once again,
Confederate hopes had been dashed in the west, and the Southern "liberation" of Tennessee, much less Kentucky, seemed farther off than ever[36]

After the Battle of Shiloh, the surviving combatants of both armies
emerged with new confidence in themselves and their regiments. Even the

Confederates could claim that they had won the fight or blame their reverse on poor training and inexperience, if not the failures of some other unit. The experience of battle also "hardened" many to the chaos and gore of the battlefield. Soldiers often wrote of their surprise in learning that despite their largely Christian values they could kill their fellow men without guilt.[37]

The civilian population reacted differently. Shiloh was the first major battle of the war, the bloodiest thus far, and the lengthy casualty rolls that followed horrified an incredulous public still primed for a short and relatively harmless contest. They sought scapegoats as well as explanations, and typically took aim at the armies' commanders, Beauregard and Grant. In striking contrast, most civilian commentators widely praised Bragg and Buell as the men of the hour. While some newspapers criticized Buell's tardiness, most journalists and even many Federal veterans of the battle credited him with "saving" the Union army at Shiloh from an allegedly incompetent and drunken Grant. Buell himself claimed the lion's share of the glory. In truth, as historian Larry Daniel convincingly maintains, Grant's men largely had saved themselves by the afternoon of the first day. Indeed, the rivalry between Buell and Grant actually hampered the Federal effort on the morning of the second day, resulting in two largely independent attacks commanded by men barely speaking to each other. Buell again proved slow and hesitant to commit himself, as had been the case throughout his march from Nashville. Overall, Shiloh enhanced Buell's reputation more than it should have— yet it blossomed nonetheless.[38]

Much of the same could be said of Bragg, although significantly he could not even enjoy the rank-and-file support Buell possessed. Promoted to full general for his activities at Pittsburg Landing, many outside the army, notably members of the government in Richmond, lauded the aggressive Bragg as one of the few bright spots to emerge from the heartbreaking defeat. His star shone more brightly than ever in the capital. The fact that he had fought foolishly and wasted lives, as bitter men in the ranks well knew, was ignored. Having agreed that he would concentrate on smashing the Federal left, their weakest point, Bragg inexplicably spent several hours launching wave after wave of piecemeal bayonet charges against the imposing "Hornet's Nest" in the Federal center. When regiments fell back in the face of heavy fire, Bragg openly questioned their courage, and when regimental colonels begged for artillery support from the most famous gunner in the old army, Bragg refused them. His only answer, Zach Taylor–like, was to press the attack. After Shiloh, Bragg ignominiously blamed the defeat on undisciplined soldiers and their cowardly officers, never acknowledging, or even recognizing, his own mistakes. Indeed, as Grady McWhiney has maintained, Bragg's worst failing at Shiloh was that he learned nothing.[39]

Yet it remained Beauregard who bore the brunt of blame in the Confederate capital, especially in an already unfriendly President Davis's office. In the weeks following Shiloh, the "Napoleon in gray" changed few minds, and what confidence in him remained waned steadily. Circumstances at Corinth did not promise any reversals of fortune either. Confronted by three Federal armies—John Pope's Army of the Mississippi arrived outside Corinth after conquering the vital Confederate Mississippi River bastion at Island No. 10 on April 7—Beauregard faced the ugly reality that not only was he outgunned, but Corinth had become, in James McPherson's words, "an ecological trap" due to a water supply laced with the army's sewage.[40] At length, he abandoned Corinth on the night of May 30 and fell back to Tupelo, fifty miles farther into Mississippi but astride a better water supply. Davis and most of the Southern populace reacted to the news with incredulous fury.[41] For Beauregard, the last straw came on June 15 when he curtly informed the president that without prior approval he was taking sick leave "about one week or ten days, or long enough to restore my shattered health," leaving Bragg in command at Tupelo while he recuperated at a south Alabama spa. Furious, Davis immediately fired Beauregard and informed Bragg, "you are assigned permanently to the command of the department."[42]

2

A BRILLIANT SUMMER CAMPAIGN

BRAXTON BRAGG TOOK COMMAND OF THE ARMY OF THE MISSISSIPPI with reluctance and, if he was being honest, grave depression. "Have a despatch from the President," he telegramed Beauregard, "direct, to relieve you permanently in command of this reluctance. I envy you and am almost in despair."[1] To his men, however, he presented a braver face. "Great events are pending," he promised his soldiers, ". . . A few more days of needed reorganization, and I shall give your banners to the breeze—shall lead you to emulate the soldiers of the Confederacy in the East."[2]

Rhetoric aside, Bragg would need more than a favorable southern wind to lift his battle flags. In fact, the new commanding general faced a formidable task at Tupelo that bordered on the hopeless. Defeat at Shiloh, the disheartening retreat from Corinth, tight rations in Tupelo, and sickness everywhere had sapped morale, with desertion the inevitable result. Freshly dug graves marked every campsite. What food was available bore the high prices of unpatriotic profiteering. Bragg also was unhappy with many of his top-ranking officers, whom he considered unfit—most notably Polk and the roughly hewn Tennessean, Benjamin Franklin Cheatham—and he adamantly expressed his belief that the practice of having soldiers elect their regimental officers dangerously undermined discipline. Beauregard also let Bragg know in no uncertain terms that he expected his staff to join him at his next assignment, which meant that Bragg had to rely on men whose loyalty and futures lay elsewhere.

To his credit, Bragg confronted his difficulties with admirable energy and considerable, still underrated skill, all but rebuilding the defeated army. The history of the Confederacy would have been much shorter had he been half the incompetent some claimed him to be. He strained to obtain food and new uniforms for the soldiers, and he ordered that wells be dug to provide healthy water. Hoping to improve morale, Bragg also encouraged regular church attendance. Many of his initiatives, however, fell flat, such as his attempt to discourage alcohol consumption. Men grumbled even worse when their enlistments ran out and they learned that the Confederate Congress had extended their terms of service.[3] Bragg's response was to institute heavy doses of drill and discipline, including executions for serious breaches of orders. The men of one Tennessee regiment nearing the end of their service found themselves facing the guns of an artillery battery, a less than subtle form of encouragement for them to reenlist. Strict obedience to orders overall, he assured his men, was "a sacred duty, an act of patriotism."[4]

Not surprisingly, his jaded soldiers found it easier to emphasize the threat of the firing squad than his more positive contributions, notably spreading the woefully exaggerated tale that Bragg ordered a hungry soldier shot near Shiloh for killing a chicken.[5] The result was that years later, Bragg the martinet became something of a stock character. "Almost every day," Sam Watkins of the 1st Tennessee Infantry remembered with embellishment, "we would hear a discharge of musketry, and knew that some poor, trembling wretch had bid farewell to mortal things here below. It seemed to be but a question of time with all of us as to when we too would be shot. We were afraid to chirp." Yet Watkins went on to confess that he himself only saw two men shot at Tupelo and two others whipped.[6] Louisianian W. L. Trask maintained that Bragg shot only "a few turbulent fellows."[7] The rest of the death toll came from exaggerated scuttlebutt.

Bragg did have his supporters. Wrote one army clerk: "When he took command at Corinth, the army was little better than a mob. The din of firearms could be heard at all hours of the day. *Now* a gun is never fired without orders. . . . Bragg had one man shot for discharging his gun on the march. . . . Since that time the discipline of the troops has improved very much. Men are not apt to disobey orders when they know that Death is the punishment."[8]

Another, Louisianian E. John Ellis, later agreed: "Many absurd stories have been told and are now ripe about the shooting of a private soldier merely for having killed a chicken, and Gen. Bragg is held up to the public as a monster who utterly disregarded the lives of his men and had them executed for the most trivial offences. Gen. Bragg did have a man shot, but that act was in direct violation of a stringent order . . . the army was fast becoming an armed mob. The firm and prompt measures of Gen. Bragg alone saved it."[9]

Although the army's fighting trim rebounded in spite of itself, Bragg still faced a seemingly insurmountable problem of numbers. At Tupelo, his roughly thirty-two thousand effectives faced an overwhelming 110,000-man Federal force at Corinth. Bragg's only advantage, as it turned out, was that his opponent was no longer the hard-driving Grant, temporarily in disgrace after the Shiloh surprise, but rather the careful Halleck. Determined to win the sort of glory that had gone to Buell and Grant, both of whom he heartily disliked and deeply envied, Halleck came from St. Louis to take personal command after Shiloh. Under his direction, the Federals inched their way the roughly twenty miles to Corinth, entrenching every night and thus taking almost a month to cover the short distance. There would be no unpleasant, Shiloh-like surprises to tarnish his reputation. When Corinth fell into Union hands without much of a struggle, Halleck saw no reason to abandon his conservative strategy. Instead, he obsessed over reports of rampant disease beyond enemy lines. If he moved deeper into enemy country toward Bragg's army at Tupelo, Halleck reasoned, disease might accomplish what the Confederates had failed to do: destroy his army. The Confederate bastion at Vicksburg briefly offered a tempting alternate target, but not only did it pose the same threat of disease, but Halleck also reasonably concluded that Vicksburg would soon fall as New Orleans and Baton Rouge had to the Union navy's Mississippi River fleets. Above all, he did not wish to displease President Lincoln, who pressed above all for the occupation of East Tennessee.

Accordingly, Halleck made the worst decision of his career. Instead of continuing forward to Tupelo or Vicksburg, he divided his force and ceased advancing south at all. One division went to Arkansas to bolster Maj. Gen. Samuel Curtis's Federal forces in that state. Grant's Shiloh army—now under George Thomas's command—and most of Pope's army as well, dispersed in garrisons behind the lines, across healthier areas of the region. There, they would cover rail routes in the rear that were increasingly vital now that the Tennessee River finally was dropping. Inertia and debilitating illness followed in northern Mississippi and western Tennessee.[10]

There still would be an offensive, though, and Halleck assigned Buell the critical and risky role. He ordered his former rival to move eastward across northern Alabama toward the vital railroad junction at Chattanooga, Tennessee, repairing and guarding the Memphis and Charleston Railroad as he went and drawing supplies from it. Major General Ormsby M. Mitchel's division of Buell's army, essentially independent thanks to Mitchel's arrogant distaste for Buell's soft war policies and Secretary of War Edwin M. Stanton's complicity, already had taken Huntsville, Alabama, on an overland march from Murfreesboro. It now would form a vanguard for Buell, and Halleck would send more troops after Buell if required. If successful, Buell might continue on as far as Atlanta. If unsuccessful, Buell rather than Halleck would shoulder the blame.

It all seemed reasonable to Halleck, but as Buell saw it, he now would have to do what he had strenuously avoided all during the previous year: lead his army into barren and rugged East Tennessee. Little had occurred there to assuage the difficulties he had enunciated upon first taking command. Typically, he balked. Buell insisted that control of Middle Tennessee remained the key, while the difficult topography of the eastern counties gave him pause. Moreover, there was the drastically changing weather, perhaps the greatest factor in the war during 1862. Having opened up regularly throughout the winter and springs, the skies over Mississippi and Alabama closed up tight in the summer, and before long drought had started to settle in across the Deep South. Once flooded, the Tennessee and Cumberland Rivers had fallen so low by June to prevent gunboats and supply vessels from coming upriver far enough to do Buell any good. He would need to rely on railroads completely to supply his men. Expressing a willingness to compromise, he counterproposed that he march first toward Nashville in order to better safeguard the two railroads stretching southward from that city to Decatur and Stevenson, Alabama. From Nashville, he told Halleck, he could easily swing to the southeast toward Chattanooga. Halleck at first agreed, but after two days changed his mind and directed Buell to follow the original orders.[11]

As historian Stephen Engle maintains, Buell's proposal was sounder from a military standpoint. Hindsight suggests that everything bad that followed for the Union cause in the west emanated from Halleck's stubborn decision to ignore Buell's misgivings and send him directly eastward across Alabama, for Buell had been correct. Not only did expected railroad repairs decelerate his advance, but Confederate horsemen such as Nathan Bedford Forrest created havoc in his rear, tearing up track, attacking isolated Federal outfits, and repeatedly raiding and wrecking his tenuous supply lines. Much energy had to be diverted to building and manning defensive works and small blockhouses at bridges and other critical points along the crucial railroad. Forage grew increasingly scarce, as Mitchel's advance column had consumed much of it earlier in the summer. As the main body moved farther from Corinth and Buell forbade foraging off civilians in an effort to rebuild loyalty to the Union, the men bitterly scraped by on half-rations. Even the hot, dry weather took its toll on the increasingly thirsty and prostrated Northerners. Morale, not surprisingly, plummeted. Even many of the freedmen who had joined the column during its march turned back to their farms and plantations. Thirty miles from Chattanooga, at the railhead in Stevenson, Buell's van finally ground to a halt, with the rest of the command still strung out across Alabama and parts of Tennessee. Years later, some veterans considered it to have been their hardest march of the war. All the while, Lincoln and Halleck pressed him to hurry up if he wanted to retain command, driving a frustrated Buell to the point of resignation.[12] "The fact that it was the home of all that was loyal to the Union in the States in rebellion," Buell later wrote bitterly, "seemed to blind the Government."[13]

Halleck's flawed strategy quite simply saved Braxton' Bragg's Army of the Mississippi. Indeed, it presented the Confederates with a golden opportunity to take the offensive and reverse the tide of the war. Unfortunately, new to command and more used to obeying orders than giving them, Bragg floundered. He knew he had to attack, but he could not decide *where*. His initial impulse, the most obvious one, was to head north in an attempt to retake Corinth—not an easy task, but within the realm of possibility with Buell's army heading elsewhere. Another possibility was to go after Buell from the rear, through Middle Tennessee. A third and more daring option involved shifting the army quickly to Chattanooga so that somewhere in Tennessee a reinforced Confederate army could confront and destroy Buell, retaking that state and perhaps even Kentucky. Choosing one option over the others, unfortunately, tied Bragg in knots; he simply could not make up his mind. Ominously, if indecisiveness often accompanies depressive disorders, so does the surrender of initiative. Bragg's tendency to allow others to make his decisions for them, leaving him the opportunity of blaming them if failure resulted, now came to the fore. In the end, confused beyond measure, he essentially allowed others to craft his final strategy for him.[14]

Four factors now combined to edge Bragg toward the bold Chattanooga option. First was the inherent real difficulty in marching either on Corinth or cross-country after Buell. Not only would he still be outnumbered by three-to-two if he went after Halleck, Bragg also lacked the requisite supplies and transportation, especially wagons. Moreover, the regional drought would hit his army as hard as it had Buell. Second, there was the temptation offered by Buell's plodding trek eastward. As long as horsemen like Forrest's and those of lesser-known bands continued to create havoc in Buell's rear, there was little indication that Buell could or would pick up the pace. Although Bragg would have to take the long way around if he shifted the army to Chattanooga, by rail via Mobile and Atlanta, the slow pace of Buell's campaign suggested that he could win the race if he chose to do so.[15]

Third, Bragg began to comprehend the political benefits of striking in the direction of Kentucky. At Tupelo, toward the end of July, a delegation of "many prominent citizens of Kentucky" visited Bragg with assurances that "Kentuckians were thoroughly loyal to the South, and that as soon as they were given an opportunity it would be proven."[16] Bragg's visitors acted within the parameters of a larger, increasingly influential group of Confederates. Despite the depressing chain of events over the previous months, many of Kentucky's true believers in the Southern cause remained undeterred. Completely exiled from their native soil, with no immediate hope of returning, refugee Kentuckians continued to serve in Confederate "Orphan" regiments, and the provisional state government, led by George W. Johnson until his death as a volunteer aide at Shiloh and then by successor Richard Hawes, continued to claim legitimacy.

More importantly, expatriate Kentuckians in the Confederate capital formed a small but highly influential power base. The "Kentucky bloc," as scholars Thomas Connelly and Archer Jones later termed it, refused to allow anyone to give up the dream of a Confederate Kentucky. To all who would listen, members of the Kentucky bloc insisted that their state was not in the Union willingly. Instead, it was a conquered province peopled by an increasingly pro-Confederate population, men like themselves who were eager to rise in support of the southern nation if Lincoln's tyrannical heel could be pushed aside. Brig. Gen. Jeremiah T. Boyle, the zealous Union military governor of the state, had conducted mass arrests and interfered in elections to the point that Unionism had acquired a bad name, they claimed, and Kentucky at last had come to its Southern senses. What was now vital, members of the Kentucky bloc insisted, was a renewed Confederate presence in the state, empowering Kentuckians to rise up en masse.

Few high-ranking Confederates wanted to dismiss the bloc's "Kentucky dream" in the spring and summer of 1862, most notably Kentucky-born Jefferson Davis. Kentucky was a slave state whose natural home was the Confederacy. For such a state to cling to the Union willingly suggested unpleasant things about the sanctity of the Southern cause. Even had Davis wanted to ignore Kentucky, he would have been unable, for his closest aide, the martyred Sidney Johnston's son William Preston Johnston, virtually acted as a one-man clearinghouse and bandwagon for the Kentucky dreamers. Ironically, that dream meshed nicely with the agendas of other Confederates who increasingly distrusted Davis and argued that the administration needed to shift its emphasis from Virginia to the west to win the war. The Kentucky dream, of course, was a chimera, based more on the wishful thinking of distant exiles and the fratricidal politics of factious Richmond insiders than an accurate sounding of public opinion. Disaffection and anger with high-handed Federal authorities was widespread in Kentucky in 1862, but it did not translate automatically into disaffection. Kentuckians might complain, but there was no real evidence that legions of the state's young men were eager to don Confederate gray. Nonetheless, an increasing number of Confederate leaders dreamed the Kentucky dream as the spring of 1862 passed into summer—a fact that an ambitious and indeed increasingly fawning Davis supporter like Braxton Bragg could not fail to see.[17]

In the end, no one came down with a worse case of "Kentucky fever" than the man who would become the fourth and deciding factor in Braxton Bragg's strategic planning:, thirty-eight-year-old Maj. Gen. Edmund Kirby Smith.[18] A native Floridian, veteran of Mexico, less-than- successful West Point mathematics professor, and western Indian fighter with Sidney Johnston's 2nd Cavalry, the wide-eyed Kirby Smith first tasted fame in July 1861 when he "saved" the Confederate army at First Manassas with his brigade's timely arrival from the Shenandoah Valley and game fighting on the Confederate left. Glory was a taste he clearly enjoyed. Adored in Richmond for his gallantry and, better still, a heroic wound, "the Blucher of Manassas" for a time eclipsed even the newly dubbed "Stonewall" Jackson as the man of the hour for his service at the battle. Indeed, as late as 1865, his old friend and mentor Jefferson Davis still credited Kirby Smith more than the martyred Jackson for the Confederacy's first victory. Not surprisingly, the young hero was promoted to major general in March 1862 and sent to Knoxville to take command of the troubled Confederate Department of East Tennessee.[19]

Troubled East Tennessee hardly was a plum assignment for an egotist like Kirby Smith in search of more martial glory. The fallen Zollicoffer and the disgraced, drunken Crittenden had preceded him, and he approached the assignment with understandable foreboding. In Knoxville, the religiously devout Floridian encountered problems that might have driven a lesser man to drink as well. He had a 180-mile front to cover, from Cumberland Gap southwestward to Chattanooga. The topography was extremely mountainous, making communications and transportation a nightmare. Worse, upper East Tennessee was strongly Unionist, especially as one moved away from the towns and the vital East Tennessee and Virginia Railroad. Over the previous months regional Unionism had metamorphosed into outright rebellion against Confederate authority. Other East Tennesseans slipped into Kentucky nightly to enlist in Union regiments, especially after the Confederate Congress adopted conscription in April. Instead of operating in friendly territory, in other words, the general essentially commanded an army of occupation. Moreover, that army was weak. Desertion had continued after Logan's Cross Roads, and transfers to other commands weakened his force still more. As a result, Kirby Smith had at his disposal only what he called "a disorganized mob" of eight thousand undisciplined and badly armed troops, most of whom had enlisted for twelve months and were about to gladly leave the service if allowed. Many were sick, and others were less-than-eager Confederates who could not be trusted.

Like Zollicoffer, a bewildered Kirby Smith zigzagged from leniency to mass arrests and military trials. Strategically, he made the decision to concentrate on his right, at Cumberland Gap, which since April had been threatened by a Federal division commanded by an old friend, Brig. Gen. George W. Morgan. The approach of Ormsby Mitchel's division forced Kirby Smith to abandon the gap and shift men toward Chattanooga. As a result, Morgan occupied Cumberland Gap on June 18. The news only got worse; Kirby Smith next learned that Buell and the rest of his force were on the way east from Corinth.[20]

Frantically, the outgunned Kirby Smith begged for help. Although reluctant initially to weaken his own outnumbered army, Bragg finally agreed late on June 26 to send Maj. Gen. John P. McCown's division of about three thousand men to bolster Kirby Smith's defenses of the city. Bragg thoroughly despised McCown, originally a brigade commander in Earl Van Dorn's Army of the West, and wanted to be rid of him if anyone. Possibly, as Grady McWhiney maintains, sending McCown was also a test of the shift-to-Chattanooga strategy as well, for if the incompetent McCown and his undisciplined men could make such a journey successfully, surely it would be possible for the rest of the army to do the same. At any rate, traveling by railroad and looping far south of Buell's army, McCown's division arrived intact in Chattanooga on July 3—remarkable time under the circumstances.

Bragg, however, remained unable to make a final decision about the bulk of his army, and he kept changing his mind almost daily. Kirby Smith, in contrast, knew exactly what course Bragg should take and, sensing Bragg's inherent passivity and confusion, began lobbying aggressively for Bragg to attack Buell. On July 20, he bluntly wrote Bragg: "it is your time to strike at

Middle Ten."[21] Kirby Smith reiterated his call for help on July 24 after receiving word from Bragg "of the impossibility of entering Middle Tennessee from [his] present position. . . . Can you not leave a portion of your forces in observation in Mississippi and, shifting the main body to this department, take command in person? There is yet time for a brilliant summer campaign . . . with every prospect of regaining possession of Middle Tennessee and possibly Kentucky." In such an event, Kirby Smith promised his full cooperation, and even volunteered to "cheerfully place my command under you subject to your orders." There was an ominous note for the future, however, that Bragg should have noticed. Complaining that Bragg's assistant adjutant general had requested weekly reports as if Kirby Smith was under his command, the younger general took pains to remind Bragg that "this department was organized independent of the Army of the West and by orders reports directly to the War Department." Despite his politic assurances, Kirby Smith rather liked independent command.[22]

What Kirby Smith could not know during his barrage of communications was that at last, Bragg had come to the same conclusion. To be sure, Bragg thus far had, in James McDonough's words, "seemed a Confederate Hamlet, unable to make up his mind."[23] Kirby Smith's desperate appeal of the twentieth, however, coupled with the promise of a "brilliant" late summer, seemed to leave little recourse. Intense and even inflexible decisiveness often follows the hopeless vacillation of depression among those suffering from personality disorders, and certainly would fit if Bragg were so afflicted. At any rate, he cast the proverbial die; Bragg finally would act by doing what Kirby Smith, the dashing Davis favorite, wanted him to do. On July 21, Bragg tersely telegraphed the president: "Will move immediately to Chattanooga in force and advance from there. Forward movement from here in force not practicable. Will leave this line defended." A day later, Bragg added a bit more: "Obstacles in front connected with danger to Chattanooga induce a change in base. Fully impressed with great importance of that line, am moving to East Tennessee. Produce rapid offensive from there following the consternation of our cavalry. Leave this State amply protected by Van Dorn at Vicksburg and Price here." Bragg referred to Major Generals Sterling "Pap" Price and Earl Van Dorn, whose two armies of roughly sixteen thousand troops each were to initially hold Mississippi and then jointly advance into western Tennessee in a complementary thrust on Bragg's left flank.[24]

Bragg confided in Beauregard rather than Jefferson Davis. He obsequiously asked the Creole for advice, still playing the subordinate and reluctant successor, although it seems more likely that he was more interested in rationalizing his decision and receiving validation for it. Most important in his conclusion, Bragg maintained, was the precariousness of Kirby Smith's position. "Smith is so weak as to give me great uneasiness for the safety of his line," he explained, "to lose which would be a great disaster." Besides that, moving against Halleck at Corinth was next to impossible. "To aid him at all from here necessarily renders me too weak for the offensive against Halleck. . . . With the country between us reduced almost to a desert by two armies and a drouth of two months, neither of us could well advance in the absence of rail transportation. It seemed to me then I was reduced to the defensive altogether or to the move I am making." What made such a move possible in the first place, Bragg added, was the success of cavalrymen such as Forrest and Kentuckian John Hunt Morgan against Buell's badly exposed supply line. "The Memphis and Charleston road has been kept cut," he wrote, "so they have no use of it and have at length given it up. Before they can know my movement I shall be in front of Buell at Chattanooga, and by·cutting off his transportation may have him in a tight place. . . . Our cavalry is paving the way for me in Middle Tennessee and Kentucky."[25]

So it was that Kirby Smith's desperate appeal of the twenty-fourth reached Bragg not in Tupelo, but rather in Montgomery, Alabama, with Bragg already riding the rails to the rescue. It was one of the boldest moments of the war. Starting on July 23 along the same circuitous, rickety, 776-mile-long path that McCown's division had traveled—which involved six separate railroads and a ferry ride across Mobile Bay—Bragg moved five thousand infantrymen per day via Mobile and Montgomery to Chattanooga. The garrison Bragg had left at Mobile spearheaded the movement. Supply wagons, cavalry, and artillery meanwhile started on overland roads across Alabama to Chattanooga via Rome, Georgia. The first of Bragg's units arrived in Chattanooga on July 27, with part of the army still in Tupelo waiting its turn. Within two weeks, the rickety Confederate railroad network incredibly had moved thirty thousand infantrymen, and in so doing altered the direction of the war.

For the men of the Army of the Mississippi, the rail transfer brought one memorable scene after another. All along the way, the soldiers were greeted with cheers, flowers, delicious food, and cold water, often supplied by pretty young women. Thirsty and enterprising soldiers also obtained burning swigs of "tanglefoot." As the army passed from Alabama into Georgia, the cheering reached a crescendo. Because of such support, not to mention the fact it at last was moving forward again instead of retreating or rotting in Tupelo, the army's once low morale skyrocketed.[26] William J. Rogers of the 13th Tennessee Infantry remembered the "women, young and old" of Mississippi "waving their handkerchiefs, wishing us success. Even the Negroes came from their work in the cornfields to see us pass." In Atlanta "women stood on the platforms by hundreds; with fruit and provisions for the soldiers."[27]

Benedict J. Semmes of the 154th Senior Tennessee remembered Mississippi less benignly but expressed only newfound devotion for Georgia. "Old Georgia beat all," he exuded, ". . . from West Point to Chattanooga was a perfect ovation, and the men were almost wild with delight, and some, I'm sorry to say, with Georgia peach brandy." His brothers in arms, he assured his wife, were now "eager to meet the Yankees, and I have no fears of the result . . . they all say that they will never forget the people of Georgia and will fight as cheerfully to defend them, as they would their own homes."[28]

Late July brought heady days indeed for the western Confederacy. While Bragg's army entrained for Chattanooga, another signal event of consequence concluded when the darling of the Kentucky bloc, Confederate colonel John Hunt Morgan, ended his daring First Kentucky Raid deep into Buell's rear. A Lexington businessman and Mexican War veteran, the dashing Morgan enlisted in the Confederate army in September 1861 and fought at Shiloh as commander of Kentucky volunteer cavalry. For many secessionists, Morgan thereafter came to personify the hope of a Confederate Kentucky. One Louisianian, for example, praising the Kentucky horseman as the "Marion of the war," assured his correspondent that "a few thousands of such men as his would regain us Kentucky and Tennessee."[29] His reputation grew still more when, on the Fourth of July, 1862, at Kirby Smith's urging, Morgan left Knoxville with close to nine hundred men. In three weeks he boldly swept through the Kentucky bluegrass, a feat that in many ways surpassed J. E. B. Stuart's celebrated "Ride around McClellan" and the Army of the Potomac the previous spring. Morgan reported that he had captured some twelve hundred Federals, whom he paroled, acquired several hundred horses, and destroyed massive quantities of Yankee supplies. He further succeeded in frightening Kentucky's Union military government.[30] Panic followed in Morgan's wake, and Washington received so many frantic appeals for help that Lincoln complained to Halleck that "they are having a stampede in Kentucky." Ultimately, thousands of troops were pulled from the front lines and detailed to protect important positions from further incursions.[31]

Morgan's dazzling success, coming just at the moment it did, had a crucial impact on Confederate military planning. "The Jeb Stuart of the West" insisted in his reports that the Kentucky dream was real, for not only had his men been cheered and supported all along the way, but great numbers of recruits had come forward as well. "The whole country can be secured, and 25,000 or 30,000 men will join you at once" he flatly promised Kirby Smith.[32] Such dispatches, coupled with Bragg's bold movement to Chattanooga, delighted and encouraged many Kentucky dreamers. General Robert E. Lee, for one, wrote the president that "if the impression made by Morgan in Kentucky could be confirmed by a strong infantry force, it would have the happiest effect."[33] No one, however, was more excited than Kirby Smith himself, who now began to consider doing just what Lee and Morgan had suggested: invade Kentucky.

While Kirby Smith pondered Kentucky's siren song of glory, Bragg's army meanwhile continued trickling into Chattanooga. Traveling from his Knoxville headquarters, Kirby Smith finally met with Bragg on the afternoon of July 31. Repairing to Bragg's hotel room/headquarters and pinning a map of Tennessee and Kentucky to the wall, they worked until after midnight drafting a campaign designed to drive Union forces from Tennessee.[34]

Kirby Smith would move quickly against Morgan's Federal forces at Cumberland Gap while Bragg waited for his artillery and wagons to arrive in Chattanooga. If Kirby Smith was successful in eliminating the Yankee menace at the gap, "our entire force will then be thrown into Middle Tennessee with the fairest prospect of cutting off General Buell." Along the way, the Confederates would pick up recruits and augment their strength, for "the feeling in Middle Tennessee and Kentucky is represented by Forrest and Morgan to have become intensely hostile to the enemy, and nothing is wanted but arms and support to bring the people into our ranks." If Grant during the interim reinforced Buell from northern Mississippi, so much the better, for then Price and Van Dorn could "strike and clear West Tennessee of any force that can be left to hold it." The reverses of 1862 were about to be avenged. [35]

Bragg and Kirby Smith's planned campaign embodied boldness but also contained serious flaws, as historian Thomas Connelly pointed out. Success depended on absolute cooperation and precise timing, qualifications often sought but rarely realized in Civil War armies. Kirby Smith had to seize Cumberland Gap and within two weeks, while Price and Van Dorn had to move at just the right moment to neutralize any Federal forces coming to Buell's aid from the west. Kirby Smith and Bragg then had to unite their outgunned armies before confronting Buell. Any number of difficulties along the way, starting with a spirited Federal defense of Cumberland Gap, would derail the campaign before it began.[36]

As it was, nothing went as planned anyway. Confusion and second thoughts developed almost immediately. Bragg's communications with Richmond clearly demonstrate that he had agreed to a campaign that first focused on defeating Buell in Middle Tennessee and liberating that state. The occupation of Kentucky was the desirable second step, but it could only be accomplished after first destroying the northern invaders of the Volunteer State. Hardly was the ink dry on the orders, however, before Bragg's old indecisiveness began to set in. Pressure from President Davis added to his distress. Upon arriving in Chattanooga, Bragg had written Davis a fawning letter ostensibly condemning the president's critics in the Alabama press, but clearly more intended to further ingratiate the general with the man with whom he once had bitterly quarreled. Replying to his "personal friend" on August 5, Davis made his desires for the impending campaign crystal clear. A signal victory in Tennessee would only be the first step in the successful campaign he so desperately needed to shore up his administration. "Buell being crushed," Davis wrote, "if your means enable you to march rapidly on Nashville, Grant will be compelled to retire to the river, abandoning Middle and East Tennessee, or to follow you. His Government will probably require the latter course, and if so you may have a complete conquest over the enemy, involving the liberation of Tennessee and Kentucky."[37]

Davis inadvertently played another role in reorienting Bragg's gaze northward toward the bluegrass, through the complicated system of military departments he had created. Although Bragg clearly was the senior officer and the commander of the larger force in East Tennessee, he and Kirby Smith officially were equals as departmental commanders under the system then existing in the Confederacy. Indeed, a recent reshuffling of departmental responsibilities had placed Chattanooga in Kirby Smith's Department of East Tennessee, an embarrassing situation that essentially forced Bragg into the uncomfortable position of being a guest in another general's bailiwick. Thus, despite repeated promises of cooperation, the two armies remained independent, with neither general given the authority to issue orders to the other. Only when the two armies joined together would the senior officer, Bragg, assume overall command and Kirby Smith revert to being his subordinate. Until that day, Davis blithely assured Bragg, friendly cooperation alone would eliminate any confusion or cross-purposes.[38]

While the once again equivocal Bragg was having second thoughts, Kirby Smith quickly abandoned the agreement altogether. The Kentucky dream beguiled him, and Morgan's escapades indicated that the time was ripe to establish a Confederate presence in Kentucky. Any resulting glory would be his and not Bragg's; it would be Manassas all over again, only better. Thus, Kirby Smith barely had returned to Knoxville when he backed away from the agreement. At first he dishonestly hid his intentions from Bragg, requesting and receiving reinforcements for the move on Cumberland Gap in the form of two of the better brigades in Bragg's army.

Tennessean Preston Smith commanded one. A Memphis attorney with no military experience before the war, the dark-haired Smith originally had commanded the 154th Senior Tennessee, whose curious name was a carryover from its origins as a Memphis militia outfit. Wounded at Shiloh, the thirty-eight-year-old Smith had recovered sufficiently to take a brigade command as "Acting Brigadier General."[39]

More promising still was the other brigade commander temporarily joining Kirby Smith, Brig. Gen. Patrick Ronayne Cleburne. Born in Ireland the son of a Protestant physician, Cleburne and his family slipped into poverty after the father's death. Intending to follow his father's profession, he apprenticed to a neighboring doctor in hopes of gaining enough practical experience to enter medical school. His plan failed, however, when he was rejected because of his inability to read Latin. Dejected and convinced that he had dishonored his kin, Cleburne at age seventeen concealed his gentle birth and joined the British army as a common foot soldier, serving over three years at home in Ireland and rising to the rank of corporal before purchasing a discharge. He then joined his family, and millions of other Irishmen, on a journey to America in hopes of a better life. Cleburne ended up in Arkansas, where he worked as a druggist, read law, and entered Democratic party politics at the elbow of his friend, future Confederate general Thomas C. Hindman. When Arkansas seceded, Cleburne followed out of loyalty to his friends and neighbors. His popularity, political connections, and military

Figure 2.1. Gen. Patrick R. Cleburne. Photograph courtesy of Library of Congress, LC-USZ62-12995.

background helped him gain the command of first a company and soon the 1st (later 15th) Arkansas. He commanded a brigade at Shiloh, where he demonstrated the aggressiveness, determination, and personal courage that would mark him as one of the great commanders in gray. His superiors, particularly Hardee, regarded the shy, tireless Irishman highly, and Kirby Smith was clearly pleased to get him.[40]

Reinforced with two of Bragg's best and most experienced brigades, Kirby Smith made his next move. On August 9 he wrote a letter in which he politely informed Bragg that he thought it might be best to scrap the Chattanooga agreement. The excuse was Morgan's alleged strength at Cumberland Gap. "I understand," he wrote, "General Morgan has at Cumberland Gap nearly a month's supply of provisions. If this be true the reduction of the place would be a matter of more time than I presume you are willing I should take." There was, however, a silver lining, he assured Bragg. "As my move to Lexington, Ky., would effectually invest Morgan, and would be attended with other most brilliant results in my judgment, I suggest my being allowed to take that course, if I find the speedy reduction of the Gap an impracticable thing."[41] Having agreed to concentrate on Tennessee only a week earlier, Kirby Smith now advocated abandoning the plan, brushing aside Morgan's division at the gap, and storming into the heart of Kentucky, Buell be damned.

Kirby Smith's letter left Bragg clearly discomfited, as his tortured reply of August 10 reveals. Bragg knew that he lacked the authority to make Kirby Smith hew to the original strategy even if he wanted to do so. Moreover, there was Davis's letter stressing the equal importance of Kentucky. Thus, with guarded optimism, Bragg expressed an initial willingness to support Kirby Smith's sudden change in strategy, even if it meant taking a secondary role. Indeed, acknowledging reports of growing pro-Confederate support in Kentucky, Bragg claimed that given the choice of marching on Nashville or Lexington, "my inclination is now for the latter."

The more he wrote, however, the more Bragg began to sound like a man trying to talk himself into accepting a dangerous dare while simultaneously hoping that the challenge would be withdrawn. Dismissing any threat from Nelson, Bragg went on to warn Kirby Smith that it would take him at least a week to get his army across the Tennessee River. During that time he recommended that Kirby Smith try to capture the gap as originally agreed upon, for "I do not credit the amount of Morgan's supplies and have confidence in his timidity." In the event that Kirby Smith crossed the border, Bragg added, going all the way to Lexington was too dangerous, for "it would be unadvisable . . . for you to move far into Kentucky, leaving Morgan in your rear, until I am able to fully engage Buell and his forces on your left." However, Bragg's mood changed yet again, and he closed on a hopeful note: "Van Dorn and Price will advance simultaneously with us from Mississippi on West Tennessee, and I trust we may all unite in Ohio."[42]

Bragg's stream-of-consciousness reply to Kirby Smith is striking for its indecisiveness, its passivity, and the author's abrupt moment-to-moment mood swings. In one letter Bragg expressed a previously unspoken inclination for invading Kentucky, suggested that Kirby Smith stick to the original Tennessee-centered plan by investing Cumberland Gap after all, and then figuratively crossed the Ohio River with Van Dorn and Price to invade the Union! In the end, he promised to do whatever Kirby Smith wished. As an army commander, Bragg clearly had no idea what to do except to attack some Federal army somewhere. Consciously or unconsciously, Bragg again had surrendered the initiative of choosing whom to attack to the junior officer, allowing Kirby Smith to draw him into Kentucky like the long tail of a small kite, just as he had been drawn to East Tennessee in the first place. At some juncture, he might well wind up facing Buell alone on the field of battle, weakened without the brigades sent to Knoxville, even as Buell's army was swelling with new recruits. It was a recipe for defeat.[43]

One wonders, what might have happened if Bragg had tried to pull rank and demanded Kirby Smith's compliance with the Chattanooga agreement? It might have worked. Historian Steven Woodworth has described Kirby Smith during the period in question as "erratic and illogical," comparing himself to Napoleon in one breath and asking to be made subordinate to some superior officer in the next.[44] He also appears to have wondered if he had pushed Bragg too far. Writing from Knoxville on August 11, Kirby Smith suddenly reversed himself, stressing his willingness to serve under Bragg and his readiness "to move at once with my troops to carry out the plan agreed upon between us." With persistence, Bragg might have secured command control after all.

Firmness, however, was not Braxton Bragg's strong suit at the time. Kirby Smith's backtracking quickly ended anyway when Bragg's August 10 letter arrived, full, as it was, with all the acquiescence the Floridian needed. Again taking pen in hand, a delighted Kirby Smith prepared his second dispatch of the day, this time promising "to move as quickly as possible and take position in Morgan's rear, where I expect to be by next Sunday evening. Should he have evacuated the Gap I will of course follow him and fight him wherever I can find him. Otherwise I will remain in his rear until you think I can move rapidly upon Lexington." He was confident that the latter was the proper course, and stressed that "every moment we delay will lessen the great advantages to be gained by an immediate move upon Lexington." Invading Kentucky had become a matter of when, not if.[45]

Kirby Smith still was not satisfied. Instead of waiting in mountainous eastern Kentucky for Bragg to get moving, he bypassed the reluctant Bragg and wrote directly to Jefferson Davis in a blatant attempt to get permission to march on Lexington. Kirby Smith had played the sycophant with Davis since his days in the old army and now he called in his favors. Stressing once again the reported strength of Morgan's position, he attempted to justify entering Kentucky. If Morgan retreated into Kentucky, Kirby Smith argued, he should of course follow. But if Morgan held fast in Cumberland Gap, then he must move into Kentucky anyway, for such an invasion "is the boldest and most brilliant in its results; it effectually invests Morgan, while it turns Buell's communications; and if Kentucky be as ripe . . . as all representations indicate it must involve the abandonment of Middle Tennessee by the Federals. Politically, now is the time to strike at Kentucky. Delay loses the golden opportunity, and fall finds her people powerless and a large army between us and the waters of the Ohio." Kentucky could be added permanently to the Confederacy, in other words, if the president would make Bragg support the younger general. Bragg's ambivalent August 10 letter apparently arrived while Kirby Smith was in the midst of writing to Davis, for he closed with the rather misleading statement that he had just heard from Bragg, who "sanctions my move on Kentucky," although "the delay which it necessitates is to be regretted."[46]

Unaware of Kirby Smith's duplicitous scheming, Bragg earnestly made ready to hold up his part of the new bargain, at least as he understood it. He sent orders to Van Dorn and Price in Mississippi "to threaten West Tennessee with about 25,000 men, thus holding the force now here or retaking the country." Bragg gave the two generals considerable leeway in methods and timing, as he would be occupied far from the scene and thus unable to take a more supervisory role. Surprisingly, considering his own dilemma, he committed the same blunder that Davis had made in East Tennessee: allowing the two generals to act independently until they joined together at their discretion under Van Dorn's overall command. Vainglorious and unimaginative, Van Dorn unfortunately was yet another of President Davis's favorites, whereas the equally vain but more solid Price was much the opposite. The two generals began to argue almost immediately on the proper course of action, with Price advising movement toward Nashville, as Bragg wanted, and Van Dorn, absolutely uninterested in assisting Bragg, replicating Kirby Smith with his insistence on a Kentucky invasion. The end result would be two disastrous Confederate defeats, at Iuka in mid-September and at nearby Corinth in early October. Aside from one day skirting along just north of the Tennessee border on the march to Corinth, the two armies would never leave Mississippi. Worse yet, they would fail to prevent reinforcements from reaching Buell.[47]

Bragg also made ready to put his own army into motion. All he asked of Kirby Smith was time. "On Friday I shall probably commence crossing the river," he wrote, "by which I shall draw their attention away from you. . . . I shall not desire to hold you longer in check than will enable me to get in motion to support you. In the mean time I hope you will bring Morgan to terms." Even that delay rankled Kirby Smith, who complained: "General Bragg does not approve of a move into Kentucky, leaving Morgan still at the Gap, until his own command is ready to move against Buell. This delay of two weeks might lose the golden opportunity of marching on Lexington."[48]

Kirby Smith's long-awaited drive toward Cumberland Gap finally began on the night of August 13. Marching on different roads, all steep and narrow, his four divisions started across the imposing Cumberland Mountains. The heat grew oppressive and the roads so treacherous that several men died slipping down the sides of ridges. Most of the locals were Unionists, many of whom took to bushwhacking the weary Confederates. Yet morale climbed, with the army exhibiting almost a missionary, hymn-singing zeal to liberate Kentucky for God and the Confederacy.[49]

According to plan, the columns converged at Barboursville, squarely in Morgan's rear, on the eighteenth. Famished soldiers feasted there on captured "bacon, salt, coffee, . . . corn and beef." William J. Rogers of the 13th Tennessee also described a bounty of captured Federal equipment, including "tents, overcoats, and cooking vessels of every description, and axes, spades, shovels, pick-axes, crosscut saws, & ordinance stores, cartridge boxes, and some guns and bayonets."[50]

Kirby Smith boasted to his wife, but he sang a different, more cheerless tune when writing to Davis and Bragg. Morgan, he claimed, not only had enough supplies to hold out at least a month, but his engineers had "rendered his position . . . impregnable." In contrast, he complained dishonestly that the area around Barboursville could not feed his army, as it was "almost completely drained of supplies," an assertion that would have come as a sur-

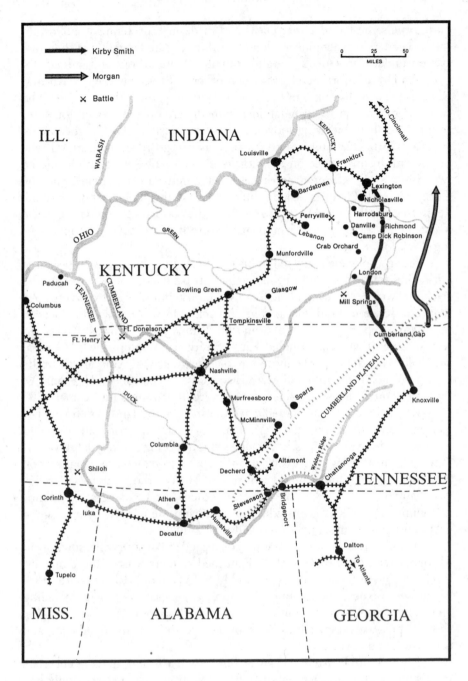

Map 2.1. Kirby Smith's Kentucky invasion route, August 1862.

prise to men with full bellies like William Rogers. The roads were worse than expected as well. Accordingly, Kirby Smith continued, he could not wait as Bragg wished. He either had to retreat back into Tennessee or push on to Lexington. "The former course," he reasoned, "will be too disastrous to our cause in Kentucky. . . . I have therefore decided to advance as soon as possible upon Lexington." Although he believed Kentuckians would rise up en masse to support him, Kirby Smith still asked for additional reinforcements—both from Humphrey Marshall, chomping at the bit to reenter Kentucky from the east, and from Bragg as well. Having left Bragg on his own to fend off Buell—he boasted of the "advantageous diversion" his Kentucky campaign provided—Kirby Smith now incredibly asked Bragg to further weaken his army by sending him more soldiers. Indeed, the Floridian encouraged Bragg "to make this the line of operations, so that you may act with our forces concentrated."[51]

· Kirby Smith played a thoroughly dishonest game. Having decided in Knoxville to march past the gap and straight on to Lexington, he deceptively withheld his full intentions from his president and his colleague until arriving at Barboursville, where he then exaggerated his difficulties to make it appear that circumstance rather than his burning ambition to accomplish something "brilliant" forced him on to Kentucky. Moreover, the duplicitous general pressured Bragg to dispatch even more reinforcements, which would have left Bragg with only enough men to serve as a shield against Buell in the rear while Kirby Smith commanded the lion's share of Confederate arms on a march to glory.[52]

Comparing himself alternately to Cortés, Hannibal, and Moses, Kirby Smith led his army forward toward the promised land that was the Kentucky Bluegrass. Staggered to learn that an unforeseen Federal force was blocking the main road to Lexington at Big Hill, south of Richmond, he initially blanched but then decided to attack. On August 30, Pat Cleburne's division, consisting of his brigade as well as Preston Smith's, spearheaded the assault. Confronting two Union brigades consisting largely of raw recruits, Kirby Smith swept the Federals from the field. The Battle of Richmond would be the most lopsided Confederate victory of the war, as Kirby Smith's men inflicted casualties so staggering that entire Union brigades ceased to exist. Once in Richmond, the triumphant Confederates feasted on captured stores, donned Federal-issue clothing, and exchanged their antiquated arms for modern Enfield and Springfield rifles. Confederate batteries appropriated nine guns.[53]

With their new weapons and wearing light blue Federal pants, and in some cases dark blue Federal coats as well, Cleburne's veterans looked particularly distinctive. That was appropriate, for the key to Confederate success at Richmond was the fighting prowess of those men borrowed from Bragg's army. Largely Shiloh veterans, Cleburne's Arkansans, Tennesseans, and Texans had made quick work of the game but unprepared and poorly led

Yankees they encountered south of Richmond. Not insignificant was the skill of their commander either, for it was at Richmond that Cleburne first fully revealed the brilliance that in time would earn him Jefferson Davis's sobriquet "Stonewall of the West." As his biographer noted, Cleburne had matured significantly since Shiloh, where, like Bragg, his every response was to attack. At Richmond, he innovatively used handpicked sharpshooters against Union guns, managed his own artillery with skill, reacted quickly to Federal movements, and counterattacked at precisely the right moment. So well arranged and prepared were his men that even when he fell, a minié ball smashing through his cheek and jaw, Preston Smith could take over command without any loss of momentum. In many respects, Richmond was as much Cleburne's triumph as it was Kirby Smith's, and Cleburne was there thanks to Bragg's willingness to cooperate.[54]

From Richmond, the army pushed on to Lexington. That city reacted with joy. William Rogers remembered that "the Rebel flag was at every door in town and every child was cheering for Jeff Davis."[55] Another of Preston Smith's men recalled that "the balconies, house tops, and windows in fact every place available for view was filled with people cheering and waving handkerchiefs while we marched through the streets as proud as peacocks to the tunes of 'Dixie' and 'The Girl I Left Behind Me.'" A soldier of the 48th Tennessee recollected free buttermilk and the clamor of "church-bells, town-bells, dinner-bells, sheep-bells, cow-bells, blacksmiths' anvils and triangles."[56] In Frankfort and as far west as Shelbyville, the reaction was more of the same. The Kentucky Bluegrass had been delivered. Few worried at the time that the crowds largely had been composed of women and children, many of the men significantly remaining indoors peeping out from behind their curtains.[57]

Fully convinced now that, like an Old Testament warrior, he was God's agent—"his hand has directed me in this movement"—an elated Kirby Smith described the scene to his wife: "My entrance into the blue grass region of Kentucky has been a perfect ovation. Old and young have flocked to me and with love in their eyes have thanked God for their deliverance from persecution." Better still, the Federals had fallen back all the way across the Ohio River to Cincinnati, leaving Louisville as the Union's only bastion in the Bluegrass. He incorrectly added that "recruits are flocking to me by thousands."[58]

Yet over the next few days a strange and sudden reversal occurred as Kirby Smith abandoned the offensive and mentally dug in. Several reasons seem to account for his sudden inertia and loss of will. Clearly he had never considered what to do once Lexington was in his hands. At various times over the next several weeks he proposed moving south toward Bragg, north to the Ohio River opposite Cincinnati, or back toward Cumberland Gap to protect his rear from Morgan. In the end, he did none of them. Instead, reports of Federal concentrations in Louisville and Cincinnati, rumored to include Grant's Fort Donelson and Shiloh veterans, frightened him so much that he spread his men out from near the gap to the Ohio in an effort to meet any contingency, as well as to collect and protect badly needed supplies. Once on the defensive, just as he had done earlier in the summer in Chattanooga, he began issuing frequent and fevered requests for reinforcements as well as for arms for Kentuckians willing to fight for the Confederacy.[59]

There were depressingly few of the latter, however, which must have given him pause as well. Despite his initial glowing accounts of enthusiasm, recruiting was going more slowly than anticipated. "The Kentuckians are slow and backward in rallying to our standard," he finally admitted to Bragg. "Their hearts are evidently with us, but their blue-grass and fat-grass are against us." Not only were arms required, he reasoned, but a Confederate state government and the presence of John C. Breckinridge and his Kentucky brigade were necessary as well if the Confederacy hoped to counter months of Federal occupation and recruit Kentuckians. All that would take time.[60] As a result, the recently aggressive general now counseled his subordinates to act with "great caution. . . . The general commanding hopes you fully appreciate the great importance of avoiding any reverse to our arms at this critical juncture."[61]

In the end, ensconced in Lexington amid the applause, Kirby Smith again shifted the responsibility for his survival to Bragg. Like a spoiled child in trouble demanding rescue from his father, he expected Bragg to extricate him from his difficulties, just as he had in July. "Unless . . . you can either speedily move your column in this direction or make with me a combined attack on Louisville before all Grant's army arrives there," he told Bragg in tones reminiscent of earlier dispatches, "I shall be compelled to fall back upon you for support. Louisville is in my opinion the great point to be arrived at."[62]

At that moment, Bragg again was on his way to Kirby Smith's rescue. Unfortunately, Buell had taken to the road as well. It was anyone's guess as to which army would arrive first.

3

THE ENEMY IS BEFORE YOU

IN THE SUMMER OF 1862, 1ST LT. HARRISON MILLARD MAY HAVE been the most contented soldier in the Union army. Normally a regular assigned to the 19th U.S. Infantry, Millard had left his regiment to serve as Brig. Gen. Lovell H. Rousseau's aide-de-camp and division inspector in garrisoned Huntsville, Alabama, after Rousseau superseded Ormsby Mitchel. Huntsville, according to Millard, was "a delightful and sympathetic little city, with a large stream of the purest water running through its center." Fully expecting to occupy the lovely borough for several more months, he happily sent to New York for his wife to join him there. The young couple moved into "a pretty little frame house which had been abandoned by its frightened owner, with all its nice furniture—even to linen and spoons—on our occupation of the town." Millard obtained a cow and hired a cook from among "the hundreds of homeless negroes floating about." A blissful month passed.

Without warning, the Millards' idyll came to a sudden and crashing end. Shocking word came that the Confederate army in Chattanooga, having only recently arrived there, was again on the move, heading north and threatening to cut the Federal army's supply lines. Millard told his wife that she had two hours to pack her trunk and catch the train to Nashville, for the army was abandoning Huntsville. "She said," he remembered, "that it was absolutely impossible, so I gave her the choice of either doing it or being left behind." Two hours later, packed trunk in hand, Mrs. Millard joined hundreds of Alabama Unionists who fled toward the presumed safety of the Tennessee capital. Her husband, along with the rest of Don Carlos Buell's army, soon followed.[1]

While Braxton Bragg's Confederate Army of the Mississippi daringly shifted its base to Chattanooga in late July 1862, Buell's Federal Army of the Ohio continued trudging toward the east, down the sun-baked roads shrouded in stifling dust clouds that ran through drought-ravaged northern Alabama and Middle Tennessee. Progress slowed to a crawl as the army fell victim to the

Figure 3.1. Maj. Gen. Thomas L. Crittenden. Photograph courtesy U.S. Army Military History Institute.

wearisome dry spell, rivers falling so fast as to endanger navigation and cut off waterborne supplies, inadequate and broken down railroads that failed to make up the difference, unfriendly partisans whose numbers swelled with every passing day, and, according to some bitter men, the willful foot-dragging of its aloof commander. Whatever the reason, Buell's Chattanooga campaign was fast proving a major disappointment to all involved.

To be sure, by mid-July two of Buell's divisions stood poised at the gates of Chattanooga. One was commanded by Maj. Gen. Thomas L. Crittenden, another son of the Kentucky senator and younger brother of the defeated Confederate commander at Mill Springs. A lawyer and businessman before the war, the rail-thin, long-haired Crittenden served ably in Mexico as an aide to Zachary Taylor before taking command of the 3rd Kentucky Volunteers, a regiment that also included John C. Breckinridge as its major. Another friend from the old days in Mexico was Jefferson Davis. A committed Unionist nonetheless, Crittenden assumed command of the Kentucky State Guard after the flight of Simon B. Buckner and the organization's second in command, Crittenden's brother George. For Thomas Crittenden, the conflict truly became the proverbial war of "brother against brother," a tragic situation seemingly reflected in his downcast, hound-dog features.[2]

Portly Maj. Gen. Alexander McCook led the other division in Buell's van and exercised overall command in the area due to seniority. One of Ohio's

Figure 3.2. "The Fighting McCooks" by Charles T. Webber. Alexander McCook is seated to the left of the painting. Wearing a hat, Daniel McCook reclines to his brother's left. To his left, Robert McCook stands behind the family patriarch. Photograph courtesy Ohio Historical Society.

celebrated seventeen "Fighting McCooks," he graduated from West Point in the class of 1852, it having taken him five years to complete his four-year studies. With frontier experience against the Indians as well as a stint as an exacting and unpopular instructor at his alma mater, he possessed valuable military experience as a regular when the war began. Nicknamed "Gutsy" at the Point for his ample waistline rather than his mettle, the inevitable result of an appetite for good food and wine, he rose quickly from colonel to major general, having fought in the east at First Manassas as well as in the west.[3] After the war, a relative described him as "enthusiastic, emphatic, impulsive with a heart of gold . . . his reading was mostly confined to books on military tactics. He was loyal and outspoken and his characteristics created strong friendships as well as strong enmities."[4]

Crittenden and McCook's men occupied the vital railroad junction at Stevenson, Alabama, only twenty miles from Chattanooga, and moved on to the mouth of Battle Creek, only nine miles from the important Nashville and Chattanooga Railroad station at Bridgeport, Alabama. The roughly nine thousand men in the command dug in there, and one Federal wrote home that "we are fortyfying this point as though we intended to hold it forever."[5] Unfortunately for the Union cause, the rest of Buell's diverted army remained far to the rear, spread over a range of more than a hundred miles in northern Alabama and southern Tennessee. Instead of driving on Chattanooga, those soldiers in the rear areas of Buell's command spent their days repairing and guarding the railroads, milling wood for bridges, building boats to serve as pontoons, and searching for something to eat and drink. Guerrilla bands constantly slowed their work, forcing Buell to detach increasing numbers of troops to build and man fortifications.

His famished army groused all the while, and morale deteriorated further as rations grew scarcer the longer the merciless summer dragged on. Widespread foraging off local civilians offset poor supply only to an extent, for even in a good year the region offered more cotton than foodstuffs, and 1862 was the second poor year in a row insofar as agriculture was concerned. Indeed, an Alabama Unionist later identified 1862 as the worst season he had seen in his forty-five years of residence. Moreover, Mitchel's men, with the encouragement of their division commander, already had taken large quantities of what food there was by the time Buell's main force moved in. What remained available came with inflated prices approaching 300 percent.

Most galling of all to his soldiers, Buell and like-minded subordinates stringently prohibited foraging, seeing it as detrimental to discipline as well as counterproductive in terms of winning the hearts and minds of the Southern people. Private property must be protected, even if it meant surviving on half-rations. His bitter men, aware that Federal troops operating elsewhere had permission to forage at will and more, defiantly ignored him.[6] "The Secesh farmers were loth to give up their produce, and grumbled considerably" Capt. J. H. Putnam of the 31st Ohio Infantry wrote, "but Uncle Sam's boys were not going to starve in a land of plenty, and it was taken."[7]

Increasingly, as Putnam's comments suggest, the war in northern Alabama also grew ugly. As elsewhere in 1862, an eye for an eye mentality crystallized into an escalating cycle of depredations and reprisals, many Federals no doubt symbolically defying their increasingly despised commander as well as punishing recalcitrant southerners. A particularly nasty incident had occurred in May when troops commanded by Col. John Basil Turchin, a Russian émigré and former colonel of the Tsar's imperial guard, went on a rampage in Athens, Alabama, raping African-American women and destroying property in ostensible retaliation for repeated guerrilla attacks. Witnesses testified that the Russian colonel vocally encouraged his men to sack Athens. Such behavior may have been acceptable along the Russo-Finnish border, where Turchin once served, but it was decidedly unwelcome in Buell's department. After General Mitchel, the division commander, slapped Turchin on the wrist, Buell relieved the Russian and had him court-martialed—punishment that only further infuriated several northern newspapers and a rank-and-file supportive of Turchin's hard-war doctrine.

Although Buell disciplined and repudiated Turchin, the area continued to seethe. On August 6, Confederate guerrillas finally retaliated for the sack of Athens, killing the popular Brig. Gen. Robert L. McCook, Alexander McCook's older brother, as he rode past in an ambulance.[8] The thirst for vengeance seized Robert McCook's brigade—particularly his old regiment, the predominantly German 9th Ohio Infantry. According to Captain Putnam: "fury was depicted upon every countenance, and revenge upon every lip . . . the 9th Ohio set about immediately executing their threat of vengeance. Seventeen men were shot and hung, and the smoke of twenty burning houses was plainly visible before the scene of blood and desolation." With that and similar retaliatory incidents, Buell's "soft" policy of conciliation all but evaporated into thin air—almost as quickly as the area's few remaining water holes.[9]

Buell's problems multiplied exponentially. In addition to local guerrillas, the long shadows of Nathan Bedford Forrest and John Hunt Morgan fell more and more across Buell's tenuous but increasingly vital overland supply lines as summer deepened. Every new exploit seemed more appalling than the last. On July 13, even as Morgan's men were galloping headlong through Kentucky, Forrest captured Buell's outpost at Murfreesboro, Tennessee. Forrest took the fourteen-hundred-man garrison prisoner, burned the depot and a nearby bridge, tore up the branch line that ran from the town to the main trunk of the just-reopened Nashville and Chattanooga line, and briefly threatened Nashville itself. Forrest also captured two hundred thousand rations at Murfreesboro, forcing Buell to put his men on half-rations again the next day. Despite the arrival in Murfreesboro of Bull Nelson's division from Alabama, Forrest struck again on the eighteenth, destroying two railroad bridges between McMinnville and Nashville, thus delaying the arrival of badly needed supplies for yet another ten days.[10]

Cavalry raids, destructive as they were, paled in comparison to the unexpected arrival of Bragg's army in Chattanooga, which presented Buell with his stiffest challenge yet. Like his sponsor McClellan on Virginia's Peninsula, Buell concluded almost immediately that his larger army must be outnumbered. Although later claiming that he found reports of Bragg's numbers highly exaggerated, Buell consistently maintained at the time that Bragg had brought at least sixty thousand men with him—roughly double the actual the number and, more to the point, double what most of Buell's subordinates and spies in Chattanooga thought the Rebels had. Having just dispatched Bull Nelson's division to confront Morgan in Kentucky, Buell made an abrupt about-face and desperately begged Washington for reinforcements. Halleck, as promised, lent his support quickly, dispatching two divisions from Grant's army to Buell's command.

Confederate cavalry harassed Buell's rear with amplified zeal after Bragg arrived in Chattanooga. On August 10, Morgan captured the entire Federal garrison at Gallatin, Tennessee, destroying several railroad bridges and, more importantly, shutting down the essential railroad tunnel north of town by setting fire to the wooden supports within the tunnel. The raid agonizingly cut Buell's hungry army off from its Louisville and Nashville bases yet again. Adding insult to injury, Morgan on August 19 routed the Federal horsemen sent out to corral him near Hartsfield, capturing their commanding officer, Brig. Gen. Richard W. Johnson, as well as many other Yankee cavalrymen.

One suspects that Buell must have wondered how much worse his situation could become. If so, he soon got his answer. On August 20, McCook reported from Battle Creek that Bragg's army was crossing the Tennessee River in force. Over the next forty-eight hours, scouts, alleged Confederate deserters, and local Unionists, notably including a "Tennessee volunteer" and a Tennessean suspiciously calling himself Andrew Johnson, reinforced the notion that anywhere from ten thousand to eighty thousand Rebels had crossed the river at three points, with some already at the top of imposing Walden's Ridge, the barrier to the Sequatchie Valley. Beyond that valley lay the Cumberland Plateau and then Middle Tennessee, including Nashville itself. Confederate deserters reported that Bragg's immediate destination was McMinnville, McCook added.[11]

Without adequate cavalry—much of it had just had been captured at Hartsville—and apparent indifference to whatever remained, Buell immediately accepted McCook's breathless dispatches without further investigation. Forced all summer to follow Halleck's flawed strategy against his better judgment; his supply lines harassed by guerrillas just as he vainly had predicted; constantly second guessed by superiors in Washington; harassed by the press as an "ass"; damned by the weather; and castigated by his own hungry, insubordinate, and dirty men, Buell now held in his hands reports that he faced a larger and aggressive Confederate army streaming toward his rear. Enough was enough. Although there was no indication if the Rebels were simply foraging, staging a diversion to assist Kirby Smith, or actively marching to cut the Yankees off from Nashville and force them to battle, assuming that the reports were reliable at all, Buell concluded immediately and perhaps thankfully that his ill-starred offensive against Chattanooga at last was done. All that was left to do, he reasoned, was what he had wanted to do in the first place: get out of Alabama and concentrate in Middle Tennessee closer to Nashville.

Buell's reaction hardly is surprising. Leading a campaign against his own wishes to begin with, he clearly had yearned to give up on it for some time, perhaps as early as the first notification of Bragg's appearance in Chattanooga. Anticipating an imminent aggressive movement from Bragg to complement Kirby Smith's Kentucky invasion, one he plainly expected to overwhelm him with superior numbers, he had issued orders a day earlier for McCook's and Crittenden's divisions to fall back into the Sequatchie Valley south of McMinnville if Bragg advanced.[12] "My plans were already matured," he admitted some years later, "and McCook had his orders for such a case, only waiting the signal to act, which was given on the 20th."[13] McCook's reports thus conveniently provided Buell with the final justification necessary to abandon the dusty morass that northern Alabama had become.

First, however, he had to try to stall Bragg in the arid Tennessee mountains long enough to assemble a defensive force strong enough to hold Nashville. That city, always central in Buell's strategic planning, could not fall. The gravity of the situation, however, combined with Buell's guiding military principles, habitual perfectionism, and hesitation, led him to demand nothing less than an ideal site to mount a defense. It had to be naturally strong but also lay along his supply lines so that he could obtain enough food and forage for a hungry army to hold out in the dry, barren hills. Without such a stronghold, he concluded, he would have to hurry back toward Nashville without contesting the enemy advance at all. Several of the orders emanating from his headquarters suggest that from the first he was pessimistic of success. Particularly indicative of Buell's state of mind is that he ordered the two borrowed divisions from Grant's army to move on to Nashville rather than toward the developing front. From the opening round, Buell anticipated failure.[14]

Buell began throwing together a defensive response with the troops he already had in the field. The exposed advance positions at Battle Creek and Stevenson had to be abandoned first. He ordered McCook and Crittenden to leave a token observation force—two regiments under Col. Leonard Harris—and fall back to the northwest with the rest of their units, where they would rendezvous with Brig. Gen. Albin F. Schoepf's brigade advancing from the mountain gap at Pelham, and three divisions under George Thomas's overall command coming down from McMinnville. Together, near Tracy City or perhaps farther north at Altamont, at the top of the Cumberland Plateau, the combined divisions were, in Buell's words, to locate "a strong position or pass in which you can repel a superior force and where you can threaten the valley . . . fight hard when you have to fight."[15]

Buell himself would not command in person, not at first anyway. After a quick visit to Stevenson and Battle Creek, Buell made his way to Decherd, Tennessee, a vital railroad junction on the Nashville side of the mountains. There, he ordered a rapid concentration of supplies as well as of the units vacating Alabama by foot or rail. Everything previously shipped to the Alabama stations, as well as hoped-for new shipments, was rerouted to Decherd. Massing his meager supplies in such a manner was crucial, Buell believed, for the army could not hold out in the barren highlands very long before privation forced a retreat. Living off the land was out of the question, he argued, for little remained after months of scraping by in the midst of a drought.[16] When the so-called Buell Commission met later in the war to investigate the general's conduct during the campaign, the defendant marshaled a host of witnesses to buttress his claims of poor supply. Notably, his chief commissary officer, Lt. Col. Francis Darr, later testified that the entire region was by late August "thoroughly foraged." An expedition launched from Decherd resulted in "but a few bushels of old corn" and two hundred head of cattle that Darr said "were in very poor condition, so as hardly to justify the trip." Faced with such conditions, Buell concluded that making a stand necessitated obtaining supplies from Nashville via the railroad, and as far as he was concerned that meant holding Decherd.[17]

Not surprisingly considering the near panic that had gripped Buell's subordinates in the Army of the Ohio, the sudden and, to the men, unexplained retreat quickly became enveloped in what Clausewitz called the fog of war. Rumors abounded that Lee had abandoned Virginia for a quick strike at Buell's army, increasing the soldiers' anxiety. On the march itself, nothing went right. Abandoning their encampments at Battle Creek, many of McCook's Federals threw away their knapsacks and burned their tents and other camp equipage, often under orders. As they retreated, carrying only a few day's rations and their blankets, many hungry Yankees foraged more than they walked, and in so doing raised doubts about the army's alleged inability to live off the country. Indeed, despite Buell's attempts to stop them, enterprising soldiers supplemented their dwindling half-rations with a cornucopia of local produce, including apples, green corn, pawpaws, potatoes, livestock, and especially roasting ears and peaches.[18] Captain F. W. Keil of the 35th Ohio Infantry remembered that "the valley into which we moved had fine cornfields, and excellent use was made of the advantages thus afforded. Never did roasting ears disappear more rapidly."

Foraging, Keil added, had an added political benefit the men quickly recognized. One of his lieutenants in particular championed the "theory . . . that there were two practical ways to put down the rebellion. The one was to whip the rebels in the field; the other to damage them in store, or literally 'eat them out of house and home.'" The lieutenant "had conceived the idea of uniting both plans so as to shorten the job!"[19] Still others pointed out that by taking food from civilians they were starving out the bushwhackers who had plagued them all summer. Certainly they were defying their commanding officer as well.[20]

Even Alexander McCook emerged, at least once, as a willing accomplice in their pillaging. Removing guards he had posted at one planter's house when he learned that the man refused to take the oath of allegiance to the United States, McCook allowed his men free reign at the man's plantation. "The soldiers 'went in' and literally swept the place of everything eatable," Wilbur Hinman of the 6th Ohio Battery remembered, and "it did not take them long to do it, either. When the storm broke upon him the planter mounted his horse and galloped to McCook's quarters and begged him that he might be permitted to swear allegiance to the government. But his sudden spasm of loyalty was 'too thin.' The gates of mercy were closed and he went away in a great rage. . . . No place was ever more thoroughly cleaned out than his."[21]

As foraging escalated and discipline broke down more and more as the pullout progressed, some Federals targeted more than food. Pillaging and outright destruction grew more frequent, especially in retaliation for bush-whacking. Captain Keil, for example, reported the theft of "an old fashioned family carriage."[22] Another column of Federals marched out of a Tennessee town allegedly loaded down with "gilded mirrors—marble tables—mahogany sofas—rose wood pianos—elegant paintings—costly statuary—cut glass chandeliers—silk dresses and oil cans, book cases and cooking stoves; hand boxes and sledge hammers; silver plate and oxhides; dry goods and groceries—and all hurrying pell mell toward the frozen latitudes—what they are unable to carry they destroy."[23]

Looting clearly provided an emotional release for the retreating army. Robert J. Winn of the 2nd Ohio Infantry noted with approval that "the boys are having a gay time forreging . . . the boys are going for things in general." On August 31, Winn added, "I didn't do anything all day, but eat and go for things."[24] Others tried to loot but frustratingly found little. William R. Stuckey of the 42nd Indiana Infantry complained that not only were rations short and water scarce, but "there is nothing to steel in this country for every thing has been taken long since."[25] Units occasionally fought among themselves for choice booty. In some cases, destruction grew to alarming levels. Soldiers in Rousseau's division defiantly set fire to much of the by then hated town of Athens as they marched through Alabama on the way back to Tennessee.[26]

Many Yankees expressed revulsion for their comrade's behavior during the retreat. Marcus Woodcock of the Federal 9th Kentucky Infantry, himself a Tennessean, angrily described "the first and I think the most blamable piece of robbery I ever saw committed." Near Jasper, Woodcock and his regiment witnessed stragglers entering a house, where they proceeded to take "anything they could find that suited them. Despite the entreaties of a tender little girl they bursted bureaus containing clothing, table ware, and anything else they had no use for, and carried off the contents—tore down ladies ward robes and carried off any and all that suited them, and what they could not carry off, they destroyed."[27]

Making matters worse, both Buell's generals and his privates exasperated him in other ways during the initial days of the retreat. McCook and Crittenden vexingly fell back from Battle Creek too slowly for his taste, and, worse yet, in what Buell deemed the wrong direction. Convinced that Confederate forces blocked the route Buell wanted them to take, McCook marched all the way to Jasper only to abort the move and retrace his steps to Battle Creek. He then embarked along a different road, one farther west and away from Bragg.[28] "We faced and flanked and countermarched and floundered among the thick bushes," wrote one of McCook's men remembering the Jasper march.[29]

From his headquarters in McMinnville, meanwhile, stolid and taciturn Virginian George Thomas contradicted Buell at every turn. Frustrated for months by Buell's hesitancy, Thomas now eyed his maps and his commander's dispositions with increasing alarm. The crux of their current disagreement was the question of Bragg's ultimate destination. The main arteries of the transportation network between Chattanooga and Nashville might be described as resembling a crudely drawn capital H slowly tipping over to the left. That stretch of the Nashville and Chattanooga Railroad extending from Tennessee's capital through the depot at Decherd to Stevenson, along with a largely parallel road, formed the left side of the figure. The road running from the Tennessee River through Sparta and on toward Tompkinsville, Kentucky, formed the right. Both routes ran roughly to the northwest, perpendicular to the mountains. Connecting the two and thus forming the H was a road running parallel to and north of the Cumberland Mountains, from Tullahoma, through Thomas's position at McMinnville, to Sparta. A just-reopened branch of the Nashville and Chattanooga additionally connected McMinnville to the main trunk. There was one additional important road, as well, one closer to Chattanooga. It extended from Decherd eastward to Altamont, which sat squarely in the middle of the H.

Shielded by the mountains, Bragg could, from various lesser roads, move onto either of the major north-south routes. Which would he choose? Victory or defeat might well depend on the correct answer. Buell automatically assumed that Bragg's real goal had to be Nashville; it certainly was what he himself would do. If so, the Confederates almost certainly would sweep down the Sequatchie Valley to the west. From perhaps Stevenson, they would move north, hoping to cut the railroad at Decherd before advancing further up the Nashville and Chattanooga toward Murfeesboro and finally Nashville. If Nashville was indeed Bragg's objective, the crucial territory in the coming days lay in the lower left half of the H, between Stevenson and Decherd. Altamont thus loomed as a vital point, since it provided Bragg the alternative of the best shortcut over the mountains to the west. Bragg would have to pass through either Altamont or Decherd, and the former provided a convenient point to prepare for either contingency. Buell therefore planned to be ready for him at Altamont.

Based on reports from his scouts and local civilians, however, Thomas remained unconvinced. If Bragg's army was out there—and, tellingly, his scouts still could not locate it—Thomas sensed that the Confederate's goal more likely was Kentucky via the Sparta Road. That made the lower right half of the H the area in which to concentrate, meaning that McMinnville rather than Altamont was the key, as McCook's informants had earlier asserted. From McMinnville the Federal army not only could move quickly in either direction, it could shift much more quickly to the Sparta Road. Altamont, in contrast, provided no direct connector eastward to Sparta. McMinnville possessed other assets as well, Thomas added. It was the stronger position in terms of terrain, and he had nearly a week's worth of rations stored at McMinnville. Altamont, in contrast, was entirely devoid of food or forage, which Thomas testily insisted Buell would know if he would pull himself away from Decherd and come look for himself. The situation was clear to Thomas: The army must concentrate at McMinnville.[30]

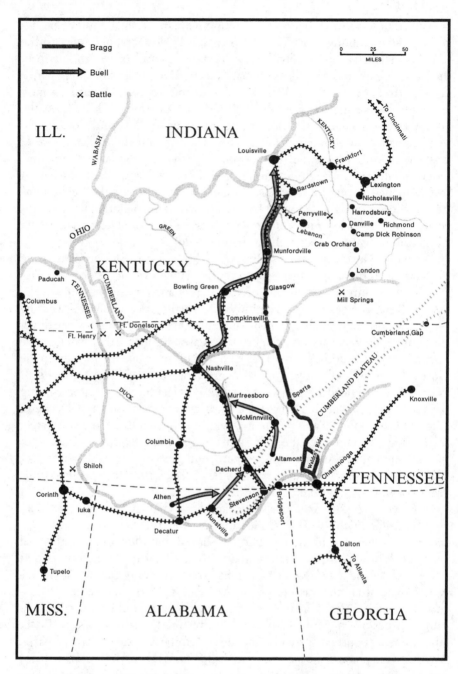

Map 3.1. Bragg's and Buell's routes into Kentucky, August–September 1862.

Buell refused to listen. He continued to order an Altamont concentration, chiding Thomas: "there is no possibility of our concentrating at McMinnville. We must concentrate in advance and assume the offensive or fall back at last to Murfreesborough."[31] Thomas complied, but only half-heartedly. Reporting that Altamont provided little water, no forage, and a road all but impassable to artillery, he immediately fell back to McMinnville. It was, he curtly reminded Buell, the better position anyway.[32]

While the generals argued and soldiers meted out revenge on Tennessee, a showdown finally seemed to be brewing after weeks of numbing railroad labor, hunger, and anxiety. James B. Fry, Buell's chief of staff, crowed that Bragg was "very slow. If he wants [a fight] he can have it. We are all ready."[33] Yet Buell continued to fret. He worried that supplies were "diminishing rapidly," communications remained impaired, and the army remained disunited. Making matters worse, "the news from Kentucky was unsatisfactory." Kirby Smith, Buell finally learned, was in the state and the Federals had only "new levies to oppose him." The dire possibility of losing Lexington and especially his Louisville base now began to loom ominously in Buell's mind.[34]

Frustratingly, he also was unable to pin down Bragg's position. Where were the Confederates? As it turned out, they were nowhere near Altamont or McMinnville, as Thomas firmly and finally reported to a skeptical Buell on August 28. McCook's initial reports of Bragg's army sweeping across the Tennessee into the Federal rear had been, as it turned out, woefully exaggerated. The simple fact was that only a few elements of Bragg's army had crossed the river on August 19 and 20, and only then to stop on the other side, where they camped for nearly a week in the shadow of Walden's Ridge. There had been no great Confederate movement from which to retreat prior to August 26, although the signs of its coming were admittedly evident. Bragg had remained in the city's environs until then.[35]

How could such a thing have happened? At Battle Creek, Union and Confederate soldiers fraternized regularly, swimming back and forth across the shallow creek until Confederate authorities clamped down on the practice. Marcus Woodcock remembered hearing "many a hearty laugh ringing across the quiet waters of the Tennessee, occasioned by the comic speeches of some sedate Yankees, or the tart replies of some specimen of Southern Chivalry."[36] Likewise, William R. Hartpence of the 51st Indiana Infantry wrote of camaraderie between the opposing lines at Battle Creek. Noting that he first heard a Confederate referred to as "Johnny" there, Hartpence described "a common necessity on both sides. Frequently the only source of fuel or water lay directly between the two armies, and neither of them could have been supplied, but for the expedient adopted by the pickets, and ignored by those in command." Temporary truces resulted, during which men exchanged newspapers, tobacco, and other items. If the brass ordered an end to the fraternization, suitable warnings were provided:

"Johnny, we've got orders to shoot."
"All right, yanks; hunt yer holes."
"Well, you rebs want to skedaddle in a hurry."
"Go to———, yanks! Let'er go!"[37]

Not surprisingly, such an atmosphere resulted in speculation, rumors, ribbing—good-natured or otherwise—and one-upmanship that abounded for weeks, cresting in late August as Bragg's army moved into its jumping-off positions.[38] On August 19, reports began filtering in that Confederates were crossing the river and moving toward Walden's Ridge. Exaggeration quickly followed. Woodcock noted "rumor though the camp in the afternoon that the Rebels had made a fresh inroad on our communication line."[39] Another Federal, George Landrum of the 2nd Ohio Infantry, wrote home on the same date, reporting that "we have all sorts of rumors of the number the enemy have on the other side of the river. . . . They are said to have from thirty to sixty thousand men; they are to cross over at different points, whip Buel's army in detail, march on to Nashville, retake it, then push on to Louisville and Cincinnati."[40] Rumors, of course, grow more distorted and inflated as they pass from one person to another. By the time they reached McCook's ears, the reports indicated a major offensive was in progress. McCook had every reason to believe such a tale, for he had received orders from Buell warning of just such an aggressive move by the enemy. In the end, without sufficient cavalry to scout Chattanooga's environs adequately enough to determine that Bragg remained there, and apparently lacking the desire to do so, a panicked Buell and his equally apprehensive generals fell victim to a self-fulfilling prophecy, and retreated from the shadow columns of rumor.[41]

For what it was worth, Bragg at least wanted to move as soon as his soldiers and Buell anticipated. Indeed, for two frustrating weeks after Kirby Smith's army marched toward Kentucky, Bragg waited impatiently to begin his march north. He already had his infantry in Chattanooga, drilling in anticipation of the strenuous mountain crossing ahead, and small band of pioneers went ahead to prepare the road, but his artillery batteries and wagon trains remained strung out far to the south.[42] Shortages of wagons and supplies further retarded his advance and created unhealthy competition among his subordinates for the little that was available.

An angry Bragg blamed "inefficient officers" for his embarrassing delay, but there was enough guilt to go around.[43] The artillery in particular had dawdled. The men of Charles Lumsden's Alabama battery, for example, paused eight days when they arrived home in Tuscaloosa, visiting loved ones and enjoying "the freedom of the city and county" before taking to the road once again. By all accounts, the subsequent line of march from Tuscaloosa to Chattanooga was whiskey-soaked, leading to "exhilaration and subsequent depression and some insubordination temporary" on the part of the Alabama

Figure 3.3. Gen. William J. Hardee. Photograph courtesy Library of Congress, LC-USZ62-14973.

gunners.[44] At least one other battery captain, Alabamian Henry C. Semple, apparently experienced headaches similar to Lumsden's, for he wrote his wife plaintively from Chattanooga, "you have no idea of the trouble and vexhations of a march when 110 horses have to be watched and 128 men . . . become children as soon as they get into the army."[45]

While he waited, Bragg reorganized the army into two wings, to be commanded by William J. Hardee and Leonidas Polk. Bragg felt great respect for Hardee, a tall, dapper, forty-six-year-old Georgian with graying hair who had served as commandant of West Point just before the war. The author of *Hardee's Tactics*, the book that under various titles officers used to train thousands of Northern as well as Southern soldiers, he had already had a tremendous impact on the war. Meticulous in dress and formal in manner, Hardee nonetheless won the affection of his men, who sensed kindness and ability beneath his prim exterior. Shiloh gained him the added reputation of being a pugnacious fighter.[46]

Bragg also thought highly of Hardee's eventual division commanders. Brig. Gen. J. Patton Anderson was a particular favorite. Although not a West Pointer, usually a black mark with Bragg, Anderson at least had fought in Mexico. After the war he won a seat as a Democrat in the Mississippi legisla-

Figure 3.4. Gen. Leonidas Polk. Photograph courtesy Library of Congress, LC-38171-1320.

ture, where he strongly opposed the Compromise of 1850. Rising quickly in national party circles, he went to the Washington Territory as a U.S. Marshal and later almost became territorial governor during the James Buchanan administration. Instead, he moved to Florida, where he supported secession and served as the first colonel of the 1st Florida Infantry. His initial service was under Bragg at Pensacola, where the two men developed a bond of loyalty. An aggressive battlefield commander as well as a strict disciplinarian like his commanding general, Anderson replaced Maj. Gen. Samuel C. Jones when Bragg determined to leave the sickly Jones behind in Chattanooga as post commander.[47]

Hardee's other division commander would be Kentuckian Simon Bolivar Buckner, who had come a long way since spearheading Sidney Johnston's occupation of Bowling Green. Dispatched to Fort Donelson just in time for U.S. Grant's assault, Buckner found himself in command when his superiors, former Secretary of War Floyd and the ubiquitous Gideon Pillow, fled the scene to avoid capture. Forced to surrender, Buckner hoped for generous terms from his old army friend Grant, who had yet to repay a loan made several years earlier. Instead, Grant demanded his "unconditional surrender." While Grant gained both a signal victory and a sobriquet, Buckner soon found himself imprisoned in Fort Warren, located in frigid Boston Harbor. Exchanged in August after five months of solitary confinement, he was promoted to major general and sent almost immediately to Chattanooga, where it was hoped that his presence would rally Kentuckians to the cause. Both Robert E. Lee and Kirby Smith campaigned for Buckner's services, but for once Bragg refused to bend, keeping Buckner for himself and assigning him to command the division originally given to Alabamian Sterling A. M. Wood, who reverted to brigade command.[48]

In contrast to his feelings toward Hardee and his subordinates, Bragg thoroughly despised his other wing commander, the genial but pompous and often incompetent Bishop Polk. Bragg considered Polk "an old woman, utterly worthless," especially at disciplining men.[49] Unfortunately for Bragg and for the Confederacy as a whole, Polk remained a great favorite of Jefferson Davis despite carefully couched hints from Bragg, which protected the irritatingly self-righteous Polk from the increasingly sycophantic Bragg and made his appointment to wing command a political necessity.[50]

However, officers closely associated with Polk were not so secure, and many bore the full weight of Bragg's scorn for the bishop. Notably, he felt nothing but contempt for Maj. Gen. Benjamin Franklin Cheatham, one of Polk's two division commanders. Frank Cheatham was a rough-hewn Tennessean who after the Mexican War went off to California to strike it rich in the gold fields. Instead, he became a Democratic machine politician, and, worse yet, he acquired a rather disreputable reputation as a trigger-happy gambler, heavy drinker, and advocate of lynch law. He returned to Tennessee in 1853, farmed, became active in the state militia, and rose to the rank of brigadier general. Although he had led his men well at Shiloh, Bragg despised him and sought to have him relieved of command shortly after Bragg took over at Tupelo. Not only was the often sinful Cheatham a favorite of the pious Polk, he also was a Tennessean. Bragg's patrician wife, Elise, who in many ways dominated her soldier husband, felt an almost pathological hatred of Tennesseans that invariably rubbed off. She wrote him constantly that men from the Volunteer State were cowards who could not be trusted. This did not bode well for Cheatham, who was the darling of the Tennessee rank-and-file. Worst of all, Cheatham had a drinking problem and quite possibly was an alcoholic. Although it had yet to affect him unduly in the field, Bragg was determined to purge his army of all its drunken generals. Several went, but Cheatham's ties to Polk and Tennessee governor Isham Harris protected him for the moment.[51]

Saddled with Polk and Cheatham, Bragg made sure that he had one dependable man in the bishop's command. That was Polk's other division commander, Maj. Gen. Jones Withers. Like Anderson, Withers had served under Bragg at Mobile. A West Pointer, Mexican War veteran, merchant, and former mayor of Mobile, the forty-eight-year-old Withers had fought well at Shiloh. Poor health, however, threatened to impede him in the upcoming campaign.[52]

All the while, Bragg's artillery and transportation continued trickling into Chattanooga. His dark mood lifted. "Bragg is in fine spirits," Henry Semple wrote his wife. "His plans are working well and he anticipates a great triump."[53] By August 25, five full days after Buell's muddled retreat began, the army finally was close enough to full strength that Bragg issued final orders for the march. Rhetorically depicting the suffering of "our old and venerated men (even the ministers of God), and . . . our women," he invoked God's help to drive the "Abolition demagogues and demons" from Southern soil. "Soldiers," he concluded, "the enemy is before you and your banners are free. It is for you to decide whether our brothers and sisters in Tennessee and Kentucky shall remain bondmen and bondwomen of the Abolition tyrant or be restored to the freedom inherited from their fathers."[54]

Such statements were more than mere bombast to Bragg, who sounded the same unhesitating note in his private correspondence. Indeed, his confidence had grown greatly, not in the least because of Buell's unexplained but welcome retreat from Chattanooga's outskirts. Bragg wrote to Price and Van Dorn and advised them that, although tardy in commencing his movement, "we hope for a successful campaign." Buell inexplicably was falling back and "will probably not make a stand this side of Nashville, if there." With Marshall in eastern Kentucky, Kirby Smith en route to Lexington, his own army now on the march, and the Yankees already retreating into Middle Tennessee, "we shall thus have Buell pretty well disposed of . . . we shall confidently expect to meet you on the Ohio and there open the way to Missouri." Bragg seemingly had imbibed fully of Kirby Smith's swaggering confidence, and now stood poised to take his assigned place on the stage.[55] The army's morale matched that of its commander. John Ellis of the 16th Louisiana wrote his father: "the army is in fine spirits and are eager to clear Kentucky and Tennessee of the invaders. This I think we will do in about 60 days and then we can go into winter quarters and await Abe Lincoln's deliberations."[56]

Delays continued to frustrate the Confederate advance, however, and it was not until the night of August 26 that Bragg truly opened the campaign. That night, Brig. Gen. Samuel B. Maxey's brigade attacked and occupied the advanced but now lightly held Federal base at Bridgeport. The next morning, the main army followed, pounding away at Battle Creek's thin blue line of defenders with artillery before driving them away and turning north. Bragg did not continue in that direction, however, but instead turned to the northeast, steering well east of a reported Federal force at McMinnville. Just as George Thomas had predicted, Bragg indeed was headed for Kentucky rather than Nashville on the Sparta Road. To be fair to Buell, as late as the initial foray across the river on the twenty-sixth, Bragg still had not made up his mind exactly what to do once he got to Sparta. His Tennesseans, augmented by an insistent Gov. Isham Harris, urged the liberation of Nashville. Bragg, however, already had promised Kirby Smith that he would bring the army north to Kentucky. Besides, without the latter's troops he lacked the force to

seize the city anyway. But what route should he take to Kentucky? Bragg finally decided that he would move from Sparta almost directly north to Albany,
Kentucky, and then on to Harrodsburg, Danville, and Lexington. J. Stoddard
Johnston, his new volunteer aide and a well-known "Kentucky dreamer," had
followed that route successfully to join Bragg's command in early August.[57]

Finally aware of Bragg's true position and intentions thanks to Thomas's
cavalry, a stubborn Buell still could not quite accept the truth of it. Trusting
his own judgment more than others' reports, a tendency that would reappear
again later in the campaign, Buell stubbornly ordered McCook's division to
Altamont to observe and hopefully retard a Confederate advance said to be
going in a different direction. Buell unrealistically hoped that McCook could
hang on for perhaps as long as a week before a lack of supplies forced him to
fall back. But McCook would have none of it. Despite an abundance of apples
and water, he immediately chimed in with Thomas on the poor quality of the
inhospitable position. It was, he explained later, "absolutely impossible" to
hold Altamont, because of all the deficiencies Thomas already had duly noted.
The Confederates further hastened his retreat when, on August 30, Confederate cavalry under the command of Col. Joseph Wheeler, screening Bragg's
left, attacked McCook's Altamont outposts. The brief skirmish convinced
McCook to flee from the mountaintop.[58]

Stymied at Altamont, his envisioned stronghold, Buell at last briefly
considered making his stand at McMinnville, which Thomas had been pleading for him to do for a week. Unfortunately, Buell's change of heart came too
late for the recalcitrant Thomas, who now warned that he could no longer
hold McMinnville either. Instead, the army must now fall back to
Murfreesboro for supplies. Thus, on August 29, the day before McCook's
final retreat from Altamont, Buell gave up for good any thought of striking a
blow anywhere in the Tennessee mountains. He ordered another retreat in
the direction of Nashville the following day. Murfreesboro, he agreed, offered a site on the railroad close to his base at Nashville, one where he could
concentrate the entire army quickly and feed it until Bragg passed. It had to
be occupied by September 5, with Thomas passing on through to Nashville
to prepare that city's defenses. Once again orders went out for supplies and
convalescents to be shipped from the front, this time from the short-lived
headquarters at Decherd and the remaining Alabama posts to Nashville itself. Hundreds of white Unionist refugees and African-American slaves followed the long, retreating blue columns—the latter hoping to maintain their
precarious, newly won freedom in the shadow of the haggard blue columns.[59]

Thomas and Buell for once agreed, but not for the same reasons. Thomas argued for a grand counterattack to be launched from Murfreesboro,
one that would annihilate the Confederate Army of the Mississippi somewhere north of Sparta. "By convenient roads," he argued, "our main force
can be thrown upon the enemy . . . overcome him, and drive him toward
Sparta, his longest line of retreat. A large force of cavalry and light infantry

Figure 3.5. Maj. Gen. George H. Thomas. Photograph courtesy Edward J. Rife Collection, U.S. Army Military History Institute.

can be pushed across the mountains . . . attack him in the rear, and completely rout his whole force."

Thomas's plan had merit, and many embittered officers who later testified to the Buell Commission expressed their concurrence that it would have succeeded. Buell, however, was uninterested; there would be no attack south of Murfreesboro. Indeed, he soon he gave up any thought of concentrating even there, for new orders suddenly redirected the army more westward to Tennessee's capital itself.[60] They were not well received. The trek to Murfreesboro in itself had been exhausting. "Hot and dry and the dust is shoe mouth deep," John A. Duncan of the 3rd Ohio Infantry recorded in his diary. "Nothing to drink except pond water and it thickened with wiggletails, dead mules and horses."[61]

"You have heard that 'Jordan is a hard road to trabbel,'" William H. Ball of the 5th Wisconsin Battery wrote his brother from Murfreesboro. "Well, Jordan is a good turnpike compared with the one we traveled yesterday."[62] Now they had to take to the road again. Many footsore, worn out men wrote bitterly of arriving in Murfreesboro only to be told to keep moving. William R. Stuckey of the 42nd Indiana, for example, complained that his regiment "only stopped there to dry clothes." Denied a fight south of

Nashville, the men in the ranks continued trudging until they reached the city itself. Exhaustion set in.[63] Wilbur Hinman recalled how "hundreds of men fell by the wayside, unable to keep up. Many of the companies stacked arms with less than a dozen men in the ranks. With aching bones and weary limbs we threw ourselves upon the ground." The following morning, "not a few of the men found themselves unable to march without absolute torture, owing to the condition of their feet, which the previous night had been blistered and bleeding."[64]

Not surprisingly in such an anger-laden atmosphere, foraging and destruction continued. Emerson Calkins of the 8th Wisconsin Battery remembered his comrades stealing honey from beehives until the bees retaliated and swarmed into the men's uniforms, forcing them to quickly disrobe and return to the column nude. When someone in a house near Murfreesboro shot a soldier relieving himself in a cornfield, Col. Edward M. McCook, yet another "Fighting McCook," ordered the corn burned, and would have torched the house as well had not the shooter fled, leaving only women and children at home. Sadly, McCook lamented, the corn was too green to burn anyway. Even the supposedly "soft" Buell finally reached his limit, ordering that civilians who made partisan attacks on his railroads be hanged.[65]

Buell arrived in Nashville ahead of his army on September 2. He immediately wrote Halleck, justifying his recent flight as "necessary" if Nashville and Kentucky were to be held. It was clear, he continued, that Bragg was bound for Kentucky. Thus, once he had secured Nashville, he would go after the Confederates. Bowling Green, once the headquarters of Johnston's Central Army of Kentucky, seemed a likely spot from which to intercept Bragg. Halleck's terse reply reflected more Washington's growing aggravation regarding Buell's lack of aggressiveness than approval: "March where you please, provided you will find the enemy and fight him.[66]

Meanwhile, Abraham Lincoln expressed growing concern with the state of affairs in Tennessee. Rumors that Bragg might have slipped Buell's noose entirely and headed to join Lee in his Maryland invasion frightened the president immensely, particularly in light of Lee's recent drubbing of John Pope at Second Manassas. "Where is General Bragg?" he asked Jeremiah Boyle on September 7. To Maj. Gen. Horatio Wright, newly commanding in Cincinnati, Lincoln wondered: "do you know to any certainty where General Bragg is? May he not be in Virginia?" Unsatisfied, the president finally wrote to Buell himself: "What degree of certainty have you that Bragg with his command is not now in the valley of the Shenandoah, Virginia?"[67] Buell's response verified that Bragg still was in Tennessee, not Virginia, and "his movements will probably depend upon mine." He offered little in the way of assurance, however. "I expect that for the want of supplies I can neither follow nor remain here," Buell told Lincoln. "Think I must withdraw from Tennessee. . . . I shall endeavor to hold Nashville, and at the same time drive Smith out of Kentucky and hold my communications."[68]

The army recovered as best it could over the next several days. Although new uniforms and equipment issued to at least some units boosted morale somewhat, the mood of the men remained sour. A lack of both mail and pay deeply embittered many.[69] Nashville's obvious secession proclivities added to the soldiers' discomfort. John Eicker of the 79th Pennsylvania Infantry remained bitter about his regiment's treatment there earlier in the year: "The ladies would look out of the second Story Windows and hiss at us, saying just wait till you meet the Rock City Guard, there won't be many of you come back." Eicker ached to avenge such treatment on the women's champions.[70]

Meanwhile, Buell's notions of a "withdraw from Tennessee" broadened and solidified. Having secured Nashville, he might have breathed somewhat easier, even though Bragg's army remained on his flank. Instead, his foreboding intensified. Nashville and Bowling Green, after all, were only links in a tenuous iron supply line that followed the Louisville and Nashville Railroad south from the army's base on the Ohio River. Kirby Smith occupied much of Kentucky east of Louisville and remained lightly opposed. Were Bragg to slip into the rear, cut that railroad, and then rendezvous with Kirby Smith, Buell's army of roughly sixty-five thousand men would be cut off entirely and both Kentucky and Tennessee effectively lost. Such a calamity nearly had happened only weeks earlier in Alabama. The only response, Buell ultimately concluded, was to fall back all the way to the Ohio, to Louisville itself. "The political effect of such a move" had led him to hesitate, he admitted, but "purely military grounds" in the end commanded it.[71]

Buell's discussion of political effects referred at least in part to the pugnacious Unionist Tennessee governor, Andrew Johnson, who had been a constant thorn in Buell's side for months. In a disagreement that quickly became common knowledge throughout the army, Johnson exploded whenever the subject of the Federal army abandoning his capital city arose. Indeed, the thought of Buell retreating into Kentucky and leaving the city unguarded sent Johnson into apoplexy. Better to burn Nashville to the ground, Johnson growled, than to give it back to the Confederacy, for the deleterious effect of Nashville's fall on the morale of Tennessee's Unionists would be enormous. Privately to Lincoln, Johnson groused that Buell was probably disloyal and certainly a coward, using the entire army as a personal bodyguard.[72]

Buell, for his part, dismissed any thought of setting fire to Nashville. He impressed slaves to dig new fortifications, and at length, not "so much from military as from political considerations," agreed to leave George Thomas's division behind to protect the city—a promise he largely reneged on as soon as he was on the move and free from Johnson's incessant complaining. He finally would leave only five thousand men to defend the "Athens of the West," while the rest of the Army of the Ohio retreated toward the river for which it was named. Buell and forty-five thousand other Yankees were Kentucky bound in pursuit of Bragg.[73]

4

THE GREAT FOOT RACE

THE CONFEDERATE ARMY OF THE MISSISSIPPI CERTAINLY HAD NOT marched to reinforce Lee, as Abraham Lincoln worried, but it meant trouble for the Union war effort nonetheless. Skirting to the east of Nashville, it had moved steadily northward toward the Kentucky border since the twenty-eighth. Hardee's and Polk's wings crossed Walden's Ridge at two different points and then dropped into the Sequatchie Valley before rejoining temporarily in Pikeville, at the head of the valley, on September 1. Two days later, the van of the army, Cheatham's division, entered Sparta, Bragg having eschewed the McMinnville Road and any direct encounter with the Yankees at Nashville. The rest of the Army of the Mississippi soon followed.

It was a hard, exhausting march on narrow, crowded roads through rugged mountains full of Unionist bushwhackers, and often staged during darkest night. The army straggled greatly at first, especially during the crossing of imposing Walden's Ridge. Men fainted in the ranks or fell out of line to sleep along the roadside. Others littered the way with blankets, knapsacks, spare clothing, shoes, and anything else deemed at the moment not absolutely essential, in order to lighten their load. The oppressive heat added to the misery, and water grew so scarce that guards had to be posted around the few pools of bad water encountered to prevent men from drinking it anyway. Some enterprising entrepreneurs, having discovered safer pools scattered along the way, took advantage of their slower comrades' thirst by selling them water at ten cents a cupful. Biscuits, meanwhile, went for a dollar apiece, for Bragg had ordered that rations carried on wagons could not be distributed until the fifth day of the march.[1] Animals, already in poor condition, suffered as well; Thomas Benton Ellis of the 3rd Florida, "detailed to assist the wagons," remembered that "we had to carry a large rock, and when the mules after a desperate struggle, would move a short distance and stop, we had to scotch the wheels with the rock."[2] Often, such measures failed. W. L. Trask, as he descended Walden's Ridge, remembered seeing "quite a number of broken down wagons, all of which were left by the road side. In many places the baggage and other plunder was piled in heaps with someone watching it, while someone else had gone off in search of means to transport it onward."

Along the brutal line of march, as straggling and foraging multiplied despite orders to the contrary, Bragg again reinforced his reputation as a stringent disciplinarian. He ordered at least two men executed, one for robbery and the other for "insulting a woman," but then reprieved them, "bidding them to sin no more. We begin to think," Trask added, "Bragg isn't nearly the inhuman, blood thirsty monster that he has been represented to me."[3] Trask remained in a distinct minority, however, as rumors within the army suggested that Bragg executed the two (or three) men after all and shot other stragglers as well—a threat that certainly encouraged men to keep up with the column if they could. Subordinate officers also meted out harsh punishment, sometimes with tragic consequences. A member of the 3rd Confederate Infantry, "a heterogenous mass of humanity, some of whom were good men while others were said to be wharf rats," found himself tied by his thumbs to an apple tree for cursing his officers while drunk. According to a witness, "he died cursing, and he was buried under the apple tree beside the road." His comrades swore that they would kill the tyrannical officer responsible, Lt. Col. Henry Keep, in the regiment's first battle.[4]

Despite such incidents, morale remained surprisingly high among most of the soldiers, especially once beyond the onerous ridge. Pretty girls began to appear along the road, the secessionists among them at least cheering. Friends and relatives of many of the Tennessee troops turned out as well. Their stories of Yankee depredations shocked soldiers and further steeled their will to battle the foe. Some local men received short furloughs to go home after Bragg halted the army in Sparta for three days of rest. For those who remained, apples, melons, and peaches materialized in abundance, as did cider. Some lucky men even feasted on home-cooked meals served on white tablecloths spread across the grass. Adding to the revival air was music; men sang patriotic songs as well as hymns all the way from Chattanooga, like Christian soldiers marching toward war and victory.[5] Best of all, the enemy offered no resistance. "We expected the enemy's forces would have met and endeavored to oppose our progress before now," W. L. Trask wrote, "but we now learn that they have pulled up and skedaddled in haste."[6]

While at Sparta, Bragg received both good news and bad. The encouraging information was that Kirby Smith had won the Battle of Richmond and was moving on Lexington. Army morale blossomed even more at word of Richmond. The bad tidings were that Bragg's planned route through Albany and Harrodsburg was reportedly so dry and devoid of food and forage due to the expanding drought as to make it all but impassable. Despite more pleadings from the Tennesseans, who again renewed their campaign for an attack on Nashville, Bragg determined to continue north but more in the direction of Louisville. Two roads emanated from Tompkinsville, either of which would take the army through the fertile valleys of the Barren and Green Rivers, usually brimming with crops. As Stoddard Johnston remembered, "the difficulty of fording the Cumberland . . . together with the scarcity of water, forage, and subsistence, were prevailing reasons for not longer considering the propriety of assuming that line of march." Forced to live off the land for long stretches of time, it made sense to march through what Johnston termed the "best country."[7] At or near Glasgow, the Confederates would move onto the Bardstown Pike, which led directly into the heart of the Bluegrass. Although the revised line of march delayed a link-up with Kirby Smith, Bragg remained confident, for the Richmond victory had lessened the need to hurry to the Floridian's aid. He reasoned that he could afford the time to take the better route. At Sparta, the army accordingly divided again, with Polk's wing moving directly north to cross the Cumberland at Gainesboro before Hardee's contingent angled to the northwest toward Carthage. The latter's movement would hopefully be enough to worry Nashville and pin down Buell. They would reunite just north of the Kentucky line at Tompkinsville.[8]

Then, on September 7, Bragg heard more disturbing news that further upset his timetable. Just as Hardee's lead column left Sparta for Carthage, Bragg received an alarming report from Forrest, who had remained in Tennessee to observe and harass the Federals. Buell was on the move, hot in pursuit, the cavalryman declared. Forrest's dispatch, as well as a later one identifying Bowling Green as Buell's goal, spurred Bragg to action. With the enemy approaching "rapidly," Bragg wrote Polk, "we must push to head him off."[9]

So far, Bragg had outgeneraled Buell consistently and proved lucky besides, but in tarrying at Sparta longer than necessary, the Confederate potentially had made a grave tactical error. Only seventy-one miles separated Bowling Green from Nashville, roughly the same distance from Bowling Green to Sparta. Stopping for three days, Bragg had allowed Buell to make up lost time. Now, it was anyone's guess which army would arrive in the Bowling Green area first. To the winner would go the prize of the Louisville Pike, which ran east of and parallel to the equally important Bardstown Pike, as well as control of the Louisville and Nashville Railroad. If Buell seized those lines of communication first, he could cut off Bragg from Kirby Smith, prevent the two from combining their forces, and wreck the campaign. Outnumbered, Bragg would face Buell alone.

Dismissing all of the by-now fruitless suggestions to march back toward Nashville, Bragg determined that the army, spearheaded by Polk's already advancing wing, first had to get to Glasgow before Buell reached Bowling Green. Glasgow was about forty miles east of Bowling Green, but because of the northeasterly turn the railroad took past the latter city, Glasgow offered the potential of cutting Buell's lines of communications to Louisville. From there the combined Confederate army could easily march the additional nine miles to the Louisville Pike and prevent the Federals from using it as well. The railroad back to Louisville could be bisected quickly and effectively by Polk's forces at Cave City and at the tunnel near Proctor's Station, between Cave City and Bowling Green.[10] With that accomplished, the army would be in an excellent position "for the purpose of striking a blow at Bowling Green" from the north.[11]

The question was whether or not they could get to Glasgow in time. Bragg's men had to try. Buell's army, according to encouraging reports, was badly demoralized and staggering toward Kentucky. Although already exhausted, the Confederate army did its part and more in a series of Herculean forced marches. As Hardee's wagons emptied of supplies, he ordered them filled with sick or worn out men in order to keep up the pace. When they broke down, the soldiers abandoned them and kept moving. It worked. Bragg's pioneers and a cavalry escort entered Glasgow late in the afternoon on September 11, followed the next day by lead elements of the infantry. The rest of the force stumbled into town on the thirteenth. Major General Jones M. Withers's division of Polk's wing continued on to the railroad, with Brig. Gen. James R. Chalmers's brigade occupying Cave City while Brig. Gen. Johnson K. Duncan's command seized the tunnel at Proctor's Station eight miles to the south. They were two days ahead of Buell.[12]

From Glasgow, Bragg issued on the fourteenth a grandiose proclamation to Kentuckians: "We come not as conquerors, but to restore to you the liberties of which you have been deprived by a cruel and relentless foe. Will you remain indifferent to our call[?] . . . Kentuckians, we have come with joyous hopes. Let us not depart in sorrow, as we shall if we find you wedded in your choice to your present lot. If you prefer Federal rule, show it by your frowns and we shall return whence we came."[13] If Morgan and Kirby Smith could be believed, though, Bragg's "joyous hopes" would not be dashed. To arm the legions of Kentuckians expected to rally now to the Stars and Bars, he sent back to Chattanooga for what Sam Jones termed "all the arms I could collect. . . . If the people of Kentucky and Tennessee rally to our standard in any considerable numbers, as I am assured they will, it is very desirable to have arms to put in their hands immediately."[14]

The occupation of Glasgow not only brought much-needed rest and a chance to acquire something to eat, it also inspired optimism, for at first Bragg's army saw few frowns indeed. Capt. Morris Wampler, Polk's chief engineer, wrote of Glasgow's ladies greeting him waving handkerchiefs and with cries of "'We are Southern! We are Rebels!'"[15] Maj. George Winchester, quartermaster of Brig. Gen. Daniel S. Donelson's brigade, likewise wrote in his diary that "the welcome to Kentucky was cheering—the shouts of the soldiers was heard swelling above the din and rattle of the wagons, and their own heavy tread, as the waving kerchiefs and—the smiling faces of men & women & even children announced the grateful welcome, with which all Kentucky received the southern soldiers."[16]

Chaplain Joseph Cross of Donelson's brigade remembered being met on the outskirts of town by "an old man . . . waving his hat over his head and bidding us a thousand welcomes." They then encountered "a pale woman" calling out "'Welcome Tennesseans! Welcome to Kentucky! Welcome to Glasgow! Welcome to our homes! You have come to redeem us. I knew you would come.'"[17] Days later, the same woman stood in the street welcoming Buckner's division with similar words.[18]

Morale buoyed accordingly, even Bragg's. He proudly reported to Richmond that his footsore army, while understandably tired, had borne up well and remained cheerful, thanks in large part to his strict discipline of course. "My admiration of and love for my army cannot be expressed," he added a few days later in decidedly un-Bragg-like tones of affection. "To its patient toil and admirable discipline am I indebted for all the success which has attended this perilous undertaking. The men are much jaded and somewhat destitute, but cheerful and confident without murmur." Coming from Bragg, it was high praise indeed.[19]

Along came more good news: reports of the Confederate victory at Second Manassas. Nonetheless, Bragg's optimism soon faded. One reason was the beginning of his disenchantment with Kentuckians. Like Kirby Smith's men in Lexington, Bragg and his soldiers soon realized that while Kentuckians might cheer, few were surrendering to the urge to enlist—not with Buell massing his forces just to the south in Bowling Green. H. W. Graber of Terry's Texas Rangers later complained, "we gathered only about six thousand recruits and they all wanted to serve in cavalry." Most of them, he added, eventually deserted.[20]

There were more immediate problems, as Bragg again was forced to reconsider his line of march, which he had altered once already. Contrary to earlier assurances, there were desperately few provisions available around Glasgow, as much of the parched Barren River Valley had been picked over by the Federals recently occupying Bowling Green. The army, Bragg believed, could not remain very long in such an inhospitable place. Coupled with Buell's pursuit, supposedly now reinforced by Maj. Gen. William Starke Rosecrans's Mississippi army, the lack of food and forage meant that Bragg had to keep moving toward a junction with Kirby Smith rather than challenge Buell with his outnumbered army. There would be no more talk of "striking a blow" on the Green River. For the first time, Bragg began to consider using the Louisville Pike, now under his control, to drive on that city itself rather than march more directly toward Lexington. Joined by Kirby Smith, the Confederates might be able to take the vital Federal base and strike a massive blow against the Union war effort. He accordingly ordered his chief engineer, David Bullock Harris, to ascertain the condition of the road and the availability of water all the way from Glasgow to Louisville. He also notified Kirby Smith of his intentions and then hoped for the best.[21]

Bragg's improvisational strategy, muddled though it had been at times, had not harmed the Confederate cause greatly thus far. Indeed, he had accomplished great things. Bragg successfully had pulled Buell's army out of Alabama and Tennessee, and had admirably placed his forces between the Federals and their base, squarely on Buell's main supply line. The ill-advised delay at Sparta had cost little thanks to the improved condition and morale of his men during the forced march to Glasgow. Even his deviations from previously planned routes reflected sound logistical judgment. If he could now persuade Kirby Smith to join him, admittedly a doubtful proposition considering the latter's previous independent and self-serving behavior, the Confederates still could defeat Buell, with haste seize Louisville, or perhaps accomplish even both. Even the enemy begrudgingly admired what Bragg had done. The Federal commission convened after the campaign to examine Buell's conduct stated that "history of military campaigns affords no parallel to this of an army throwing aside its transportation, paying no regard to its supplies, but cutting loose from its base, marching 200 miles in the face of and in reality victorious over an army double its size."[22]

Nonetheless, Bragg's indecisive lack of vision, combined with Kirby Smith's massive and touchy ego, remained a constant threat to the campaign. Moving without a coherent strategy or even a clear-cut reason for being in Kentucky other than to support Kirby Smith, Bragg, increasingly feeling the strain of command, changed his mind almost daily about goals, tactics, and now whether to first fight Buell or effect a junction with Kirby Smith. It was as if he needed someone to push him in one direction or the other, as Kirby Smith had done from Tupelo to Chattanooga. That general, however, was so preoccupied with his own affairs that he offered Bragg little in terms of support or direction. Richmond, meanwhile, was consumed with Lee's Maryland raid. As a result, Bragg found himself truly on his own in the midst of a campaign he initially had opposed, and he was not sure what to do next. His indecision had not hurt him thus far, but the specter of disaster remained to shadow the army like its train. It caught up with them at a place called Munfordville.

Having occupied Cave City per orders near midnight on September 12, the men of Chalmers's brigade proceeded to accomplish their assignment, tearing up track and occupying the telegraph office. Control of the telegraph wire proved crucial, for almost immediately the Confederates began intercepting Federal messages. Several dealt with nearby Munfordville, a dozen miles to the north. The hometown of Simon B. Buckner as well as one of Buell's division commanders, Buckner's boyhood friend Thomas J. Wood, Munfordville occupied a crucial point on both the railroad and the Louisville Pike. The bridge there, eighteen hundred feet long and 115 feet above the Green River, was the most vulnerable point on the entire Louisville and Nashville line. For that reason, an entrenched Federal garrison of indeterminate size defended the town and the bridge. Alexander McCook, who had ordered the fort built during the previous year on the south side of the Green River, had feted Anthony Trollope there eight months before. Now, alarmed that an overestimated body of more than seven thousand Confederates had cut the railroad, the current Federal post commander, Col. John T. Wilder, a former Indiana businessman, requested reinforcements from Louisville. Late in the day, still another intercepted telegram revealed that Col. Cyrus L. Dunham's 50th Indiana Infantry would leave that evening to reinforce the town's defenders, and, more importantly, Buell himself was closing to the rescue. However formidable Munfordville's defenses might be, they were about to grow stronger.[23]

At about the same time, Chalmers received information of a different sort. Kirby Smith had sent Col. John Scott down from Lexington with a brigade of three hundred horsemen to keep tabs on Bragg and Buell and to destroy Louisville and Nashville Railroad bridges if the Yankees got in front. The most important of those bridges was the one at Munfordville. Coincidentally arriving in town that evening, Scott bellicosely demanded that Wilder surrender the town, which he assumed was lightly held. When the Federal refused, Scott sent a messenger to Chalmers. According to Chalmers, Scott claimed that the town contained "not more than 1,800 men, entirely raw troops, and that they were fortifying their position, but that the railroad and telegraph had been destroyed in their rear, cutting them off completely from all communication and re-enforcements. He also told me that he intended to attack them at daylight on the following morning, and desired that I would co-operate with him with a part of my force."[24]

Whether it was because of reports of large quantities of wheat near the town, or more probably his own ambitions for glory and a promotion, Chalmers decided to march his entire brigade to Munfordville that night to assist Scott's cavalrymen. He expected an easy victory; the Yankees probably would surrender without much of a fight. Accordingly, he did not bother to inform his superiors of his decision, an incredible lapse in judgment. Unfortunately for the Confederates, in the cool early morning fog of September 14, Munfordville did not look so ripe for the taking after all. Chalmers could not see all of the Union works through the gray mist, but what he could observe seemed much more imposing than what Scott had suggested. Despite his reservations, he nonetheless launched his attack at 5 A.M. as agreed. For the next four and one-half hours, Chalmers's men, mostly fellow Mississippians, launched repeated charges against the deadly earthworks. All were viciously repulsed. Confounded, Chalmers then tried a bit of bluff himself, sending a note to Wilder demanding his surrender. Not surprisingly, the Federal commander again refused, for not only had he held his position, but Dunham was arriving with the reinforcements Scott had promised would never come. Better still, Buell hopefully was marching to the rescue from Bowling Green. Wilder did consent to a truce for gathering the wounded and burying the dead, but that was all.[25] Satisfied "that I had been deceived as to the strength of the enemy's works, as well as their numbers and disposition and the possibility of being reinforced," Chalmers gave up and returned to Cave City, leaving thirty-five dead, 253 wounded, and the pride of the army bloodied.[26]

Back in Glasgow, it had been a day of rest. Many of Bragg's men took the rare opportunity to attend church on the fourteenth, some of them receiving Holy Communion for the first time since they had first donned their uniforms. Others less inclined to worship indulged in whiskey to the point that by evening their officers ordered them bucked and gagged.[27] Toward evening, however, Bragg learned of Chalmers's "unauthorized and injudicious" repulse and reacted with unchristian anger. Worse yet, at about the same time, he also found out that Buell and much of his army finally had arrived in Bowling Green.[28] What to do? While he could bypass Munfordville easily by remaining on the Bardstown Pike and keep moving toward Kirby Smith, Bragg worried that doing so "was calculated to throw a gloom upon the whole army." It had been defeated in its first encounter, and the Stars and Stripes still flying above Wilder's works added salt to the wound. Thus, he made a fateful decision. He would detour the entire army to Munfordville, reduce the position before Buell could get there, "and turn defeat into victory."[29]

Starting in the early afternoon, the army made a grueling night march of between twenty-five and thirty-five miles, depending upon its various starting points, to Munfordville. Many soldiers fell by the wayside, and confusion invariably occurred in the darkness—most notably when men in Donelson's brigade killed one of their officers after mistaking his party for Federal cavalry. Still, by the hot, steamy morning of September 16, the Army of the Mississippi confronted the Federal works that had stymied Chalmers. Realizing their strength, Bragg sent in a note asking the Federals to surrender. Dunham initially expressed defiance, but then requested a suspension of hostilities in order to hold a council of war. Confused as to what to do next, Dunham wired headquarters in Louisville, whose bizarre response was to relieve him and put Wilder back in command. Wilder stalled as long as he could, but in the end agreed to surrender if Bragg could prove he possessed the superior numbers he claimed to have. Bragg at first chafed at any conditions, but in the end allowed Buckner, the hometown boy, to give Wilder a tour of Hardee's wing. Counting forty-five cannon and upward of twenty-five thousand veteran Rebel soldiers, Wilder agreed that surrender just might be a good idea after all.[30] Anything else, he later explained, would have been "no less than wilful murder." At six the next morning, the paroled defenders of Munfordville donned new uniforms and marched out "with all the honors of war, drums beating and colors flying," for Buell's lines in Bowling Green.[31]

Bragg expressed unwarranted jubilation over the little victory. "We get 4,000 prisoners, 4,000 small arms, pieces of artillery, and munitions of war in large quantities," he reported to Richmond. "My position must be exceedingly embarrassing to Buell and his army. They dare not attack me, and yet no other escape seems to be open to them."[32] Indeed, so confident was Bragg that Buell would remain behind his works in Bowling Green that, echoing a general policy proclaimed by President Davis, he set aside September 18 as a day of thanksgiving and prayer. The haste to slip Buell and rendezvous with Kirby Smith was forgotten temporarily in the unreasonably overconfident glow of his first victory as army commander.

His men, hungry and ill equipped though they were, also sounded sassy after the fall of Munfordville.[33] Louisianian John Ellis lamented that Wilder "surrendered so soon. His fort would have been blown to atoms in half an hour."[34] John Inglis of the 3rd Florida compared the defeated Federals to his comrades, noting that "they looked fat, clean & had new uniforms an we dirty ragged, barefooted and hungry, and skins dark our burned."[35] Likewise, W. L. Trask remarked that Munfordville's defenders in blue were a fine look-ing set of men. . . . To look at them, one would have not thought that they had ever robbed a hen roost or burned a barn. Some had been in service but four weeks and non more than twelve months. They were well clothed, looked fat and sleek clean and neat and were in strange contrast to our own hungry, ragged and dirty looking rebels." Yet in the end it had been the ragged men who triumphed.[36]

The Army of the Mississippi thus rested on its laurels. Men joyously acquired coffee, hardtack, beef, clothing, and shoes from the stocks that the Federals surrendered. The cost in the end was high, however. Buell had not halted behind Bowling Green's fortifications as Bragg confidently expected. On the night of September 16, just as a rare rainy spell set in, spies reported that Buell instead had left the city and, using roads west of the Louisville Pike, seemed to be trying to slip by the Rebels at Cave City. They reported that his initial destination was Hawesville or even Owensboro, the latter a hundred miles west of Louisville on the Ohio River. From there, Buell could swing back to Louisville without confronting Bragg, perhaps even on the Indiana side of the river. If true, his army was woefully out of position.[37]

Dumbfounded again by Buell's unexpected aggressiveness and appar-ently unorthodox tactics, Bragg grasped for a response. It was, he told a local man, "a very ugly position" to be in, caught between Buell and the Federals in Louisville. Buell, he added, was sure to swing to the west just as Wheeler indicated, for the Yankee general was a "smart man" who would not wait to be caught between Bragg and John C. Breckinridge's column—the latter presumably advancing northward to join the army with reinforcements—nor risk a headlong attack on Munfordville. Indeed, Bragg advised the man not to flee with his family; there would be no further fighting in the town. The man recorded that Bragg "would not consider it more than a breakfast spell to take General Buell's army, if he would attack him, and that his army could eat Buell's up alive."[38]

Confident that he had deduced Buell's plans, Bragg concluded that he still had time to complete the junction with Kirby Smith. After a council of war with Hardee and Polk, he dispatched Stoddard Johnston to Lexington with a verbal request to send "a heavy train of provisions" to Bardstown, to be followed by Kirby Smith and his army. Bragg, meanwhile, would move toward Bardstown and the junction rather than turn to fight Buell then and there. Together, they then would approach Louisville, ready to hit Buell in the flank as he veered toward the city. The reportedly strong Louisville garrisons, like Morgan's Federals at Cumberland Gap, would be left marooned. Bragg added that Kirby Smith needed to keep an eye toward Cumberland Gap in case Morgan emerged.[39]

Bragg's mental floundering unfortunately had not ended. As he had done ever since taking command from Beauregard, Bragg started giving in to his doubts, second-guessing his own conclusions to the point that they hardly could be called decisions at all. After midnight, Bragg abruptly decided to stand and fight after all. Cavalry skirmishing at Cave City indicated that Buell, contrary to Wheeler's earlier reports and Bragg's overconfidence, was pushing directly toward Munfordville and battle. Bragg decided to give it to him and ordered his army, including Forrest's far-flung cavalry, to concentrate at Munfordville. They would use Wilder's works to anchor an imposing defense, one that would shred Buell's army just as Chalmers had been bloodied. Having defeated Buell, the army might even descend on Nashville, an odd notion in that Bragg had rejected similar plans for days.[40] Meeting with Bragg that morning, Wheeler found the army commander "never . . . more determined or more confident. The entire army was in the best of spirits. I met and talked with Generals Hardee, Polk, Cheatham, and Buckner; all were enthusiastic over our success, and our good luck in getting Buell where he would be compelled to fight us to such disadvantage." Bragg particularly was "anxious for a fight," Wheeler later wrote.[41]

The new day brought no heavy push from the Yankees, only more sporadic killing by the horse soldiers. Bragg again vacillated. If Buell was moving that slowly, or not at all, he still had time to link up with Kirby Smith. Accordingly, he ordered Buckner's division to Cave City to feel the enemy out while the rest of the army prepared to march for Bardstown at dawn.[42] To a staff officer, Bragg commented "with emphasis, 'This campaign must be won by marching, not by fighting.'"[43]

Leaving behind the Louisville Pike for Buell, Bragg's army, exhausted from marching and countermarching according to its commander's whim and disappointed at not fighting Buell, stepped back onto the Bardstown Pike early in the morning on the twentieth. The Green River bridge burned behind them. Traveling slowly through Hodgenville, Abraham Lincoln's birthplace, the van of a tired, famished army arrived in Bardstown on the twenty-second. It was a difficult and disappointing march made by jaded, hungry soldiers driven at least initially by the notion that they were racing Buell to Louisville but who in time realized the discouraging truth. Some feasted on fresh beef, but most made do with little besides parched corn, stolen apples, and whatever they could find at nearby homes.[44]

One Alabamian remembered that the biggest problem was a lack of water, which recent storms had done nothing to alleviate. "At times," he wrote, "we obtained water under deep limesinks, some of these being partly full of water, and Federals had utilized some of the partly filled sinks as a place to butcher cattle and dumped offal into them, making the water unfit to drink."[45] Likewise, James Iredell Hall of the 9th Tennessee Infantry remembered suffering "for the want even of drinking water, the only water accessible was pond water and that was warm and muddy. The water we were compelled to drink, was so muddy that we could not wash our faces in it."[46] That lack of potable water would become a critical factor in the days to come.

Abandoning Munfordville for Bardstown and thus allowing Buell a straight path to the Ohio River up the Louisville Pike would loom as one of the most controversial moments of the campaign in the months and years to come. Starting with officers such as Wheeler—who in truth had served his commander poorly, providing more confusion than accurate information—generations have castigated Bragg for not making a stand at Munfordville. The "Munfordville myth," the idea that Bragg could have defeated Buell and in so doing held Kentucky in the Confederacy, after the war became akin to gospel in the church of the lost cause. Many recent historians, however, have dismissed the notion. Remaining at Munfordville, they point out, hardly would have resulted in automatic victory. First of all, Buell easily could have flanked Munfordville without giving battle at all. Had he gotten into Bragg's rear at Elizabethtown, there would have been no junction with Kirby Smith, and probably no further Confederate advance as well.

Moreover, without cooperation from Kirby Smith, Bragg would have been outnumbered even if attacked, and Kirby Smith almost certainly would have left Bragg to his own devices. After the war, Kirby Smith insisted that Stoddard Johnston had garbled his chief's orders upon arriving in Lexington, telling him to *prepare* to move to Bardstown rather than ordering him to move immediately. The only actual orders he received, the general continued, were to keep an eye on George Morgan. When that officer finally abandoned the Cumberland Gap on the night of September 17 and headed into the mountains of eastern Kentucky, Kirby Smith moved instead to meet Morgan's threat. He offered little more to Bragg than Cleburne's and Smith's borrowed brigades at Shelbyville, a little cavalry, and advice for Bragg to seize Louisville on his own if possible. And what if Buell had attacked and been defeated? He almost certainly would have fallen back initially to Bowling Green, where formidable defenses would have preserved his army, forcing Bragg into either a suicidal frontal assault like Chalmers's at Munfordville, or a siege he did not have the strength to maintain.[47]

The Munfordville myth also never took into account the destitute condition of the Army of the Mississippi. Thanks to the drought, the valleys of the Barren and Green Rivers were almost entirely devoid of supplies. Brigadier General St. John Liddell, one of Bragg's brigade commanders and still a Bragg loyalist in 1862, wrote four years later that at Munfordville, the army had at best two days' rations. "I have frequently heard it said," Liddell added, "that Bragg *ought* to have fought Buell at Munfordville. But the truth is that he could not wait without starving. There was nothing in that section in the way of provisions at that time. . . . Bragg decided upon the best course held out to him."[48]

Instead of avoiding battle at Munfordville, Bragg's real error was going there in the first place. Unless he intended to fight it out along the Green River, an idea that flickered only briefly under duress, Munfordville was a three-day distraction the Confederate cause could ill afford. Bragg's first priority, as he usually but not always remembered, was to join forces with Kirby Smith and negate as much as possible Buell's numerical advantage. Once the armies were united, Kirby Smith's ego-driven independence would have been subverted to Bragg's command as well; he would have been a loose cannon no longer. Thus strengthened, Bragg could well have kept Buell out of Louisville and fought on his terms somewhere in the Bluegrass. That, however, did not happen. Bragg's spur-of-the-moment decision to "turn defeat into victory" at Munfordville severely limited his options from then on. The shadow of disaster, like the dust clouds following Buell's Army of the Ohio, now threatened to envelop the disappointed Confederates as they plodded into Bardstown.[49]

While Bragg's Confederates marched into Kentucky singing songs and tasting victory, Don Carlos Buell's veteran Federals pursued them in exhausted agony. Occasionally marching over thirty miles a day, sometimes until midnight only to rise again at two or three, the ragged, footsore, and often barefoot Army of the Ohio stumbled insensibly northward like drunken men along the path of the Louisville and Nashville Railroad toward Bowling Green. They moved on roads choked with limestone dust and past cotton, tobacco, and wheat fields devoid of rain. Traffic clogged the road too, at times so much that units filed onto the railroad bed to march. The days were hot and the nights cold, yet having left their tents in Tennessee, they slept on the hard ground. Aside from a rare spring, green, scum-covered ponds—often containing "waggletails" if not putrid animal carcasses—provided the only source of water for the parched lips and dry throats of most of the men. The rare working wells were often reserved "for headquarters." Half-rations and then quarter-rations sufficed, and when the hardtack ran out, commissary officers issued wormy flour without the requisite utensils to make bread, leading the men to heat dough wrapped around their ramrods and mix it with salt in their tin cups, or place it on barrel staves before open fires. One soldier compared the result to the unleavened bread Moses and the Israelites ate during their flight from Egypt, while another less devoutly likened the bread produced to cannonballs. Meat was scarce as well. Not surprisingly, foraging continued, with apples, green corn, and potatoes the chief supplements to army fare. Camp guards proved unwilling or unable to stop hungry and determined foragers, who sometimes boasted of aid from "contrabands" who helpfully identified secessionists possessing full smokehouses.

Because of the heat, their diets, and the stagnant water they were drinking, many Yankees grew ill on the march into Kentucky. One soldier complained that he spent two days riding on the axletree of a wagon because the ambulances were full. For others, the wounds were psychological. Hungry, thirsty, trudging past destroyed Federal works, bridges, railroad cars, and telegraph wires, defeat seemed to stare from every vacant door or dried up pond. Constant rumors of Confederate ambushes and potshots from bushwhackers wore away at morale, and a few real skirmishes with Rebel cavalry drew enough blood to keep everyone on edge. Many straggled, and a few soldiers, especially Kentuckians, deserted.

Most of the boys in blue persisted and persevered, however, and then slowly discovered renewed pride in their doggedness. Indeed, perhaps the most significant result of Buell's long march was how the beaten-down army's morale rose as it drew nearer to Louisville. Much was at stake, the soldiers realized, during what many called "the great foot race" or "the race to Louisville." Captured Confederate stragglers reinforced the notion that their army was bound for Louisville and planning to winter north of the Ohio in Indiana. Some camp rumors depicted the battle for Louisville as already under way. Lacking faith in Buell, whom they believed never should have allowed Bragg to enter Kentucky in the first place, they nonetheless determined not to allow the Confederates to ravage their midwestern homes. Confederate deserters and runaway slaves joining the columns also reinforced the beliefs of many that they suffered for a righteous cause. They stubbornly willed one foot in front of another, both Bragg and Buell be damned.[50]

South of Bowling Green, Buell's advance saw another dust cloud in the distance: Bragg's army. They had caught the Rebels, and, despite their condition, itched for a showdown. Buell, however, would not attack. For five days the army stopped in Bowling Green before taking to the road in the direction of Cave City, once again granting Bragg precious time. More dispiriting still was news of the fall of Munfordville, which many blamed on their commander's unwillingness to fight despite the urging of his subordinates. According to one unfounded but widespread rumor, the fall of the town led to a near duel between the villainous Buell and the common soldier's hero, Thomas. Buell, they complained, did not want to catch Bragg. The sight of the paroled defenders of Munfordville, passing through the lines with dejection, filled many Federals with indignation, while others openly wept.[51] "It would be just throwing away money to get our lives insured," one soldier bitterly quipped, "as the safest place in the world, so far as getting hurt was concerned, was Buell's army."[52]

Not completely safe, however, for Buell momentarily determined on September 16 to give battle. Learning of the Confederate detour to Munfordville, Buell had indeed veered from Glasgow toward Cave City, seemingly still determined to fight. The following evening, however, Colonel Wilder, the other paroled men, and several Munfordville Unionists entered his lines. Wilder reported that Bragg had drawn up in line of battle behind the Munfordville defenses, and was expecting the arrival of Kirby Smith's force as well. Although hungry and ragged, Wilder and the others added, Bragg's Confederates exhibited perfect discipline and would make a formidable foe. Newly concerned about being outnumbered, Buell pulled up and ordered Thomas's division to hurry up from Nashville. He would wait in Bowling Green.[53] According to Col. William P. Carlin, a brigade commander in Mitchell's division, Buell's chief of staff, Col. James B. Fry, explained "that Buell did not wish to fight there, or anywhere, until he had reached Louisville and received reinforcements of new troops that were assembling there."[54]

By September 20, when Thomas arrived, Bragg had abandoned Munfordville for Bardstown. Initially, Bragg's latest movement confused Buell. Years later, he wrote that at that point, "there was no reason to hesitate . . . as to the course which I should pursue." Kirby Smith certainly was out there, and united, the Confederates "would outnumber me very greatly. Louisville, also, in the presence of this combined force, might be in danger. Besides, our provisions were nearly exhausted. . . . I therefore pushed forward to Louisville."[55] In truth, Buell did "hesitate" for a day. He wrote to Bull Nelson in Louisville on September 22 that Bragg had three options. He could "go rapidly through to attack Louisville, or, if he thinks you too strong to be easily beaten, he may go to Bardstown to effect a junction with Smith, or he may halt at Elizabethtown to complete the junction and fight me there. The latter I think the most probable, considering that I am so close on him. . . . My own movements depend so much on those of the enemy that I can hardly tell you what to do." Instead of moving quickly toward Louisville, then, Buell determined to move on Elizabethtown on the Louisville Pike, fully expecting a fight. He did ask Nelson to erect a bridge over the Salt River so that Buell's army could cross it if need be. Only the next day did Buell accept that fact that Bragg had gone to Bardstown and was letting him pass by to Louisville unimpeded. Concerned about supplies as well as meeting the combined forces of Bragg and Kirby Smith, Buell decided to speed for the Ohio.[56]

The army now pushed hard, driving to reach Louisville before the Rebels. All the miseries of the previous march now were exacerbated. A sudden thunderstorm at Bowling Green soaked men who had left their tents in Alabama and Tennessee. Three days' rations issued before the march all but ran out. Buell ceased to issue orders prohibiting foraging, but it mattered little, for, as one soldier put it, everyone knew there was little or nothing left to steal anyway. Water grew scarcer as well, and the overwhelming drought meant dust everywhere, occasional thunderstorms and a few acquired bottles

Figure 4.1. Soldier of the 10th Indiana Infantry, on the march to Louisville. From James Birney Shaw, *History of the Tenth Regiment Indiana Volunteer Infantry.*

of applejack doing little to ease the situation. Stragglers lined the roads. Nonetheless, stimulated by commissary-issue whiskey and crowds of cheering, flag-waving Kentucky Unionists, the army struggled on until its forward units reached West Point, a town on the Ohio River twenty miles from the city, where rations requested by Buell reportedly waited. The steamboats carrying the food arrived late. When they arrived, a riot nearly ensued, but was stopped short when the crew began to throw food onto the shore for self-protection. On September 25, the first units began to enter the city in a scene that was repeated for the next two days.

The men of the Army of the Ohio were justly proud of what they had accomplished. Foot racing remained a popular pastime in antebellum America, and in the minds of Buell's men at least, they had won the greatest American race ever, a vital marathon of several hundred miles to Louisville. In so doing had saved the North from Braxton Bragg's veterans. Reinforcing their cheer was welcome news that McClellan had defeated Lee in Maryland along Antietam Creek. Along the banks of the Ohio, worn out but proud men ate roasted beef, bathed, soaked their feet, and at night sang patriotic songs such as "Rally Round the Flag" and "John Brown's Body," entire regiments swelling in tune.[57]

Men from nearby Indiana were particularly affected. Colonel Benjamin F. Scribner of the 38th Indiana remembered that

> many of my men could look across the river and behold their homes which, for twelve long, lagging months. They had so wistfully yearned for. . . . It was a rare and touching sight to see these poor fellows so covered with limestone dust that their garments, beards, hair, and visages were all of the same color, all seeming old and gray with the dust and bending under the burden of their guns and knapsacks, limping along on blistered feet. They appeared more like grim spectres than young and sturdy men, whose hearts were beating with tenderness and love for the dear ones they were passing by without a word or caress.[58]

George H. Alverson of the 10th Wisconsin Infantry felt the same way but put it less poetically. Writing to his father, Alverson exclaimed, "thank the Lord we are out of Alabama and in old Kentucky once more and we have had the damdest time a getting here that ever was." All the army needed, he assured his father, was a respite and some new clothes before pursuing Bragg again.[59]

There was only one sour note. Their general had let the enemy get away unmolested to fight another day. Hatred of Buell had been building for months, but the march to Louisville was for many the final straw. Buell had starved them while protecting Southerners, driven them to exhaustion, and then refused to fight when presented with the opportunity, allowing Bragg to escape "as usual like a scared mink."[60] To many angry or humiliated soldiers, Buell's refusal to fight Bragg suggested that he was nothing less than a traitor. "Old Buell is a coward or a Rebel," one Hoosier complained. "Shoot him let us go."[61] Another, a Kentuckian in blue, wrote that as the army entered Louisville, "free use was made of epithets 'traitor, tyrant, fool, and coward' with references to Gen. Buell."[62] One widespread rumor provided an explanation for their general's treachery. "Genl's Buell and Bragg were brothers in law," wrote an angry Emerson Rood Calkins of the 8th Wisconsin Battery, "and there began to be a good deal of dissatisfaction among the Soldiers because he Buell, dident force Brag to give battle, the boys used to declare that they slept together nights."[63]

"Great God!" still another soldier calling himself "Seventeenth Regiment" complained in the *Cincinnati Daily Commercial*. "[W]ill the Government permit this, and not sink him as low in the eyes of foreign nations as he is in the eyes of his own men? Let Abraham Lincoln send secret agents into our ranks, and ascertain in what light Gen. Buell is held by the men who have marched through the dust, over the mountains, and upon half rations . . . and if he does not remove him, the American people will damn *him*."[64]

Once rested and refitted, the Army of the Ohio would never be more eager to fight. But would it fight for the despised Don Carlos Buell? That question remained to be answered.

5

A BABEL OF CONFUSION

IN MAY 1862, HARD ON THE MUDDY HEELS OF ANTHONY TROLLOPE, yet another curious Englishman arrived in Louisville hoping to understand and describe Kentucky's Civil War. Journalist Edward Dicey, a fervent supporter of the Union unlike the pro-Southern Trollope, entered a city that in his estimation already had "suffered terribly" from a year of conflict. Instead of the lovely provincial city Trollope described, Dicey's Louisville reeked with stagnation. Because of the loss of its once lucrative Southern trade, as well as much of the profitable nonmilitary shipping that plied the Ohio River before Fort Sumter, the town's storefronts sat largely boarded up, he wrote, and factories largely remained idle. Workers from those establishments complained to him of inflation and unemployment, and lamented about their struggles to make ends meet. Meanwhile, quiet streets and a dormant waterfront gave the city a "sleepy, drowsy look."

Dicey also expressed surprise that supporting Federal armies, the one activity still thriving, remained an unwelcome enterprise to that minority of secessionists who still chafed under Federal occupation. They were, he added, foolishly allowed too much liberty to express their opinions. Thousands of mourners turned out for the funerals of local Confederates. They then would retire to taverns to vent their frustrations and hatred for Lincoln and abolitionists. Yet even Unionists expressed growing disillusion with Washington's handling of the war, he added. Thus, he agreed on one point with Trollope: "The result was that the state was still halting between the North and South. Its sentiments drew it toward the latter, and its interest toward the former."

About the only thing in forlorn Louisville that still brought a smile, Dicey admitted, was the lovely spring weather, which reminded him "of an English summer." Outside the city "the pasture lands were as green, and the crops as rich, and the fields as carefully tilled and hedged in, as they would have been in Warwickshire."[1] That, however, was about to change, as the drought that had been torturing Bragg and Buell's armies to the south slowly expanded toward the banks of the Ohio in the van of those dust-covered

hosts. John Jefferson, a twenty-six-year-old Louisville merchant and Unionist, most meticulously recorded its onslaught in his journal. June was both
rainy and unseasonably cool, and as late as June 19 Jefferson thought a fire
necessary at night. July, while hotter, generally brought more of the same,
and it rained five times during the first two weeks in August. Then, just as
Kirby Smith was enticing Bragg into Tennessee and casting his own eyes
northward to glory, the sky over Louisville all but closed shut. Only twice
more in the month and four times in September did but "litt rain" fall in the
city. Dust clouds filled the streets, and the Ohio River, at flood tide when
Trollope crossed it months earlier, fell so low that at some spots upriver
people could walk across to the free states.

Jefferson recorded more in his diary than temperatures and rain mea-
surements that summer. An ardent observer of the war, he almost daily wrote
in growing horror of the one gray cloud rising over the Bluegrass.[2] He was
not alone either, for Louisville's soldiers and Unionist citizens alike greeted
each new report of the Confederate advance with growing alarm and increasing dread. Bustle and eventually bedlam superseded the lethargy Dicey
observed as the city bestirred itself in anticipation of Bragg's onslaught. Louisville would not appear drowsy come September.

As the spring of 1862 faded into summer, Confederate partisans on horseback had continued to comprise the major problem for the Union cause back
in Kentucky. Having remained in command of the extensive Department of
the Ohio despite increasing distance and more pressing responsibilities in
Alabama and lower Tennessee, Buell ordered cavalry around the state hoping to stymie the partisans, while simultaneously requesting more troops
from the governors of the Midwest. Faced with more immediate problems,
however, Buell left much of the day-to-day running of the state to Princeton-
educated Jeremiah T. "Jere" Boyle, the prewar attorney and iron-fisted military governor whose blatant political ambitions and draconian rule had not
only disillusioned Unionists but emboldened the Confederacy's Kentucky
dreamers.

Not surprisingly, Bragg's unexpected advance, coupled with Kirby
Smith's more immediate march toward Kentucky in late August, shook to its
foundations the tenuous chain of command that traversed three states. With
little real faith in Boyle, Buell ordered someone he trusted, the competent
and more popular Bull Nelson, home to organize the state's defenses. Buell
acted just in time, for Boyle buckled under the pressure almost immediately,
dispatching sheaves of anxious telegrams to Washington and across the commonwealth about the imminent loss of Kentucky while simultaneously attempting to shift responsibility to whomever would take it. The political
waters remained choppy, however. Buell's already strained relationship with
Republican politicians of the Old Northwest, particularly Ohio's Tod and
especially Indiana chief executive Morton, proved harder to overcome, for

they constantly bickered over when and how requested reinforcements were to be sent to Kentucky. Ultimately, Halleck and Secretary of War Stanton had to endorse Boyle and Buell's urgent demands for soldiers before the governors would comply. Many would be the rawest of new recruits, sent south without the guns they had not yet learned to fire.[3]

Meanwhile, increasingly dissatisfied with Buell's "apparent want of energy and activity"[4] and Boyle's frightened dithering, the Lincoln administration acted decisively in the face of the Kentucky invasion. Halleck reorganized the Department of the Ohio on August 19 and gave most of it to Maj. Gen. Horatio G. Wright. Buell, for the time being at least, would remain in command of the army as well as in charge of most of Tennessee, but everything north of Kentucky now was Wright's responsibility. The new commander, a forty-two-year-old career officer hailing from Connecticut, graduated second in the West Point class of 1841 and spent his prewar service in the Corps of Engineers and at West Point. After Fort Sumter, he fought in Virginia at Norfolk and First Bull Run before a promotion took him to the South Carolina and Florida coasts. His actions as a division commander at Secessionville, South Carolina, a bitter and controversial repulse for Federals arms, nonetheless resulted in both a promotion and command of the new Ohio department. According to Albion Tourgée, who served under Wright before going on to a successful postwar career in law and letters, Wright was no Grant or Stonewall Jackson, but rather a carbon copy of his sponsor, Halleck. "As a cool, level-headed organizer . . . his administration of the short-lived Department of the Ohio will always remain a testimony to the highest soldierly steadfastness and remarkable executive ability," Tourgée wrote. ". . . He had not, however, the power to inspire men to supreme exertion."[5]

Under Halleck's direct instructions, Wright reluctantly headed west, making his headquarters at Cincinnati rather than Louisville at Halleck's urging, for the latter city remained a hornet's nest of political intrigue.[6] "There are two factions there, the Speeds and the Guthries, very jealous of each other," Halleck wrote. "It will be difficult if at Louisville for you to keep clear of these factions, so as not to offend one or the other. Be on your guard against them even at Cincinnati." The duplicitous Halleck held out an added carrot: Buell's command. "The Government," Halleck wrote, "or rather I should say the President and the Secretary of War, is greatly displeased with the slow movements of General Buell. Unless he does something very soon I think he will be removed. . . . There must be more energy and activity in Kentucky and Tennessee, and the one who first does something brilliant will get the entire command. I therefore hope to hear very soon of some success in your department."[7]

Wright got the message, but when he arrived in Louisville on August 23 on the way to Cincinnati, he immediately discovered such pandemonium that he must have despaired. He found a city still without enough troops to defend it. Soldiers in the units he did possess were either unarmed or poorly equipped with ancient flintlock muskets, and poorly equipped with other accouterments as well due to military red tape and clashes between the army and various state governments. A burgeoning political crisis growing out of Boyle's unauthorized decision to draft all men between the ages of eighteen and twenty-one into military service had flared up as well. Rumor was rampant and reliable information hard to come by, Wright lamented to Halleck. Guerrillas, seemingly everywhere in the surrounding countryside, extended their raids right up to the city's picket lines. Moreover, the local authorities seemed either ignorant or indifferent to the crisis. Nelson, insubordinate and angry because he had been passed over in favor of Wright, presented still another problem. He remained loyal to Buell and wanted out of the department.

Beset with such difficulties, the new commander of the Department of the Ohio rolled up his sleeves. Seeking support for Boyle's draft in Washington and giving the Kentuckian immediate military command of Louisville as well, Wright turned to the more immediate need to put enough armed men in the city to defend it. He badgered the Midwest governors for more troops while simultaneously fending off their meddling and complaints about the treatment of the soldiers already sent to Kentucky. His patience faded quickly, and soon he was sounding the same exasperated notes as Buell. Answering Ohio's Tod for example, who had complained about his men's lack of knapsacks and tents, an exasperated Wright shot back that the rebels were without similar equipment but seemed to be doing just fine. Perhaps Tod's Ohioans could deign to put up with the same deficiencies in order to defend the North.[8]

Strategically, Wright initially focused on George Morgan's straits at Cumberland Gap and Buell's growing need for support. Kirby Smith's sudden appearance south of Richmond thus took the new Federal commander completely by surprise. Like Jefferson Davis and Braxton Bragg, Wright had expected Kirby Smith to go by the book and first lay siege to the gap. Hurriedly dispatching many of his newly raised regiments directly to Lexington from their camps of instruction in hopes that they would reach Nelson's equally raw force in time, Wright reacted with disbelief when news of the debacle at Richmond first trickled in, and at one point assured newly appointed Kentucky governor James F. Robinson that the reports could not be true. When the facts no longer could be ignored, Wright first wrote a letter to Halleck, making sure that the general in chief realized that the defeat was the result of Buell's man Nelson disobeying orders and not because of anything he himself had done. Only after placing the blame squarely on Nelson's shoulders did Wright ride to Lexington to survey the damage, no doubt worrying all the way that the dangled army command was slipping away.[9]

He immediately concluded that Lexington could not be held. The battered survivors of Richmond, as well as those who arrived too late for the battle, had to be organized quickly so that they could fall back toward Covington or Frankfort in hopes of at least stalling Kirby Smith in front of Cincinnati or Louisville as he chose. Complicating matters further, Nelson had been wounded, so someone else would have to take command of the retreat. When brigadier generals Charles Cruft and James S. Jackson both ducked the assignment, Wright turned in desperation to an unusual alternative candidate both officers suggested: Capt. Charles Champion Gilbert. The forty-year-old Ohio native brought much to the crisis that seemed to recommend him. A West Pointer and veteran of the siege of Veracruz during the war in Mexico, Gilbert spent the following years both at West Point and in active service on the southwestern frontier. After the war began, he led a company of regular troops at the Battle of Wilson's Creek, where he was wounded. Later, at Shiloh and Corinth, he served as inspector general of the Army of the Ohio, and in August he journeyed to Kentucky with Nelson. In the moment of crisis following Richmond, the game Gilbert must have seemed a godsend to Wright. The only problem was his rank. Straightaway, and without any legal authority to do so, Wright accordingly promoted Gilbert on the spot to "Acting Major General" and gave him command of the column.

Wright's reasoning remains murky, but clearly he had more faith in an experienced fellow veteran of the old army, one at least willing to take the job, than he did in the beaten cast of characters who greeted him in Lexington, even if the former was a captain who had commanded no more than a company in battle.[10] One supporting clue came several days later. Appealing to Halleck for the services of Brig. Gen. Philip Sheridan, then serving under Brig. Gen. Gordon Granger, Wright complained that "we have no good generals here and are badly in want of them."[11] In the case of Gilbert, he decided to make a major general out of whole cloth to outrank Boyle, Cruft, Jackson, and the others. President Lincoln would quickly follow up with an appointment of brigadier general for Gilbert, but congressional approval awaited his performance in the days ahead.[12] The two stars Gilbert proudly began to wear almost immediately in time became one of the most fractious elements of the entire Kentucky campaign.

The forced march from Lexington to Louisville brought intense suffering. It was the first hard marching for most of the new men under Gilbert's command, and they quickly tossed aside freshly issued and heavy knapsacks, overcoats, blankets, underwear, drums, and anything else that seemed expendable. Water was scarce, ankle-deep limestone dust rose above the roads in yellow clouds until it blocked the sun and the stars, and the heat became so oppressive that soldiers died of heatstroke or else straggled far enough behind to be captured. Sick men filled the ambulances. Some worn-out soldiers wanted to stop and fight in Frankfort, for not only did the state capital offer a good defensive position, but many also believed they could go no farther. They preferred to die in battle rather than of heatstroke. Among them were many men of the 105th Ohio Infantry, who removed their shoes upon arriving in the state capital and discovered the next morning that their feet were so swollen that they could not put them back on. They would henceforth march barefoot.[13]

All along the march route, neighborhood slaves "came, one by one, and offered to bring water, to carry guns or knapsacks,—anything, if they could only follow us." Some bluecoats proved perfectly willing to employ the so-called contrabands as porters. Others expressed a more defiant brand of sympathy. In Frankfort, constables and slaveholders attempted to seize their runaway human property, only to be met in many cases by the lowered guns of the men in blue, sending brigade commander and native Kentuckian Jackson into a fury. The "Hell-March" finally ended when the column straggled into Louisville on September 5, only to be reproved by comrades for their disgraceful retreat and condemned by the recovering Nelson as cowards.[14] Wright, however, pronounced himself so pleased with Gilbert's performance that, with Boyle's acquiescence, he gave him command of all forces in and around Louisville, including the nervous loose cannon Boyle, thus apparently nullifying another problem.[15]

Although much of the Federal army escaped Richmond, panic spread all across the lower Midwest after the crushing defeat. Few expressed faith in the rookie force gathering in Louisville and Cincinnati, least of all Boyle, who wrote directly to Lincoln: "Lexington will be in their possession to-morrow. We must have help of drilled troops unless you intend to turn us over to the devil and his imps."[16] Nor did he mince words with Halleck, writing that the only way to preserve Kentucky for the Union would be to send for U. S. Grant's veterans, as the new levies pouring south across the Ohio could not hope to stop the Rebels alone, and Buell still was miles away. Others—including Nelson, Cincinnati commander Lew Wallace, and ultimately Wright himself—took up the call for either Grant's or Samuel Curtis's armies, the latter currently in Arkansas, although Wright tactfully asked for the former's troops without Halleck's old rival Sam Grant in tow. In response, Grant agreed to send Brig. Gen. Gordon Granger's division to Wright from Corinth. He could, he said, spare no others.[17] If nothing else, Grant's veterans would, in Halleck's words, "give confidence to the new levies."[18]

For the time being, until Buell or Granger arrived, Wright remained largely dependent upon the new recruits from the Old Northwest. Along with civilians and impressed slaves, they threw up a few breastworks and dug rifle pits to retard any Confederate assault. According to later accounts, they made little headway. Officers spent more time drilling their raw charges than using them as laborers, hoping to prepare them for the anticipated Rebel onslaught. Many citizen-soldiers, unused to drill, succumbed to heatstroke and died in the narrow, suffocating streets of Louisville, as did at least four others engaged in a grand review through the city ordered by the increasingly unpopular James Jackson in hundred-degree weather on September 16. Some men swore to murder Jackson and other officers during their first battle in retaliation for the review deaths. Diarrhea resulting from poor camp conditions sent more men to the hospitals, and a few others fell in random skirmishes with Confederate horsemen on Louisville's perimeter.[19]

Nonetheless, the boys in their new blue uniforms innocently exuded confident pride. Thomas Frazee of the 73rd Illinois Infantry wrote home as if describing a pleasant holiday in the country. Camped "in a very pretty place" amidst yellow poplars and beech trees, Frazee assured his reader that "we have first rate times here we have plenty of peaches and melons & have had good times ever since we came here." He also expressed pride in his new regiment, which was, he promised, "as good a regament as their is in the service." Jay Caldwell Butler of the 101st Ohio Infantry, writing from a Louisville rifle pit, assured his parents that "it would be almost impossible to take us," for cannons and breastworks encircled the city. Still another, German-born John Weissert of the 1st Michigan Engineers and Mechanics, consoled his wife that he might be home soon, for the battle at Louisville would end the war. "If it comes to an attack." Weissert wrote, "the rebell army will be destroyed and peace will come again to the land, and men will be able to go home from their bloody work."[20]

Despite their boasts, nervousness also prevailed among Louisville's green troops. John A. Boon of the 85th Illinois Infantry complained that his officers swore at the men too much, leaving them on edge and unhappy. Levi Adolphus Ross of the 86th Illinois Infantry meanwhile described a telling incident that occurred while half of his company was on picket duty the night of September 15. A storm blew up, with wind strong enough to break dry limbs out of the surrounding trees. Hearing the snapping of dry wood, the Illinoisans jumped to the conclusion that they were under attack and formed up into line of battle. Tardily, their swords left lying beside their warm bedding, the regimental officers scurried over to take command of the skirmish with the wind.[21]

In the meantime, with Kirby Smith's intentions still unclear, Wright shifted physically and mentally back and forth between Cincinnati and Louisville, while the leaders of both cities simultaneously demanded the lion's share of troops. Such disorder reigned in Cincinnati that shops and schools closed, forcing Wright to order all except the liquor sellers to reopen. When hysterical mass arrests of African Americans began, Wright asked the mayor to stop harassing those who had so cheerfully undertaken much of the manual labor required to fortify the city. Adding to the chaos were the wildly undisciplined groups of "Minutemen" or "Squirrel Hunters"—the uncontrollable militia Governor Tod had inflicted on Lew Wallace to supplement the thin blue line opposite Cincinnati at Covington.[22]

The situation deteriorated still more as the moment of truth seemed to approach. Kirby Smith sent Henry Heth's infantry division and Morgan's cavalry troopers northward from Lexington toward Cincinnati. Unaware of Heth's true strength, or lack thereof, Wright understandably expected the rest of the Army of Kentucky to follow. As a result, he made defending the Ohio city his most immediate priority. Louisville, he reasoned, had enough force to hold out, whereas Cincinnati's chances remained doubtful. Accordingly, on September 10, Wright ordered Gilbert to send two regiments to Cincinnati. Louisville reacted to the orders by panicking anew as many Kentuckians became convinced that the entire army was about to abandon the city to Kirby Smith or Bragg.[23]

A *Louisville Daily Journal* editorial writer suggested on September 16 that the city could no longer depend upon the military to defend it; townspeople must do the work themselves. With a passing jab at Nelson's performance at Richmond, he continued:

> How is it with Louisville? Are her prominent men and her military commanders making the proper preparations for her defence? We see nothing of the kind, except that masses of brave but undisciplined Indianians are thrown upon her suburbs . . . as well as untaught soldiers of Illinois, equally brave and courageous, but all of whom have yet to learn the art of war. The consequences of this inactivity are manifest. . . . If we do not prepare ourselves— if Louisville is not fortified, it will be taken and given up to Confederate pillaging and magnanimity. . . . In God's name, why do not our people wake up to a sense of danger?[24]

Local and state officials such as the brand-new Governor Robinson agreed. So did Boyle, who should have known better. Instead, he again went over Wright's head to write directly to President Lincoln, warning this time that Wright's decisions were "creating a panic and will ruin the state. The enemy cannot be so foolish as to move on Cincinnati. . . . It is a trap in which General Wright will suffer us to be caught or suffer Buell's army to be cut off." To the general himself, Boyle complained that "withdrawing the troops from here is creating a panic and inviting the enemy to attack here and it will be done. If Louisville is taken the State is gone. There is much too much nervousness about Cincinnati. The enemy are marching . . . in this direction."

Concerned by what he read in the letters pouring in, Halleck sent a telegram to Wright telling him not to abandon Louisville if that truly was his plan. Wright wearily pointed out in his response that he had withdrawn only two regiments, leaving twenty-five others as well as batteries of artillery in place. More support and sanity quickly emanated from the president, who wrote Boyle: "Where is this enemy which you dread in Louisville? How near to you? What is General Gilbert's opinion? With all possible respect for you I must think General Wright's military opinion is the better . . . for us to control him there on the ground would be a babel of confusion which would be utterly ruinous."[25]

One wonders what might have happened had Kirby Smith continued his pressure on Cincinnati. He did not, at any rate, pulling back Heth's columns to meet George Morgan's apparent threat on September 18. With the city seemingly safe, headquarters' attention shifted back to Bragg and Louisville, where news of the fall of Munfordville had unleashed still another round of alarm and recriminations. Munfordville at least galvanized Wright to action. He decided that Nelson must march south from Louisville to link up with Buell, creating a combined force that would allow the Federals to whip Bragg in the field long before it reached the city. Nelson commanded at that moment about twenty thousand soldiers in Louisville. To bolster his force, Wright ordered three dozen additional regiments, including Granger's veterans, to move quickly from Cincinnati to Louisville for the operation. Nelson sent reconnaissance forces down the Bardstown Pike, resulting in erroneous reports that the great battle of the campaign already had begun somewhere on the Green River. Such misinformation convinced Nelson and Wright on September 22 to hold their ground and wait for further news.[26] Meanwhile, the city prepared for the worst. "Intelligence has reached me that the rebel hordes who are now ravaging the fair land of Kentucky are advancing to attack this city," Nelson wrote to his troops in orders that were also published in the newspapers. "We will give them a bloody welcome . . . shoulder to shoulder we will meet the enemy, and rival on the plains of Louisville the glory won by our fellow-soldiers at Fort Donelson, Shiloh, Pea Ridge, and other memorable fields of honor."[27]

Many of Louisville's now thirty-two thousand defenders vowed to comply. J. Lincoln Conkey of the 79th Indiana Infantry assured his correspondent that the Rebels would get a "warm welcome" from the city's entrenched defenders. Others, however, were less sanguine. Cold, sick, and hungry, Garret Larew of the 86th Indiana Infantry wrote in his diary that "I want to see Eliza and Johney so bad that I hardly know how to keep going, pass or not, if I knowed that I would not be taken as a deserter. . . . If I was at home and had not volunteered I would let them draft me fifty times for none months before I would volunteer." With battle approaching, Larew vowed that he would not again play cards or drink any more whiskey "unless it is for medicine."[28]

Two chaotic days passed in Louisville, the troops and every other able-bodied Unionist male black or white using the time to tardily augment the city's expanding earthworks, construct abatis, clear fields of fire, and organize hospitals before Bragg's blow fell. New units continued pouring into the city from across the Ohio to bolster the garrison. "It has been drill, guard, chop and dig, dig chop, guard and drill, all the while," Job Barnard of the 73rd Indiana Infantry scribbled, while Ohioan Bliss Morse wrote his mother that "the woods sing with the sound of axes about here." Louisville's few remaining businesses finally closed up shop, joining the barrooms shut down by Nelson five days earlier. When Nelson also ordered all women and children across the Ohio into Indiana, panic again ensued. He eventually needed sixteen ferries running around the clock as well as three pontoon bridges to handle the traffic. According to John Jefferson, Nelson "says he will shell the city before he will give it up—this is for effect I think. Hundred are leaving, mostly for Indiana." Soldiers transferred hospitals and military supplies to the Indiana side of the river as well. On September 24, according to Jefferson, "all business houses closed all day" as work on the fortifications continued.[29]

Later that day, however, came the word that every Union supporter had longed to hear: Crittenden's corps was across the Salt River; Buell's army had arrived. "Louisville is now safe," Bull Nelson exulted to Wright. "We can destroy Bragg with whatever force he may bring against us. God and liberty."[30]

The men of the Army of the Ohio entered Louisville, recorded T. J. Wright of the 8th Kentucky Infantry, "the hungriest, raggedest, tiredest, dirtiest, lousiest and sleepiest set of men the hardships of this or any other war ever produced."[31] Not surprisingly, Louisville to them resembled Paradise Found, and they embraced it with boisterous enthusiasm. Greeted with unfamiliar cheers, cigars, fluttering flags and handkerchiefs, baskets of cakes and pies offered by young women and mothers longing for their sons, and welcomed water carried to the ranks by children, the tired soldiers of the Army of the Ohio straightened their lines as they entered the city. They rested once they reached camp; ate their fill for the first time in weeks; collected new uniforms, shoes, and months of back pay; attended religious services; posed for photographs and basked in the glow of the city's relief—despite a rare rainstorm on the twenty-seventh and chilly nights throughout. How much happier the citizens seemed to see them, one soldier noted, compared to the year before. Southern Indianians particularly reveled, for home was just across the river, making visits from friends and loved ones frequent. Temptation beckoned them as well, as thousands of Hoosiers, officers as well as men, took the opportunity to slip out of camp and sneak home for a spell of "French leave"—some of them actually wading or swimming across the Ohio in order to get home. Kentuckians did much the same. Still others disobeyed orders by seeking liquor in the city's barrooms and more successfully from enterprising women who boldly and bawdily sold canteens full of whiskey from underneath their skirts.[32]

All in all, Buell's men cut loose. Fully one-third went absent without leave, particularly Hoosiers,[33] and those soldiers who remained in Louisville proceeded to raise all the hell they could muster. According to Marcus Woodcock:

> The Provost Guards were quickly subdued after the approach of daylight by some of our . . . boys and we had full liberty to roam over the city during the whole day . . . the effects of this began to be plainly visible by now in the numerous "turning up" of canteens by almost everybody; the numerous whoops and huzzas, and jovial speeches and comical remarks, and staggering forms of our boys all told but too plainly that ardent spirits had in a measure got the better of martial spirit, and was waging a fearful war with good order and military discipline."

Some regiments went even further. While Woodcock's 9th Kentucky apparently indulged only one day, the inveterate forager Robert Winn indicated that many of his comrades in the 2nd Ohio staged a four-day drunk.[34] Angry both because of their dirty campsite by the river and a perceived favoritism for volunteers, half of the regulars of the 16th U.S. Infantry defied orders to the contrary and went absent without leave into the city to drink. "A laggard of my company," Edgar R. Kellogg remembered with more amusement than anger: "and the first sergeant of D company, both exhibiting the outward and visible signs of an inward and spiritous peace, were standing over a fire a few yards distant, and bombarding each other with quotations from Shakespeare. My man was firing chunks from Macbeth, and the sergeant was replying with missiles from Hamlet."[35]

Andrew F. Davis of the 15th Indiana Infantry indicated that some of his comrades never returned from drinking bouts. Wrote Davis, "a great many of Our Regt. took the opportunity to take a Spree and many of them were not on hand when we were ready to march consequently were left be hind."[36] Once the dust cleared, however, "good order and military discipline" not only survived the battle of the bottle in most cases, it emerged much stronger. Coupled with their much-needed breather, the attention the army received in Louisville and the opportunity to blow off steam augmented its already blossoming morale.

The effect of hordes of drunken soldiers out on the town on Louisville's patriotism and morale remains open to question. Merchants could not have appreciated the fact that some soldiers were unable to break the foraging habit, as when John A. Duncan of the 3rd Ohio Infantry stole a shirt from a "Jew store" after he convinced himself that the proprietor planned to cheat him.[37] John Jefferson was much more impressed with the "Pea Ridge men" sent from Grant's army, Phil Sheridan's veteran division of mostly Missourians and Illinois Suckers, than he was with Buell's ragged band.

As for the new recruits who had filled Louisville's entrenchments and now continued to dig, they looked upon the hardened veterans entering the city with a mixture of wonder, admiration, and horror.[38] Notably, they found the veterans filthy. "Such jaded men!" Mead Holmes Jr. of the 21st Wisconsin Infantry wrote his parents. "Some have marched all the way from Alabama. At home they were old acquaintances; here we could not recognize them. The pleasure of a bath I am sure they have not known these weary months; and such a tale!" A. J. Jones of the 24th Wisconsin Infantry agreed, marveling at men "so covered with the soil of Kentucky that it was impossible to tell whether they were white men or black, many of them barefooted, we wondered if we should ever look like that disreputable appearing aggregation."[39]

In contrast, Buell's veterans generally regarded the newly recruited, freshly scrubbed "fresh fish" or "troopees," as they called them, as objects of great amusement and derision, as well as sources for free coffee and unwilling suppliers of newly issued war materiel.[40] To be sure, many veterans had made up their minds even before they sighted any of the new regiments that their men had to be worthless. Writing of the reported new recruits from Bowling Green, a bitter William R. Stuckey of the 42nd Indiana told his wife that "I was glad to here that those fellows at home had to turn out and fight for there country as well as I there homes was no dearer than mine it was no worse for them to leave there loved ones at home than me to leave you and my sweet little babe."[41]

Once in Louisville, Buell's men saw little that changed their minds. James Birney Shaw of the 10th Indiana Infantry remembered: "all kinds of lies and improbable stories were told the new men. They stared with wide open eyes to see the boys coming in with hardly anything in the shape of equipments, while the new troops were loaded down with all kinds of trumpery." Much of that fine new equipment soon started to disappear. "The nights began to grow cool and as we had no blankets the boys went to foraging among the 'fresh fish' and in due course of time they were comfortably fixed and the new fellows relieved of considerable weight."[42] The 10th Indiana hardly was alone. Jesse Connelly of the 31st Indiana recorded the theft of cooking utensils from the rookie 90th Ohio Infantry. When men of the newly raised 88th Illinois Infantry complained to the veterans of the 36th Illinois about similar thefts, the veterans "called us 'sixty-dollar' men and told us to go spend our bounty." Veteran John Sipe of the 38th Indiana Infantry excused such behavior by noting that men like himself regarded many of the new regiments as "inflicted" with Rebel sentiments.[43]

Only occasionally did the new men dare to resist their treatment at the hands of the veterans, and then with dire consequences. One notable incident involved the 21st Wisconsin Infantry, a spunky, outspoken outfit initially known for its unusually tall soldiers but soon to gain the reputation of being the most troublesome regiment in the entire army. Angered by repeated incursions through their camps, Maj. Frederick Schumacher ordered that the next unit cutting through his territory be stopped. As luck would have it, the next group of offenders came from the veteran 44th Illinois of Phil Sheridan's command. Ordered to halt at the outskirts of the camp, a contingent of men from the Forty-fourth refused, their captain telling the officer of the guard, "Damn your halt I will blow your brains out." Turning to his men, he added, ""boys charge bayonets upon them and let us see if they will not give away." The veterans then forced their way past the camp guards "yelling through our camp kicking the knapsacks of our men some of which they destroyed." Then, for good measure, they came back through and did it again.[44]

As far as Buell's veterans were concerned, there was no greater insult than to be compared with the "fresh fish" of Louisville. On September 27, John W. Tuttle of Buell's 3rd Kentucky Infantry and his captain went into town to get a bath and haircut and look for new uniforms. Unfortunately, "we were mortified as we passed along the streets by being called '*new troops*' '*band box soldiers*' '*never seen hardship*' etc. until we wished we had southern soil an inch thick all over us."[45]

While his army rested and reveled, General Buell wrestled to maintain command of it. Various stumbling blocks stood in his way, some larger than others. At a public dinner in honor of Nelson, several toasts given by subordinates and local notables suggested that Alexander McCook would be a better army commander than Buell, further undermining the commander. The ambitions of Horatio Wright, who thanks to Halleck had hoped to take command of the army rather than serve under Buell, presented another minor problem. Disappointed in his ambitions, Wright dragged his heels at taking commands from Buell. Only repeated dispatches to and from Washington established that Buell would exercise command by virtue of rank over the entire assembled force. Wright then took a different tack, complaining that he and Cincinnati were being abandoned to face both Kirby Smith and Marshall without necessary aid from Buell. Meddling from his old bêtes noires, the Midwest governors, still threatened to undermine Buell's authority as well. Indiana's Oliver Morton in particular irked Buell, for he now openly campaigned for Buell's dismissal. Arriving in Louisville, still furious over Buell's treatment of the Hoosiers who had defended Munfordville, Morton gave a rousing speech to his assembled constituents in uniform, demanding that every Hoosier in the army receive new uniforms and shoes, as well as a bath.[46] "'Give Indiana soldiers less marching and more fighting,'" Morton proclaimed in a direct jab at Buell's retreat.[47]

On a fateful September 29, the fragile command structure of the army, and Buell in particular, suffered a more substantial blow. Again, the ubiquitous Governor Morton played a supporting role. Earlier in the month, before Buell arrived in town, Wright had sent Brig. Gen. Jefferson C. Davis to Louisville to help Bull Nelson organize the city's defense. From the first, the Davis-Nelson relationship proved a marriage made in hell. A proud Indianian, Davis was bristling even before he arrived at the Kentuckian Nelson's widely discussed contempt for Hoosiers, especially the incendiary comment that Indianians essentially were the children of "white trash" from the Appalachian Mountains. More recently, Nelson supposedly had made scapegoats of his Indiana troops for the disaster at Richmond. According to sensational but widely believed newspaper reports, he had beheaded several Hoosiers during the rout. For his part, Nelson remained loyal to Buell and immediately concluded that Davis was an incompetent toady of Halleck's minion, Wright. Tensions grew until a shouting match between the two men on September 25 resulted in Nelson arresting Davis and ordering him back to Cincinnati. Matters might have ended there had not Wright, who already had clashed with the prickly Nelson himself, advised Davis to return to Kentucky. Buell was in charge now, he counseled. Stay well clear of Nelson and everything will be fine. Governor Morton, a friend of Davis's, suggested the same course and even agreed to take Davis with him when he traveled to Louisville to greet the army.

All went well until the morning of September 29, when Davis, Morton, and Louisville attorney Thomas Gibson saw Nelson in the lobby of the Galt House, the Bull's headquarters and Louisville's finest hotel. Looking for redress, Davis lost control and impetuously stormed over to Nelson, demanding to know why he had been placed under arrest and ordered out of the state. Nelson responded by ordering the "damned puppy" out of his sight. Davis instead flicked a crumpled calling card into Nelson's face, whereupon the Kentuckian slapped the Hoosier hard across the face and stormed off. Davis shouted a threat as Nelson disappeared. Then, taking a pistol from Gibson, the irate Davis pursued Nelson, confronted him again, and shot him once in the chest. He died within the hour.

Nelson's murder convulsed the army's command structure. His friends—most notably generals Thomas Crittenden, William B. Hazen, William Terrill, and James Jackson—demanded Davis's arrest and execution, and threatened Morton as well. Regiments that had served under Nelson at Shiloh also mourned their old commander, and Buell ordered at least one placed under guard lest its men attempt to take revenge.[48] However, sentiment in the ranks almost universally favored Davis, the men respecting him as a brave officer who, according to the grapevine, had incurred Nelson's wrath by standing up for the common soldiers. Nelson, in contrast, emerged in diaries and letters as a profane bully, tyrant, and, worst of all, confidant of the despised Buell. He was seen as an officer who abused his men and in the end got what he deserved. Any legal niceties aside, Davis had reacted in the manly way. Indeed, some regiments defied Buell and cheered upon hearing his general order announcing the Old Bull's death. Bluecoats with abolitionist leanings further condemned Nelson's alleged cruelty to African Americans. Meanwhile, a few befuddled soldiers expressed joy thinking that someone had just shot the president of the Confederacy.[49] More typical was the reaction of the 9th Ohio Infantry's A.T. Coburn, who wrote his father that "General Nelson was shot yesterday by Gen Davis of Indiana and it is one of the best things that has happened in this department he was shot and repented and was babtised and went to heaven in about twenty minutes, but then I have my doubts of him a going there."[50]

On the heels of Nelson's murder, the Lincoln administration provided a still greater challenge to Buell's authority, and in so doing only added to the "babel of confusion" the president earlier had said he wanted to avoid. Long unhappy with Buell's performance and attitude, the administration also had to mollify angry Old Northwest Republicans who wanted Buell, Halleck, and McClellan fired and replaced with more energetic generals. Those new men would hopefully be westerners, non–West Pointers, and, most crucially, members of the Republican Party. Lincoln's incomprehensible loyalty to incompetent and suspect officers like Buell, they warned, tarred him with the same brush in the eyes of disgruntled and war-weary voters. Looming congressional elections in the North added urgency to Republican pleas for action, for many feared a Democratic sweep. Like-minded Secretary of the Treasury Salmon P. Chase, the Radical Republicans' favorite in Lincoln's cabinet and a man who coveted the presidency, served as an effective conduit for party faithful fed up with Buell's retreats.

At length, concerned with nothing less than the survival of the administration, Lincoln, Secretary of War Stanton, and Halleck on September 24 dispatched confidential orders to Louisville relieving Buell of command and replacing him with George Thomas. Only if Buell "should be found in the presence of the enemy preparing to fight a battle, or if he should have gained a victory" would he retain command. Separate orders to Thomas demanded he conduct "energetic operations," something Buell clearly had not done in Washington's view.

Buell immediately and professionally complied upon receiving the orders on September 29, the same day Nelson died. At that moment he may have felt well rid of command. Thomas, however, quickly proved less than energetic himself. He simply did not want the job. "General Buell's preparations have been completed to move against the enemy," he wrote Halleck, "and I therefore respectfully ask that he may be retained in command. My position is very embarrassing, not being as well informed as I should be as the commander of this army and on the assumption of such a responsibility."

In reply, Halleck dissembled. Claiming that "the order . . . was not made by me nor on my advice," he wrote that he had sent telegrams trying to stop the issuance of the new orders. At any rate, they were now "suspended." Buell would remain in command for the time being; the murder of Nelson on the day the orders arrived already had shaken up Kentucky's Unionists enough without adding to their consternation by changing commanding generals on the eve of the battle for Kentucky. Still, the net effect of the episode was that Buell now stood on shakier ground than ever. Lacking support in Washington as well as among Republicans, and with rumors of his aborted ouster spreading rapidly through the officer corps of his army, he realized that only a quick victory accomplished before the Union chose a new Congress would allow him to maintain command. Unfortunately, his innate perfectionism and dependence upon well-laid plans, heightened as a result of his dilemma, stood at loggerheads with the need for haste. Worse yet, in his hour of need he turned increasingly to favorites, men whose loyalty and support could not be doubted.[51]

As Thomas indicated, Buell already had laid the groundwork for a campaign against Bragg. On the hectic twenty-ninth, with the last of his units finally arriving in the city but Nelson dead, he hastily restructured his total force, incorporating the new and old units into a hopefully cohesive whole. With two fateful omissions, each brigade was to contain one raw regiment and three veteran ones. He then parceled out his twenty-five brigades among

three corps. Thomas rose to second in command of the army, just the powerless place for a sometimes argumentative heir-apparent. Buell at least did
share fully his plans with Thomas, and, as the latter later pointed out, the
two men got along well enough in the days ahead, although a chill remained
evident.

Buell's top two choices for corps command were obvious. Alexander
McCook would command I Corps while Thomas Crittenden took over II
Corps. Both had served well under Buell in positions of increasing authority,
and despite McCook's privately expressed preference for Thomas and his
prominence in the wished-for coup, Buell felt he could count on both of
them in the coming campaign. Buell tapped James Jackson, Lovell Rousseau,
and Ohioan Joshua W. Sill to serve as McCook's division commanders, with
Sill taking over McCook's old division. A native Kentuckian and lawyer by
profession, the hot-tempered Jackson served in the military during the Mexican War but resigned as the result of a duel he instigated. He returned to
Kentucky, involved himself in politics, and served in Congress until the end
of 1861, when he accepted the colonelcy of the 3rd Kentucky Cavalry. Since
that time he had done little to endear himself to the soldiers under his growing command. Many of those who followed him back to Louisville from
Richmond on the "Hell March" despised him as a tyrant, and those who did
not soon learned to do so after the much-maligned Louisville grand review.
Nonetheless, Jackson would command no veteran troops in his division; all
would be drawn from the ranks of the raw levies, men who already hated
him.[52]

Rousseau's background was quite similar to Jackson's, but his reputation differed greatly. Kentucky born as well, and largely self-educated,
Rousseau moved to Indiana in 1840 and served two years in the state legislature before enlisting to fight the Mexicans. He returned to Louisville in 1849
to practice law. By the time of Fort Sumter, fellow attorneys recognized him
as the city's leading trial lawyer. He returned to politics as well, serving in the
state senate. As commander of the Louisville Home Guard, he emerged as a
leading Unionist during the secession crisis. After Polk's invasion, Rousseau
accepted the colonelcy of the 3rd Kentucky Infantry, and he rose steadily
thereafter. Although a strict disciplinarian, his men grew to adore him during the long summer of 1862. One of them, "Sparta," effusively praised his
general not only as a soldier but also as a "statesman" who had commanded
occupied Huntsville with a fair but stern hand. Moreover, "Sparta" insisted,
Rousseau's tireless labor and determination to instill discipline and order in
demoralized units all but redeemed the army during the Alabama ordeal.[53]

G. N. Bachelor, a member of the 1st Michigan Engineers and Mechanics, remembered a story, probably apocryphal, that nevertheless illustrates
Rousseau's popularity with his troops:

"No officer in the army was more beloved than the gallant General
Rosseau, and whenever he was seen by the men there was always a shout of

Figure 5.1. Brig. Gen. Lovell H. Rousseau. Photograph courtesy William Prince Collection, U.S. Army Military History Institute.

applause sent up. During those days we were often camped in the woods where rabbits were abundant, and the boys had a good time chasing them and hurraing. Upon hearing a prodigious shout one evening at his headquarters, Gen. Jeff. C. Davis inquired the cause. 'Well,' said his orderly, 'I can't exactly say, but I guess the boys are either after general Rossuau or a buck rabbit.'"[54]

William Sooy Smith, Horatio P. Van Cleve, and Thomas J. Wood would serve as Crittenden's division commanders. Despite a twenty-year differential in their ages, Smith and Van Cleve had in many respects led parallel lives. Both Smith, a thirty-two year old Ohio native, and the fifty-two year old New Jersey–born Van Cleve were West Pointers who had left the military after brief stints in uniform, moved farther west, and worked as civil engineers. Van Cleve additionally had farmed, first in Michigan then Minnesota. After Fort Sumter, both raised regiments and eventually rose to brigade command in the Army of the Ohio, Smith having fought at Shiloh and Van Cleve joining the main force at Corinth.[55]

Wood, however, was a much different character. A native Kentuckian, Wood grew up in Munfordville alongside his best friend, Simon B. Buckner. Graduating from the Military Academy in 1845, Wood went on to be bre-

veted for bravery at the Battle of Buena Vista. The young engineer transferred to cavalry after the Mexican War, and spent most of the interwar years
on the western frontier fighting Indians. Once the Civil War came, he rose
steadily in rank, and commanded one of Buell's divisions at Shiloh.[56]

If Crittenden and McCook were noncontroversial choices for corps
command, Buell's choice to lead his third and final corps was anything but.
The trusted Bull Nelson originally was to have commanded III Corps, but
his sudden and unexpected death demanded that another officer fill the role.
Forty-year-old Albin Schoepf, who had been an officer in the Austrian army
until defecting to the Hungarian rebel forces during the revolutions of 1848,
was the obvious choice to replace Nelson, having served in an equal capacity
to Crittenden and McCook back in Tennessee. In addition to his European
experience, he already had fought in Kentucky at Wildcat Mountain and
under Thomas at Mill Springs.

Scheopf, however, was too closely linked to Thomas for Buell's comfort. Worse yet, as the Buell Commission's deliberations later embarrass-
ingly revealed, Scheopf and Buell hated each other passionately. Back at
Corinth, when some of Schoepf's brigade commanders went to Buell in an
attempt to have him fire the Austrian, Buell lent a sympathetic ear. Scheopf
responded by questioning Buell's loyalty and calling for his ouster, opining
that any Union commander whose conciliatory policies had won the esteem of
Southerners could not be trusted. A confrontation seemed sure, and one finally exploded in Pelham in late August when Buell ordered Scheopf arrested
after he rode through the latter's lines one night without being challenged by
sentries. Making matters worse, the brigade commander—Kentuckian Speed
S. Fry, a Schoepf loyalist—pulled his revolver on Buell that night, later claiming that he thought him a Rebel. Indignantly, Fry and Schoepf charged that
Buell had sneaked into the camp in order to embarrass them.

Now, with his planned command structure already in disarray, it hardly
seemed the time for Buell to give corps command to an open enemy. Accordingly, he fatefully turned instead to the former captain, Charles Gilbert. Buell knew and respected Gilbert as a former staff officer and friend,
and Wright thankfully had provided enough faux stars for Gilbert's collar to
allow Buell to supersede characters such as the untrustworthy Schoepf. Dis-
ingenuously claiming that he really believed Gilbert was a major general—
an assertion the Buell Commission later found difficult to swallow—Buell
assigned him to corps command.

Schoepf, Davis, and Boyle originally were to have been Gilbert's division commanders. Little went as planned, however, in what immediately
became the most troubled of the three corps. The arrest of Davis led Buell to
replace him with the aggressive former Ohio and Kansas politician Robert
B. Mitchell, whose division had joined the army from Mississippi at
Murfreesboro.[57] Phil Sheridan, meanwhile, reacted poorly to news that he
was to serve under both Boyle and Gilbert as a brigade commander. A newly

appointed brigadier general, Sheridan imperiously "insisted that my rights in the matter be recognized." Buell gave in and assigned Sheridan to command what was to have been Boyle's division. Boyle would remain behind in Louisville.[58]

With ham-fisted zeal, an inflated ego, and no doubt some private insecurities, the inexperienced Gilbert immediately set to work alienating the men under his command. F. W. Keil of the 35th Ohio remembered that his new corps commander "soon became noted for 'nosing' through baggage wagons to see what effects officers and men placed in them." James Birney Shaw of the veteran 10th Indiana Infantry described a near-mutiny that took place on that most tumultuous of all days for the army, September 29. When his regiment and the 10th Kentucky Infantry were not paid along with the other regiments in their brigade, the angry soldiers set off a "rumpus," shoving their bayoneted rifles into the ground and demanding their money. Until then, they refused to move. When their colonels as well as brigade commander Speed Fry failed to convince the men to give in, "a 'feller' by the name of Gilbert . . . rode up and began a tirade of profanity and abuse, and finally ordered Battery C [1st Ohio Light Artillery] to unlimber and throw a few charges of canister into the two regiments and 'blow them to ——.'" When the battery refused to obey his orders, Gilbert "was boiling over, ripping, raring mad." In the end, it took their beloved "Pap" Thomas to diffuse the situation.[59] Having failed in his first test as corps commander, Gilbert grossly compounded his error the following day, ordering the soldiers in his corps "to stand to arms every morning from 3 oclock until daylight," with all division and brigade commanders forced to circle their commands every thirty minutes to make sure the order was obeyed.[60] Small wonder that Gilbert soon grew as despised as his mentor Buell.

While he reordered his command, Buell also decided what to do with it. Typically, the tactical plan he developed had much to recommend it. Dismissing earlier reports that Kirby Smith had moved to join Bragg, and confident as well that Humphrey Marshall remained east of Lexington, Buell ordered that on October 1 Sill's division of McCook's corps would move against Kirby Smith on the Confederate right, directly east through Shelbyville toward Frankfort. Supported by a second division of new recruits under Brig. Gen. Ebenezer Dumont's command, Sill's demonstration hopefully would "mislead [Bragg] as to the real point of attack, and prevent him from moving upon my left flank and rear." That real attack aimed at Bragg's last reported position at Bardstown. Taking three separate routes from the city, the Bardstown, Shepherdsville, and Taylorsville Pikes, the three corps would converge at Bardstown, force Bragg back and away from "any convenient line of retreat," and finally crush the Confederate invaders somewhere south of Lexington. All Buell required Bragg to do was take the bait and patiently allow his army's demise. That he would do so seemed obvious to Buell.[61]

While the Army of the Ohio girded for battle in Louisville, its opposite number prepared for the anticipated collision about forty miles to the south at Bardstown. Best known as the inspiration for Stephen Foster's popular prewar minstrel tune "My Old Kentucky Home, Far Away," Bardstown was home to about two thousand people in 1862. Site of the historic first Roman Catholic cathedral erected west of the Appalachians, Bardstown likewise claimed well regarded Saint Joseph's College, a Catholic institution that had produced among its graduates Confederate brigade commander Sterling Wood.

When the first elements of the Army of the Mississippi marched into Bardstown on September 22, townspeople embraced them as deliverers in a tableau reenacted for days.[62] The 3rd Florida's John Inglis, for example, vividly described the scene on the evening of September 24 as John C. Brown's brigade arrived in town for a grand review of the army: "slow going men came up, took places. Colors, unfurled, bayonets fixed. 'Right Shoulder shift,' dressed files Bands to Front, and fine order & Style at a quick swinging step we went through B. Town streets lined with citizens & Ladies, waving nekchfs 'Dixie' & 'Bonnie Blue Flag' playing, artillery booming with, Old Bragg, Gens. Polk, Chalmers, Pat. Anderson, Buckner, all in full uniform, our Staffs soon making speeches, we swept along, our road to Coast, this high regalia gold, braid brass buttons and pomp & parade behind us, the Ladies looks so sweet, we camped, on Louisville Road."[63]

Thus began a brief summer love affair between the town and the army that lasted at least until overwhelmed merchants closed their doors rather than accept Confederate money.[64] Few sang Bardstown's praises more than Dr. George Little, a former Mississippi chemistry professor more recently serving as orderly sergeant in Lumsden's Battery. Visiting the college library, Little "saw a volume of Humboldt's Kansas and on telling the Librarian that he had breakfasted with Humboldt in 1858, at the home of the American Minister, Gov. Wright of Indiana, at Berlin, Prussia, he told him that this was an odd volume and he could have it." Bardstown had won over Little for life.[65] For those of less cultivated tastes, Bardstown offered a bounty of eatables to famished men and animals, not to mention cheap and plentiful whiskey. Young officers paid expectant calls on the area's young ladies, universally described as extremely attractive. News of Nelson's murder meanwhile rang like God's welcome judgment on the wicked and invited thanks. All in all, Bardstown's only notable disadvantage as far as the rank and file was concerned was its dwindling water supply. With the drought that already had bedeviled them having spread across the Bluegrass, little remained for the soldiers to drink but the warm, muddy pond water they had grown accustomed to and the ever-present barrels of liquor.

Still, despite Bardstown's many assets, a cloud of disappointment hung over the Confederate camps, refusing to dissipate fully. Unlike the gritty, rising morale of Federals in Louisville, Confederate confidence waned noticeably in Bardstown. The army had expected to fight Buell for Louisville, not stop miles short of the city in order to let the Yankees waltz in uncontested. In terms resembling those used by their foe against their general, bitter soldiers concluded that Bragg was either a fool or a traitor for allowing the Yankees to occupy the city without a battle, perhaps both.[66]

Worse yet, with Louisville firmly in Union hands, pro-Confederate Kentuckians continued to fearfully hold back from joining the army, despite the southerners' best efforts. Wrote one disgusted Alabama trooper, "There was no hope of arousing a general sympathy in Kentucky for the Confederacy with the enemy in final possession of Louisville." However much they might cheer, Kentuckians still would not fight.[67]

The Louisianians of Austin's Sharpshooters agreed. Unit humorist Andrew Devilbiss got the best of a Kentuckian who said: "'Hello—is that a Confederate flag? If it is please bring it out here—I want it to wave over me one time.'"

"Devilbiss," related a comrade sourly, "told him if he would come and join our command we would let him wave it over him all the time. Of course the country cousin was taken down a bit and didn't say a word more."[68]

Indeed, very few Kentuckians seemed eager to march under the Stars and Bars. Increasingly concerned by their reluctance, Bragg first pinned his hopes on the popular Buckner, sending him to the former Camp Dick Robinson in Garrard County, which had been renamed Camp Breckinridge after the Confederates seized it, to raise recruits. Hoping that he could rally the entire commonwealth, the Kentuckian also wrote a stirring address to the state's citizens. Depicting in some detail what he called the "despotism" of the Lincoln administration, and concluding with the outrages of Turchin and Boyle as well as Lincoln's preliminary Emancipation Proclamation, Buckner begged the men of the state "to join the standard of freedom. If you are worthy of freedom you will win it. We have arms for all who will join us."[69]

Fine words availed little, however, for only about fifteen hundred responded, and most of them demanded to serve in the more glamorous cavalry. Wondering what was wrong with Kentuckians soon occupied a great deal of the soldiers' time in Bardstown. Louisianian John Ellis wrote home that "the people of this section are nearly all secessionists—They received us with the wildest demonstration of delight—The women all kissed Gen Buckner and strong men wept like infants." Nonetheless, "the people of this state seem scarcely to know what to do—They put me in mind of men half asleep—They talk enough and strongly enough but talking will not wrest Kentucky from the hands of Lincoln." Like Buckner, Ellis hoped that Lincoln's freshly issued preliminary Emancipation Proclamation would finally "fix the state firmly on the side of the south."[70]

Former resident Sterling Wood took a different tack, attributing recruiting failures to religion. "All the Catholics in this county are Secesh," he wrote his wife. "The Protestants Union." Unfortunately, there were more

Protestants.[71] "Press," writing to the *Atlanta Southern Confederacy*, countered that the real problem was gender. "It is painful to acknowledge," he wrote, "the marks of the Federal yoke are too visible in the temper of the men. But the spirit of the women is irrepressible. Our troops are every where met with the smiles and tears of the women and they display the Southern flag and wave their handkerchiefs wherever we go. I have no doubt of the Southern sympathies of the men, but time and a large exhibition of Southern ability to defend them are necessary to assure them."[72]

Whatever the cause, the Kentuckians' refusal to take up arms seriously threatened the campaign. Unhappiest of all with the situation was Bragg himself. When he first arrived in town, the general spoke to the townspeople with feeling, assuring them that "he did not come here to arrest men, imprison women, or rob peaceful citizens of their property; but to give Kentucky the chance to express her southern preferences without fear of northern bayonets—that if Kentucky will rally to his standard, he will stay and defend her soil:—but if she declines the offer of liberty, he will withdraw his army and leave her to her choice."[73]

As even casual bystanders could attest, however, Bragg seethed at the state's apparent response. "'I never saw such terrible eyes,'" a woman told John Ellis at a church service as Bragg passed by, "'they look as if they burn whatever they rest upon.'"[74] At that moment, Bragg particularly wanted to sear Kentuckians. All the way from Chattanooga, Bragg had expected pro-Confederate Kentuckians to swell his ranks, allowing him to offset the Federals' numerical advantage once he arrived. Had not Morgan and Kirby Smith promised as much? If the Kentucky dreamers were somehow wrong about the commonwealth's loyalties, his army was in greater trouble than he already believed, outnumbered and a long way from home. "I heard Bragg feelingly deplore the inaction of the state and the indifference of the people," St. John Liddell wrote in 1866, "from whom he had been led to expect great efforts. Kentucky, of all the Southern states, had less to complain of and more to be ashamed of." What was the problem?[75]

Bragg poured out many of his fears and frustrations in a September 25 letter to Richmond. In many ways, what is most striking about the missive is its blatant mendacity. He had wanted to fight at Munfordville, he claimed, but Buell "declined" and instead raced toward the Ohio. "For want of provisions," he wrote, "it was impossible for me to follow or even stay where I was, the population being nearly all hostile and the country barren and destitute. . . . It is a source of deep regret that this move was necessary, as it has enabled Buell to reach Louisville, where a very large force is now concentrated."

Whether or not Bragg actually convinced himself to believe such revisionist history is open to conjecture. Perhaps he simply felt he needed excuses as far as Richmond was concerned. Then again, perhaps he really believed it. He had, after all, wanted to fight at Munfordville—briefly. At any rate, what emerges even more is his determination to duck responsibility and blame all his problems on a wide range of scapegoats. Van Dorn and Price were in part at fault, he insisted, for not moving into Tennessee as ordered, so as to tie down Union forces in western Tennessee and northern Mississippi. "We might have made some headway after arriving here," he continued, "but we find the armies of generals Grant, Rosecrans, Curtis, and Buell, with many of the new levies, opposed to us. In this condition any advance is impossible . . . we may be seriously embarrassed." Curtis, Grant, and Rosecrans were nowhere near Louisville, of course—Rosecrans had just defeated Price at Iuka back in Mississippi—but Bragg must have felt as if he was facing every Yankee west of the Appalachians. Price and Van Dorn still must come up, he declared.

Beyond the two recalcitrant generals, who in truth had faltered, the real villains were the Kentuckians, who with rare exceptions unmanfully refused to enlist. "We have 15,000 stand of arms and no one to use them," Bragg complained. "Unless a change occurs soon we must abandon this garden spot of Kentucky to its cupidity. The love of ease and fear of pecuniary loss are the fruitful sources of this evil. Kentucky and Tennessee are redeemed if we are supported, but at least 50,000 men will be necessary, and a few weeks will decide the question. Should we have to retire, much in the way of supplies and *morale* will be lost, and the redemption of Kentucky will be indefinitely postponed, if not rendered impossible."[76]

This letter, for the first time in the Kentucky campaign, reveals the Braxton Bragg familiar to later historians. Up to Munfordville, he had shown initiative, determination, self-confidence (occasionally too much), and real ability. To be sure, he already was in his men's minds the brutal disciplinarian of legend. Worse yet, he had proven such a passive personality that Kirby Smith had been able to drag Bragg along in the wake of his Kentucky adventure, resulting ultimately in an invasion without a firm raison d'être. Passive-aggressiveness remained a constant. Only at Munfordville, however, did depression overwhelm him. Indecision, irascible frustration, and the need to blame everyone but himself quickly followed. Buell's entrance into Louisville made everything worse, for the foe now would be resupplied and reinforced. The Federals certainly outnumbered him—although not as badly as he claimed—yet no one would help him. Anything bad that followed thus was not his fault, he told the high command. Blame Van Dorn and Price. Blame his soldiers, some of whom he demanded be court-martialed on one charge or another. Most of all, blame Kentucky. Psychologically speaking, Bragg clearly was drifting into dangerous straits. Abrupt mood swings, barely restrained anger, and a total inability to act decisively without second-guessing himself would characterize his generalship from then on. Just when his army needed a clear-headed commander most, Braxton Bragg began breaking under the strain.[77]

In the short run, he continued to despairingly flounder over what to do next. As had become commonplace, Kirby Smith only added to his agitation.

Arriving in Bardstown, Bragg found a letter from the general waiting for him, finally informing him that Kirby Smith cavalierly had decided to ignore Bragg's pleas and not come to Bardstown with his army as requested. There could be no concentration of forces. Instead, the Floridian, following earlier suggestions more to his liking, deployed to meet George Morgan's force finally moving up from Cumberland Gap. Indeed, the Army of Kentucky at that moment was moving in the opposite direction, eastward, to join Humphrey Marshall's three-thousand-man force at Mount Sterling.

Unable to even count on Kirby Smith's reinforcements, Bragg foundered all over again. The next day found him briefly reconsidering an attack on Louisville after all, even directing his owlish chief engineer Harris to scout routes from Bardstown to Louisville in order to locate water holes and ascertain the mileage between them. Perhaps he still could get there before Buell. His resolve to fight, however, evaporated within twenty-four hours as sense again set in; the time to take Louisville long had passed. On September 25 Bragg told a shaken Stoddard Johnston that he would allow Buell to reach the city after all. It would take the Federal commander weeks to prepare for an offensive, Bragg rationalized—time he could use to build and train an effective force with which to meet him. Johnston had heard such brave words before, indeed only recently at Munfordville, and he found both them and Bragg's mood disquieting.[78]

Not surprisingly, Bragg's list of scapegoats widened as disappointments multiplied. One prominent name added to the list was that of John C. Breckinridge. As the hero of the lukewarm pro-Confederate Kentuckians, guilt by association made Breckinridge suspect enough. Still, it was his inability—Bragg unfairly maintained his disobedient refusal—to join him in Kentucky that elicited his greatest contempt. In truth, it hardly was Breckinridge's fault. Like the Kentucky soldiers of his "Orphan Brigade," he yearned to get home. A division commander in Van Dorn's army, the former vice president had encouraged Bragg and, more importantly, promised to bring his command north to support Bragg as he entered the Bluegrass State. The difficulty was Van Dorn's selfish and stubborn reluctance to let them go. Once that commander relented, more problems ensued. Breckinridge raced to Chattanooga, where, to his amazement, Sam Jones promptly pulled rank and ordered Breckinridge to remain in East Tennessee. In the end, one hardly can fault Breckinridge. Considering Bragg's state of mind, however, it was easy for him to assign blame to still another Kentuckian.[79] Breckinridge, Bragg charged, had used every excuse to delay, aided and abetted by a "self willed, rather weak minded & totally deficient" Van Dorn. "The failure of Genl Breckinridge to carry out his part of my programme has seriously embarrassed me and marred the whole campaign to some extent," Bragg complained to Jefferson Davis in a letter damning Breckinridge.

Nonetheless, Bragg continued, "the results are still not small, and I hope we may yet retrieve all that is lost."[80] But how? Groping for a solution to his dilemma, Bragg by September 27 had reached two tentative conclusions, conditional in the sense that every decision he made over the next few days was subject to his own repeated reexamination and amendment. First, he would abandon offensive operations and assume a safer defensive posture. Clearly expecting the worst, he accordingly prepared for it. On September 27 he wrote Kirby Smith, telling him to establish a supply depot at Camp Dick Robinson/Breckinridge, on the opposite bank of Dick's River just northeast of Danville. Such a base would serve as a central "rallying point for us in case of necessity" during a retreat. Moreover, he wanted another depot established farther south at London, on the road to Cumberland Gap, "so that in case of absolute necessity we could make the gap with our haversacks."[81] At the gap itself, John McCown, still commanding in Knoxville, would create a third base "in case we should fall back" that far. Bragg further ordered McCown to scour the countryside and collect at least ten days' rations for twenty thousand troops.[82]

Prepared, almost expecting, to abandon Kentucky altogether and fall back to Tennessee, Bragg proceeded with the second part of his plan. There still might be a glimmer of hope. If Buell would just drag his heels long enough, Bragg could increase his force and offer the Federals an even fight. If the fainthearted Kentuckians chose not to join him voluntarily, he now would make them. Having proclaimed conscription in Tennessee earlier in the month, Bragg decided he now should do the same in Kentucky. The one sticking point was the lack of a legal Confederate government in the state. Providentially, Richard Hawes, the provisional Confederate governor of Kentucky, had just arrived in the state from Richmond. Bragg seized upon the idea of taking Hawes to Frankfort for a formal installation so that conscription could proceed on a legal basis. Kentuckians, he claimed, seemed to want him to do so. "I see no hope but in the conscript act," he wrote Davis, "and I propose to enforce it immediately after installing the provisional civil government on Saturday the 4th inst. The people themselves assure me they prefer it, as they hope thus to escape the penalty of confiscation if we are obliged to retrograde."[83] In the meantime, Bragg's men posted proclamations advising Kentuckians that their last chance to volunteer had come, or else they would be drafted. In places like Danville, many men who did not "prefer it" reacted by fleeing immediately to Union lines.[84]

His mind made up, Bragg acted quickly. His lethargy became a thing of the past as activity and enthusiasm returned. On September 28, he turned temporary command of the army over to Polk and headed for Danville, where Hawes waited. Their ultimate destination was Frankfort, but Bragg first planned a side trip to Kirby Smith's headquarters at Lexington, where he finally would assert his authority over that elusive younger officer, thus solving another problem.[85] Riding east with a small escort, he passed through a small, Boyle County town called Perryville at midday. Bragg had heard of it, for earlier his engineer had drawn attention to it as one of the few towns in the drought-plagued region still enjoying a ready supply of water. Serenaded by students of the Ewing Institute, a school for young ladies, the party dined with "a widow lady in moderate but very comfortable circumstances." Their conversation soon turned to war.

"'Do you think, General,'" the hostess asked at one point, "'I can dig up my silver mugs and spoons now?'" Yes, Bragg confidently assured her, she indeed could do so, for the danger of Federal occupation had passed. Without further fanfare, Bragg and his entourage finished eating and rode on toward Danville. Bragg's advice, as it would turn out, was a wrong-headed as anything else he did that week. Ten short days later, the woman's house would reek with stench and horror after being impressed into service as a Federal hospital.[86]

Bragg and his party arrived in Danville later in the afternoon. From his hotel veranda he again attempted to rally the people of Kentucky, telling them that he was not there "to arrest men, imprison women, and rob peaceable citizens of their property; but to give Kentucky a chance to express her Southern preferences without fear of Northern bayonets—that if she will rally to his standard, he will stay and defend he soil; but if she decline the offer of liberty, he will withdraw his army, and leave her to her choice." His words had little impact according to Chaplain Joseph Cross, for Danville, hometown of Jere Boyle and prominent Republican cleric Robert J. Breckinridge, "contains the worst community in the State. The faculty of Centre College, and the professors of the Theological Seminary, are a nest of unclean birds, all of the Breckinridge plume and bill."[87]

Nonetheless, later that night Bragg heard enough good news to lift him completely beyond his debilitating depression. George Morgan's column had eluded the Confederates, but only as it turned out to veer deeper into the rugged mountains of eastern Kentucky. That was good news, he assured Polk in a dispatch, for "our cavalry under [John Hunt] Morgan is harassing him and getting many prisoners, besides destroying his trains." George Morgan's Yankees would not be a factor in the coming days. Better still, Brig. Gen. Carter Stevenson and eight thousand troops had arrived in Danville under orders from Kirby Smith. Having followed Morgan's Yankees from the Cumberland Gap, Stevenson now would continue on to Shelbyville so that Cleburne's and Smith's brigades could finally rejoin the main army. Another bit of encouraging news was that Brig. Gen. William Preston had arrived in Danville as well. Bragg expressed confidence that the popular Kentuckian might help with recruiting.

Thus buoyed by events, Bragg not only recaptured his old aggressiveness, but his good mood soared to unreasonable and unhealthy heights, as exemplified when he confidently and entirely unrealistically mentioned in a letter to Davis his pending invasion of Ohio! Largely eschewing the defensive stance he had just ordered, as well as any discussion of retreat, Bragg reversed himself completely and directed Polk to "move your troops forward. This will serve the better to invest Louisville and to cover important mills in our front from which to draw supplies. Reconnoiter the ground well, and if favorable encamp your main bodies on the Seven Mile Creek, holding Taylorsville, Shepherdsville, &c.; drive the enemy from Elizabethtown and hold that, so as to cut off communication with Munfordville; then feel that, so as to see what they have there and if we may not pick it up." Such a movement, if carried out, would push the army halfway to Louisville. Along with Cleburne and Smith at Shelbyville, the Confederates would control all the main roads leading south and east from the city. Such an aggressive order was a far cry from laying the groundwork for a retreat to Knoxville, and it says much about Bragg's increasingly abrupt mood swings. Bad news, such as the capture of the entire 3rd Georgia Cavalry south of Bardstown at New Haven on September 29, did not sway him now.[88]

On October 1, an increasingly self-assured Bragg continued on to Lexington to meet with Kirby Smith. It was the first time the two men had seen each other since the barren session in Chattanooga the previous August, and much had changed since then. Certainly the Lexington meeting proved less cordial than had the previous one. Confident now, and no doubt tired of Kirby Smith frustrating his designs as well, Bragg finally pulled rank on the troublesome younger officer, asserting his authority over him and his forces as soon as he arrived in town. "Gen Bragg is in command," Kirby Smith sniffed to his wife after the conclave, "I am no longer at head of affairs but have only to obey orders."[89] Serving as a subordinate proved a hard pill for a would-be Moses to swallow, and with it Bragg earned Kirby Smith's undying enmity.

As it was, they had much to discuss. On the following morning, October 2, Bragg received a stunning report stating that Buell's army was on the march, "moving in force" toward Shelbyville. The armies' respite had ended, and suddenly the battle for Kentucky loomed. Unfortunately for the Confederates, a "babel of confusion" of their own making would continue to dog their response.

BLISSFUL IGNORANCE

IN 1781 OR THEREABOUTS, ACTING UPON THE ACCOUNTS OF THE explorer Dr. Thomas Walker, a party of Virginians led by Walker's son and one James Harberson fled their war torn state and crossed the Appalachian mountains into Kentucky. Settling among the rolling green hills of the central Bluegrass near Harrodsburg, then seven years old and Kentucky's oldest surviving white settlement, the group constructed a fort on the western bank of the Chaplin River near a spring and above a cave, and dubbed their new home Harberson's Station. Trouble followed. Although they had left behind the set-piece violence of the American Revolution, bloodshed quickly found them nonetheless. Central Kentucky remained Shawnee country, and like the more celebrated settlers just to the east led by Daniel Boone at Boonesborough, the Harberson party encountered its share of resistance at the hands of the region's original owners. One day in 1783, James Harberson, having grown lame, apparently tarried outside the fort too long and was captured. Although his body never turned up, survivors later discovered his head about a mile away. His wife carefully preserved it to remember him by.

Born in the midst of war, Harberson's Station survived as peace slowly descended over central Kentucky and the Shawnee slowly and defiantly fell back deeper into the Midwest. Just after the War of 1812, with the indigenous threat finally extinguished, local landowners Edward Bullock and William Hall drew up plans to construct a town on property they controlled near the fort site. They renamed the settlement Perryville in honor of naval hero Oliver Hazard Perry. While Bullock and Hall certainly envisioned a favored future for their venture, reality ultimately must have dampened their boosterism. In the years that followed, Perryville never became a rival to Louisville or Lexington, or even nearby Danville for that matter.

After 1836, when the state legislature chartered a turnpike to run from Springfield, through Perryville, to Danville, the hamlet grew into a comfortable Southern market town. By 1860, Main Street, which ran along the west bank of the Chaplin River, boasted six ornate buildings that comprised

"Merchant's Row," Perryville's heart. Area farmers raising hemp, potatoes, wheat, corn, and livestock on holdings that averaged between one hundred and five hundred acres, routinely came to Merchant's Row to trade. After completing their transactions, they could refresh themselves and talk politics at Abraham Fulkerson's tavern, or spend the night at the Barker Hotel. Other townspeople also vied for their business. Besides the merchants and hoteliers, the town's 1860 population included fifteen blacksmiths, fourteen carpenters, seven stonecutters, six clergymen, five doctors, and numerous other tradesmen, including brick masons, cabinetmakers, cobblers, mechanics, millers, mule traders, saddlers, and tailors. There was at least one cooper, gunsmith, harness maker, hatter, machinist, and attorney. Two residents described themselves simply as "gentlemen," while W. S. Bork taught the art of dancing. Only four men described themselves as common laborers, suggesting perhaps that Perryville did not contain a sizable underclass, drawing instead upon the ranks of the rural poor and slaves for basic labor.

Culture as well as business defined Perryville. Townspeople pointed proudly to Perryville Seminary, a Presbyterian academy founded in 1850 on the eastern edge of town. Educating over seven hundred students by 1861, its principal changed the institution's name that year to Harmonia College. Another point of pride was Ewing Female Institute. Founded in 1858, the well-regarded institution's students one day would sing for Braxton Bragg. Like many other towns in the upper South, Perryville also contained several churches, Masonic and Odd Fellows' lodges, and an active Temperance Society.

One element of the population might be excused from singing Perryville's praises. African Americans as well as whites called Perryville home in the antebellum years. Boyle County ranked twenty-fifth among Kentucky's slaveholding counties in 1860. Thirty-five percent of the county's population in that year, 3,279 residents out of a total of 9,304, remained enslaved. Another 435 African Americans possessed a tenuous freedom; only three Kentucky counties contained more free Blacks at the time of the 1860 census. A few freed African Americans from Boyle had continued on to Liberia.

Historian Richard C. Brown attributes the relatively high number of free Blacks in Boyle County to a widely held local belief in gradual emancipation exemplified by several local leaders, notably Centre College's Robert Breckinridge and wealthy businessman Charles "King Charley" Henderson. A few residents actively worked to assist escaping slaves. Be that as it may, 88 percent of Boyle County's Blacks remained enslaved on the eve of the Civil War. The average Boyle County slaveholder owned one bondsman, and half of the county's slaveholders controlled five or fewer. On the other hand, twenty-four slave owners possessed more than twenty slaves, earning them the right to be called planters. Despite occasional trouble, few slave owners imagined, or at least admitted to imagining, that their bondsmen were anything but well treated, content, and inferior. Emancipation could come one

Figure 6.1. Perryville in 1862. From *Harper's Weekly*, Nov. 1, 1862. Photograph by Tom Beggs.

day in the future, many maintained, but only with adequate compensation followed by African colonization. For the foreseeable future, Perryville and Boyle County remained part of the slave South.

The slave issue inevitably influenced politics in prewar Perryville, as it did everywhere in the nation. Politically, Boyle County, like much of Henry Clay's state, was Whig territory. Whigs routinely took home two-thirds of the vote in presidential elections from the time of their party's founding. Although the party collapsed nationally due to the furor caused by the Kansas-Nebraska Act of 1854, its successors continued to squash Democratic hopes under various temporary guises, with the same basic results. In 1860, Constitutional Unionist and former Whig John Bell won 64.4 percent of the county's ballots—697 votes—just as he captured Kentucky as a whole. John C. Breckinridge, in contrast, captured only 331 votes in Boyle County, about a third of Bell's totals. Stephen Douglas garnered just 52 votes, and only three hearty souls voted for Lincoln.

Voting loyalties often make it difficult to separate traditional party allegiance from the issues at hand, but subsequent events do reinforce the notion that most Boyle County residents were, in fact, archetypical Kentuckians who remained loyal to their party, supported legal slavery, and desired the preservation of the Union. Certainly the leading lights championed Unionism. Danville's Joshua Fry Bell represented Kentucky at the Washington Peace Conference while his neighbor Robert Breckinridge rose to prominence in the Republican Party. Among those in uniform, Jere Boyle notably was a native of the county, as was Speed Fry, the officer who drew his revolver on

Buell at Pelham in support of Albin Schoepf. More to the point, however, two-thirds of the local men who enlisted to fight donned Federal blue, although the Union occupation undoubtedly suppressed Confederate enlistments somewhat. Ultimately, only the Emancipation Proclamation in 1863 would drive Boyle County Unionists toward the Democracy. Support for the Union remained disassociated from ending slavery for most white Kentuckians, Boyle Countians included.[1]

Perryville and Harrodsburg, however, regularly provided something of an exception to the rule, for Democratic loyalties and secession sentiment in those two towns was stronger than anywhere else in Boyle County. Dr. Jefferson J. Polk, a Methodist minister as well as a Perryville town doctor and a Unionist, remembered with some chagrin the numbers of townspeople who turned out to welcome Bragg's Confederates in October 1862. "Many of the citizens showed the greatest signs of joy;" he complained, "many shouted for Jeff. Davis and the Southern Confederacy; rebel flags were displayed by women and children; and some were heard to exclaim, 'O, I am happy! My savior has come!" To a clergyman like Polk, such cries bordered on sacrilege.[2]

Two factors combined to bring those would-be saviors in gray to Perryville in the early autumn of 1862. One was desperately needed water, which Perryville still could provide in at least limited quantities. In normal years, water seemed to flow everywhere in and around the town. Perryville by 1862 had grown to straddle the shallow and sluggish Chaplin River, which approached from the southeast, meandered roughly northward through town to a point about two and one-half miles beyond, and then turned abruptly to the southwest. There, Walker's Bend, named for the family that resided within, formed a narrow, thumb-shaped peninsula pointing southwest before the river eventually turned north again. A tributary of the Chaplin, Doctor's Creek, branched off toward the southwest from Walker's Bend. About a mile and a half southward along that creek, a third waterway, Bull Run, entered it from the south. Farther up the Chaplin itself, Wilson's Creek also branched off, flowing to the southwest as well.

At least that was the case most of the time. The autumn of 1862, however, fast was becoming one of the driest on record, and all that remained of Perryville's normal bounty of irrigation were a few springs and stagnating, scum-covered pools in the deepest recesses of otherwise dusty riverbeds.[3] "There was no water in the channel of this creek about the town," Thomas Head of the 16th Tennessee Infantry remembered, understandably mistaking the normally shallow and now dry Chaplin River for a mere creek. "Two miles below Perryville there was a depression in the channel of the creek. This depression was about two hundred yards long, the width of the entire channel, and filled with water to the depth of from two of four feet." It might as well have been gold.[4]

Perryville's position along a critical crossroads invited further attention. Perryville could be reached from the west by any of three converging

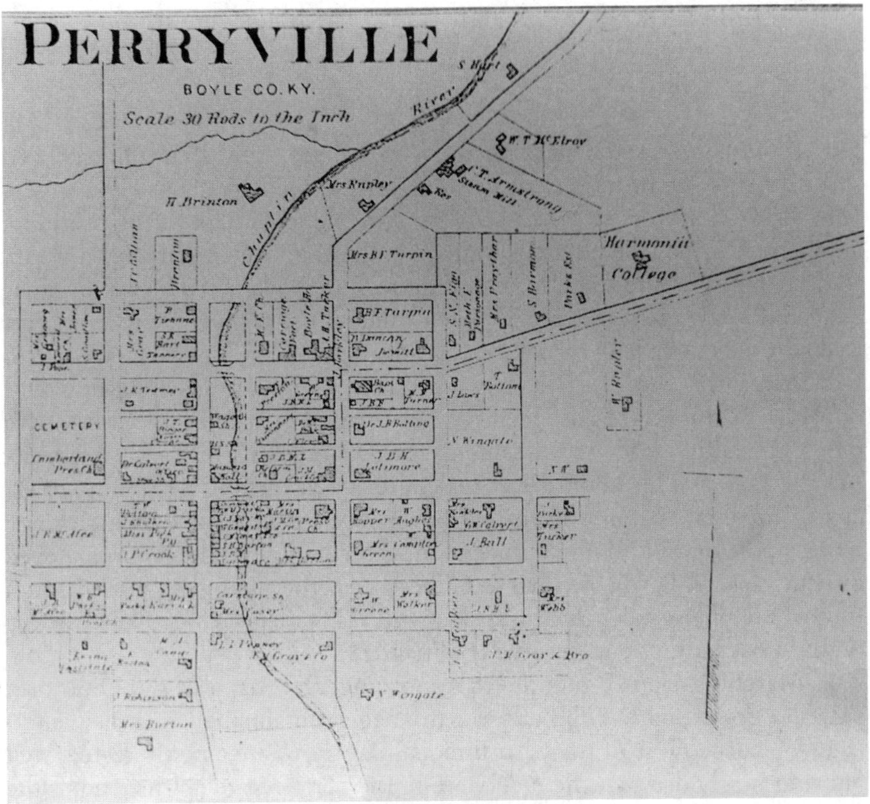

Map 6.1. Perryville, about fifteen years after the battle. Detail from "Map of Boyle and Mercer Counties," courtesy Perryville Enhancement Project.

roads, all of which normally funneled rural farmers and travelers toward Main Street and Merchant's Row. The Springfield-Danville Pike extended through town along an east-west axis. The important connector that had given the town life, the retreating Confederate army would use it in early October as it fell back toward Danville and ultimately Harrodsburg. The turnpike from Lebanon to Harrodsburg additionally bisected the immediate area from northeast to southwest, although in town it ran directly north-south along Main Street. An attentive observer also would have noticed two additional roads, the Mackville Road, which entered Perryville from the northwest before terminating, and the Mitchellsburg Road, which ran directly south out of town.

October 7 saw all three roads west of town choked with the dusty, exhausted, and rapidly dehydrating soldiers of Buell's Army of the Ohio, which was again in pursuit of the Confederate army. In Perryville, William J. Hardee's wing of the Army of the Mississippi, joined by Frank Cheatham's division of Polk's wing, expectantly waited for the enemy to show themselves. After decades of placidity, Perryville, born in bloodshed, hesitantly greeted war again.

On September 30, 1862, the soldiers of the Federal Army of the Ohio cooked three days' worth of rations, drew supplies, and made ready to leave Louisville. Provost officers swept the city for stragglers. The following morning, augmented by new levies, the seventy-five-thousand-man army left the city to do battle with the Rebels. According to Buell's plans, Sill's two divisions headed directly eastward toward Shelbyville on the main route to Frankfort to divert the enemy away from the real advance. The rest of McCook's corps moved out first onto the Bardstown Pike but then six miles out swung left, onto the Taylorsville Pike. That road in turn divided at Plum Creek, with one fork leading to Shelbyville and the other branching off to the southeast toward Taylorsville. Until the corps chose the latter route at Plum Creek, any Confederate cavalry on the road probably would assume that McCook was supporting Sill. Completing the movement, Crittenden's corps moved directly toward Bardstown while Gilbert's, on the far right, headed south toward Shepherdsville. Buell traveled with Gilbert, perhaps to keep an eye on his most inexperienced corps commander.[5]

Marching from Louisville that morning, the Army of the Ohio presented a grand sight. "The entire army had been supplied with new equipage," George Herr of the 59th Illinois Infantry wrote, "newly rested, well fed, and newly dressed, the men were in the very best of spirits, and as the host moved gayly forward the air trembled in the throes of martial music, the spectacle was grand, inspiring, magnificent. Proud stepping men, proud stepping horses, blaring trumpets, flashing sabres, burnished guns, gleaming bayonets blazing in the day, with plumes and spurs and banners dancing in the sunbeams and spangling the air, presented a fine picture of the pomp, panoply and circumstance of war."[6]

Very soon, however, the pomp gave way to frustration, fatigue, and occasional drunkenness. Many men had not eaten breakfast, and as the day wore on they grew increasingly hungry, which in turn inevitably led to widespread straggling and scattered foraging in farmers' fields and storehouses. The day itself was suffocating. Roads soon grew clogged, halts became frequent, and the columns lengthened over several miles. Ankle-deep road dust rose to clog nostrils. Dust clouds hovering above a tree line once alive with the bright hues of autumn soon enveloped the four separate columns, leaving only scattered acorns and walnuts along the road to remind one of surrounding red and gold forests. Soldiers soon found that the only water available along the roadside lay in shallow, muddy streams or green, stagnant pools. Fruit proved to be a godsend in the search for moisture, and men greedily sucked the juices from every fruit they encountered along the way. Afternoon storms did little except make the men even more miserable. Some units only marched six or seven miles before dark, and quite a few soldiers ended the day riding in an ambulance.

The inexperienced "troopees," the new recruits, suffered most of all. Some collapsed by the wayside and lost contact with their regiments until morning.[7] Others littered the roadside with "surplus baggage . . . whenever a halt was made the men took the opportunity thus offered of relieving themselves of needless articles which they had loaded themselves with under the erroneous impression that they were necessary for a soldier's comfort. Whole knapsacks, filled with kits—from shaving appliances and shoe brushes to portable writing desks—were thrown away."

Old soldier Wilbur Hinman of the 6th Ohio Battery left a particularly vivid account of the new regiments on the first day out. Noting that the new men "were going to show the old soldiers that they could march as well as anybody else," Buell's veterans soon had a great laugh at the expense of the raw troops when they faltered, calling out jests as the "fresh fish" limped by. "'I say,'" they called, "'ye better give that knapsack a dose o' physic!'"

"'Brace up, there, young feller!'"

"'Don't ye wish ye were home?'"

"'How's yer sweetheart?'"

"When one of these suffering pilgrims lost his temper," Hinman continued, "—as he was very likely to do—and snapped and snarled in reply, he made a mistake, for the boys only redoubled their efforts to make his life a burden, if, indeed, it could be made any greater burden than it already was. But it was only fun." That night, the veterans engaged in even more "fun," stealing the rookies' blankets to leave them shivering in the cold.[8]

More serious matters than hazing occupied some soldiers. On the Shelbyville Road, Sill's column encountered considerable resistance in the form of John Scott's Confederate cavalry, still attached to Kirby Smith's Army of Kentucky, while crossing Floyd's Fork. A short skirmish ended with the gray-clad horsemen driven back. Similar skirmishes occurred at the head of the other columns as well, with the Army of the Mississippi's horsemen again giving way, especially in the face of Gilbert's column. Colonel John Wharton, the tall, gaunt Texas Ranger who only recently had superseded Forrest, reported that the Yankees "have appeared in strong force on all the roads, chiefly on the Mount Washington Pike, with cavalry, infantry, and artillery." The fighting had begun. What the Confederate brass would make of such reports was anyone's guess.[9]

On the Union left the following morning, October 2, McCook's corps minus Sill's contingent continued down the Taylorsville Pike, ordered by Buell to seize the junction of the Shelbyville and Taylorsville Roads. The day again proved hot and the men grew more desperate for something to drink, for as McCook wrote George Thomas, "there is no water in Plum or Elk Creek for man or beast."[10] Mead Holmes of the 21st Wisconsin Infantry wrote home

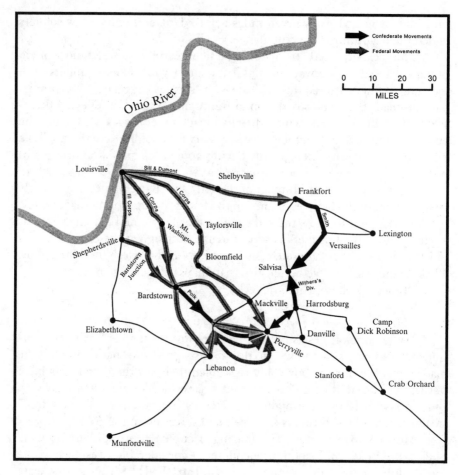

Map 6.2. Roads to Perryville, October 1-7, 1862.

that what water they found was so dirty that he could not see an inch into it. One of Holmes's comrades further remembered that tempers in the regiment flared again over water, most notably when the adjutant rode his horse into a slimy pond as the men tried to drink. Angered, they threw stones and clods at the horse, driving the officer from the waterhole. Much to the soldiers' satisfaction, Col. Benjamin Sweet, a thirty-year-old politician and heretofore-unpopular colonel, ordered the adjutant placed under arrest. Nonetheless, the incident was an ominous sign of things to come.[11]

In fields along the way, local farmers and more numerous slaves worked at cutting corn and preparing the soil for winter wheat. Many of the latter rushed to the roads to watch the men in blue march by. McCook finally ordered the column an additional five miles past the crossroads to the town itself, where his worn-out men rested all day on the third despite an ironic torrential downpour overnight, endured without tents left back in Louisville. Frequent alarms occasioned by the sound of distant artillery occurred as elements of Wharton's Confederate cavalry doggedly challenged the corps' forward units, creating further uneasiness. Nevertheless, McCook's soldiers greeted their respite, as well as fresh beef, mail, and Unionists along the roads, with enthusiasm. Thousands of them, according to Henry Fales Perry of the 38th Indiana Infantry, bathed and washed their clothing in the clear and cool river, immersing themselves decadently in what normally was a precious commodity. A few, such as a member of the 3rd Ohio Infantry who died during an impromptu wrestling match, exerted themselves too much.[12]

"Taylorsville is a fine little place," Hoosier Ormond Hupp wrote approvingly, "the country from Louisville to here is beautiful and well adapted for farming." Charles W. Carr of the 21st Wisconsin agreed, writing his wife that night: "such a splendid evening I never saw. It was as light as day, and troops moving as far as the eye could see over the hills, for it is a hilly, roaling country here in old Ky. It was magnificent scenery." The 123rd Illinois Infantry's James A. Connolly disagreed, however, seeing only "the peculiar marks of indolence and slow decay seen in all these southern towns."[13]

To men like Connolly, there was an even uglier side to Taylorsville that was peculiar to the South—as the already agitated soldiers of Col. John Starkweather's brigade soon discovered. Sergeant John Henry Otto of the 21st Wisconsin, a veteran of the Prussian army barely coping with his largely untried officers and men, watched as two runaway slaves entered his brigade's camp at Taylorsville, soon followed by two local men "each with a long whip." Colonel Sweet, having already earned the admiration of the men in the ranks once for punishing his adjutant, now rose again in their eyes as he ordered the slave owners to leave. When a threatening group of soldiers gathered around the Taylorsville men, some pelting them with corn cobs, Sweet reluctantly reversed himself and allowed the slave owners to search the premises after all, afraid that any sign of personal weakness might result in his men killing the Kentuckians.

Unfortunately, the slave catchers seemed to possess a death wish, at one point cursing the Federals as "damned blackguards, Abolitionists, thiefs and beggars. This," Otto added, "was too much for the boys," especially the raw Wisconsinites of the Twenty-first and some of the veterans of the 24th Illinois Infantry, who now cried out for lynching the Southerners. Lovell Rousseau, alerted by his fellow Kentuckians as well as an orderly who had ridden to the camp and been pelted with corn cobs by the Badgers, arrived on the scene at that moment and angrily "ordered the 21st to stake arms and march 20. paces backwards." Rousseau then ordered the 79th Pennsylvania Infantry to stand between the Illinoisans and their weapons, the Pennsylvanians "ordered to load, facing toward us. The 24th Ill. Was placed in our rear; the 1st Wis on our right along the road and Capt Stones Kentuky batterie on our left flank."

"'Now 21st Wis . . . ,'" Rousseau declared, "'will you obey my orders or not?'"

"'Yes general,'" a voice called out, "if consistent with our duty and our Concience, but no slave catching."

"'Who said that?'" demanded a now-furious Rousseau. At length, five men stepped forward and admitted to harassing the slave owners. The situation quickly defused. The common soldiers were well pleased with themselves, and the brigade threw itself a party, complete with singing, bands, a barrel of bourbon, and, ironically, a minstrel show attended by, among others, Generals Mitchell, Terrill, and Starkweather. The highlight of the evening, however, occurred elsewhere when the homes of the two slave owners went up in flames. Smuggled out of camp in an ambulance, the escaped slaves remained with the regiment as servants and "pack mules." Lovell Rousseau's opinions of the Wisconsin regiment remained an open question.[14]

In the meantime, urgently seeking information as to the disposition of the enemy, McCook only disoriented himself more while at Taylorsville. Just as he had back in Tennessee at the beginning of the retreat, McCook gullibly and impulsively placed great reliance on reports from Confederate deserters, which again proved erroneous if not downright misleading. On October 4, he reported: "two deserters of the First Louisiana came to my pickets. They left camp at Bardstown yesterday morning . . . they say Bragg's entire force is there, and that they intend to fight. They have no intrenchments, and the force as far as they know is 60,000. They say they have had a great many recruits since they came to Kentucky, and that they have a considerable number not armed. . . . The plan was to draw Buell to Bardstown; then Kirby Smith to come in our rear between us and Louisville." Little of it was true, of course, but it disturbed McCook greatly and increased his hesitation.[15]

Having duly reported the deserters' tale, McCook proceeded to Bloomfield before daylight. An initially clear and sunny day turned rainy again. The temperature dropped as well until, in the words of Alfred Galpin of the 1st Wisconsin Infantry, the day became "cold as fury." Nerves remained taut, and Galpin added that the regiment's Company C fired a few dozen shots as the result of one false alarm. Straggling also worsened as hungry men searched for food, an activity boosted by the reputed prosecession sentiments of the locals. All the men of Bloomfield save one, Robert Taylor reported, had fled the town, leaving only angry women.[16] One unidentified member of the increasingly notorious 21st Wisconsin wrote home: "I took dinner at a house on the route, the man of the house being one of those sleepy, 'I reckon' sort of men, said all he wanted was 'peace' and did not care which side came out ahead. One or two of the boys heard what he said, so they of course concluded to 'confiscate' some of his property, the whole amounting to the following: —One boy (colored), 18 years old, three turkeys, one pig, two sheep, chickens, apples and *sich* like in large quantities."[17]

Meanwhile, "in blissful ignorance" of Buell's orders or other dispositions, McCook informed Thomas that his cavalry had reported Hardee near Chaplin. By then he knew from Buell that the enemy had abandoned Bardstown. Confused by conflicting reports, however, McCook could not decide whether the enemy was concentrating at Frankfort or Harrodsburg. He thus decided not to move at all until he received positive orders.[18] Instead he spent the day personally seeing to the rounding up of stragglers. Robert B. Taylor remembered seeing a regiment approach town with fixed bayonets and return two hours later with an estimated fifteen hundred Federals under guard. At his headquarters, McCook reprimanded the officers among the prisoners and as he frequently "discharged them; but ordered the men to take each a rail upon his shoulder, they were formed into companies and placed in command of an orderly sergeant of their number, were put in motion, and marched around a circle of about a quarter of a mile in circumference to the infinite amusement of the whole army." Others, Taylor added, fared even worse, notably three men executed for "committing some serious depredations on a man."[19]

The awaited orders finally came on the sixth. The enemy was definitely retreating toward Danville, McCook learned. Accordingly, Buell ordered him to march to Harrodsburg, with Sill following so as to rejoin the corps. McCook absolutely had to be in position there by October 8, Buell added. The column moved out with Starkweather's brigade in the lead, followed by Terrill's brigade. Marching quickly through Chaplin and as far as Beaver Creek, the van arrived in a state of near exhaustion and camped in bramble-filled, hilly fields. Foraging continued all along the route, the perceived secessionist proclivities of the locals providing an excuse, and tempers between officers and enlisted men flared yet again, especially when men of the feisty 21st Wisconsin cut loose a gunner from Stone's Kentucky Battery who had been tied to the wheel of a gun carriage for stealing a turkey.

That night, however, a staff officer rode into McCook's camp with drastically revised directions. Buell had received information that Sill remained at Shelbyville rather than Frankfort, concerned by reports that Kirby Smith, Marshall, and Stevenson were massing at Frankfort to strike him. Sill's immobility made a junction at Harrodsburg much more difficult. Instead, Buell now wanted McCook to march as quickly as possible toward Perryville, by way of Mackville if possible, with Sill to follow when he could. The Mackville Road thus brought McCook's two divisions toward Perryville from the northwest.[20] Ormond Hupp of the 5th Indiana Battery took an instant dislike to the country as soon as he spied it. "Here the country became more hilly and rough," he wrote, "the timber scrubby and mostly oak, the enterprise of the people much less, and it looked about twenty five miles from nowhere."[21] In fact, it was roughly that distance to the town of Perryville.

In the Federal center, Thomas Crittenden's II Corps, accompanied by second-in-command George Thomas and occasionally by Buell as well, had encountered more determined Confederate opposition than had McCook. The bulk of Wharton's Confederate cavalry, considering the Federal force on the Bardstown Pike the major threat of the three Federal advances, had quickly concentrated north of Mount Washington to hinder it. On the rainy, steamy morning of October 2, Crittenden's lead elements, spearheaded by cavalry and Col. Samuel Beatty's brigade of infantry and artillery, pushed ahead deliberately on choked roads and in the defiant face of the bulk of Wharton's horse soldiers. Late in the afternoon, the rain stiffening, Federal artillery firing from high ground battered the bulk of Wharton's horsemen across Floyd's Fork of the Salt River and back toward Mount Washington. The next day brought a gray, rainy morning that gave way to sunshine as Crittenden's men took the town and, in the face of a masked Confederate battery, forced a crossing of the Salt River—dishonorably under a Federal flag of truce, Wharton complained. One Federal countered that the Rebels held on to the flag bearer as long as possible to buy time, and in so doing got what they deserved.[22]

Only three days out of Louisville, Crittenden's men nonetheless were again exhausted. An Illinoisan wrote: "the turnpike being very hard, notwithstanding a dust carpet an inch thick, the weather being warm, the water scarce and impure, made the march extremely wearisome. The result was fruitful of sore feet and aching limbs, and a unanimous verdict that 'Jordan am a hard road to travel.' Other ailments still more disabling were produced, and the ambulances were in demand. Many guns and accouterments were piled on, or hanged on, the wagons in the train." Straggling escalated as well, and some men, particularly Indianians, lagged behind, never to be seen again by their officers. The nearby presence of enemy cavalry and increasingly harsh punishments nonetheless convinced most of the men to keep up.

Hazing of new troops also went on unabated in II Corps. One member of the 100th Illinois Infantry later remembered that veterans confiscated foraged delicacies from them and routinely stole their new hats as well.[23] "There seems to be a feeling very much akin to animosity prevailing amongst the old regiments toward the new," wrote a member of the 26th Ohio Infantry. "Some of the old regiments make a practice of insulting the new levies whenever they meet them, ridiculing their movements, accusing them of cowardice in not having volunteered sooner, and of selling themselves to their country for ninety or a hundred dollars. Officers of old regiments frequently encourage men to make these taunts."[24]

Bloody skirmishing continued on the rainy fourth of October as both Wharton's and Wheeler's cavalry continued to put up surprisingly effective but ultimately vain resistance in front of Bardstown, which fell late in the day to Thomas Wood's division. "We have several hundred prisoners sick in hospital," Thomas wrote Buell, "all of whom I will have paroled tomorrow." Better still, the town's civilians, having feted the Confederates earlier, now put out the welcome mat for the Yankees, who universally praised Bardstown for its revived Unionism. Some townspeople helpfully added that Bragg's army, retreating on the Springfield and Little Beech Fork roads, was both sickly and depleted.[25] Many Federals, while pleased with the foodstuffs they found in town, expressed disappointment that no fight occurred. "We had expected to find the rebels in full," Marcus Woodcock of the 9th Kentucky wrote, "and rather desired than dreaded to give them a fight, hoping it would in some way terminate the long and heavy marches we were almost daily being compelled to make; but we had learned that the last of the Rebels had left Bardstown just as our advance came in sight."[26]

Early the next morning, Crittenden, Thomas, and Buell held a brief meeting. The enemy could not keep retreating, Buell suggested. Somewhere they had to make a stand. He believed the most likely spot was the town of Perryville, which offered a likely location for a junction of Bragg and Kirby Smith's armies.[27] William C. Johnson, the newly appointed chaplain of the 13th Kentucky Infantry, wrote in his journal that the dawn of October 5 brought "one of the most beautiful Sabbath mornings . . . that I ever beheld," but no respite from the campaign. Buell ordered Crittenden that morning to pursue the rebels toward Glenville on the Springfield Pike. Alerted by a local Black man that as many as sixteen thousand Confederates had camped in Glenville the previous night, Crittenden moved "cautiously" toward the town, arriving himself about six in the evening. More witnesses confirmed that the Confederates looked "distressed, weary, and harassed."[28] "The road we were following was beaten smooth by the tramp of the retreating Rebels," Chaplain Johnson wrote, "and we . . . picked up about fifteen stragglers; we captured from them about a dozen muskets and three horses. I pitied the poor fellows, and talked particularly with three of them, all of whom said they did not enter the army voluntarily. Two of them expressed a willingness to take the oath of allegiance."

Johnson's flock collapsed in exhaustion along Beech Fork, near the village of Lynchburg, at the end of the day. "I proposed to preach at night, but the poor, hungry soldiers, as soon as they had eaten their scanty meal, wanted to lie down to sleep, and I felt so too. A few of us got together and sang a few hymns, and thus ended my first Sabbath in the army."[29] They were not alone, for the general lack of potable water, the bad road, and long day combined to produce much straggling, especially among the worn out new regiments. Some had no more to eat than parched corn.[30]

The next day, October 6, Crittenden's tired men marched "over very bad road"[31] toward Springfield despite a sporadically furious series of skirmishes with Wheeler's cavalry that delayed the advance much of the day. Stragglers fell out by the hundreds. Water continued to be a scarce commodity, creating much distress in the ranks. Members of the 6th Ohio Battery and then others attempted to compensate with a discovered cache of from twenty to fifty barrels of whiskey until their division commander, Wood, ordered what was left of the coveted liquid poured out on the ground, a decided waste the men complained. Foraging continued as well, with beef cattle particularly prized.[32]

   That night they slept in or around Springfield, "hungry, tired, leg weary and foot-sore, shoulder tired and tender with knapsack, gun, and cartridge-box, and not in the best spirits or humor." Captain Francis B. Mattler of Company B, 86th Indiana Infantry, already hated "for his extreme officiousness and petty, tyrannical conduct on numerous occasions" discovered as much when he ordered some of his men out of a potato patch. Only the intercession of a more popular captain as well as their colonel prevented the irritated and ill-fed Hoosiers from attacking the despised Mattler. "This was the situation of the Eighty-sixth on the evening of October 6 at Springfield, Kentucky," wrote its regimental historians. The same sad fact held true more or less throughout Crittenden's corps.[33]

By October 6, the combination of tension between old and new soldiers, insubordination, hunger, and especially maddening thirst had devitalized Crittenden's and McCook's corps. In Charles Gilbert's already troubled III Corps, the result was much worse.

   Four days earlier, before sunup on October 2, Gilbert's column again took to the road and headed almost directly south toward Shepherdsville on the Salt River. They reached the town without opposition early the next day. Turning eastward toward Bardstown, Federal cavalry under Col. Minor Milliken of the 1st Ohio Cavalry skirmished with elements of Wharton's brigade at Cedar Church, inaugurating a series of cavalry skirmishes that swirled between the armies for the next several days.[34] Marshall Thatcher of the 2nd Michigan Cavalry described the cavalry's war: "Firing, then retire to give the alarm . . . cavalry attacking skirmish lines; sometimes mounted, oftener dismounted, steadily moving forward, pressing the enemy's rear guard, and a continuous running fight of seven days followed." Fighting by night as well as day, sleeping irregularly, desperate for water and something to eat, "was it any wonder that men swallowed Kentucky apple-jack in draughts that would have killed a man under ordinary circumstances?"[35]

   The infantry, largely deprived of the cavalry's alcohol, remembered only the heat, dust, thirst, and distant sound of artillery as they tried to sleep. "Our water is very poor," Abraham Ulery of the 17th Ohio Infantry wrote his aunt and uncle, "it would almost make on sick to drink it if it was not maid in to coffy, it is nothing but pond watter that we have hear and it stinks at that." Levi A. Ross of the 86th Illinois agreed. He described what little water they found as "almost nauseating even to the stomach of a soldier . . . water blue and thick from the slime of frogs and hogs."[36] "It was a fearful hot day—the Second of October," A. M. Crary of the brand-new 75th Illinois Infantry later added, "—and the dust so thick that it almost smothered a man. . . . It was march, march, march, fifty minutes by the watch, then, with a ten minute's rest in order to take breath and reflect upon soldier life."

As elsewhere, hazing from the veterans remained pointed: "We were often accosted by 'Hello Boys, How do you like it anyway? Oh, never mind, you'll get used to it after a year or so. Keep a stiff upper lip and you'll come out all right'."[37] Veterans such as David Lathrop of the 59th Illinois Infantry who were behind the hazing maintained that such treatment of the "fresh fish" was entirely justified, for in terms hinting of implied homosexuality he branded the new men as weak and unmanly. "The old troops were anxious to overtake the rebel army and give battle," he wrote three years later, his contempt for the latecomers still tangible. "The new troops were also willing to encounter the foe if necessary—but was as soon have remained in Louisville, with their paper collars and black boots, and their nice light bread and butter." Having looked down upon the dirty, ragged veterans in Louisville, Lathrop went on, the "mincing" new men finally were receiving a necessary education in soldiering.[38]

When foraging for food, however, the green soldiers demonstrated they could learn quickly the ways of veterans, especially when their veteran officers supported them. Colonel Dan McCook, for example, continued to prove particularly adept at encouraging foraging, personally commandeering and ordering five beeves slaughtered to feed his new brigade. "We are in the land of Secessia," John A. Boon wrote home, "and we are not going to starve as long as we can find anything fit to kill and eat."[39] Another member of the brigade, Levi Ross of the 86th Illinois, recorded that "we have nothing to eat unless we 'jayhawk' it from rebel farmers—they deserve to lose it for being traitors, we deserve it for sacrificing to save our country." Accordingly, the rookie Illinoisans swept the vicinity of their route looking for anything edible on two or four legs.[40]

On October 4, Gilbert's corps turned eastward. Sheridan's division marched onto a muddy and slippery Bardstown Pike, skirmishing and marching through the rain to support Crittenden in case the Confederates decided to fight for the town, while the others moved up Cox's Creek, parallel to the pike.[41] The reported nearness of the enemy stirred emotions, especially among men facing their first combat. Long after dark that evening, members of the 88th Illinois Infantry, marching with Col. Nicholas Greusel's brigade of Sheridan's division near the rear of the column, began singing "John Brown's Body" as they marched. "Very soon," remembered Charles Lewis Francis, "our whole regiment, then another, and in a short time the whole division caught up the strain, and then—the occasion defies description." Among the hills and valleys, Francis maintained, the sound grew "unearthly."[42]

Late on the morning of October 5, the van of the corps reached Bardstown, Sheridan's Pea Ridge veterans almost running the last three miles in hopes of cornering the enemy. Stragglers, however, either foraging or simply overcome with fatigue, stretched out behind the corps like a tail for miles, taking all day and part of the night to come in. The next morning, Gilbert's corps left Bardstown for Springfield. It was the most grueling day yet for his men, some of whom walked as far as thirty miles through and past the town, amidst sporadic skirmishing, before arriving at their destination hours after sundown.

On the march to Springfield, Gilbert's disquieted and ill-managed corps finally began coming apart at the seams.[43] Unit cohesion all but disappeared along the torturous road. "Our regiment was stretched out for miles," George Morris of the 81st Indiana Infantry wrote, "the men completely worn out. Every fence corner had one or two men lying in it. . . . Company organizations were represented in some cases by only a half-dozen men, a mere corporal's guard, and in some cases hardly that. Officers coaxed and threatened their men to move forward, but it was of no avail, nature could not stand it in some cases." The chief culprit, Morris contended, was the lack of water. "We suffered a great deal for water," he remembered. "The enemy drank up all the streams and wells on each side of the road. Some of the men went three and four miles from the road to get water."[44] Much of what they found, added Capt. Allen L. Fahnestock of the 86th Illinois Infantry, stank. Others reported paying a dollar for a full canteen from some enterprising comrade in arms. Food was in short supply as well; one Hoosier recorded receiving only two crackers at the end of the day. He admitted to being too tired to eat them anyway.[45]

Insubordination followed in the wake of exhaustion. According to Jay Caldwell Butler of the raw 101st Ohio Infantry:

> About one-half of the regiment have fallen, one man reported fallen in his tracks, dead. Large, stout, able-bodied men give out. . . . The old regiment say they never experienced such marching and fall out by the roadside. Two men, friends, in our company fall out, the one can't hold up his head, the other stays, partially to take care of him, the officer of the day, Capt. McDonald (a brute) ordered the latter to go on. He told him he couldn't and wanted to stay and take care of his friend. McDonald ordered the guard to drive him along at the point of the bayonet.

Butler added ominously, "they will revenge it."[46]

Most hated among the officers remained the corps commander himself. His reputation as a profane and petty martinet grew incessantly during the week-long march. Although Gilbert apparently realized that he at least had to cultivate his brigade commanders—he wrote a fawning letter to Sheridan complimenting him on the beauty of his camp—he showed no similar skill in dealing with his enlisted men.[47] As a result, like Confederate veterans discussing Bragg, men who had worn blue seemingly vied with each other for decades to relate the most outrageous Gilbert story. "Stringent orders against foraging were promulgated by Gen. Gilbert," a member of the 36th Illinois Infantry remembered, "and much of that officer's time, and by far the most onerous of his duties, was the protection of hen-roosts and 'truck patches' of the fellow citizens of his native State." Gilbert accosted members of a company of that regiment, for example, as they gathered apples from an orchard, allegedly ordering his escort to open fire on the trespassers. "The order was scarcely uttered, when every man by the wayside sprang to his feet, seized his musket, and the ramming of cartridges and click of gun-locks was fearfully ominous, and warned the escort to desist from putting the order into execution."

"'Where is the officer in command of these miscreants?'" Gilbert demanded, proceeding to unleash a "torrent of abuse."

"'General,'" the captain in charge responded, "'one word from me will call the boys out of that orchard a d——d sight sooner than you can shoot them out; and should it come to that, I have the honor to assure you, General, that my boys never allow themselves to be outdone in this shooting business.'" The corps commander did not force the issue. He instead placed the entire regiment under arrest.[48]

Gilbert, however, did not learn anything from the encounter. Thus, on the long sixth, a similar incident occurred. James Birney Shaw of the 10th Indiana Infantry, a unit that already had experienced one run-in with Gilbert back at Louisville, had just fallen asleep when a party of horsemen rode into camp. "A man sang out to Captain Boswell, 'What regiment is this?' The captain replied that 'it was the Tenth Indiana.' "D——d pretty regiment. Why in —— don't you get up and salute me when I pass?' Boswell said 'Who in the —— are you?' 'Major General Gilbert, by —, sir. Give me your sword, sir, you are under arrest.'"

Nor had Gilbert finished. After arguing with the regimental colonel, Gilbert rode over to the color bearer "and demanded the colors, that he would disgrace such an armed mob. Dave gave him a cursing and told him if he polluted the colors by touching them he would kill him. Finally the boys began to get mad and thought they had enough of his insults. Jim Luddington, Company H, said, 'Now here, you d——d son——, get out of here or you are a dead man, go—git.' At this point someone fired a musket, and at the same time Lud jabbed Gilbert's horse with a bayonet. The horse reared and plunged and nearly threw Gilbert off—and they went off in a gallop." Left in the dust, many of the Hoosiers promised themselves to kill Gilbert in battle themselves if the opportunity ever presented itself.[49]

So it was that a troubled Federal army neared the town of Perryville.

TO STRIKE A BLOW

BRAXTON BRAGG FIRST LEARNED OF SILL'S DIVERSIONARY ADVANCE on October 2 while consulting with Kirby Smith in Lexington. As Buell hoped, it completely disoriented his opposite number. Days earlier, the news would have immediately precipitated the planned retreat, but now, brimming with the unreasonable confidence he found between Bardstown and Lexington, it only served to stir Bragg's fighting blood. He hurriedly sketched out a plan to crush the Yankees. While Kirby Smith held the line against Buell, Polk would bring the army north and hit the Federals in the flank. "It may be a reconnaissance," he warned Polk, "but should it be a real attack we have them. We shall be at Frankfort to-morrow with all our force. Hold yourself in readiness . . . to strike them on the flank. With Smith in front and our own gallant army on the flank I see no hope for Buell if he is rash enough to come out. I only fear it is not true . . . if you discover a heavy force that has moved on Frankfort strike without further orders."

Just after noon, Bragg wrote Polk again. There was no question now, Bragg asserted, Buell clearly was moving against Frankfort in force. The Federals already had driven back Cleburne at Shelbyville, and he was falling back to the state capital. "Put your whole available force in motion by Bloomfield," Bragg urged, "(and) strike him in flank and rear. If we can combine our movements he is certainly lost."[1]

With the major battle for control of Kentucky seemingly about to occur west of Frankfort, Bragg abruptly turned to other matters and quickly made a stupendously illogical decision. The inauguration of Richard Hawes as the Confederate governor of Kentucky must go on as scheduled, he announced, battle or no battle. Most scholars attribute Bragg's curious decision to a natural rigidity. His unhealthy, euphoric overconfidence, however, probably contributed to the decision in some manner as well. After the war, a defensive Kirby Smith claimed that both he and Buckner begged Bragg to instead concentrate the armies immediately and set aside the political pomp for later. Instead, Bragg insisted on first installing Hawes. Kirby Smith's army would consolidate in Frankfort to protect the inauguration, but the ceremony would go on. "'I can crush Buell with my command at Bardstown alone,'" Bragg supposedly declared.[2]

Assuming that Kirby Smith reported the conversation honestly—admittedly a major assumption considering his previous conduct—he clearly misunderstood Bragg's plan, which most certainly did not rely solely on the Army of the Mississippi. As Thomas Connelly wrote, Bragg envisioned something of a Second Manassas, with Kirby Smith in the Stonewall Jackson role, holding the line until Polk, like James Longstreet, smashed the enemy in the flank.[3] One major difference, however, was that Lee did not attempt simultaneously to establish a government behind Jackson's thin gray line. Dealing with John Pope proved enough of a challenge without playing kingmaker. Kirby Smith, moreover, was no Jackson, and as events were about to prove, the often querulous Longstreet paled in comparison to Polk when it came to second-guessing commanding officers.

Still, Kirby Smith was on to something. What is most fascinating about his recollection is Bragg's cocky remark that Polk could defeat Buell alone, even without the force at Frankfort. Only a few days earlier, Bragg despaired that the *combined* armies could stop Buell without falling back to Tennessee. To be sure, Stevenson had come up to free Cleburne and Preston Smith, and Morgan was lost in eastern Kentucky. Still, the anticipated return of two brigades hardly canceled out Buell's numerical advantage. One must conclude that Bragg's decision ultimately emanated from the same mental confusion that caused him to briefly and impetuously want to give battle at Munfordville and then to attack Louisville just as Buell reached the city. On both occasions, second thoughts won out within a day. This time, actions took on a life of their own before Bragg could change his mind, setting in motion a tangled chain of events that led inexorably to battle in a place never anticipated.

Aside from his own apparently troubled psyche, Bragg's biggest problem was and would remain faulty information. The Federal column approaching Frankfort consisted only of Sill's and Dumont's divisions, misleading Kirby Smith's pickets just as Buell had planned. Bragg had heard nothing of the simultaneous Federal movements toward Polk at Bardstown, although a courier with a dispatch from Polk was belatedly on the way. Left in the dark by his subordinates, he thus continued making plans for the installation of Hawes and the destruction of Buell's army.

Finally arriving in Frankfort on the evening of October 3, Bragg's enthusiasm rose to new heights. Waiting for him were letters from Polk and Hardee written the previous day. Polk's earliest letter, written at 10 A.M., was admittedly disturbing, for it brought the first indication of Buell's other troop movements. Polk confessed first of all that he had never moved forward as Bragg earlier had directed him. The army remained at Bardstown, facing a "forward movement in this direction." Federal columns marched on all three of the area's major roads, with strong forces reported at Shepherdsville, Taylorsville, and especially Mount Washington on the main road to Bardstown. "If an opportunity presents itself," Polk wrote, "I will strike. If it shall be clearly inexpedient to do that I will, according to your suggestion, fall back on Harrodsburg and Danville on the roads indicated by you, with a view to a concentration with General E. K. Smith, Stevenson, &c."

For that brief moment, Polk's understanding of the dilemma facing him, and through him, Bragg's, was clear. The ink was not dry, however, on what would be his clearest dispatch of the campaign before the fog of war settled in again on Confederate headquarters. "Since beginning this note," he added, "I have a dispatch from Colonel Cleburne at Shelbyville inform- ing me that the enemy last night at 10 o'clock were in strong force within 5 miles of his position, Rousseau commanding one of the divisions."[4]

Polk's letter might well have created a stir had it arrived by itself, al- though Bragg's euphoria might have led him to minimize its import. At the very least though, an alerted Bragg might have stopped to take stock. As it was, Bragg read it at the same time as Polk's later and very different letter, along with a dispatch from Hardee. Polk's second letter, while again men- tioning the Federal advance toward Bardstown, went on to indicate that the enemy, McCook's corps in actuality, had stopped at the Salt River. Polk instead stressed the pressure Cleburne had received at Shelbyville. The Federals clearly were concentrating with an eye toward Lexington, he advised. Hardee agreed, adding that Confederate forces needed to concentrate to meet the apparent threat to Lexington; as it was, they were too spread out. Neither officer indi- cated the seriousness of the Federal pressure coming to bear on their army at Bardstown, apparently because they did not appreciate it themselves.[5]

Not surprisingly, the mixed signals coming from Bardstown confused an already bedeviled Bragg still more. Both generals implied that the real Federal threat was aimed at Frankfort. If true, there was no cause for worry because recent information obtained from Kirby Smith indicated that no danger awaited him there, either. The Federal movement on Frankfort, Bragg reassuringly wrote Polk, really had been only a feint itself, one now appar- ently abandoned by the foe. Buell's movements did not indicate a real push but rather merely probing. There was no immediate danger. After canceling the anticipated flank attack, Bragg warned Polk to be prepared to move at a moment's notice so as to effect a concentration of Confederate forces in the Bluegrass as he and Hardee had advised. Place one flank at Taylorsville, he added, forgetting that Polk already had indicated that Taylorsville might well already be in enemy hands, as in fact it was.[6]

The following morning, the weather rainy and miserable, Bragg re- ceived yet another murky dispatch from Polk that should have given him pause. The earlier orders commanding the flank attack had arrived. Due to unspecified problems "on my front and left flank," however, compliance was "inexpedient and impracticable." What Polk inexplicably did not explain was that strong Federal columns had all day maintained pressure on the Shepherdsville and Taylorsville roads, with at least a Federal division on each. Backed by a council of the army's wing and division commanders, with only Bragg-loyalist Patton Anderson dissenting, Polk determined to ignore Bragg's orders yet again, confident that the Louisianian would concur once all the facts were known. Instead of advancing, he instead had ordered the army to retreat toward Camp Breckinridge at Bryantsville, away from Frankfort instead of toward it.

Near dawn on the rainy morning of the fourth, not long before Bragg opened Polk's dispatch, the Army of the Mississippi moved out, a day ahead of the enemy. Hardee's wing trudged toward Harrodsburg while Polk's marched in the direction of Springfield and Danville.[7] "We were aroused last night about two o'clock by our pickets," Texan John Street wrote his wife on October 4, "and told that the advance of Buell's army was within a mile of us coming down from Louisville and that the whole army was advancing on Bardstown." Street at that time was eight miles north of Bardstown on the Louisville Pike. Falling back to the town, his 9th Texas Infantry found the entire army in motion. Sore-footed and exhausted, the army stumbled east.[8] Despite drenching rains, potable water remained scarce, as did other liquids. "People all kind to us," Floridian John Inglis wrote, "lots of Whisky offered but officers, emptied it all out, none allowed."[9] Despite such precautions, many members of the 5th Confederate Infantry's rear guard managed to get drunk. Some refused to march; others fell out and were captured.

Few men could understand why they were retreating at all, and a lack of urgency characterized still more. Some stopped to forage, others deserted.[10] After the skies cleared, intense heat added to the men's misery. William E. Bevens of the 1st Arkansas Infantry recalled several men dying "on those long sunny pikes, with never a sign to mark the grave of a hero, noble sacrifice to their cause." Odd, ironic moments of humor set the men's tribulations in sharpest relief. Bevens particularly remembered an assistant surgeon "carrying an umbrella . . . when General Hardee came along. The General had nothing to shield him from the sun but a little cap. He rode up to the surgeon and said, 'What is your name?' The man told him his name, rank, and regiment.

"'Well sir,' said General Hardee, 'just imagine this whole army with umbrellas.' The doctor shut up his parasol and pitched it over into a field."[11]

Meanwhile, Polk's magnificent vagueness continued to contribute mightily to the growing crisis within the Army of the Mississippi's high command. What exactly was happening on his left and center to cause him to give way? He never told Bragg. Thus emerged one of the better known "what if" questions of the Civil War. Did Polk act correctly in ordering the retreat, or should he have obeyed his orders, as Patton Anderson advised, and move north despite the threat approaching him? Most modern Civil War scholars—including Herman Hattaway, Archer Jones, Grady McWhiney, and

Stephen Woodworth—argue that if Polk had moved as Bragg desired, he still could have united with Kirby Smith and crushed Sill's and Dumont's isolated force, dealing Buell a serious blow. Others, notably Thomas Connelly and Stanley Horn, disagree, maintaining that Polk behaved properly. Not only had Bragg already called off the attack, admittedly a fact Polk could not know, the Federal advance made following Bragg's orders tenuous at best and probably impossible. McCook's corps was already across the Taylorsville Road and in possession of the town, as both Polk and Kirby Smith knew. He could not follow orders without opening up his left flank to a devastating attack.

Connelly's interpretation in the end has more to recommend it; Polk probably chose rightly. Nonetheless, like so many similar queries, the question obscures as much as it enlightens. Whatever he *should* have done, Polk did choose to retreat. More important is the basic fact that Confederate communications were in such disarray that Bragg's figurative right hand had no idea what the left hand was up to, a situation inevitably resulting in the sort of confusion now being produced. His failure to unite the armies of the Mississippi and Kentucky, despite repeated lip service, now came home to roost as both armies independently fell back into a defensive line under well-applied pressure by the enemy. Not surprisingly, they considered the enemy closest to them to be the major threat. What occurred ultimately happened because of Davis's brittle department system, Kirby Smith's inflated self-importance, and Bragg's passivity and mental confusion. Other than his incredible ability to write much and say little, Polk hardly was solely responsible. Retreating was justified given the power vacuum at the top of the Army of the Mississippi.[12]

Nor, one must note, was Bragg all that upset when he learned of Polk's retrograde maneuver—itself a telling clue. To be sure, after the Battle of Perryville, Bragg claimed that he reacted to Polk's dispatch with dismay, as it "necessitated an entire change in my plans, the abandonment of the capital, and the partial uncovering and the ultimate loss of our stores at Lexington."[13] By then, however, most every Southerner except Jefferson Davis had condemned Bragg for losing Kentucky, and the unpopular general reacted characteristically by again seeking scapegoats. The truth was that when he first received Polk's communication, Bragg acquiesced without a murmur of disapproval, simply ordering Polk to concentrate at Harrodsburg. There, Bragg promised, a brigade from Stevenson, Cleburne's division, and ultimately the rest of Kirby Smith's Army of Kentucky would join him.

How does one explain Bragg's consent? One must assume that by then, Bragg had learned from Kirby Smith about the Federal occupation of Taylorsville, for he continually pressed the latter for news from the front. In addition, as Connelly suggested, Bragg's natural rigidity may have prevented him from deviating from his course. October 4, after all, was Inauguration Day in Frankfort. Fighting the Federals would have to wait until a Confederate governor took office and proclaimed conscription. Bragg's overconfidence played a role as well. Admittedly unsure of whether the enemy planned primarily to attack Polk or, as he more supposed, move on Frankfort, Bragg nonetheless expressed an overconfident conviction that the combined Confederate host would crush Buell wherever he turned up once the festivities ended. All would be well.[14]

Accordingly, a large but nervous crowd gathered in Frankfort that morning to witness the formal ascension of Confederate power in Kentucky. The Stars and Bars whipped proudly over the statehouse, the red, white, and blue banner displayed starkly against a wet, Confederate-gray sky. When anxious secessionist Kentuckians expressed worries that the Confederates might abandon them once they committed themselves, leading local heroes such as Buckner and Stoddard Johnston reassured the throng that Bragg's army had come to stay. Hawes, a sixty-five-year-old attorney still recovering from a bout of typhoid fever, arrived just before noon, escorted by Kirby Smith and a band of cavalrymen and serenaded by the martial music of an artillery salvo. The soaked assembly proceeded to crowd into the Kentucky statehouse, those unlucky enough not to obtain seats in the House chamber spilling out onto the puddled floor beneath the rotunda. In the wet hall, Brig. Gen. Humphrey Marshall briefly spoke first. Bragg followed, attacking the Lincoln administration with rhetorical flourishes while promising Kentucky greater liberties under the Stars and Bars. Hawes then took the stage. He took no oath, having done so months earlier, but he did proceed to give an inaugural speech, reading slowly in measured tones. When he finished, a cry went up for native son Marshall. Just at that moment, the distant sound of artillery rent the air.[15]

Couriers soon arrived with grim news for Bragg. The Federals were across the Kentucky River, on the Shelbyville Road and advancing on the town "in heavy force . . . only 12 miles out." Without sending out a reconnaissance, Bragg assumed that it had to be Buell with the main Yankee army; Frankfort must be evacuated immediately. While guests at a select dinner dined unaware, secure in the knowledge that Bragg would hold the town, the general himself hurriedly scratched out a note to Polk, again directing him to Harrodsburg: "Shall destroy bridges and retire for concentration and then strike. Reach that point as soon as possible."[16] With Polk already pulling back toward the east, Harrodsburg offered the best place for a concentration of Confederate forces, as it secured both Confederate communications and the supplies at Camp Dick Robinson. Indeed, Harrodsburg, according to Johnston, was "the key to all the blue grass region."

In the midst of panic and dismay, Hawes fled, as did Bragg and his staff, who galloped from town late in the afternoon as smoke and red flames from the burning bridges formed a backdrop to the dismal scene. "The evacuation of the state was regarded as a fixed fact," Stoddard Johnston bitterly remembered. "A paralysis of gloom settled . . . and the name of Bragg became odious." Bragg's much anticipated inauguration,[17] "this premature and absurd formality" St. John Liddell later called it, had backfired beyond reckoning, and the gathering of Kentucky prominent secessionists, despite brave promises only a few hours old, found themselves fleeing before the Federal army after all.[18]

Bragg raced southeast to the town of Versailles, west of Lexington, veering east away from the main road to Harrodsburg for fear of running into Federal cavalry. He spent the night there before continuing on, reaching Harrodsburg after noon on October 5—roughly the same time that the Federals occupied Bardstown. His own army had not yet arrived in Harrodsburg, and it looked at first like it might not anytime soon. Hardee had found the road to Harrodsburg so "hilly, rocky, and slippery" due to the continuing storms, that, with Polk's permission, his column joined the latter's on the better Springfield Pike. Unfortunately, that road led to Danville rather than Harrodsburg. Bragg, clearly annoyed by Polk's and Hardee's constant disregard for his orders, instructed them to forget about Danville and march to Harrodsburg as he twice had ordered.[19]

Kirby Smith created more confusion still. Bragg ordered the concentration of all Confederate forces in Kentucky at Harrodsburg before leaving Frankfort. However, left on his own again, Kirby Smith immediately reasserted his willful independence. Only following Bragg as far as Versailles and the Lexington side of the Kentucky River near Salvisa, he halted and then wrote his commander on the fifth, expressing his reluctance to cross the river. Only Sill's division, he admittedly now confessed, had comprised the recent threat to Frankfort and Lexington. "Our friends in Shelbyville," however, reported that both McCook and Rousseau were at or near Taylorsville, and so Lexington remained in great danger. "If a move is to be made to cover Lexington," he argued, "my position is good. The moment I cross the river Lexington . . . will be lost."[20]

Kirby Smith, hungry to maintain independent command and hang on to the scene of his great triumph, was again up to his old tricks. His resentment of Bragg was palpable, for glory was not something Kirby Smith easily shared. Lexington, his great triumph, could not be surrendered without a fight. He also misunderstood McCook's intentions; those Federals already had gone south rather than east, as Scott's cavalry should have known. Buell already knew about the abandonment of Frankfort via Sill and had ordered McCook accordingly.[21] Bragg, unfortunately, proved all too gullible to the younger man's sleight of hand despite recent experience. Receiving Kirby Smith's letter, he concluded without further evidence that a sizable Union force indeed must be threatening Kirby Smith's army. Instead of ordering him to Harrodsburg then, or even sending out cavalry to better pin down Buell's position, Bragg again overreacted, just as he had done throughout the campaign in pressure situations. Reversing himself completely, he decided to call off the Harrodsburg concentration and instead move his army north to join Kirby Smith.

Such a move would be tricky, for his own army remained strung out like a caterpillar. Polk, along with Cheatham's and Withers's dusty and ragged divisions, plodded into Harrodsburg on the sixth, finding "more Southern sympathy in Harrodsburg than at any other place on our march thus far."[22] Cleburne's men arrived as well, finally rejoining their old comrades after weeks under Kirby Smith. Patton Anderson's division remained on the road south of town, however, camped at Salt River. Hardee, traveling with Buckner's division, had only reached Perryville. Wheeler's cavalry, bringing up the rear, reported no one but Yankees behind.

Exhausted stragglers lined the roadside between Harrodsburg and Perryville, looking for something to eat or a place to rest. One Harrodsburg Unionist recalled: "for some days there could be no thicket treaded, or by-path ventured into that some grey spectre was not met straggling from the main body, but with full intent of rendezvous at the battle; and the highways presented a spectacle, at a distance, of a murky grey river flowing . . . in all the grime and rags with which time and hard service had covered them and which their sympathizers were powerless to clothe with their well earned— a treasonable uniform."[23]

Few Confederates took much notice of Perryville as they dragged themselves through town; it looked little different from those through which they already had marched. One exception, Texan John Street, pronounced it " a beauty ful village . . . in one of the finest country's I ever saw you cannot travel in this portion of Ky. without being all the while in a lane—all the country is fenced up & is nearly as open as the prairies of Tex all the timber nearly being cut away." John Magee of Stanford's Battery likewise thought the area "well settled and improved," if rocky, but most remembered a little girl named Prewit who helped him forage for corn.[24]

Over in Harrodsburg, according to St. John Liddell, morale in the ranks had rebounded, for the day of battle seemed near. Kirby Smith must be nearby, the men reasoned, and once the two Confederate forces were joined, victory was all but assured. "It was the general belief that Bragg would *refuse* battle until he had effected a junction. No one . . . knew precisely where Kirby Smith's command was," he wrote. "Common opinion was reduced to every confidence that it was within striking distance, at least, or sufficiently near to turn any doubtful scale. . . . there was no uneasiness."[25]

Sam Watkins agreed: "This good time we were having was too good to last. We were in ecstasy akin to heaven. We were happy; the troops were jubilant; our manhood pulsated more warmly; our patriotism was awakened; our pride was renewed and stood ready for any emergency; we felt that one Southern man could whip twenty Yankees. We went to dances and parties every night."[26]

While the men danced and courted, Polk clumsily added to Bragg's determination to move north, indicating to him with a supremely regrettable phrase that the threat created by the Federal force pursuing Wheeler's cavalry did not seem great. "I cannot think it large," Polk wrote Bragg from Harrodsburg near midnight. Nonetheless, Polk ordered Anderson's exhausted division, which had only just arrived in Harrodsburg at dusk, as well as Cleburne's original brigade and Wharton's cavalry, back to Perryville to support Hardee. His assignment on the seventh was "to ascertain, if possible, the strength of the enemy which may be covered by his advance."[27]

Much has been made since the event of Polk's ambiguous "I cannot think it large" comment. What did "large" mean to the bishop? And did he refer to an entire force or only an advance column, as his biographer-son later claimed? Certainly he thought it was more than a mere feint. On the night of the sixth he essentially ordered half of the gray-clad army, Hardee's entire wing supported by additional cavalry, to hold Perryville while his own wing waited near Harrodsburg. Such a disposition indicates that he feared at least a division and probably two was approaching Perryville from the west. Buckner's division could have dealt with anything smaller by itself. That he suspected most of Buell's army lay somewhere nearby as well, an assertion often dismissed, also is clear in a letter written to his wife the next day. In it, Polk maintained: "we have come here to concentrate our army with that of E. Kirby Smith. It has been done and now we shall give the enemy battle wherever he presents himself." There was no mention of moving north to reinforce Kirby Smith; Polk obviously believed him to be nearby. One thing Polk was sure of: The great battle would be fought in the vicinity of Harrodsburg.[28]

Bragg's reports of his conversations with Polk in regard to the matter differ entirely from his chief lieutenant's. According to Bragg, Polk indicated to him that the Union force behind them was truly small and nonthreatening, convincing him to continue with his plans to withdraw to the north. Kirby Smith, meanwhile, had reported to Bragg in Harrodsburg, telling him that the Federal pressure in his sector had increased dangerously. Most of Buell's army, Bragg concluded, had to be with the Frankfort force.[29] As Bragg aide George Brent put it: "The enemy front seems extended & dispersed. A good opportunity to strike a blow."[30]

The weight of the evidence rests with Polk's account. The letter to his wife is clear, and, like Hardee, he continued to maintain after the campaign that he had informed Bragg that a sizable Federal force was approaching. Bragg, in contrast, displayed selective memory on several occasions after the campaign, as with his later recollection of Polk's initial retreat from Bardstown—"it necessitated an entire change in my plans"—as compared with the bland reaction apparent in contemporary dispatches. But the question still begs: If Polk had indeed informed Bragg as he indicated, why did Bragg persist in moving the army toward Versailles and Kirby Smith? One possibility is that Polk proved too obtuse to understand, an interpretation a reader of his correspondence might readily believe. Then again, Bragg had to be confused because both Kirby Smith and Polk indicated they were facing the larger Union force. One of them had to be wrong, and Bragg long had felt contempt for the bishop, whereas Kirby Smith seemed to possess a gift for mesmerizing Bragg. Whatever the reason, Bragg concluded to take his army north of the Kentucky River.[31]

Accordingly, on the morning of October 7, Bragg issued new orders putting in motion his previous decision to take the army north. Spearheaded by Withers's division, Polk's wing would march through Lawrenceburg to Versailles, where it would "follow General E. Kirby Smith's command." Hardee would follow "as circumstances allow"; Bragg could not have expected that to take very long. Combined at last, the Confederates would "strike a blow" and defeat Buell. Boldly pointing to a map, Bragg told his staff that the great battle for Kentucky was about to occur at Versailles. He could not have been more wrong, for the bulk of the Union army was in his rear, approaching the village of Perryville even as he spoke.[32]

In Perryville on the morning of October 7, Hardee hurriedly prepared to meet his pursuers. Until the expected reinforcements arrived, he had only three of the four brigades of Buckner's division with which to work. The men of Bushrod Johnson's, St. John Liddell's, and Sterling Wood's brigades had spent the night west of town sleeping on their arms. Hardee now pulled them back through town. He anchored Wood's left north of the Harrodsburg Pike on Seminary Ridge, which ran in a northwesterly direction along the northeastern edge of Perryville. In the middle of the brigade, on the higher ground called Seminary Hill, Capt. Henry C. Semple's Alabama Battery unlimbered four twelve-pound Napoleons and two six-pound rifles. Johnson's brigade further extended the Confederate battle line northward along the high ground on the east bank of the Chaplin.[33]

With those brigades in place, Hardee rode out with his staff and Liddell to survey the ground north and west of town, concentrating particularly on the triangle created by the Springfield and Mackville roads. Liddell would remain in an advanced position out there somewhere. As the men rode, Hardee told Liddell that they must fight, that "the enemy must be driven back or checked to save the supplies we had in Danville"—roughly the same language he used in his official report two months later. Liddell concurred, pronouncing Perryville with its surrounding hills an ideal place to fight a defensive battle, especially against a tired and thirsty foe desperate for what little water the Confederates controlled. As the men rode, they particularly noted a wooded, hilly area located between the Springfield and Mackville roads, about a mile to the rear of Liddell's original position, which controlled both pikes as well as Doctor's Creek and Bull Run.

Returning to town, Hardee's party climbed a hill on the northern edge of town that seemed the perfect site for a battery, for it provided such a fine view of the town that a few days later a *Harper's Weekly* artist would use it to sketch a cover illustration of Perryville for his employers. After introductions, the owner of the home located there, Nancy Tadlock, "expressed her sincere sympathy for the General that one so advanced in years should be engaged in the dangers and troubles of war."

"'Why Madam,'" exclaimed the vain Hardee, "'how old do you take me to be?'"

"'Well, Sir, I am seventy-two and I think you are about a year younger.'"

Gesturing incredulously to Liddell, Hardee cried out, "'How! What! Why, Madam, I am not as old as that man.'" Hardee vainly spent the next few minutes attempting to convince the woman of his true age, even calling upon witnesses, all to no avail. A bemused Liddell in the meantime bided his time sketching out a map of the Chaplin Hills.

Finally acknowledging the futility of correcting the stubborn widow, Hardee got back to business and ordered Liddell to place his brigade on the wooded hill they earlier had noted just to the right of the Springfield Pike. Home to prosperous forty-five-year-old farmer Sam Bottom, whose newly rebuilt house stood on the hill's cleared western face, Bottom Hill, as it was called by the locals, sloped rapidly away to the west past a spring into the nearly dry bed of Bull Run. From there the ground rose again into another, higher wooded hilltop about three quarters of a mile away. That was Peters Hill, named for Jacob Peters, a farmer who lived in a log house at the western base of the hill on the Springfield Pike. The more impressive wooden-frame house on the western brow of Peters Hill actually belonged to farmer Jacob Turpin. Only two hundred yards of open country separated woodland that covered most of both eminences, an area containing the creek but also a cornfield to Liddell's left and open ground to the right as he peered west. The meandering Springfield Pike connected both hills like a loose thread.[34]

Liddell's Arkansans quickly moved into line on Bottom Hill. All were hardened veterans of Shiloh. The hard-luck 8th Arkansas Infantry, serving under Sterling Wood on the first day of the battle, had absorbed heavy casualties when friendly fire raked their lines, yet the men had rebounded for one of the many assaults against the Federal "Hornet's Nest." Liddell's other regiments—the 2nd, 5th, 6th, and 7th Arkansas—also had paid a price in that bloody Shiloh debacle. Now, as the sun rose behind them far to the north in Kentucky, Liddell placed his veterans into line on Bottom Hill, with the 6th, 2nd, 5th, 7th, and 8th Arkansas arrayed from left to right, a brown-and-gray line stretching in front of Sam Bottom's large, two-story house. Captain Charles Swett's Mississippi Battery unlimbered to the front and left so as to command the open fields as well as the road. That battery anchored Liddell's left while a precipitous drop-off protected the line's right. Broken down stone fences and numerous trees provided extra cover.

Liddell remained unsatisfied. The wooded Peters Hill to his front worried him. Shaped like an animal's paw clawing at his position, it commanded the sector. Any Federal battery situated there might well drive him to the rear, he fretted. In addition, Peters Hill overlooked the small pools of water

Figure 7.1. Peters Hill, as seen today from the ruins of the Sam Bottom House. Photograph courtesy John Walsh Jr.

in the bed of Doctor's Creek, which normally skirted past its western slope in a north-south direction. Anxious to obey Hardee's orders but unwilling to abandon the western hill completely, he thus sent the 7th Arkansas back to Peters Hill as skirmishers to occupy the crucial high ground. Scarcely had they moved into the woods and out of sight before Federal artillery rounds began exploding amongst them.[35]

The morning of October 7 found Buell's army converging on Perryville via three separate roads. McCook's I Corps awoke at dawn along the banks of the Chaplin River to continue southeastward toward Mackville via Willisburg, stopping every mile or so on the narrow and hilly route and thus not passing through the town and halting until sundown. Water remained scarce and slimy, but most of the local people along the pike were Unionists, and they greeted the men with enthusiasm. Mackville, in contrast, while lively enough, unfortunately seemed full of secessionist Kentuckians. Long after dark there, many of McCook's anxious men remained awake. The soldiers of Starkweather's brigade camped far enough in front to be denied fires, but others in the rear busied themselves roasting freshly killed beef or chickens for the morrow.[36]

From Springfield, Crittenden's II Corps moved almost directly south at a rapid pace toward Haysville, from which it was to turn to the east and approach Perryville from the southwest via the Lebanon Pike. For Crittenden's men, the hot, dry day spent on the narrow, rocky, hilly route local people called the Wilderness Road proved excruciatingly grueling, the worst yet. Shrouded by clouds of dust, men fell out all along the road until, in one soldier's estimation, half the corps had fallen behind. Knapsacks and even guns littered the pike. Those who had sampled Springfield's hidden whiskey suffered the most. Entire units did not stumble into camp until 3 A.M. on the eighth, and sometimes then only at bayonet point. The lack of water remained key. Thirsty men that day found even less than usual, leading Thomas to take the corps over two miles past Haysville—and almost two miles farther away from Perryville— to the Rolling Fork of the Salt River, in hopes of camping along a water supply. Only a series of stagnant pools remained in the bed of what had been the waterway, but men consumed it greedily.[37]

By that time, thirst had driven many men to the brink of madness. One sufferer, Asbury L. Kerwood of the 57th Indiana Infantry, wrote that "to increase the torture, as soon as the eyes closed, visions of home, well-filled tables, downy beds, and clear, cold water, fresh from the hands of loved ones there, came before us with such striking clearness that we bounded to accept the proferred gifts, only to find, when fully aroused, that we were getting into line, perhaps to travel but a dozen paces, and then renew the scene."[38] Another Hoosier described "mutterings and questionings of the need for such marching, then lagging, irregular, tottering footfalls. All were tired and some were sleeping. . . . The men were well-nigh famished, in fact they became almost frantic. They could scarcely articulate. The topic of conversation was without exception of the one thing on all minds, water, water, water."[39]

With Robert Mitchell's division in the lead, Gilbert's corps moved slowly eastward after sunup on the Springfield Pike, heading directly toward Perryville. Although the day would turn out to be cooler than the previous one, water remained a rare treasure. One soldier commented that his comrades were drinking water that was so bad they would not have allowed their farm animals to imbibe of it had they been at home. The men noticed that the countryside grew increasingly hilly and more difficult as the Chaplin Hills began to roll up westward from the river. There were compensations, however. Welcome evidence of Unionism, mingled with a survivor's pragmatism, appeared along Gilbert's line of march as well as McCook's.[40] Jay Caldwell Butler of the 101st Ohio reported "one very fine looking, young lady [who] waved her handkerchief and cheered for the Union. . . . At another place where the whole family were out in front waving, one little boy shouted, 'Hurrah for the Union! Hurrah for Bragg!' showing that they had been learned two stories."[41]

Suddenly, at about 7:30 A.M., the booming of cannon and the cracking of small arms fire began reverberating through the hills from the east. At a point six miles west of Perryville, near the Boyle County line and just east of the village of Pottsville, Joe Wheeler's horse soldiers, sent about a mile beyond Liddell's position on Bottom and Peters Hills to screen the Arkansans, had ambushed Ebenezer Gay's cavalry brigade as it advanced along the pike. Like Gilbert, Gay was another controversial officer placed in a position far above his normal rank at Louisville. Legally a captain, Gay held the dubious rank of "Acting Brigadier General" and served as inspector and chief of cavalry in the Army of the Ohio. No one seemed to know how he acquired the position. Most blamed Wright, but that general later absolved himself of any blame. Gay's rise to power remains murky, but it probably was Wright's doing.

Allowing the Federals to approach within two hundred yards before firing, Wheeler's men, augmented since Munfordville with a section of six-pound smoothbores of Calvert's Arkansas Battery commanded by Lt. S. G. Hanley, opened up with surprising fury on the advancing enemy from a dominant hilltop.[42] In the words of Michigan cavalryman Marshall P. Thatcher, "A wreath of smoke; a sharp crackling report; a whizzing, screeching sound, followed by a bursting shell close to out lines, warned us that the enemy had found a good place to make a stand."

Gay quickly ordered his five companies of the raw 9th Kentucky Cavalry—the balance of the regiment rode with Sill—to charge the gray line down the Springfield Pike.[43] The Kentuckians galloped "in good style" straight into the enemy position, but a shower of grapeshot and canister from Wheeler's guns soon drove them back in confusion, so "hatless and completely demoralized," that fellow troopers of the 2nd Michigan Cavalry laughed aloud. It was a reaction they soon regretted, for in the wake of the collapse of the Kentuckians the crack Wolverines, who had been led by Gordon Granger and Phil Sheridan before their promotions, "were immediately given an opportunity to do better." Dismounting, a few companies of Michiganders gingerly moved forward but soon halted and then gave way. The artillery firing that followed often overshot the target, and Federal shells killed several of Liddell's men in the rear. Holding on to their position on the other side of the field, Wheeler's men rounded up prisoners, picked up supplies left in the dust by the retreating Federals, most notably fifty Colt revolving rifles and ammunition abandoned by the 2nd Michigan, and settled in to wait for the Yankees next move. Wheeler scratched out a brief report, which found its way into Hardee's hands by 9:30.[44] It clearly concerned Hardee, who sent the report on to Polk in Harrodsburg along with a request for help. A strong force was developing in his front, he warned. One prisoner supposedly had reported that Buell was present and in command.[45]

Horse artillery boomed sporadically over the next several hours. Then, between two and three in the afternoon, Gay's cavalry—supported by Mitchell's division drawn up in line of battle a mile to the rear, and Schoepf's farther to the left and behind in reserve—advanced carefully up the road again. Slowly, the larger Federal force pushed the rebel horsemen back to a ridge roughly three miles west of Perryville. When Confederate sharpshoot-

Figure 7.2. Joseph Wheeler later in the war, after his promotion to general. Photograph courtesy Division of Military & Naval Affairs, New York State Adjutant General's Office, and U.S. Army Military History Institute.

ers along the ridge checked the Yankees, two companies of the 2nd Michigan dismounted and began creeping forward through the cornfields located on both sides of the pike. Unexpectedly, Wheeler counterattacked. He boldly led several companies of the 1st and 3rd Alabama Cavalry Regiments straight down the road in a column of fours, directly into the Federals' dismounted skirmish line, whose members took cover behind the wooden stake-and-rider fences on either side of the narrow lane. Again, the dismounted Federal horsemen gave way. Confederate artillery opened up on Gay after Wheeler raced back to the safety of the ridge.

Wheeler momentarily had regained control of the ground. It was not to last, however, for once again the tide turned. Without warning, unexpected return fire opened up on the Confederate left flank. Buell had ordered Col. Nicholas Greusel's brigade forward to support Gay. Confronted with a brigade of infantry and an artillery battery, Wheeler gave way at last. As darkness fell, he retreated to the safety of Liddell's position, flanking the Arkansas infantry before retreating back to town.[46]

One interested observer of the late-afternoon skirmish was Buell, who had ridden forward with Gilbert's infantry. As he neared the scene, the general's well-known and widely despised concern for Southern civilians, overriding momentarily even his interest in the fighting, finally got the best of him, resulting in the most critical incident of insubordination yet in the Army of the Ohio. Noticing a party of stragglers from the 75th Illinois Infantry cleaning out a garden, Buell stopped to order the men to return to their regiments. Angry words passed, and at length Buell bore down on one particular back-talker who had further enraged the general by wiping his sweaty face with precious water from his canteen. The soldier sprang to his feet in his own defense and grabbed Buell's bridle, jerking it hard. The general's horse reared and fell over backward with Buell still aboard. He was not seriously hurt, but he could neither sit up nor ride, so he observed the rest of Gay's fight from an ambulance. "But a few sympathized with Buell for his fall," J. W. Sheaffer of the 75th Illinois commented, "while many gave expression to the thought that a broken neck would not have proved a disaster to the service." It was another bad omen for Buell's troubled army.[47]

Meanwhile, at exactly 3:20 P.M., as the cavalry skirmish renewed itself, a worried Hardee dashed off a report to Bragg informing him that "there is a sharp cannonade in front between Wheeler's forces & the enemy. He is advancing this evening to gain position. Tomorrow morning early we may expect a fight. If the enemy does not attack us, you ought to unless pressed in another direction send forward all the reinforcements necessary, take command in person, and wipe him out. I desire earnestly that you will do this."[48]

Hardee later claimed that he had reported that he faced a "heavy force," presumably much if not all of Buell's army. Perhaps he really thought he had done so, but in truth his message contained the same wordy ambiguity that characterized Polk's correspondence. At no point did he indicate the size of the opposing force or express grave concern. Moreover, his request for only Buckner, to command his division in person, reinforces the notion that he and Polk suspected that one or two divisions—at most an enemy corps— were approaching Perryville on the Springfield Pike. With what he now had, as well as the units already on the way, Hardee implied, Bragg would have enough manpower on hand to wipe out the Federal column. Moreover, Hardee's caveat about "being pressed elsewhere" further reflects the confused belief that much of Buell's army confronted Kirby Smith elsewhere. In truth, no one in the Confederate high command had an adequate grasp of the situation.[49]

Bragg responded to Hardee's report at 5:40 P.M. in a brief message to Polk: "You had better move with Cheatham's division to his support and give the enemy battle immediately; rout him, and then move to our support at Versailles." Withers, with the balance of Polk's wing, would continue moving toward the junction with Kirby Smith, as would Bragg himself. The great battle for Kentucky, Bragg continued to believe, would come near Versailles.[50]

That response greatly worried Hardee, who received Bragg's dispatch sometime after seven. He drafted his response carefully, clearly wary of upsetting the mercurial Bragg. "Permit me from the friendly relations so long existing between us," he began at 7:30 P.M., "to write you plainly." Unfortunately, the rest of Hardee's pedantic letter smacked less of friendship than it did a classroom lecture. "Do not scatter your forces," he continued. "There is one rule in our profession which should never be forgotten; it is to throw the masses of your troops on the fractions of the enemy. The movement last proposed will divide your army and each may be defeated, whereas by keeping them united, success is certain. If it be your policy to strike the enemy as Versailles, take your whole force with you and make your blow effective if, on the contrary, you should decide to strike the army in front of me, first let that be done with a force which will make success certain." Hardee expressed his willingness to support Bragg in either event, but "if you wish my opinion it is that in view of the position of your depots you ought to strike this force first."[51]

In giving full rein to the side of his personality that had once administered West Point, Hardee created only more confusion. Never did he state a clear opinion about what sort of force or "army" opposed him on the Springfield Pike. Hardee himself obviously was befuddled, for he continued to believe that a sizable Union army threatened Versailles, and as a result counseled Bragg to unite Confederate forces against a "fraction," be it in Perryville or Versailles. What Bragg was supposed to make of such a letter was known only to Hardee.

Slowly, the fierce afternoon gave way to evening and night. Activity continued until well after midnight as tired Confederate troops trudged into town and assumed their assigned positions in Hardee's extending defensive line. Patton Anderson's division began arriving at about 3 P.M. Some of Anderson's men expressed anger at retracing their steps for no known reason, while others, aware of Wheeler's running fight with the enemy, anticipated a battle. Adams's and Powell's brigades of Anderson's division continued on through town and formed up on the left of Wood's brigade, with the extreme left anchored in the hills south and east of town and the bulk of the three brigades extending up the Mitchellsburg Road. Later in the evening, Brown's and Jones's brigades would come, halting about two miles from town and taking up a position on Johnson's right, their camps stretching along the north side of the Harrodsburg Pike.

Pat Cleburne's brigade arrived next, having left Harrodsburg at daylight; it also took a position on the Harrodsburg Pike.[52] Finally, around midnight, three brigades of Frank Cheatham's division arrived in Perryville, having left Harrodsburg at about 7 P.M. Leaving their baggage train behind, encumbered only by the ambulance and ammunition trains, Cheatham's men had moved quickly and enthusiastically, brimming with confidence. Five miles from Harrodsburg, Preston Smith's brigade unaccountably received orders to return to Harrodsburg. The others continued on west.

"The night was beautiful," Maj. George Winchester wrote, "—the moon with full beams shining from an unclouded vault, revealed the close column and its unfaltering tread, as it moved to the scene of the morrow's action." In Perryville itself "the scene was unusually quiet." With the full moon and Federal rockets providing adequate light, Cheatham's tired men formed into a rough line of battle on the extreme Confederate left and slightly to the rear, extending Hardee's overall line farther southward beyond the town limits, and feel asleep on their arms.[53] A few worn-out soldiers seem to have wandered on across the riverbed into the town cemetery.[54] The night, however, carried uncomfortable portents of what was to come. Sam Watkins remembered the sight of a dead aide who had ridden out too far and unhappily encountered a Federal picket. "He was very bloody," wrote Watkins, "and had his clothes riddled with balls." Surrounded by other silent men holding candles against the darkness, the dead man's body presented a chilling scene.[55]

Three miles to the west, tired and thirsty Yankee soldiers also tried to sleep. Gilbert's corps bedded down for the night with Mitchell's division in the center astride the Springfield Pike, Shoepf's to the rear of Mitchell, and Sheridan's late-arriving division slightly to the front and right of Mitchell.[56] It was a beautiful evening to Northerners as well. In the eyes of one soldier, a scene of pastoral splendor, sadly marred by man's callousness, unfolded: "The sunset hues were filling the west with gorgeous beauty. The eye took in a varied landscape of hill and vale, field and woodland, alas! Soon to echo the roar of artillery, and the rattle of musketry, to be seamed and defaced by plunging shot and shrieking shell."[57]

Fitfully, and vainly, soldiers tried to sleep. "They expected the enemy," one war correspondent wrote of Buell's Federals, "and were impatient for his appearance. Every sound was noticed and commented upon, eyes were strained in peering away far into the dim distance beyond the reach of the moonlight illumination; cartridge boxes are . . . re-examined; stories of former campaigns were told, and in this manner the night wore away."[58]

Elsewhere, conversation turned to another topic: Buell. His leading enemies within the officer corps finally had had enough. Despite the fact that battle beckoned, or perhaps because of it, they determined that the moment had come to overthrow their commander. Quietly, word circulated among Crittenden and Gilbert's corps about a meeting that night in a private home on Rolling Fork. Witnesses before the Buell Commission were not always forthcoming, fearful of incriminating themselves or angering Albin Schoepf, the ringleader at Rolling Fork who now sat in judgment of Buell. About two dozen high-ranking officers attended, including Schoepf, all his regimental and brigade commanders, and division commander and Schoepf loyalist Speed Fry. James Steedman also was there. Several of those in attendance, most notably his bête noire Schoepf, accused Buell of incompetence and disloyalty. The end result was that the conspirators signed a previously prepared letter to President Lincoln, asking him to remove Buell from command in favor of Thomas.[59]

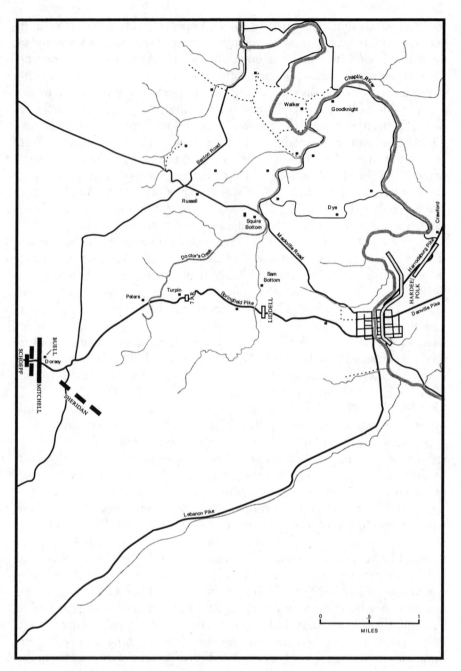

Map 7.1. Troop positions at Perryville, 1 A.M., Oct. 8, 1862.

Completely in the dark as to the designs of some of his officers, a bruised and embarrassed Buell sat up late that night at his headquarters, a tent set up near the log home of John C. Dorsey, located on the Springfield Pike in the midst of Gilbert's fitfully sleeping soldiers. Most of the day he had assumed that the enemy would concentrate at Harrodsburg, but the gathering gray host at Perryville forced him to rethink his plans. Clearly the Rebels held Perryville with a "strong force," and only a general engagement would drive them away. That he had to attack at the first opportunity had been certain ever since the almost-removal in Louisville, but he also had to be careful, precise. He would use all of his available force the next morning to overwhelm the enemy, all three corps, just as Jomini and the Comte de Saxe taught. Buell wrote Thomas at 7 P.M., telling him that Crittenden's corps must march "without fail" precisely at three the next morning, so as to come up on Gilbert's right. Report as soon as possible once you are in position, Buell added. Orders for a similar movement on Gilbert's left went out to McCook an hour later. The army would attack no later than 8 A.M.

One nagging problem remained: water. Buell stressed to both McCook and Thomas that the men had to fill their canteens before they marched. He further directed that they be instructed to use what little they could carry sparingly. "There is no water here," he warned, "and we will get but little, if any, until we get to Perryville."[60] However, there was water not far away in the bed of Doctor's Creek and in the shadow of the 7th Arkansas on Peters Hill. The Federal discovery of that fact soon would alter Buell's plans significantly.

ENOUGH BOYS, FOR THIS MORNING

AS BOTH ARMIES CONVERGED ON PERRYVILLE ON OCTOBER 7, MOST of the town's citizens hastily loaded up whatever they could carry on their backs or in their wagons and fled. Sam Watkins remembered the town as all but deserted by the early morning hours of October 8—a handy fact when he and another man ransacked "a citizen's pantry, where we captured a bucket of honey, a pitcher of sweet milk, and three or four biscuit. The old citizen was not at home—he and his whole household had gone visiting, I believe. In fact," Watkins continued, "I think all of the citizens of Perryville were taken with a sudden notion of promiscuous visiting about this time; at least they were not at home to all callers."[1]

Watkins never realized how close he was to the truth with his last clause. Not all of Perryville's residents had fled. Many hearty or terrified souls remained in their homes that night, hunkering down in the darkness to avoid uniformed "callers" like him. The morning brought new terrors. The frightening sounds of gunfire from the west at dawn, coupled with the growing presence of hungry soldiers at their doors, all but completed the civilian exodus the following morning. Indeed, panic ensued. According to local tradition, many fled south toward the hilly area near Mitchellsburg called the Knobs, a hearty Unionist enclave from which they would watch the day's battle. On the Lebanon Pike, another line of escape led toward the southwest. There, Yankee Eastham Tarrant of the 1st Kentucky Cavalry encountered "wagons loaded promiscuously with household goods, apparently thrown in at random, with youths, maidens and children riding on top of the plunder, getting away from the threatened carnage in the greatest haste possible." Tarrant remembered "one handsome maiden in particular—or at least she would have been handsome if her features had not been so contorted with fright—whose heartrending screams haunted him for many days."[2]

The chaotic scene was much the same to the west on the Mackville Road, where frightened Methodist minister W. D. Campbell proved so eager to race his loaded wagon through Perryville's crowded streets and get out of town that only once free of the traffic jam did he realize that he had left one of his daughters behind.[3] Nearly all of those who, like Campbell, initially had planned to ride out the storm changed their minds by late morning. Well-to-do slave owner Harriet Karrick had intended to remain at home with her eight children and slaves until Confederates camped in her yard finally convinced her that "there would be fighting" after all. According to family tradition, "they got what jewelry, silver, bedding and clothes they could get on a two horse wagon" and had their slaves drive them to safety.[4]

"Deserted and left desolate by its once happy inhabitants," Perryville by noon largely belonged only to the soldiers who already had begun to fight and die in order to possess it and its water. Only a handful of stubborn inhabitants, such as druggist Wilson Green, said by many to be the spitting image of Abraham Lincoln, lay low in their homes and shops to wait out the impending iron and lead storm.[5]

The gunfire Perryville's residents heard at dawn came from out on the Springfield Pike. As they had begun their flight on the evening of October 7, the worn-out men of Gilbert's corps filed into line of battle astride the pike, unrolled their blankets on the hard, cool ground, and settled in to wait anxiously for morning. Rest would not come for many of them. One of the officers, Speed Fry, returned from the mutinous Rolling Fork meeting long after dark only to discover that Gilbert had made him officer of the day. The choice of Fry made sense, for aside from his recent clandestine plotting with Schoepf, which neither Buell nor Gilbert knew much about, he was the perfect choice. Born only a few miles from Perryville, Fry knew the lay of the land intimately. That knowledge would come in handy almost immediately, for ahead of the corps that night lay both opportunity and danger—not to mention the pride of firing some of the first shots in the Battle of Perryville.[6]

A mile and a half to the east of the Federal camps that evening, glistening with the light of a reflected full moon shining in a clear sky, shallow pools of water lay in the otherwise dry bed of Doctor's Creek, "where one, with a spoon, could dip water enough into a canteen to keep down thirst yet possessing sand and mud enough to pave the throats of those who drank."[7] Since midafternoon, when dry-throated Federals first spotted them, the puddles had enticed Gilbert's dehydrated column; it was the first water most men had seen all day. After dark, desperate men crept alone or in small groups down to the creek to drink. However, thanks to a Confederate presence on the heights above, most of Gilbert's soldiers, like Sisyphus in Hades, could not reach the water resting so close to their lips as to madden them. On the hill above the creekbed drab forms had been seen sporadically during the day along the crest—the 7th Arkansas, sent forward by Liddell that morning in advance of the rest of his brigade. No one had seen them in several hours, however. As the moon reached its pinnacle in the night sky, the Federal high

Figure 8.1. Brig. Gen. Speed S. Fry. Photograph courtesy U.S. Army Military History Institute.

command wondered if the Rebels remained up there. Could the precious water be secured? Buell ordered Fry to find out.[8]

He moved quickly, the water drawing his men like a magnet. Stealthily, their shadows silhouetted by the bright moonlight, the veteran 10th Indiana Infantry followed Fry toward Peters Hill. Reaching the Peters house at the base of the high ground, he sent the Hoosiers off to the left, north toward the shimmering water. They moved quietly through the dry brush, first skirting the base of the hill and then slipping around to the left of the last-seen Confederate position. Reaching the location Fry initially indicated without encountering any of the enemy, Lt. Col. William B. Carroll pushed two companies of skirmishers farther forward, hoping to firmly locate the Confederate lines. Flanking Peters Hill to the north, the two Indiana companies stumbled eastward between the hills through the dark, wooded, rolling valley of Bull Run, then moved obliquely toward Liddell's main line on Bottom Hill. As the Hoosiers drew close to the Confederate position, shots unexpectedly rang out in the night. The Federals briefly returned fire. However, convinced by the voluminous muzzle flashes and the clamor of opposing fire that they were woefully outnumbered, they scampered back to rejoin their regiment without losses.[9]

Considering Liddell's earlier fears for the safety of his position, as well as his earlier acknowledgment of the key role Peters Hill played in the entire Mackville Road–Springfield Pike sector, the brief encounter oddly provoked little response from him or anyone else on the Confederate side of the line. What the 7th Arkansas was doing on Peters Hill remained anyone's guess, for their guns remained strangely silent during and after the encounter to their rear. Liddell himself nonetheless expressed no concern then or later regarding the firing, and indeed never bothered to mention the exchange in his official report or his later memoirs, except to note in the latter that "all was quiet except an occasional shot between the advanced pickets. This proved to me that my own men were on the alert, which rendered a night surprise improbable." He of course was grossly in error; his "advanced pickets" not only had allowed two Federal companies to slip by undetected, but seemingly remained unaware of the 10th Indiana huddled at the base of Peters Hill. In retrospect, Liddell may simply have been too exhausted to think clearly. Worn out but unable to sleep, the general remembered lying restlessly at the base of a tree, turning over in his mind possible events of the next day. A few pickets shooting at each other in the darkness hardly justified immediate concern.[10]

Unfortunately for Liddell and his Arkansans, a "night surprise," as he called it, proved to be exactly what the Federal high command had in mind. Fry duly reported the Confederate position on Bottom Hill and confirmed the presence of water at the base of Peters Hill to Gilbert, who in turn passed along the crucial information to Buell. Possession of the strangely quiet and thus presumably unoccupied Peters Hill now seemed vital to gain and maintain control of the invaluable water, looming as so necessary for the coming day's expected action. Based on the amount of fire coming from Bottom Hill, however, it would take more than one regiment to hold it if the enemy contested its occupation. Accordingly, Buell directed Gilbert to send forward a brigade to seize the hill. Gilbert handed the assignment to Sheridan, who in turn gave it to Col. Dan McCook.[11]

McCook, at age twenty-eight three years younger than his brother the corps commander, nonetheless was a solid veteran of the western theater. Once considered by his relatives the most "delicate" of the McCook brothers, the young man before the war had been a bookworm who especially favored history and poetry, often quoting the latter at length. Plagued by ill health, McCook ironically attended Alabama University in Florence for the climate. He became known as an athlete there before relocating to Kansas, where the Ohio native briefly toiled as William Tecumseh Sherman's law partner. Beginning the war in 1861 as a Kansas infantry captain, McCook fought at Wilson's Creek and Shiloh before returning home in May 1862 to raise the 52nd Ohio Infantry, or "McCook's Avengers"—so named because of his brother Robert's recent murder in Alabama. His new brigade, created by combining the raw 52nd Ohio with three equally green Illinois regiments, had learned to forage well under their popular brigade commander's tutelage, but remained absolutely untried in battle. That Sheridan chose it for the assignment rather than one of his veteran brigades suggests that he not only wanted the new men to "see the elephant" before the expected a major clash, but also felt that the task should not prove difficult and thus did not require veterans. All McCook's fresh fish had to do after all was take an unoccupied hill and hold it until morning.[12]

McCook nonetheless reacted with justifiable nervousness. It was his first important assignment as brigade commander, and his men were raw. Told to consult with Gay as to the location and terrain of the position, McCook grew still more jittery. He ordered that his men be awakened and then placed onto the pike, with all baggage left in camp, and galloped off in the darkness in search of Gay, apparently without a clear idea as to where to find him. During his self-described "meanderings," he somehow stumbled into Buell's headquarters at the Dorsey House, where the commanding general himself heard the subordinate's plaintive plea for Gay's whereabouts and invited him in. There, as Buell well knew, sat Gay himself. During the brief discussion that ensued, Buell displayed a pointed and even fatherly interest, reminding McCook at one point to ask Sheridan for a battery of artillery to go along on the mission, something the shaky younger man apparently had not previously considered. At the conclusion of the brief council, McCook galloped back to his column and put it into motion on the Springfield Pike. Soon thereafter, thanks to Buell, two sections of Capt. Charles Barnett's six-gun Battery I, 2nd Illinois Light Artillery, gobbled up a hasty breakfast and rattled up the dark road to catch the brigade.

Reaching the forward outpost of Col. Nicholas Greusel's brigade at the eastern edge of the Federal camps at about 2 A.M., McCook learned unwelcome information from that brigade commander as well as Fry. Silent as it had been during the recent picket firing, Peters Hill apparently remained occupied after all. Greusel warned that a Confederate picket line had been clearly visible from time to time all evening against the bright night sky, and despite current appearances might well still be there. Taking the hill as a result might require more effort than originally anticipated. Consequently, as carefully and silently as possible, Fry joined McCook in aligning the now more dangerous Federal advance.

To support his tenuous foothold on the left, Fry borrowed the 86th Illinois Infantry from McCook and sent it out to reinforce his own 10th Indiana, which it did by forming to the left of the Hoosiers.[13] Exhausted from the day's march and apparently expecting little action until sunup, the worn-out Illinoisans immediately stacked arms and lay down to catch a few winks while Capt. Allen L. Fahnestock of Company I and one of his lieutenants paternally watched over them. Resting against a tree, a single blanket draping both officers, Fahnestock gazed expectantly on the horizon as shadowy figures moved back and forth on Peters Hill. Few others expressed concern, however. Lt. Col. D. W. Magee walked over to Fahnestock, laid his head in the captain's lap, and quickly drifted off to sleep.[14]

McCook in the meantime placed the 85th Illinois Infantry on the right of the pike and then formed his own Ohio regiment to the left. With bayonets fixed, four companies from those regiments began inching toward the front and flanks as skirmishers to probe the hill. As McCook turned to the 125th Illinois Infantry, preparing to form it into a second reserve line straddling the road, two cracks of musketry rent the still air. For a moment the Federals held their breaths, then Peters Hill blazed with the yellow-orange flames of musketry. Watching McCook's three remaining regiments ominously deploy in the bright moonlight,[15] the riflemen of the 7th Arkansas finally had come alive, opening "a severe and galling fire" upon the Yankees. There was no mistaking it now; there would indeed be a fight for the water.[16]

Although they had never before faced the enemy, McCook's green Federal skirmishers reacted surprisingly well, putting their heads down like farmers caught in a sudden shower of hail and forging ahead as ordered. On the left, Companies A and H of the 52nd Ohio moved steadily up the open slope of the hill. To the wooded right, however, the 85th Illinois's skirmishers found their ascent tougher going, for most of the Arkansans defending the summit were crowding over into the protective cover of the trees near the road and on the south side of the hill. Hurriedly, McCook ordered his Buckeyes to change direction, veer to the right, and hit the Rebels in their flank. Soon more help came, as Fry led skirmishers of the 10th Indiana and the 86th Illinois about half a mile across an open field to the north. They too soon scrambled up Peters Hill from the extreme left. The balance of McCook's brigade then concluded the assault, sweeping up the western slope as it bore down on the woods. In fifteen minutes the hill was theirs, at a cost of six men killed and twenty-seven wounded. Throwing skirmishers forward into the trees and cornfield east of the hill, McCook ordered his remaining men to lie down on the western slope, where they would be safe from enemy fire. He then brought up Barnett's tardy sections, placing two guns on the left of the road and two to the right. Looking toward the Confederate lines on Bottom Hill, the men saw the roses, grays, and blues of dawn appear in the eastern sky as Barnett's Federal guns opened up on Liddell's position.[17]

Having abandoned Peters Hill in a hurry, the soldiers of the 7th Arkansas, outnumbered five to one, fled down the reverse slope into the partially wooded valley of Bull Run.[18] Alarmed at last, Liddell turned to the regiment's commander, Col. D. A. Gillespie, who had been with Liddell on Bottom Hill, and ordered him to rally his men and retake the position. The brigade commander then dispatched the 5th Arkansas to assist Gillespie. Finally, he directed his battery, stationed in two sections on the left and right of the hill just behind Sam Bottom's house, to open up on the Federals in the woods atop Peters Hill. The Mississippians of Swett's Battery, temporarily commanded by Lt. Thomas Havern, promptly began lobbing spherical case shot, antipersonnel projectiles particularly effective at longer ranges, as well as solid shot over the Federal lines. The 85th Illinois immediately began taking

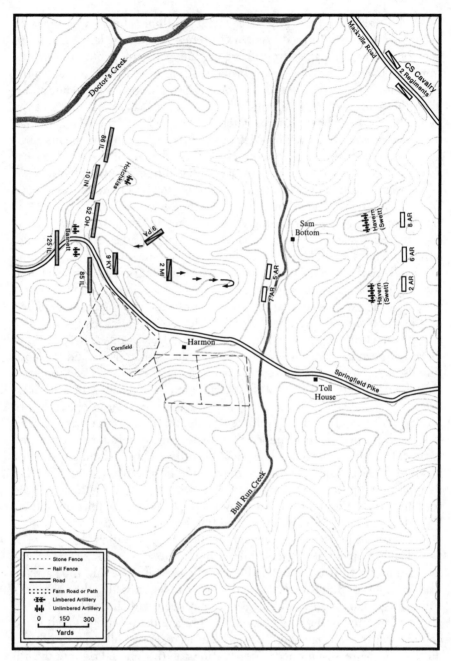

Map 8.1. Peters Hill-Bottom Hill fighting, 7:15 A.M.

casualties from the shell fragments. The 125th Illinois, supporting Barnett's battery, suffered to a lesser extent. However, the major effect of the bombardment, as was often the case, proved psychological. Such a spirited resistance, combined with hot, jagged iron raining from the dawn sky, combined to offer an already hesitant Dan McCook more than he had bargained for. Indicative of his anxiety was his crucial overestimation of enemy strength. In the gray twilight, observing the 5th Arkansas move down Bottom Hill to form in line behind their fellow Arkansans, the nervous brigade commander swore that he saw two full brigades of Confederate infantry moving toward his position. He was, McCook concluded, badly outnumbered.[19]

For almost an hour, Barnett's and Swett's batteries dueled, the superiority of the four Federal guns and their crews quickly beginning to tell as they repeatedly zeroed in on the inferior Confederate guns. Three times, Havern shifted his pieces out of range before Barnett's still-unscathed gunners finally disabled one and drove the others behind the hill. Meanwhile, the men of the Federal brigade hugged the ground. Then, just as the Confederate fire slackened, the 5th and 7th Arkansas moved forward to retake Peters Hill in what many described as two parade ground lines stretching across the cornfield north of the woods and pike. An eerie calm momentarily filled the morning air as the veteran Arkansans, marching with as much precision as the difficult terrain allowed, slowly advanced up the slope to within two hundred yards of the hilltop. McCook later guessed that the enemy "supposing from the quietness which I required my men to keep [believed] that they had run us out of the woods." He probably was correct.

Aching like all green troops to open up on the closing enemy immediately, McCook's apparently well-trained infantrymen nonetheless reacted well again, managing to hold their rifle fire while Barnett's James guns and twelve-pounder Napoleons tore huge gaps in the Confederate line. Undaunted, the veteran Arkansans closed up their ranks and kept moving. Then, when the gap between the lines finally closed to within a hundred yards, the 85th and 86th Illinois, 52nd Ohio, and at least the right-flank companies of the 125th Illinois, joined by Barnett's guns firing double-shot canister, rose up and delivered a crushing volley of lead and steel that ripped terrible smoky holes in the advancing gray lines, almost immediately driving the attackers back into the valley.[20] "They wavered, broke and retreated to the woods," one of Barnett's artillerymen remembered. "It was more than they could stand, and no soldiers could stand that terrific fire from infantry and artillery at such short range."[21]

As his Arkansans fell back, Liddell to his horror grasped for the first time that a considerable Federal force held Peters Hill. "The force of the enemy had been increased so largely and suddenly as to force back both lines," he wrote, "the officers and men contesting the ground with resolute determination, unwilling to yield it to even the great odds against them."[22] Across the Bull Run valley, however, McCook was in no mood to use numbers to his advantage—much to the consternation of his men, who thirsted for a counterattack. He continued to believe that he was woefully outnumbered. On his right and extreme left, dust clouds rising in the morning air signaling Rebel troop movements augmented his hesitation. Confederate cavalry, probably Wheeler's, suddenly appeared out of nowhere on his left along the Mackville Road. McCook ordered Barnett's section of James guns to fire on the horsemen. That forced them back for the time being, but he nonetheless anxiously began envisioning a numerically superior enemy flanking him and turning his position. Accordingly, he sent an urgent request for reinforcements.

Thanks to the brittle chain of command in the Army of the Ohio's III Corps, support proved agonizingly slow in coming. Unwilling to trust McCook completely, Sheridan rode forward to survey the position for himself. Then Gilbert briefly joined the rapidly expanding council, offering his views but giving no orders. Before riding off to Buell's headquarters to seek his advice, Gilbert firmly ordered McCook not to advance. On the way to see Buell, however, the corps commander had second thoughts and dispatched Gay's cavalry to the scene with orders to clear the woods in front of Peters Hill.[23]

It was now almost 7 A.M. Acting on his own without informing Gilbert, Sheridan had, during the interim, sent back word to bring forward Col. Bernard Laiboldt's brigade, as well as Capt. Henry Hescock's Battery G, 1st Missouri Light Artillery, from Gruesel's brigade. As Sheridan placed his newly arrived veteran infantrymen into a reserve line, ordering them bluntly to shoot McCook's rookies if they ran, another eerie silence fell over the field, disturbed only occasionally by a skirmisher's rifle and then by a notably fierce argument among two hesitant officers. When Gay finally arrived on Peters Hill with his cavalry, he took one look at the shadowy wooded valley below and summarily refused to go any farther alone. If McCook wanted those woods cleared of Confederates, Gay maintained, he was welcome to use his own infantry to do it. McCook in turn refused. Gilbert had ordered him to sit tight; the corps commander wanted Gay to accomplish the task. Which was just fine with McCook, who continued to worry that two enemy brigades were lurking in the trees beyond. Miffed and equally apprehensive about attacking a reported two brigades of infantry with three cavalry regiments, Gay continued to balk. He scribbled a note to Gilbert asking the corps commander to order McCook forward. After a tense pause, the answer arrived. Gilbert still wanted McCook to stay put. The argument summarily ended; Gay had no choice but to attack the woods alone.[24]

He did so without enthusiasm. Gay's horsemen tentatively rode forward. No sooner had they passed McCook's skirmishers than a volley of musketry rang out from the woods to the left of the road. Gay, expecting as much if not worse, instantly halted. Dismounting the 2nd Michigan Cavalry, his best unit, Gay sent six companies to the left and forward toward the woods, supported to the rear by the 9th Pennsylvania Cavalry. His five companies of the 9th Kentucky Cavalry, having broken the day before, remained in reserve behind the Pennsylvanians. As the Wolverines nervously advanced, a hail of shots emanated from the woods, cutting down close to two dozen troopers.[25] So accurate was the fire that one Michigander later swore the regiment had not encountered a run-of-the-mill body of infantry but rather "an unusually large body of sharpshooters . . . decimating our ranks." Stopped cold at the foot of the hill, the Michigan men responded by nervously firing their revolving rifles into the trees.

"'Under cover' was shouted along the line," Michigan cavalryman Marshall Thatcher remembered, "and every puff of smoke was met by another. Two regiments of sharpshooters confronting each other was no boys' play. . . . A hand, a hat, or the smallest part of the body exposed, on either side, were sure to receive a bullet." At first, the fight was equal, but the Federals' superior firepower from their Colt revolving rifles quickly began to tell. "We had five bullets to one," wrote Thatcher, "and their fire was very soon silenced by our steady pouring of lead into their hiding places, and the enemy were glad to creep rapidly along the ground, and behind trees until the brow of the hill put them in temporary safety."[26]

Gay responded to the temporary stalemate by sending his Pennsylvanians farther to the left, intending to flank the enemy position. They nervously advanced about a quarter of a mile along a fence fronting the woods, shooting sporadically at shadows with revolvers and carbines borrowed from the 9th Kentucky, before Liddell ordered the right section of his artillery to open up on them from atop Bottom Hill. "The loud-mouthed cannon," Pennsylvanian George W. Bowers remembered with understandable exaggeration, "coughed up balls as large as buckets. Our regiment was drawn up in line of battle to charge that cannon, and we maneuvered around awhile, but the order was countermanded, to our salvation." After a few minutes, the 9th Pennsylvania gave up and making a right wheel fell back at a walk on Peters Hill.[27] "Captain Gay started his cavalry into the woods," McCook later said laconically, "and they came back very rapidly."[28] All Gay could do now was order Capt. William Hotchkiss to place a section of his 2nd Minnesota Battery, temporarily attached to Gay's force, opposite Havern's guns in hopes of providing his dismounted troopers some cover. Soon the Minnesotans' brass twelve-pounders began firing at the battered and woefully outnumbered Confederate battery.[29]

Abandoned for the moment, the troopers of the 2nd Michigan hung on for dear life. Desperation then begat a desperate response bordering on the suicidal. Watching as the Arkansans regrouped behind a fence, the pinned-down Federals, "as if seized by sudden impulse," seized the initiative and without orders rose up suddenly and madly charged their tormentors, climbing over a fence and racing up the hill after Liddell's surprised and temporarily discomfited Confederates. Providentially it seemed, the Confederate line melted before them. When the 2nd Michigan topped the hill, however, the Confederates, having formed a workmanlike new line on the protected reverse slope, unleashed a wicked volley into their too-ardent pursuers. "It was too hot for so small a number," Thatcher admitted, "even with revolving rifles." The Michiganders fell back, at first in an orderly manner, but then running for dear life as the pressure mounted.[30]

As the 2nd Michigan ran back into the protecting trees along Bull Run, the artillery battle intensified over their heads. On Bottom Hill, Federal grapeshot and shell continued taking such a toll that Liddell finally decided to pull back both of his gun sections and then mass them on his right. He had just completed giving the order when an orderly rode up with a message. General Buckner, Liddell's division commander, had arrived on the field and wanted to see Liddell immediately. "All things in my front seemed to be going right," Liddell later wrote with some exaggeration, "so I rode off hurriedly to find General Buckner." Liddell found him just to the rear on the Springfield Pike, but the excited brigadier either proved unable to provide a coherent report or Buckner was particularly dense that morning. Failing to explain his predicament adequately verbally, a frustrated Liddell took a sheet of paper and tried to sketch a map of his position while grapeshot and shells fell around them. Liddell's map apparently made no sense to Buckner either, for at length he gave up and begged Buckner just to ride forward and see the situation for himself. The two generals trotted along the chaotic pike at the base of Bottom Hill and then turned to the right, in Liddell's words "passing between the opposing lines unharmed." The position had to be held, Liddell stressed as they ducked whistling shell fragments, for it was "the key to the whole field." Comprehending Liddell's dilemma at last, Buckner agreed, then raced off to find Polk, promising that he would "get him to hold the position in the event of its being decided to fight."[31]

Nearly another hour had passed; it was now almost eight o'clock. John G. Cavis of the 36th Illinois noted that it was becoming "a fin day not very warm Just a Breze."[32] As that breeze blew, Cavis's division commander, the aggressive Sheridan, made a major decision. Gay's cavalrymen alone obviously could not do the job assigned to them, and McCook and his "troopees" were spent, not to mention otherwise untrustworthy. Holding the hill had become a bigger job than he originally anticipated. He concluded that the celebrated veterans of his old brigade, Laiboldt's Pea Ridgers, must now take over the struggle. Captain Walter Hoppe, acting commander of the 2nd Missouri Infantry of Laiboldt's command, soon stepped up and volunteered for the dangerous assignment of seizing the valley. "If you can do it," Sheridan responded, "do so."[33]

The 2nd Missouri was a German-speaking outfit from St. Louis, "brave little 'dutchmen,'" F. B. James of the 52nd Ohio later wrote, "not one of whom seemed to be much, if any, taller than the huge brass-handled sword bayonet which dangled at their side."[34] Supported by the 44th Illinois Infantry as well as Hescock's guns, which clumsily peppered them in the back with friendly fire as they advanced, the skirmishers and then the main line of the Missouri regiment poured down Peters Hill and dove into the treacherous

Figure 8.2. Bottom Hill today, as seen from Peters Hill. The clump of trees in the center marks the Sam Bottom House site. Photograph courtesy John Walsh Jr.

woods.[35] "You have done enough boys, for this morning" a confident Missourian called out to Gay's horse soldiers as they passed, but some horsemen nonetheless tagged along, eager to take another swing at the Rebels. The Pea Ridgers pressed ahead steadily in the face of heavy fire. "Not a waver along the line," Marshall Thatcher remembered with admiration, "but that steady tramp! tramp! tramp! Moving on up over the hill the scattering ceased and the only sound to be heard was the muffled tread of armed men. Again the rattling fire, but not a step was broken, and now we see those men with iron nerve raise their polished arms to a level with their eyes and—Woo-o-o! As if one hand had moved the whole; and forward upon double quick they go—loading and firing at will, as they run."[36]

After a brief but spirited resistance, the exhausted Confederates emerged from the rear of the forest cover and poured back up Bottom Hill, a section each of Barnett's and Hescock's batteries pounding the unlucky Arkansans still more as they fled. The Pea Ridgers surged over the brow of the ridge in pursuit, their long and unusual Enfield sword bayonets gleaming in the morning sun, past Sam Bottom's house and into the apple orchard that lay behind it.[37] From the left, dodging Hescock's friendly fire, Fry's two brigades simultaneously swept toward Liddell's lines, adding to the Federal pressure. Moving up the hill at the double-quick, Fry's regiments brushed by a squad of sharpshooters, losing only one man. "When our boys gained the crest of the hill, with a yell they poured in a tremendous volley upon the enemy," wrote G. W. Brown of the 86th Illinois. "They did not wait for a second, but ran precipitately from the field." The 86th Illinois figuratively as well as literally had come a long way from that night outside Louisville when it panicked at the sound of cracking tree limbs.[38]

Momentarily shocked by the ferocity and speed of the attack, Liddell's brigade buckled for a moment, fell back, and again rallied to form a new line behind a stone fence. "It was soon plain enough that I could not maintain my skirmish line against the division before me," wrote Liddell. "I drew it in and got ready to receive the attack in line with the three remaining regiments. My skirmishers obstinately contested the ground. Not withstanding the fire from the line of battle, they slowed the enemy's approach."[39]

Meanwhile, on Peters Hill, Sheridan hurried to secure the hard-won position. The men of the 15th Missouri moved forward to support their home-state comrades. Sheridan also sent up Hescock's battery with the 86th Illinois in support to occupy a new position in front of the timber from which it could enfilade Liddell's gunners. On Sheridan's extreme left, the 9th Pennsylvania Cavalry returned to action, throwing down sections of the stone fence along Bull Run, crossing the watercourse, and obliquely proceeding half a mile forward until assailed and driven back by Confederate artillery fire. Increasingly overwhelmed all along his line, Liddell responded by again turning to Havern and ordering him to concentrate on the more dangerous Yankee gunners. The two batteries blasted away at each other at short range for about ten minutes. The superior Federal marksmanship finally won out, once again forcing Liddell's game but exhausted gun crews to the rear.

Whether Liddell ultimately could have halted Sheridan's growing momentum is anyone's guess, although in retrospect it seems most unlikely without reinforcement. At any rate, he never got the chance. Concerned with the escalating action, Buckner had returned to headquarters as promised and reported the situation to Polk. The action had grown so heavy, Buckner maintained, that he either had to commit more troops or withdraw the Arkansas brigade. Against Buckner's expressed wishes, Polk chose the latter. Orders from Buckner soon arrived on Bottom Hill directing Liddell to fall back. Withdrawing under fire in surprisingly good order, Liddell's veteran Arkansans backed off Bottom Hill and left it to Sheridan and his Pea Ridgers.[40]

Why did Polk refuse to fight for Bottom Hill? The answer has much to do with Polk's dawning realization of what he was up against. Simply put, by 10 A.M., the last thing he wanted to do was instigate a general engagement west of the Chaplin River.

Polk had not always felt that way. Arriving in Perryville still full of fight during the night, Polk had written Bragg an aggressive note at six the next morning in response to the first stages of the Peters Hill action. "The enemy seem disposed to press this morning," Polk reported. "Understanding it to

Figure 8.3. Maj. Gen. Philip H. Sheridan in 1863. Photograph courtesy Massachu-setts Commandery, Military Order of the Loyal Legion, and the U.S. Army Military History Institute.

be your wish to give them battle we shall do so vigorously."[41] Handing the letter to one of Wharton's cavalrymen, Polk advised the courier, "Do not let any grass grow under your horse's feet."[42]

Not long after dispatching the report, Polk rode out to examine the rough line of battle his subordinates had laid down in the darkness of the night before. What he saw shook him. For the first time, Polk dimly per-ceived the reality of his army's task. A large Federal force, at least a corps, lay beyond his lines west of the river. To cross the dry riverbed and attack such a host with three outnumbered and below strength divisions seemed inadvis-able to say the least. Yet Bragg, unaware that most of Buell's army lay in wait at Perryville, had ordered just such an assault. Such orders, Polk concluded, should not—could not—be obeyed. Exactly as he did at Bardstown when he had wanted to disobey Bragg's orders, Polk immediately called a council of war to back him up. Bragg, Polk rationalized, had only *suggested* an assault after all, leaving him leeway to do otherwise if necessary. After receiving the support he desired from Hardee, Anderson, Buckner, and Cheatham, Polk resolved "to adopt the defensive-offensive, to await the movements of the enemy, and to be guided by events as they developed." There would be no "vigorous attack" unless Buell launched it. Polk would fight a defensive battle at Perryville. The first result of Polk's "defensive-offensive" mind-set came when he ordered Liddell to fall back into the relative safety of the thin gray line hugging the east bank of the Chaplin River.[43]

In the years to come, many participants and scholars would excoriate Polk and Hardee as well for not doing what Bragg wanted that morning. Hindsight suggested that given a few more hours of daylight, the Confederates could have completed what they almost accomplished anyway, the destruction of at least a Federal corps. Such a decisive victory might well have changed the course of the war in the west. Writing in the influential *Battles and Leaders* series, for example, Joe Wheeler maintained that he had begged Hardee either to attack early on the morning of the eighth or otherwise find a better place to fight a defensive battle, one that offered the enemy less opportunities for flanking. Had they attacked as ordered, Wheeler went on, the army could have destroyed Gilbert's advanced corps before the others could come to their assistance.[44] Several recent scholars agree that Polk and the other senior commanders failed miserably, both in canceling the attack and then in not bothering to inform Bragg about the change.[45]

In regard to the latter charge, there is no excuse; Polk was derelict. The other issue, unfortunately, is more problematic. It is the accepted duty of every soldier to obey orders unless compelling reasons force disobedience. Was that the case at Perryville that morning? Probably. It is unfair to censure Bishop Polk and the others for their inability to see into the future, to know that the planned Federal attack would break down later that morning or that a division of raw Yankee troops soon would occupy a critical place in their army's line. At daybreak on the eighth, what did Polk know? He finally realized that he faced a superior force, one he was supposed to assail. Should he have known sooner? Better utilization of his cavalry would, without a doubt, have provided more detailed information. Nonetheless, he did not know. As a result, one cannot fault Polk for assuming a defensive posture that morning anymore than one can criticize Robert E. Lee for doing the same thing a few weeks earlier in the face of a numerically superior enemy along Maryland's Antietam Creek. Polk's force was outnumbered, and it lay miles from both its commander and desperately needed reinforcements. Bragg's assurances regarding Buell's supposed drive to the Kentucky River also must have seen dubious to Polk as he observed the long blue lines of Gilbert's corps. In that light, insubordinately and furtively to be sure, Polk in fact made the best decision possible.

Interestingly enough, given his way, Phil Sheridan would have acted exactly as Polk expected. Full of fight, he prepared to march his brigade down the Springfield Pike after Liddell. Sheridan snapped to one of Buell's aides who had ridden forward, "Tell Buell that they are fighting with a good deal of vim in my front, but if he will let me go, I can drive them to ——!"[46] However, he would never get the chance, for, as in Liddell's case, the high command's plans soon overrode the recommendations of the generals on the scene. A little before 10 A.M., as Sheridan prepared to pursue Liddell, Gilbert returned to Peters Hill and discovered to his horror that it was "vacant." That would not do; Buell's attack was to commence at ten; Alex McCook's corps tardily was moving into position on Gilbert's left. Accordingly, Gilbert ordered Sheridan to fall back onto Peters Hill "and limit himself to its defense until a general advance to attack in force should be ordered. To this order was added the explanation that General Buell was particularly solicitous that nothing be done to bring on a general engagement until after the junction of the flank corps."[47]

Sheridan had no choice but to abandon the pursuit. The battered Pea Ridgers fell back to Peters Hill and began digging shallow rifle pits while Daniel McCook's 52nd Ohio moved into the valley to hold the dry channel of Bull Run. McCook halted his Avengers east of the woods and brought the rest of his brigade forward into two lines of battle, the right resting on the Springfield Pike. Not long after, around ten, McCook spotted elements of his older brother's corps moving east on the Mackville Road, preparing to form a continuous Federal line anchored on Peters Hill.[48]

Like bloodied boxers retreating to their corners after the first round of a prizefight, Laiboldt's, McCook's, and Liddell's contending brigades fell back to lick their wounds. Stopped short by Gilbert and Buell, many bluecoats ached for another go at the foe. A Cincinnati war correspondent noticed that Laiboldt "seemed restless, uneasy, repeatedly declaring that he 'could not rest that night without another bout with the enemy.'"[49]

Others could not fight again that day, if ever. Confederate casualties had been surprisingly light under the circumstances, largely confined to the 5th and 7th Arkansas. Liddell eventually reported seventy-one total casualties for the day, most but certainly not all a result of the Peters Hill fighting. The Federals, who had attacked most of the morning, paid a higher price. In about fifteen minutes the 2nd Missouri alone lost as many troops as Liddell's entire command in its assault on Bottom Hill—including Captain Hoppe—while McCook's brigade counted about as many casualties again. Gay suffered, too. Surgeons, joined by a minister and Springfield businessman E. L. Davison, owner of the whiskey looted by Crittenden's men in Springfield, would spend the rest of the day operating on the wounded of both sides. Few Federals could disagree with the exhausted member of the 2nd Missouri who reportedly told an Ohioan at the conclusion of the struggle, "I fights mit Lyon, I fights mit Gurtis, und I fights mit Sigel, but dish es hail." Yet, to Buell's overall effort, the fight for Peters Hill had been well worth it. For the next two days, the Army of the Ohio survived on the pools of water in the bed of hard-won Doctor's Creek, as well as a wondrously discovered spring found near the creek bank in front of Sam Bottom's house. The opening round and a great liquid prize belonged to the men in blue.[50]

9

A SMALL SIZED HELL

BY LATE MORNING, UNITS OF GILBERT'S III CORPS HELD PETERS HILL and for a brief time Bottom Hill beyond it, and the combatants were now drinking from the precious water. Still, the struggle for the hills mattered little to Don Carlos Buell as he watched his overall battle plan fall apart. Sore, still unable to ride due to his fall the previous evening, Buell lay on his cot reading a book during the Peters Hill fighting, confident that he had perfected his plans. He expected to launch his attack at ten o'clock, commanding from an ambulance if necessary. As that hour came and passed, however, only Gilbert's corps stood ready for the fray.

To Gilbert's left, the head of McCook's column was just coming up into line at ten, at best two hours behind schedule. As Buell saw it, many more hours would pass before all of I Corps could be ready to fight. An egregious staff error coupled with the previous week's hard marching occasioned McCook's lateness. Although Buell had written I Corps's orders at eight the previous evening, McCook convincingly maintained that they did reach him until 2:30 that morning. The question of why it took one of Buell's staff officers six and one-half hours to ride ten miles down an important if narrow and twisting road illuminated by a full moon remains frustratingly unanswered. Perhaps he became lost, fell asleep under a tree, or most likely just could not find McCook's headquarters. We probably will never know. Whatever the reason, the incident reflects poorly on the army commander's staff.

At any rate, McCook did not receive his orders until the predawn hours. It then took two and one-half hours more to get the exhausted corps on its feet and moving as McCook allowed his men to fill their canteens and eat at least hasty breakfasts if their brigade and division commanders saw fit. Not until about five, with the sun rising in the east, did two of Lovell Rousseau's brigades, Col. William Lytle's followed by Col. Leonard Harris's, take to the road. An interval then appeared in the column, for many of the men in Rousseau's third and final brigade, commanded by Col. John Starkweather, had spent much of the night west of Mackville guarding the division's supply train. Starkweather needed extra time to move up, and after that wanted more to draw supplies. Once he did, the plan called for Jackson's rookie division to follow. Expecting a fight that morning, McCook warned Rousseau to exercise great caution as he advanced by using skirmishers as well as flankers to screen the march. To help make up lost time, McCook ordered everything in his train except the ambulances to remain at Mackville.[1]

Some of them eager to fight the Confederates at last, others fearful and hesitant, McCook's tired and by now dehydrated men stumbled toward the front. The narrow dirt road from Mackville to Perryville proved to be steep, winding, and wearisome. Distant guns, the sounds of the Peters Hill fighting, grew more distinct as the column neared the front, causing the fatigued and thirsty men to pick up the pace to the double-quick as they drew closer. A little before ten, Rousseau's lead elements reached the ridge-top intersection of the Mackville and Benton Roads, called the Dixville Crossroads by Boyle Countians. From that high, wide ground a mile northwest of Peters Hill, a summit commanding the entire area, the column first observed the silhouettes of Gay's horsemen and the smoke of artillery as it rose from the distant horizon of Peters Hill to the right front.[2] Told by men drifting to the rear that Sheridan had engaged the enemy, many of Buell's veterans initially expressed confusion. "An occasional straggler on being asked where he belonged would reply, 'Sheridan's division'," Angus Waddle of the 33rd Ohio Infantry remembered. "'Who the devil is Sheridan?' would be the next query, for no one seemed to know this coming man."[3]

McCook as of yet had no idea what was happening before him, but the fight on the right, coupled with the sight of Confederate scouts in the woods to the east, worried him that the Confederates might be attacking unexpectedly. The corps commander accordingly ordered Rousseau to place his artillery on the high ground near the crossroads and then send cavalry and infantry to probe carefully forward in reconnaissance. While the six companies of Col. Buckner Board's 2nd Kentucky Cavalry trotted forward, Rousseau led an unspecified "portion" of Lytle's infantry in Board's wake. The horsemen soon reappeared with an alarming report that the Confederates to their front indeed were advancing. Rousseau immediately halted his force and sent for McCook. Together, the two generals rode ahead toward the handsome, white, two-story frame home of prosperous farmer John C. Russell, which stood on the ridge south of the Mackville Road and east of the intersection. Russell was a prominent local Unionist whose eighteen-year-old daughter Isaphena recently had married a local man named May, who was serving in the 63rd Indiana Infantry. With her father out of town, Isaphena May had charge of the home. The area around the Russell House, the "white house" of so many after-action accounts, provided a sweeping view of the fields below, overlooking a valley with woods to the front and left as well as open fields to the right.

Russell owned about 150 acres of land that was about to become battle-

Figure 9.1. The Russell House, about 1927. Photograph courtesy Special Collections: Photographic Archives, University of Louisville.

field. Farther down the hill to the east, "Squire" Henry Bottom's deceptively modest frame home could be seen along the west bank of Doctor's Creek where the watercourse crossed the road. Bottom was a wealthy farmer, cabinetmaker, local justice of the peace, slave owner, and the most prominent secessionist in the area, a fact that had apparently estranged him from his cousin Sam. He owned almost eight hundred acres of land, fields and pastures that included nearly everything the Federals could see between the Russell property and the creek. Just beyond the creek ran the equally dusty bed of Bull Run as it broke off from the creek and ran in a parallel fashion to the south.[4]

From the Russell House, by far the highest eminence in the area, McCook watched Liddell's Arkansans to the south melt before Gay and Sheridan's assault. He surmised almost immediately that Board had jumped to conclusions; no Rebel advance could be seen. Later, at least one Federal opined that Board, as unfamiliar with Sheridan's Pea Ridgers as Rousseau's other men, must have mistook Little Phil's veterans for the enemy. McCook at that moment could not be completely sure, however, so he dispatched an aide to confirm his impression. In the interim, just to be safe, McCook and

Figure 9.2. Henry P. Bottom Farm, as viewed from near the Russell House in 1885.
Photograph courtesy Massachusetts Commandery, Military Order of the Loyal Legion, and the U.S. Army Military History Institute.

Rousseau also agreed to form Lytle's and Harris's brigades into a line of battle anchored on the Russell House and its commanding heights and then running in a north-south direction almost parallel to the Benton Road. Happily, such an alignment also essentially served to fulfill Buell's orders to form up on the left of Gilbert's line, which now could be easily seen from the Russell House some four or five hundred yards to the right.

While Rousseau's brigades hurriedly swung into position on the best ground in view, McCook called Capt. Cyrus O. Loomis's 1st Michigan "Coldwater" Battery up from the crossroads and personally placed it to the left of the Russell House, where it could control a wide expanse of ground. Loomis and his men were veterans of the fighting in western Virginia. Acting as skirmishers, the Cincinnatians of the crack 10th Ohio Infantry of Lytle's brigade meanwhile moved deliberately forward into the woods and down to Doctor's Creek. Answering a written request from Gay for support, Rousseau then sent the 42nd Indiana Infantry down the hill to support Hotchkiss's battery. Finally, when the Confederates began pulling back from Bottom Hill for good, Rousseau dispatched a section of Loomis's battery farther down the road toward an exposed hill that commanded the west bank of Doctor's Creek from the left of the pike in order to hurry the Johnnies along. Equipped with longer-range Parrott rifles, Loomis could accomplish more than Hotchkiss, whose battery had smoothbore field howitzers. Satisfied that his position was secure for the time being, McCook rode off to report to Buell, having ordered an aide to stay behind to assist Jackson's division into line when it finally came up. McCook wanted Jackson to place his brigades in column just to the right of the Mackville Road, ready to move to the left or to the right as needed. Without informing Rousseau, McCook then rode away.[5]

Other than the artillerymen, who continued throwing an occasional round into the woods, McCook's men relaxed. Every indication suggested to their hopeful minds that the enemy had retreated.[6] "We all supposed they were leaving, as we could see nothing of them," wrote Lt. George W. Landrum of the 2nd Ohio Infantry. The excited anticipation of battle gave way to relaxation as men pulled food from their haversacks and ate an early meal. "With a feeling of disappointment," the 3rd Ohio Infantry's Col. John Beatty wrote, "the boys lounged about on the ground and logs awaiting further orders." Added another of Rousseau's soldiers: "all became quiet. A few skirmishers were seen between us and the creek, and a squad of cavalry"—Gay's men—"passed between us and the [Mackville] Road, going towards Perryville. These soon disappeared; the coast seemed clear."[7]

Rousseau was not so sure. An hour passed with no word from McCook, and he grew increasingly fidgety. At one point he rode down the hill to confer with Cyrus Loomis, the eccentric former attorney and milling equipment salesman who had accompanied his forward section. As the general reigned in his horse, Loomis noticed a cloud of dust rising above the eastern horizon. He "gruffly . . . roared 'General, what is that away up the pike across yonder.'"

"'Well, I should say it's dust.'"

"'I should say so. Oh, I'm not so full but I could tell that, ha!ha!'" Watching the dust cloud rise, Loomis added, "'General, that's a large body of troops, and that's—yes, Harrodsburg pike. I guess we have tread on the tail of Mr. Bragg's coat, ha ha!'"

Taking Loomis's telescope, Rousseau "gazed long and carefully. . . . 'Well Loomis,'" he concluded at length, "'you are right, you can give them a small sized hell right here. I'm a *little lame*, reckon I'll have to be going.'" Rousseau then rode away, convinced like Loomis and everyone else that the dust cloud represented Bragg's army fleeing before them in full retreat.[8]

That confidence and miscalculation conditioned Rousseau's next, fateful decision. As noon approached and the sun directly overhead grew hotter, the men's thirst grew increasingly more unbearable. At the bottom of the hill, in the otherwise dry bed of Doctor's Creek to the right of the road and Loomis's position, small pools of scummy but nonetheless cherished water cruelly enticed them. Rousseau knew that he should maintain his position on the commanding high ground, but he also knew his soldiers had to have water. The enemy, moreover, was retreating again; there was no danger. He had no way of knowing that back at Buell's headquarters, where confidence also brimmed, the commanding general, acting at McCook's request, was about to sanction just such a movement. Rousseau thus made the ultimately momentous decision to march his two brigades down to Doctor's Creek without McCook's permission. The 42nd Indiana, already forward supporting Hotchkiss, would go first, while the rest of Lytle's brigade formed into column with the 3rd Ohio in front and began advancing, snaking slowly downhill to the waterway. Harris would go after Lytle. Although ordered to fill their canteens as quickly as possible so as to make room for the next regiment, the Hoosiers seemed to be in no hurry; the Rebels, after all, were retreating. Stacking their arms and crawling down into the creek bed north of the road, they looked forward to boiling water, making some coffee, and eating dinner in peace. As fate would have it, the Hoosiers went into the creek where its western bank was stony, high, and indeed almost perpendicular. Entering there was a simple matter. Extricating themselves would be another thing entirely.[9]

If Rousseau's two forward brigades presented a picture of calm during the late morning of October 8, the third found itself enmeshed in a maelstrom of a traffic jam back down the Mackville Road.

The men of John Starkweather's brigade came to Perryville with chips on their shoulders. A rear-echelon brigade whose military experience had largely involved safeguarding Buell's railroads, Starkweather's men had yet to prove themselves in battle. "During the first year of our service," Elias Hoover of the 1st Wisconsin Infantry later wrote, "we thought we were somewhat abused, as we were in the rear guarding railroad bridges and watching John Morgan's command, with occasionally a little skirmish, and the boys were really itching for a fight."[10] A comrade in arms agreed. "It was our first chance in a regular battle," L. E. Knowles remembered, "though we had been in the service a year, chasing John Morgan's 'critter company' over the best part of Tennessee, and the boys were . . . eager for the fray."[11]

At first, however, such eagerness seemed misplaced, for once again that morning bad luck seemed to seek out Starkweather's hard-luck regiments. After abandoning the train they had guarded the night before, Starkweather's men came up from the rear of the division to draw commissary stores in Mackville as ordered. That took time, too much time in the opinion of the always volatile James Jackson. With every minute's delay, Jackson grew hotter. Eager for battle, and showing the same consideration for his charges that always marked his tenure, he had awakened his rookie division at 3 A.M. and had it in line so quickly that most of his men had no time to eat breakfast. Most of their canteens remained empty as well. Jackson ached to move, but now he had to wait as Starkweather's men lined up for supplies before moving out. At length, he could take no more. Around 8 A.M., Jackson ordered his division toward Perryville despite McCook's orders, and in so doing cut off Starkweather from the rest of Rousseau's division. Rousseau therefore could not expect that brigade's support any time soon. Starkweather's men thus were the last to come up the Mackville Road. Some wondered if once again they had missed the fight.[12]

McCook's tardiness, while great, was not Buell's major problem, however. As slowly as McCook's I Corps had advanced, it still in the end had moved more promptly than Crittenden's, which to Buell's consternation remained even farther from its designated position down the Lebanon Pike. All the staff and command problems that had bedeviled I Corps that morning had occurred in spades on the Federal right. As a result, at 10 A.M. II Corps was nowhere near where it was supposed to be.

Buell had dictated his orders for Thomas and Crittenden at seven the previous evening, an hour before he composed McCook's. For the day at least, the corps would be Crittenden's in name only. As second in command of the army, Thomas in actuality would command the corps during the impending battle, and so Buell's orders went directly to him. One result was that Crittenden would remain in the dark for months after the battle insofar as the events of the previous night were concerned. He did remember Thomas first showing Buell's orders to him at three the following morning, having apparently just received them himself. Once again, Buell's staff somehow had let him down; it had taken the commanding general's dispatch almost eight hours to travel at most fourteen miles.

Compounding II Corps's difficulties at that hour, Crittenden's rear division, Thomas Wood's, did not begin arriving in camp until around 3 A.M. after its hellish march to and beyond Haysville to Rolling Fork. To ask men so worn out to keep moving seemed unwise if not heartless to Thomas. As a result, without informing Buell, and despite the clearly audible sounds of cannon fire coming from Peters Hill, Thomas decided that all the men needed more rest than Buell's orders allowed. Crittenden's cavalry, Col. Edward McCook's brigade, did not ride out until daybreak, and the lead infantry division, W. S. Smith's, did not march until seven the next morning, the men breakfasting on roasted corn while their officers enjoyed a better fare of ham and eggs. That essentially put the division four hours behind Buell's schedule, with the other two divisions set to follow behind at two-hour intervals and thus come up even later.[13]

Edward McCook's cavalry finally pushed up the road after sunrise. All along their path, the bluecoats encountered refugees hurriedly fleeing town. Then, around ten o'clock, the Federal 1st Kentucky Cavalry and 7th Pennsylvania Cavalry confronted pickets from Joseph Wheeler's command on a long ridge near the Williams House, and drove them back a mile to where the main body of Confederate cavalry was positioned. Advancing behind the retreating enemy, the Federal horsemen formed into line on the brow of the ridge and unlimbered an artillery battery, which promptly opened fire on Wheeler's troopers. The 1st Kentucky's Company A then dismounted and descended into a steep ravine to develop the enemy line.

As the bluecoats advanced, Wheeler received orders from Polk telling him to keep the road clear and protect the army's rear. That was all the aggressive Wheeler needed to hear. The Confederates counterattacked quickly and without warning. Covered by their own artillery, the 1st and 3rd Alabama Cavalry Regiments, heroes of the previous day's encounter on the Springfield Pike, charged down the road in column, sending the surprised and confused Federals reeling a full two miles in retreat, back to the safety of Smith's infantry. Wheeler reported "capturing many prisoners and horses in single-combat . . . the enemy also fled panic-stricken from a battery placed in advance of their general line and left it at our disposal." Unfortunately, not everything went well for Wheeler, for behind the Alabamians, Lt. Col. John Hart's Georgia cavalrymen somehow took a wrong turn and disappeared from the scene. Outnumbered and confronted with a superior mounted force, Wheeler had no choice but to fall back. He deployed his men in a line along the high ground and unlimbered his artillery to further stall the Federal advance. Unaware of the size of the force he truly faced, Wheeler would try to hold the road as ordered.[14]

Down the road, Smith's division advanced slowly toward the Confederate cavalry, encumbered on the march by a supply train Smith foolishly refused to leave behind. In the distance, muffled artillery announcing Gilbert's struggle at Peters Hill occasioned yet another agonizing delay as Smith's gunners stopped to transfer baggage from their guns and caissons to baggage wagons. Thereafter the pace quickened. Many soldiers expressed their yearning to fight Bragg, and Smith himself prodded the less willing. Between ten and eleven, as his column reached a point three miles from Perryville and eight miles from the previous night's camp, Smith halted his men, advanced them again, and halted them for good in a line of battle stretching across the pike along a roughly north-south axis. Smith intended to wait there while Van Cleve's and Wood's brigades came up and accomplished the linkup with Gilbert's right flank. For the time being, a sizable gap still remained between Smith's units and Gilbert's corps. Thanks to hard marching over the course of the last three miles—"quick time" occasioned only by the sounds of fighting to their front—Van Cleve's regiments moved with more dispatch than Smith's, finally racing up to form on his left around eleven o'clock. As they filed into line in a wooded area to the left of the road, a thick pall of smoke rising from Gilbert's front blanketed them. Battle, they believed, would find them soon as well.[15]

Just after Smith's column reached its assigned point on the Lebanon Pike, Thomas dispatched his artillery chief, Capt. O.A. Mack, to report the news to Buell and request further orders. Mack's tardy report constituted the first communication from Thomas to Buell that morning, which greatly perturbed the commanding general. Thomas's failure to keep Buell informed over the previous few days had already annoyed him so much that he had referred to it in his orders of the previous evening. "Nothing has been heard of you since we parted this morning," Buell complained. Lest there be a continuation of Thomas's silence, Buell wrote expressly that Thomas needed to report directly and in person once Crittenden's corps arrived in its appointed position on Gilbert's right. Yet throughout the morning of the eighth, the sphinxlike Thomas again maintained his aloofness, following more the letter than the spirit of Buell's instructions. As a result, Buell knew nothing definite about Thomas's whereabouts until Mack rode into his camp at around eleven. Even then, Thomas did not bother to report in person as ordered.[16]

Why did Thomas act as he did? One can only speculate. James McDonough has suggested that Thomas's silence that morning reveals the "subtle tensions" that had existed between the two generals since Halleck attempted to give the army to Thomas. Then again, McDonough continues, "perhaps something about the wording, the tone of [Chief of Staff James] Fry's message to Thomas from Buell, did not set well with Thomas. The stalwart Virginian could be touchy at times."[17] Perhaps. Then again, tensions between Thomas and Buell predated events in Louisville, and indeed were evident at the campaign's genesis. When the retreat from Tennessee began, an increasingly frustrated Thomas had given Buell what he deemed good advice without a favorable response. Instead of consolidating at McMinnville when the movement began as Thomas had urged—an eventuality Thomas clearly still believed would have kept Bragg in Tennessee and prevented everything ill that had followed—Buell insisted instead on Altamont, a position so devoid of food, water, and forage as to be practically indefensible. Buell had asked too much of his men at that time and since. Perhaps "Old Pap," the soldiers' general, now saw in Buell's orders the same breezy unconcern for the army's basic physical needs. His men were exhausted, hungry, and thirsty. They were in no shape to march, much less fight. Yet if Thomas reported that to Buell, he was certain the latter would demand an immediate movement anyway. Thomas thus may well have reasoned that it was better not to report that he had delayed the march contrary to orders until the corps reached its position, presenting Buell with a fait accompli.

One point must be added. Such a literal interpretation of Buell's words makes sense only if Thomas did not expect a battle that day, negating the need for haste. That, sadly, is reasonable as well. How many times over the previous few weeks had Buell avoided offering battle to Bragg? Thomas may well have regarded Buell much like the boy in the fable who cried wolf. If so, the end result was a self-fulfilling prophecy. With McCook late on the left and Crittenden even later on the right and out-of touch most of the morning thanks to Thomas's borderline insubordination, Buell concluded between 10:30 and 11 A.M. that he could not strike the enemy at all that day with the overwhelming force his understanding of war demanded. Rear brigades would require all afternoon to come up. He thus made the momentous decision to postpone the attack until morning. The army would use the rest of the eighth to perfect its lines and hit Bragg the next day. In the meantime, the men could relax. A bruised Buell certainly intended to do so.

If Thomas indeed equated Buell with the boy who cried wolf, he sadly missed the moral to Aesop's fable. In the end, a real-life wolf killed the boy in the story at a moment when no one took his cries seriously. Three miles to the east, the gray wolf that was Braxton Bragg was throwing together an attack Don Carlos Buell scarcely anticipated. Thanks to Buell's overconfidence and habitual perfectionism, as well as to the strained command structure within the Army of the Ohio, initiative now dangerously shifted to the Confederates as the sun climbed toward its zenith.

Poor communication and weak links in the chain of command hardly confined themselves to the Union army at Perryville. All morning, a similar leadership crisis crippled the Confederate Army of the Mississippi. That imbroglio developed as the latest manifestation of the poor communication between a confused Braxton Bragg and his obtuse subordinates, Generals Hardee and Polk.

Nothing that occurred during the evening of October 7, including several reports from Perryville, had deterred Bragg from continuing to believe that Buell had moved toward the Kentucky River in the vicinity of Versailles with most of his force. Indeed, scattered reports throughout the night reinforced Bragg's disorientation. At 8 P.M. an unidentified citizen rode into Bragg's camp and reported to the general that McCook's corps was at Mackville. More critically, the civilian added, advance Federal pickets had reached Cornishville, located only five miles northwest of Harrodsburg. Their presence seemed to indicate an advance to the northeast toward Kirby Smith. Bragg immediately dispatched his aide Stoddard Johnston with fifty cavalrymen to confirm the report. Johnston returned at 2 A.M. and authenticated the McCook part of the story. He could not, however, confirm the presence of Union cavalry in Cornishville.

Bragg nonetheless believed all of it. To Bragg, the two reports taken together proved conclusively that Buell and the bulk of his army indeed threatened Kirby Smith to the north, most likely near the town of Salvisa. That McCook might be moving from Mackville southeast toward Perryville rather than in the direction of Harrodsburg and Salvisa apparently never occurred to Bragg. The reported but unconfirmed presence of Union cavalry at Cornishville indicated a northeasterly line of march, exactly the sort of movement McCook would make if Kirby Smith's reports were accurate. In contrast, nothing from Perryville indicated the presence of a Federal corps there. Hardee's 7:30 dispatch, the most recent report from that front, arrived at midnight with its pedantic "do not scatter your forces" advice but no firm indication of Federal troop strength. Kirby Smith must be right, Bragg reasoned.[18]

In the end, as Bragg explained to Jefferson Davis in May 1863, "General Kirby Smith's appeals to me were more frequent and much more urgent than Polk's or Hardee's, for a concentration of the whole forces in front to him, and I did all I could, by personal labor and orders, to accomplish that object."[19]

Accordingly, Bragg told Johnston after the latter returned from his reconnaissance that they would rise at six and make their way to Salvisa, joining Kirby Smith in preparations for the great battle for Kentucky. To assure that victory, he added, Polk needed to dispose quickly of the apparently smaller Federal force at Perryville and then move with haste to combine the armies on the banks of the Kentucky. Typically, however, it was not a firm decision. Bragg continued to second-guess himself as he had done for days. One suspects that he slept fitfully, if at all. Hardee's dispatch, vague as it was, bothered him. How strong was the enemy force at Perryville? Strong enough to push by the army and seize the supply depot at Bryantsville's Camp Dick Robinson/Breckinridge? That would be devastating. In contrast, Kirby Smith seemed safe enough after all, at least for the moment. If McCook was camped in Mackville, he could not reach Salvisa before the ninth at the earliest. The silence coming from the south on the morning of the eighth further concerned Bragg, for the all-out attack he had ordered Polk to make against the Federal force there should have been audible in Harrodsburg. What was wrong? In the end, Bragg gave in to his doubts, announcing to his staff that instead of going to Salvisa, they would ride to Perryville instead and join the bulk of the army there.[20]

Leaving at seven, the party intercepted a courier from Polk bringing his 6 A.M. dispatch with its promise of a "vigorous" attack. There was little evidence of it, however, as Bragg and his aides arrived in Perryville about half-past nine, just as the Peters Hill fighting reached its climax. Meeting his surprised subordinates at the handsome brick home of John M. Crawford, just north of town on the Harrodsburg Pike and near the camps of the previous night, Bragg first learned of their decision to "adopt the defensive-offensive" in violation of his direct orders. He was, by all accounts, furious. After an angry discussion, Polk petulantly offered to turn immediate control of the army back over to Bragg. The latter declined, but he did reassert his original orders: The army must attack as soon as possible, complete the task, and march for Kirby Smith, Polk's concerns notwithstanding. He then rode out to survey the line for himself while his willful subordinates prepared for battle.[21]

Heading north along the Confederate line, Bragg soon saw something that made his blood boil even more. Polk's battle line, as an aide wrote in his diary with singular understatement, "was not so good."[22] On the south side of Walker's Bend, where Doctor's Creek branched off from the main channel, Polk's right flank was "in the air," unanchored by a hill, waterway, building, or anything else. Bragg quickly grasped the danger of Polk's casual disregard for inspecting his own lines there. A Federal force, moving unopposed into the unoccupied breach between Buckner's division and the dry bed of the Chaplin River at Walker's Bend, could easily flank and then turn the entire army out of its position, cutting it off from its base of supplies. More dangerous still, just such an attacking force seemed to be gathering for that purpose precisely at that moment. "Extending to the forks of the creek," Stoddard Johnston remembered after the war, "there was a gap, which already the enemy was aiming to possess . . . and it was not long before the enemy effected a lodgement on a portion of the bluff with his sharpshooters, while on the slope beyond the creek could be seen long lines of infantry, with their glistening bayonets, as if preparing for an advance. It was evident that with the enemy in this position, we could make no fight."[23]

The troops Bragg saw were Harris's and Lytle's brigades of Rousseau's division, formed up in line of battle as their division commander and McCook had ordered after first arriving on the scene near the Russell House. They had no intention of attacking as Bragg feared, for at roughly the same moment Buell was deciding to postpone his advance until the morning. Bragg, however, had no way of knowing that. All he could see was Polk's egregious error, an unanchored line of battle, and an enemy force apparently poised to exploit it. No time could be lost, the gap had to be filled before he could crush the Yankees and head north to support Kirby Smith.

Back at the Crawford House, Bragg went to work with desperate haste. The main Federal threat, as far as he could tell, remained on the Springfield Pike in front of Bottom Hill, where Sheridan most recently had forced back Liddell. Clearly, though, Bragg believed the enemy also was in the process of extending its line to the north from the Mackville Road to exploit Polk's inattention. In contrast, Bragg for the moment knew nothing about Crittenden's approach to the south, up the Lebanon Pike. Indeed, he expected to hear nothing since most of Buell's army was supposed to be elsewhere. Although he had sent Wheeler to picket that road and clear it of any enemy horsemen, Bragg was confident that Wheeler alone would, in the young cavalryman's words, be "able to hold their own against the enemy on that part of the field."[24] In other words, Bragg refused to believe that there could be a sizable force coming up the Lebanon Pike, and as of yet Wheeler had said nothing to dissuade him. Thus, Polk's poor deployments, Wheeler's silence, and Bragg's grasp of the overall situation directed his attention northward, where Rousseau's presence anchored it.

Based on that conception of Federal dispositions and plans, as well as the immediate need to do something about the danger at Walker's Bend, Bragg hastily but confidently gambled, ordering two complementary but time-consuming movements. While Hardee's wing crossed the dry bed of the Chaplin River and advanced closer to the enemy, Cheatham's division on the far left would pull out of line, move at the double-quick through town behind the screen created by the rest of the army, and reform two miles north on the extreme right, in the gap at Walker's Bend. Extensive woods and the rolling, swelling character of the terrain theoretically would conceal from the bluecoats everything but perhaps Cheatham's trail of dust as he marched. Wharton's cavalry would screen Cheatham as he approached the enemy left. After a thirty-minute artillery bombardment, set to begin at 12:30 P.M., Cheatham's division, acting under Polk's orders, would launch a surprise attack in echelon, brigade by brigade, turning the exposed and hopefully confused Federal left and then rolling up the enemy brigade by brigade from north to south. Hardee then would advance his divisions into the fleeing blue mass to finish the job.

All morning, Confederate soldiers drawn up in Perryville had listened to the sounds of the Peters Hill fight, the artillery of that engagement reverberating particularly along the expectant gray line. They occupied their time engaging in the several pursuits soldiers embrace before fighting. Some conversed, others prayed or picked lice from their clothing. The men of Brig. Gen. Daniel Adams's brigade donned new uniforms, leaving their lousy and tattered old ones in heaps in the woods where they camped.[25] "They are fighting for water now," Chaplain Charles Quintard told Rev. Joseph Cross as he listened to the guns, "I am informed they have had none for two days."

"I hope," a third man broke in, "they will never get a drop till Father Abraham sends it to them by Lazarus."[26]

Suddenly, Bragg's orders came, and they were up and moving. Hardee's wing lurched forward across the Chaplin River's dry course after 11 A.M. and moved directly to the west "so as to take position on the space between the two streams [the Chaplin River and Doctor's Creek] on the west of town, extending across the Mackville Road, with its left toward the Springfield turnpike." The two smoothbore-equipped sections of Capt. Henry Semple's six-gun Alabama Battery, detached from Wood's brigade, remained east of town on Seminary Hill, allowing Semple to sweep the ground between Hardee's left and the road as the infantry advanced. Supported in that manner, the two brigades from Patton Anderson's division that until Cheatham's arrival had comprised the left of the army marched up the Springfield Pike, once again on the far left. Colonel Samuel Powell's brigade took the extreme left, south of the road, while Adams's brigade formed to Powell's right.[27]

An aggressive officer and the victor of one of Mississippi's most notorious duels before the war, the Kentucky-born Adams lost his right eye at Shiloh but recovered to take command of the brigade in Chattanooga. Marching in column, screened by Maj. John E. Austin's battalion of sharpshooters, his brigade moved parallel to the Springfield Pike and approached unoccupied Bottom Hill, Liddell's former position and the site of the morning's struggle, from the rear. Using Bottom Hill as a shield, Adams, following Anderson's orders, then turned off the road and began moving obliquely northward across generally open country, brushy and full of stumps but largely treeless, in the direction of Bull Run and its intersection with the Mackville Road at Squire Bottom's house a mile distant.[28]

Instead of marching briskly, Adams's brigade lurched forward in fits and starts, much to its commander's growing consternation. As Adams understood his orders, Anderson's two brigades were to move up to the front in tandem, but from the first, Powell's brigade lagged considerably behind Adams's Louisiana veterans and finally disappeared in their dust. Before long, Anderson sent orders to Adams telling him to stop, or at least slow down, so that Powell could catch up. Adams did so, but when Powell still failed to appear, Adams sent him a message to hurry up and start moving again— "very slowly" in Adams's words. Farther across the pie-shaped triangle of land formed by the Springfield and Mackville roads and Bull Run, Adams halted again, sent another dispatch, and began moving again. Indeed, by his own admission, Adams stopped to wait on Powell "several" times.[29]

Adams waited in vain. Powell's brigade had halted for good, stopping on the first eminence it came to west of town along the Springfield Pike. Captain Overton W. Barret's Missouri Battery of four six-pounders unlimbered on that tree-covered hill near J. F. Edwards's house, masked from Sheridan's position on Peters Hill by two intervening ridges, while the infantrymen went into line. Powell clearly planned on holding the position for the foreseeable future. Why? Powell's dawdling unfortunately remains unexplained. Inexperience might well be one factor. Powell, previously the colonel of the 29th Tennessee Infantry, rose to brigade command when Bragg cashiered Brig. Gen. Lucius Marshall Walker of Tennessee for incompetence and drunkenness. Perryville was to be his first combat assignment in charge of a brigade. Then again, perhaps Powell only obeyed bad orders. Patton Anderson's whereabouts during the late morning remain foggy, but his orders to Adams strongly suggest that he rode with his more inexperienced brigadier. Later in the day he would be at Powell's shoulder on Seminary Hill, having essentially abandoned Adams's brigade to Buckner's control. Perhaps Anderson and not Powell thus was at fault. Unwilling to expose his position and bring on a fight precipitously, Anderson may well have ordered Powell to halt sooner than he needed to stop. Whatever the reason, a widening gap soon separated Hardee's two left-flank brigades, leaving Adams's left exposed and Powell dangerously alone. A serious breakdown already had occurred on the extreme Confederate left.[30]

Simon B. Buckner's center division, the Confederate unit closest to Adams on the right, began marching toward the enemy roughly at the same time as Anderson's left brigades. On Buckner's left, Brig. Gen. Bushrod R. Johnson's six-regiment brigade hiked three-quarters of a mile from John Dye's impressive looking two-story house, which Buckner had claimed as his headquarters, southwest and more or less downhill toward R. F. Chatham's more humble hillside home, orchard, and fields. Reaching the brow of Chatham Hill, Johnson called a halt. The tableau that lay spread out before him to the west and southwest fairly chilled the general. Past the Chatham House and outbuildings, open fields sloped unevenly 150 yards down to the banks of Doctor's Creek, just north of its intersection with the Mackville Road at Squire Bottom's house. Approaching the creek under fire would be difficult at best. A marked "undulation" running parallel to the hilltop seemed sure to cause problems. Farther on, two hundred yards before reaching the creek, marching soldiers would encounter a split rail fence running north to south that divided Chatham's sloping field in two. Once they reached the creek, his men would be forced to scale its nearly vertical bank, well over five feet high in some places, and then surmount a stone fence on the other side. Beyond the creek and toward Squire Bottom's yard, another stone fence ran parallel to the watercourse. Yet another fence, partially stone and partially of split rails, ran from east to west past the house along the Mackville Road, further enclosing Squire Bottom's premises. More stone fences ran across the squire's fields to the rear of the house.

Worst of all, the ridge west of the creek already was occupied in force. Johnson already could see Rousseau's thirsty blue lines on the slopes below the Russell House, and the 42nd Indiana in the creek, presumably acting as skirmishers. From the heights above and right of the Bottom House, Federal artillery could create havoc in any attacking lines all along the slope. Small wonder that Johnson later wrote: "the position was a very strong one. There was perhaps none stronger in the enemy's lines."

Johnson nonetheless forged ahead as ordered. He told Capt. Putnam Darden to place sections of his Mississippi Battery on the finger-like north and south spurs of Chatham Hill in preparation for the planned barrage.[31] According to one observer, what was left of Swett's pugilistic battery unlimbered there as well, its brigade withdrawn to a reserve position. Leaving the 37th Tennessee to support those batteries, Johnson pushed the 44th Tennessee Infantry forward down the slope toward the Chatham House as skirmishers.[32]

Meanwhile, to Johnson's rear, Pat Cleburne's reserve brigade came onto the ridge behind Johnson and halted. Cleburne's men reacted to the Federal position in a manner that mirrored the men in Johnson's command. The sudden sight of the long blue line in the distance impressed veteran Robert Smith of the 2nd Tennessee. "All drawn up in battle array," he wrote, "it was a very imposing sight, the most magnificent line I ever saw."[33] Behind the crest of Chatham Hill the two brigades minus skirmishers lay down to await the impending artillery bombardment.[34]

Farther north, Buckner's other frontline brigade, Wood's, advanced along with Brown's and Jones's orphaned brigades from Anderson's division, moving from the vicinity of the Webb House toward the high ground above Doctor's Creek as it approached Walker's Bend. Archeological evidence suggests that Semple's section of rifled three-inch guns traveled after them but did not catch up immediately. The advance continued without incident for a while, but suddenly the unexpected happened. Without warning, Wood's skirmishers encountered Federals where there should have been none. The 10th Ohio of Lytle's brigade, still skirmishing in front of Rousseau's division, had crossed the creek there and with enthusiasm had penetrated so far into the woods on the Confederate right that Lytle's aides could not find them to deliver recall orders. A few random shots drew Wood's men to the right, across Jones's front and toward a prominent hill. The unanticipated sound of gunfire also attracted both Buckner and Bragg, the latter having ridden to a point east of the creek behind Buckner's advance as the movement began.[35] Concerned, Bragg ordered Wood to veer even more to the right and seize the heights "immediately, or else that the enemy would be firing down upon you in five minutes." Moving at the double-quick with skirmishers and sharp-shooters to the front, Wood drove away the blue-coated skirmishers and seized the hill in ten minutes time. While they did so, Bragg ordered Jones to fill the gap created between Wood's brigade and the rest of Buckner's division.

Surmounting the hilltop, Wood saw the same ominous scene across the valley that had stunned Bushrod Johnson: two of Rousseau's three brigades in all their martial glory. Because of a northeasterly turn in Doctor's Creek, Wood actually stood farther from Rousseau than Johnson, but to the former the enemy nonetheless seemed close indeed. As his aide later wrote, "at that time the enemy—moving obliquely from right to left across the field in front of us—were almost if not quite within point blank gunshot range."[36] A more sober observer, Col. Mark Lowery of the 32nd Mississippi Infantry, esti-mated the distance to be six hundred yards.[37]

Whatever the range, Wood knew the formidable Federal line meant trouble, especially with an alerted Federal battery, Cyrus Loomis's, appar-ently preparing to bear down on his men. As Semple's rifled guns had not yet caught up, Wood sent an aide to Polk with an urgent request for help. Polk responded by dispatching Capt. William Carnes's battery from Brig. Gen. Daniel S. Donelson's brigade to support Wood's infantry. Wood was lucky to get Carnes, an 1861 graduate of the Naval Academy, for only an accident had made him available. During Cheatham's movement from left to right, Carnes had become delayed when one of his teams, "in passing through a big gate one of my pieces was carelessly driven so as to run the right wheel against the gate post." Unwilling to wait, Donelson's lead infantrymen tore down a sec-tion of fence and kept moving, leaving Carnes stranded. Polk's aide ran across the battery just as it extricated the piece from the fence and dispatched it to the left. Two regiments from Donelson's brigade, the 8th and 51st Tennes-see, remained as well, and they were diverted as Carnes's support. Going into battery on the high knoll Wood occupied, his back to the forest but an open valley before him, Carnes calmly estimated the distance to Loomis's battery while others cut fuses in preparation. Once ready, he opened fire.[38]

Across the no-man's-land west of Doctor's Creek, Rousseau and his Federals reacted to the sudden flurry of musketry with surprise and even disbelief, for by then Cheatham's dust clouds had convinced Rousseau that Bragg was in full retreat. While Carnes drew careful aim, some "fifty or sixty" officers, including Rousseau, Gay, Jackson, Lytle, and several regimental officers, had gathered around Loomis's battery north of the Squire Bottom House to get a closer look at the woods and hills east of the creek, and, according to at least one witness, circulate a bottle of liquor. All were convinced that the Confederates were in a full retreat, and the mood thus was light.[39] One of Rousseau's aides, the same Harrison Millard who lived in style with his wife in Huntsville, remembered that his chief and Jackson were in particularly good moods, and had been joking ever since Jackson came up at 10 A.M. in advance of his division. "'Well, General,'" Rousseau had asked jokingly of Jackson when the latter appeared, "'how do you like this kind of life?'"

"'Oh, it just suits me,'" Jackson replied, "'this sloshing 'round—this constant excitement of being always on the go.'"

While the brass kidded each other and passed the bottle, Millard grew concerned. Riding forward and presumably northward to the creek with *New York Herald* correspondent W. F. G. Shanks, Millard saw a Confederate soldier lying in the woods, apparently one of Wood's men wounded in the skirmish with the 10th Ohio. "I asked him what he was doing there," Millard remembered, "and he replied that he was wounded, and had been left there by his regiment, which only a short time before had gone on. We were greatly surprised at our near proximity to the enemy." The aide rode back to warn Rousseau, but the general refused to take the report seriously. "'Oh bosh!'" Rousseau exclaimed, "'it is impossible. There is no one anywhere near here.'"

"'Well,' said I, (looking through my field-glass), 'please look there. What is that?'"

Millard pointed to a body of Confederate soldiers in the distance, probably members of Johnson's brigade passing through a clearing near the Chatham House.[40] Lieutenant Landrum of the veteran 2nd Ohio Infantry, a First Manassas regiment, saw them too. Landrum wrote home that he "saw a man *pop* out of the woods, and then another, and another." Landrum warned Rousseau that he had spotted rebel skirmishers in the woods opposite them, and Rousseau took Landrum's glass to see for himself. But by then they were out of sight. Convinced that Landrum had seen the 10th Ohio, he stubbornly concluded again, "'No, they are our own men.'"

"'If so,'" the lieutenant dissented, "'they were dressed in "Butternut" clothes.' After looking a long time," he continued, "I was perfectly satisfied of it, but could not convince anyone else of the fact." A new dust cloud rising at the point where Landrum had seen the skirmishers did not add credence to his warning, nor did the sight of "the wheels of some kind of carriage"— most likely a section of Darden's battery on the hill opposite them. Buell's overconfidence seemingly had filtered down through the entire I Corps command structure.[41]

If Landrum and Millard seemed to be Cassandras, now so did Ebenezer

Gay. Watching a dust cloud rise in the north, concerned that it indicated arriving Confederate reinforcements, the cavalry chief remarked to Rousseau that "the enemy were in view again." Then one of Gay's aides, still jumpy from the fight for Bull Run, exclaimed, "Look yonder! There's fifty thousand of them!" Unimpressed, the general rode over to Captain Hotchkiss, took his glass, and "was putting it to my eye [when] they opened some two or three batteries and there was a rapid and accurate firing of shells." "Now you know where they are," Rousseau cried out.[42]

"All were then convinced that they were Rebels," George Landrum later noted with undisguised I-told-you-so satisfaction, "and such a skedaddling to get out of range I never saw before . . . *all* scattered in every direction. I could not help laughing; at the same time I felt as though I would be safer a little further off."[43]

S. F. Horrall of the 42nd Indiana, still down in the tunnel-like bed of Doctor's Creek with his regiment, remembered the moment differently. "The first intimation we had of the immediate presence of the rebels," wrote Horrall, "was a shot from their cannon, which passed directly over the heads of the field and staff officers, cutting limbs and branches away, which fell with a crash upon 'headquarters' mess.' The next was one aimed lower, which knocked away a stack of guns."[44] A comrade wrote home: "shot and shell flew thick and fast over our heads. Very many of the enemy's shell burst over the heads of our men while grape fell thick all around. Loud thundered the rebel artillery and promptly was it replied to by that brave officer, Captain Loomis."[45]

To counter the enemy artillery and any unexpected attack that might follow, Rousseau first called forward the rest of Loomis's battery and then Capt. Peter Simonson's 5th Battery, Indiana Light Artillery, attached to Harris's brigade, to join Hotchkiss and Loomis in battling the Rebel guns.[46] "'Captain Loomis,'" a Cincinnati reporter asked as the gunner rode back toward the Russell House to retrieve the rest of his battery, "'don't you intend to reply to that fire?'"

"'Yes,' said he, 'I'll fetch em!'"[47] He spoke too soon. While Carnes's fire from the first fell effectively, particularly among the infantry, Loomis's and Simonson's rifled guns at first shot high, "making a great noise with bursting shells in the tree tops," according to Carnes, "but really doing no harm to any of my men." Indeed, shells from Loomis's guns have been found six hundred yards behind Carnes's position. Hotchkiss in contrast could not reach Carnes. It did not take long, however, for the Federals' superior rifled guns to find their range, particularly Simonson's James rifles. Exploding shells from those powerful tubes drew increasingly closer to Carnes's outnumbered and exposed battery. Fortunately for Carnes's Tennessee gunners and Wood's men, at that juncture at least two additional Confederate batteries opened up: Capt. Charles Lumsden's Alabama Battery of Jones's brigade, and the section of Calvert's Arkansas Battery commanded by Lt. Thomas J. Key, which still was attached to Cleburne's brigade. Darden's battery and perhaps Semple's detached section joined in as well. Wrote Carnes: "these helped to divide the fire from the enemy in time to prevent my getting the concentrated fire of the . . . Federal batteries after they got well down to business."

The artillery duel continued for nearly an hour, the deafening booming heard as far away as Danville. Local civilians hid in cellars or, like the Russells, took to the woods to escape the cross fire. At its height, Cheatham dispatched Capt. Thomas J. Stanford's Mississippi Battery, equipped with rifled guns, to replace Carnes's less-effective short-range smoothbores. As Stanford wheeled his pieces into place, Carnes withdrew behind the heights to repair damage to his harness and replace fallen horses.[48] The Mississippians soon discovered the dangers of their position, as they were raked with effective fire. "The Yankees had perfect range on us," wrote gunner George Jones. "Had one of our ammunition chests to explode. Pitt McCall and Charles Boycroft killed and several wounded before we could fire a gun."[49] Still, "we fired for one half hour," John Euclid Magee added, "doing great execution." After a while, Stanford shifted his guns roughly a hundred yards south to gain more cover.[50]

Aside from horses and a handful of artillerymen, the Federal barrage caused relatively few casualties among the Confederates hugging the earth on the east bank. One notable exception was General Wood, who went down when his mount, either hit or frightened by Federal fire, threw him. It was a painfully familiar experience for Wood. At Shiloh, a wounded horse had thrown him and dragged him through the abandoned Federal camps, leaving him senseless for three hours. Now, something similar had happened again. Confusion inevitably followed. Although Col. Mark Lowrey of the 32nd Mississippi, a former minister who had served in Mexico and the senior regimental colonel, took command, many of the men now under his charge never realized it, and indeed remained convinced long after the war that they had fought the rest of the battle piecemeal without a brigade commander.[51]

Across the field, beneath the screaming, flying shells and antipersonnel canister thrown up by the batteries, Col. William Lytle struggled to arrange his infantry to receive the now-anticipated Confederate attack. A native Cincinnatian and son of a Democratic congressman with strong Kentucky ties, the urbane, thirty-six-year-old as a youth had yearned to attend West Point but did not because of his parents' opposition. Turning instead to the law and Democratic Party politics, Lytle won further renown as a poet. The itch to be a soldier never quite disappeared, however, and when the war began he formed the 10th Ohio and led it at the Battle of Carnifex Ferry in what became West Virginia.[52] Perryville, however, would prove the first major test for the Byronic, hard-drinking Lytle.

While the 42nd Indiana hunkered down in the dry bed of Doctor's Creek and the 10th Ohio reappeared at last and fell back up the ridge to the safety of Loomis's guns, Lytle dispatched the 3rd Ohio Infantry to form a line of battle to the right of the Mackville Road and roughly parallel to the creek. The Ohioans went into line behind the stone fence that ran along the brow of the hill behind Squire Bottom's house. Near the center and just in front of the regiment's formation stood Bottom's wooden barn, recently stuffed with wheat and oats. Before them lay a partially harvested cornfield as well as the house and yard. A hundred yards farther back, the rest of the brigade formed a second battle line straddling the Mackville Road. The 15th Kentucky Infantry formed up behind the 3rd Ohio there, while to its right the 88th Indiana Infantry extended Lytle's reserve line down a slight valley. Farther to the right, Gay arrayed his dismounted cavalry so as to occupy the area between the two present corps.[53]

While Lytle arranged his brigade under fire, anticipating an infantry assault momentarily, Rousseau galloped back up the Mackville Road toward the Russell House to bring up Harris's brigade. While Harris's men waited there, a few shells had fallen among his regiments, doing little damage other than wounding the pride of a group of officers who had scrambled from a stricken and falling tree as their men laughed in amusement. Together, Harris and Rousseau now moved the brigade forward and placed it in two lines on the higher ground to the left of Lytle and the road. The 10th Wisconsin Infantry and 38th Indiana Infantry formed a line in a cornfield to support Simonson's battery, the 33rd Ohio Infantry moved forward as skirmishers, and the remainder of the brigade—the 2nd Ohio Infantry and 94th Ohio Infantry—formed on a prominent ridge to the rear. Expecting an attack momentarily, the men lay down in the open field to await the bombardment.[54] "We had just got into position," wrote Frank M. Phelps of the 10th Wisconsin, "when the solid shot & shell commenced to whistle through the air over our heads but every shot we could see that the rebels were getting a better range on us & pretty soon the balls commenced falling thick and fast around us. I spoke of one boy in Co. 'A' having half his head taken off & another in Co. E being hit in the brest." Shaken by the accuracy and noise of the Confederate guns, Phelps convinced himself that the enemy somehow had brought up thirty-two–pounders against his brigade.[55]

For the next hour, "a continuous roar of cannon, intermingled with the screeching of shells and the whistling of balls" created "a pandemonium of discord and terror" in Rousseau's ranks. As among the Confederates, however, casualties were surprisingly few. "Occasionally," wrote the *New York Herald's* Shanks, "a poor fellow would be struck down by a passing ball, and more frequently an exploding shell would make a gap in the ranks, and stretch a dozen strong men, mutilated and in agony, on the ground." Still, "our loss was but trifling in this duel; scarcely a dozen men were killed and certainly not over fifty wounded." As the fight went on, the reporter added, fewer infantrymen and more artillerymen fell as the Confederates improved their aim.[56]

A war correspondent from a Cincinnati paper concurred with his colleague's assessment: "A few of the men belonging to these brigades were killed and wounded by the fire from the rebel cannon, but generally the shot passed harmlessly over their heads." One exception was Lytle's orderly, a Cincinnatian named Robb, who endured the barrage with the 3rd Ohio. Robb died when a cannonball "struck him in the side, passed entirely through his body, and buried itself in the ground beyond. He died instantly, and almost without a gasp. Not a man of the regiment he was with, in this stage of the battle, was either killed or wounded."[57]

George Landrum, having fallen back to the vicinity of Squire Bottom's barn, described the scene there: "Suddenly a shell came whizzing over us and exploded almost under our horses' feet. Then another came so near Capt. Grover's head that he could feel the wind rush by, and a third took off the corner of the roof of the barn over our heads. . . . Our horses were jumping and plunging about almost uncontrollable, and as it was no use keeping our position as mere spectators, we skedaddled again."[58] At length, Lytle's front line could take no more, and the brigade commander ordered his men to abandon the crest of the ridge and fall back to its foot, out of the line of fire.[59]

As 1:30 P.M. approached, the gunfire on both sides slackened and "a dull, dead calm" descended.[60] After firing rapidly during the previous hour with what historian Matthew Switlik has condemned as "an excess of enthusiasm," Loomis, who had run out of long-range ammunition, announced that he must fall back to the Russell House to replenish his caissons. As he withdrew with permission from Rousseau—but without informing Lytle—the 10th Ohio advanced to the crest of the hill to hold it. When the Confederate fire stopped soon thereafter, a cheer ran down Rousseau's line, and Simonson fired one last shot to claim the last word.[61] When no gray lines appeared on the horizon, many men concluded that the gunnery's purpose had been merely to cover the hoped-for enemy withdrawal. "After that time, the firing ceased," wrote George Landrum, "except now and then a musket could be heard; and I supposed they had brought the Battery there to cover their retreat, as I had lost all faith in their fighting us."[62]

Still marooned in the dry bed of Doctor's Creek, apparently forgotten by Lytle, the isolated men of the 42nd Indiana also welcomed the odd and sudden silence. Major James Maynard Shanklin calmly began sharing a sweet potato with one of his captains as the latter remarked, "'Loomis must have dismounted some of their guns; they have quit firing.'"

Shanklin jokingly replied, "'suppose a couple of regiments of cavalry come down on us through this ravine, wouldn't we be in a nice fix.' We talked several minutes in this way," Shanklin continued, "not dreaming that our conjectures were soon to be realized. The truth is our Generals never dreamed any thing of the kind either, or we should have never have been put down into such a slaughter trap as we were in."[63]

FORWARD

AT 11:00 A.M., JUST AS HARDEE'S WING BEGAN MOVING WEST TOWARD Buell's Federal army, Frank Cheatham's division pulled out of line on the Confederate left and marched rapidly toward the army's extreme right, heading for the critical gap Bragg had located at Walker's Bend. Spearheaded by the brigade commanded by sixty-one-year-old planter and West Pointer Brig. Gen. Daniel Donelson, the late president Andrew Jackson's aging nephew, Cheatham's soldiers jogged through town on the Lebanon-Harrodsburg road as far as Bragg's headquarters at the Crawford House. There they turned off the main road to the west and marched down a narrow, wooded path, past a rare and precious supply of potable water in the springs of Crawford Cave, to the dry bed of the Chaplin River. After crossing the sun-baked ditch that until recently had cradled that waterway, Cheatham's men followed the road north as it snaked along the west bank of the Chaplin until they passed behind and beyond Wood's brigade. At that point, as the Chaplin began its leisurely turn to the west, the column most likely left the road and took a shortcut across gently sloping meadows and fields directly toward the infamous gap.

Deceived by the rolling nature of the landscape and distracted by their own overconfidence, the Federals across the valley either remained completely unaware of Cheatham's flanking march or misinterpreted what few clues they possessed. Both Cyrus Loomis and Lovell Rousseau had observed the dust clouds Cheatham's column produced as it shifted position, but like others dismissed them as evidence of a much-desired Confederate retreat. Still, Cheatham's hurried march was not without incident. When still a mile from the designated jumping-off point, stray cannonballs and shells from the nascent artillery battle began falling in and around the column. Few casualties resulted from those projectiles, but the rare exceptions were grisly indeed. Stoddard Johnston remembered a Federal cannonball beheading a man who had left the column to scoop a drink of water from the creek. Such grisly deaths, coupled with the roar of the guns and the sounds of exploding shells, could not help but heighten the division's apprehension.

At length, the column reached the vicinity of Jacob Goodknight's home, tucked into the curving south bank of the Chaplin near where the river again briefly turned north to complete the thumb of Walker's Bend. Cheatham and Polk quickly formed the attack force into a column of brigades. Donelson's brigade would lead the assault at 1 P.M., followed at 150-yard intervals by Brig. Gen. Alexander P. Stewart's and Brig. Gen. George Earl Maney's brigades. Every attacking infantry regiment in the column save one, Maney's 41st Georgia, hailed from Tennessee. Cheatham now dispatched Stanford's battery to take over for Carnes, hoping that Stanford's superior rifled arms would drive the annoying enemy batteries farther to the rear than Carnes's smoothbores could, and thus ease the pressure mounting on his waiting infantry. At the same time, doctors commandeered the Goodknight House for a field hospital and began tending the first unlucky casualties.[1]

A strong, steady wind blew up in the men's faces from the west, scattering dust and autumn leaves. As 1 P.M. neared, Polk completed his final preparations to send Cheatham forward as ordered. Just a few minutes before the hour, however, John Wharton rode up to the bishop with a disturbing report that gave him pause. Wharton's troopers originally had trailed the three infantry brigades during the movement toward the Goodknight House. When the artillery fight began, Wharton first led his men farther to the Confederate rear in order to get out of harm's way, and then out onto a wooded ridge on the extreme Union left, beyond Wilson's Creek. From there they could keep an eye on the Federal flank Bragg had targeted. While there on the ridge, Wharton discovered a previously unaccounted-for column of Federal infantry moving up the Mackville Road to reinforce the Federal left.

His report to Polk regarding that unanticipated column startled the bishop. To attack now as ordered, Polk reasoned, might well lead to mass suicide. The Federal column could hit him in his own flank just as he tore into the enemy's.[2] Better to delay yet again, he reasoned, for "our chances of success were greater against the line in my front even when re-enforced than it would be by attacking it as it stood and exposing my flank to the approaching force, [thus] I awaited until the re-enforcements got into position." Thus, for the second time that day, Polk disobeyed Bragg and postponed an ordered attack. He would wait for the rest of the Yankees to come up into line before he attacked them.[3]

Having made his decision, Polk somehow never bothered to inform Bragg about the newly sighted column of blue-clad soldiers. Perhaps he did not want to risk another angry confrontation like the one that morning at the Crawford House. Then again, communication never was Polk's strong suit anyway, as the previous week had conclusively proven. Bragg nervously watched as the hands of his watch marked one o'clock and then waited anxiously for the sounds of musketry. Noticing none, he dispatched first one staff officer and then another to order Polk to begin the assault. At 1:30 P.M., still with no answer or explanation forthcoming and the artillery duel petering out, a furious Bragg rode over to find out for himself why Polk had again disobeyed. He arrived just as the bishop sent Wharton out to locate and sweep around the Federal flank one more time. Only then did Polk proceed to explain what had happened. Hopefully, he added, the new units had taken their places and the way was clear for the tardy infantry assault to begin.[4]

Bragg went along with Polk's decision to hold back. Indeed, he had no choice but to concur. However, he made one thing very clear: He wanted no more delays, the attack must begin as soon as possible. A march north to Versailles still beckoned that evening. Bowing to the bishop's very real concerns, he acceded to Polk's slightly modified orders. Instead of driving straight ahead into the gap as originally envisioned, Cheatham's division would first cross the dry riverbed, then double-quick a few hundred yards farther north into Walker's Bend and attack the enemy from there. By shifting farther north, a flank attack would be assured despite any added Federal presence on the heights beyond—assuming, of course, that no more Federals showed up to extend their line even more.

Although it all looked sensible on a map, as is so often the case when leaders have not walked the ground themselves, Walker's Bend proved a nightmare for the men of Cheatham's division who had to make the orders a reality. While the ground ascended more or less gently from their original position south of the river's bend through generally open fields up to the bluff, the wooded, tangled bank just within the bend was nearly vertical. In some places the sheer face of the bluff reached a height of from twenty to fifty feet. A rough farm path leading from the Walker House in the center of the bend to the top of the bluff, unnamed at the time but long after the war improved and named the Dug Road, would help some lucky infantrymen surmount the natural wall. Unfortunately, most of the others faced a strenuous, taxing climb even before they sighted the enemy.[5]

As Cheatham's infantry entered Walker's Bend and established their lines, Wharton's horsemen formed into a column of fours and thundered north along the so-called County Road, the Goodknight's and Walker's connector north to the village of Dixville. Wharton intended to make a counterclockwise circle around the Federal flank, take one last observation, and screen Cheatham's assault from any enemy skirmishers. Once across a wooden bridge spanning the deep, dry channel of the Chaplin, Wharton ordered "left front into line." Five lines of gray-clad cavalry galloped first northward and then, reaching a fork, to the west, along the ridges that roughly paralleled Wilson's Creek as it meandered westward.[6]

The Federal troops Wharton had observed belonged to Col. George Webster's brigade of James Jackson's division, moving up to bolster the line of McCook's I Corps. Returning from his meeting with Buell, who had ordered him to advance a reconnaissance force to the river, McCook rode back to the Russell House sometime before one o'clock only to discover that Rousseau already

Figure 10.1. The bluffs above the Chaplin River, as seen from near the "Dug Road" in Walker's Bend today. Photograph courtesy John Walsh Jr.

had undertaken just such a movement without approval in his absence. Rousseau himself was nowhere to be found, having finally ridden off himself to search for Starkweather's lagging brigade after several aides were unable to do so. Meanwhile, Loomis's and Simonson's batteries continued firing into the eastern hills. Before McCook rode away, Buell's chief of staff warned him that intelligence reports indicated that Hardee was in Perryville with two divisions.[7] The corps commander, seeing no infantry across the river at that moment, "ordered no more ammunition to be wasted."[8]

As the cannons' booming ceased, McCook quickly turned to aligning Jackson's division, which had finally arrived at the Dixville Crossroads with Webster's brigade in front. Webster's weary, hungry men first heard the foreboding cannon fire from miles away. As a result, their officers had advanced their unbloodied charges slowly behind a screen of skirmishers, retarding their arrival by as much as an hour according to one of Jackson's aides. This annoyed the division commander immensely. Once Webster's men reached the rear of Harris's brigade, occasional stray balls and shells falling around them, Jackson ordered the brigade to move into line to the right of the road, behind Rousseau's division. Brigadier General William R. Terrill's brigade would form on their left, Jackson's largely rookie division thus creating a second, reserve line behind Rousseau's veterans. For the moment, however,

Terrill's men remained to the rear, separated from Webster's brigade by a tangle of ammunition wagons and ambulances.[9]

On the high ridge dominated by the Russell House, Webster ordered Capt. Samuel J. Harris's 19th Battery, Indiana Light Artillery, to unlimber in front and well to the left of the Mackville Road. Taking advantage of the commanding heights, the battery could overlook the undulating country below and retard any enemy advance against the Federal line. Apparently with Webster's permission, Harris promptly renewed the artillery fight on a smaller scale, neither men willing to miss the opportunity to lob a few long-range shells at the enemy. A veteran of the Mexican War's famed Ringgold Battery, Sam Harris was a tough regular who deplored what he lamented as "babyism" in his rookie volunteer gunners. If true, they began to grow up quickly, for a Confederate battery soon answered with a few rounds of its own, one cannonball nearly killing Jackson as it rolled within a foot of him.[10]

Meanwhile, Webster dispatched the 98th Ohio Infantry up to the right of the Harris's battery to support it, but "owing to the nature of the ground it was found impossible for them to form in line of battle." He quickly improvised, shifting his brigade more to the left and rear of Sam Harris's battery, so that his men could lie down in the relative safety offered by the western slope of the Russell House ridge. Indeed, aside from the 80th Indiana Infantry, which eventually would move into line to the right of the battery, Webster placed all of his command in a second line to the rear of Harris's guns, and to the left rather than the right of the road. Because of the topography, Webster's resulting line ran at an angle to Leonard Harris's farther toward the front, rather than parallel to it. Webster's and Harris lines drew closest together at their northern termini, near the tenant farm of young Mary Jane Bottom Gibson, Sam Bottom's sister and the recent widow of Milton Gibson. At that point, the so-called Widow Gibson House and farm, only about a hundred yards separated the two lines. Harris's battery anchored that position. As the lines stretched to the south, the width between them steadily increased.[11]

Anticipating their first battle, many of Webster's men waited nervously behind the rail fence that separated them from the large cornfield below. None worried more than the new recruits of the 121st Ohio Infantry, for about four hundred of them went into battle knowing that the old Prussian muskets they carried were useless except as clubs.[12] Others felt exuberance. A comrade of Joseph Glezen of the 80th Indiana Infantry asked, "'Isn't this terrible?' I replied," wrote Glezen, "that it was really sublime. He said he was unable to discover anything sublime about it." That feeling must have deepened when, just at that moment, a cannonball slammed to earth, knocking off Glezen's hat and then killing the man lying on his other side, ending any discussion of sublimity. Taken aback momentarily, Glezen rolled the ball farther down the hill, afraid that it might explode. Under fire, the rest of Webster's men continued to wait for whatever sublimity would come next.[13]

Webster was now up and in line, but not where McCook originally wanted him. Seat-of-the-pants improvisation continued on the Federal left as McCook next decided what to do with Terrill's brigade, still waiting on the Mackville Road near the Dixville Crossroads. Should he place the brigade in a reserve line behind Rousseau as he had originally intended, or instead use the brigade up front to extend Webster's line further to the left, taking full advantage of the terrain? Leonard Harris and Capt. Beverly D. Williams, McCook's guide, argued for a third option. They insisted that the ideal position for the brigade lay a few hundred yards farther along the ridge to the northeast, on Harris's left. At the northern end, they counseled, the high ground of the ridge rose to an imposing crest on a high, open knob overlooking Walker's Bend to the east and a deep valley to the north. Riding over to the area they had indicated to see for himself, a delighted McCook found the spot and immediately agreed that troops placed there would command the Chaplin River and especially the pools of water sighted in the river's bend six hundred yards below. The site was ideal ground, save for the fact that it threw any troops occupying it would be well forward of Harris's and Lytle's line, not to mention Webster's. As fate would have it, those troops would belong to the corps' least-experienced brigade. McCook, however, could not pass up occupying such imposing ground.

To secure the Open Knob, McCook ordered two companies from the 33rd Ohio Infantry of Harris's brigade into the woods below and to the right, where they would join skirmishers from the 2nd Ohio already out there and feel for Rebels on the ridge above Walker's Bend. He then sent for Jackson and Terrill. McCook told Terrill that he wanted him to occupy the ridge from the Open Knob south toward the Widow Gibson's house. He further instructed Terrill to place his artillery battery on the knob and make sure that it had strong support. Once Terrill had accomplished that, McCook told him to advance a line of skirmishers down to the river to further secure the position.[14]

Assuring McCook that his men already were on their way up, Terrill promised his corps commander that he would obey. "I'll do it, and that's my water," Terrill avowed.[15] He had much to prove that day. A Virginia native, graduate of the West Point class of 1853, and later a mathematics instructor at the academy, Terrill crushed his father in 1861 with his decision to fight in Union blue instead of Confederate gray like his brother James and cousin J. E. B. Stuart. The thought of one son killing another so upset Terrill's mother that she secured a transfer to the West for her older son so that her two boys might never meet on a battlefield. He went on to fight with distinction as an artillery battery commander at Shiloh. During a critical Confederate assault that day, facing the brigades of George Maney and Preston Smith, Terrill held his ground until so many of his men fell that he began loading and firing one of the pieces himself. After his Shiloh heroics, Bull Nelson called Terrill's regular battery the best in the army. Serving again with Nelson at Rich-

Figure 10.2. Brig. Gen. William Terrill. Photograph courtesy Brian Pohanka and the U.S. Army Military History Institute.

mond, Terrill received his general's star after that fight at the behest of Cruft and Jackson.[16]

Back in Louisville and in command of a brigade, Terrill did little to endear himself to the new volunteers he led. His participation in Jackson's infamous Louisville review remained a bone of contention weeks later, and some men frankly hoped to see both generals fall in battle. "Our Brig. Gen. Terril is a tall light haired man with a coarse voice," Bliss Morse of the 105th Ohio Infantry wrote home, "which makes him quite a target for the boys to mock at. He loves good liquors and beef for his table. . . . The boys rather dislike him since that *review* down in Louisville. Some of them swore they would take his life."[17]

Terrill had one more formidable enemy in the army. For years, Phil Sheridan had despised Terrill more than any foot soldier ever could. Since their West Point days, when a nasty brawl between the two cadets resulted in the younger Sheridan's yearlong suspension from the corps, Sheridan had abhorred the Virginian. Then, the evening before the battle, Sheridan encountered him along with Terrill's friends Jackson and Webster. Beneath the clear night sky, Sheridan later claimed, the two men ended the feud. The evening that followed passed pleasantly. When the topic of death in battle came up, Sheridan remembered, Terrill expressed confidence and assured the others of their chances. Mathematically, he explained that the probability of his death remained small. The chances of all of them dying, he added, were next to impossible.[18]

Now, a little before 1:30 P.M. the following day, Terrill began moving his men toward the Open Knob as McCook wanted. He first ordered forward the 123rd Illinois Infantry and Col. Theophilius Garrard's detachment, the latter composed of one company each drawn from the 7th and 32nd Kentucky and 3rd Tennessee Regiments, to secure the position and then advance companies as skirmishers to the left of the 33rd Ohio. Terrill then ordered up his artillery. Like the rest of his brigade, Lt. Charles Parsons's eight-gun battery was infinitely raw, having been formed at Terrill's request in Louisville just weeks before from among the new recruits of his various infantry regiments, particularly the 105th Ohio. It quickly became the former gunner's pet project, if not his obsession. Armed with five smoothbore brass Napoleons, two other twelve-pound howitzers, and one Parrott rifle, the battery had rapidly come together under the tutelage of its captain, a West Pointer and regular artilleryman who, like his brigade commander, also had won acclaim at Shiloh.[19] Parsons "was a man of singular purity and sincerity," one of his subordinates later wrote, "an able and accomplished officer . . . and in every respect a man of most admirable qualities and character."[20]

Now, Parsons's men and horses moved toward the exposed position on the Open Knob. "They were in fine fettle," Albion Tourgée remembered, "and one did not wonder at the flush of pride on the gallant Parsons' face as the guns filed past him and took their way along a narrow country road toward the left front. The fire of battle was in his eye and one guessed that the trot the bugle sounded was less because of any emergency in the order he had received than of his own impatience for the fray."[21] With Parsons on the way, Terrill then called for the rest of his brigade, the 80th Illinois Infantry and the 105th Ohio. All of the men were tired, hungry, and thirsty, but Terrill sent orders for them to push ahead the roughly three-quarters of a mile distance as rapidly as possible.[22]

His dispositions complete, McCook prepared to leave the Open Knob. Everything was falling into place, and there was little indication that there would be any trouble the rest of the day. "The only enemy in sight at that time," he remembered, "was about 400 or 500 cavalry on the other side of Chaplin River."[23] Unable to fathom that he was about to come under attack, McCook sanguinely concluded that Wharton's galloping line of gray-clad horsemen had to be up to nothing more than "threatening my train in the rear."[24]

To the rear of Terrill's designated position on the Open Knob, John Starkweather's frustrated brigade finally reached the front as well. It had been a long, confusing morning for them. Realizing that his men worried that they once again would be unable to prove their mettle in battle, Col. Henry A. Hambright of the 79th Pennsylvania Infantry had called out to his men in Mackville as they prepared to march, "Boys, you have longed to meet the enemy on the battle-field, and you will have a chance to-day, or do without water, as the enemy holds the spring that we will have to encamp at." The men cheered, many crying out "a fight and water we will have."[25]

As they moved out, the rumble of cannons at Peters Hill ominously began to shake the earth "like distant thunder far of towards the East among the hills," veteran sergeant John Henry Otto of the green 21st Wisconsin wrote. "Some of the boys thought of a regular, good sized thunder storm and jokingly remarked that would settle the dust and give us pure water. But not the sign of a cloud could be detected on the horizon. Well did I know the meaning of all but I kept my peace. Soon enough the men would know the real cause."[26]

The column moved as quickly as possible, the men aching to catch up with the rest of the division. Some companies were so anxious to "see the elephant" that regimental formations began to break down as the men surged forward in anticipation.[27] "'Free admission to the circus, boys!'" called out one man. "'McCook is tickling Braggs hinder,'" responded another. The men's enthusiasm soon began to get the better of them, however, for the growing heat, coupled with haste, quickly produced fatigue and a dire need for water. Indeed, coming up from the other side of Mackville where they had spent the night protecting the supply train, the soldiers of the 21st Wisconsin grew parched even before they reached the village. John Otto, who had made many a march while a soldier in the Prussian army, begged his captain to send out a half-dozen men with canteens to find water now that the regiment brought up the choking, dusty rear of the advancing column. When that officious officer refused, Otto angrily took a dozen canteens and stormed off to look for it himself.

Reaching a small house a half-mile off the road, Otto entered and discovered a man and woman, "both smoking a corncob pipe, with just enough raggs dangling about them to cover the greater part of their hide. Three dirty, almost nacked urchins of about the same size sat digging holes in the clay floor." The family gave Otto a drink from a jug, but when he asked if any more water could be found nearby, the man of the house "shook his head sadly and replied: 'I reckon not stranger; been as it is so dry right smart along, the well is gin out this jer long time, but I calkerlate you mout get some in that that gully.'" He pointed toward a ravine. Otto gave each child a hardtack cracker and strode off. As he walked away the man called after him: "'Say stranger! Mought you b'long to the yanks crawling o'er that ther pike yonder al this morn?'"

Otto replied that he did.

"'Waal, Stranger, I used ter think a heap on Bragg aforn this, but been as it is, an he cum along hair thater day but what wud he do as he sent a lot sojers hiar who toted my ceow along an I have nary live beest of my own. I reckon you uns is spilling for a tussel with that thar Bragg and I tell you stranger, if you uns get a mite chance mak it blazing hot for em, hotter'n hell.'"

Filling the canteens at a spring, the sergeant returned to the road a half-hour later only to find his regiment long gone. Anxious to catch up, he began to stride cross-country toward Mackville. As he entered town, he noticed stragglers already dropping back. Miles up the road, another congregation of stragglers attempted to steal the canteens, but Otto scared them off by leveling his rifle at the men. Later he laughed at them, for only new men would assume that he carried a loaded rifle. Finally, Otto encountered men from his own company. In the road ahead, west of Perryville, their ambulances and ammunition wagons sat halted, and beyond them he finally found the 21st Wisconsin, "the arms stacked, the boys squatted on the ground chewing hard tack and raw bacon."[28]

Leaving John Otto and many others behind, Starkweather had moved as hastily as possible in Jackson's rear. Three miles from the field the latter's column ground to a halt, creating another traffic jam. Unwilling to dawdle in the crowded road and wait for Jackson to disperse while the sounds of artillery fire up ahead suggested a battle already in progress, Starkweather decided on his own to get to the front the quickest way possible. That, he concluded, meant leaving the road and taking off cross-country across fields and through woods. Unaware that the balance of his division lay directly ahead, he chose to go left. The column began to move at roughly 1:15 P.M. Eventually, most of the brigade—the 21st Wisconsin remained in the rear, the last to move—came to a halt on the long ridge to Webster's left and rear. Starkweather promptly dispatched a messenger to Rousseau to inform him of his actions and position.[29]

Rousseau greeted the message with relief. Starkweather's brigade, he later wrote with undisguised admiration, had occupied "the very spot where it was most needed." That was not quite true. Starkweather had the 24th Illinois Infantry and 79th Pennsylvania Infantry Regiments, both largely composed of native German speakers, in the front line.[30] He also already had positioned Capt. David C. Stone's Battery A, Kentucky Light Artillery. Stone was a rigid and unpopular disciplinarian whom Simon Buckner drove from the Kentucky State Guard in 1861 for his open Unionism and refusal to follow orders. Starkweather had turned to position his other battery, Capt. Asahel K. Bush's 4th Battery, Indiana Light Artillery, when Wharton appeared on the Benton Road. Using his two Parrott rifles, Stone fired off fifteen or twenty well-placed shots before the horsemen disappeared into woods, presumably driven off by the fire but in fact merely following the road as it took a sharp turn. Archeological evidence suggests that Bush got at least one shot off as well. Starkweather, McCook, Jackson, and Terrill on the

Open Knob stopped to admire the Federal gunnery. While his gun crews fired at the enemy horsemen, the rest of Starkweather's hungry, footsore, and desperately thirsty men wearily stacked their arms, sat down on the ground, and began to eat their dinners.[31]

As Wharton's horsemen disappeared into the distance at about 1:45 P.M., Rousseau galloped onto the scene. The men stood and cheered as the general rode up and down their lines waving his hat. Starkweather remained at the rear of the brigade, icily watching his superior's grandstanding. "'Why don't you tell the General that he is out of place?'" he complained to Rousseau aide Harrison Millard.[32] Their relationship could only have soured further in the next few minutes. Despite his later praise, Rousseau at the time did not like what he saw of Starkweather's dispositions, and he quickly pulled rank and altered them. Roughly a hundred yards farther forward was the northern extension of the same long ridge that Lytle and Harris occupied, one Rousseau must have ridden across earlier. At the northern end of that ridge, a junction with yet another crest formed a right angle of high ground overlooking the Benton Road from the west, the northernmost ridge angling diagonally toward the front. Beyond that, in a narrow valley below, was a cornfield that rose to the western face of the Open Knob, where McCook at that moment was preparing to leave Terrill to bring up his brigade. Desiring to hold that high ground, Rousseau immediately ordered Starkweather's two batteries forward to the extreme left of the second ridge, accompanied by the 1st Wisconsin to support them. Bush would unlimber farthest on the left. The turbulent, often insubordinate 21st Wisconsin, thrust ahead of the others to the foot of the hill and the cornfield, would hold the center. It was an important and dangerous position for a raw unit, especially one as undisciplined as the 21st Wisconsin. Although Rousseau clearly disliked the regiment, one suspects that haste prompted his decision. Meanwhile, the 79th Pennsylvania and 24th Illinois on the right were to take their positions on the sloping face of the ridge. "This formation gave a cross-fire," Rousseau explained.[33]

Indeed, despite the fact that McCook and Rousseau continued making troop dispositions on the fly without consulting each other, the final, almost serendipitous placement of the corps' entire front line would, as it turned out, facilitate a cross fire that would devastate any attackers. Instead of the two parallel division lines one might have found drawn on a classroom map at the academy, McCook's five brigades, once Starkweather took the new position, would constitute a formation resembling an × from the air—the two key ridgelines intersecting each other more or less at the center of the corps. Harris and Lytle to the south and Terrill to the north formed the eastern side of the ×, while Starkweather and Webster together in the rear made up the western half. Haphazard and potentially dangerous as it was in terms of divisional cohesion and command, the end result splendidly utilized the rolling high ground of the Chaplin Hills.

Two major drawbacks existed, however. First was the unlucky positioning of Terrill's brigade in the front ranks. Considering the haphazard placements of the forenoon, Starkweather's more seasoned and better-fed veterans almost certainly would have occupied the ridges around the Open Knob with two batteries had not Jackson impatiently pushed his men ahead. In contrast, Terrill's men were rookies anchoring an ad hoc battery. Worse yet, thanks to the division commander's eagerness, Jackson's men already had been up for almost eleven hours and, unlike most of the day's combatants, had eaten no breakfast. Historian Lawrence Babits has argued convincingly that the combination of hunger and sleep deprivation severely limits the effectiveness of even veteran campaigners. The addition of combat stress, which increases a soldier's metabolism, quickly depletes reserves of energy and lessens the ability of men to deal with the rigors of battle. Terrill's men, fatigued, hungry, thirsty, and only a few weeks from home, were ripe to collapse if pressed.[34]

A second problem existed. The two divisions did not intersect completely at the center of the ✕. Because each brigade had lined up from the outer end inward, and because none possessed enough men to control the hills completely, a breach existed squarely in the center of the formation, near Widow Gibson's farm. As fate would have it, Leonidas Polk and Frank Cheatham in Walker's Bend were aiming their opening assault at that very spot.[35]

Suddenly under unanticipated fire from Stone's battery, Wharton's reconnaissance element withdrew up the County Road and turned south into the shelter of woods. From there his men galloped south along the summit of the ridge overlooking Walker's Bend, down what is now the New Mackville Road as it passes in front of the modern battlefield park. Nearing the stone fence that marks the modern entrance to the battlefield park, the gray-clads unexpectedly encountered the two companies of the 33rd Ohio McCook had sent toward the river. They sent the Federals reeling back up the ridge from whence they came with revolver fire. Exuberantly, the cavalrymen continued advancing.

Alarmed by a report of Confederate infantrymen in line of battle atop the bluff, McCook had in the meantime dispatched the balance of the 33rd Ohio to support their comrades in the skirmish line. Angus Waddle rode ahead with orders from the corps commander not to fire until the entire regiment was present, but as he neared the bluff he heard the volley of fire ahead and realized that he was too late. His horse frightened by the fire and uncontrollable, he later claimed, Waddle rode swiftly to the rear without delivering the now moot orders. As the bulk of the regiment crossed the valley west of the Walker's Bend ridge and approached a line of stone fences, the skirmishers fell back. Then Wharton's horsemen topped the hill.[36] "A volley from our regiment," Angus Waddle remembered, "emptied many of their saddles and caused them to quickly disappear."[37]

Wharton fell back into Walker's Bend and reported to Polk and Bragg about what he had seen. Polk, delighted with the cavalryman's obviously exaggerated account, later wrote: "Wharton charged the enemy's left with great fury, passing over stone walls and ravines and driving back the enemy's infantry several hundred yards." Wharton, of course, had not driven back the 33rd Ohio at all, they instead had forced him to the rear with a single volley. The rest of his report proved equally misleading. To be sure, the Confederate cavalry could claim success for clearing the ridge above Walker's Bend of Federal pickets who might have seen and reported Cheatham's approach as his men topped the bluff. Wharton's movement, Polk agreed, "placed in our possession a skirt of woods and an eminence of great importance to our success on our right." Cheatham would launch his attack against the Federal left from that "eminence."[38]

In a larger sense, however, Wharton's reconnaissance failed miserably. It was not all his fault, but rather a function of timing, topography, and perhaps fate. The entire basis of the Confederate attack was a surprise flanking movement against an unanchored Federal left. Had Wharton ridden out five minutes later, he would have seen the first of Starkweather's and Terrill's brigades moving onto the northern hilltops and might have concluded that the northern flank extended much farther to the north. Wharton, however, rode out when he did, and so saw only a few mounted men—conceivably cavalry, but in fact several generals with their staffs—on top of the Open Knob.

Topography, like timing, bedeviled the young cavalryman. From his viewpoint on the County Road where it veered sharply, the point where Stone's battery fired upon him, the hill that was Starkweather's first position masks perfectly the ridge behind it where Webster's brigade formed its lines. The result is an optical illusion. Today, a barn on the former hill and a house on the latter appear to be side-by-side in the same yard. Looking at Stone's battery on October 8, 1862, Wharton could easily conclude—and did decide—that the gunners firing on him belonged to Sam Harris's battery of Webster's brigade, which he had seen during an earlier sweep of the area. But Wharton saw neither Starkweather's men moving onto the ridge above the Benton Road nor Terrill's brigade beginning to come into line on the open knob—the entire northern extension of McCook's × formation. The end result of Wharton's seemingly doomed reconnaissance would be an attack not into a weakly defended flank, as the Confederates anticipated, but straight into the vortex of a Federal corps.[39]

A little before two in the afternoon, secure in the notion that the enemy's unsuspecting flank waited to be turned thanks to Wharton, Polk at last sent Cheatham's division climbing out of Walker's Bend. Neatly dropping their packs and blankets, the men formed into lines of battle and began scrambling up the bluff. Toward the right of the bluff the present three regiments of Donelson's brigade—two remained in the rear with Carnes's battery—

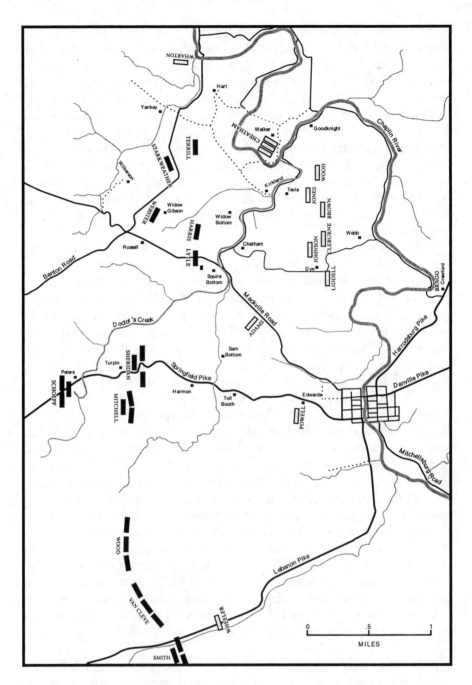

Map 10. 1. Perryville battlefield, 2 P.M.

went up first. Stewart's would follow up the more imposing left face. Not surprisingly considering the terrain, their neat lines broke down immediately. Individuals or small groups ascended the steep incline with whatever speed and dexterity they could muster. Aided to an extent by the "Dug Road" path, the 15th and 16th Tennessee Regiments of Donelson's command reached the summit first, reformed their lines, and sat or lay down for a moment to rest in the open field on the eastern face of the bluff as the 38th Tennessee continued climbing up to join them.[40]

Shielded by the rolling Chaplin Hills, particularly the ridge swept by Wharton, the Confederates still largely escaped detection. At least one jumpy Federal continued watching the eastern horizon with trepidation, however. Having established a signal station toward the Federal rear, the 2nd Ohio's George Landrum returned to the front "to see if I could see anything of the enemy. . . . They had removed their Battery, and for some time I could see nothing of them, and felt sure they had retreated. Looking again, however . . . I could see about a dozen men on horseback. They were evidently taking a survey of the field. They wheeled around and disappeared in the woods, and for about ten minutes nothing more was seen of them."[41]

Landrum almost certainly saw Donelson, his staff, and three regimental colonels with their aides as they took a look at the ground over which they would attack. Among them was Col. John H. Savage of the 16th Tennessee, who observed the rolling valley below with foreboding. As the balance of the brigade climbed onto the field, Donelson rode over to his right where Savage had just rejoined his command. Verbal fireworks flew immediately. Donelson and Savage, the latter a former Tennessee congressman and veteran of combat in Florida and Mexico, hated each other fervently and had tangled frequently in the past. For that matter, getting along with John Savage tested the patience of many men less thin-skinned than Donelson. Even Savage's friends admitted that the old bachelor was gruff, hard to get to know, and downright peculiar, a "semi-barbarian" in the Rev. Joseph Cross's mind. Savage enjoyed boasting that he was a sworn enemy of Cheatham; his patron, Tennessee governor Isham Harris; of Jefferson Davis; and of anyone who followed the lead of the late South Carolina senator John C. Calhoun. But Savage hated Donelson most of all. Convinced that his Seminole War and Mexican War service helped him understand military tactics better than his immediate but less-experienced superior—a well-connected nephew of Andrew Jackson who had resigned from the army a year after graduating from West Point to embark on a political career—and further despising Donelson as a drunkard, Savage often had disobeyed Donelson's orders, resulting in his arrest and unsuccessful court-martial. Egocentric if not paranoid, Savage usually imagined that everyone was against him, and he personalized every situation.

Thus, when Donelson approached him and directed him to assault the only Federal battery barely visible on the horizon—Sam Harris's Indiana battery—Savage interpreted it as his death warrant. Donelson, he believed, literally wanted to murder him. "I believed that the battery was supported by a strong line of infantry concealed by a fence," Savage later explained, "and a forest not more than eighty yards in its rear, and that it had been placed in the field as a decoy to invite a charge. I believed that a charge would end in my death and the defeat and ruin of my regiment."

"'Colonel, I am ordered to attack,'" Donelson stated. Ready to believe that Cheatham and Donelson both were drunk again—no one else made that allegation about that October day—and just as persuaded that both hated him enough for his previous insubordination and political outspokenness that they were willing to order him and his men to their deaths, Savage refused to respond. Donelson repeated the order again, and then a third time. Savage "then said: 'General, I see no enemy to attack except that battery over there in the field. Do you mean, sir, that you want the Sixteenth to charge that battery?' He said, 'Yes.' I replied, 'General, I will obey your orders but if the Sixteenth is to charge that battery you must give the order.' He raised his voice in a rather loud and excited tone and said, 'Charge.'"[42]

Hostile as usual toward his brigade commander, keyed up even more with a fight impending, Savage clearly misconstrued Cheatham's intent, which was to have all of Donelson's present brigade flank the battery, which presumably anchored the northern terminus of the Federal line, and thus turn the enemy force out of its position. In the front line from left to right, the 15th and 16th Tennessee would proceed together against the Hoosier battery. The 38th Tennessee would follow the 16th Tennessee, giving added weight to the Confederate right as it struck and hopefully turned the enemy flank. Stewart and Maney then would complete the turning movement and the rout would be on. No one asked the 16th Tennessee to win the battle itself, but in Savage's mind that was his forlorn task, and he proceeded to act accordingly.[43]

The moment arrived. Polk galloped up the Dug Road path and rode down the rising line, exhorting Donelson's Tennesseans to fight so as to honor their native state.[44] Cheatham, in contrast, sat quietly in his saddle, smoking a pipe.[45] "'Forward,'" Donelson cried.[46] Many of the men cheered or gave the rebel yell, still others shouted "'Victory.'"[47] Donelson's three regiments strode across the field and up to the flat, narrow summit of the bluff, in Stoddard Johnson's memory "as if on dress parade, with a spirit not excelled by anything I afterwards witnessed."[48]

"With . . . composure and without a sound," agreed an Atlanta newspaperman, "the whole line moved forward in beautiful order. All my conceptions of the hurrah and din and dust of battle were confounded by the cool, business-like operations going on before me. Those badly clothed, some shoeless, dirty and ragged-looking men walked into the harvest of death before them with all the composure and much less of the bustle that a merchant would exhibit in walking to his counting-room after breakfast."[49]

Figure 10.3. Maj. Gen. Benjamin Franklin Cheatham. Photograph courtesy National Archives and Records Administration.

Most of Donelson's men were veterans of Shiloh, hence their "composure." Nearly all wore ragged and faded gray or butternut uniforms, although a hostile observer in the 80th Indiana complained some men were in captured Union uniforms as well. The latter uniforms, plus the Stars and Bars waving over some Confederates' heads, looking so much like the Stars and Stripes on a smoky field, convinced the Hoosier that Donelson's men had unethically broken the rules of war.

Ahead of them the rippled, irregular terrain gradually descended for almost four hundred yards toward a deep trough or hollow that lay about halfway between the two armies. From the trough, the ground rose irregularly again through cornfields and an open belt of beech trees to the ridge held by the now fully visible left of Leonard Harris's brigade and part of Webster's behind it. However, a north-south ridge blocked any view of Lytle to the south. Offering little resistance, the 33rd Ohio's skirmishers, still in the area, unleashed about twenty rounds and retreated toward their regiment and a skirt of woods on Harris's left, where it fronted Widow Gibson's farm.[50]

For the first time, Donelson's men on the summit of the bluff saw fully what they were up against. A half-mile ahead in the distance, Carroll Henderson Clark of the 16th Tennessee gazed upon what "looked to me like the whole face of the earth . . . covered with Yankeys."[51] The Confederates

Figure 10.4. Confederate attack on Harris's brigade. From *Harpers Weekly*, Nov. 1, 1862. Photograph by Tom Beggs.

advanced steadily at first, but within moments regimental lines began to break down. Stone fences running along the top of the ridge momentarily slowed bunches of attackers as they began descending into the valley, staggering their lines. Savage's interpretation of Donelson's orders added to the confusion. He drove his regiment at a furious clip directly at Sam Harris's distant battery, angry for the rest of his life that the 15th Tennessee did not keep up with him. As a result, the 16th Tennessee approached the hollow all but alone, moving far out in front of the remainder of the brigade. Hungry and dehydrated men struggled to keep up their mounted colonel's wicked pace.[52]

Across the valley, Buckeye George Landrum gasped when he saw Donelson's attackers running toward him, having seemingly appeared from out of nowhere thanks to the rolling terrain. "Suddenly," he wrote, "there emerged from the wood the head of a column of men, and as they came out, their bayonets glistened in the sun, and then I knew they were coming for us. . . . They advanced at 'double-quick' and formed in line of battle under cover of a small knoll." Landrum drew Peter Simonson's attention to the brown-gray line, and almost instantly the latter ordered his crews to fire canister into the advancing enemy. "The line wavered an instant," Landrum continued, "but again advanced in fine order. Another charge of Canister and the line was broken, but they immediately reformed, and on they came in the most gallant manner."[53] The men of Harris's battery also had watched the Confederates come on, their bayonets shining from that angle as well, and now they turned their guns on the 16th

Tennessee, inflicting more damage with well-aimed spherical case shot and explosive shells as well as canister.[54]

Despite the storm of steel balls and iron shrapnel, caught in an artillery cross fire "that seemed to make the earth quake,"[55] the 16th Tennessee pressed on toward the trough and Harris's battery, Savage riding in front. The depression would provide shelter from the enemy batteries, he hoped, but his men needed to get there quickly. "I thought as soon as I moved into that hollow I would be out of reach of the battery and that I could come up on the other side within sixty or seventy yards of the battery," he later reported. "I was in no hurry; got in front of my regiment and said, 'Forward, march!'" As the Tennesseans poured into the hollow, Savage halted them momentarily in order to dress his lines. The time was roughly 2:10 P.M.

Suddenly, without any warning, seven unlimbered guns of Charlie Parsons's freshly arrived battery on the Open Knob unexpectedly fired lengthwise into the hollow from Savage's right with every sort of projectile they carried in their caissons, enfilading the attackers with deadly precision. Although Parsons seems to have fired a couple of rounds of canister at Donelson as he began his approach, no one on the Confederate side realized it in the confusion, or even suspected that the battery was there. As a result, men fell like wheat mowed down by a scythe.[56] "The boys were falling dead & wounded all around me," Carroll Henderson Clark remembered with sorrow, "& I thought all would be killed. Some of my school mates & playmates, neighbors and friends lost their lives there. . . . If you wish to know how a soldier feels in such a battle as that, you must ask someone else. I cannot explain, but I had no hope of getting out alive."[57]

Dozens of men fell dead or dying within seconds, others collapsed with wounds of all descriptions. As he shouted above the din, two cannister balls fired from opposite directions collided into each other in H. I. Hughes's mouth, knocking out all his lower teeth and lodging in his neck. "His face was not marked on the outside," Thomas A. Hughes later wrote with some wonderment.[58] Another projectile from Parsons's guns passed through the head of Savage's horse, wounding it severely without killing it outright. Shocked years before over the sight of dozens of riderless horses running back and forth at the Battle of Molino del Rey in Mexico, Savage leapt from the falling animal and tied it to a stump before continuing on.[59]

In the hell that the hollow suddenly had become, one of Donelson's staff officers somehow caught up with Savage. With horror Donelson had seen Parsons's unexpected fire from the right. "I did not have the proper direction," he later lamented. Obviously something had gone wrong, for they had not struck the Federal flank but rather had charged head-on into a formidable line. Now they were trapped in the cross fire of three batteries: left, center, and right. Donelson ordered Savage to shift to the right and halt while he brought up the balance of the brigade on the run. Together they would storm the unmasked battery on the knob and secure the flank. Savage

Figure 10.5. Lt. Charles Parsons as a West Point cadet. Photograph courtesy U.S. Army Military History Institute.

for once agreed with Donelson, and he began sliding his men more to the right while Donelson raced to hurry up the rest of his brigade. More confusion followed. Reacting differently to the same scene, an excited Cheatham bypassed Donelson in the chain of command and personally sent both regiments straight ahead to support Savage. He would send Stewart as well, he promised, while Maney would move to the right flank and attack the new battery. Donelson should continue pushing straight ahead.[60]

In the meantime, the 15th Tennessee had caught up and entered the hollow to Savage's left. It too began taking heavy casualties as murderous fire from the Federal batteries swept the Tennesseans from three directions. Savage pulled his revolver from its holster and ordered his men forward, hoping to escape the killing fire from at least Sam Harris's guns. Up out of the hollow and down the other side of the hill the bloodied Tennesseans raced,[61] "one solid mass, on a double quick, trailing their arms and yelling like fiends."[62]

Farther ahead lay the ridge where the northern end of Harris's lines waited, near the breach in the Federal line at Widow Gibson's farm. The Confederates stopped less than fifty yards from the blue line at the edge of the beech grove, stabilized their line as much as possible, and fired the first of several volleys toward the strong enemy position. James Thompson, bal-

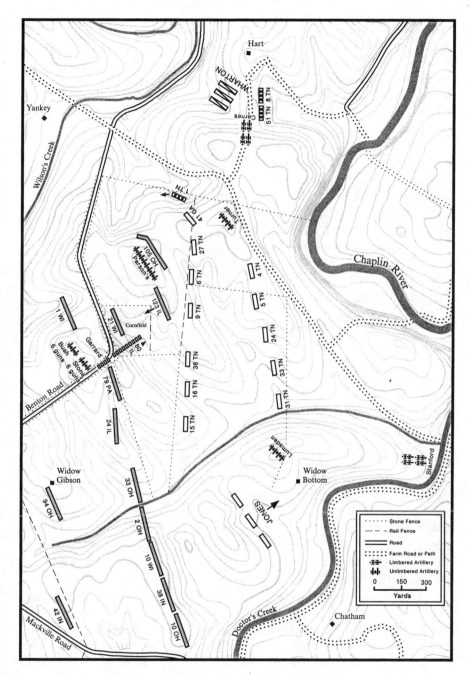

Map 10.2. The fight for the Open Knob, 3 P.M.

ancing his rifle on a stump in order to take better aim at his tormentors on the hill above, shivered as friendly fire struck the stump from behind, barely missing him. "I stormed out at them that if any of them shot me, I would come back there and kill him," wrote Thompson.[63]

Unfortunately, nothing went right for Savage, who had led the two Tennessee regiments into another cross fire at the nexus of the Federal lines. The bluecoats up on the ridge poured volley after volley into the gray-clad attackers. "We all bounded to our feet like so many parched peas," Hoosier Joseph Glezen wrote, "determined to pour the contents of our muskets into the ranks of our ungodly opposers . . . they kept so well concealed behind trees that only a few could be seen. Notwithstanding this our bullets found them in their hiding places and strewd the ground with their mutilated carcases—the legitimate fruits of [their] own treason and folly."[64]

To make matters worse, the attacking Tennesseans began taking fire in their right and rear from the 33rd Ohio, which having retreated now deployed as skirmishers behind a rail fence running perpendicular down from the ridge and opened fire. Their fire was particularly galling, so Savage wheeled to the right and ordered his men to charge the skirmishers behind the fence. Moving across the Federal line in the general direction of the Open Knob, the Tennesseans swept forward, firing as they went. The Ohio regiment exchanged several volleys with the Confederates but, after taking heavy casualties, fell back rapidly toward the main line with the Confederates on their heels. Left on the ground near the fence were the regimental colonel, Lt. Col. Oscar F. Moore, who had been shot in the leg, and dozens of his men.[65]

Advancing as far as two outbuildings belonging to the Widow Gibson, Savage spotted Sam Harris's battery between fifty and a hundred yards obliquely to the right. Using the two log structures for cover, the Tennesseans hunkered down momentarily in the face of Harris's canister as well as musketry emanating from the left of Leonard Harris's brigade. Between the two structures lay a space no wider than fifteen feet through which the Yankee gunners fired. "I stood between the cabins," Savage reported, "would watch the gunner ram home the charge, and say, 'Lie low, boys; he is going to fire,' and step for protection close to the cabin nearest the battery."[66]

Pandemonium reigned on the Federal side of the battle as well. In the center of the firestorm, near the Gibson outbuildings, McCook personally ordered the 2nd Ohio up to support the 33rd Ohio on its left and thus fill the treacherous gap. However, both soon came pouring back into Webster's rear lines in the face of Savage's desperate charge. Turning to Rousseau, who had just raced over after placing Starkweather into position, McCook told him to bring one of Starkweather's regiments from the left up to plug the gap and support the staggering 33rd Ohio. Wasting little time, Rousseau rode back, pulled the 24th Illinois from Starkweather's right and personally advanced it as skirmishers toward Harris's left. Harris himself dispatched the 38th Indi-

ana Infantry to help the 10th Wisconsin Infantry support Simonson's battery. The rookie 94th Ohio waited in reserve behind them.

To the rear, mortified that the enemy might flank Harris's brigade on
his left, Webster ordered the raw 50th Ohio Infantry from its place in the
second line behind the 80th Indiana, supporting Sam Harris's battery, and
sent it into line to the left of the Hoosier regiment. In the chaos of their first
battle, many of the men in the 50th Ohio froze. Only Company A moved as
ordered; the rest of the confused unit remained in place behind the 80th
Indiana while its colonel, Jonah R. Taylor, shoved a wounded soldier from
behind a tree and took his place. Company A's Capt. Thomas P. Cook, however, would not hide. Instead, he left his company to go back and retrieve the
rest of the regiment. Company F moved up promptly and went into line as
ordered under the captain's guidance, but for the time being the rest of the
regiment remained in disarray. Eventually, other companies, not all, would
drift to the firing line. Unwilling to call up the equally untried and badly
armed 98th or 121st Ohio Regiments until absolutely necessary, Webster
roused the 2nd Ohio and pushed it back into the gap in the front line.[67]

Along the ridge, the old and inferior weapons issued to the newest Federal recruits hindered the Federal defense. Fear worsened the situation. Civil
War soldiers under fire often displayed a disturbing tendency to continue
loading their weapons without firing. Never was that more true than in
Webster's brigade at Perryville. John Glezen nervously loaded his rifle a second time and discovered to his chagrin that it would not fire with a double
load. Failing to make it operational, he picked up a second weapon from
among the wounded only to find that it was in the same condition. He tried
another, then another. The fourth rifle he picked up "had lead just about one
foot from the muzzle." Bewildered, Glezen lay down behind a stump for two
minutes before his courage got the best of him and he again began searching
for a workable weapon among the fallen. The next two had "loads halfway
down the barrel." At last, on the seventh try, Glezen found an operational
musket and reentered the fight.[68]

Despite such difficulties, the combined fire from parts of two infantry
brigades and three artillery batteries continued to decimate Donelson's outnumbered brigade. One attempt to shift around to the right and attack
Parsons's battery went nowhere when the man leading it, a private named
Andrew Dow, realized that he was attacking alone. As he shouted to counter-
mand Dow's one-man flanking maneuver, a minié ball ripped through Savage's
leg even as a steel canister ball hit a cabin and struck off a chunk of wood that
then ricocheted into the colonel's back, felling him and leaving him temporarily paralyzed. Savage remained sensible long enough to turn over command to Donelson, who had personally brought up the 38th Tennessee, and
to urge him to attack Parsons. Unit cohesion all but disappeared in the madness that followed as the fresher men of the 38th began intermingling with
the already blended 15th and 16th Tennessee Regiments. After about fifteen

minutes, Donelson could take no more. Casualties in the brigade already probably surpassed 20 percent, and losses among what was left of the hard-hit 16th Tennessee were staggering, amounting to perhaps half its strength a half-hour earlier. Wounded and dead men lay everywhere. He still had no artillery support. Two of his regiments, the 8th and 51st Tennessee, remained lost in the rear with Carnes, all useless to him. Stewart had not come up either. Left all but abandoned, Donelson's brigade finally fell back, perhaps as far as the ridge where the men had first gathered before their attack. By 2:30 P.M., the Confederate attack on the Union left had foundered.[69]

Back in Walker's Bend, Frank Cheatham quickly redeployed the remainder of his division to meet the unanticipated threat from Parsons's battery on the Open Knob. Leaving Stewart to go in as planned to support Donelson, Cheatham ordered Maney's brigade to move farther north, where it would take possession of the wooded heights on the far bank of the river and then hit Parsons in his left flank. "'Advance as rapidly as possible through the woods toward the enemy, attack, drive and press him,'" Cheatham told Maney, using no uncertain terms.[70]

In October 1862 George Maney was the best brigade commander in the Army of the Mississippi, the right man for the job Cheatham now gave him. A thirty-six-year-old Nashville lawyer, he had fought in Mexico, served more recently under both Robert E. Lee and Stonewall Jackson in western Virginia, and received honors for his service at Shiloh.[71] Filing as quickly as possible through a frustrating defile tangled with underbrush and trees, and further impeded by Wharton's horsemen as they recovered in the safety of the woods from their recent scrape with the 33rd Ohio, Maney and his men approached and crossed the dry riverbed where it came out of Walker's Bend with some difficulty, then reassembled on the northern end of the bluff. Wooded high ground two hundred yards farther west of the bend continued to hide the brigade from the enemy on the Open Knob. Once in the strip of woods Cheatham had indicated as his assembly point, Maney arrayed the first three of his regiments to arrive into line, the 9th and 6th Tennessee and the raw 41st Georgia, extending from left to right.[72] Without waiting for his other two regiments, determined to rescue Donelson without delaying another second, Maney "pressed on with all rapidity practicable" through more dense forest toward the sound of Parsons's guns. A staff officer stayed behind with orders for the remaining two regiments to form into line and follow as hastily as possible. Ahead of the attack galloped Wharton's refreshed horsemen, who had been flushed from the trees. As they rode out into the open, Parsons ordered his still deploying battery to face north. At least one gun, perhaps more, opened fire on the gray-clad cavalry as they rode beneath the precipitous northern slope of the Open Knob.

Aiming at a cleared field beneath the knob, Maney hurriedly approached the enemy battery, still screened by the intervening ridge. Less than two

Figure 10.6. Brig. Gen. George Maney. Photograph courtesy Library of Congress, LC-B812-2727.

hundred yards from the knob, Maney's right regiment, the 41st Georgia, suddenly emerged into view just as Wharton's cavalry disappeared on the western horizon. On the Open Knob, Parsons's gunners and the supporting infantrymen of the 123rd Illinois could barely believe their eyes as the Georgians, followed by the rest of Maney's line, marched into view.[73] A correspondent from the *Cleveland Plain Dealer*, standing in the rear of the Illinois regiment, wrote that he "saw from behind his tree the several lines of the enemy as they advanced to the attack. The sight was most magnificent. He felt as if the single brigade of Terrill would be swept away."[74] Staff officer Samuel M. Starling added that the Confederates' faded uniforms looked so much like dry October weeds that he believed the enemy had camouflaged themselves, thereby escaping detection until the last moment.

Faced with the new threat, Terrill summarily ordered Parsons to wheel his pieces around yet again and open fire on the advancing foe. That took time for the rookie gunners, and by the time at least some of their cannon were facing east, Maney's oncoming line had strode to within a hundred yards of the battery, marching through a strip of brushy woods that extended from the foot of the knob, partially up its eastern face, to a high split-rail fence shrouded in bushes and briars. The gray line came to a halt at the fence

Figure 10.7. Maney's approach as seen today from Parson's position on the Open Knob. Photograph courtesy John Walsh Jr.

like a wave crashing into shore. The brigade's officers shouted above the din in a desperate effort to shift the entire line more to the Confederate right, around the fence and the enemy flank, but to no avail.[75] More confusion ensued on the right of the line when Lt. Col. John W. Buford of the 9th Tennessee ordered a captain to "'oblique his company to the right,'" only to watch in amazement as it veered back to the left instead. "'Captain . . . I told you to oblique your company to the right,'" shouted Buford. "'If you don't know what I mean by "right oblique," sir, then gee them, sir, gee them, gee them.'" Moments later, Buford fell seriously wounded.[76]

Unconcerned with the technicalities of proper artillery practice at that desperate point, Parsons's inexperienced gunners continued jamming down their muzzles whatever they found first in their caissons, just as they had against Donelson, and let fly at the nearby woods as quickly as possible.[77] Shooting like veterans, the high ground giving them confidence, the green 123rd Illinois meanwhile poured enough musketry into the enemy below to convince George Maney that an entire brigade defended the guns. In his words, the enemy "concentrated a most terrific and deadly fire . . . the Enemy Battery together with his entire infantry force (a full Brigade) were pouring destruction upon us. Casting more shots and to better advantage than ourselves."[78]

"Now the fight became general," a member of the 41st Georgia remembered, "and looked like the whole world had been converted into blue coats, whistling balls, bursting shells and brass cannon. Right here it was almost impossible for mortal men to stand up in the face of such a rain of lead and our lines wavered a moment. . . . At the same moment the clear voice of brave Frank McWhorter rang out, 'Die, my comrades, rather than give it up.'"[79]

"It seemed impossible for humanity to go farther," the colonel of the 6th Tennessee added, "such was the havoc and destruction that had taken place in their ranks. A temporary halt was the inevitable result."[80] Stymied for the moment, the two lines fired away at each other with abandon. "Most of the bullets went over our heads," Illinois major James A. Connolly wrote home, "and sounded like a swarm of bees running away in the hot summer air overhead."[81]

Up into the maelstrom rushed Maney's fourth regiment, the 27th Tennessee, hard on the heels of the 6th Tennessee until it neared the strip of woods and the fence. "During the whole time of passing through the woods," Lt. Col. William Frierson reported, "the battery was playing upon us with terrible effect; but as soon as the fence was reached, in full view of the battery, such a storm of shell, grape, canister, and Minie balls was turned loose upon us as no troops scarcely ever before encountered. Large boughs were torn from the trees, the trees themselves shattered as if by lightning, and the ground plowed in deep furrows."[82]

Federal reinforcements raced to the scene simultaneously. From a half-mile to the Federal rear, the second of Terrill's regiments, the 105th Ohio, double-quicked toward the open knob to bolster the line. Exhausted from their sprint, the panting Ohioans neared the top of the hill only to confront chaos. "On a little knoll to our right front," Albion Tourgée remembered, "the battery was firing with frenzied rapidity. The shells from the enemy's battery flew over our heads and cut the limbs of the trees by which we stood, sending down a shower of acorns. Bullets pattered about us. We could see the artillerymen dashing back and forth as the smoke lifted from the guns. Men were coming back from the hell which the crest hid from our view, some wounded, some stragglers."

Just to the rear of the battery, Tourgée continued, stood generals Jackson and Terrill. Most shocking of all to Tourgée was that, after no more than fifteen minutes of combat, his brigade commander clearly had broken under the strain, all but abrogating his responsibilities. Leaving the disposition of his infantrymen for his aides to worry about, the former artilleryman focused obsessively on Parsons's battery, shouting encouragement and orders to his pet gunners as if he were their captain. "He was by training, almost by instinct, an artilleryman," Tourgée remembered, "and his battery's action eclipsed in interest the maneuvering of his brigade. . . . its peril absorbed his whole attention." An aide had to guide the 105th Ohio to a position along the crest of the hill.[83]

Figure 10.8. Modern view of Parson's position, as seen by Maney's attackers. Photograph courtesy John Walsh Jr.

Terrill's concern for his battery now led him to commit an egregious error. At about 2:50 P.M., just as the 105th Ohio neared the hilltop, he launched a pathetic, ill-advised attempt to turn the tide and save his beloved eight guns. Unable to deduce Maney's strength in the dark woods behind the fence except by counting flashes of smoke, he ordered the raw recruits of the 123rd Illinois to rise up from where they lay to the left and rear of Parsons's guns and charge the enemy's three regiments with bayonets while Garrard's little detachment approached the guns. Barely drilled before marching out of Louisville, the Illinoisans poured down the hill in confusion to their right front, moving toward the 6th and 9th Tennessee Regiments, the fence, and the trees. Unable to maintain order, the regiment's rear line overtook and stumbled through the more hesitant front rank as momentum outpaced dread and inexperience. Halting halfway between the battery and the fence, the Illinoisans squeezed off one volley before nearly point-blank Confederate fire delivered by Maney's Shiloh veterans blasted them and drove the survivors back up the knob, to the protection of the battery and the 105th Ohio, which in the interim had formed a line on the crest of the hill.[84]

Terrill had blundered, asking the impossible of his willing but painfully raw troops. The 123rd Illinois left a quarter of its strength dead or wounded on the eastern slope of the Open Knob. "Such an order," Albion Tourgée of the 105th Ohio wrote of the bayonet charge, "was justifiable only to gain time to withdraw the battery or for the arrival of expected succor. As an attempt to carry the enemy's position, or repel their attack, it was simple madness. . . . The fear of losing his battery evidently blinded General Terrill to all other considerations."[85]

Still poised beside the guns on the summit, Jackson and Terrill vainly called out to the Illinoisans to halt and stand their ground as they fell back up the hill. "'Well,'" Jackson remarked to Samuel Starling, "'I'll be damned if this is not getting rather particular.'" As he turned to Maj. James Connolly of the 123rd, advising him to dismount, a Confederate ball hit Jackson and he tumbled to the ground. "We ran to him," wrote Starling, but "his eyes were closed, with a tightness preternatural his eye brows almost rested on his cheeks, his mouth was open, and he gave several short spasmodic groans, but I am sure he breathed *not once*. There was a hole in his coat surrounded by blood ½ an inch all around it, immediately below his right nipple." The aides picked Jackson up and lugged him to the western foot of the knob before halting. "He was a heavy man," Starling explained, "and here [assistant adjutant general Percival P.] Oldershaw who had been very much complaining of his back for several days broke down, and proposed to send for an ambulance to take him off the field. We laid him down *dead*, and scattered to find one." Oldershaw ran off in a different direction to find Webster so that he could take command of the division.[86]

Back on the Open Knob, chaos reigned as the fight intensified. About 3 P.M., Maney's Confederates finally began receiving tardy support in the form of the two iron six-pounders and two twelve-pound bronze howitzers of Capt. Melanchon Smith's Mississippi Battery, temporarily commanded that day by Lt. William B. Turner. Delayed by repairs near the Goodknight House, Turner, under Cheatham's supervision, had forded the Chaplin, crossed through Walker's Bend on the County Road, and, after following Wharton's previous path, unlimbered less than three hundred yards northeast of the Open Knob.[87] The gunners promptly enfiladed the Federal position with canister from the right and rear of Maney's line. The bodies of wounded and slain horses and men by now lay everywhere from the top of the hill to its base, including a considerable number of Parsons's gunners. Without Jackson at his shoulder, Terrill, in the midst of the anarchy, mentally buckled even more, losing interest in everything except the battery and its dwindling firepower. Meanwhile, its lines so confused by unfamiliarity with close-order drill that its nominally left companies ended up on the right, overlapping the battery, the 105th Ohio's refused left flank extended along the crest northward and then down the steep northern face of the knob to the open field below. Shooting from their knees, the Ohioans fired at will as they ducked Confederate musket fire. Farther to the right, eight companies of the 80th Illinois as well as Garrard's three companies arrived and moved into line to the right of the Buckeyes, where they immediately began taking casualties.[88]

As in Webster's brigade, faulty weapons combined with the first sight of the proverbial elephant lessened the effectiveness of the hilltop's defenders. "Those with guns [that] were loaded fired; the others made haste to load," Tourgée remembered. "Men fell, sometimes with a groan, sometimes without a sound. It was slow work loading and firing with the old muzzle-loaders. The air seemed full of flashing ramrods."[89] Another member of the regiment, Bliss Morse, wrote after the battle that "we were drawn up on the left wing of the line of battle with the right wing of our reg. Where the left should have been, the rebels had the start of us by two rounds while we were forming and loading our pieces. There was no cessation of firing . . . it was a perfect hail storm of balls all the time."[90]

Down the hill within the lines of Maney's brigade, bedlam held sway as well. "It was a fearful time," Georgian John Knight later wrote.[91] Maney turned to aide Thomas H. Malone and asked what he thought of it. "I told him I didn't think our position could be maintained. . . . he asked me what I thought should be done, and I told him I believed our only chance was to take those guns. He asked if I thought it was possible for our men to do it. I said, 'I think so.'"[92] Maney agreed and mounted his horse. Oblivious to the danger, or at least determined not to show any fear, Maney rode the length of the line exhorting his men to charge forward and seize the guns "as it was our last and only chance of safety and success."[93] When his mount went down, Maney continued on foot, shouting encouragement up and down the line. At the same time, Malone rode along the brigade's rear shouting orders to regimental officers. Those commands were simple: charge bayonets and do not fire until reaching the crest of the knob.[94]

Led by Malone, the four regiments quickly threw down portions of the fence, screamed the rebel yell, and scrambled up the knob's steep eastern face or else bypassed it to the north.[95] As the gray line rushed toward him, Terrill responded by ordering another bayonet charge, shouting to his men: "'Forward! . . . Do not let them get the guns!'" Albion Tourgée bitterly added that the brigade commander's face "was flushed with agony at the thought of losing the battery of which he was so proud."[96] The companies of the 105th Ohio surged forward on the right in front of the battery as Capt. H. H. Cummings fired two last charges of double-shot canister from his section and then abandoned his guns and moved to the rear of the Ohio regiment. No one else obeyed. The rest of the blue line remained hunkered down on the knob, pouring volleys of iron and steel into the attacking line. Fifty feet from the crest, the attackers wavered again and fell to the ground, searching for cover amid the writhing or still casualties of the 123rd Illinois, Federal fire from the knob proving too much to bear.[97] "The butchery was something awful," Thomas Malone wrote later. "I remembered thinking at the time that I could walk upon dead bodies from where the enemy's line was established until it reached the woods, some three hundred yards away. Of course, in making this charge we lost a great number of men."[98]

Meanwhile, Maney, who had found another mount, rushed back toward the rear to bring up his last regiment, the 1st Tennessee, "which I deemed by this time would have arrived." Stopping halfway, pleased to see the tardy Tennesseans finally advancing, Maney turned and "observed to my great surprise and anxiety my front line halted about one hundred yards in advance of me . . . lying on the ground and hotly engaged in firing against the Enemy's Battery support which was protected by the crest of the hill." He galloped north to consult with Cheatham, who had taken a position on the extreme right flank, and returned to align his second line.[99]

Returning fire from their prone positions, the Confederates hesitated only a few moments, for in such an exposed position they absorbed heavy casualties. A third of the men who got that far never went any farther according to Malone. Accordingly, up and down the line, orders rang out, generally from junior officers replacing men who had fallen only moments before, "to make a charge and take" the battery.[100] Some men never heard the fresh orders above the din, but instead advanced entirely on their own.

As Maney's men made one last desperate lunge for the hilltop, the exhausted Federal defenders broke. Wrote one Buckeye, "It was useless to stay there and be annihilated."[101] Another commented, "by this time every man seemed to be looking out for hisself as we were all broken up for my part I could not tell whether we had any regiment or not."[102] With no alternative left, Terrill spiked the gun closest to him and ordered a general retreat to a skirt of woods at the western foot of the hill, about fifty yards to the rear, where he tried to rally his broken men around another rail fence. From there they fired at Maney's Confederates as they topped the hill, as did John Starkweather's men on the high ground above the Benton Road,[103] "a fire that opened their ranks with the wildest havoc."[104]

One man who did not obey Terrill's orders, at least at first, was Charlie Parsons, who proved even more stubborn than Terrill in his determination to save his battery. Parsons was famous among recent West Point graduates for stubbornly continuing a fist fight even though his larger opponent knocked him down seven times. Now he showed the same tenacity. The last Confederate assault came just as Parsons struggled to reorient his seventh gun to the east. The gun crew promptly abandoned the piece and fled. What happened next remains shrouded in legend. Confederate chaplain Charles Quintard, who ironically after the war won Parsons to Christ in New York City and then ordained him an Episcopalian priest, told a noble story in which the captain drew his sword and stood at parade rest as the Confederates swarmed onto the hill. So impressed were the Southerners with Parsons's courage, Quintard claimed, that they allowed him to walk back to his lines unscathed. No corroborating evidence exists for Quintard's knightly tale, however, and it seems that Parsons either retreated voluntarily or more likely was dragged away. He saved one gun, four caissons, and two limbers as the last remnants of Terrill's line melted away. Confederates, most likely men of the 9th Tennessee, captured seven of his guns.[105]

Parsons survived, but hundreds of other men died or fell wounded in the struggle to control the Open Knob. "Never perhaps did troops fight more desperately than did these on this occasion," wrote the 41st Georgia's John Knight.[106] The butcher's bill certainly supports his assertion. Parsons's battery lost perhaps two-thirds of its number as well as seven of its eight guns, and would be disbanded after the campaign. As it retreated, the 105th Ohio left over two hundred soldiers, almost a third of its number, spread across the hill. The 123rd Illinois lost over 180 men, 25 percent of the regiment. Confederate regiments paid just as high a price as they charged the muzzles of the often-maligned recruits of Terrill's brigade. The 41st Georgia lost about 150 men, including several color bearers, in the fight for the knob. Casualties in the 6th Tennessee and 9th Tennessee were comparable.[107]

The fight for the Open Knob "was a complete triumph of resolute courage and determined fighting over every odds," according to William Frierson of the 27th Tennessee. "The enemy had every advantage of position, and were superior to us in numbers by at least two, and probably three, to one. His battery was composed of large Napoleon guns, and still the Third Brigade, tired and alone, with a bright sun shining in their eyes to bewilder them, overcame all these obstacles and took the battery." Courage there was in abundance, but bravery alone did not account for the results. Maney's men, excluding the 41st Georgia, were ably led Shiloh veterans. Moreover, topography allowed them to approach the knob without being seen until it was almost too late for Terrill, and the strip of woods along the rail fence offered further protection from which to launch the final assault.

In contrast, Jackson and Terrill had poorly served the willing but hungry, thirsty, exhausted, and largely untrained men under their command—soldiers who had not even mastered the manual of arms or the skill of marching in formation before entering battle. When Maney's line appeared, Terrill's men already suffered from exhaustion thanks to Jackson's driving them since well before dawn. Neither general was to blame for not having the entire brigade in position before the fighting started, but Terrill blundered from then on, and Jackson did nothing to stop him before he fell. So obsessed was Terrill with his battery, so panicked did he become, that he committed his regiments piecemeal in two fruitless bayonet charges. Those assaults clearly marked turning points in the battle for the Open Knob. Confederate testimony speaks volumes about the effectiveness of Federal fire raining down on them from above; nearly every officer in Maney's brigade reported that they faced an entire brigade from the first. Had he hunkered down on the heights, Terrill might have used the terrain and his superior numbers to hang on indefinitely, all other errors aside. However, as Colonel Frierson suggested, the general did not take advantage of what few good cards he held, much to the consternation of his men. Worse yet, once the first charge failed, Terrill broke down completely. When he should have been arranging his men to receive and repel the enemy's assaults, he reverted to his previous role of captain of artillery and, according to some witnesses, worked a piece like a common gunner as he did at Shiloh when facing the very same Confederates. The fog of war obscures much, but better leadership might have held the Open Knob. The men certainly fought better than should have been expected of them.

Unfortunately for Maney's weary soldiers, there could be no resting upon their laurels. Their fight was far from over. Ahead of his bloodied regiments beyond the fenced-in cornfield lay another hill crowned with two additional batteries and Starkweather's fresh, more experienced brigade of Federal defenders. Having achieved nearly the impossible, the Tennesseans and Georgians would have to do it all over again against worse odds. Although beaten back, the Federal left flank remained unturned at 3:30 P.M.[108]

11

A SQUARE, STAND-UP . . . FIGHT

FROM A CEDAR-STREWN BLUFF HIGH IN THE CONFEDERATE REAR, Braxton Bragg and his staff looked on with unfeigned pride as Cheatham's division opened the army's assault against the Federal left. As Donelson's thin ranks slammed into the fulcrum of the enemy's lines, a new flourish of musketry drew Bragg's eyes farther to his left as Hardee's divisions commenced their part in the terrible drama. Bragg aide Stoddard Johnston described "the air filled with the sound of battle, while shot and shell were screaming overhead or plowing up the ground around us." Hoping for a better view, Bragg rode closer to the edge of the bluff. Dodging the occasional stray shell or minié ball, the wind gusting in their faces from the west, the general and his aides observed to the right Donelson's blunted attack, Maney's desperate and ultimately more successful assault on the Open Knob, the death of James Jackson, and the seizure of Parsons's battery. "Upon our left and center," Johnston added, "the fighting was severe and stubborn. I recall, with a feeling of horror, the sight which presented itself to view from our position. It was a square, stand-up, hand-to-hand fight. The batteries and lines of battle of both sides could be seen distinctly, except occasionally obscured by the dense smoke, which alternately hung over the scene or was blown off by the western breeze."[1]

As he watched the attack unfold, Bragg remained perilously unaware that he faced the entire Federal Army of the Ohio. Acting more as mounted infantry than cavalry, their mounts all but worn out by the long incursion, Bragg's horse soldiers still failed to provide him with adequate reconnaissance. Wharton remained on the far right while Wheeler, consumed with dueling Edward McCook's Federal cavalry for control of the Lebanon Pike, reported nothing about the additional Federal corps to his front. As a result, Bragg continued to believe, despite mounting evidence to the contrary, that he faced only a portion of the enemy's army.[2]

At least Bragg knew that there was a battle in progress. Three miles to the west at the Dorsey House, Don Carlos Buell could not even say that.

Nature as well as habitual overmanagement, overconfidence, and the consequences of his bruising fall the previous evening now combined to play a cruel joke on Buell. Due to that "western breeze" Stoddard Johnston described, as well as the rolling nature of the Chaplin Hills, an atmospheric phenomenon called "acoustic shadow," or more properly "sound refraction," bent the sound waves produced by the musketry west of the field. As a result, only some of the big guns could be heard at Buell's headquarters. No smoke rose along the horizon either, as the wind drove it north or east. The booming of "a heavy and furious cannonading . . . in front," the opening of the battle, brought the sore, aching Buell from his tent at the Dorsey House. However, unable to fathom that the Confederates might not wait for him to perfect his lines and attack on the morrow as planned, Buell immediately concluded that either another artillery duel or at worst a skirmish had flared up. Certainly he could hear no musketry. Annoyed at what he perceived to be nothing more than "a great waste of powder there," Buell turned to Gilbert, whose headquarters tent stood nearby, and crustily ordered him to "stop that firing."

Gilbert dictated an order to his orderly and dispatched it to Sheridan, for presumably either he or Gay was the culprit. After the aide carrying the order disappeared, Gilbert decided to ride to the front and see for himself what was happening. No, stay, Buell responded with confidence, dinner was nearly ready. Eager to please his mentor, Gilbert agreed. The two generals walked to the mess together to enjoy a leisurely meal and make plans for the next day's battle.[3] "As the firing suddenly subsided," Buell later explained, "and no report came to me, I had ceased to think of the occurrence."[4]

How could Buell and the others at his headquarters dismiss the sound of artillery so cavalierly? Previous experience seems the most logical answer. "Most of the remarks made in regard to the firing," Capt. J. H. Gilman later testified, "were that they were probably shelling the woods or firing at skirmishers and that the enemy probably intended to make a stand."[5] Years later, Gilbert expanded upon why "shelling the woods" would bring no reaction. "From Shiloh to Corinth," he later wrote, "they learned to distinguish between . . . 'shelling the woods' and the rapid firing of a couple of sections of artillery in a conflict for position on the cavalry lines. On both sides, before reaching Corinth, picket firing had come to be a nuisance. . . . 'Shelling the woods' by batteries was now fast nearing the same point."[6]

Dismissing the sound of battle as no more than a common, recurring "nuisance," too sore to ride out and see otherwise, and his judgment clouded by his own overconfidence, Buell ignored the clamor. Two hours more would pass, hours marked constantly by the sporadic distant thunder of cannon, before he finally learned that both his army and his career were in for the fight of their lives.

Like a giant swinging door hinged at its south end, Bragg's attack continued opening to the west with Hardee's initial assaults. Yet confusion and disappointment attended Hardee's opening gambit as much as it plagued Polk and Cheatham's earlier foray.

If his after-action report is any indication, Hardee had intended for Bushrod Johnson's veteran, six-regiment brigade of Buckner's division to lead his wing's advance against the enemy at Squire Bottom's house, despite the fact that two of Anderson's brigades plugged the gap on Johnson's immediate right, and thus should have moved first in a classic echelon attack. Just minutes before Johnson marched out, however, a little before 2:30 P.M., one of those two orphaned brigades, Col. Thomas Jones's undermanned, poorly armed, and largely unbloodied brigade of three Mississippi regiments, went forward against Leonard Harris's right, troops on imposing high ground anchored by Simonson's Indiana battery.

Why Jones attacked at all, much less ahead of Johnson's stronger and more experienced brigade, remains a question whose answer lies shrouded in the fog of war and the passage of time. The most obvious explanation is that Jones attacked first simply because he was supposed to do so. Supporting such a contention, Buckner later straightforwardly wrote: "the signal for my movement was the advance of our troops on our right." Incorrectly identifying the brigade as Wood's, not Jones's, Buckner added that the brigade "advanced with Cheatham's force on my right." Seeing those troops move out, Buckner would order Johnson's brigade forward.[7]

If that was the case, however, Hardee's after-action report suggests that he and Buckner misunderstood each other. In Hardee's report, the wing commander still maintained that Johnson "gallantly led the advance," and implied that the role of Jones's brigade as well as Wood's was only to safeguard Buckner's right flank. Still convinced after the battle that Johnson and not Jones opened the assault in his sector, indeed apparently unaware of the Mississippians' efforts, Hardee at least did not give the command for Jones to lead any attack. Nor, by his own admission, did Buckner. Jones's immediate superior, Patton Anderson, away on the extreme left and overly preoccupied with Powell's brigade at the time, surely did not order Jones to attack at that moment either. It is conceivable of course that Anderson had advised Jones earlier, before Polk's second thoughts, to anticipate an echelon attack. Then again, Buckner's comment that the brigade to his right advanced with Cheatham could be taken literally. Cheatham could have dispatched orders to Jones to attack along the beleaguered Donelson's left just as Maney was going forward to rescue him on his right. Donelson certainly needed the help.[8]

Then again, perhaps no one ordered Jones to attack. Jones may well have "jumped the gun" and led his men forward entirely on his own. It is conceivable. A thirty-year-old, Virginia-born West Pointer who graduated near the bottom of his class in 1853, Jones normally commanded the 27th Mississippi, but on this day filled in for Col. Edward Cary Walthall. Inexperienced at commanding formations larger than a regiment, perhaps wishing to prove himself in battle, or assuming that his superiors expected him to attack with battle raging to his right, according to this theory Jones either ignored or misunderstood orders to stay put. That he never commanded a brigade again, and indeed ended up doing garrison duty on the North Carolina coast, might well support an allegation that Jones mishandled his brigade at Perryville. The major problem with this interpretation is that neither Buckner nor Cheatham expected Jones to remain in place. If Jones was mixed up, then so were they.[9]

In the end, about all one can say with certainty is that the confusion seemingly inherent within the Army of the Mississippi, enhanced that morning by Bragg's wholesale shifting of brigades and divisions, placed Jones's men in a dangerous position. Whoever determined that they attack at that moment, they "moved forward with a shout."[10] Supported from the rear by Lumsden's Alabama battery, the little brigade gamely advanced toward Harris's line. Initially it passed the small home and apple orchard of Mary "Polly" Bottom, Squire Bottom's aged and widowed mother. As it drew closer to the enemy position, the brigade briefly descended into a swale that ran from north to south between the Widow Bottom's property and another long ridge that intervened between Confederate and Union lines. Still another ridge running at right angles to the others separated Jones's front from Donelson. Thus shielded momentarily from enemy fire in a three-sided box, the Mississippians marched westward through the swale and up the eastern side of the steep ridge to their front, frustratingly unable to see the foe that waited so near until the last minute due to the steep angle of the hill.

Skirmishing ahead of the Confederate brigade thanks to their privately purchased Enfields, the only rifles in the otherwise smoothbore musket–carrying regiment, the raw men of Company K, 27th Mississippi Infantry, were the first to top the ridge and see the enemy position. The sight that suddenly greeted their eyes astonished them. Before them lay yet another imposing ridge, packed with Harris's and Lytle's men. Simonson's battery ominously sat almost directly ahead of them, the linchpin of the two brigades. In between them and the Yankees ran a narrow, steep ravine thirty feet deep, its most notable feature a foreboding sinkhole. The Bottoms had grown corn in the ravine that summer, and had cut all of it except an acre that remained standing immediately around the sinkhole. Jones's brigade would have to advance through that golden, open valley of despond up to the bayonets of two brigades and a battery arrayed on high ground and shielded by a worm fence. It was too much for Company K's captain, John Sale, who stopped dead in his tracks and shouted back to his colonel that they had encountered "a precipice thirty feet high." Unmoved, the colonel replied, "'Forward the skirmishers!'" Meanwhile Jones, at least according to one source, ducked into a ditch and out of harm's way.

Over the ridge top went the skirmishers, with the well-remembered exceptions of Jones and Sale's manservant John, who had marched to the front with the regiment but now mounted his master's horse and abandoned him with haste. After a moment of surprise—the terrain shielded Jones's men to the last minutes as well—Simonson's gunners gathered their wits, switched to canister, and began emptying their guns into the attackers. Almost simultaneously, the 10th Wisconsin of Harris's brigade, supporting the Federal battery on its left, and the 10th Ohio of Lytle's brigade to Simonson's right unleashed three wicked volleys at a range of 150 yards.[11] "Now there is nothing but the thunder of our artillery poring shells & canister into the rebel ranks," wrote Frank Phelps of the 10th Wisconsin. "We layed still . . . & watched our battery throw *death* into the rebels, we could see awful gaps in their ranks & then they would close up & march over their comrads, never stopping untill they got within 30 rods of us & just as they got on the top of a knowl the col. called out for us to *up & at them* & we pored in a deadly fire into them."[12]

For what must have seemed like an eternity in hell, Jones's brigade twitched along the brow of the ridge, regiments attempting no less than four times to descend into the ravine before finally giving up. Together, the brief explosion of close-range Federal fire killed fifty Mississippians outright, wounded perhaps four hundred, and ultimately drove the rest out of the ravine and back over the ridge. With a casualty rate approaching perhaps 50 percent, what was left of the Mississippi brigade finally reeled back toward friendly lines, so battered that it would not fight the rest of the day.[13]

The Mississippians' sacrifice had not been completely in vain. Not only had they drawn some fire away from Donelson's brigade as those Confederates fell back to safety—their real purpose, if Cheatham was in fact the man who ordered them forward—Jones's brigade did manage to bruise Harris's right flank, loosening it up it for later attack waves. Most of the Federal defenders finished the fight with lighter cartridge boxes, rounds they would miss desperately later in the afternoon. More crucially, those Federals would not have Simonson's battery with them at the front. During the attack, Jones's muskets and counterbattery fire from Lumsden's battery hit Simonson hard. The Federal battery lost fourteen men and sixteen horses before it was over. Finding it in bad shape, McCook's chief of artillery, Maj. Henry Cotter, immediately ordered Simonson to fall back about three hundred yards toward the high ground southeast of the Russell House, there to join Loomis's battery. McCook already had rushed the 38th Indiana up from a quarter-mile back to rescue Simonson, telling them "for God's sake to save that battery." Now, as Simonson withdrew, Harris pushed those Indianians forward to take the battery's place in line and anchor his weakened right. He did so not a moment too soon, for to his right, Bushrod Johnson's attackers appeared almost immediately to continue the contest.[14]

Bushrod Johnson was an anomaly, a Northerner in the Confederate army. Born in Ohio in 1817 of Quaker abolitionist parents, the West Pointer left the army after Seminole and Mexican War service under the cloud of a clumsy bribery attempt and black-market corruption. His options limited, Johnson taught at and eventually presided over struggling military schools in Kentucky and Tennessee. Embracing the latter state and eventually its cause, Johnson in 1861 followed Tennessee into the Confederacy. According to his biographer, the promise of advancement and martial glory in a new army, as compared to dimmer prospects in the army that had demanded his resignation, probably appealed to him more than Southern ideology. That glory proved slow in coming. Roundly criticized for approving the grossly inadequate site for the future Fort Henry, Johnson barely escaped from Fort Donelson before its surrender, returned to the army, and suffered a serious wound at Shiloh. Like his prewar career, Johnson's Confederate service thus far had been passable in most respects but hardly exemplary. Generally able if introverted, personally courageous in battle, Johnson unfortunately also could be diffident, irresolute, and downright unlucky under fire, unwilling to act without the approval of his superiors. On those occasions, his eagerness to win praise and advancement and to escape the stigma of his past led him to go along with his superiors even when he privately disagreed with their decisions. All of those negative qualities were about to shape his planned attack on Lytle's Federal line.[15]

As Johnson prepared to move out against the enemy, Buckner presented his brigade commander with hastily modified orders. Concerned with safeguarding his left flank, Buckner first shuffled Johnson's lines, detaching the 17th Tennessee Infantry to safeguard the left and support the left section of Darden's battery. Noting the strength of the enemy position and especially its batteries, something of which Johnson already was painfully well aware, Buckner then directed his subordinate to move the balance of his force obliquely down the slope about twenty degrees to the left, rather than straight ahead to the west as Bragg had intended. Such a march, taking advantage of all the cover provided by the hills opposite the creek, would bring them to the intersection of that creek and a country lane used by the Chathams to reach the wider Mackville Road at a point diagonally opposite Squire Bottom's house. In that manner he might avoid much of the fire sure to come from the Federal batteries on the heights above Doctor's Creek. "This was the key point on that part of the field," Buckner explained. "It was a strong position, the enemy being well covered by a natural parapet caused by an accident of the ground and several stone fences. A battery of artillery occupied its right, and its front was protected by the fire of another of his batteries towards his right, which swept partially the ground in front of his position."[16]

Unfortunately, not every regiment received those new orders, and chaos followed their nondelivery. Advancing in the first line across a wide front, the 5th Confederate Infantry and 25th, 44th, and 37th Tennessee Regiments— so arrayed from left to right—quickly became separated. On the far right of the line, completely unaware of Buckner's recent orders to move obliquely, the 37th Tennessee advanced steadily westward as originally ordered, toward the Jones-Harris front. However, the 44th Tennessee, in receipt of the new orders, wheeled obliquely to the left, creating a sizable gap between it and the 37th Tennessee.

Similar confusion existed farther down on Johnson's left. The 25th Tennessee emerged into the open in good order, but a series of rail fences immediately slowed and to degree broke up its approach. Nearing the stone fences at Doctor's Creek, Col. John M. Hughes reluctantly ordered his regiment to execute the ordered left oblique, even though he thought it a bad idea. Like the regiments on the right, the 25th Tennessee was now all but isolated as well, for the 5th Confederate Infantry had disappeared from sight. That regiment, in another condemnation of Johnson's clarity of expression, had somehow veered right, not left, and in so doing was passing from the left flank of the 25th Tennessee to its right rear.

Worse was still to come. Without warning, Johnson's three left regiments suddenly came under fire, but not from their front as expected. Instead, musketry to their left, at first scattered and then sustained, was followed by antipersonnel fire from a battery located to the south, east of the creek. As canister began whistling through the left flank of Johnson's front line, his Tennesseans realized that their attack had gone horribly and dangerously wrong.[17]

Neither Johnson nor his troops had any reason to know that the battery enfilading their exposed flank was Capt. Cuthbert H. Slocomb's 5th Battery, Washington Artillery, of Adams's Confederate brigade. What was Adams doing so close to Johnson's flank, and without Johnson's knowledge? And why was Slocomb firing on fellow Confederates? The answers again have much to do with the confusion rampant at the army's brigade and division levels. Still moving slowly in a stop-and-go manner thanks to Powell and Anderson's tardy advance, Adams's brigade had veered away from the Springfield Pike and crossed in front of Sheridan's Federals at Peters Hill, mostly shielded by intervening ridges. During and after the noontime artillery duel, Adams had continued moving northwest, toward the developing salient at Squire Bottom's house. "We were now getting close enough," John W. Headley wrote of the approach to the house, "to see that the Federal line extended away to the right with a gap to the left."[18] Like his comrades, Headley could not know that the "gap" actually divided Gilbert's corps from McCook's. Headley at least had a better grasp of the peril than Adams, who expressed confidence that he was still moving through secure Confederate territory. The men up ahead on the ridges must be fellow Confederates, he reasoned.

W. L Trask, screening the front of the column with Maj. John E. Austin's two-company battalion of sharpshooters, remembered the major result of Adams's wishful thinking. During the march, Adams ordered his skirmishers not to fire on anyone lest they kill fellow Southerners. Reaching a prominent hill southeast of Squire Bottom's house and south of the Mackville Road, from which "a long line of battle could be plainly seen . . . on top of a sloping hill beyond," Austin's sharpshooters moved into the valley below, up toward the banks of Bull Run. Slocomb's battery unlimbered back on the hilltop, a mere two hundred yards from the Mackville Road–Doctor's Creek intersection. The balance of the brigade followed and began forming into line on an east-west axis at the foot of the hill, hidden from both Federal lines by an intervening plateau just west of the creek. While they did so, Adams sent one of his aides, Lt. E. M. Scott, back to the rear with yet another message to Powell insisting that he hurry up. Whether Scott delivered the message or not is unknown, for he was never seen again. Powell would never arrive in that sector.[19]

Little had gone right for Adams thus far that afternoon, and now yet another unanticipated stumbling block appeared. A small, thirsty detachment from the 42nd Indiana had shifted farther south along Bull Run in search of water, and the men were drawing it from a spring near the run's banks when Austin's sharpshooters first emerged from the woods into the creek bottom. Promptly disobeying their brigade commander's orders, Austin's men opened fire the moment they saw blue. Continuing to believe that the line ahead of him was friendly, Adams reacted with anger, shouting at his men that they were firing on their fellow Confederates. "General Adams would not believe it was the enemy, and contended it was our own men," W. L. Trask remembered incredulously. "Our men knew better than Adam's did, and in spite of him, would fire a few shots at a party getting water from the spring in the ravine, killing five of them at the first volley." The men at the spring immediately grabbed their own rifles and returned fire.[20]

Sources differ as to just what Adams did next. According to one contemporary report, the general called out to Austin to cease firing. Austin refused. "'I tell you, sir, they are Yankees,'" the major replied.

"'I think not,'" Adams replied, "'and you had better go forward first, and ascertain.'"

Austin continued to argue. "'I go sir,'" he replied, "'but I don't think it necessary, for I know they are Yankees.'"

"'Well,'" Adams huffed, "'I'll go myself.'" Spurring his horse, Adams raced ahead a hundred yards, only to come under fire from the same Federals. Driven back to his lines, a chagrined Adams admitted his error and allowed Austin to continue the skirmish.[21]

In another, slightly less dramatic version, Adams was sighting one of Slocomb's guns when a Federal bullet fired by the water party flew over his head and crashed into the trees. At that, according to W. L. Trask, Adams finally admitted that the enemy lay just beyond the woods at Bull Run and Doctor's Creek. "By God, those are Yankees," he cried out to Slocomb, "*Fire!*" Slocomb recorded the exact time as 2:35 P.M.[22]

Whatever the details, Adams's battery and skirmishers coincidentally opened fire on the 42nd Indiana roughly at the same moment that Johnson's

Figure 11.1. An 1885 photograph of Doctor's Creek, showing the position of the 42nd Indiana. Photograph courtesy Massachusetts Commandery, Military Order of the Loyal Legion, and the U.S. Army Military History Institute.

brigade was launching its attack. Most of the Hoosiers still remained in or near the creek, down in the "slaughter trap" that had so worried James Shanklin. The Hoosiers had heard Johnson coming—Shanklin remembered someone in the woods ordering companies forward into line "by company left half wheel"—but he and most of the others mistakenly assumed it had to be comrades in blue, as the Rebels supposedly had retreated. When the regiment's commander, Col. James G. Jones, finally realized the error, he briskly ordered his men to pick up their stacked rifles and fire by file. As they did so, enfilading musketry and grapeshot from Darden's and Slocomb's batteries began careening through the deep ravine that was the dry creek bed, followed almost immediately by the uncoordinated but threatening approach of the 37th Tennessee on the Indianians' left. Still unable to see the enemy in the woods but well aware of the enemy presence on both regiments' flanks, Jones realized that he was in a bad fix. As he considered a retreat, one of Lytle's staff officers arrived on the scene and directed the regiment to "break by companies to the rear," starting with those on the left, and reform on the 10th Ohio on the high ground to the rear. At first orderly, the retreat quickly degenerated into every man for himself. Men raced down the creek bed or else climbed the precipitous bank of the ravine and then fled uphill as fast as they could run.[23] "Oliver [Buzingham] was killed by my side as we retreated up the hill," William Stuckey wrote his wife of one comrade, "he was struck with a ball in the back he fell and ask me for help but there was no place to stop and help wounded men."[24]

As the 42nd Indiana hastily fell back to safety, Adams noticed the bulk of Johnson's first line moving across his front in the same direction, directly into Slocomb's line of fire. Now far from confident that he was in friendly territory, and blinded by the thick woods separating the two brigades, Adams easily assumed that Johnson's regiments were more Yankees falling back from forward positions. He acted accordingly, directing Slocomb to continue his fire. Adams thus unleashed exactly the sort of "friendly fire" he initially had sought so assiduously to avoid.[25]

As solid shot and fragments from exploding spherical case shot began tearing into his exposed flank, Johnson's already collapsing line went to pieces in confusion. Encountering the 42nd Indiana just after the Federals opened up on Adams's brigade, the 37th Tennessee fired into the bluecoats and kept moving to the creek as the Hoosiers began to fall back. Only when he emerged from the woods did Col. Moses White of the 37th Tennessee discover, as he put it, "that we were separated from the brigade, which was to us a matter of no little surprise, as we had received no command but forward."

The 44th Tennessee was still wheeling to the left when Slocomb opened fire on it. Colonel John S. Fulton, not anticipating the presence of a battery on his left, understandably assumed that the barrage came from Union guns. Several men fell instantly. The regiment wheeled even more sharply to the left in response, away from Lytle's Federal line and almost directly south, toward the battery. As men continued to fall, there seemed to be no alternative but to take the guns. Accordingly, Fulton ordered his men to fix bayonets and charge the concealed, presumably Federal battery.[26]

The 25th Tennessee also received fire from Slocomb's guns. When the 44th Tennessee appeared on his front, moving south toward the battery, Colonel Hughes decided to turn south and follow in support. At roughly the same moment, Col. James A. Smith of the 5th Confederate, having crossed behind the 25th Tennessee, also ordered his men to wheel toward the forested hill. Thus, instead of advancing west against Lytle's lines on the ridges above the creek, three of the four regiments in Johnson's first line now independently wheeled south to assault a battery none had expected to encounter.[27]

Their bayonets shining, the angry men of the 44th Tennessee tore through the woods and stormed the hill from which the galling fire emanated. Gaining the crest, the Tennesseans discovered to their amazement none other than Adams's Confederates. No record of their subsequent exchange survives, but it could not have been pleasant. At least the guns ceased firing. The tragi-comedy of errors then continued over the next few minutes as the 25th Tennessee appeared as well, followed at least to the base of the hill by the 5th Confederate. Completely dumbfounded by that juncture, and still nervously unwilling to admit that a Federal assault on his guns was not brewing somewhere in the woods below, Adams pulled rank on the Tennessee regiments. He held the 44th Tennessee in reserve and ordered the 25th Tennessee to advance in support of Slocomb's battery to a point a hundred yards forward, in the creek bottom to the rear of the Bottom House. From there, the now-exposed Louisiana gunners opened up on the stationary enemy visible to the left, Sheridan's troops on Peters Hill. A brief artillery duel lasting perhaps ten minutes ensued between Slocomb's gunners and Capt. Henry Hescock's Union battery, stirring up a great deal of dust without injuring anyone seriously.[28]

While Johnson's first line came unglued, apparently without his knowledge, he ordered his second into action as Buckner directed, thus adding to the bedlam. On the left, the 23rd Tennessee moved slowly in the wake of the 5th Confederate, impeded by the broken nature of the ground as well as several stone and rail fences. As they neared the front, the regiment shifted more to the left so as to come up on the left flank of the 5th Confederate as it moved away from Adams's lines and resumed its westward trek toward Lytle's brigade. Meanwhile, the flanking 17th Tennessee, given no definite orders but now simply told by Buckner, not Johnson, to advance, moved toward the Bottom House. Finally realizing that the enemy had fallen back across the creek, and with no further word forthcoming from his brigade commander, Col. Albert S. Marks decided to occupy a prominent hill visible ahead to the right of Squire Bottom's house. From there he thought he could assail the enemy from the left. As he drew closer, however, he saw the 5th Confederate emerging from beneath the bluff. Hoping to cooperate with that regiment, and surprised by the steepness of the banks of Doctor's Creek below the hill he had fixed upon, Marks veered left as well, unintentionally occupying the gap between the 5th Confederate and 37th Tennessee.[29]

Thus, as it lurched toward Lytle's Union line, Johnson's muddled and poorly commanded brigade had flown apart like a crazy carnival ride, spinning out of control. Two regiments, the 25th and 44th Tennessee, temporarily remained under Adams's control, while the other four again approached Squire Bottom's house, the original first and second lines intermingled beyond recognition. The 23rd Tennessee, 5th Confederate, 17th Tennessee, and 37th Tennessee formed a rough line of battle from left to right, the right flank regiments out in front and the line probably angling back somewhat to the southeast. Johnson might have straightened out the mess had he been up front, but he had remained in the rear while Buckner ordered his regiments about piecemeal.[30]

Across the creek, with a sizable enemy force coming right at him, William Lytle ordered the bulk of the 3rd Ohio back up to the rail fence on the ridge crest above the Bottom House, the position it had abandoned during the artillery fight. From there it hopefully would join the 10th Ohio to the left in

Figure 11.2. "Squire" Henry P. Bottom House in 1885. Photograph courtesy Massachusetts Commandery, Military Order of the Loyal Legion, and the U.S. Army Military History Institute.

blunting the enemy assault. They retook the position in the face of withering artillery fire from Darden's and Slocomb's batteries. Loomis's and Simonson's batteries and Hotchkiss's section responded from the Russell House, but largely shot over the heads of the attacking Confederates. As the Confederate line approached to within rifle range, about 150 yards distant, the men of the 3rd Ohio rose from prone positions behind the rail fence and emptied the first of many volleys into it. From the heights to the Confederate right, the 10th Ohio opened fire as well.[31] "The shock was terrific," Capt. C. W. Frazer of the 5th Confederate later wrote, ". . . the line swayed as one body, leaving a track of dead and wounded to mark its former position."[32]

Recovering from the shock, Johnson's men responded, and soon both sides were firing at each other with furious abandon. Lytle remembered that the sound thus produced was "deafening," so loud in the bowl-shaped depression created by the hills that he could not discern the location of the enemy artillery.[33] "For a time," John Beatty, the unpopular colonel of the 3rd Ohio, remembered, "I do not know how long thereafter, it seemed as if all hell had broken loose; the air was filled with hissing balls; shells were exploding continuously, and the noise of the guns was deafening."[34] Men fell all around as the Confederates raked the Federal position "with destructive effect. Capt. H. H. Cunard, Company I, was one of the first to fall," Beatty reported, "shot through the head . . . A little later Capt. Leonidas McDougal, Company H, while waving his sword and cheering his men, fell pierced by a ball though the breast."[35]

The stand-up fight continued for several minutes. Then Colonel Marks of the 17th Tennessee begged Johnson for permission to charge forward to the stone wall running parallel to the western bank of the creek, as the enemy fire was cutting his regiment to pieces in its exposed position. At first reluctant, Johnson finally approved the order. Shouting the rebel yell loudly enough to be heard over the cacophony of battle as far back as Bragg's position, Marks's Tennesseans double-quicked up to the wall, followed by the 5th Confederate.[36] The 37th Tennessee simultaneously filed to the right toward a rail fence that ran diagonally toward the road from the stone wall. "Here," Colonel Moses White reported, "we were met with an almost overwhelming storm of lead from a corn or cane field near by"—fire most likely coming from the 10th Ohio on the heights to the 37th's right. Desperate for better cover, White ordered his men to climb the rail fence and advance another fifty yards through Squire Bottom's yard and past his house, toward a second stone wall running parallel to the one the 17th Tennessee held. Over the fence the Tennesseans charged, gaining the western stone fence after a brief hand-to-hand struggle despite heavy casualties inflicted by the 3rd Ohio. To their left, six companies of the 17th Tennessee crawled over the eastern wall and raced toward the second stone wall, arriving at roughly the same time. More pressure on the outnumbered Federal regiments quickly appeared in the form of the 23rd Tennessee and 5th Confederate Infantry, which also now advanced under Johnson's orders to the wall at a midpoint between the 17th and 37th Tennessee. Shielded solely by the rail fence and Squire Bottom's barn, which helped anchor the Ohioans' position near the road, the Federal defenders absorbed heavy casualties.[37] "All along our front," wrote Captain Frazer of the 5th Confederate Infantry, "a solid line of dead and wounded lay, in some places three deep, extending to the right from the barn."[38] In contrast, the stone walls, cane, tall corn or cut shocks on the slope below the Federal position, and the slope itself all combined to limit the Federal fields of fire. However, pinned down behind the relative safety of the wall, the two Confederate regiments blasted away at the enemy but could go no farther. Johnson's men alone could not dislodge the Federal defenders. Plagued by poor leadership on Buckner's and Johnson's part, a tangled and treacherous terrain that defied advancing lines, and Lytle's position on the commanding heights above, Johnson's attack had ground to a halt.

To some Confederates not directly involved at the moment, like Louisianian W. L. Trask of Adams's brigade, the scene seemed marvelous. Trask called it "the grandest but the most awful sight, ever looked upon. . . . the enemy stood firm . . . pouring heavy fire into our lines with considerable

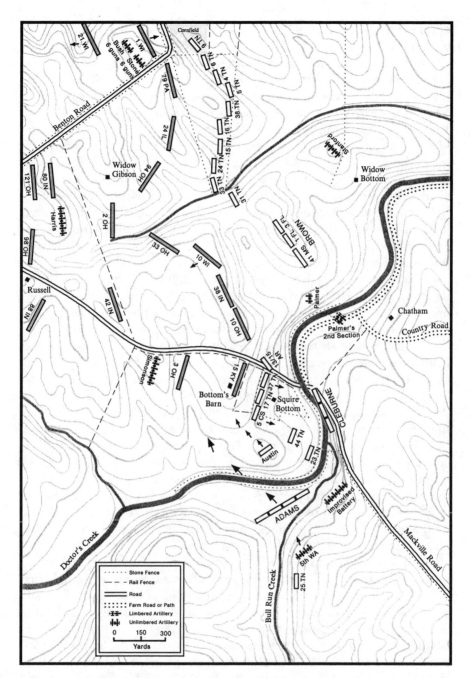

Map 11.1. Squire Bottom House sector, 3:45 P.M.

effect but not half so damaging as would have been supposed considering the closeness of the range."[39]

Watching from the rear, Buckner saw nothing "grand." Indeed, he realized to his dismay that the brigade had bogged down above the creek, having engaged "a heavier force of the enemy than when it first conjectured." The Tennesseans clearly needed assistance. Accordingly, Buckner called for Pat Cleburne's brigade and sent word for St. John Liddell to move forward his tired Arkansans from their reserve position in the rear in order to safeguard the division's left. As Cleburne started moving forward, Buckner finally learned that his left was safe, for Adams's entire brigade was on the scene at the Bottom House, across the road from Johnson in the bottom of Bull Run. He rode there quickly and ordered Adams into action. Encountering Johnson's 44th Tennessee, temporarily detained by Adams, Buckner ordered the regiment to form into line of battle and move forward as well, probably behind the 23rd Tennessee.[40]

From the creek bed, Slocomb's battery took aim at the Federal batteries at the Russell House. An exploding shell crashed into one of Simonson's limber chests, the subsequent eruption sending the battery for cover. Historians Charles Bishop and Ralph Wooster maintain that the experience on the part of Confederate batteries, notably action at Shiloh, meant that Bragg's gunners consistently out shot their less-experienced Federal counterparts all day. That was not always true, however, as William Carnes and Thomas Stanford might attest from their experience in the earlier artillery duel, but it was the case along the front in the vicinity of Squire Bottom's house. Despite their inferior weapons, the Confederate gunners held the edge in skill.[41]

With such support, Adams's infantry entered the fray. The Louisianians moved quickly northwest toward the Bottom House, along a front forming a ninety-degree angle with Johnson's lines. Austin's sharpshooters formed the right of the Louisiana brigade's line, fired one volley into the enemy, and then splashed through the dank puddles of Doctor's Creek to the rock wall on the opposite bank. "A perfect storm of bullets was rained on us, " John Headley remembered, "or rather on the fence."[42]

Meanwhile, Adams's main line continued advancing to a point within three hundred yards of Lytle's position. Still forward of the rest of their brigade, Austin's sharpshooters drew up to the south side of Squire Bottom's stone walls at the double-quick and opened up on the Federals along the rail fence. At roughly the same moment, a Confederate shell struck Squire Bottom's barn. Stuffed with threshed wheat and oats for the oncoming winter, as well as with some of Lytle's wounded, the barn ignited and quickly blazed into an inferno hot enough to blister the faces of those close to it and burn alive the men within. Flames shot from the door, windows, and from between the logs. As the men inside the fiery furnace shrieked in agony, the companies closest to it could not help but shift away. Smoke soon enveloped the compressing line as the west wind shifted to the south.[43]

Twice already, the 3rd Ohio's Colonel Beatty had rebuffed Col. Curran Pope of the reserve 15th Kentucky, who eagerly hoped to exchange places with the Buckeyes. The veteran Ohioans had little confidence in the inexperienced outfit they derisively called "The Paper Collar Regiment" because of its excessively neat appearance. But now, with its supply of ammunition already running out, numbers rapidly mounting against it, and the blazing barn confusing his line, Beatty reluctantly agreed to fall back to the bottom of the ridge and let the Kentuckians have a go at the enemy. As the 15th Kentucky moved up to the crest with fixed bayonets, Beatty's Ohioans gave way in good order, as their colonel later boasted. They left a third of their comrades behind, dead and wounded men strewn about the smoky ridge in windrows.[44]

It was now Pope's turn to face the steel and lead whirlwind. "The roar of musketry and artillery which greeted its appearance," wrote a 42nd Indiana soldier, "sounded not like successive volleys, but like the continued rattle of ten thousand drums."[45] It was a deadly rattle. Almost immediately after moving forward, men began to fall, and enemy riflemen soon shot the regimental colors to tatters. Pope himself was hit in the left shoulder, although not seriously it seemed, and his horse fell dead beneath him. Many other Unionist Kentuckians fell in the chaos. Shot in the arm, Coleman Spencer fell back to the rear carrying his rifle. Pursuing the wounded private, Lt. Col. George P. Jouett "considerately told him to drop his gun, and support his wounded arm with his right hand."[46] At that moment, Jouett promptly went down himself with a more serious wound. "Lt. Col. Jouett was shot in the leg," Pope wrote after the battle, "and Lieut. [James A. T.] McGrath went to his assistance. After raising him, he himself was shot dead through the head. Major [William P.] Campbell was shot through the body about the same time, and was borne from the field to a house where he died immediately afterwards." Nonetheless, Pope continued, "the firing of the regiment had not been interrupted by these events at all, but was kept up with overwhelming effect, and we had succeeded in driving the enemy entirely beyond the stone fence."[47]

Hoping to flank the 15th Kentucky as it came into position, Austin ordered his sharpshooters to double-quick farther down the fence line to the left, to a clear spot of ground just past the house. From there they could turn right and enfilade the enemy. Pope observed the flanking maneuver, however, and the 15th Kentucky responded with heavy fire into Austin's Confederates. "It was a clean spot of ground outside of the farm between the creek and the enemy," according to John Headley. "We went yelling about half way, aiming to flank the enemy at a large barn. Major Austin was right along on my horse. I did not see how he escaped. The fire in front of us and from both flanks was too hot and Major Austin ordered us back behind the rock fence." Headley's mention of fire on "both flanks" suggests yet another friendly fire incident involving Confederate artillery.[48]

Figure 11.3. Col. Curran Pope. Photograph courtesy U.S. Army Military History Institute.

Austin, Adams determined, had the right idea but too few men. As the sharpshooters retreated to safety, the balance of Adams's line crossed the creek behind them and formed up on the sharpshooters, creating a brigade line running in a generally east-west direction, almost parallel to the Mackville Road, and well past the 15th Kentucky's exposed position. Lytle's right-flank regiments now found themselves caught in a butternut-and-gray nutcracker that threatened to snap shut at any moment. To at least partially blunt the new threat, three companies from the 3rd Ohio and two from the 15th Kentucky changed front and formed perpendicularly along a rail fence facing the Louisianians.[49]

Of particular interest to W. L. Trask and some others at that moment were a "few Negroes" seen fighting alongside Lytle's men. African Americans clearly participated in the fight between Lytle's and Adams's brigades, but while at least a few Black soldiers are known to have fought with at least the 13th Louisiana on the Confederate side, the identity of the men on the Federal side of the lines remains unknown. Union sources do not mention their presence, which might suggest postwar racism, but could also theoretically mean that their presence was unremarkable or even protected. "Contrabands," escaped slaves who had fled to the Union lines, supported the Federal military in a host of ways during the Civil War, from driving wagons to cooking to burying the dead. Many left farms and plantations to join the Yankee columns during the marches from Nashville and Louisville, in some cases to be hidden and shielded by Northern soldiers in defiance of their officers. Others probably fell in at Perryville. Preston Sleet, a neighborhood slave, later claimed to have fought in the battle there. A number of Blacks accompanied slave-owning officers as personal servants, and some of them escaped across the lines as well. Whatever their status or point of origin, African Americans fought and died in the vicinity of the burning barn and Squire Bottom's house, most of them for the Union.[50]

Despite the added contribution of a few Black combatants, possibly for the first time in the American Civil War, Lytle's brigade, the nut in the Confederate nutcracker, remained in serious trouble. His outnumbered line also had ammunition problems. Having gone into combat with forty rounds, the men were running dangerously low, and Lytle had no idea where the ammunition train was. Even worse, two of his staff officers sent to the rear to find Rousseau and seek help, returned and informed him bitterly that with Jackson's division in such trouble on the left, Rousseau could furnish no additional men.[51]

Watching it all unfold, Gilbert's Federal III Corps, although so near on the ridges to the right, frustratingly remained little more than spectators to the contest. Concerned with his own front, Phil Sheridan sat passively on Peters Hill. How could that be? Yet again, command confusion and personal rivalries plagued Gilbert's troubled corps—and in so doing endangered the army as a whole.[52]

Well past noon, hours after the fight for Peters and Bottom Hills, Dan McCook's tired rookie brigade had remained in the woods east of Peters Hill, while the rest of Sheridan's division dug in. During the artillery fight at midday, Hescock's battery on Peters Hill joined in with "occasional escapades of artillery," but the Missouri artillerymen largely left the affair to McCook's gunners. Then, at about 2 P.M., the worst time possible in retrospect, Gilbert sent orders pulling Sheridan's forward units back onto Peters Hill with the rest. After a clumsy retreat occasioned by McCook's rookies, Sheridan formed an arcing line along the eastern crest of the hill. From there, the dry bed of Doctor's Creek and about 150 yards separated McCook's left from the right of his older brother's corps, which greatly concerned the young general. Despite Gay's cavalry and two howitzers, which lay in the depression between I and III Corps in a static, dismounted line, young McCook remained worried about his flank. Gay, after all, had displayed little energy in protecting McCook's position that morning. With Gilbert's permission, McCook sent the 86th Illinois into the intervening woods, placed them behind a wooden fence, and ordered them to shoot anything that moved.[53]

The 86th Illinois barely had reached its new position on Dan McCook's left when the Confederate attack on I Corps commenced to the north. He watched with horror as the enemy wheeled artillery onto the heights beyond and opened up on his brother's corps. Then Johnson's infantry advanced against Lytle. Sheridan, for his part, later claimed that upon seeing Johnson's Confederates advancing, he had tried to warn Alex McCook by signaling to him. If true, no one responded. Sheridan's men then noticed between the trees Adams's brigade moving into its position on the hill above Squire Bottom's house, followed by puffs of white smoke that warned of incoming fire.

"Their guns were admirably handled," one Federal remembered, "and began to throw shot among us too lively for enjoyment." Despite Slocomb's accurate shooting, however, no one was injured and nothing was lost other than two haversacks, a deck of cards, and a backpack, shot from the man wearing it without harming him.[54] Sheridan responded by ordering Hescock's battery forward to a position from which it could more effectively assail Slocomb. McCook's brigade and two additional regiments would support Hescock. Captain Charles M. Barnett's Illinois battery, still on Peters Hill, also opened fire. Together, the two batteries dueled with Slocomb's gunners for a few more minutes while Dan McCook's infantry shifted to their left. However, when Slocomb moved up again and shifted his aim back to Lytle's brigade, Sheridan's batteries fell silent. Many assumed that their batteries had driven the Confederates off the hill entirely; perhaps Sheridan did too. At any rate he did nothing else to help I Corps, even after receiving a message from McCook dispatched at 2:30 asking him "to look to my right and see that it was not turned."[55]

Why did Sheridan act—or rather not act—as he did? Even if one absolves him of the standard but unfair charge of allowing Adams to pass in front of his position—there is no evidence from Sheridan's men that suggests Adams marched by in full view, and a simple examination of the terrain demonstrates how easily that brigade could pass by unobserved—his passivity is still worth consideration. Some of it, as Kenneth Hafendorfer correctly argues, had to do with his adverse relationship with Gilbert.[56] The corps commander, as usual, was in a testy mood that afternoon, and Sheridan, a subordinate who had openly questioned Gilbert's right to command, remained the object of his greatest ire. Anxious to keep a tight rein on the impetuous and obviously jealous "Little Phil," whose bellicosity Gilbert worried still might bring on a general engagement before Buell wanted it, Gilbert had sent nagging messages by signal flag from his headquarters to an increasingly annoyed Sheridan, repeatedly ordering him to remain in place.

In doing so, however, Gilbert only wasted his signalmen's time. Sheridan by early afternoon had lost the aggressiveness that immediately followed the exciting storming of Bottom Hill. More than Gilbert's orders ultimately chained Sheridan to Peters Hill. Increasingly convinced that he faced an overwhelming force gathering to renew the fight, Sheridan later admitted that he needed no reminders from Gilbert to hold the line and sit "snugly fixed in the rifle pits. . . . I replied to each message that I was not bringing on an engagement, but that the enemy evidently intended to do so, and that I believed I should shortly be attacked."[57]

The simple tenacity exhibited by St. John Liddell's Arkansas brigade earlier in the day clearly had given Sheridan second thoughts. In the absence of good intelligence from Gay, whose troopers now essentially functioned as no more than mounted infantry, Sheridan might be excused for expecting a momentary assault against his position, one that might turn McCook's right were he not cautious. Seizing Bottom Hill had required effort, and its defenders that morning remained out there somewhere. Moreover, the Confederate attack clearly was cascading in echelon from north to south, suggesting that the enemy would next assail Sheridan's lines, hitting him with a punch equal to that which Lytle was receiving. It made sense. Sheridan had no way to know that the enemy's command structure reeked with as much ineptitude as his own, and thus assumed that Peters Hill was only lightly held. As a result, Sheridan clung to his "snug" rifle pits, awaiting the hammer blow he expected to fall on his division. The best way to protect McCook's right, he concluded, was to hold Peters Hill.[58]

To a degree, Sheridan was right to hesitate. Hardee did plan to seize Peters Hill. Hardly realizing that an entire corps lurked behind its heights, however, he prepared to accomplish the job and deliver the coup de grâce with Powell's lone brigade. Since initially lurching forward late in the morning before falling behind Adams, Powell's slow-moving regiments had remained on Edwards House Hill, supporting Capt. Overton Barret's battery of six-pounders and keeping track of the battle's progress as best they could. At length, around three o'clock, an aide arrived with orders from Bragg for Powell to seize Peters Hill and silence the battery on its crest. The brigade formed into line and slowly began moving forward overland toward the hill and Hescock's battery. To an anxious Sheridan, Powell's regiments seemed a juggernaut, or at least the tip of one, and he braced for the attack. Any thought of supporting Lytle dissolved once and for all when Powell's little brigade slowly marched into view. He quickly ordered Dan McCook back to his starting point and turned his guns to answer the new threat.

As far as Sheridan was concerned, he could give no assistance to Alex McCook. The men on the heights behind Squire Bottom's house were on their own.[59] That was not the answer I Corps's commander needed to hear. With no help coming from Sheridan, he desperately cast about elsewhere. McCook sent staff officer Capt. Horace N. Fisher to look for "the nearest commander of troops" and ask for assistance. Racing southwest into Gilbert's rear, Fisher found Gilbert's reserve division commander, Albin Schoepf, first. It was about 3:30 P.M., and Schoepf was leading Col. Moses B. Walker's and Brig. Gen. James B. Steedman's brigades up the Springfield Pike to go into line on Sheridan's right. Explaining the situation, Fisher begged Schoepf for assistance. Expressing his willingness to help, the touchy Schoepf nonetheless refused to do so unless Gilbert approved. He had had enough problems with Buell already. Gilbert, Schoepf indicated, was with Buell at the Dorsey House; only he had the authority to change his orders. Chagrined, Fisher spurred his horse and headed for Buell's headquarters.

With no sign of Fisher, McCook then sent another of his staff officers, Capt. W. T. Hoblitzell, ironically, to locate Schoepf. If he could not find Schoepf, McCook told Hoblitzell to locate "the commander of the nearest troops in the rear to inform him of my condition and ask for troops." At the same time, ninety minutes into the battle, McCook also sent his first report directly to Buell, dispatching his aide, Maj. Caleb Bates, to headquarters. Why did McCook wait so long? That question has intrigued many, including Buell himself, ever since the battle. McCook never answered it before the Buell Commission, or anywhere else for that matter, leading scholars such as Buell biographer James Robert Chumney to place the blame for what occurred that day squarely on McCook's shoulders. Somewhat more charitably, Kenneth Hafendorfer suggests that McCook was simply spoiling for a fight and probably worried that Buell would order him to fall back if he reported his dilemma. Several soldiers in the ranks that day later would agree that McCook acted rashly, and McCook himself castigated Buell in his testimony for not reinforcing him so that he could continue the fight in the morning. However, McCook later claimed to have little ill will for Buell himself. His real anger flared up when he execrated Gilbert for not helping him on the right flank.

While aggressiveness may well have been a factor, a more immediate explanation suggests itself: sheer panic. Confronted by a surprise attack, engaged on all sides, McCook without warning faced the fight of his life. Tunnel vision, much like that displayed by Terrill on the Open Knob, forced him to concentrate totally on the immediate task at hand: saving his corps. Gilbert's brigades lay to the south in full view, so close. Why waste time with the chain of command when a brother officer stood in a position to help? McCook needed help then and there, and Gilbert could easily provide it. Only when elements of III Corps refused to help, a memory that still incensed McCook months later, did he think to inform Buell. Like a drowning man, McCook groped for the closest life jacket available. Only when it eluded his grasp did he think to shout to shore for help.[60]

Although nowhere as near to the scene of the hardest fighting as Gilbert's III Corps, Thomas Crittenden's command also stood in a position where it conceivably could have turned the tide of battle and rescued I Corps. Once again, however, Buell's overconfidence and personality problems within the army's leadership combined to undermine the Union cause and endanger the army that defended it. As a result, II Corps offered no direct assistance either.

Since eleven that morning, when Smith's and Van Cleve's divisions had reached their designated place on the Lebanon Pike three miles from town, the officers and men of Crittenden's corps had occupied themselves with extending the line on the Federal right. Thomas, unwilling to meet with Buell personally, had sent his chief of artillery, Capt. O. A. Mack, to headquarters to report the corps' tardy arrival and ask for instructions. The noise of cannonading on the left worried both Thomas and Mack as the latter officer rode off, but a satisfactory explanation was soon forthcoming. Arriving at headquarters about 12:30, Mack encountered Gilbert and told him that he "thought there was a battle . . . going on." Gilbert, falling back on the explanation favored at headquarters, disagreed, responding that the noise represented nothing more than Gay skirmishing with the enemy. Both Buell and the officer of the day, Speed Fry, concurred with Gilbert's assessment. The Federal commander then told Mack that he had put off the planned attack until morning. Leaving the details up to Thomas, Buell instructed Mack to tell Thomas to leave two divisions astride and right of the Lebanon Pike, but to dispatch a third farther south so as to advance east down the Mitchellsburg Road with a brigade of cavalry, prefatory to an attack on the ninth. As Mack prepared to return to his post, Buell cautioned him that while he did not want an overall attack that day, Thomas had permission to push forward cautiously if it would result in more water for the army.[61]

Despite the stiff west wind, many of Crittenden's men heard the clash of artillery that signaled the Confederate attack on McCook's corps. At times the soldiers of Van Cleve's northernmost division could also hear musketry. Occasional frightened, riderless horses ran through the lines of the 44th Indiana, increasing those men's anxieties. Crittenden himself heard no musketry, however, and he expressed little concern about the artillery. Like so many others, he dismissed it as comparable to the "shelling the woods" he had heard during the stationary siege of Corinth. He too assumed that an artillery duel or skirmish with cavalry had broken out. The battle would begin the next day, he reasoned, just as Buell wanted.

Somewhat more concerned with the clamor than the nominal corps commander, Thomas persuaded Crittenden to at least send a staff officer to ask Gilbert about the source of the commotion. The officer rode off; he would not return until almost sundown. In the meantime, no other information arrived from headquarters. Out of touch with headquarters all morning, Crittenden's corps never established a link with Buell's signalers either. Without additional orders or information, or even a clear sense of what was happening to the north, Thomas accordingly began putting Buell's most recent orders sent via Mack into effect. He dispatched Smith toward Mitchellsburg, away from Perryville, as Wood neared the front. At about three, Wood's brigade came up, the men's pace quickening with the distant sounds of battle, and the brigade began shifting to the left of Van Cleve's division and moving into line of battle. The men in Van Cleve's ranks interpreted the hustle and bustle as clear signs of impending battle, and wondered why it did not come.[62] "The regiment lay . . . in line all day except while engaged in throwing down a fence in its immediate front," one Hoosier remembered. "Batteries came galloping up to the line and wheeled into position. Hither and yon staff officers might be seen galloping in hot haste with orders for the different parts of the line. 'The rumble and roar' of battle on the left could be distinctly heard. . . . But the regiment only waited, that was all."[63]

A modicum of danger did exist for at least some in II Corps. In front of Smith's lines on the Lebanon Pike, Joe Wheeler's cavalry continued tormenting the Federals with cavalry dashes and artillery. As the hours passed, the cavalry fight slowly rolled south toward Mitchellsburg and Brumfield Station. Scattered skirmishing involving the infantry also continued with regularity, the men expecting heavy action at any moment. At one point, Wheeler's artillery opened up on Edward McCook's cavalry but overshot into Col. William B. Hazen's brigade, "the shells bursting about a quarter mile from us, wounding several. . . . some balls from skirmishers came close" as well, according to Eden P. Sturges of Battery B, 1st Ohio Artillery, attached to Cruft's brigade. Cruft's gunners, joined by Capt. Daniel T. Cockerill's Battery F, 1st Ohio Artillery, from Hazen's, responded in kind as Smith's division advanced in front of Cockerill's guns and pushed back the Confederate cavalry.[64]

On another occasion, a company of mounted rebels rushed forward in what seemed to be an attempt to capture Thomas, who had ridden to the front with his staff to survey the scene.[65] "As they wheeled and put spurs to their horses," Eastham Tarrant of the Federal 1st Kentucky Cavalry wrote, "we opened a scathing fire on their advance, which caused them to retire."[66]

Nonetheless, Wheeler's contributions, as significant and annoying to II Corps as they were, have been exaggerated. Never one to hide his candle under a basket, Wheeler set the tone a few days after the battle when he claimed that his men had held off at least two enemy divisions.[67] That Wheeler would think that makes sense, but little evidence exists that Crittenden's men were fooled by Wheeler, or even took much notice of him. Buell's orders and the strained communications between Buell and Thomas did more to keep II Corps out of the battle, much to the consternation of the men. Those factors probably would have held the corps in position Wheeler or no Wheeler. Indeed, the diminutive "War Child's" determination to hunker down and keep the enemy force off-balance may have injured the Confederate cause more than it helped. For hours, Wheeler believed that he faced only cavalry. Not until around three did Bragg receive word that Wheeler in fact faced a sizable force on the Lebanon Pike, and Wheeler's report was so vague as to offer Bragg little useful information. The Battle of Perryville might have been quite different had Bragg known that an unbloodied Federal corps waited to the south. And Bragg should have known—it was Wheeler's job to tell him. However, because he did not, the Confederate attack continued unabated.[68]

One can say this for Wheeler's cavalrymen: Without their efforts on

Figure 11.4. Brig. Gen. William Lytle. Photograph courtesy Cincinnati Museum Center.

the Lebanon Pike, Edward McCook's horse soldiers would have been free to ride straight into Perryville and provide *their* commanders with more accurate information. Had they done so, they would have found a wide-open Confederate flank ripe for a II Corps attack. The entire battle, indeed the course of the war in the West, might have changed. But that would have required Buell to react promptly, or Thomas to act upon such information and move without Buell's express orders. Even that seems unlikely, however. In the end, it was Buell and Thomas who kept the bulk of II Corps out of the Battle of Perryville, not Wheeler. The scattered fighting along the Lebanon Pike remained a sideshow.

While the men of II Corps waited and Sheridan's division braced for an attack, the Confederates maintained the pressure on Rousseau's bending division. At the Bottom House salient, the "square stand-up . . . fight" involving Lytle's Federals and Adams's and Johnson's Confederate brigades continued into its second hour. By 4:30 P.M., Lytle's men were about out of ammunition. Johnson's regiments, who had been engaged longer than the Louisianians, were also running low.[69]

Help was on the way to Johnson, however. First came renewed pressure on Lytle's left, at the brigade's juncture with Leonard Harris's brigade, in the form of the three-regiment brigade commanded by thirty-five-year-old Brig. Gen. John Calvin Brown. Like Thomas Jones's brigade, Hardee had detached Brown from Patton Anderson's division earlier in the day to fill the gap between the two Confederate wings. Now, Brown's new assignment must have seemed close to impossible: advance over the same ground that had bedeviled Jones's brigade less than an hour before with a brigade of similar size, cross the deep valley and sinkhole that had stymied Jones, and cut off Harris's brigade from Lytle's. Brown brought competence but relatively little experience to the task. Enlisting as a private at the beginning of the war, the former attorney quickly rose to command of the 3rd Tennessee Infantry. After being captured at Fort Donelson while commanding a Tennessee brigade, Brown was exchanged in August 1862. The Confederate War Department promptly promoted him to brigadier general. He subsequently led a new, mixed brigade consisting of the 1st Florida Infantry, the 3rd Florida Infantry, and the large 41st Mississippi Infantry from Chattanooga into Kentucky. Also attached to the brigade at Chattanooga was Capt. Joseph E. Palmer's Battery A, 14th Battalion, Georgia Light Artillery. Known as the "States Rights Battery," it previously had been stationed in north Georgia. So raw were Palmer's men that one later expressed amazement at seeing body lice for the first time at Perryville. Indeed, aside from the 1st Florida, Brown's entire command remained untested in battle, and men such as company officer John Inglis of the 3rd Florida longed to prove their mettle in a fight.[70]

More than an hour into the battle, however, Brown's brigade remained in reserve, his men flat on their faces as artillery shells intended for Lumsden's nearby battery on the right and their own on the left fell around them, wounding several and frightening the rest. Jones's brigade to their front advanced and retreated, while off to the left, Johnson's battle with the Federals at Squire Bottom's house flared up and raged. Like most Civil War soldiers, Brown's men found waiting for their first combat to be maddening, an emotional combination of fear and excitement stimulated by a plethora of stimuli. Undergoing an artillery barrage only made it worse. "We could see for miles in front," Inglis confided to his diary, "men getting enough of this, no way to hit back, and battery not replying to enemy."[71]

William Ralston Talley of Palmer's battery recalled the experience of "the first shells I ever heard passing over my head. I tell you they sounded terrible to me. We went out of the woods into a field on the side of a hill where the corn had been cut down and shocked. We stopped on the brow of the hill and could see the battle across on hills beyond . . . in a meadow near a fence as I was looking that way, I saw a man fall—the first man I ever saw shot down."[72]

At last, around 3:30 P.M., after an agonizing hour under artillery fire, Brown ordered his men to stand "as if on drill, raised his sword, and with the command 'forward, guide right, march,'" led them forward in line of battle. As was the case with Jones earlier, there is no indication as to who ordered the brigade into action. With division commander Anderson at Powell's shoulder on the far left and Cheatham engrossed on the far right, the best guess is Polk. Neither Hardee nor Buckner indicated any knowledge of the movement. At any rate, down the hill the brigade advanced, first walking, then at a "trot," and finally running, the men screaming the rebel yell as they went to relieve their pent-up emotions. As they neared the dry bed of Doctor's Creek, the shouting, inspired mass came to an uninspiring dead stop when the 3rd Florida, having gotten ahead of the other two regiments, encountered a field of "brambles, high as our heads." Furious that his compact lines had given way to an aggressive thicket of black locust, Brown halted the attack, dressed his line, and, in Inglis's words, "*cussed* us for being too quick[. 'Dress] up or you will be cut to pieces in such order.'"[73]

The steep creek bank north of the 42nd Indiana's previous position, ten feet high on the far side according to Georgia gunner William Talley, provided cover from Federal small-arms fire. Unfortunately, the bank also frustrated the advance, forcing the brigade to file to the right through a shallow ravine to a place where the men could cross and reform their lines. The first section of Palmer's battery followed and unlimbered on the hill above the creek, but because "there was not enough room on the battle line for all of our guns," Palmer's second section remained in the creek bed, two hundred yards from enemy lines. Palmer immediately opened up with canister. The 10th Wisconsin and 38th Indiana of Harris's brigade responded with a barrage of small-arms fire that shot down most of the forward section's men and horses in a matter of minutes. Palmer ordered the men of the second section to drag the first's guns back into the relative safety of the creek bed.[74]

As Brown's infantry reformed their one line and advanced, the 41st Mississippi on the left of the two Florida outfits, Harris's two right-flank regiments opened up on them, forcing the Confederates farther to the right, behind the same ridge that had shielded Jones's advance. On Harris's right, however, the men of Lytle's 10th Ohio, lying flat on their faces, refused to fire in assistance. Nonplussed, Col. Benjamin Scribner of the 38th Indiana sent an aide to Harris in hopes of getting the 10th Ohio's spectators to act. Harris then dispatched an aide of his own to stimulate the Ohioans, only to discover that, with his right in turmoil, Lytle had ordered the regiment to hold its fire, as he would soon need its help on his beleaguered front. For the moment, the 38th Indiana and 10th Wisconsin were on their own.[75]

While the two Federal brigade commanders sent aides back and forth vying over control of the 10th Ohio, Brown's brigade steadily drew closer to the same ridge top where Harris's right had stopped and mangled Jones's brigade. This time, however, the Federals faced a harder task, for they had expended much of their ammunition against Jones and, in the case of the 38th Indiana, Daniel Donelson's brigade as well. As a result, the attack soon degenerated into a stand-up affair, the Federals again benefiting from the treacherous ravine and sinkhole to their front. The two lines slugged it out for perhaps half an hour. When Thomas Benton Ellis of the 3rd Florida—who had deserted his position as a wagon guard to go into battle with his brother, the regimental color-bearer—fell wounded, his captain asked him to carry *his* brother to the rear. Both men later would spend a month in a Federal hospital. William A. Bryant of the 3rd Florida wrote his mother that one friend went down with a shoulder wound while another was mortally wounded in the face. Brown himself went down with a bullet in the thigh, and Col. William F. Tucker of the 41st Mississippi took temporary command of the brigade. After Tucker suffered a wound in the arm, Col. William Miller of the 3rd Florida took over.[76] One of the wounded, John Inglis, so anxious to enter the battle only minutes before, described the horror of the afternoon in his diary: "I, hit in shoulder, colar bone broken, the groans of dying & the cries for water of the wounded was terrible, I am nearly killed."[77]

Before long, both sides complained that they were running out of ammunition. Among the Federal regiments, the 10th Wisconsin was the first to empty its cartridge boxes. Harris decided that he had no choice but to withdraw the regiment, even though it would create a two-hundred-yard gap between the 38th Indiana and Lytle's left regiment, the inactive 10th Ohio. He sent another dispatch to Lytle, informing him of the decision, and simultaneously sent a second aide to bring up ammunition and reinforcements. In the meantime, the men of the 38th Indiana ran out of ammunition, leaving them with only bayonets to brandish at Brown's Confederates.[78] "Our ammunition gave out," John Sipe of the regiment wrote home, "and we had to stand some time and let the Rebels shoot at us without being able to return the fire."[79]

Brown, however, was in no shape to immediately take advantage of the situation. His men were fast depleting their cartridge boxes. Incompetence and dereliction of duty also hampered their effort, at least according to Colonel Miller, who complained that "the Ordinance Officer, a nephew of general Brown was drunk, and supplies of ammunition had not arrived." Regimental officers went up and down the line, telling their men to cut off the cartridge boxes of the wounded and dead; many of them fell in the process. The fight continued but with slackened fire as both sides proved unwilling to give up. Miller particularly remembered one soldier, "a boy" he found wounded in the leg. When Miller told him to go to the rear, the "brave little fellow said, with some surprise in his eyes, 'Colonel, I am not going to quit for that,' and he went to his place and was again wounded and left the field."[80]

The rest of Brown's and Harris's men tenaciously hunkered down and hung on, as unwilling to quit the field as the wounded boy from Florida. Both of their brigade commanders desperately sought ammunition; victory would go to the one that found it first.

Dwindling ammunition was a problem farther south along the battle line as well, for the men of at least three of Bushrod Johnson's regiments were down to their last few cartridges. An ominous silence descended on the field as Johnson told them to hold their positions and then rode over to Patrick Cleburne, "suggesting the propriety of an advance upon the enemy." Cleburne's brigade now began moving up toward the stone walls around Squire Bottom's house to take Johnson's place and to launch a fresh attack on Lytle's battered right. With Adams to the left, Brown on the right, and Cleburne replacing Johnson, the Confederate nutcracker was about to snap shut.[81]

UP THE HILL CAME THE REBELS

AS THREE O'CLOCK CAME AND WENT ON THE CONFEDERATE RIGHT, Brig. Gen. Alexander Stewart might well have pondered what thus far had proven to be his unlucky stint as a brigade commander in the Army of the Mississippi. Nicknamed "Old Straight" by his men, Stewart was a forty-one-year-old Tennessean, West Pointer, and former mathematics instructor who commanded artillery early in the war and first led a brigade at Shiloh. Everything at that bloody battle seemingly had gone wrong for the new brigadier. Sent in relatively late after Tecumseh Sherman's front line broke, Stewart quickly lost control of his units upon reaching Col. Everett Peabody's abandoned Federal camps. When the 4th Tennessee Infantry went off in the wrong direction in the confusion of battle, Stewart personally chased it down instead of sending an aide. Returning to the scene with his lost sheep, he discovered to his horror that all three of his other regiments had disappeared while he was absent. One of Polk's aides had led away the 13th Tennessee Infantry, the 33rd Tennessee Infantry had become involved in a firefight with another Confederate regiment, and a second incident of friendly fire resulted in Sterling Wood being wounded. Stewart's only non-Tennessee regiment that April morning, the 13th Arkansas Infantry, took so many casualties that after the battle it was temporarily consolidated with the 15th Arkansas and placed under Cleburne's command. Bad luck followed Stewart and his men all day April 6. It was not an auspicious beginning as a brigade commander.[1]

Now, six months later in the Chaplin Hills west of Perryville, everything was going wrong again, the stiff breeze in his face seemingly an ill wind. Earlier in the day, Frank Cheatham had taken Stewart's brigade into Walker's Bend and placed it in line behind Donelson's, the second of three waves to be launched against the enemy flank. Cheatham told Stewart to remain four hundred yards behind Donelson as he pushed ahead on Donelson's left. The men's spirits were high as they ascended the bluff behind the latter's regiments.[2] Discovering a Federal flag abandoned there, most likely lost by the 33rd Ohio in its brief fight with Wharton's cavalry, several members of the 5th Tennessee Infantry began ripping it into souvenirs. Observing Polk riding by, one called out to him, "'Look here, General, what we have.'" Polk was delighted. "'Come on and let's get one apiece,'" he replied heartily as the men shredded the Stars and Stripes.[3]

However, the unexpected Federal resistance to Donelson's attack quickly dampened such high spirits and spawned confusion at Walker's Bend. Eager to flank Parsons's unanticipated battery, Cheatham peeled off his third line, Maney's brigade, and sent it farther to the right. Having given those orders, the division commander rode to the far right to watch the attack on the now critical Open Knob, at one point personally placing Turner's battery in position to assist his Tennesseans. Indeed, according to one gunner, Cheatham gleefully aimed and fired one of the guns himself, as happy as a schoolboy. Judging by the general's own account, he remained on the right throughout the rest of Maney's attack. Consumed by the fight for the flank, Cheatham either forgot about Stewart or, more likely, assumed that "Old Straight" would advance as originally determined. Stewart, however, refused to move without positive orders. Huddled beneath the bluff atop Walker's Bend, its brow swept by enemy fire, Stewart's men lay down and waited impatiently for almost an hour for the command to advance. Donelson and Maney's lines disappeared in the clamor and smoke of battle, and Cheatham and Polk rode off out of sight. But Stewart, not knowing what to do, still did not move.

Finally, an urgent message from Donelson begging for reinforcement spurred Stewart to act. Unsupported by artillery like Donelson before him—Cheatham had commandeered Stanford's battery earlier to replace Carnes's and it remained several hundred yards to the left supporting Hardee's lines—Stewart's five Tennessee regiments descended in an orderly row into the smoky valley to help rescue Donelson's brigade.[4]

Up ahead and to the right, Maney's brigade pounded up the Open Knob like gray autumn waves against a rock, each succeeding one closer to shore than the last. Their hopes renewed by Maney's support on their flank, and with Stewart finally approaching to the rear, Donelson's battered regiments also regrouped and around 3:15 P.M. renewed their assault against the Federals at the edge of the Widow Gibson's cornfield. For the second time, they approached the Gibson outbuildings, driving terrified sheep and rabbits before them. The 2nd Ohio and 33rd Ohio were still on the left of Leonard Harris's front line there. To their left, Starkweather's 24th Illinois, "the invincible Dutch 24th" personally placed there by Rousseau, deployed as skirmishers, loosely plugging the gap between Harris's and Starkweather's commands. To the rear of the front line regiments, several companies of the 50th Ohio, still in confusion after the cowardice of its colonel, joined all of the 80th Indiana of Webster's brigade in supporting Sam Harris's battery. The untried 98th Ohio and 121st Ohio remained farther back, behind the battery in reserve. Brigade lines remained indistinct after Donelson's initial attack as the 80th

Figure 12.1. National colors of the 2nd Ohio Infantry. Photograph courtesy Ohio Historical Society.

Indiana of Webster's brigade edged forward toward the 2nd Ohio of Sam Harris's command.[5]

At about 3:30 p.m., Terrill's brigade on the Federal far left finally abandoned the Open Knob to Maney. While many of Terrill's men tried to make a stand at the foot of the hill, others fell back toward Starkweather's lines. Meanwhile, the 80th Illinois collapsed on the right, falling straight back toward the protection of Leonard Harris's position, and then fled through the 2nd Ohio and 38th Indiana on the Buckeyes' right. Tearing through Webster's lines, the regiment continued on into the woods to their rear.[6] Having spoken briefly with Terrill as the latter worked to establish his new line at the western base of the Open Knob, Rousseau galloped toward the broken unit and began striking the frightened men with the flat of his sword until he broke it, hoping to stop their flight. When that failed, he turned to the men he still had in line. Sticking his hat on the end of his broken sword, he rode down Harris's brigade line, hoping to inspire the remaining combatants. Stopping before the 38th Indiana, he called out, "'Here comes Indiana; she always stands by Kentucky.' To another group he cried out, "we will whip them yet."[7]

The moment was well remembered, but not as Rousseau probably wanted. According to one witness, "Gen. Rousseau came galloping along the line of the 80th Indiana and 2nd Ohio with his hat on the end of his sword, and was enthusiastically cheered by the officers and men. The general rode to the rear and center of the 80th Indiana, where he was met by Maj. _____ [Anson G. McCook] of the 2nd Ohio. The General said: 'Major, I will remember this day.'"[8] Despite his bravado, the sort of thing so popular with civilians and the popular press, Rousseau's display of personal courage apparently did little for the men to whom it was directed, soldiers who fully understood their responsibilities and the situation without needing a general to tell them. According to one member of the 38th Indiana, his regiment's response contained not cheers but cries for Rousseau to "'get out of the way, so we can fire.'" The General reportedly replied, "'Shoot under my hat.'"[9]

Waiting anxiously behind the rail fences that cordoned off the Gibson field from the barn lot, the Federals braced themselves for the renewed attack they saw coming. Donelson's line drew within twenty yards of Leonard Harris's, angling again toward Sam Harris's battery. "'Up the hill came the rebels,'" wrote one Federal, "'and made as gallant a charge as ever was met by brave men. But, O! so terrible and bloody was the repulse! Along the line of the 2nd Ohio and 38th Indiana and Captain Harris's battery, I saw a simultaneous cloud of smoke arise. One moment I waited, the cloud arose, and revealed the broken column of rebels flying from the field. . . . The shout that arose from our men drowned the roar of the cannon, and sent dismay into the retreating, broken column.'"[10]

The Confederates felt dismay all right, but not because of shouting alone. With better ground and more guns at their disposal, albeit faulty weapons in too many cases, the Federals simply held the advantage over Donelson's sadly diminished brigade, and for a second time the battered Confederates fell back to relative shelter. "With our numbers now much weakened," J. J. Womack of John Savage's mangled 16th Tennessee admitted, "we rallied and charged them a second time, with about the same success as the first."[11] Alone, Donelson's rapidly diminishing brigade could never dislodge Harris and Webster from the Widow Gibson's cornfield.

Luckily for Donelson's Tennesseans, help from their home state drew near at last, as Stewart's line finally closed on them. Exhausted and nearly out of ammunition, Donelson's men fell back toward their fellow Volunteers and began to replenish their cartridges from the boxes of the dead. Donelson himself dispatched two aides to the rear, both to bring up more ammunition and to locate his two still-missing regiments, the 8th and 51st Tennessee, last seen going off in support of Carnes's battery.[12]

Stewart deployed his brigade in a single wide line, with the 31st, 33rd, 24th, 5th (including one orphaned company of the 46th Tennessee), and 4th Tennessee Infantry Regiments arrayed from left to right. Although Cheatham's original orders directed Stewart to bear to the left of Donelson, as it drew near the scene of action the brigade essentially enveloped the "fragments" of retreating regiments from Donelson's brigade on both sides, while simultaneously plugging the gap between Donelson and Maney. Whether Stewart directed such a movement or, as at Shiloh, regimental colonels such as the 4th Tennessee's Otho Strahl acted independently, the 4th and 5th Tennessee veered right into Maney's sector, linking up with Maney's 6th Tennessee near the Open Knob and passing down its western face through Parsons's abandoned limbers and caissons. Stewart's other regiments came up on Donelson's left. Meanwhile, Turner's battery moved forward to the Open Knob and began lobbing shells into the Federal line.[13]

Now faced with a much more dangerous threat, the Union commanders responded as best they could. About to face Maney's onslaught as well as Stewart's and Donelson's, Starkweather reeled the 24th Illinois back into his lines. "Facing the enemy's right," the Illinois regiment refused its flank by shifting somewhat to the rear to protect the brigade's right on the ridge.[14] Deprived of the cover Starkweather's Illinoisans had provided on his left, and facing a bolstered Confederate attack as well, Harris anxiously sent for the 94th Ohio, which he had left to his right and rear. Again he was disappointed. To Harris's chagrin, he discovered that the regiment was no longer where he had stationed it, for in the interim McCook already had dispatched the raw Ohioans a half-mile to the left in a vain attempt to save Parsons's battery. Only their knapsacks remained in position.[15]

A stroke of luck, good for Harris if bad for William Terrill, strengthened Harris's line nonetheless. Arriving too late to save Terrill's broken brigade, Col. Joseph W. Frizzell placed his 94th Ohio just where Harris had needed him: in the widening gap between Starkweather's brigade and his own. Frizzell had barely gotten his raw recruits into position when Stewart's left regiments, joined by what was left of Donelson's brigade, advanced toward them, "making a dash for the breach" according to the Ohio regiment's historian.[16] "With yells and cheers," Donelson reported, the combined line advanced directly against the enemy, centering on the "breach" now held by the 94th Ohio, whose presence Donelson interpreted as "the Enemy . . . making a forward movement in the direction of the Captured Battery evidently with a view to retake." Firing rapidly, the Confederates advanced on Harris's left regiments—the 94th, 2nd, and 33rd Ohio—and began pushing them farther back up the ridge toward Webster's reserve line.

Although bending, especially on the flanks, Harris's men still would not break. As the Confederates drew near his refused flank, Starkweather offered support, Stone's battery and the 24th Illinois enfilading their right flank. The men of the 80th Indiana kept up their fire as well. With the 94th Ohio's rookies fighting as gamely as veterans, supported by some of Webster's and Starkweather's guns, the Federal line stubbornly gave ground and then solidified. After about forty-five minutes, the Confederate attack stalled below the ridge top and left of the cornfield to the west of the Open Knob.[17]

Federal fire took a severe toll on Stewart's ranks throughout his opening advance. John Gold of the 24th Tennessee remembered that "as we advanced unfortunately Company F . . . came to a gap that had been made in a very high rail fence most of the boys crowding through the gap but it made a solid mass for the enemy to shoot at and they made good use of the opportunity for several of the boys were killed in that gap. I realized the danger of doubling up and got over the fence."[18]

The Federal line held. Still, despite inflicting so much damage on the enemy, Harris's brigade had reached its brink. The condition of his left regiments now was as bad as those holding off Brown on the right. The 2nd and 94th Ohio were all but out of ammunition and, like their comrades to the right, were hastily stripping the dead and wounded of their reserves. The desperate Harris again sent an aide to McCook with a plea for more ammunition, and wondered how much longer he could hold out.[19]

Despite recalling the 24th Illinois, Starkweather was in as much trouble as Harris. The combined Stewart-Donelson attack on his right could easily turn into disaster if Harris's men faltered. Worse yet, having seized the Open Knob and Parsons's seven abandoned guns, Maney's front line, although "much broken" and "greatly disordered," had not paused. Rather, it continued moving quickly down the hill's western slope, through a thin belt of woods toward the cornfield below and Starkweather's position on the ridge above it. The 9th Tennessee, victor in the race for Parson's guns, and the terribly battered 6th Tennessee remained on the left, linking up with the approaching 4th and 5th Tennessee of Stewart's brigade on the wooded border of the cornfield. To their right, the mangled "Tigers" of the 27th Tennessee and what was left of the 41st Georgia, the latter regiment's ranks as badly depleted as the 6th Tennessee's, moved forward as well.

Erroneously convinced that the enemy had devoted most of its strength to holding the Open Knob, Maney and his officers expressed confidence that "one strong and spirited Regt might do much toward his rout." Accordingly, he rode back to bring up the 1st Tennessee, which barely had missed the fight for the knob, in order to throw it forward in pursuit. Reaching the regiment, he discovered that Polk had already ordered it to deploy into the valley to the right in order to flank and capture Bush's battery on the north flank of the Federal position. While discussing the matter with the regiment's lieutenant colonel, Cheatham rode up and reiterated Polk's orders. It was just as well, Maney concluded. With Stewart's fresh troops on the left and the 1st Tennessee on the right, he believed that Cheatham's division soon would sweep the enemy before them.[20]

Much that occurred in the next few minutes reinforced such confidence. As they poured over and around the crest of the Open Knob, Maney's and Stewart's reinforced Confederates first encountered the remnants of Terrill's brigade, which had rallied sixty yards back in the belt of trees and

Figure 12.2. Starkweather's position as seen today from the Open Knob. Photograph courtesy John Walsh Jr.

behind a rail fence. Most of Parsons's limbers, caissons, and sixty-odd living and dead horses were there as well, further jamming the narrow back slope like so many barricades. As the Confederates swept over the knob, elements of the 105th Ohio, firing at will, hit their pursuers with a withering if ragged volley that opened holes in the rebel ranks. Taking fire from Turner's battery almost immediately, however, Terrill led his forlorn hope farther back into a gully in the cornfield.[21] "The enemy followed sharply," Albion Tourgée remembered, "and their bullets cut stalk and leaf and rattled the kernels from drooping ears beside us, every now and then claiming a victim." Faced with such fire, Terrill quickly abandoned the notion of making a stand in the gully. He now ordered his men to fall back again, flanking to the right, into Starkweather's rear.[22]

Not everyone heard the order in the commotion, however, and some men from Terrill's tenacious 105th Ohio continued to hold their ground. One of them, Lester Dewitt Taylor, "kept at work till turning my head a little when sending a bullet home I saw but one man in sight—Charley Hitchcock, turned my head the other way, & saw three men. I delivered that fire, & fell back to the Reg. We did not see Charley alive again."[23] Others retreated after a Federal volley from the rear and fire from Stone's battery crashed over their heads into Maney's men. "As we flung ourselves upon our faces and crept around the flank out of this maelstrom of fire," wrote Tourgée, "we

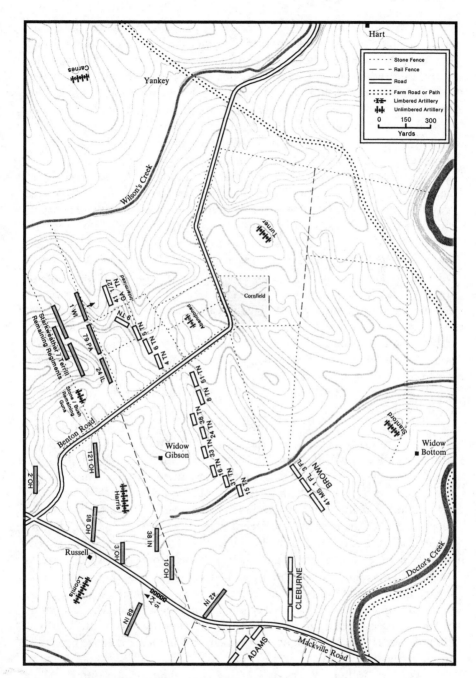

Map 12.1. Starkweather holds the Federal left, 4:15 P.M.

could but exult in the skill of our comrades whose level volleys cut the serried stalks in their front like a sickle of flame." Some, like Joshua Ayre, shot through the left calf, made it no farther than the cornfield, but fell dead or wounded there. Ignored by pursuing Confederates other than one who cut away his cartridge box and left him, the lame Ayre lay low as the battle swept around him. Most of Terrill's survivors eventually managed to make it back on their own or in small groups to an imposing ridge point overlooking Starkweather's position from two hundred yards away. There, their officers began cobbling together a makeshift line from the residue of the brigade.[24]

Terrill's line dissolved into the high corn only to expose another raw and untried outfit, I Corps's notorious abolitionists and high-principled troublemakers, the 21st Wisconsin. When the division commander hastily shifted Starkweather's brigade forward from ridge to ridge, Rousseau also had thrust the Badgers' eight present companies over a hundred yards forward, past the Benton Road to the western edge of the cornfield. Ominously, the regiment's best-trained companies, B and C, remained in the rear guarding the brigade supply train from reported guerrillas. Starkweather's front regiment was so new that it had no colors around which to rally if necessary, and with only four days of drill before the battle, its inexperienced men probably would not have been able to rally on the colors even if the regiment had some. Their flanks lay completely open and unanchored. Perhaps Rousseau remembered that he had nearly ordered the regiment shot for disobedience a few days earlier. At any rate, he seemed to have taken pains to place it in harm's way.

Tall corn, ten to twelve feet high according to Sgt. John Otto, restricted the regiment's vision even when standing. As the attack on the Open Knob heated up and several men fell to overshot balls intended for Terrill's men, the regiment, acting on orders, lay down in the field. Stone's battery booming from directly behind them further encouraged the men to stay close to the ground. Unable to see more than a few feet to the front, it came as a surprise to the balance of the regiment when the skirmishers raced in from the belt of trees and through the field into the main line, chased by many of Terrill's panic-stricken troops and then by shells from Turner's battery. As Terrill and his men ran past the frightened Wisconsinites, they warned that the enemy was right behind them. Meet them with the bayonet, Terrill called out as he sped past. Worried about his inexperienced men, Maj. Frederick Schumacher, essentially in command that afternoon while an ill Col. Benjamin Sweet lay in an ambulance to the rear, called out for them to keep cool and aim low.[25]

As Maney's Tennesseans drew closer, according to John Otto, "bullets came zipping and whizzing through and over the corn in a lively manner, the first time the men became acquainted with that peculiar hissing 'zipp' a bullet can only make." Behind them, Starkweather's main line opened up with what Otto called a "lively fire . . . the noise became almost deafening. Half a dozen batteries were roaring, shells exploding everywhere; thousands of rifles kept up an incessant rattle. Still we did receive no order, or if we did we could not hear it." He stood up to look at his comrades then, but when he turned to the front he saw with chagrin "a rebel flagg, that is, the upper part of it above the cornstalks and not far away either. I sat down on my right knee and said as loud as I could: 'Boys be ready! They ar coming!'" Expecting orders but hearing none above the din, Otto leveled his heavy Austrian rifle and fired at a man wearing a "butternut coleured jacket" about forty yards away. His company and the rest of the regiment followed suit.

The 21st Wisconsin held long enough to fire two effective point-blank volleys into the enemy ranks. The 5th Tennessee lost two color-bearers in the twin explosions of flame and lead. Another man, Benjamin Hagnewood, fell wounded when a ramrod fired by a frightened Badger impaled him. Thrown from his horse and seriously injured, the regimental commander, Col. Calvin D. Venable, continued on with the aid of two of his men who carried him forward. Nonetheless, the fight in the cornfield was never a contest. With a rebel yell and plenty of adrenaline, the 9th and 27th Tennessee and 41st Georgia slammed head-on into the out-manned Badgers with gunfire and bayonets. Simultaneously, the 1st Tennessee on the right and the increasingly disorganized 4th, 5th, and 6th Tennessee to the left swept around the Union flank. In a last-ditch effort to stop the enemy tide, both Stone's battery and the 1st Wisconsin, the latter back up on the ridge to the left, opened fire into the melee, canister and musketry killing and wounding friend and foe alike. Men from both armies fell in droves among the cornstalks. The 9th Tennessee lost every company commander. The 5th Tennessee lost its colonel, acting major, and three captains in the bombardment. Colonel Charles A. McDaniel of the 41st Georgia fell mortally wounded. Two successive musket balls hit the 21st Wisconsin's Schumacher while others killed two horses beneath him, still another killed the regiment's major instantly a few moments later. To the rear, in his ambulance, Sweet was hit in the shoulder and elbow.

"Now was the moment to fix bajonet and charge," the Prussian Otto lamented. "But no order of any kind." In fact, Starkweather cried out just such an order from the ridge in the rear, but with the regiment's field officers down and the men inexperienced, few heard him in the cacophony and fewer still responded. As the companies on the right gave way and ran for the ridge, Sweet, who true to form had debated Rousseau's posting of his regiment there in the first place, stood and cried out a commonsense but unmilitary order that William J. Hardee never thought to include in his tactics manual: "break and rally!" Whether following the order or, more likely in the din, following the collapsing companies, the balance of the regiment took off for the rear, the sickly and bleeding Sweet their rear guard as they crossed the road, leapt over a fence halfway up the hill, and sped up the ridge. Dozens more fell, shot in the back as they retreated, most of them while scrambling over the fence. Racing through the ranks of the 79th Pennsylvania, the survivors did not stop until they reached Starkweather's batteries,[26] many crying aloud as they ran, "The Secesh are coming, run for your lives."[27]

As the balance of their regiment faltered, Companies B and C of the 21st Wisconsin double-quicked to the scene, hurried by Chaplain Orson P. Clinton, who ran up to them shouting "Captain hurry up your men, your comrades are fighting and need your assistance." Stampeding riderless horses, balls and shells, and finally their bloodied and maimed "pards" from Wisconsin met them in the rear as they approached the front. Faced with "destruction and hell in front of us," Evan Davis later admitted, "it required considerable courage to move forward." Indeed, Davis began to pray as he ran forward, only to be upbraided by a friend who told him that the battlefield was no place for prayer. It was the last thing the man ever said, as a ball immediately struck him in the forehead. Arriving finally on the ridge top, confused as to what to do next, they obeyed Rousseau, who ordered them to line up and lay down to the left of the 1st Wisconsin, which lay behind Bush's battery. Also scattered among the battery's defenders at that moment were a contingent of stubborn soldiers from Terrill's 105th Ohio and 123rd Illinois. According to one witness, Charles Parsons was there as well, working a gun that might have been the one he rescued when Maney seized the rest of his battery. Rousseau later reported that the men placed their caps on the ends of their bayonets and shouted at the Confederates in defiance.[28]

In the valley below, Stewart's 4th and 5th Tennessee joined Maney's veterans as they poured across the cornfield and up the ridge toward Starkweather's brigade, hard on the heels of the broken 21st Wisconsin. On the left, the 5th Tennessee outpaced the 4th and 6th Tennessee up the slope to a rail fence that ran in front of Stone's battery. To their right, the 9th and 27th Tennessee made for Stone's battery as well. Although Stone unloaded canister directly into their faces, many men in those regiments reached the crest and fired a murderous volley into the battery's gunners. As they did, panic seized Stone's men, and possibly Stone himself, who at least according to his lieutenant ran to the rear and lay down behind his limbers and caissons. Unwilling to take the time to limber up, those gunners still standing and game enough grabbed their pieces by hand and for a moment tried to pull them to the rear, Colonel Sweet's fleeing men providing human shields as they worked. Before long though, they abandoned the guns entirely and fell back.[29]

"When we came to the battery we found it silent and deserted," wrote John Otto of the 21st Wisconsin. "Most of the artillerie men being dead, or wounded. The Capt. and some of the unhurt gunners had deserted the battery."[30] Still full of fight, Otto and another Prussian veteran, an ex-gunner named Loewenfeld, grabbed a few men and somehow managed to load four of Stone's pieces with double-shot canister. Acting with surprising quickness, Otto and Loewenfeld unloaded the guns into the gray mass. At the

Figure 12.3. Site of Stone's battery as seen from the Benton Road in 1885. Photograph courtesy Massachusetts Commandery, Military Order of the Loyal Legion, and the U.S. Army Military History Institute.

same time, the 79th Pennsylvania and 1st Wisconsin opened fire into the flanks of the depleted gray ranks with several heavy volleys. Together, the Federals killed many of the pursuers and staggered the rest, driving the others back down the ridge into the cornfield, where they barely missed a second blast of canister from the infantrymen-turned-gunners of the 21st Wisconsin. Loewenfeld then loaded a round of exploding shells and unleashed them. At that moment, Starkweather approached the battery and, according to Otto, asked, "'Who runs this concern?'"

"'Colonel,'" Otto claimed to reply, "'We are running this business on shares; but here Loewenfeld serves as a Captain without commission.'"

"'Well,'" Starkweather told him, "'give them hell!'" Loewenfeld dished out no more "hell," however, as Otto soon wisely led his charges to the rear to rejoin the regiment. As they did, Stone's artillerymen returned to their guns and opened fire, aiming at a new threat that had just appeared on their left flank.[31]

That new threat was Carnes's battery. Earlier in the afternoon, after Cheatham had withdrawn the battery from its position during the artillery duel at midday, Captain Carnes had pulled back to replace his killed or wounded horses, feed his animals, and repair his equipment. Cheatham had told the captain to stay there and await orders. He had done so, but with considerable impatience. At length, with the sounds of battle rolling toward him from the front, Carnes could take no more. Convinced that Cheatham had forgotten about him—he probably was right—he and his officers debated what to do. Just then, Bragg and his staff rode by in the distance, heading for the front to order a more energetic advance. Chasing down the general, Carnes secured permission to go forward and rejoin Donelson's brigade.

Riding forward with his battery, Carnes followed the County Road out of Walker's Bend and headed toward the sound of the fighting. As he reached the fork in the road near the Open Knob and rode ahead alone, he saw Turner's guns already operating in support of Cheatham's attack against that eminence. Unsure of what to do next, Carnes located Donelson and asked him where he should deploy his guns. Donelson replied that since there was no place he could use at that moment, he should return to his battery and await new instructions. Carnes had heard that before, and he did not like it. As the frustrated battery commander rejoined his men, he saw Wharton conversing with one of his lieutenants. Wharton explained to Carnes what he had just told the junior officer, namely that he had discovered a spot where some battery "could do great execution at some risk." Leaving the lieutenant in charge again, Carnes rode down the County Road with Wharton, past the Open Knob and the Confederate right, to a hilltop overlooking the Federal left. Wharton was right: the position gave Carnes command of the entire sector, including Starkweather's brigade.

With permission from Donelson's staff, accompanied once again by the unbloodied 8th and 51st Tennessee as well as Wharton's troopers, Carnes moved his battery to the hill and promptly "sailed into them."[32]

Carnes had not been engaged long when Cheatham ordered the units on his far right to resume the attack. The 1st Tennessee crossed the cornfield and the Benton Road, and then bore down on Bush's battery from the north. According to some Federals, the Tennesseans carried a black flag, signifying that they would give no quarter. Starkweather's men probably mistook the 1st Tennessee's navy blue regimental "Polk flag" for the black flag. In any event, they responded accordingly. Supporting the gunners on the crest, the 1st Wisconsin, Companies B and C of the 21st Wisconsin, and some of Terrill's orphans shifted their aim and opened up on the new wave of attackers. Aside from a few Badgers who picked that moment to rejoin their regiment in the rear, the Federals delivered a heavy volley of lead into the 1st Tennessee. At the same time, Stone's battery and the 79th Pennsylvania to the south enfiladed the Confederates' exposed left flank, finally giving Pennsylvanian John Eicker the chance he had waited for since Nashville to humble the city's beloved Rock City Guard. Men fell by the dozens, including at least two color-bearers. Somehow, the dogged Tennesseans kept moving anyway, charging to the base of the hill where the Federal gunners, unable to depress their guns enough, could no longer hurt them.

Bush's men did not have long to wait. Up and over the brow of the hill and into the muzzles and smoke of the battery popped the 1st Tennessee.[33] As the Confederates reappeared in his sights, Bush hit them with canister at thirty yards. Sam Watkins remembered the "mangling and tearing men to pieces. . . . We did not recoil, but our line was fairly hurled back by the leaden hail that was poured into our very faces. Eight color-bearers were killed at one discharge of their cannon. We were right up among the very wheels of their . . . guns."[34]

Among those to fall at the cannons' mouth was the man leading the assault, Lt. Col. John Patterson, who was hit, according to Marcus Toney, in the mustache. A fifteen-year-old Tennessean went down beside him. The brutal killing went on. Around the guns, back and forth, the men of the 1st Wisconsin and 1st Tennessee now fought hand-to-hand, brutally stabbing their enemies with bayonets and more often swinging their empty rifles as clubs. Captain George Bentley of Company B, 21st Wisconsin, emptied his revolver into the Confederates, threw it away, killed another Confederate with his sword, and shot still another with the rifle of the first, only to fall himself immediately after. Orderly Edward T. Kirkland of the same company shot a color-bearer. As he exulted "I have fetched him," two other Confederates shot Kirkland in the mouth and shoulder. A Federal shot a Confederate lieutenant in the face, blinding him for life. While the infantrymen battled, Bush's men continued loading and firing into the melee until most of them had fallen. Many of the battery's horses lay dying on the slippery, blood-soaked hilltop, and the others grew all but unmanageable in their panic, to use Starkweather's phrase.[35] "The very air seemed full of stifling smoke and fire which seemed the very pit of hell, peopled by contending demons," Sam Watkins recalled. "Our men were dying right in the very midst of this grand havoc of battle. . . . The sun was poised above us, a great red ball sinking slowly in the west, yet the scene of battle and carnage continued. I cannot describe it."[36]

Slowly, ferociously, the Confederates slugged the men in blue back away from the guns, only to break and fall back to the base of the hill in confusion just as quickly, and without Bush's cannon. Colonel Hume Feild, who had acted thus far as Maney's adjutant general, blamed "some mistake," for the sudden reversal, whereas Cheatham later attributed their retreat to the regiment's heavy losses. Captain Thomas Malone, on the other hand, ascribed it to the death of Patterson. The colonel was on horseback when hit, Malone explained, and when his uncontrolled horse galloped back toward Confederate lines, the regiment followed. There is, no doubt, some truth in each explanation. Most likely a combination of casualties, exhaustion, disorganization, and the lack of immediate leadership on the ridge after Patterson fell were responsible. At any rate, the 1st Tennessee gave up the guns and hurriedly fell back. While the Tennesseans rallied at the base of the hill, Feild reasserting command, the 1st Wisconsin staggered back to Bush's guns.

At the same time, the 79th Pennsylvania and 24th Illinois reinforced the position from the right and waited for the next assault. It was now about 4:15 P.M.[37]

William Terrill's men had already started to rally on and in front of the ridge in Starkweather's rear after their ouster from the cornfield. According to Albion Tourgée, the brigade commander himself initially seemed both dazed and depressed as he halted his flight and sat down on a log. One can hardly blame him. His brigade had broken and fled, abandoning all but one of Parsons's guns. Indeed, the entire scene in the rear at that moment was dispiriting. Wounded and dying men begged for water, while the living swallowed whiskey to wash away the bitter taste of gunpowder and moisten lips made dry by fear. As individuals and groups trickled in, some refused to stop but instead kept walking away from the battlefield, chased by the occasional overshot minié ball. Others, including line officers, took a rifle, slipped past Terrill, and headed back to the front on their own. Still others tried to form companies and call rolls, but lacking orderly sergeants as well as rosters, settled for grouping the men as best they could. So mangled was the 21st Wisconsin's chain of command that Starkweather dispatched Capt. John C. Goodrich of the 1st Wisconsin to take over the regiment.[38]

This was the situation when Carnes's flanking fire began to enfilade their fragile line. The effect was terrific, their already asymmetric ranks coming fully unglued as alarmed men scrambled for cover. Although they fared somewhat better, Carnes's unexpected barrage from the left, coupled with Maney's fierce attack, temporarily unnerved Starkweather's men as well. Many of them immediately concluded that Kirby Smith had arrived with his army, and they feared the worst. Starkweather certainly did. Hammered from two sides, and possibly facing sizable Confederate reinforcements on his flank, he made a crucial decision. Having almost lost his batteries once, he decided to withdraw both of them to the steeper and higher ridge behind him—the position he had first occupied before Rousseau ordered him forward. He reasoned that his guns would be there. Just as importantly, the steep ridge, running roughly parallel to the Mackville Road, could provide a formidable last stand for defending the Dixville Crossroads from the north. Were that junction to fall, I Corps would be totally cut off from the rest of Buell's army. The plan that followed was simple. While the 79th Pennsylvania, 24th Illinois, and elements of the 1st Wisconsin held the ridgeline, Starkweather would order his artillerymen, detachments from the 1st Wisconsin, and the two orphaned companies of the 21st Wisconsin to throw down everything but their rifles and drag the pieces back down the road to the steep, narrow ridge in the rear. To support the batteries there, Starkweather would leave the reunited 21st Wisconsin as well as whatever was left of Terrill's brigade.[39]

Ironically, the new threat shook Terrill out of his funk. Unfortunately, he typically directed his renewed energies not toward the men in his command, but rather to the closest operating artillery battery, which happened to be Bush's. Bush and Stone, together with Loomis and possibly Simonson as well, according to Carnes, had responded to his bombardment with blistering counterbattery fire. That was the sort of action that stirred William Terrill. Suddenly realizing that he should have succeeded Jackson as division commander, he rose and ordered Garrard's little three-company detachment back to the front to support Bush. Then, "indignant" according to Robert Taylor over the way Bush was handling his pieces, Terrill decided to go back to the front himself and take over. "Drawn as it seemed by irresistible magnetism," Albion Tourgée wrote bitterly, "he walked toward the battery now hotly engaged upon the opposite hill three hundred yards away."[40]

What happened to Terrill next is elusive. Most scholars have accepted the account of Maj. James Connolly of the 123rd Illinois, the same man who claimed to have been conversing with James Jackson moments before he fell on the Open Knob. Connolly wrote that Terrill approached him about rallying his regiment once he reached Bush's position. As Terrill advised Connolly, shell fragments struck the general in the breast, tearing much of it away. "I was the only one with him," Connolly wrote his wife. "I raised him to a sitting position. . . . he recognized me and his first words were: 'Major do you think it is fatal?' I knew it must be, but to encourage him I answered: 'Oh I hope not General.' He then said: 'My poor wife, my poor wife.'"[41]

Not exactly, according to Kentuckian Robert Taylor of Garrard's detachment, who maintained that Terrill arrived on the ridge only to assert his command of the division, pulling rank on Starkweather. Then, removing his jacket and rolling up his sleeves, Terrill inexplicably began working on one of the guns, possibly the one rescued by Charlie Parsons from Terrill's beloved battery. Shortly after, the shell hit him. Considering Terrill's previous behavior on the Open Knob, not to mention the long odds against James Connolly speaking to not one but two generals just as they were hit, Taylor's narrative must be taken seriously. However Terrill fell, the effect was that he had been mortally wounded. A group of men picked him up and carried him to a makeshift hospital located behind his brigade's position in the home of David Wilkerson, John C. Russell's brother-in-law.[42]

After a long, bloody day, the sun finally began to dip toward the horizon as soldiers bore William Terrill to the rear. The battle, however, was far from over. Back at the front, the Federals' superior guns increasingly took a toll on Carnes's battery, which could not respond in kind with smoothbores. Turning to Polk, who had ridden to the battery to observe the fight, Carnes told him that he could not remain where he was. He either had to retreat or advance, and Carnes preferred the latter. Polk agreed. Carnes summarily ordered his pieces limbered and they bounced and thundered several hundred yards farther forward to "a commanding ridge with a barn at one side and a small grave-yard at the other. . . . Some of our infantry officers remarked that it was the first and only battery charge they ever saw." If anything, the position was better than their last, giving the young gunner a clear shot at every Yankee between Starkweather's left and the Dixville Crossroads. The only drawback was that he had come much farther into Federal range. Hoping to minimize the danger to his pieces as much as possible, he ordered his gunners to scatter and unlimber along the ridge, well beyond the regulation distance between battery guns. Thus arrayed, Carnes again began pouring shrapnel into the Federal lines, his jagged metal rain reaching as far as the disputed crossroads.[43]

Carnes proved enough trouble, but the aggressive intentions of other Confederates further upset Starkweather's planned withdrawal. Just as Stone began pulling his guns to the rear, Maney, along with Stewart's right regiments, renewed his assault. Leaving Carnes after giving the young Tennessean permission for the original advance to the flank, Bragg and his staff had ridden on to the Open Knob, where they encountered "a ghastly scene of dead and dying," according to Bragg aide Stoddard Johnston. Concerned by Starkweather's movements, which Bragg, as he had done all day, mistook for a pending attack, the Confederate commander dispatched Johnston with orders for Cheatham to "hurry forward over the hill and drive the enemy back." He found him with Maney's resting men, the general's demeanor "calm and cheerful" according to the aide, and delivered Bragg's orders.

Cheatham needed little prompting. Already prepared to resume the attack, he wasted no time carrying out his new orders. On Maney's extreme right, the 1st Tennessee, along with forty or fifty stragglers from other regiments, presumably the now-shattered 27th Tennessee and 41st Georgia, once again moved up the ridge in an attempt to seize Bush's guns. "In an instant," Johnston remembered, " his line was in motion, sweeping over the hill."[44] At roughly the same time, Maney's remaining regiments, along with the 4th and 5th Tennessee of Stewart's brigade, rolled up the ridge toward Stone's pieces. Slashing and clubbing their way back to Bush's guns, in Maney's admiring words "fighting with the desperation inspired by their memory of invaded and outraged homes," the 1st Tennessee seized them once more and drove back their protectors at bayonet point, aided at an opportune moment by enfilading fire provided by their 9th Tennessee comrades on the left. Just as quickly, however, the 79th Pennsylvania and 24th Illinois decimated the regiment with several volleys, killing or wounding a dozen men with each, according to Feild. "Just then," he continued, "I discovered Hardee's battle-flag coming up on our left about 500 yards in rear. Expecting that regiment that carried the flag would engage the enemy that were cross-firing upon us I determined to hold the hill at every cost, thinking that they would drive the enemy before them."[45]

Reality soon dashed Feild's hopes. The Hardee regiment he glimpsed continued driving straight ahead toward the west rather than angling toward him; it would render no assistance to his beleaguered men. Instead, the situation worsened in the last few minutes as the 1st Wisconsin mounted a charge

Figure 12.4. "Polk flag" of the 1st Tennessee Infantry, captured by the 1st Wisconsin at Perryville. Photograph courtesy Wisconsin Veterans Museum.

to retrieve Bush's guns. The melee that followed, again in Maney's words, was "perhaps one of the bloodiest and fiercest contests of the war for the numbers engaged." During the struggle the 1st Tennessee lost its "black" battle flag, which fell among Bush's guns and eventually ended up in Starkweather's possession.[46]

The 1st Tennessee, or rather what was left of the regiment, finally had no choice but to fall back again into the cornfield and prepare for another counter-attack. The equally battered 1st Wisconsin did not pursue, but instead returned to the desperate task of pulling Bush's guns back to the next ridge.[47] On the 1st Tennessee's left, the rest of Maney's brigade, joined by elements of Stewart's, made more progress. The 9th Tennessee came up on their left and pushed on through at bayonet point, past four of Stone's guns that had been abandoned by their fleeing gunners, and into the open woodlot on the opposite slope. The 5th and 4th Tennessee followed on the left, with the 6th Tennessee in between.[48] The Stewart-Maney line slowly pressed Starkweather's dogged but beleaguered forces away from their position, through a thin strip of woods, down into the cornfield that filled the steep ravine that divided the two ridges, and up the slope of the rear ridge, where they joined Terrill's brigade and their batteries three hundred yards to the rear of their previous position. Bush's surviving gunners dragged caissons and limbers while the 1st Wisconsin manhandled the cannons. One Federal wrote his father that the men on Starkweather's left fell back in small groups

Figure 12.5. Starkweather's earlier position as seen today from his last line at the "high water mark." Photograph courtesy John Walsh Jr.

rather than in one line as they ran out of ammunition. Once the guns were well on their way, the 79th Pennsylvania and 24th Illinois, joined by orphaned men of a half-dozen other regiments, followed, defiantly holding the enemy off as they pivoted away. Many of them already should have been in the hospital. Pennsylvanian William T. Clark, for example, complained of three flesh wounds in the side, elbow, and shoulder, yet he and many others continued to fight. Taking a position on the brow of the hill behind a low stone fence, Starkweather's conglomeration of regiments opened fire into their pursuers while Bush and Stone's guns, divided into three ad hoc sections, hammered Carnes and Turner.[49]

Bedlam reigned. Evan Davis remembered lying on the ground watching Colonel Sweet, sick and twice wounded, who refused to prostrate himself but remained sitting behind his regiment. Davis also remembered a comrade who nervously tried to lower his rifle's hammer only to have it slip and shoot a friend through both his legs. "The agonizing cry of the wounded and pitiful heart-rending moan of the one that caused it will never be eradicated from my memory," Davis said years later. "The wounded by bullet died a few days later, and the wounded in mind and heart of the one that caused it never regained self again, soon sickened, died, and was buried at murfreesboro."[50]

Stewart's and Maney's tired and thin line pursued the retreating Federals into the ravine and began to scale the slope, the steepest they had encountered that day. Adding to the natural strength of the position, Federal soldiers stood six deep behind the stone wall at its top, exchanging firing positions. As they ascended the hill, the Confederates encountered a murderous barrage of rifle and canister fire, especially from Bush's battery on their right. The 9th Tennessee veered and drove to within fifty yards of those Federal cannons before halting, but then received orders from Stewart to fall back and let him have a go. Maney's 6th Tennessee and the 4th and 5th Tennessee of Stewart's brigade now were in position to supersede the 9th Tennessee. With all ten of his company commanders down, the 9th Tennessee's Col. George W. Kelsoe ordered the remainder of his battered regiment to withdraw. Unfortunately, many of his men did not hear him and instead continued to charge up the ridge with the other regiments. Somehow, a forlorn few reached the summit, but devastating fire either killed them or drove them back down the ridge. Ordered by Maney to try again, the Confederates again began their deadly ascent, only to be driven back a second time. The end result of a third attempt to take the hill proved horribly similar. Firmly checked by the enemy and low on ammunition, Stewart finally pulled the men under his control back to Starkweather's previous position. Unsupported on the left by the Donelson-Stewart mixed line, which was stymied for the moment in a stationary fight, the Maney-Stewart attackers could make no headway against such an imposing position manned by a mass of desperate men, and fell back for good.

The high-water mark of the Confederacy in the western theater, no less important than the Angle at Gettysburg, had been reached. The Union army, as it would at Gettysburg a year later, held.[51]

As the sun sank toward the horizon a few minutes after 4:30 P.M., the Battle of Perryville was over for George Maney's mangled brigade. It had bent back the left flank of Buell's army almost ninety degrees, but in the end, aided by topography and hard fighting, that flank had not broken. Worse, in accomplishing what they did, every regiment on the Confederate right had suffered tremendous losses. The 1st Tennessee lost 179 men killed, wounded or missing. Its command structure was devastated; Company D left the battle commanded by its nineteen-year-old fourth corporal. Maney's brigade as a whole had lost 722 troops, roughly forty percent of its strength when the assault began. The two regiments of Stewart's brigade fighting alongside Maney's men in the sector fared almost as badly. The 4th Tennessee suffered 50 percent casualties, 85 men, while the 5th Tennessee lost an additional 94. Their Federal opponents were in about as bad a shape. Three of Starkweather's four frontline regiments—the 79th Pennsylvania (216 casualties, 51.4 percent), the 1st Wisconsin (204 casualties, 50.1 percent), and the 21st Wisconsin (198 casualties, 49.0 percent)—lost more or less half their strength. The 24th Illinois lost almost 30 percent of its men. Terrill's smashed brigade, really no more than associated companies by the end of the day, had fared

Above, figure 12.6. The "high-water mark" of the western Confederacy today, as seen from just below. *Below*, figure 12.7. The "high-water mark": a Federal perspective. Both photographs courtesy John Walsh Jr.

nearly as badly. The 105th Ohio suffered a 31.5 percent casualty rate (203 men down), Parsons's battery a 28.7 percent rate (39 men), and the 123rd Illinois 24.5 percent (189 casualties). Few Civil War clashes demanded a higher price in men's lives than the fight for the northern flank at Perryville.[52]

Nor had the bloodletting ceased. The killing continued farther to the south. Convinced that Starkweather had saved his left at last, McCook rode away and raced down to the Dixville Crossroads on his right. Those crossroads were the prize, that and the survival or annihilation of his corps.[53]

The flag Hume Feild briefly and hopefully noticed remains unidentified but it most likely belonged to the 13th/15th Arkansas of Pat Cleburne's command. Cleburne's sudden appearance on Cheatham's left indicated that Hardee's wing, like Polk's, had finally been successful in driving back the first enemy line it faced. At that moment McCook's I Corps was crumbling all along its front.[54]

At the junction of the two Confederate wings, John Brown's brigade had continued applying what pressure it could to Leonard Harris's right-flank regiments. Farther left, faced with a continuing stalemate at Squire Bottom's house, Bushrod Johnson at length had requested to pull back his worn-out brigade in favor of Cleburne's veterans. Throughout the afternoon, Cleburne's men had waited on the ridge above the Chatham House watching the fight along the Mackville Road and waiting for their inevitable entrance into it. W. E. Yeatman of the 2nd Tennessee Infantry, Memphis's "Irish Regiment," recalled the view as something "like you see in pictures. For a mile we could see them, their splendid looking lines."[55]

Finally, around 4 P.M., the call to battle came. With brass bands playing, the veteran brigade double-timed forward in two lines, the 2nd Tennessee and the 13th/15th Arkansas in the first and the 35th and 48th Tennessee Infantry in the second. Although Johnson's men tenaciously maintained their fire as best they could considering their emptying cartridge boxes, enemy balls raked Cleburne's men as they descended Chatham House Hill. Crossing the nearly dry bed of Doctor's Creek just left of the sheer rock bank that had nearly spelled the doom of the 42nd Indiana, the Confederates dropped out of range and enjoyed a momentary reprieve. The 2nd Tennessee bizarrely encountered there a confused and frightened flock of geese that somehow had navigated through the flying lead in its search for water and safety. Without pausing, two presumably hungry men named Terry and Smith grabbed two geese each, tied them to their cartridge boxes, and kept moving.

The sight of Cleburne's lines descending the hill and rising from the creek bottom initially gave some Confederates pause. Colonel Smith of the 5th Confederate took one look at Cleburne's men over his shoulder, many still dressed in Federal-issue blue uniforms they had scavenged at Richmond, and lamented that the enemy had gained his rear. Turning to Capt. C. W. Frazer, Smith stammered, "'Captain, have you a white a handkerchief? I am afraid we will need one.'"

"'There's not one in the regiment;'" Frazer replied, "'and you have on the only *"biled shirt,"* the lower end of which will answer if occasion requires.' Just then," he added, "they raised a *yell* (Federals always *cheered*)." With relief, Frazer and Smith realized the identity of the men in blue.[56]

Crossing the creek, the brigade scaled the bank and moved west, closely following Johnson's line of advance. An inferno literally awaited them ahead, for not only did renewed infantry and artillery fire greet their arrival, but a grassfire whipped up by the wind spread northward from Squire Bottom's blazing barn, engulfing the hilly field and rail fences with smoke and flame. Cleburne reacted quickly to the hellish vista before him, and with the same innovative skill that had won the Battle of Richmond. To cover Johnson's withdrawal, he first ordered the 13th/15th Arkansas farther to the right, and then up the opposite side of the road. From there, protected by the stone walls and rail fences that partially lined the road, the Arkansas regiment poured unwelcome flanking fire into the 15th Kentucky. The topography thoroughly protected the Arkansans from the 10th Ohio on the ridge to the north, but at that moment the Buckeyes remained on their faces, per Lytle's orders.

Cleburne's fresher troops could not immediately replace Johnson's. Not only was the maneuver difficult at best under fire, but also some of Johnson's men refused at first to give way. Colonel Marks of the 17th Tennessee hotly quarreled with Cleburne when told to give up the hard-won position at the stone wall before he finally relented.[57] During the inescapable lull, an increasingly active Buckner did what he could to support Cleburne's pending assault. First, he ordered Adams to renew his northwesterly push against the Federal right flank. Adams shifted farther up the Kentuckians' right, past Squire Bottom's small orchard, and toward their rear. Buckner then ordered a section of Slocomb's Washington Artillery battery, Semple's rifled section, and Cleburne's section of Calvert's battery farther forward to support the renewed attack. Crossing the creek to a position just south of the house, the improvised six-gun battery began enfilading the already battered 15th Kentucky's right.[58]

Battered terribly by Johnson, enfiladed from both sides, and now facing a potential threat to the flank and rear, the Kentuckians' Col. Curran Pope hastily consulted with the 3rd Ohio's John Beatty. For the moment, Adams's flanking movement seemed the most serious threat of all to both Federal regiments, for unchecked he could well cut off their line of retreat. They thus decided to fall back across the road and form a second line bent into a right angle, in hopes of blunting both Adams's flank attack and the enemy at the stone wall. The regiments slowly fell back from the barn and crossed the road, probably company by company. Five companies, three from the 3rd Ohio and two from the 15th Kentucky, initially took positions along rail fence to form the new line.[59]

Watching the Federals retire from the rail fence and burning barn, Cleburne's Confederates below the stone wall assumed that the Yankees were

Figure 12.8. Burned barn site today. Photograph courtesy John Walsh Jr.

retreating. Now was the time to move if they were not going to get away. Cleburne, having already pulled the 13th/15th Arkansas back into line and completed his other preparations, immediately launched his attack up the hill. His skirmishers marched ten paces to the front of his main line, unconventionally carrying their regimental battle flags. Brilliantly using the terrain, as well as information provided by a captain from the 15th Arkansas, Cleburne hoped that the enemy behind the hilltop would empty their guns into the flag-waving skirmishers, perceiving them to be the first line. Then, before the Federals had a chance to reload, the genuine front rank would decimate them.

As the brigade started up the hill, moving at an angle toward the road and away from the burning barn rather than straight up the hill, a key Confederate error nearly derailed the attack. Without warning, artillery fire hit Cleburne's lines from the rear. Like those worn by the men of the 5th Confederate, the blue uniforms Cleburne's men wore fooled some unidentified gunners of the newly improvised battery, part of which opened up on the defenseless brigade, killing and wounding several men and forcing the rest back down the hill in search of cover. Cleburne hurriedly dispatched an aide to stop the firing, even as Johnson ordered the artillerymen to cease firing and advance forward in support. Another regrettable friendly fire episode had nearly caused disaster in the Bottom House sector.[60]

With the guns silenced and limbering, Cleburne tried it again. The

Confederate nutcracker finally was snapping shut, for as Cleburne drew nearer to the enemy, Adams on the left continued pressing them as well, crossing through a corn field. Still consumed with Adams's more immediate threat, Beatty and Pope shifted the rest of their companies to the road fence, creating a line perpendicular to the original. Dangerously low on ammunition, the Buckeyes fixed bayonets and prepared to meet the Louisianians.

William Lytle, however, had seen enough; without full cartridge boxes his men he knew could not withstand another attack on that line. The brigade commander thus ordered both of his frontline regiments to fall back up the Mackville Road to their ammunition wagons, which were parked in the ravine in front of the Russell House. The 10th Ohio, now to their left, and the reserve 88th Indiana farther back would support their withdrawal. Orders went out to both regiments to hurry, but none reached the 10th Ohio. Meanwhile, the 3rd Ohio backed off first, followed by the 15th Kentucky. However, the narrow avenue of escape, made narrower every second by Adams's approach, delayed the Kentuckians' retreat, and some companies remained helplessly near the fence line as Cleburne drew near.[61]

While the 3rd Ohio and 15th Kentucky gave way and marched to the rear under pressure from Adams and Cleburne, Leonard Harris faced a similar crisis on his front. The men in Brown's brigade had at last been able to replenish their cartridge boxes, ultimately making the difference in the standup fight Harris's right-flank regiments had conducted with the Confederates. Finally able to renew the fight, William Miller, still in command of Brown's brigade, determined to advance it through the ravine. "As we went towards the fence," he remembered, "a young fellow, almost a boy, tried to shout. His excitement was so great that he only brought out a squeak. The effect was electric. The shout commencing on the left swelled along the line until it became a great roar. At the command, the brigade broke into a double quick for the fence."[62]

Miller charged the brigade at the best possible moment, for he had not only more ammunition but reinforcements as well. Seeking to apply the coup de grâce to Rousseau's division on both its flanks, the ubiquitous Buckner had already dispatched Sterling Wood's reserve brigade to fill the gap between Brown's command and Donelson's battered regiments. Buckner hoped that a "combined attack" all along the Federal line would break it at last.[63] Commanded by Col. Mark Lowrey of the 32nd Mississippi since Wood's injury during the noontime artillery duel, the men of the brigade—and, according to a Federal staff officer, at least one woman, fighting alongside her husband—had moved when the battle commenced to a position about 250 yards from the enemy lines, near a section of Semple's battery and the Dye House and to the rear of Jones's brigade. It waited there for two hours, enduring a heavy bombardment.[64] Jesse Cheeves of the 32nd Mississippi described how his friend W. H. Rees "lost his lift arm . . . by a cannon ball. The man in the rear rank behind Rees was struck by the same ball and knocked ten or twelve feet and instantly killed. . . . We were exposed to a terrible fire of solid shot and shell." Hickory nuts and bark also peppered the men whenever a shell hit one of the abundant trees behind them.[65]

Now they advanced quickly, with pent-up emotion and bayonets fixed, into the hazardous gap. The 32nd Mississippi Infantry occupied the right of the first line, the 33rd Alabama Infantry the left. With a narrow front ahead of them, file closers kept the flanks of the two regiments so crowded together that, according to one Alabamian, "the pressing together caused some of the boys to use language they did not learn in church." The 45th Mississippi Infantry, which included surviving elements of the 27th Alabama Infantry, most of which had been captured at Fort Donelson, followed, as did the 15th Battalion Mississippi Sharpshooters, an outfit made up of men previously drawn from nearly every regiment in the brigade. The 16th Alabama Infantry remained behind in reserve.[66]

As the brigade drew near the scene of battle, shells from Sam Harris's Federal battery and then small arms from supporting infantry ripped through the attackers' lines, taking a terrible toll, especially on mounted officers. Increasing their pace to the double-quick and shouting the rebel yell, the two lead regiments reached the base of hill and methodically started up the slope, headed straight for the battery. As they drew near a low rail fence running across their path some thirty yards from the guns, Harris switched to canister while Federal infantry enfiladed the 32nd Mississippi from the right. Reaching the fence, the brigade line twitched in the steel rain, wavered, and then fell back in disorder to the foot of the hill, where the men lay down momentarily for cover. However, seeing Donelson and Stewart's mixed line coming up on their right, Lowrey and other regimental officers almost immediately rallied the men for a second attempt at the guns.[67]

Lowrey's Confederate reinforcements came at the worst possible time for Leonard Harris. He had just received the bad news from his aide that there were no reserve troops available for reinforcement and that the only available ammunition remained in his rear. After personally consulting with Lytle, whose own right was crumbling at that moment, Harris concluded that holding his position any longer was hopeless. Indeed, it is conceivable that Harris and Lytle jointly decided to fall back at that time. Harris's right flank now consisted of no more than the 38th Indiana, a regiment without ammunition, facing Brown's entire brigade. To its right, the men of Lytle's 10th Ohio remained inertly on their faces.

Harris's left was in nearly as bad a shape. Anxious to renew the fight, Donelson earlier had sent aides to track down the two regiments last seen supporting Carnes: the 8th and 51st Tennessee. They now double-quicked across the field to rejoin their comrades. Thus, augmented with perhaps eight hundred shouting and reasonably fresh riflemen, Donelson's brigade, accompanied by Stewart's left contingent of three regiments and Wood as well, pressed home the attack. Sam Harris's battery yet again served as a focal point for the attackers, and as the Confederates drew near for a second time his artillery horses began to fall in agony. Captain Harris himself went down twice, hit by spent balls, although the wounds proved minor enough for him to remain in action. Running low on ammunition after firing more than nine hundred rounds, with his horses dying all around him and his men so exhausted that soldiers from the 98th Ohio had come forward to move the guns for firing, Harris finally decided to fall back before the enemy seized his battery as it had Parsons's. He hurriedly issued orders for the withdrawal. While three men hastily broke apart several Enfield rifles they had collected from fallen men behind the battery, the others limbered up as best they could and raced to the rear with two guns and six caissons, nearly trampling many members of Webster's 80th Indiana as they thundered through the infantrymen's lines. Four silent guns remained at the scene.[68]

Abandoned by Sam Harris's battery, cartridge boxes empty or nearly so all along his battered line, and with Lytle's brigade giving way to his right, Harris ordered his brigade to retire into the woods at the eastern edge of the cornfield, past the Widow Gibson's house and farther up the slope toward the Russell House. The 38th Indiana had retreated about a hundred yards when Brown's men skirted to the left of the abandoned battery and advanced upon their vacated position. Meanwhile, their lines apparently mixed, Donelson's and Wood's regiments tore down the rail fence and raced past Sam Harris's guns and over his dead and wounded.[69] They continued in pursuit, "over the ridge, down the slope, and across the second valley in pursuit of them."[70]

In between Harris's retreating brigade and Lytle's collapsing line south of the Mackville Road remained the stubborn 10th Ohio, once the keystone of the two brigades and now the last Federal regiment still in position. Its immediate future was grave. Not only was Brown bearing down on the regiment's left front, but Austin's sharpshooters of Adams's brigade, well ahead of the main body, were also approaching their flank. The latter Confederates moved as "stealthily as a cat steals upon he prey," according to an anonymous 42nd Indiana soldier. "Great heavens!" the Hoosier continued, "will no one tell the 10th of their fearful peril?"[71]

At last, Lt. Col. Joseph W. Burke responded to the chaos around him. Still with no orders from Lytle but aware that the situation was rapidly disintegrating, Burke ordered his men to rise from the ground and charge down the hill. They temporarily checked the tired 3rd Florida's effort at bayonet point despite suffering severe casualties. As the survivors began to fall back to their ridge-top position after a volley of fire, they encountered so many bodies lying on the slope that company formations began to break down. Out of instinct, the veteran Ohioans rallied toward the colors, creating even more disarray. Watching his lines break down, Burke impatiently grabbed the bugle from his bugler, sounded the halt himself, and calmly redressed his lines. Then, deploying his flank companies as skirmishers, Burke ordered a retreat up the Mackville Road.[72]

As the 10th Ohio fell back, Brown's brigade swept up the ridge, took the position, and pursued the Ohioans as far as Simonson's second position. There the Confederates halted and turned their guns to the northwest, for the collapse of the 10th Ohio nicely supplied Brown's men with enough room to enfilade Harris's Federals as they continued falling back toward the Russell House. Unfortunately, the men of the 3rd Florida also hit some of Wood's pursuing Mississippians, creating hard feelings between the regiments ever after. A section of Palmer's battery followed, hoping to hit the retreating Federals in the flank as well. After an afternoon of gallantry, Leonard Harris's men fled for their lives.[73]

Finally moving toward the rear, the men of the 10th Ohio fell back until they encountered their brigade commander in a ravine north of the Mackville Road, just to the rear of the line recently abandoned by the 3rd Ohio and 15th Kentucky. Lytle halted the regiment there, hoping to throw together a new line with the approaching 88th Indiana and what remained on the scene of the 15th Kentucky. He never had the chance. Within moments, Cleburne's skirmishers and color-bearers topped the ridge at an angle. As Cleburne expected, the Federals gathered behind the ridge opened fire into his skirmishers and color-bearers at first sight. Before they could reload, Cleburne's front line topped the ridge and fired down into the mass of Federals from point-blank range. Approaching from the flank at a steady walk, firing as they went, Adams's men also pressed against the Federal flank, until a distance of no more than thirty yards separated the two lines. After what Adams called "a short but spirited contest," Lytle's thin, exhausted, and outgunned rear guard broke, many throwing away their guns as they fled. Others, including an African-American combatant who identified himself as a cook, perhaps in order to survive his capture, surrendered rather than be driven into the flames of the spreading grassfire. Several wounded and dead men already lay burning in the flames.[74]

Indeed, W. L. Trask of Austin's sharpshooters had trouble remembering a more horrible scene. From the burning barn to the site of the 10th Ohio's brief stand, the dead lay "in two straight lines as they had fallen . . . I could have walked on their bodies without touching the ground several hundred yards. Scarcely a man could be seen out of his place in line."[75]

His new line smashed, Lytle tried to rally his men, but he had halted only a hundred or so when he too fell, wounded in the head. The last remnant fled as the poet Lytle reportedly said to a comrade, "*You may* do some good yet, I can do no more, let me die here.'" He did not die, however, as Austin's pursuing men captured the wounded but very much alive general. A squad carried him to the rear, where Johnson sent him on to his surgeon for care. Cleburne in the meantime attempted to keep moving, but, finding his ranks disorganized, he stopped to dress his line of battle with his left flank anchored on the road. Adams briefly ordered his men to lie down and fire. Then, with Adams on the left and a little forward, and Cleburne lagging a bit on the right, the two brigades again pressed up the Mackville Road toward the Russell House.[76]

Now only the already bloodied 42nd Indiana and the fresher but still raw 88th Indiana stood between the approaching Confederate wave and the Russell residence. The latter regiment had moved forward about three hundred feet before the front line broke and Lytle went down. It had held there, a little less than 250 yards from the woods in front of the house. Under orders from Buckner, who had joined Adams momentarily at the front, the Louisiana brigade veered farther to the right and bore down on the flank of the 88th Indiana's rookies, whose line at that moment lay at a forty-five-degree angle south from the road. His hat still on the end of his broken sword, Rousseau desperately rode before the raw Hoosiers, trying to rally their spirits as the enemy approached. Enthusiasm alone could not stop Adams's attack, however, as Rousseau soon realized. To bolster his flank, he more realistically shifted the 42nd Indiana to higher ground and placed its men in a line behind a rail fence, at a right angle to the 88th Indiana but directly facing Adams's men. The Hoosiers of the 42nd Indiana lay down to await the expected onslaught.[77] According to one of the regiment's soldiers:

> They advanced in heavy lines toward our position. Their appearance, as regiment after regiment, and mass after mass, came forth from beneath the woods and advanced down the slopes of the hills, was imposing in the extreme. Distance concealed the rags composing their uniforms; the bright sunbeams glancing from their bayonets flashed the lightning over the field, and the blue flag with a single star waved all along their lines, as proudly as though it were not the emblem of treason, slavery and death. . . . However one might hate these traitors, he could not help admire this conspicuous and daring valor.[78]

Supported by the massed guns of the Confederates, which had advanced to the ridgeline vacated by the 15th Kentucky under Buckner's personal supervision, Adams and Cleburne swept toward the Federal line "in beautiful style," according to James Shanklin of the 42nd Indiana, "cheering as though the victory were won."[79] Including five companies of Avegno Zouaves who still wore their once dashing blue jackets, red caps, and red baggy trousers, the "hard looking set . . . of Irish, Dutch, Negroes, Spainiards, Mexicans, and Italians" in the ranks of the 13th Louisiana faced off directly against Shanklin's regiment.[80] They had much to prove. At Shiloh, Bragg had accused all of them, but especially their commander, Col. Randall L. Gibson, of cowardice. Three times that April, Bragg had ordered them to attack a seemingly impregnable position with cold steel while simultaneously refusing Gibson the artillery support for which he begged. All three attacks failed. After the battle, Gibson lost his brigade command and barely survived a Bragg-induced court-martial. His personal friendship with Albert Sidney Johnston's son, and through him influence with Jefferson Davis, may have been all that saved him. Their honor questioned once, the "Louisiana Tigers" as Lytle's men would always remember them, would not risk similar condemnation again.[81] "They moved on steadily; apparently, as if on drill in camp," S. F. Horrall of the 42nd Indiana later recorded. Sharpshooters went forward with orders to "keep the rebel flag down. Three times it, with its bearer, fell, and was taken up again. The fourth time it fell within seventy-five yards of our line."[82]

Lined up behind a rail fence at the edge of a stand of trees, the 42nd Indiana also took heavy casualties. Under Buckner's direction, supported by the resupplied 17th and 37th Tennessee of Johnson's brigade, along with the brigade commander himself,[83] the massed Confederate guns began "throwing shell and grape furiously. "The scream, the wild terrible, demon yells of the bombs that whizzed past us, and the snake-like hissing of the bullets, made that march . . . decidedly the most interesting trip I ever took."[84] While Dick Nash of Company A swore loudly at the enemy, "the rest of us were hugging the ground," recalled George Kirkpatrick, "for the bullets were coming up thick and fast. I saw Dick get up on his knees and offer up a prayer as fine as any minister, could do."[85]

"The battle, in the mean while, was a perfect storm," wrote Confederate John Headley, "the sound of musketry never ceasing and the roar of cannon rolling without a break. And the yelling was continuous along the line of our army. We passed through camps and over the dead and dying. Loose horses were running in all directions and wounded men were crying for help."[86] As the Tigers strode halfway up the hill, the 42nd Indiana rose from the ground, unloaded a volley into their ranks, and desperately charged down the smoke-covered ridge in bayonet-tipped files. Captain Charles G. Olmstead of Company A fell at the outset, a ball drilling into his forehead just as he cried out to his men, "This is as good a place to die as any other." His brains splattered Kirkpatrick in the face, blinding him momentarily. Meanwhile, James Shanklin fell stunned when a shell exploded just above his head. Two of his men carried him to the rear as the rest of the regiment double-quicked toward the Confederates. The Federals formed into line in a stand of heavy timber, and, using the woods as cover, opened up at close range, firing, according to Shanklin, until they had all but exhausted their ammunition. It worked, for Gibson's surprised Louisianians scattered and fell back to the safety of the Confederate guns. When two Confederates caught in the trees attempted to surrender, Kirkpatrick and another man clubbed them to death with their rifles. The 42nd Indiana had stopped Adams, at least for the moment.[87]

No sooner did the worn-out 13th Louisiana fall back, however, than Cleburne's first line drew a bead on the Hoosiers, threatening to envelop them. Worried about his exposed left, Col. George Humphrey of the 88th Indiana gave up and fell back all the way to Loomis's battery. His own left flank exposed, Cleburne meanwhile first dispatched a handpicked band of twenty sharpshooters, men equipped with Kerr rifles and commanded by Capt. Charles H. Carlton of the 15th Arkansas. With his left secured as best as possible, Cleburne bore down on the isolated 42nd Indiana. Suddenly confronted by another strong force and facing the enemy alone, the Hoosiers' fragile morale understandably began to waver. Lieutenant Colonel Charles Denby, wounded in the mouth and spitting blood, rode along the line and ordered his men to cease firing at Adams and retreat. When Kirkpatrick refused and fired again nonetheless, frightening Denby's horse and causing it to rear, the colonel took a swing at the soldier with murderous intent with his sword, catching instead the barrel of Kirkpatrick's sergeant's gun.[88] Just then, yelling "like a thousand savage wolves," Cleburne's line hit the 42nd Indiana with a savage volley. Their cartridge boxes empty, the Hoosiers fled up the ridge into the woods, taking more casualties as they retired. Among them was Denby, who became separated from his men when his dying horse fell on him.

Cleburne was now within a hundred yards of the Russell House and the Dixville Crossroads.

Up at the house, the reforming Federal line hunkered down for a last-ditch stand. What was left of the 3rd Ohio and the 15th Kentucky had arrived, rested, and replenished their cartridge boxes. Survivors from the fleeing 10th Ohio and the 88th Indiana had followed, the latter hightailing it all the way to Loomis's battery before moving back up to the coagulating line near the main house. Leonard Harris's retreating columns were there as well. Believing Lytle dead, John Beatty reported to Harris for orders. General McCook also arrived on the scene at that point, after having quickly ridden over from Starkweather's newly stabilized sector to find his corps still in jeopardy. Alarmed by the heavy Confederate attack rolling toward his flank, McCook ordered Loomis to hold his fire until the Rebels closed, and then galloped to the northeast front to find Webster.[89]

Instead he found chaos. The retreat of Harris's brigade and the collapse of the 10th Ohio had for the first time fully exposed Webster's line to the Confederate onslaught. Riding down from the Russell House, McCook ordered Webster to shift his brigade to the right to blunt Adams's approach on that flank. Webster's men would never comply. Instead, the inexperienced and drained brigade began to break down almost immediately. Having avoided being crushed under the wheels of guns and caissons, Webster dispatched the already battered 80th Indiana and 2nd Ohio to the rear. The 50th Ohio followed the Hoosiers in such haste that the hard-luck regiment grew more

Figure 12.9. National colors of the 121st Ohio Infantry. Note the use of "Chaplin Hills" rather than "Perryville" as a battle honor. Photograph courtesy Ohio Historical Society.

separated than ever and would not be reunited until morning. That left only the two inexperienced reserve regiments, the 98th and 121st Ohio, to face the enemy fully for the first time. Poorly armed and largely undrilled, the result was all but mass murder. They immediately began absorbing heavy casualties, the men falling in almost neat rows that later aided in burying them.[90]

Among those who went down was the brigade commander. The night before, William Terrill had assured Jackson, Sheridan, and Webster that the chances of all four of them dying were mathematically negligible. Now Jackson was dead and Terrill, at the Wilkerson House, was about to follow him. On his front, Webster remained with his rookies, trying to steady them and direct their fire. Sergeant Major Duncan C. Milner of the 98th Ohio was fumbling through a dead comrade's cartridge box when the brigade commander collapsed "about 20 feet from me" to the rear of the firing line. Milner dropped his musket and ran to his brigadier's side. "He told me he thought he was mortally wounded, and prayed for God to have mercy on his soul. He also said: 'Tell my dear wife and children they were last in my thoughts.'" Milner and several other soldiers carried the fallen colonel to the rear and lay him beside a tree. "I examined his wound," Milner continued,

"and found the ball had entered his right hip, and he was bleeding profusely."
The soldier ran to find a surgeon; failing in that, he procured some brandy
and water. Returning to his commander he encountered several men carrying Webster to the rear. He joined them and remained with his colonel at a
field hospital, for, he explained, "I had no particular friends in the regiment."[91]

With Webster's mortal wound, the last fight went out of the 98th and
121st Ohio. Just as hungry and fatigued as the men in Jackson's other brigade, under increasing pressure all afternoon, unable to mount much fire of
their own due to their inexperience and defective muskets, and understandably fearful of being trapped between the pincers of Brown and Wood on
their right and Donelson and Stewart on their left, the rookie Ohio regiments broke and quickly beat a path back to their comrades on the high
ridge to the west. In the words of the 121st Ohio's Jonathan McElderry, the
rookies had faced " a criticall moment [and] we left the field to the more
experienced souldiers."[92]

As McCook had ridden off to locate Webster, Lovell Rousseau galloped up
to the Russell House, shouting "for Old Kentucky." Already informed of
Lytle's collapse, Rousseau found the brigade's two exhausted and desperately
thirsty frontline regiments lying down in line on the brow of the Russell
House hill, the 15th Kentucky south of the road and the 3rd Ohio to its
north. The 88th Indiana extended the line farther right; other men milled
about all along the front. Many of the Kentuckians rose and cheered their
home state general as he rode by, but his battered Ohioans apparently exhibited less enthusiasm.[93]

As the enemy drew closer, Rousseau hastily did what he could to
strengthen the makeshift and exhausted line for the final tug. He first hustled
up some supporting infantry for Loomis's battery, driving between one hundred and two hundred stragglers from various regiments to the right of the
guns with the broad side of his sword. McCook had also found an additional
hundred men who could help—bridge builders from Companies A, C, and
H of the 1st Michigan Engineers and Mechanics, who had been watching
the battle from behind the lines until the corps commander ordered them
forward. As Rousseau placed the mechanics into line to the right of Loomis's
guns along Russell's log outbuildings, he told them to ignore the minié balls
zipping around their heads. "Oh, never mind those little things!" he exclaimed.
Just then, a shell flew over the position and nearly took his head off. "We
commenced to laugh and shout," G. N. Bachelor remembered, "as only soldiers can, and the general finished his speech with "but d—n the big ones.""[94]

In the meantime, Loomis's battery sat silently. Non-plussed, Rousseau
impatiently ordered Loomis to open fire, but in Rousseau's words Loomis
"replied that he was ordered by General McCook to reserve what ammunition he had for close work. Pointing to the enemy, I said it was close enough,
and would be closer in a moment."[95]

Figure 12.10. Position of Loomis's battery at the Russell House. Photograph courtesy Massachusetts Commandery, Military Order of the Loyal Legion, and the U.S. Army Military History Institute.

The enemy was close indeed, about seventy-five yards from the guns, when Loomis begrudgingly opened fire. Cleburne's approach had already slowed by that time. His units had grown separated in their swift pursuit of the 42nd Indiana and were physically spent from exertion. The general himself had been wounded twice, though not seriously, and the Yankees had shot one horse from beneath him. His flanks again were exposed and ammunition was running low. At that moment, Loomis hit his ranks with point-blank fire. Cleburne, realizing that his men could do no more, reluctantly drew up his tired line in a ravine a little to the rear of the valley, out of the line of fire. His brigade was done.[96] "Not being discovered owing to the darkness," W. E. Yeatman of the 2nd Tennessee wrote, "we had the novel experience of witnessing a grand artillery duel fought over our heads."[97]

After more than two hours of battle, charging up one hill or another, the Confederates had broken McCook's line all along his front. The men of I Corps, low on ammunition, clung to desperately drawn second lines along the Benton Road, leaving many of their comrades on the field. Even though Starkweather had held on McCook's left, the corps remained in peril. If Rousseau had to fall back past the Dixville Crossroads, the Confederates would be in Starkweather's rear, dividing McCook's two divisions from one another. I Corps as an organization might well cease to exist.

Nonetheless, McCook still had three factors in his favor. Time was one. Behind his lines, the sun was dipping behind the horizon. Having started the attack so late, daylight was a precious commodity to the Confederates, one that fast was running out. Everyone on the field knew that if they could just hang on until dark, I Corps probably would survive. Rousseau expressed it best when he exclaimed to one of his aides, "Will that sun never go down!"[98]

The ground also continued to favor McCook. If anything, the ridges where his new lines waited, curling around the crossroads to the north and east, were the highest and most imposing yet. To destroy McCook, the Confederates had more hills to climb. Finally, not four hundred yards to his right, a powerful and largely unbloodied Federal corps lay on its arms. With some assistance from Charles Gilbert's III Corps, the day still could be saved. Would Gilbert at last come to his rescue?

13

I Want No More Night Fighting

ALL AFTERNOON, WHILE THE BATTLE WAS SWIRLING TO HIS LEFT, Phil Sheridan had kept his division hunkered down on and behind Peters Hill, nervously anticipating that the enemy would confront him in force as it had Alexander McCook. Despite I Corps's increasingly dire position, Sheridan had done little more to help than to occasionally enfilade the enemy's advancing lines with artillery and permit a ten-minute artillery duel with Slocomb's battery of Washington Artillery. Frustrated beyond measure, his men lay flat on their bellies, raising their heads only slightly to watch with horror as Lytle's and Harris's shattered brigades gave ground and finally fell back before Adams and Cleburne's lines. "When Rousseau's line was broken," one observer remembered, ". . . every glass was directed thitherward, and when our lines went down before the irresistible charge, many a prayer went up to heaven, 'God help our poor boys now!'"[1]

At last, as the sun sank toward the horizon behind Sheridan, the threat he expected finally seemed to materialize against the southeastern sky. Colonel Samuel Powell's four-regiment brigade, numbering no more that twelve hundred men, had been just as immobile as Sheridan's since halting and forming into line on Edwards House Hill just after noon, much to Brig. Gen. Daniel Adams's consternation. Some time before 4:00 P.M., orders finally arrived from Bragg sending Powell west toward Peters Hill, his mission to silence Hescock's enfilading battery three-quarters of a mile distant. No one on the Confederate side of the line realized that the annoying battery fire represented only the tip of an entire Federal corps. The batteries presumably anchored the right of a Federal line that kept shifting ever northward. Indeed, some captured Confederates later told their captors that they did not think any infantry supported the batteries at all.[2]

Between the two hills lay open, rolling, broken meadows and cornfields, bisected at an angle by the Springfield Pike. Their line of march would take them up and over the southern extension of Bottom Hill, into the narrow Bull Run valley, and up the slope that earlier that morning was the scene of the repulse of Liddell's brigade. Urged on by their regimental officers, three of Powell's four regiments—the 45th Alabama Infantry, 24th Mississippi Infantry, and 29th Tennessee Infantry—moved quickly forward in two lines. The 1st Arkansas Infantry remained behind to support Barret's Missouri Battery, which immediately opened up on the Federal battery some three quarters of a mile away.[3]

The sudden booming of incoming and accurate cannon fire, coupled with the first glimpses of flag-waving, shouting Confederate troops moving obliquely in his direction, checked for good any momentary impulse Sheridan might have had to render assistance to I Corps. Indeed, fooled by their expectations as well as the rolling terrain, he and his men immediately and woefully overestimated the strength of the column bearing down upon them, as they had all day in that sector. Sheridan immediately assumed it to be a major threat carried by at least two brigades if not a division, and he responded quickly. As Powell's Confederates shouted the rebel yell and commenced their advance, Hescock hurriedly moved his battery to the right of the road to meet the new threat. Simultaneously, Barnett shifted his guns slightly to the left, bringing them close to Hescock's. Both immediately opened up with counterbattery fire. Meanwhile, Dan McCook's brigade on Sheridan's left raced back into the freshly dug rifle pits atop Peters Hill. McCook's redrawn front line consisted of the 52nd Ohio, in front of Hescock's battery, and the 85th Illinois to its right. The 86th Illinois remained in reserve, directed to keep watch on the left for any spillover from the attack against Rousseau.[4]

To McCook's right, most of Greusel's brigade, comprising Sheridan's center, began moving forward to straddle the Springfield Pike in anticipation of action. The 21st Michigan Infantry supported Barnett's battery. To its left, hard against McCook's right and Hescock's battery, the rookie 24th Wisconsin Infantry, jaded from a quarter-mile sprint from the rear, flopped down on the road as it ran up to the hill's western brow, just out of the line of direct fire. More than a thousand men strong, the "Milwaukee Regiment's" inexperienced line overlapped the 52nd Ohio from behind. The raw 88th Illinois Infantry moved up and over the exposed crest of the hill into an even more vulnerable position to the artillery's right.

The brigade's 36th Illinois Infantry, however, was dangerously out of place. Earlier it had veered too far to the north as it withdrew from the cornfield below back into the timber fronting the hill. As a result, it ended up well to the left of the rest of the brigade and, as the Rebels approached, to the left and a little forward of the 52nd Ohio. McCook thus did not have to worry about anchoring his left, for as luck would have it, the 36th Illinois already was there.[5] Yet while McCook could depend on one of Greusel's regiments for added support, he had lost in the confusion one of his own. To the right of Gruesel's brigade, Laiboldt's brigade hurriedly prepared for action as well. While the fresh 73rd Illinois Infantry fell back up the hill from an advanced

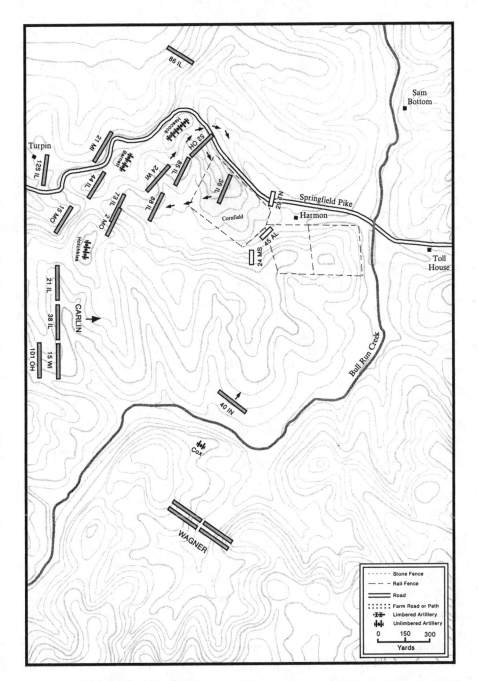

Map 13.1. Powell's attack and repulse, 4 P.M.

position in the corn, going into line with a section of guns with the 44th Illinois farther on its left, the battered 2nd Missouri on the left and the 15th Missouri on the right formed a reserve line. For still unexplained reasons, McCook's out-of-place 125th Illinois remained well to the rear, bolstering Laiboldt's defense. Sheridan's line thus betrayed signs of anxious confusion, but it nonetheless presented a formidable front.[6]

Taking the range of the Confederate guns quickly, Barnett and Hescock answered them shot for shot. When Powell's infantry finally drew within effective range, the Federal gunners quickly shifted their fire to them, exploding hollow-cased shells above and then canister into the twin gray lines. To the Federals' considerable dismay, the attackers kept coming, closing up the gaps in their lines as men fell.[7] Later, one Federal soldier could not help but express his admiration: "They advanced most gallantly marching in splendid order, not a man wavering or falling on line [despite the Union artillery] . . . tearing great rents in their lines which were instantly closed up, the column sweeping steadily onward. Their line of march could be traced by the dead and wounded thickly scattered along the way, laying where they had fallen and weltering in their blood."[8]

As they crossed into the Bull Run valley and the cornfield in front of the Federal position, still aiming toward the batteries on the hilltop above, Powell's men began "yelling like fiends broke loose from pandemonium." As the first line, consisting of the 24th Mississippi on the left and the 45th Alabama on the right, started up the hill and drew within fifty yards of the batteries, the men of the out-of-place 36th Illinois rose up and opened fire on them. Surprised to encounter infantry, the two Confederate regiments momentarily wavered but then recovered, doggedly pushing ahead another fifty feet. Despite growing numbers of casualties, they reached a rail fence on the crest that cordoned off the western edge of the cornfield and separated the 36th Illinois from Powell's men. The 29th Tennessee moved up from behind to the right of the 45th Alabama to form one continuous front. About a hundred feet separated the two lines.[9]

Powell's men quickly grasped that they had walked headlong into a nightmare. "We found ourselves confronted with more than ten times our numbers," Col. William F. Dowd of the 24th Mississippi remembered with only slight exaggeration. "The crest of the ridge we occupied was very sharp with a rail worm fence running along nearly its whole length. Finding it impossible to charge the overwhelming odds of the enemy strongly posted, my regiment was placed behind this fence and we opened fire." Thinking quickly under pressure, Dowd ordered his men to lie down and begin taking careful aim at their targets, instead of the usual practice of firing by volleys, in hopes of maximizing their limited punch. The west wind, by blowing the smoke thus produced back over their heads, aided their accuracy while simultaneously providing some cover. To the Mississippians' right, the 45th Alabama and then the 29th Tennessee followed suit. Under Dowd's direction, the men of Powell's brigade essentially metamorphosed into a prickly phalanx of sharpshooters.[10]

Caught in a cross fire between the ends of the wider Federal front line, yet partially shielded by the rail fence, trees, and smoke, Powell's three undermanned regiments maintained a surprisingly heavy and effective fire. Federals fell amid a torrent of lead in the lengthening afternoon shadows, but Powell's inexperienced marksmen often as not shot too high.[11] The psychological effect of their fire was considerable, however. One member of the 24th Wisconsin echoed other participants in describing "balls flying like hail," while comrade Eugene Comstock wrote home that "the bulletts flew around us thick and the boys were as excited as possible." Comstock added that at first he could only think of "heaven home and friends, but soon got used to it and was cool as could be under the circumstances."[12]

Nonetheless, Sheridan's three brigades simply had more guns than Powell's three regiments, and the numbers soon began to tell. Double-shot Federal canister ripped through Powell's line from four angles, the two sections of Hotchkiss's 2nd Minnesota Battery not detached to Gay's cavalry now having joined the fray from the far Union right. Meanwhile, other Federal infantry units started shooting, their fire cascading quickly from north to south. The 52nd Ohio and 85th Illinois opened fire soon after the 36th Illinois, rushing forward to the rail fence and unleashing several volleys before heavy return fire sent them back to the top of the hill for cover. As they opened up, the 24th Wisconsin moved up over the hilltop, just to the left of the Gruesel's 88th Illinois, shifted back a tad for safety, and began firing as well. To their right, the 73rd Illinois and 2nd Missouri of Laiboldt's brigade commenced firing obliquely into Powell's left flank. After a few moments, the 73rd Illinois started to retreat. The regimental historian attributed the withdrawal to a misinterpretation of orders, but the bitter veterans stationed behind the Illinoisans said cowardice caused them to fall back.[13] The men of the 2nd Missouri, heroes of the morning's fight, derisively cried out, "Shame!" Ordered forward to replace the undependable fresh fish, the veteran Missourians quickly found themselves "all mixed up" with the 73rd Illinois, which had halted in embarrassment. Together, the two regiments returned to the front and gave the Confederates "a double dose" of fire.[14]

Sheridan soon received even more assistance, this time from Crittenden's II Corps. Discovering earlier that a half-mile gap still extended between his division, on Crittenden's left, and Gilbert's corps, Thomas Wood had ordered Col. George D. Wagner's brigade to form in line of battle. As skirmishers from the 40th Indiana Infantry spread out into the gap, they discovered Powell's brigade just as it advanced from Edwards House Hill toward Peters Hill. When word reached Wood, he ordered Wagner to send the balance of the regiment forward to occupy the hill lying between the two occupied positions. The Hoosiers took off at a dead run, followed by the balance of the brigade.[15] "Again we were in motion," wrote Asbury Kerwood of the 57th Indiana Infantry, "—now no longer a march, nor double-quick, but a run—an actual race—to see which should first reach the hill."[16]

Reaching a low ridge facing north and running roughly parallel to Powell's line of march about three hundred yards from the Confederates, Wagner's skirmishers arrived too late to intercept the enemy. Undaunted, the Hoosiers continued advancing toward Sheridan's right while a section of Capt. Jerome B. Cox's 10th Battery, Indiana Light Artillery, stopped atop the ridge, tore down a fence line, and unlimbered two Parrot rifles. Barret fired several rounds at the new threat, but Cox soon managed to silence the incoming fire. Soon thereafter, Cox's Parrotts began adding to the artillery hell Powell's infantry faced, while the rest of the brigade waited on or behind the ridge in line of battle, fearful that the Confederates would turn on them.[17] In contrast, Wagner groused that Wood would not permit him to pitch into the enemy with his full brigade. "The boys of the Second Brigade will remember what a terrible man to swear Gen. Wagner was," D. M. Osburn reminisced, "and how he exercised his talent because he was not permitted to go into the fight."[18]

Meanwhile, the din on the front line had reached terrific levels. "The roar was terrific," wrote John A. Boon of the 85th Illinois. "The best thing I can compare it to is for you to take a pan of popcorn, put it in the fire, leave it until it is doing its very best. Now just suppose you have twelve pans all doing the same thing, every crack of corn a musket with a ball flying, you'll have a slight insight how the fight went on our part for half an hour."[19]

Sheridan watched on horseback a few feet behind the 52nd Ohio as the fight raged on, frequently conferring with Dan McCook, his newest brigadier, and Barnett. At first, he displayed great nervousness and agitation, sending hasty messages to Gilbert and Mitchell asking for reinforcements. I Corps had broken, he warned, and he doubted if he could hold on either without assistance.[20] "Sheridan's right leg was excited," recalled the 52nd Ohio's J. B. Work, "and frequently he rested heavy on the stirrup to stop the 'buck ague,' as I thought. Later on it all left him, and he seemed calm. Though his face was flushed, he appeared as though no unusual excitement existed."[21]

Sheridan's changing demeanor and increasingly steady leg had much to do with the rapidly changing fortunes of his division. Although he never admitted it, Sheridan had to realize at some point during the fight that he had overestimated the Confederates' strength. Faced with devastating fire from elements of four batteries and five brigades, Powell's gallant but undermanned brigade could not hang on much longer. It did try, though. Rallying several times, one Alabama color-bearer at length tied his flagstaff to the rail fence, refusing to let the colors retreat or fall again. Meanwhile, the 29th Tennessee on the Confederate right shifted farther north in a desperate attempt to flank and enfilade the 36th Illinois. Already running low on ammunition, their gun barrels so hot that many men could not ram down the few cartridges they did possess, and taking fire from the flank as well, the cut-up Illinois regiment fixed bayonets and fell back obliquely through the 88th

Illinois, "cursing and swearing because they had no more ammunition." The unexpected retreat unnerved the men of the new regiment, a few of whom began to take off for the rear. To plug the hole and preserve his suddenly wavering line, Sheridan shifted the 24th Wisconsin across the road to his left flank to meet the Tennesseans while McCook rushed the 52nd Ohio directly forward to take the place of the 36th Illinois. After steadying words from their officers, the 88th Illinois also pushed down the hill and resumed firing.[22]

Sheridan's numerical superiority ultimately proved too much for the Southerners. Powell's woefully outgunned regiments could take no more. Nearly out of ammunition, the sun setting at last, the 24th Mississippi began to fall back from the fence, "first in squads then in companies."[23] As their left gave way, the 45th Alabama and 29th Tennessee followed. On the Union left, amidst Federal cheering, the 24th Wisconsin advanced behind them, pursued the Tennesseans briefly, and then deployed skirmishers to take prisoners. Over on the extreme right, Wagner's 40th Indiana followed suit.[24] The advancing Federals found the slope of Peters Hill and the cornfields below once again full of dead and wounded men and their equipment. "Knapsacks, guns, cartriges, haversacks, and duds were laying around thick as hops," recalled Eugene Comstock.[25]

"Their dead and wounded lay in swaths," an Illinoisan later remembered of the same scene. "All through the field bodies attired in Confederate gray were scattered among the long aisles of corn. No matter in what direction one walked, the shocking picture of death in its most revolting form was presented, touching the heart, awakening pity, filling the soul with horror and the eyes with tears."[26] Powell left between two hundred and three hundred soldiers on the hill, most of them wounded. Federal losses, in contrast, were apparently light in terms of percentages of men engaged, the 36th Illinois probably suffering the most.[27]

Having survived the Confederate assault, one more threatening in his imagination than in grim reality, Sheridan hesitated to mount a pursuit. Despite his later assertions, he also initially vacillated in regard to doing anything to help I Corps. A lull fell across Peters Hill. Not content to dawdle with more fighting to be done on the left, Greusel soon took matters into his own hands, calling out to Henry Hescock, "'Captain Hescock, those fellows over yonder are using McCook's boys rather roughly. Can't you reach them with your shot?'" Obeying the implicit order, Hescock made ready to fire.[28] Meanwhile, a shaken Dan McCook pleaded directly with Sheridan to do something to rescue his brother's command now that his was secure. "By marching 250 yards over an open-plain corn field," McCook later complained, "I could have taken the rebels in rear and flank and had them between Lytle's battery and my own." Sheridan nonetheless refused to allow it. Frustrated, McCook "begged General Sheridan to at least allow us to open on them with artillery, for . . . I felt satisfied that the rebels were concentrating their whole force against our left wing." Sheridan was more willing to do that, but only with

Gilbert's approval. Only then could Hescock and Barnett begin firing solid shot and shell into Adams's vulnerable flank. But by then it might be too late.[29]

In his partial defense, Sheridan could let Powell get away because another component of III Corps already had a pursuit under way. Between 1 and 2 P.M., as he had adjusted his corps' front, Gilbert had ordered Brig. Gen. Robert B. Mitchell forward to a position closer to and somewhat to the right of Sheridan's. Mitchell, an aggressive and impatient Mexican War veteran and Free Stater from Kansas, was an angry man that afternoon. He had already argued once with Buell, the night before the battle, vehemently maintaining that he could move forward and occupy Perryville if Gilbert and Buell would only allow it. The enemy seemed little disposed to put up much resistance, he said.[30] Buell brushed the prickly Kansan off with a laugh, joking that Mitchell was too "rash, intimating that I was exceedingly eager. . . . General Buell replied to me that I could have not done it with twice my number; and furthermore told me that if I could go in there with my division he would put another star on my shoulder." Buell was tactically correct—the enemy held Perryville in force—yet his clumsy attempt to deal with Mitchell backfired. It was no joke to Mitchell, and he burned with resentment throughout the next day, convinced that the town should have been occupied, and that Buell had treated him with disrespect.[31]

Now, itching for a fight more than ever, Mitchell placed Col. Michael Gooding's brigade to the left of the Springfield Pike and Col. William P. Carlin's to its right, along a wooded hill. Colonel William Caldwell's brigade took up a position behind Carlin. Confederate troops, presumably Wheeler's cavalry moving on Carlin's right, in the gap between Gilbert's and Crittenden's corps, gave Mitchell momentary pause, leading Carlin to send out skirmishers in their direction. The cavalry threat was more apparent than real, however, and soon the men of the brigade settled into line.[32]

Mitchell's division remained there in position throughout the Confederate attack on I Corps and the initial stages of Powell's assault, anxious but unable to join the fray in support of their comrades. "I could see the whole Battle field at a time it was raging the hardest," wrote Col. Hans Christian Heg of the 15th Wisconsin, "Heg's Norwegian Regiment." "It was a sight I shall never forget. . . . The smoke and dust filled the air a great deal—and a constant rattle of cannon and muskets, and now and then a ball whistling by me so near that I would sometimes bow my head down without hardly knowing it myself."[33]

Convinced like Sheridan that a Confederate division was concentrating in front of him to assail Little Phil's position on his right, the more aggressive Mitchell was already preparing to strike when Sheridan's panicked plea for reinforcements arrived. Good as his word, within ten minutes he had ordered Carlin's brigade forward to Sheridan's right, telling the men of the 15th Wisconsin that he expected to hear good reports about his Scandinavians. Hoping to surprise the supposedly superior force, Mitchell told Carlin to remain out of sight in the trees for as long as possible and then to shock the Confederates at bayonet point. He added that they should pursue them without stopping to fire.[34]

Carlin advanced quickly, the former Indian fighter's largely veteran brigade led by a company of skirmishers from the 15th Wisconsin. Leaving the balance of the Wisconsin regiment and the new 101st Ohio in column on the flank, he formed the 21st Illinois and the 38th Illinois into line, with Hotchkiss's battery to the Illinoisans' right. He soon encountered difficulty. After crossing through a skirt of timber and moving up to the brow of a hill, Carlin discovered an old rail fence, buried in hedges and laced with thorns, running across his line of march. One hundred fifty yards away lay the ripe, open flank of the winnowed 24th Mississippi as it retreated toward town through the smoky valley. Trapped in the thorns, however, Carlin could not fall upon them quickly, and he lost the element of surprise as his men tried to extricate themselves from the thorny hedgerow. When Colonel Dowd of the Mississippi regiment saw them he ordered a change in front and fired into Carlin's approaching line. Misinterpreting the Federals' gyrations in the brambles as a retreat, and probably partially blinded by the setting sun on the horizon as well, Dowd confidently ordered the retreat to continue.[35]

Carlin's men suffered more from the thorn bushes than from the Confederate gunfire, and they most certainly were not retreating. Once through the hedge, Carlin obeyed Mitchell's orders to the letter, ordering his brigade to charge the enemy with cold steel at the double-quick and "overpower him." On Edwards House Hill, the men of Barret's battery opened up on the advancing blue line in an attempt to cover Powell's retreating brigade, but their erratic fire did little damage. As Carlin's brigade quickly drew closer on a dead run, Powell's battered regiments faltered and then broke for the protection of their guns.[36]

The race was on. Carlin's front line chased the routed Confederates as fast as their legs would carry them, across a rolling, broken course strewn with bodies and equipment. "It was like running a marathon," Arthur Siver of the 15th Wisconsin wrote, "over fences and ditches and corn fields, the enemy ahead and we in pursuit." Carlin's Norwegian skirmishers soon caught up to Powell's slowest stragglers. "At times," Siver continued, "we were so close that I was once able to give a Rebel a kick in the rear. He fell full length and we gagged him."[37] Other exhausted Confederates fell captive in the next few minutes. In the meantime, Carlin's main lines and then Hotchkiss's limbered battery followed in support.[38]

As Powell's men melted before the enemy and drew near their earlier position on Edwards House Hill, Barret's battery, accompanied by the 1st Arkansas, fell back through town to prepare a secondary line of defense on the other side of the Chaplin. The rest of the winded brigade soon jogged across the in-town bridge after them, poured through town, and fell into line on the eastern slope of Seminary Hill. Preston Smith's brigade formed by files into a second line a hundred yards to their rear. The last brigade to leave Harrodsburg, and the only unbloodied brigade remaining at Bragg's disposal, Smith's contingent had arrived in town at midmorning and held a reserve position just south of the town limits. The brigade nominally belonged to Cheatham's command, but with command responsibilities in the army thoroughly mixed up he now received orders from Patton Anderson to move through town and back up Powell. The two howitzer sections of Semple's battery still on Seminary Hill shifted forward and opened up on Carlin. Fearing the worst, Powell also ordered his teamsters to hurry out of town. Taking him at his word, they skedaddled several miles down the Harrodsburg Pike.[39]

Not long after the mule skinners began cracking their whips in fury, Carlin's men raced up the hill Barret had vacated. The 15th Wisconsin and elements of the 21st Illinois continued the pursuit down the hill and over the next to the cemetery on Perryville's western outskirts, shouting at the top of their lungs as they went. They held the line alone for what seemed an eternity. Finally, thundering up from behind them came the main line and then Hotchkiss's gunners, who quickly unlimbered and opened fire on Barret. Establishing his position on the hill above town, facing the Perryville cemetery and Merchant's Row, Carlin placed the balance of the 21st Illinois to the left of his battery and the 38th Illinois on its right, its line extending as far as the Springfield Pike and "the garden stone fences on the north side of Perryville." The 101st Ohio remained in reserve behind the hill, its ranks augmented by ninety-two-year-old "volunteer private" Thomas Stewart, a survivor of British navy impressment during the War of 1812 and spry son of the oldest living man in America at that time.[40]

When Hotchkiss opened up from his new position, Barret's and Semple's batteries responded with counterbattery fire. The noise was deafening. "I heard a voice of command order 'double charge of canister boys;' 'Ready,'" Louisianan John Ellis remembered, "then the last word was drowned. I saw a flame of fire and heard a sound as if an earthquake for it sounded as if all the pieces were discharged simultaneously. The enemy responded with a cheer but their line wavered."[41] The Confederate canister momentarily forced Carlin's men to the ground for safety. In between the batteries, the pacesetting skirmishers of the 15th Wisconsin and 21st Illinois fell to the earth for cover or else hid behind trees and buildings as shells noisily but harmlessly flew over their heads or fell around them. Soon realizing their relative safety, they then opened fire on Powell's new line as it advanced back toward the riverbed, shooting well enough to convince one Arkansan that they were trained sharpshooters. Hotchkiss caused more damage still, raking Powell's already ragged line with canister. So confident did the Federals become that during the firefight many crept down into the bed of the Chaplin River after water, filling their canteens and even gun barrels with the precious commodity.

Observing the scene from just to the Federal rear, Robert Mitchell sensed his chance to change the course of the battle. For almost twenty-four hours he had seethed over Buell's failure to seize Perryville, Now, miraculously it must have seemed, another chance presented itself. The town was his. Hoping to break Powell's line completely, capture the town, flank Bragg, and then move into the enemy's rear, he first sent orders for the 15th Wisconsin to bear left across the Mackville Road in hopes it could get behind Powell. Mitchell then hurried forward a section of Capt. Stephen J. Carpenter's 8th Battery, Wisconsin Light Artillery, of Caldwell's brigade, to help Hotchkiss batter the enemy position. Finally, he decided to ride back a half-mile to bring up Caldwell's infantry and throw them into the fight.[42]

Providentially, the tip of the iceberg that was II Corps now waited in a position to supply Mitchell with even more punch. After Powell's retreat, Wagner, acting on orders from Wood, advanced his brigade toward town. Stumbling over fallen Confederates in the lengthening shadows, the brigade came to a halt on Edwards House Hill, to the right and slightly to the rear of Carlin's position, the 40th Indiana in the lead. Encountering more wounded Confederates along the pike as well as the abandoned knapsacks of the 24th Mississippi, Wagner formed a new line of battle, ordered Cox's battery to open up on the enemy's battery, and awaited additional orders. Colonel Charles G. Harker's brigade moved up in support to his rear, strengthening the Federal presence south of town.[43] On the hill itself, J. S. Mavity of the 24th Kentucky Infantry discovered among the groaning wounded and captured enemy there "the face of a young man who was working for my father when I went into the army. He looked straight at me and then covered his face with a blanket. I thought he did not want me to recognize him."[44]

As the sun disappeared behind the western horizon and darkness fell, elements of II and III Corps stood poised to roll up Powell, capture Perryville and with it the Confederate line of retreat, seize Slocomb's battery from behind, and perhaps even tear into Bragg's exposed left flank. Perhaps a dusky hour of twilight remained, but it might be enough to relieve McCook and even change the course of the battle. With only two brigades still uncommitted, Liddell's and Smith's, Bragg would have to fight hard to stop a determined onslaught from Mitchell and Wood. Mitchell, however, had not accounted for Charles Champion Gilbert.

After Buell extended the dinner invitation, Gilbert had spent most of the afternoon with him at headquarters, both men still ignoring the scattered sounds of cannon fire emanating from the east. What happened next depends on what version of Gilbert's story one wishes to believe. Long after the battle, Gilbert claimed that the first sounds of Sheridan's fight with Powell spurred both him and the commanding general to action. At around 4:15, he wrote, "the cannon firing became so continuous and was so well sustained and so different from the irregular shots . . . that it was readily recognized as a battle." Turning to Gilbert, Buell said, "'That is something more than shell-ing the woods; it sounds like a fight.' I at once mounted," Gilbert continued, "and set off at a rapid pace down the road in the direction of the firing."[45]

Such a melodramatic ride almost certainly did not happen. In the re-port Gilbert filed just after the battle, he admitted as much, telling a story both less exciting and more discreditable. There was no mention of rapid firing or any dramatic Sheridan-at-Cedar Creek ride to the front mentioned in 1862. Having merely reported his position and dispositions to Buell—there also was no official mention of their leisurely dining—Gilbert, accord-ing to his contemporary report, simply and routinely rode forward toward his headquarters. While cannon fire of increasing volume certainly could be heard at Buell's headquarters at the time Gilbert rode away, there is no indi-cation in either Gilbert's report—or Buell's for that matter—that they im-mediately realized that a major battle was in progress. Indeed, when Gilbert met II Corps staff officer O. A. Mack in the road after leaving headquarters, he assured him that the gunfire represented not a battle but merely "Captain Gay operating on the rebels." That also was the prevailing view at headquar-ters once he got there, Mack testified.[46] Gilbert proceeded to write Crittenden a note that stated, according to George Thomas, "that he had met some little resistance himself, but was then camping his troops for the night; that General Rousseau had been engaged—I think he said driven back slightly, but had regained his ground."[47]

In fact, Thomas's recollections were favorably hazy. More damning still, Gilbert actually had written Crittenden that his "children were all quiet and by sunset he would have them all in bed, nicely tucked up, as we used to do in Corinth."[48] That the author of such words was at the time racing forward to battle is beyond credibility. Eager to defend himself from continuing attacks in later years, Gilbert stretched the truth to the breaking point in order to put himself in the most favorable light possible. He obviously did not learn of the battle until someone near the front told him. Indeed, all of the aides bringing back bad news seemingly converged on a frazzled Gilbert within minutes of each other in a dizzying whirlwind of disaster. Riding east on the Springfield Pike, Gilbert first encountered Captain Fisher of Alexander McCook's staff. Fisher reported the Confederate attack and his general's dire need for reinforcement. That news alone admittedly flabbergasted Gilbert. In 1886, referring to himself in the third person, Gilbert wrote:

> He had no knowledge of the subsequent forward movement
> [of I Corps] and descent to the Chaplin River, and he at first re-
> ceived the astounding report brought by Captain Fisher with much
> abatement. That a battle could rage for two hours or more on
> high ground like that, and nobody in camp hear it, was not to be
> credited at once. . . . The situation was difficult of realization.
> McCook's command was reported from all quarters as suffering

defeat, and yet it appeared to General Gilbert to be fighting in front of the line of battle, an odd place for a beaten wing of an army to be still fighting."

Gilbert claimed to be unaware of Rousseau's advance to the creek, and thus did not grasp that I Corps had given ground. I Corps, after all, still was forward of the Russell House, the last position he associated with it.[49]

Hardly had he digested Fisher's report when Sheridan's aide rode up with his report of Powell's attack and Sheridan's dire straits. As if on cue, increasingly rapid cannon fire from Sheridan's front reinforced the bad news. Gilbert instinctively grasped for ways to save his own corps before rushing any assistance to McCook. Persuading Miller to ride on and inform Buell, Gilbert first ordered Albin Schoepf forward into the gap on the left between the two corps, and then sent a message to Mitchell ordering him to close up on Sheridan's right.

Leaving the road, still largely worried about Sheridan, Gilbert galloped cross-country to his left to the bank of Doctor's Creek, where Col. Michael Gooding's brigade of Mitchell's division still waited for orders. Without bothering to inform Mitchell, Gilbert immediately ordered Gooding's infantry to bear right so as to bolster Sheridan's left. When Schoepf rode up at the head of his division, Col. Moses B. Walker's brigade in the lead, Gilbert immediately ordered Walker to deploy into the area just vacated by Gooding. Then more bad news arrived. As Walker's men hurried forward, McCook's other aide, Captain Hoblitzell, found Gilbert "with the information that the troops, though fighting stubbornly, were falling back everywhere, and that if assistance was not speedily afforded they must be soon driven from the field." Jackson was dead, the aide added, and Terrill was dying.[50]

Concerned largely with Sheridan and his own front, and still unconvinced McCook was in jeopardy, Gilbert responded to the new report with neither the speed nor the manpower Hoblitzell's words demanded. Instead, he ordered the aide to wait with him until Powell's attack against III Corps was decided. Curiously, despite his concern, at no time did Gilbert ride forward to observe Sheridan's front for himself. Relying instead on Sheridan's initial, panicky report and the apparently untrustworthy sounds of cannon fire, Gilbert waited in the rear until the sounds of battle ahead began to diminish. Only when assured of his own corps' safety did he agree to assist McCook. Planning initially to send Walker's brigade, Gilbert soon expressed second thoughts: "I discovered it had not yet deployed and, moreover, did not seem to be sufficiently familiar with the tactics to make the simplest movements with promptness and intelligence."[51] Reports from within the brigade suggest instead that Walker's men had succumbed to the lure of the springs near Bull Run, using the opportunity to fall out of formation and get water. Whatever happened, a disgusted and nervous Gilbert abandoned them there as useless, dispatching his adjutant general to recall Gooding. Under Hoblitzell's guidance, Gooding's brigade instead would march to I Corps's assistance. Within a few minutes Gooding had countermarched back to his starting point, but precious time had been wasted. This time taking his brigade's battery, Capt. Oscar F. Pinney's 5th Wisconsin Battery, Gooding followed Hoblitzell toward I Corps's collapsing front.[52]

Gooding barely was out of sight when Buell aide Maj. J. M. Wright rode up with additional orders. Having been sent on to headquarters by Gilbert, Captain Fisher of McCook's staff had proceeded on to inform Buell of I Corps's impending collapse. In his own account Buell said he had expressed some concern about the increased volume of cannon fire coming from Sheridan's front, but after Gilbert's departure he apparently slipped back into complacence, assuming like Gilbert that Gay alone was responsible. One witness remembered him still on his cot, reading. Thus, when Fisher came riding up with his breathless report of I Corps's battle and impending doom unless reinforced, Buell was, by his own admission, "astonished."[53]

Despite the aide's assurance, Buell refused to fully believe what he now heard. Most notably, Fisher claimed that I Corps had been in battle for three hours, yet Buell had not heard the slightest hint of musketry from the front during that time. "It was so difficult to credit" Fisher's report of that, Buell admitted in his after-action report, that he had trouble swallowing the rest of the captain's wild story. Firmly convinced that McCook could not be in the dire straits Fisher claimed, unwilling even to accept the possibility that the captain might be telling the truth, Buell sent him back to his commander with a statement "that I should rely on his being able to hold his ground, though I should probably send him reinforcements." Only after a few minutes of deliberation did Buell decide to send help—just in case there was some validity to Fisher's tale. He accordingly dispatched orders to Gilbert telling the III Corps commander to send two brigades from Schoepf's reserve division immediately to McCook's assistance. He then sent off another aide to find Thomas "with orders to move forward quickly and press the Confederates on their left flank, hoping to relieve some of the pressure on McCook and Gilbert.[54] As Kenneth Hafendorfer convincingly maintains, sending only two brigades to McCook's immediate assistance—II Corps was miles away—demonstrates more conclusively than anything else Buell's inability to accept reality. Trusting his own acoustically addled senses more than the men under his command, he simply refused to believe that I Corps could be fighting for its life.[55]

Gilbert proceeded to make a bad situation worse. When Wright arrived with Buell's orders to dispatch two of Schoepf's brigades to bolster I Corps, Gilbert, still largely concerned with his own front, balked. Gilbert told the aide he had already sent one of Mitchell's brigades with a battery, so surely only one of Schoepf's need follow. Buell, after all, had intended to send two brigades, not three. Gilbert, expressing eagerness to be of assistance, told the major to pick the brigade he wanted. Getting little real help from the corps commander, Wright rode off to find Schoepf, encountering him in a cornfield as the latter slowly rode to the front in an ambulance ahead of two of his brigades, the third still in reserve near headquarters. Without hesitation, Schoepf calmly selected the larger of the two, Brig. Gen. James Steedman's five-regiment brigade, whose men were raring to go after an afternoon of impotent observation. Satisfied, Wright galloped off to find McCook to relay the word that help was on the way. Moving quickly cross-country toward the scene of fighting after receiving their orders, Steedman's men had traversed a valley to reach the Benton Road in the Union rear. There, McCook had met them and ordered the brigade into line on Rousseau's right.[56]

Preoccupied with his own front without bothering to reconnoiter it in person, Gilbert had begrudgingly supplied McCook with the least amount of help possible. Having done so, he now for the same reason threw away whatever slim chance Buell's army had of reversing the course of the battle. At the western edge of Perryville, Robert Mitchell hurriedly had thrown together a force to turn Bragg's flank. He did so in clear violation of Gilbert's wishes. As he initially aligned his troops, one of Gilbert's aides arrived with orders for him to fall back in line with Sheridan, telling the general "that I was acting rashly and would not be sustained." Furious, Mitchell refused. Already indignant with Gilbert's staff—"his staff annoyed me from the time I went into the corps till I left it" he bitterly told the Buell Commission— Mitchell told the aide that if Gilbert wanted him to give up the town, he had better put it in writing. "I had received a great many orders from his staff officers that were not sustained by him," Mitchell angrily continued, "and if he desired me to fall back he must bring me a written order from General Gilbert." He further instructed the aide to tell the corps commander that he was "in the rear of the enemy batteries" and needed instructions.[57]

The aide disappeared, leaving a relieved Mitchell to order the 15th Wisconsin into Powell's rear and bring up more guns. Mitchell clearly expected that Gilbert, if accurately apprised of his position and prospects, would allow him to move forward. He was to be disappointed. As Mitchell rode back to bring up Caldwell's brigade, the staff officer returned in smug triumph, with a pencil-written note from Gilbert again ordering Mitchell to fall back to Sheridan's right. Incredulous and disgusted, Mitchell at last agreed to retreat, but he did so only with Caldwell's men and his batteries. He insubordinately sent word to Carlin to remain in position until he received further orders. He also said nothing of Wagner's approach on the right.

In Perryville itself, sporadic fighting continued in the lengthening gloom despite the cessation of artillery fire. Company K of the 38th Illinois encountered and, much to the men's delight, captured several wounded Confederates accompanied by Cuthbert Slocomb's surgeon, an ambulance, and a caisson dispatched by Slocomb's battery to Anderson's headquarters on Seminary Hill to bring back more ammunition. A half-hour later, the men of Company G trumped their comrades, seizing a dozen wagons full of rifle cartridges being hurried forward in the opposite direction to Adams's brigade, as well as all the men detailed to guard the train. Meanwhile, placing his artillery on a hilltop, in position to cover both the town and the Springfield Pike, ready for any contingency and still desperate for a fight, Mitchell sent one of his aides to Gilbert with a hastily drawn map of his front. He was still hoping that the corps commander would see the error of his ways. The aide, however, returned empty-handed; he could not find Gilbert at all. Mitchell himself would not speak with his corps commander face-to-face until early the next morning. His men, meanwhile, held their positions all night.[58]

So ended perhaps the last chance Buell's army had to achieve victory at Perryville. To be sure, the odds were stacked against Mitchell. Darkness had fallen. Apparently unaware of Preston Smith's fresh veterans behind Seminary Hill, Mitchell would have encountered something more than twice the enemy guns he expected to face in town. Even had the three brigades at his disposal managed to drive back Anderson's two, reinforcements from an enthusiastic Gilbert or Thomas would have been necessary to cut and firmly hold the Harrodsburg Pike in Bragg's rear, and thus cut off any Confederate retreat. That eventuality was unlikely in any event. All in all, it would have been a near-run thing. Yet any unexpected pressure at all on Bragg's flank would have served at least to lessen the pressure on I Corps. At the very least, St. John Liddell's brigade would not have been able to enter the fight for the Dixville Crossroads.

As the sun fell behind those key crossroads, the October sky turning a brilliant red, the climactic hour in the Battle of Perryville arrived. McCook's hard-pressed right had fallen back to form a desperately makeshift line on the heights between the Russell House, hastily converted into a hospital, and the Dixville Crossroads. McCook fell back with them after Webster went down and personally took charge of pulling together a new line. Taking advantage of the high ground originally occupied by Rousseau, the new line ran parallel to the Benton Road, protecting the vital road junction. Loomis's and Simonson's guns, driven back by heavy fire from the massed Confederate batteries, anchored McCook's forlorn hope. Down the hill ahead of them, Cleburne's exhausted brigade finally had pulled up, out of ammunition, as had Brown's. But Adams and Wood continued advancing, despite heavy artillery fire from the vicinity of the Russell House, into the bloody glare of that red western sky.[59]

Riding toward the crossroads hoping to find McCook, Major Wright took one look across the field and pronounced it "the finest spectacle I ever saw. It was wholly unexpected, and it filled me with astonishment. It was like tearing away a curtain from the front of a great picture. It was like the sudden bursting of a thunder-cloud when the sky in front seems serene and clear."[60]

To Adams, however, the field was decidedly less picturesque, for his advance bogged down like Cleburne's. He had tried to get his brigade moving again after the rebuff handed it by the 42nd Indiana, but the closer the Louisiana brigade moved toward the Russell House, the more iron and steel the now-active Federal batteries on the Benton Road poured into its front. Minié and smoothbore musket balls rained down the slope as well. Seventy-five yards from the blue line, heavy fire from the enemy position halted Adams again.

Almost immediately, just as the two stationary lines began exchanging musketry, unexpected artillery fire tore into the Confederate left flank. At last receiving tardy permission from Gilbert and Sheridan, the latter boasting that he had "whipped them like hell" on his own front, Barnett's and Hescock's batteries on Peters Hill opened up on the exposed Confederate flank with pent-up rage, peppering the left of the exposed massed battery as well as Adams's brigade with shot and shell.[61] Bushrod Johnson, whom Hardee had sent to supervise the massed artillery, later complained of "a direct and enfilading fire from the enemy's batteries. Balls and shells here continued to fall thick and fast from the enemy's guns, while our own batteries replied with great rapidity."[62]

From their vantage point on Peters Hill, Sheridan's men cheered on the bombardment with delight. One recalled that "shot after shot enfiladed their line; shells bursting in the midst of closed ranks caused great rents which were promptly closed. . . . How eagerly we watched the effect of shot hurled seemingly in the center of their squares; and when the dust was seen to fly, and men scattering in every direction, loud shouts broke from our ranks, and men grew hoarse with cheering."[63]

Concentrating on the enemy to his front, lulled into a false sense of security by the silence to his left, Adams and his men reacted with shock to the unexpected and heavy flanking fire. Looking south through his telescope, Adams saw, apparently for the first time, Dan McCook's brigade in line of battle as well as the offending batteries. Understandably convinced that the newly sighted enemy meant to launch an infantry attack—just as Dan McCook correctly but vainly had yearned to do—Adams sent a messenger to Cleburne informing him that he was falling back to his line, and then proceeded to do so.[64] In truth, he had little choice by then anyway, for many of his men had already made a similar decision on their own. "Little squads started off to the rear," a Federal remembered, "followed by whole battalions, seemingly excited and panic stricken. Officers were seen running hither and thither, waving their swords, gesticulating and undoubtedly threatening their men with due punishment for this exhibition of cowardice."

"In a little time," the Federal continued, "the panic seemed to subside."[65] Adams's veterans quickly regained their composure as they fell back to Slocomb's battery, and together they continued retreating all the way back to the relative safety of Squire Bottom's house and down into the dry bed of Doctor's Creek. There they encountered an angry Hardee, who immediately ordered Adams to move his brigade back up to the top of the hill he and Cleburne had earlier wrested from Lytle. While Slocomb moved his battery

Figure 13.1. Russell House site as seen from Peters Hill today. Photograph courtesy John Walsh Jr.

back out of the creek bed forward to a hill to the right and promptly resumed his fire on the enemy at the Russell House, Adams retraced his steps up the bloody ridge.[66] Once it was occupied, the brigade's fighting was done, although the dying continued. As W. L. Trask remembered, "we had to endure a heavy fire from front and flank. . . . the grape and solid shot flew thick and fast around us."[67]

Adams's brigade lost seven men killed and 152 casualties all together that afternoon, significant but relatively light figures when compared to those of Donelson's or Maney's Confederate brigades. Those statistics largely reflect its observer status during most of the fight on the Confederate left, Austin's battalion of sharpshooters being the exception, but they also indicate the deep emotional shock that Sheridan's guns must have provided at the worst possible moment. The unanticipated flanking fire had stunned the tired brigade psychologically more than it had battered it physically. In historian Earl Hess's words, Adams's veterans had reached the reasonable "limits of bravery" fighting men on both sides recognized. Retreating in the face of heavy fire, but regaining their order once in the rear, Adams's Louisianans retained their honor according to the standards of Civil War enlisted men. Nonetheless, Hescock and Barnett had rendered them at least temporarily unusable as an attacking force. Like Cleburne, Adams was done for the day.[68]

With Adams falling back, only Wood's brigade on the right continued toward the crossroads, angling toward it from the northeast. With most of the brigade's officers down, including acting brigade commander Mark Lowrey, Perryville had truly become a soldier's battle for Wood's Alabamians and Mississippians. Pouring through the abandoned flotsam of Webster's retreating brigade, Wood's men made their way quickly across the field and reached the foot of the last ridge in their way. Without orders they began scrambling up into the timber, the vital junction now within reach. It was slow going.[69] "Our line had been very perceptibly thinned by the time we reached the foot of the hill," recalled a member of the 45th Mississippi, "and the ascent was slow and laborious in the face of a terrible fire from an enemy two or three times our number."[70]

Providentially, that "heavy fire" came not from Webster's broken regiments, whose men were at that moment fleeing farther to the rear, but rather from the fresh troops of Michael Gooding's brigade, who had just arrived at the crossroads. Having received his orders from Gilbert, Gooding had double-quicked his men almost a mile cross-country through woods in a general northwesterly direction, finally reaching the Benton Road a quarter-mile from the crossroads. It had taken them about twenty minutes. Turning right onto the road, the column hurried on to the scene of the fighting, passing the wounded and other retreating men as well as two of Gay's cavalry regiments, who had arrived to bolster the position and were now drawn up in line. Gooding found McCook at the crossroads, where Major Wright from Buell's headquarters had just cheered him with word of Steedman's approach.

After a hurried discussion, McCook ordered Gooding's men into line. The rookie 75th Illinois relieved John Beatty's battered 3rd Ohio on the left and went into line north of the Mackville Road, using a split-rail fence for partial cover. Its colonel, George Ryan, stood in the ranks after having been arrested during the march for failing to have properly supplied his men with enough ammunition. On the Illinoisans' right, the 22nd Indiana formed up to the right front of Leonard Harris's 38th Indiana in an open field behind and slightly above the Russell House and its outbuildings. Although it was Gooding's former regiment, many had come to consider the Hoosier outfit a problem command, especially after hundreds of men deserted temporarily to visit loved ones during the Louisville interlude. Now, a weeping Benjamin Scribner wanted to hug them all. Gooding then placed the 59th Illinois to the right of the 22nd Indiana. As Gooding's men moved into position, shouting defiantly, fire from Wood's brigade and the Confederate batteries drove what was left of Rousseau's division back across the road.[71] Unaware of the exact identity of the newcomers, Rousseau nevertheless breathed a slight sigh of relief. "The reinforcements were from Mitchell's division, as I understood," he later reported, "and were Pea Ridge men. I wish I knew who commanded the brigade, that I might do him justice. I can only say the brigade moved directly into the fight like true soldiers. . . . It was a gallant body of men."[72]

While Gooding's infantry rushed into position, the rest of Rousseau's exhausted veterans fell back beyond the road into the woods, leaving the fight entirely to the new arrivals. Major Wright wrote that the survivors of the 15th Kentucky in particular "seemed to stagger and reel like men who had been beating against a great storm. . . . They filed into a field and without thought of shot or shell they lay down on the ground apparently in a state of exhaustion."[73] Loomis's gunners also fell back to the road, abandoning their guns and blocking Pinney's men as they put their pieces into position. Pinney unlimbered with difficulty opposite the road at a position chosen by McCook: the brow of a small, heavily wooded hill three hundred yards behind the Russell House. So narrow was the available clearing on the otherwise forested hill that only five of the battery's six guns could be used. As the artillerymen prepared for action, McCook told Pinney: "We have whipped them on the right and center, and I think this brigade will turn the scale on the left. You are just in the nick of time."[74]

Pinney hoped so. A former regular with Florida service, California prospector during the 1849 gold rush, and Wisconsin farmer since 1852, Oscar Pinney ached to prove himself to the folks back home, some of whom had publicly doubted his capacity to control and command their rambunctious sons. Growing darkness, coupled with the ubiquitous smoke of battle, nonetheless hindered him at first. "D—— 'em," he exclaimed, "where are they!" Unable to see the enemy's batteries, Pinney opened fire in their general direction, aiming at "a heavy bank of smoke and a continual flash of flame . . . [that] poured forth a storm of lead and iron hail."[75]

"The battle now raged furiously," Gooding reported, "one after one of my men were cut down, but still, with unyielding hearts, they severely pressed the enemy, and in many instances forced them to give way."[76] Thirty yards from the rail fence, and not much farther from the crucial crossroads, Wood's tired men realized that something had gone wrong, for they clearly had encountered a sizable number of fresh troops. Protected to a degree by the tree line and slope, the Confederates halted, hunkered down, and returned the fire. As the sky darkened, fiery muzzle flashes lit up the growing darkness. After several minutes of musketry, a few members of the 45th Mississippi on the left gave up and fell back down the hill. They were soon followed by others and finally by most of the rest. Their retreat dangerously exposed the flanks of the 32nd Mississippi and 33rd Alabama farther to the right.[77]

Back up the ridge, Major Wright asked McCook if he had anything to report to Buell. His line seemingly stabilized by Gooding's reinforcements and with the enemy beginning to fall back, McCook told him "to go back and tell General Buell he thought he was all right and could hold his ground." As Wright rode away with the good news, he "saw the great yellow moon rising out of the tops of the hills I had left, and across its face and through the background of dark blue sky, from opposite directions, I saw the shells of opposing batteries cross and fall like meteors toward either line. It was a

Figure 13.2. "Hardee flag" of the 33rd Alabama Infantry. Photograph courtesy Alabama Department of Archives and History.

beautiful view—the enchantment of which was considerably heightened by distance."[78]

Wood's two remaining regiments, the 32nd Mississippi and 33rd Alabama, enjoyed no such luxury. They hung on for perhaps twenty minutes longer, unwilling to surrender ground for which they had paid so heavily in blood. A. M. Crary of the 75th Illinois remembered that the 33rd Alabama "rained their leaden hail upon us," while supporting Confederate artillery simultaneously hit the ridge top with canister fire.[79] Hoping to break the stalemate, the Illinois regiment shifted toward the Alabamians' right and began flanking the regimental line, shoving the 33rd Alabama's right companies in behind those on the left. Reacting to the pressure, the entire regiment then pivoted back on the 32nd Mississippi, roughly forming a right angle, and backed up some more, so much so that the Alabama regiment's left flank rested in the midst of the Mississippians' right-flank companies.[80]

At that inopportune moment, the 22nd Indiana rose up and charged down the hill, bayonets fixed. Shocked, the men of the 32nd Mississippi broke for the rear, invariably carrying the 33rd Alabama down the hill with them in a snowball of human confusion. Together, they fell all the way back to Sam

Harris's now-silenced guns before those officers still on their feet managed to check the panicked mob and form a new line behind the split-rail fence defended earlier that afternoon by Webster's brigade. Behind them, the 22nd Indiana pursued until a volley of gunfire stopped its men in their tracks and sent them back up the ridge. Marching beneath their blue "Hardee flags," St. John Liddell's Arkansas brigade had once again taken the field.[81]

Back at Squire Bottom's house, watching Wood's men come to a halt on the sloping ridge, William J. Hardee also could see momentum slipping away from his army, even as the sun set and darkness began to spread over the field. The situation, he would soon tell Stoddard Johnston, was "'Nip & Tuck' & he once thought 'Nip' had it."[82] Brown, Cleburne, Adams, and now Wood had ceased advancing. Time was running out. Desperate to deny "Nip" a victory, Hardee decided to play his last card: Liddell's Arkansas brigade, which had started the battle for the Confederates so many hours before. Liddell's men had waited in reserve all afternoon. Before Cleburne's assault on Lytle, Liddell, acting on orders from Hardee, had brought his brigade forward to Chatham House Hill. There, Buckner had ordered him to hold it at all costs in case the enemy somehow successfully counterattacked. From the vicinity of the Chatham House, Liddell and his men watched their comrades' assault on the burning barn and dodged overshot Federal shells that killed a private in the 2nd Arkansas and wounded a handful of others. Liddell compared the sight before him to "a great amphitheater. The arena was encircled by the high ridge for use of spectators. Hardly high enough, however, to be indifferent to the danger."[83]

As Cleburne halted and Adams at length fell back toward Squire Bottom's house, the volume of shells careening into Liddell's position increased, killing and wounding several more dodging Arkansans as they bounced and ricocheted through his lines. Liddell sensed his men's growing dread, and he felt it himself as he saw what he called "an ill omen." Across the "arena" at the Russell House was an American flag, flapping against the horizon as the red sun sank behind the ridge. "Shining through the folds and stripes," Liddell wrote just after the war, "gave the sun the appearance of a flame of fire. I could not suppress the sudden misgiving that the Union *flame* would yet consume the Confederacy. . . . Perhaps it would have been better for us to fight for our rights in the Union under the same flag."[84]

Liddell, however, had little opportunity to debate the wisdom of secession that evening. One of Hardee's aides rode up and shook him from his dark reverie. Hardee, the aide announced, wanted him to move forward immediately. The aide, Col. Hardin Perkins, rode with Liddell's column as it snaked down into the valley of Doctor's Creek by the right flank. "'I had like to have forgotten,'" Perkins added as the column moved up the opposite bank. "'The General says go where the *fire is hottest*.'"

"I looked around for the hottest place," Liddell added. "It seemed to be

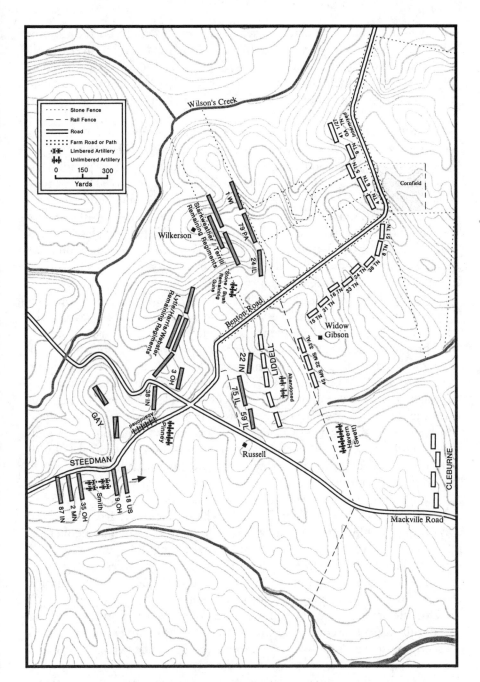

Map 13.2. Fight for the Dixville Crossroads, 5:45 P.M.

everywhere." Liddell quickly focused on Loomis's battery on the extreme southern end of the Union line, to the left of the road as it ran over the red horizon. "I spoke a few cheering words to the men," Liddell remembered. "I assured them that their vigor and bravery would decide the battle. I felt confident that they would not fail. A cheer and a voluntary fixing of bayonets was the answer."[85]

Still in column, the brigade moved quickly over the ridge held by the enemy earlier in the day near what had been the junction of Harris's and Lytle's brigades, brushed by Wood's stragglers, and came up past the new position just taken by the remainder of Wood's brigade. There the Confederates fired their volley into the 22nd Indiana. Despite the help, some of Wood's men resented what they regarded as Liddell's tardiness. "Had some of these or other troops been moved in on our right earlier in the evening and kept the Federals off our right flank and from getting in our rear," one bitter Alabamian wrote, "we might have carried the line behind the fence in our first front."[86] A few others fell into line, however, eager for one more try at the enemy.[87]

In hastily ordering Liddell forward himself, Hardee bypassed Buckner in the chain of command. Necessity certainly counted for only part of the slight. Hardee felt great confidence in Liddell and his men, whom he had first brought to Kentucky from Arkansas the previous year, and clearly still thought of the Arkansas brigade as his to command when push came to shove. They were his "Old Guard." Had Hardee consulted with Buckner, however, he might well have reconsidered, for Buckner had learned that the Federals near the Russell House had been reinforced from somewhere on their right. Buckner in fact dispatched two aides to his superior warning of the unanticipated reinforcement, with a strong recommendation that Liddell hold his position to counter the potential threat. Too late, Buckner learned that Liddell already was in motion.[88]

Liddell by that time had reached Sam Harris's abandoned guns. There he encountered Cheatham and Polk, who had ridden over from the right. According to Liddell, Cheatham was so bellicose as to be all but incoherent. "General," Cheatham exclaimed, "you can save the fight! Go on and save it!"

"I shall try, General," Liddell replied with less enthusiasm, "but come and show me your line. It is now getting too late to distinguish colors clearly. I might fire by mistake upon your men." Liddell clearly had mistaken Wood's line for one of Cheatham's brigades, and he assumed more Tennesseans must be ahead. Instead of correcting him, however, Cheatham could only incoherently bluster more. "No—go and save the fight," he replied. "You will find the line."[89]

Liddell, more uneasy than ever after his conversation with Cheatham, resumed his march, accompanied by perhaps three dozen of Wood's men. Polk tardily followed as well. Behind them, a full moon rose in the evening sky, the image symbolically represented in their blue flags. Whether that would prove to be a good or bad omen remained to be seen. The brigade

essentially retraced the steps of Wood's men, moving back toward the sloping ridge and Gooding's left regiment, the rookie 75th Illinois. Meanwhile,
painfully aware of the new Confederate effort to seize the crossroads thanks
to Liddell's volley in defense of Wood, a still-mounted Gooding pulled the
22nd Indiana out of line and ordered it to the 75th Illinois's left, intending to
blunt the new assault. Unfortunately, the Federals lost sight of the new threat
in the gathering darkness. Desperate to locate the Rebels, Gooding rode
away to his left.

Liddell's line was, in fact, much closer than Gooding realized: within
thirty yards of his line and starting up the final slope.[90] Without orders, some
of Liddell's nervous men fired directly into the shadows of the 22nd Indiana
as the Federal regiment took its new position on the brigade left. Equally
nervous Federals responded. The Hoosier regiment's Lt. Col. Squire Keith,
confused enough by the darkness and terrain to assume that the raw 75th
Illinois and not the enemy had fired into his line, cried out, "You are firing
upon friends; for God's sake stop!"[91]

The plaintive plea froze Liddell, who still worried that some of Cheatham's
regiments were ahead of him. What should he do? Finally deciding on a bayonet charge, Liddell gave way to Polk, who by then had caught up with him.
After assuring Liddell that the men to his front could not be Cheatham's, Polk
admitted in his next breath that he was not sure of their identity. Unable to
locate any of his aides, Polk without another word disappeared into the darkness, eager beyond good sense to prove his point. Simultaneously, Col. John
H. Kelly of the 8th Arkansas, who was also concerned about what lay ahead,
rode up the ridge from a different spot to identify the other line.

Reaching the dim line at the top of the ridge, Polk took center stage in
a brief, grim farce. After momentarily convincing himself that the mystery
men *were* Confederates after all, the bishop gave the man who was obviously
the officer in charge a quick tongue lashing for firing into friends and demanded an explanation. Chagrined, the equally bewildered Keith plaintively
replied, "I don't think there can be any mistake about it, for I am d—d certain that they are the enemy."

"'Enemy!'" Polk spat, "'why, I have only just left them myself. Cease
firing!'" Continuing in the same vein, Polk demanded that the officer identify himself. Before Keith could answer, another rider appeared from a different direction. It was Colonel Kelly. The situation began to seem very odd
to Keith. Identifying himself as the colonel of the 22nd Indiana, the beleaguered officer asked the identity of his guests. Only then grasping his danger, Polk realized that his best chance was to bluff. Hoping that his dark gray
blouse would continue to conceal his allegiance in the dim light of the trees,
he growled, "I'll soon show you who I am sir; cease firing, sir, at once.'" He
slowly pulled on his reins and rode away, remembering to shout "cease fire"
one or two more times as he cantered off. Then, after telling Keith to "stay
where you are," Kelly officiously followed Polk like any good aide would.[92]

Only after reaching the safety of the trees did Polk and Kelly spur their mounts. "General," Polk blurted out to Liddell as he galloped up, "every mother's son of them are Yankees." "Yankees!" the Arkansas men cried out, "Yankees!" Liddell ordered his bugler to sound the command to fire. As he did, "a tremendous flash of musketry" rent the darkness,[93] looking to one of Liddell's men like "a long sheet of fire."[94]

Still confused by the mysterious riders, Keith and his men were awkwardly milling about when the first devastating volley—fired by the 2nd, 6th, and 7th Arkansas—hit the Hoosiers at point-blank range. Dozens of men went down instantly, and still more fell in successive volleys of flashing gunfire unleashed over the next few minutes into the dazed and hapless Indianians. Among them were Gooding, whose horse fell in the first volley as he rode up in search of the enemy, and Lieutenant Colonel Keith, who died within minutes. Gooding survived only to be taken prisoner a few moments later by Colonel Kelly as the 8th Arkansas ceased fire and advanced through the newly created gap. Bodies lay everywhere before the attackers; almost two-thirds of the 22nd Indiana's complement of troops, 195 men, lay dead or wounded along the top of the ridge, some shot three or fire times. The regiment's 65.3 percent casualty rate was the highest suffered by any regiment at Perryville. Instinctively, the survivors retreated from the Arkansans and collapsed back across the Benton Road and into a cornfield, losing their shredded colors in the process. There they took cover behind a rail fence, reforming under the command of Maj. Thomas Tanner but refusing to fire into the dark and smoky woods, shaken and afraid of shooting their comrades in the back. There was little they could do to stop Liddell anyway. One of the regiment's companies now consisted of its captain, a noncommissioned officer, and two enlisted men.[95]

The collapse of the 22nd Indiana dangerously exposed the 75th Illinois's flank, and it too retreated to the presumed safety of the fence, followed in turn by the 59th Illinois. Both units took casualties as they fell back. Reunited at the fence, the brigade's three regiments, having suffered a total casualty rate of perhaps 35 percent, regrouped and fell even farther back to the west into a ravine. They then left the field, abandoning Pinney's battery to its fate. Meanwhile, Pinney's guns had grown so hot that the battery had ceased firing. As the brigade collapsed around him, Pinney unloaded a few rounds of canister into the approaching Confederate line and then ordered his crews to limber up and follow the infantry.[96]

The sudden silence blanketing the field as Gooding's men retreated, coupled with the unknown terrors of the smoky night, baffled Polk and Liddell. Instead of quickly following up his advantage, Liddell first paused to secure his position. He called up Swett's battery so that it could command the dark woods before him. He then dispatched skirmishers toward the woods. After that, well ahead of his now stationary main lines, Polk and Liddell rode cautiously into the coveted crossroads to survey the scene. Both Confederates expressed shock at the magnitude of the slaughter their men had committed.[97] "The Federal force had disappeared everywhere," Liddell remembered. "The ground before my battle line was literally covered with the dead and dying. I returned to the line and announced the cheering fact that the field was ours. It was answered with repeated cheers and then followed loud cheering *far to our left*, which we supposed to be from Anderson's Division."[98]

Liddell was wrong, and he soon realized his error. The cheers he heard, which came from a few hundred yards to the southwest down the Benton Road, were from the men of Steedman's brigade, the only other reinforcements Gilbert had permitted to go to I Corps's assistance. Moving quickly northward toward the scene of the fighting after receiving their orders, Steedman's men made their way through the Union rear to the Benton Road, while their commander rode ahead. He found McCook standing near Loomis's battery. "Here come the Pea Ridge men," McCook called out to Buell's aide, Major Wright, "tell the General I am all right now."

"He recognized me immediately," Steedman later testified, "and approaching me remarked that he had never been so glad to see me in my life." While overjoyed to have more help, McCook nonetheless remained overwhelmed with the task before him, and he began to dash off without telling Steedman where he should place his men. When the brigade commander requested positive orders, McCook could only reply, "'You remain here for a short time and watch the front, and if you see anything going wrong take care of it. . . . I will return in a few minutes and give you orders.'"[99]

Much to Steedman's consternation, he never saw McCook again until the battle was over. Waiting in vain "for some time," he watched with growing reservations as Lytle fell back before Adams and Cleburne toward his position near the Russell House. Loomis's battery was unsupported, and Steedman worried that if he did not do something, it too would fall to the enemy. Finally, he gave up and went back for his brigade, determined that he would hold the position if no one else would. Racing back down the road, Steedman encountered his men coming onto it from a cornfield, the 18th U.S. Infantry regiment in the lead. To his surprise, Steedman learned from that regular regiment's Maj. Frederick Townshend that McCook had ridden by minutes before and already had told Townshend to take the brigade to a position on the right of Loomis's battery.[100]

Steedman led his men up the Benton Road to the Russell House. As they raced to the front, his men saw evidence of the rout everywhere. "The valley presented a scene of bustle and commotion;" recalled F. W. Keil of the 35th Ohio, "ammunition trains were pushing toward the front; ambulances passing to the rear with wounded men; aids and orderlies were urging onward their jaded steeds, while stragglers seemed intent on but one idea—getting to the rear." Suffocating clouds of dust rose from the road.[101] Turning off of it to reach Loomis's guns, Steedman ordered his men down the slope

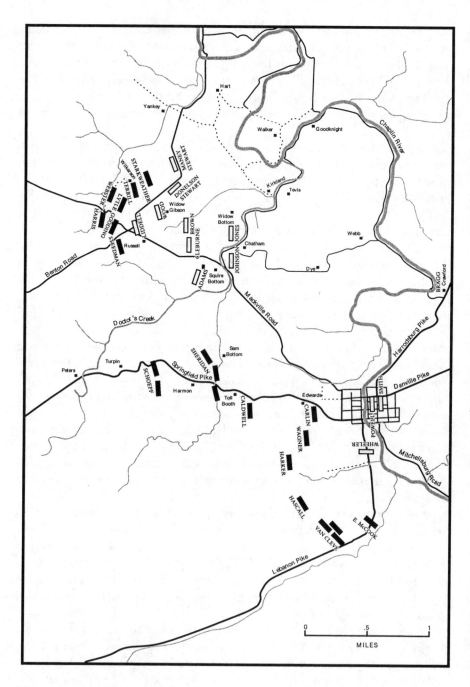

Map 13.3. Perryville battlefield, 8 P.M.

to its brow, the 18th U.S. Infantry, the 9th Ohio, and Battery I of the 4th U.S. Artillery, commanded by Lt. Frank G. Smith, forming the first line from left to right. Backing them up in the woods were the 35th Ohio and, supporting the battery, the 2nd Minnesota. Coming up last, the rookie 87th Indiana would take a position behind the Minnesotans. While Smith's men unlimbered and opened up with counterbattery fire, skirmishers advanced and the balance of the infantry lay low as Confederate shells and rifle balls screeched over their heads.[102] Searching for an appropriate simile, Minnesota farmer D. B. Griffin remarked that the enemy shells provided "deathly music. Some of them sounded like a threshing machine cylinder when they went through the air."[103]

"Don't fire until you can see the whites of their eyes," Steedman barked.[104] Obeying such a melodramatic order, however, was by no means easy in the heat of a night battle, as the men of the 2nd Minnesota learned when the 87th Indiana came within a moment of opening fire into their backs, thinking them the enemy. "We had no experience in the whole war more startling than the cocking of muskets behind us," Minnesotan Judson Bishop remembered, "knowing as we did, that they were in the hands of friends who were not informed of our presence in front of them."[105] Nonetheless, as night fell, the guns of Steedman's infantry remained silent. Only their unexpected voices could be heard as Liddell rode into the crossroads.

Finally realizing that another enemy contingent lay to his left, Liddell prepared to maintain his advantage and continue the fight. The enemy batteries must be taken, he reasoned, if he was to hold the crossroads. Accordingly, he dispatched orders to Havern telling the artilleryman to bring his guns up to the junction, and he put his riflemen to work clearing bodies out of the way. Skirmishers from the 6th Arkansas quickly advanced toward the dark woods across the road. Polk, however, learning of Liddell's determination to continue the fight, objected. "'I want no more night fighting,'" Polk told the brigade commander. "'It will be a waste of ammunition. Await orders just as you are.'" Stunned, Liddell disagreed vehemently, telling the bishop that only confused and panic-stricken men lay before him, ripe for the taking. Polk still refused to budge. The advance was over. As far as Liddell was concerned, there was nothing left to do but care for the wounded, gather prisoners, collect Federal small arms that lay in abundance on the ground, and down a swig of rotgut reportedly taken from McCook's captured ambulance.[106]

Across the road, the Federals listened expectantly for renewed shooting. When a handful of Confederate horsemen rode by Pinney's limbered battery, the bellicose artilleryman ordered his number three gun to "Unlimber, and give them canister by G-d." A few last shots echoed over the dark Chaplin Hills as the mounted men galloped away, followed by a silence punctuated only by the screams and moans of the wounded. The Battle of Perryville was over.[107]

14

SCENES OF BLOOD AND SUFFERING

HIGH ABOVE THE CHAPLIN HILLS WEST OF PERRYVILLE, THE BRILLIANT harvest moon that illuminated Liddell's attack reached its apex near midnight, shining so brightly that Louisianan W. L. Trask paused to pick up and eventually read a copy of the *St. Louis Republican* he discovered on the ground. Tragically, that silver moon also revealed a grimmer harvest that sickened Trask and drove him to the rear. All across the once peaceful fields and pastures, from the lines of early morning to the final fronts of night, men and animals lay dead or dying by the thousands, their bodies often hideously disfigured by shot and shell. Groans, pitiful cries, the banging of ambulances, and occasional shots from pickets broke the silence of the mournful night. Stretcher bearers crisscrossed the ridges and valleys searching for the living, their lanterns making them seem like the ghosts of the slain already haunting the field. Despite the objections of officers on both sides eager to maintain order in the face of a still dangerous enemy, the carnage inevitably drew other men, some weeping or shouting names as they sought out relatives or friends, others hoping to find water, still others to scavenge, and many more simply attempting to comprehend the horrors of the day.[1]

On the Confederate right, where Cheatham's division had battled McCook's Federal I Corps all afternoon, death and suffering were omnipresent. Hundreds of men, including Cheatham himself, swept the field for survivors. Dead soldiers, some in blue, others in gray, lay in what Sam Watkins of the 1st Tennessee called "inextricable confusion." Helping to retrieve the wounded of his regiment, Watkins observed horrendous sights that still chilled him twenty years later. The enemy had shot off one man's jaw, leaving his tongue to hang in the cavity. Vomiting blood, a captain begged Watkins to lay him down and let him die. A lieutenant lay blinded, both eyes shot out. "I cannot tell the one-half," Watkins observed bitterly, "or even remember at this late date, the scenes of blood and suffering that I witnessed on the battlefield at Perryville."[2]

"It was a sad sight that night as I gazed upon the upturned, ghastly faces of our dead;" comrade-in-arms Marcus Toney agreed, "and the cries of the wounded for 'water!' 'water!' 'water!'" was heartrending."[3] Many indeed had died horribly. One of Toney's officers, Thomas Malone, remembered "seeing what appeared to me a great bundle of rags. . . . It proved to be a body in which, it seemed, a shell had exploded, leaving no trace of humanity except blood and bones and shattered flesh."[4] Nearby, William Carnes and one of his lieutenants, having left their guns, searched for friends in the 1st Tennessee. Instead, they happened upon what turned out to be the wreckage of Parsons's battery on the Open Knob. As he surveyed the dead artillerymen still sprawled across the hill, Carnes brooded on whether his guns could have caused such horrible havoc.[5]

The situation was no less terrible on Hardee's front. As soon as the firing died down, the men of Wood's brigade moved back up toward the Benton Road to search for comrades and gather the personal effects of the slain. Discovering scores of wounded, they gathered straw on which to place those who could not be moved and brought up full canteens to slake their thirsts. "Although we were thoroughly tired out," one soldier of the 33rd Alabama wrote, ". . . we were up with the wounded boys and assisting the doctors nearly all night. . . . some complained of being cold, their clothing being wet with blood. We wrapped our blankets about them."[6]

While the firing lines reeked with death, the rear areas offered no comfort either. Wharton's cavalrymen rode into a nightmare as they searched for something to drink at Crawford Springs. According to W. H. Davis of the 4th Tennessee Cavalry, "no man ever experiences such a night of torture as we did listening to our wounded comrades, prostrate on the hot earth, crying for water."[7] An even more ghastly encounter shook the men of Slocomb's battery as they pulled their guns back into Bushrod Johnson's lines and began their desperate search for water. Rediscovering the same small pool in the channel of Doctor's Creek occupied by the 42nd Indiana hours before, the Louisiana gunners elbowed their way past other men and horses to its edge and began to drink. One man was so thirsty that he crawled in on his belly and lapped up the water like a dog. Only after slaking their thirst did the Louisiana gunners notice that many of the men around then in the pool were dead, Federals "who had been killed in the pool or had dragged themselves there to die." Only a similar experience at Shiloh, one artilleryman remembered, kept Slocomb's veterans from vomiting all they had imbibed.[8]

Such terrible episodes were hardly peculiar to Bragg's men that night. Like their Confederate counterparts, many Federals wrote of similar experiences on the moonlight-bathed battlefield. I Corps's survivors, having borne the brunt of the Confederate assault, had fallen back into unoccupied areas west of the Benton Road. As their officers cobbled together a new line, the men, dreading another assault, held their muskets close. Some bowed their heads as Capt. Edward V. Bowers of the shattered 105th Ohio began an impromptu prayer service and led his bloodied congregation in a hymn. Largely denied access to the battlefield, most of McCook's survivors experienced at least its aural horrors. John Beatty of the 3rd Ohio remembered listening to the moans and cries of their friends within the Confederate lines. "Their thoughts are on the crest of that little hill," Beatty wrote, "where . . . scores . . . lie cold in death. They think of the wounded and suffering, and speak to each other of the terrible ordeal through which they have passed, with bated breath and in solemn tones, as if a laugh or a jest, or frivolous word, would be an insult to the slain."[9]

Some men, unable to bear the waiting, slipped back to the front. Among others, members of the 79th Pennsylvania and 121st Ohio went out to find their dead. The Pennsylvanians dragged theirs away and buried them that night behind the lines in a hundred-yard-long, blanket-lined mass grave.[10] Mead Holmes of the 21st Wisconsin recalled his captain asking for volunteers to go forward and do likewise. Carrying a handkerchief tied to a stick, Holmes and a handful of others crossed the lines went back into the bloody cornfield. The first man they found was their fallen major, his body stripped and left behind, among other Badgers who had been killed or wounded. "I helped carry off four, and then gave out from exhaustion," Holmes wrote home. "The moon shone full upon the scene; it is utterly useless to describe the sight,—men and horses dead and wounded, wagon-wheels, arms, caissons, scattered, and the moans and shrieks of the wounded. Oh, may you never see such a sight! I helped carry off one poor fellow with his mouth and lower jaw shot off—stop, stop! I can't say more."[11]

Although the Confederates had hammered McCook's corps back more than a mile, they had failed to dislodge Gilbert's at Peters Hill. Instead, elements of II and III Corps had counterattacked and advanced to the edge of town, where they remained. Still in possession of that part of the field along the Springfield Pike, those Federals enjoyed greater access to scenes of battle than did McCook's hunkered-down lines. Their accounts are tragically similar to those of the Confederates to the north. Emerson Rood Calkins of the 8th Wisconsin Battery in Caldwell's brigade wrote that "the moon was full, and I tell you it was a ghastly sight, dead men so close that one could walk on them for rods and not touch the ground."[12] One of his brigade comrades, George W. Morris of the rookie 81st Indiana, remembered his great sadness as he surveyed the dead of Powell's brigade: "Their faces were very pale, and the light of the moon glittered in their eyes. It was fearful to behold."[13] Meanwhile, back on Peters Hill, Phil Sheridan's exhausted men lay down and slept among the dead and wounded "whose cries of anguish ascended from every part of the blood-stained battle ground."[14]

Arguably the most ghastly sights of all were to be found at local homes, churches, and barns, all of which surgeons had converted to hospitals during the afternoon. There, doctors toiled through the night, professionally unconcerned as to the allegiance of their patients.[15] Conditions remained primitive at best. "One must not expect to much of a hospital behind a battlefield," John Henry Otto of the 21st Wisconsin bitterly cautioned. "In this case the hospitals consisted of a few small houses in Perryville, two small log barns in the rear of the battlefield and one big hospital tent. The barn nearest the line was used as an amputation room; that is wher arms and legs were sawed off. The boys called it the 'butchershop, or barnjard.'" The other barn, Otto added, served those with other wounds requiring "probing for bullets and dressing of wounds." All around the buildings lay treated men "covered with a blanket and left to themselfes to indulge in wholesome meditations over the beauties of patriotism and liberty."[16]

S. K. Crawford, regimental surgeon of the 50th Ohio, probably would have agreed with Otto's caustic assessment of medical care in the Army of the Ohio. Lacking any real organization or support from Buell, a general serenely uninterested in the medical arm, regimental surgeons largely had been on their own since the beginning of the campaign, when Buell ordered them to leave behind all their hospital and medical wagons save one per brigade to make up time. During the afternoon at Perryville, Buell again left them to their own devices when it came to setting up hospitals. Several surgeons in Rousseau's division pooled their resources and commandeered the Wilkerson House and its outbuildings. Before long, the buildings and surrounding yard teemed with wounded men like Terrill and Webster, stragglers, and local slaves seeking safety and protection. Convinced that they were well behind the lines, Crawford and the others did not realize how elusive their safety was until Carnes began lobbing shells over their heads at Loomis's battery late in the afternoon. Three rounds of solid shot hit a nearby cabin crammed with frightened slaves, sending the occupants in all directions.[17] There was worse to come. As night fell and the battle ended, the enormity of their task finally confronted the doctors at the Wilkerson House. As the wounded poured in, Crawford realized "the awful fact" that he could supply no more water, no food, "no medicines, no dressings, no rations."[18]

Confederate hospitals to the east coped no better with the onslaught of wounded. Chaplain Joseph Cross spent the afternoon at the Goodknight House at Walker's Bend, which fast became the major aid station for Cheatham's division. The condition of the wounded there left him "sick at heart." The first man to come in, recalled Cross, was "a poor fellow from one of the batteries, with both legs crushed by a cannon-ball. Another has a hole through his body, which would admit a man's arm; yet, strange to say, he lives a full hour. A third, smeared with blood and brains, presents no semblance of the 'human face divine.' Some are shot through the breasts, through the lungs; others through the arm, the hand, the shoulder."

Cross remained there for hours after dark, his "hands and clothes . . . besmeared with blood," when the ambulances began to bring new waves of wounded gathered from the moonlit field, rendering the hospitals more horrible than before. "Nothing is heard except the rumbling of the ambulance, the groans and cries of the sufferers, the slash of the surgeon's knife, and the harsher sound of the saw." Only after hearing that his friend John Savage of the 16th Tennessee remained alive but dangerously wounded did Cross escape the hospital, hoping to find the colonel before the Yankees did but undoubtedly desperate to get away from the Goodknight House as well. Two miles out, he came across Savage, alive and as ornery as usual, herding in a company of Federal prisoners while mounted on the same wounded horse he had ridden into battle. "'Well, Doctor,'" Savage exclaimed, "'I have got all my wounded men off the field, I believe; and now I am coming off myself.'"[19]

Donelson's quartermaster, Maj. George Winchester, also remembered the Goodknight House with pathos. At the beginning of the battle, Winchester gave in to curiosity and went forward to observe the fight. As the sun went down, the division's surgeon tracked him down and asked him to find lanterns. He rode five miles into the rear to get them. Returning around nine, Winchester found "a scene revolting to humanity—the house, yard, and every available space upon an acre of ground were covered with the wounded—The night was quiet, and the moon shone as calmly and as placidly as if nature looked with approving smile upon the terrible drama which had just been enacted." As he walked stunned among the wounded, the quartermaster could not help but wonder "why Christian men could approve and encourage, such a wholesale butchery."[20]

No one could have had worse memories of Perryville's hospitals than the wounded themselves. Among those Cross and Winchester pitied that long night lay James Irdell Hall of the 9th Tennessee, who fell during the afternoon on the reverse slope of the Open Knob. Left behind by his comrades, Hall waited anxiously for them to come back for him as they had promised. In the meantime, a Mississippian herding a prisoner to the rear ordered the captured Yankee to climb a tree and cut down branches to use for an arbor that would shield Hall from the sun. That evening, as he grew increasingly weak from the loss of blood, his friends finally returned and carried him to an ambulance, which reached the Goodknight House around midnight. A surgeon judged his wound mortal, dosed him with morphine, and ordered him to an area around an apple tree where two equally drugged mortally wounded men waited to die. According to Hall, the others "kept me awake for a long time by asking such questions as, 'how I felt,' and 'whether I thought I would last through the night.'" He did; they did not.[21]

One cannot be sure, but Hall's surgeon could well have been Charles Todd Quintard, who already was exhausted by the time Hall came in. He had been operating steadily since three in the afternoon, never stopping to eat, and he continued to work on the wounded until near dawn the next morning. Later, he wrote that "it was a horrible night I spent,—God save me from such another. I suppose excitement kept me up. About half past five in the morning of the 9th, I dropped,—I could do no more. I went out by myself and leaning against a fence, I wept like a child."[22]

The sight of so many mangled men and the voices of so many wounded, whether still on the field or at hospitals, affected soldiers differently that night. All across the battlefield, some of the men who earlier had sought to kill one another practiced simple acts of kindness. Prisoner A. J. Herald of the 3rd Ohio remembered a captain from Adams's brigade dragging the bodies of dead Federals from a still-burning rail fence near the charred ruins of Squire Bottom's barn. As William Woodward of the 79th Pennsylvania lay in the darkness along Starkweather's line, wounded four times and desperate for water, a passing member of the 41st Georgia stopped and exchanged his full canteen for Woodward's dry one before exchanging a bit of small talk and disappearing forever into the shadows.[23]

Farther south at the Russell House, which had been abandoned by Federal doctors and transformed into a Confederate field hospital for Hardee's wing, W. L. Trask and some of his comrades from Austin's battalion attempted to aid suffering Federals as well as Confederates. Trask and his lieutenant covered several men with blankets and supplied them with water as best they could. Most tragically, they found a twelve-year-old boy, severely wounded in the thigh and vomiting from nausea. He was the son of a Confederate cavalryman, the boy said, forced into Federal service. He begged for someone to carry him to the Confederate lines. After comforting the boy and leaving the hospital, the Trask party wandered over to Simonson's now silent guns. More unattended wounded lay there, among them an Ohioan who begged the rebels for water. "He told me he had a wife and two sweet children in 'Ohio,'" Trask wrote, "—that he was wounded through the bowels and knew that he could not live until morning. He complained of cold and we placed two blankets over him." After that, Trask could take no more. He and his comrades "next turned toward our command."[24]

Federals likewise attempted to relieve the suffering of the wounded enemy. Discovering some of Powell's downed men around a campfire, Hoosier George W. Morris and his companions joined them in conversation, for they "seemed very friendly." On a battlefield after a fight, he explained, "human nature becomes milder and soldiers will give an enemy a drink of water, when a few moments before they were seeking each others lives."[25] Several members of the 33rd Ohio, only slightly less hospitable, traded Confederate pickets whiskey for water.[26]

Others proved less charitable toward the foe. Prisoners found themselves particularly vulnerable to abuse that night. Many in both armies had been captured during the day, while patrols took more after dark as they roamed the field. Wharton's horsemen in particular gobbled up prisoners as they skirted the Federal lines. Many men allowed themselves to be taken. Their treatment varied. A slightly wounded member of the 98th Ohio later complained to his sister that after he was captured, the Rebels took his shoes and picked his pockets. In contrast, an Ohioan from Lytle's brigade wrote that the enemy "caught some of our men, who went on the field to rob, and treated them far better than the rascals deserved." Indeed, the soldier added, Confederate doctors routinely dressed the wounds of slightly injured Federals, gave them coffee and whiskey, and freed them to return to their regiments.[27] Likewise, Lt. Col. Oscar Moore of the 33rd Ohio later praised John Savage and his 16th Tennessee for their kind treatment while a wounded prisoner. Several members of that regiment were apparently less charitable toward others, however, as they angrily charged that some prisoners were parole violators from Munfordville.[28]

Although their fate is uncertain, one Federal prisoner who certainly came close to death was Michael Gooding. Soldiers of the 8th Arkansas took the stunned colonel prisoner after their attack on his brigade. As they brought him in to their general, the unidentified colonel of another Arkansas regiment rode up and attempted to kill the Yankee. The angry Confederate believed that Gooding, rather than Squire Keith of the 22nd Indiana, had deceived his men by ordering the Confederates to cease firing. Seizing the officer's sword arm, Liddell angrily chastised him and ordered him back to his regiment. Chagrined, the colonel offered Gooding satisfaction; Gooding wisely declined.[29]

While the abuse of prisoners seems to have been scattered, another form of disrespect became commonplace. As the night turned cold, hungry and poorly clad Confederates began to strip the enemy dead of clothing, shoes, blankets, food, weapons, and anything else they could use. Several Federals later accused Wharton's Texans of such looting, but many other units engaged in robbing the dead. Confederate soldiers routinely exchanged their less effective smoothbore muskets for Enfield and Springfield rifles found on the field, sometimes acting under direct orders to do so. Cheatham and Liddell specifically told their men to collect superior enemy arms. Liddell later claimed that his men brought in at least four thousand, while Cheatham wrote that every ambulatory man in his command left the field with two weapons each. Cheatham also gave orders to his artillerymen to swap inferior guns where possible with some of the thirteen he had captured, and to haul away as many of the others as available teams made possible. Buckner directed the men in his division to fill their cartridge boxes from those of fallen men; others no doubt did the same.[30]

Some men, of course, walked away with more than small arms. Thomas R. Hooper of the 16th Tennessee, although wounded in the jaw and heading for the rear, stopped long enough to strip a fallen Federal of his shoes, cup, and canteen, regretfully leaving behind some peaches he could not chew. Several men from Lumsden's battery ransacked Federal knapsacks for canteens, items that were far superior to those issued to Confederates, and secured blue overcoats to keep out the cold. Some later sold extra coats for profit. Meanwhile, their captain ransacked Federal carriages to reequip a gun dismounted during the fight. Liddell himself shared with his staff some of Alexander McCook's captured rotgut whiskey, which he claimed to abhor, and sent on to Bragg the general's letters, papers, overlarge clothing, and two ambulances.[31]

At other times, robbing the dead became purely symbolic, the victors searching for trophies among the vanquished. Encountering the abandoned body of James Jackson, Confederate Thomas Malone stooped to cut a button from the general's uniform as a souvenir. Malone's companion, ironically an old friend of Jackson, walked up and exclaimed: "'Why, damn it! that's Jim Jackson! . . . Well, Jim, old boy, you ought to have had better luck!'" Malone continued, "It strikes one now as very unfeeling, but at the time it seemed to me all right." A Federal officer later reported that he found Jackson's body the next day, undisturbed except for missing boots, hat, and buttons.[32]

In such an atmosphere, it is not surprising that a few soldiers even robbed their own. Much to the disgust of the men of the 33rd Alabama, for example, Confederates in the rear stole the knapsacks they had left behind while they scoured the area around the crossroads for brothers in arms. Thomas Moore of the 50th Ohio charged the men of the 2nd Minnesota with the same crime. An aura of every man for himself drifted over the field like the shadows of the full moon.[33]

While the last tragic hours of October 8 passed on the battlefield, Braxton Bragg at the Crawford House grew increasingly concerned. It appeared his men had won a great victory, having driven the enemy back at least a mile, yet something was not right. Continued if scattered artillery fire strongly suggested that the enemy stubbornly remained near the field, prepared to fight again at first light. More ominously, dispatches from Wheeler that began coming in around sundown indicated large numbers of Federal troops rumored to be commanded by Thomas Crittenden were on the Lebanon Pike. Aides' nearly unbelievable reports of Carlin's unexpected counterattack against Powell on his left, coupled with descriptions of the loss of Slocomb's ammunition wagons in town, added fearful credence to Wheeler's warnings. Federal prisoners' claims to represent a plethora of units further indicated a sizable force beyond the western horizon. Unwilling to consider the possibility that he had erred so egregiously as to take on all of Buell's army with only part of his—surely the Federal commander would have used all his available force given the chance—Bragg understandably concluded that heavy reinforcements had appeared on his left. Buell indeed must be arriving with the rest of his army, his numbers allowing him to renew the fight with the odds in his favor. Even worse, he could flank the Confederates and reach Bragg's supplies at Camp Dick Robinson in Bryantsville, the dire possibility that had brought Bragg to Perryville in the first place.[34]

In sharp contrast, Bragg had to admit that the battle had terribly diminished his force. By his rough estimate, he had lost 30 percent of his available troops. Kirby Smith, meanwhile, remained miles away with Withers's division, waiting for an enemy that would not be coming his way. Convinced that the enemy now must outnumber him, Bragg rushed out aides with orders for his chief lieutenants to assemble for a hasty council at the Crawford House. Polk and Hardee soon arrived, full of elation at their hard-won success. At about 9 P.M., Bragg laid out the situation for his generals, insofar as he understood it, and markedly dampened their spirits. He told them that they would have to abandon the field. After midnight, using darkness to cover their pullout, the army would fall back to the lines it had occupied that morning. At daybreak, it would retreat toward Harrodsburg and concentrate with Kirby Smith, leaving only a picket line behind to delay pursuit. Faced with Bragg's dire assessment, his chief subordinates agreed. Bragg briskly wrote orders directing his men to bury the dead, prepare the wounded for the move, and hasten the collection of enemy small arms. Bragg further ordered Wheeler to form a rear guard along the Danville Pike while Wharton, accompanied by two of Wheeler's battalions, brought up the rear on the Harrodsburg Pike. Finally, he sent a courier to Kirby Smith with orders to rendezvous with him in Harrodsburg.[35]

Between 1 and 2 A.M., officers began telling the men on the Confederate front lines to get up as quietly as possible and prepare to march. W. L. Trask and his comrades in Austin's battalion assumed they would be making a night attack on the broken Federal left flank, which was said to have been driven back a mile. Likewise, the artillerymen in Stanford's battery arose expecting to renew the battle. Instead, the Confederates marched toward the rear and stacked arms. Most concluded that they would resume the battle at dawn.[36]

Haste inevitably led to upheaval in the moonlit darkness. Notably, in the confusion of the retreat, the acting commanders in Brown's brigade never received the new orders. Not until after two o'clock did they realize that the rest of the army had abandoned the field and left them behind. They hastily awoke their men, still sleeping among the dead of the 10th Ohio, and ordered them to gather up the Federal's abandoned rifles and destroy them. That task accomplished, they finally pulled out around 3 A.M. Unable to grasp that they were surrendering the field to a beaten enemy, Brown's troops decided that they must be giving way to fresher men.[37]

As they prepared to evacuate, Confederates hurried their attempts to provide for their fallen comrades. Scattered groups hastily buried their friends as best they could near where they fell, or else piled them up and surrounded them with fence rails in hopes of protecting the bodies from the rooting wild hogs found everywhere in rural America. Marcus Toney laid the remains of twenty-seven fellow members of the 1st Tennessee in a gully underneath the guns of Stone's battery and thinly covered their bodies using a scoop he fashioned from a dead Federal soldier's breastplate. Others sought to care one last time for the wounded, many of whom had lain on the battlefield all night. Constrained both by haste and a shortage of wagons, the army left behind perhaps nine hundred wounded compatriots hurt too badly to take along. Cheatham ordered two of his doctors to remain with his wounded, but by and large the Confederates had to hope that Federal doctors would care for their friends.[38]

At daylight, the beginning of what Stoddard Johnston remembered as a "clear and bright day," Bragg, Hardee, Polk, Anderson, Buckner, and Cheatham held a last brief conference before the retreat began. With not enough wagons even to carry all their wounded, Cheatham's men broke and threw away most of the Federal guns they had picked up as they formed ranks. As the first troops stepped away at about 7:30, a few enemy guns opened up with scattered fire from the west, killing one of Preston Smith's Texans, but the Federals did nothing more to contest the pullout, much to the surprise of the men in gray and brown. Indeed, all morning, as Bragg's regiments waited their turn to move, no opposition developed to stop them. Adams's brigade, acting as the rear guard, did not leave until after noon. When it did march, it did so uncontested.[39]

Bragg led the way as the vulnerable army retreated toward Harrodsburg. He could not believe that Buell would let him get away so easily. On the contrary, the expectation that Buell still might hit him while his army marched strung out along the Harrodsburg Pike worried him greatly, despite all appearances to the contrary. Liddell remembered that as Bragg rode by him, "he said, 'Be ready, General, to fight at any moment.' Great anxiety seemed to be depicted on his face. His look was so unusual that I feared some unforseen calamity."[40]

Bragg need not have fretted, for there would be no pursuit that day, no attack on his bloodied, strung out, and outnumbered force. He would manage to slip away thanks to Don Carlos Buell's dogged stubbornness, the lingering psychological aftereffects of acoustic shadow, and the muddled command structure of his army.

Phil Sheridan was one of the first outsiders to witness the dangerous dissonance reigning at Buell's headquarters. Not long after the shooting stopped, Gilbert and Sheridan rode to the Dorsey House. There they found the commanding general nonchalantly preparing to eat his supper. A famished Sheridan remembered Buell's generous offer to share, just as he had enjoyed his leisurely dinner with Gilbert several hours earlier. In retrospect, food seemed to have been uppermost in Buell's mind all day; as Sheridan biographer Roy Morris pithily observed, Buell "seemed to be running a restaurant more than a headquarters."[41] Sheridan eagerly accepted the offer and took his place at the table. Conversation regarding the battle inevitably followed, and increasingly it disturbed Sheridan as much as the meal pleased him. Still unwilling to believe that a great battle could have been fought without his hearing it, Buell consistently dismissed his generals' accounts of a full-scale battle and persisted in planning the attack he already had intended for the morning of the ninth. To Sheridan, "the conversation indicated that what had occurred was not fully realized, and I returned to my troops impressed with the belief that general Buell and his staff-officers were unconscious of the magnitude of the battle that had just been fought."[42]

Sheridan was not alone; Lovell Rousseau experienced a similar encounter. Hoping to find McCook, whom he had not seen since before Liddell's assault, Rousseau rode off at last to headquarters. He apparently arrived not long after Sheridan left. Thwarted in his original quest, Rousseau took the opportunity to explain the afternoon's actions to Buell, calling the fight "an exceedingly hard one. . . . the hardest fight I had ever seen." Considering the enemy's élan, he added, they almost certainly would attack again in the morning, mandating reinforcements for McCook.

To Rousseau's surprise, Buell seemed "pretty cool about it," telling him that I Corps needed no reinforcements. Indeed, he dismissed all the general's fears out of hand, saying, "'We will not wait for them to attack, I will attack them at daybreak.'" While that satisfied the aggressive Rousseau somewhat, Buell's overconfidence nonetheless continued to bother him. In regard to the day's fighting, Rousseau marveled that Buell would not accept that the fight was as bad as he claimed, and bluntly told him so. Buell snapped back, telling Rousseau that he understood what had happened perfectly and had responded appropriately by dispatching two brigades from III Corps. Rousseau remained unconvinced, especially after Buell said that "there seemed to be no advance of the other side, or words to that effect. . . . It was very clear to my mind . . . that he did not fully appreciate the fight we had had." Silently blaming an inefficient staff for Buell's haziness, Rousseau departed with orders for McCook to come to headquarters for a council of corps commanders.[43]

Back on I Corps's confused front, McCook had been searching for Rousseau. Like many of his officers, he initially expected Bragg to renew the assault that night, owing to the light provided by the full moon. Only slowly did he accept that his corps would enjoy at least a temporary respite, allowing him time to prepare his lines for a renewed struggle. Worried all evening about the closeness of the Confederates' lines, in some places no more than forty yards away, McCook between nine and ten o'clock determined to do something about it. He would pull back and create a new line on high ground south of the Mackville Road, anchored by the pike on the left and Steedman's troops on the right. Such a move was admittedly risky, for he imagined that the Rebels would be on him in a heartbeat if they sensed he was pulling out. What he needed, McCook concluded, were more fresh troops from Gilbert's command to provide cover. When Rousseau rode up with Buell's orders for him to come to the Dorsey House, he immediately advised the division commander of his plans. As he did, a new communication from Buell arrived, disturbing McCook greatly. Buell informed McCook "that if I had to retreat to retreat by the Dicksville and Springfield road, which led to his headquarters therefore the Mackville road was of no importance to me."[44]

Buell obviously had misunderstood Rousseau, adding to the fog of war encircling the Dorsey yard. McCook now also realized that Buell underestimated the tenor of fighting that afternoon and evening. Buell incredibly continued to assert, as he had since late afternoon, that I Corps had given up little if any ground. If so, how to explain the excited reports coming in from the front? Buell must have concluded that I Corps's generals had overreacted to the Confederate attack and panicked. Robert Mitchell's later testimony before the Buell Commission adds credence to this supposition. Mitchell had ridden to headquarters hoping that Buell would override Gilbert and allow him to advance. As he walked up, Buell told him he "had the only face that looked like victory since the commencement of the fight." By implication, Rousseau and even Sheridan earlier must have looked like defeat. Hence Buell's new orders. Although he wanted I Corps to sit tight, as beaten as its generals must be, they might very well fall back still more. If so, then they should fall back toward the rest of the army, reducing the gap that existed between McCook's and Gilbert's corps.[45]

McCook and Rousseau, of course, saw it differently. After reading the retreat order, McCook told Rousseau that Buell's plan invited just the sort of danger he hoped to avoid by opening his flank to the enemy. Confused and concerned, McCook told Rousseau to begin the movement he already had planned, and then rode off to headquarters to meet with Buell. He arrived at Buell's tent around midnight. Thomas was already there, again acting as de facto commander of II Corps. The council marked Buell's first face-to-face meeting with Thomas since before the battle, and one gathers that it was not a pleasant encounter. As McCook approached the gathering, Buell and Thomas were discussing whether to launch an attack in the morning. McCook did not say more about the conversation, but subsequent events suggest that Buell favored an attack more vehemently than Thomas. McCook, however, did not pause to listen, but rather immediately launched into a detailed description of his corps' fight, jabbing at a map to illustrate his narrative of events. The enemy nearly had him surrounded, he concluded. If the Rebels attacked in the morning, I Corps would be destroyed. McCook begged for the use of two brigades for two hours to cover his move to a better line. Buell, more concerned with the gap between I Corps and headquarters, curtly refused. McCook then asked for one brigade; Buell again declined, and told the general he "should not have another man. I was at that time very much vexed and provoked," McCook added.[46]

Buell dismissed McCook's concerns because he already had made up his mind. Indeed, with a few necessary modifications, Buell would doggedly stick to the plan he had crafted for the previous day. Again he asserted that Bragg would not attack him; as he told McCook, "he did not think he could be attacked."[47] To insure that conclusion, he needed Gilbert's men for something far different. Assuming that Bragg must have concentrated with Kirby Smith to offer battle in the first place, Buell explained to McCook that he fully expected Bragg to stand and fight the next day, but that this time he would not give him the time to launch offensive operations. Buell then gave careful orders for a counterattack in the morning. McCook was to shift south until he made contact with Gilbert's main line, feed his men, and wait in reserve. At 4 A.M., Crittenden's fresh corps would begin moving forward in column toward Perryville. As II Corps's ranks came up abreast of his lines, Gilbert would join the movement. Together, the two corps would hit the Confederates in their apparently weak left flank at daylight. As a result, McCook presumably would be relieved of Confederate pressure before the enemy had a chance to renew the contest on his front. He would then advance on Gilbert's left.[48]

Thomas sent Buell's orders to Crittenden via the Signal Corps. Instead of following them up personally, he remained with Buell until four o'clock. When he finally arrived back at II Corps's headquarters at about 6:30 A.M., confusion reigned. First of all, two brigades, Harker's and Wagner's, remained separated from the rest of the corps, still in their advanced position southwest of town supporting Carlin's forward lines. Thomas summarily ordered Wood to recall the two brigades and move into a reserve position behind Smith and Van Cleve in the rear of II Corps.[49]

Thomas, although he could not know it, had made a crucial error, for his orders threw away the last realistic chance to hit the enemy hard in Perryville. Indeed, in many ways it was a reprise of Gilbert's reigning in of Mitchell the evening before. The brigades in question already were in the best position to force Bragg to hold up and fight. Wary and anxious, Wood after midnight had ordered his two forward brigades to be ready to move at daylight. He then retired to the rear and somehow lost contact with them. As sunrise brightened the eastern sky, increasingly concerned about the sound of wheeled vehicles in the night that suggested a Confederate retreat, a troubled George Wagner rode forward personally to see what the Rebels were doing. From a hilltop he was able to observe enemy troops moving through town. He paused apprehensively, waiting to determine whether the enemy was shifting right for a flank attack or retiring. Finally concluding the latter, he raced back to his lines and ordered Cox's 10th Indiana Battery to open up on the vanishing rebel column, an action his men mistook for simply shelling the forward woods, but one that worried the retreating Confederates. Simultaneously, he ordered his brigade forward. To his right, an alerted Carlin advanced his brigade in unison. On the left, young Charles Harker, greatly concerned about the gunfire yet less eager for a fight, more guardedly moved his troops forward to the hilltops before halting in Wagner's rear. Carlin and Wagner continued to advance cautiously without him, their skirmishers entering the western edge of town a little after sunup. Observing the tail of the Confederate column as it passed through Perryville, Wagner again ordered Cox to unlimber and open fire on it. As the last infantry disappeared, elements of Wheeler's cavalry emerged from a line of woods and menacingly formed into line.[50]

Already well ahead of where he knew he was supposed to be, Wagner hesitated to attack until he received the orders he expected from Wood. The cavalry, whose allegiance remained undetermined, gave him pause him as well. The more circumspect Harker behaved likewise, and dispatched an aide back to Wood requesting direction. The aide returned a half-hour later and reported that Wood could not be found. The Federal brigades froze in place. Another hour passed before one of Wood's aides arrived with Thomas's orders to fall back a full two miles to Crittenden's main lines. Because of the breakdown in division communications, Wood still knew nothing of the situation in town, and simply sought to carry out Thomas's instructions. Incredulous, Harker argued that the enemy was escaping, but in the face of the aide's intransigence, he gave in and fell back as ordered into a cornfield, where his men stacked arms while he waited for orders. Wagner proved more resistant, refusing to obey orders that seemed to require him to fall back only to advance over the same ground. He told the aide that he had better inform Wood that he occupied Perryville and the enemy was retreating. The aide at length gave up and returned to his general as Wagner fell back half a mile and stopped. He and his men watched with frustration as Confederate infantry and a baggage train disappeared to the east. The Rebels were getting away scot-free.[51]

Wood did not receive Wagner's verbal message until later in the morning. Not convinced even then, he rode forward to see for himself before accepting the truth. He then galloped back to find his superiors. Encountering Crittenden and Thomas, he informed them that the enemy was indeed gone. By that point, however, it mattered little. Other troops had entered town, but by then Thomas's grand advance already had failed to accomplish its mission. The last critical moment had passed thanks to the breakdown of communication in Wood's division.[52]

All that remained in the near future. More immediately contributing to Thomas's consternation when he arrived at Crittenden's headquarters was the fact that Crittenden was only then getting the balance of his corps ready to move out after breakfast. Thomas later would blame Crittenden for misconstruing his orders, while the upstaged corps commander would fault Buell's much maligned Signal Corps, claiming that the signalmen garbled Thomas's directions and told him only that he should be ready to move at six. Once again, Buell's chain of command had broken down along the II Corps link. Whoever should shoulder the blame, the end result was that II Corps characteristically was already more than two hours behind schedule. Thomas immediately ordered Crittenden to get moving. Screened by the "Wild Riders" of the 1st Kentucky Cavalry, Smith's lead division tardily began snaking up the Lebanon Pike, marching as slowly as it had the previous morning.

Contrary to Buell's orders, the apprehensive Smith marched his men in line of battle rather than in column, screened by a cloud of skirmishers. Van Cleve's division followed in a similar alignment. While a safer formation if attacked, their decision to ignore Buell's wishes upset his timetable even more. Moving cross-country in line rather than down the pike in column, regiments encountered fences, hills, hollows, and tangles of forests, all serving to retard their pace and exhaust the men.[53] "Marching in line of battle is usually very slow," L. A. Simmons of the 84th Illinois complained, "and always terrible tiresome, and when . . . the impression is fixed in the minds of all, that an important advantage had been lost, that the commanding officer has been outgeneralled, the useless effort and exertion becomes doubly onerous and disagreeable."[54]

The topography, coupled with the widespread trepidation abroad in the corps, hindered the advance, but so did the Confederate rear guard. Joe Wheeler's cavalrymen did as much as they could to enhance II Corps's hesitation. Deftly employing his horse soldiers as skirmishers and making good use of the woods, Wheeler managed to stop Smith's lead division in its tracks several times until falling back under fire for good at about 9 A.M. Wheeler's men thus prevented the enemy from gaining immediate access to desperately needed water found in springs along their path. Smith's division did not enter the deserted town until around ten o'clock. In adding to Smith's distress, Wheeler earned the praise usually accorded him for his activities during the battle.[55]

The other corps, largely unopposed, accomplished no more. Gilbert's officers awakened their men at three o'clock and formed them into line. At first light, on orders from Mitchell, Hotchkiss's battery shelled a body of Wheeler's cavalrymen moving toward the Lebanon Pike, eliciting only a brief response. With Carlin still farther up front and Gooding's brigade back along I Corps's lines, Mitchell ordered William Caldwell's brigade to advance parallel to Smith's in support of the battery. Before long, however, the brigade halted and stacked arms.[56]

Gilbert at least made the effort. McCook, in the meantime, had done nothing to conform to Buell's wishes. Indeed, after leaving headquarters, he did not return to his men with the new orders, but instead stopped along the Springfield Pike, dismounted, and went to sleep. When Maj. J. M. Wright of Buell's staff found him there on the cold ground sometime after 8 A.M., the groggy McCook proved unresponsive. Continuing on to the crossroads area, Wright found I Corps still in the positions ordered by McCook before he left for Buell's headquarters, drawn up along a skirt of timber in lines running almost parallel to the Mackville Road. Wright later testified that McCook's men were as lethargic as their commander. No one had advanced, he complained, despite the absence of the enemy, and no one had eaten. In fact, only a Captain Wickliffe seemed to have any interest in advancing, drawing Wright's attention to three or four of Parsons's captured guns that the

Rebels had abandoned several hundred yards ahead. Wright awakened Rousseau, who replied that if the aide wanted the guns, McCook would have to make the decision. Frustrated, Wright rode down McCook, but the general remained as somnolent as before. While he floundered indecisively, Wickliffe and Parsons took a small body of men and retrieved the guns. They were exceptions. Like their exhausted, battered, and shaken corps commander, McCook's fatigued men had reached their limit. They could do no more than they had already.[57] "The boys were all fierce for a fight before they got it," wrote John Holbrook Morse of the 105th Ohio, "but now they say that they never want to see another and I am sure that I do not."[58]

Meanwhile, Buell had begun to sense that his grand counterattack was floundering, although he did not as yet know why. Attempting to monitor the situation from headquarters, again relying upon the questionable skills of his signalmen, the still bruised general grew increasingly frustrated with II Corps's dawdling as the morning progressed. He also began to worry, for according to Mitchell a Confederate prisoner had claimed that the army was shifting north to Dixville to continue the fight. Twice he sent messages to Thomas asking if the advance had begun, but received no reply. Thomas, as usual, remained closed mouthed. Only late in the morning did Buell receive positive information from the right, and it was not good news. Two Confederate regiments, one cavalry and one infantry, had crossed the Danville Pike and were moving south. The sender of the unsigned note, almost certainly Thomas, added that he had ordered Edward McCook to ride out and investigate.[59]

The news, the first intimation of a Confederate retreat, alarmed Buell. Which way were they going, toward Danville, Dixville, or Harrodsburg? He responded quickly, ordering two II Corps divisions to Crawford Springs up the Harrodsburg Pike, where they would be in position to move toward Dixville or Harrodsburg as well as to assist McCook in case of another unexpected attack on the left. He sent an additional division from Gilbert's corps south of town to Walker's Springs. Then, just after noon, another communication arrived from Thomas, this one sent at twelve o'clock. A civilian's report indicated that the enemy definitely was not on the Danville Pike. Rather, he suspected that the Rebels were moving toward Harrodsburg. Thomas again had sent Edward McCook's cavalry to investigate. In the meantime, all of II Corps continued its advance on Walker's Springs. It met no resistance. At two, Thomas sent another message, again asserting that the enemy was in retreat toward Harrodsburg. Only cavalry operated on the Danville Pike. He added that, in his opinion, Bragg was probably making for Camp Dick Robinson.[60]

As the rest of the morning and early afternoon passed, Buell's army gradually occupied the ground the Confederates had held the previous day. After halting for a leisurely dinner, the balance of II Corps followed Smith's division through Perryville through the afternoon, sometimes to the triumphant strains of band music, before encamping along the Harrodsburg Pike north and south of town. To the left, Gilbert's corps got moving again around 11 A.M. Angling northward toward Squire Bottom's house and the Mackville Road, the van continued moving cross-country to the vicinity of the Goodknight House and Walker's Bend before crossing the river. Gilbert's men bivouacked along the road there, happy to have abundant water at last. Worn out and occupied with their dead, McCook's I Corps did not begin moving forward until late in the afternoon, to the left of Crittenden and behind Gilbert, and then did not get very far. Once past Squire Bottom's house, the men bivouacked in the fields between Doctor's Creek and the Chaplin River.[61]

Wherever Buell's men marched that day, daylight and an absent foe allowed stunned observers to wander the bloody field in awe. Only then did Buell's men feel the full weight of the battle. The wreckage stunned even veterans, but especially affected rookies like Marcus Woodcock of the 9th Kentucky, who had missed the bulk of the fighting in Crittenden's corps. Woodcock wrote that he nearly vomited as he gazed upon the dead left behind where a Confederate battery had fought. The sheer number of dead men overwhelmed many others, he added. The fallen "could be found lying almost in columns, sometimes U.S. and C.S. being piled promiscuously together . . . the dead of both armies could be found almost anywhere either were laying."[62]

The condition of the killed added to the horror. An Indiana captain described men "mangled in every imaginable manner." Some had been decapitated; others lay without limbs or faces. One Confederate lay "too helpless to move, and near him lay one of his dead comrades, with the top of his head torn off, and hogs eating his body—the wounded man unable to drive them away."[63] Ole Johnson of the 15th Wisconsin wrote of "seven rebels killed by a single shell."[64] "I volunteered . . . to go on the field and help gather up the wounded," John Sipe of the 38th Indiana wrote his wife, "and of all the horrible suffering, I hop I may never witness the like again. Union and rebel lying side by side with their limbs blown off or shattered to pieces. One Rebel with boath his arms blown off told me if he were in his grave he would not suffer so."[65]

Some Federals maintained until their dying day that more than uniforms distinguished their comrades from the enemy. Many claimed that a prebattle diet of whiskey and gunpowder, allegedly intended to inflame the enemy for the coming fight, caused the Confederate dead to bloat and discolor more quickly. Although dismissed by men such as the 2nd Michigan Cavalry's Lt. John Robinson, commander of a burial detail on October 9, the legend of green or blackened Confederates survived and in time became one of the more enduring memories of the battle. The whiskey-and-gunpowder myth neatly explained the sheer ferociousness of the Confederate attack, and in so doing somewhat excused McCook's Federals for their performance.[66]

Another discussed difference in the dead was their state of dress. Many

Federals lay only partially clad, their bodies stripped of shoes, uniforms, and personal effects by the enemy. The sight of so many robbed corpses angered their living comrades. "By the side of every one of our dead men," Ohioan George Landrum wrote to his sister, "you would see an old pair of shoes and a greasy, filthy pile of clothes. . . . I never hated them till now. I have now a thirst for vengeance."[67]

Not surprisingly, a few unlucky Confederate prisoners paid the price for their comrades' actions. Ole Johnson of the 15th Wisconsin, among others, described a Confederate prisoner discovered with two old paroles still in his pocket. With the approval of McCook and Rousseau, riflemen immediately executed the Confederate. William Clark of the 79th Pennsylvania may have been discussing the same incident when he wrote of a "spy" captured and shot behind Federal lines, the body then thrown among other Confederate dead.[68]

Such scapegoating seems to have been rare. More often, the soldiers expressed their anger when dispatched from every regiment to bury the dead. Generally, burial details concentrated first on their own regiment's casualties, and then fellow Federals. Aside from some officers whose remains were prepared for shipment home, as well as those who received more personal attention from relatives and friends, most went into long, shallow trenches dug into the rocky limestone soil near Peters Hill. Many details left crude wooden grave markers, sometimes made of emptied cracker boxes, while others drew maps to aid with future identification and relocation. A short prayer and rifle volley completed what little ceremony there was.[69] The sheer volume of dead men, however, coupled with a relative lack of tools and hard, rocky soil baked by drought, stymied any efforts to bury them all immediately. As night fell, many Federal dead remained on the moon-soaked field, still so numerous in some places, according to a soldier from Wisconsin, "that one could walk on them for rods and not touch the ground."[70]

If all the slain Federals could not be committed to their graves immediately, Confederates certainly would not. While details from at least Greusel's and Dan McCook's brigades apparently buried friend and foe alike, Federals more often than not left the enemy dead where they fell, to rot or else be consumed by crows and the ravenous wild hogs that swarmed over the field. Indeed, along his front, Rousseau ordered that no Rebels would be buried in retaliation for the stripping of his dead. Some Federals exacted an added measure of revenge on the dead by searching and stripping them of valuables, just as the hated Confederates had done the night before. A major from the 9th Pennsylvania Cavalry complained to his men that he was getting his fingers bloody as he removed a gold watch and chain from the body of a Confederate officer. Eugene Comstock of the 24th Wisconsin rifled a Confederate's knapsack for a new blanket. Like their Confederate counterparts, Union officers also ordered their men to collect anything that might be of use to the army. Julius Birney Work of the 52nd Ohio served on a detail

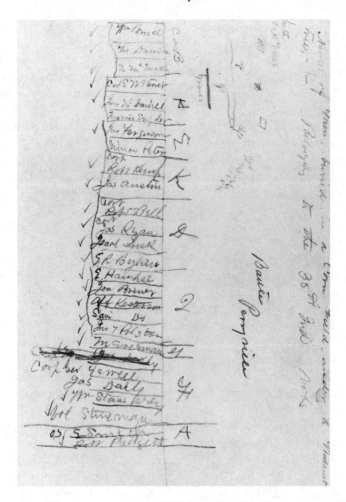

Figure 14.1. Hand drawn map of the 38th Indiana's battlefield cemetery. Photograph courtesy Indiana State Archives.

that gathered enemy weapons. One large stand of muskets, he wrote, remained unused, their barrels stuffed with paper on which someone had written "Home or Hell."[71]

Still, compassion sometimes outweighed the desire for revenge. Many Federals sought to aid all the suffering wounded still on the field, Confederate as well as Union, although such kindness emanated generally from troops who had seen less action. While their major robbed a dead Confederate of his watch, for example, other members of the 9th Pennsylvania Cavalry retrieved a wounded man from beneath a pile of fence rails and revived him with whiskey.[72] George Morris of the 81st Indiana and his "pards" shuttled water from Doctor's Creek to wounded Tennesseans from Bushrod Johnson's command. "Some of them deserved no compassion," Morris claimed, "for they spoke impudently and disdainfully. Nevertheless, on account of their wounds, no notice was taken of it."[73]

Even Rousseau's anger had its limits. One Federal aide described riding along the front with Alexander McCook, Rousseau, and Cyrus Loomis. Near Wood's last position they discovered a wounded woman dressed in a Confederate uniform. Shocked by the sight, the generals sent for a stretcher and had her taken to the recaptured Russell House hospital. Her husband, who had been captured during the battle, later explained that his wife had run away from her disapproving parents to be with him.[74]

Dealing with the wounded invariably involved a trip to one of Perryville's ubiquitous hospitals. In addition to barns and farmhouses near the scene of the fighting, nearly every home, business, and church in or near Perryville proper had been converted into a hospital. Sights seen there often seemed more sickening to observers than those on the field. Outside many, severed limbs piled up like cordwood. A captain in the 81st Indiana described one hospital as "harrowing. The surgeons were provided with boards on which their patients were lain, and where legs and arms were sawn off with the same *sang froid* which a butcher would manifest in dissecting a beef."[75] At the Bottom House, George Morris described a "yard full of wounded men, lying in rows, covered up with blankets, shrieking with pain, and some lying their dead. . . . At a short distance to the left was another house used for the same purpose, the yard of which was filled with dead laid in rows. Close to the fence was a pile of arms and legs. It was a ghastly sight to look upon."[76] Viewing the same scene, L. W. Day of the 101st Ohio noted that the "surgeons of both armies were very busy. . . . Doubtless they were kind-hearted and careful, but to us it seemed like brutality. There were several piles of amputated limbs, to which accessions were being made constantly."[77]

Late in the afternoon, Harker's brigade moved through town to the vicinity of the Crawford House. Nearby the men discovered Cheatham's Goodknight House hospital. The sight of it amazed Wilbur Hinman of the 6th Ohio Battery: "Lying on the ground, with no shelter from the fierce heat of the sun by day or the dews by night, were some three hundred rebel wounded. They had as yet received no care from the surgeons. Many of them were in the most horrible condition that the mind can conceive." Shocked, the Ohio gunners brought the wounded enemy water and gave them the food they carried in their haversacks. "There was nothing else we could do."[78]

The wounded themselves remembered the hospitals no more fondly. David J. Ryan of the 21st Wisconsin went down in the cornfield fighting with a gunshot wound in the hip. Carried to a hospital behind Starkweather's lines, probably the Wilkerson House, Ryan lay outside all night because the building was full. The next day, ambulances relocated Ryan and others to a hospital established at Antioch Church, two miles farther back. Discovering that it too was full, a comrade organized a field hospital for the regiment "in a shady place" nearby. Ryan and the other wounded Badgers remained there in the open air for five more nights, their only caretakers fellow soldiers and "an old man."[79]

Adam Johnston of the 79th Pennsylvania had made a similar journey to the Antioch Church hospital the night before. "Thrown out like a pile of wood," Johnston rolled downhill toward a fence and passed out. When he awoke, he was still outside. Worse still, a dying soldier had pinned him to the fence. A local man removed the other soldier at Johnston's pleading and covered him with a blanket. He too lay there for another five days, and recorded bitterly that doctors dressed his wound only once during that time.[80] Faced with such conditions, the wounded soon exhibited both shock and despair. Wrote Samuel Potts of the 105th Ohio: "In the hospital at the Church . . . there 200 wounded men and you might go all around the Church and in it, and you would not hear a groan escape from those brave men's lips."[81]

As evening fell and campfires flared up, the Federal survivors of Perryville feasted on chicken, turkey, and pork, washing down the meat with the seized water. Discussion around the fires turned to other topics. Many wondered what the battle would be called. Some began campaigning for promotion, hoping to fill the slots of slain or wounded comrades. Wisconsin men embarrassed by the 21st Wisconsin's performance attempted to distance themselves from their unfortunate comrades.[82] The main topic, however, was who to blame for the mismanaged battle, for those horrible sights that, according to Marcus Woodcock, caused "the very blood" of his comrades "to boil with indignation."[83] While a minority censured Alexander McCook for bringing on battle too hastily, most condemned Buell, especially for his inability to bring all of his troops into action and his lack of immediate pursuit. Why were they sitting there while the Rebels escaped? Some went so far as to accuse their commander of treason, maintaining that he deliberately kept most of his army out of the battle and then allowed Bragg to escape after consulting with the Confederate.[84] "All the old charges of incompetency, traitor, and communicating with the enemy, were revived and sounded over the land," wrote a member of the 86th Indiana.[85] Likewise, Levi Adolphus Ross of the 86th Illinois recorded that "Gen. Buell, lay on his back in his tent, reading, cooly indifferent to how the battle was going. . . . he is branded as a traitor by nearly every soldier in the Union Army." Such behavior had to be expected, Ross added, from Bragg's brother-in-law.[86]

15

TRAMP, TRAMP, TRAMP

SLOWLY AND SULLENLY, THE ARMY OF THE MISSISSIPPI RETRACED ITS steps down the Harrodsburg Pike. It moved in three columns, wagons and artillery occupying the road while the infantry hugged the edges in two parallel columns. Wharton's cavalry continued to serve as the rear guard. The morale of many soldiers remained surprisingly good, especially when assured by their officers that they were only falling back to link up with Kirby Smith and "make Buell's annihilation complete." Some expected a fight even before reaching Harrodsburg. The more pessimistic, however, expressed anguish at surrendering the battlefield or passing up an opportunity to finish off the Yankees then and there. A few actually wept with despair.[1]

By the time Bragg's van arrived in Harrodsburg, roughly at noon, the town already was in a state of uproar. Twenty-four hours earlier, Harrodsburg's residents began transforming their town into a vast Confederate hospital complex, one that would be the last stop for many of Perryville's wounded. They readied public buildings, notably churches and the Harrodsburg Springs resort, to serve as hospitals. Others marshaled carriages to function as ambulances. The women of the town hastily made bandages and prepared lint. The first wounded started coming in around sunset, and by 10 P.M., according to one resident, "the legs and arms, that had been amputated, rose like a pyramid to the floor of the second story gallery of the Spring's ball room."[2] Scattered groups of deserters passed through town that night; others made their way toward Danville, further agitating residents of both towns. "They are much scattered and faded," a local civilian reported to the Federals, "and a great many stragglers [are] on the road and in the woods."[3]

Tired, dusty, and hungry, the remainder of the army followed. For a few, Harrodsburg brought a smile. Bushrod Johnson enjoyed a brief reunion with a sister-in-law there. Others seized upon the amenities the town willingly or unwillingly offered. William E. Bevens of the 1st Arkansas and a friend purchased jeans cloth in Harrodsburg intending to make trousers. Others apparently acquired new garb without payment. Bragg's "horses drank our town branch absolutely dry," Unionist Maria Daviess complained, "and few sympathizers had more clothes when they left than they stood in. The commissary department was certainly the most efficient wing of Bragg's army."[4] One Federal later observed: "the Rebs have robbed every store on the whole route."[5]

While the army trudged in brigade by brigade, Bragg continued to wrestle with indecisiveness. He remained alert to the danger Buell posed, particularly in regard to his base at Camp Dick Robinson. The question was, how best to defend it? That morning he had advised his lieutenants and Kirby Smith that he intended to concentrate the two Confederate armies and offer battle at Harrodsburg, but once in town he developed second thoughts. According to Stoddard Johnston, Bragg that afternoon decided instead that the army would move on to Danville the next morning. From there he could screen his vital supply depot at Bryantsville just as well as from Harrodsburg. Moreover, possession of Danville, located farther south on the army's line of escape to the Cumberland Gap, lessened the possibility of being caught in a trap.[6]

Within a few hours, however, Bragg changed his mind again. Frequent skirmishes during the day between Federal cavalry and Wheeler's horsemen on the Danville Pike indicated a possible threat to the town, the road to Tennessee, and finally his depot. Camp Dick Robinson needed immediate security, and the army required a better defensive position if Buell was flanking him with dispatch. He accordingly directed Polk to get the army moving again, pass through Harrodsburg, and continue on several more miles in the direction of Bryantsville and the high rocky bluffs above Dick's River. They would cross the river in the morning and reach the vital depot well before Buell's horsemen could seize it. Bragg, in the meantime, would wait in Harrodsburg for Kirby Smith, while Wheeler continued to delay the Federal force approaching Danville from the west.[7]

Exhausted and confused, the army took up the march again—some in the rear of the column had never stopped marching—and trudged on until it reached the river around midnight. After sleeping restlessly for a few hours, disturbed by the clamor of Wharton's and Wheeler's artillery to the south and west, the tired Confederates set out again at first light. Advanced units crossed the river and covered the short two to three additional miles to Bryantsville by midmorning. The day was miserable, colder temperatures and driving rain heralding both the coming of winter and the end of the Kentucky drought. Despite the storm, Bryantsville and the much-discussed stores at Camp Dick Robinson drew hungry soldiers like ants to a picnic. Morale rose accordingly as the men stopped, spread tent flies in the mud, stuffed their empty bellies, and wrote letters home.[8] Boosting morale even more was the simple fact that the men expected another battle, one in which they and not the Yankees would hold the topographical advantage. Camp Dick Robinson, as Confederate John Inglis wrote, was "a natural Sebastopool."

The imposing natural palisades formed by the Kentucky River cliffs protected the position from the north, while somewhat smaller cliffs along the
Dick's River guarded the western approach. Together, the two rivers created
an angle of water and stone that opened only to the southeastern rear. Within
that angle, fed with the mountains of supplies that had been accumulated, the
army could make a stand that easily rivaled the Yankees' in the Chaplin Hills.[9]

While Bragg's army lurched away from Harrodsburg, Kirby Smith arrived
there with his. Much to his chagrin, answering Bragg's call for a concentration had not gone anything like the ambitious young general desired. On
October 8, as Bragg's and Buell's armies battled at Perryville, Kirby Smith
and the bulk of his small army remained southwest of Lexington, aligned in
an arc from Versailles, through Salvisa, toward Lawrenceburg on the Salt
River. During the day, he learned that Sill's Federal column had abandoned
Frankfort to Dumont just after midnight, pushed Scott's Confederate cavalry aside, and was moving south toward Jones Withers's orphaned division
at Lawrenceburg. Sill clearly intended to cross the river and rendezvous with
Federal forces to the south. For the first time, Kirby Smith grasped that not
he but Bragg had faced the bulk of Buell's army. Hoping to hit Sill in his
flank while Withers's division occupied the Federal front and defended his
river crossings, Kirby Smith resolved to march quickly and secure another
victory for himself on the morning of the ninth. As he dispatched orders to
Withers and otherwise readied his men to march, he also sent word to
Humphrey Marshall, halted east of Lexington with his small force, to move
on the city and screen his rear.[10]

As it turned out, Sill's head start enabled him to move too fast for his
pursuers. Kirby Smith arrived in Lawrenceburg at 3:30 the following morning only to find Sill long gone. His column already had made a forced march
through town around midnight, and by the time Kirby Smith appeared the
enemy was ten miles farther down the Bardstown Pike. Rather than confronting the Federals as ordered, a hesitant Withers had let the enemy slip
by, finally hitting them only in the rear at daybreak, in the vicinity of Dry
Ridge. The four-hour rear-guard action that followed resulted in the capture of a small supply train and some prisoners, but failed miserably in its
larger purpose to impede Sill's march. Without the rations required to continue an independent pursuit into Buell's rear, Kirby Smith directed his cavalry to pursue and harass Sill's train while he led the rest of the army to
Harrodsburg. He hoped that he, along with his lead division, would reach
there by morning, but he warned Bragg via courier that his men were much
fatigued.[11]

For once true to his word, Kirby Smith arrived in Harrodsburg on the
morning of the tenth, only to find that aside from Bragg, his staff, and seventeen hundred hospitalized Confederates, the rest of the army had moved on
to the east. Bragg, in the eyes of one Army of Kentucky observer, seemed in

unusually high spirits as they entered town. According to his own later account, Kirby Smith, having learned of Polk's march to Bryantsville, begged Bragg to call back his army, unite the two forces, and fight the grand battle for Kentucky then and there. Bragg supposedly agreed enthusiastically, telling Kirby Smith to choose the ground while he called back his army from Bryantsville.

As usual, however, the younger man's ego got in the way of the whole truth. Hoping to cleanse his reputation in Kentucky after the war, Kirby Smith neglected to mention that while he conferred with Bragg, couriers arrived from Wharton with news of a sizable Federal advance on the Harrodsburg Pike. Bragg had no choice but to order Kirby Smith to form into line of battle two miles west of town on the rolling west bank of the Salt River, to act as a delaying force while he attempted to hurry his army back from Bryantsville. As it was, only Preston Smith's brigade, at the rear of Polk's column and still west of the Dick's River four miles from Bryantsville, made the countermarch to Harrodsburg. As the afternoon and evening passed, no Federal attack materialized to warrant more, leaving Kirby Smith with nothing more to do than follow Polk's lead and seek solace from Chaplain Quintard in Harrodsburg's Episcopal Church. Later in the evening, additional messengers rode up with dispatches from Wheeler warning that a large Federal force was also moving up the Danville Pike. In the early morning hours of October 11, faced with the threat of being caught within a Federal pincer, Bragg wisely decided to abandon Harrodsburg. He would escape Buell's developing trap and fall back to Camp Dick Robinson, his Kentucky "Sebastapool," at first light.[12]

The Federal forces pushing toward Harrodsburg and Danville, confounding Bragg more than once, initially belonged only to Edward McCook's cavalry on the Danville Pike and Gay's horsemen on the Harrodsburg Pike. Despite the wishes of his men, Buell had kept his army largely stationary in Perryville all day on the ninth, refusing to mount any pursuit beyond cavalry once he learned with certainty that Bragg was gone. Only on the following gray morning did Buell half-heartedly pick up the chase. Now, as convinced as Thomas that Bragg was falling back through Harrodsburg on Camp Dick Robinson, he ordered Thomas to take II Corps minus Harker's absent brigade down the Danville Pike as far as the Salt River, while the 1st Ohio Cavalry scouted the road connecting Harrodsburg and Danville. Crittenden remained out of the loop as Thomas maintained de facto corps command. With any luck, Thomas would flank the enemy from the south and cut off his escape to Tennessee. Meanwhile, Harker's separated brigade pushed a few miles on up the Harrodsburg Pike from its encampment to support Gay. Behind Harker's II Corps orphans, Gilbert later in the day began advancing the fresher elements of his corps, moving cautiously, as Buell had ordered, so as to not bring on an engagement. Buell remained in Perryville with his most bloodied units, those of I Corps as well as Sheridan's division and the balance of II Corps, and waited for Sill's imminent arrival. If at all possible, he wanted to avoid a fight until Sill's troops augmented his numbers.[13]

Shaking himself from his curious two-day lethargy, Thomas had II Corps up at daybreak and moving quickly despite the worsening weather. As the men passed through town, they noticed that nearly every building showed the effects of being riddled with shot and shell. Despite the stop-and-go of a jammed and rocky road, sporadic cavalry skirmishing, and a short halt to deploy artillery, Thomas by early afternoon had arrived on the banks of the Salt River, three miles from town, and had arrayed his three divisions into a line extending from the road to the river. Seeking shelter from the worsening rainstorm that also tormented Bragg's Confederates, his tentless men that night crawled under hemp stacks, threw blankets over upright guns bayoneted into the ground, or constructed shelters of straw and fence rails to ride out the night.[14]

Moving northeast from Perryville, Harker's isolated brigade also marched early in the day, stirring up enough dust to frighten Wharton, force Kirby Smith into line of battle, and momentarily upset Bragg's pullout. Unfortunately, in contrast to the alacrity of Harker and Thomas, Gilbert got a late start. Schoepf's division led the way but at a snail's pace, leaving a gap of several miles between their ranks and Harker's. Indeed, well after dark much of the corps remained queued up in Perryville. Caldwell's brigade, the least bloodied in Mitchell's division, did not take to the road until 10 P.M. By then, however, the weather had grown miserable. George Morris of the 81st Indiana remembered that as they marched out of town the low clouds and rain combined with the pungent odor of the still unburied Confederate dead to produce a horrible stench. An hour after midnight, Gilbert's column halted for the night, with Schoepf miles from Harrodsburg and Mitchell's rear division still stuck in the mud near Perryville.[15]

The next morning brought no letup in the weather. Still supported by Harker to their rear, Gay's horsemen shoved Wharton's rear guard back through town and around noon rode in to find the soggy town all but deserted of ambulatory Confederates. Kirby Smith, under orders from Bragg, had begun his retrograde march to Camp Dick Robinson only hours before. At 2:30 P.M. Gay reported that the Rebels had crossed the Salt River, leaving the bridges burning behind them, and had left Harrodsburg to him. The river, he hastened to add, was fordable just a bit upstream, rendering the damage caused by the loss of the bridges relatively slight. A few hours behind Gay, Harker's brigade, deployed in line of battle, followed the cavalry up to the edge of town. Isolated and unsure of the enemy's intentions, deeply concerned as well over prisoners' reports that Bragg's army still lurked in the vicinity, Harker determined to employ a stratagem. After sundown, he had his men set huge campfires, hoping to deceive the enemy as to his numbers, and then advanced them another mile into town. In occupying Harrodsburg, they seized the major Confederate hospital as well as a few dozen stray cavalrymen before falling asleep in the cold, dark streets.[16]

Harker and his soldiers held the town tenuously that night, for Gilbert had continued to advance hesitantly, with Mitchell's division finally following the rest of the slow-moving III Corps up the Harrodsburg Pike that morning. Buell, meanwhile, had selected a token force from Webster's division to hold Perryville, and at last ordered the balance of his remaining army to take to the road. McCook's I Corps, drastically reorganized to account for the loss of three generals, followed Gilbert, while Sheridan's division moved in a different direction to catch up with the rest of II Corps at Danville. As they left Perryville behind, the battle's survivors took a last sad look at those who had fared worse. The hospitals remained jammed, and large numbers of the dead remained unburied. Some scenes they saw that day would haunt them the rest of their lives.[17] Nixon B. Stewart of the 52nd Ohio remembered passing a building where a Confederate drummer boy lay dying. "Some one had leaned a broad plank against the side of the building where he lay," Stewart wrote, "to keep the drip of the eaves of the house from falling in his face, for it was raining as it always did after a battle. I shall never forget that sweet, childish voice; he said in his delirium; 'mother, dear mother, why don't you come and take me home?'"[18]

In the midafternoon, Buell, still in Perryville awaiting Sill, received Gay's dispatch regarding the occupation of Harrodsburg. With Gilbert and McCook already on the move, theoretically keeping pressure on Bragg, Buell ordered Thomas to push at least one of II Corps's divisions across the river at the fords and then move the rest of his available force cross-country to the Danville-Harrodsburg road in support. It was late in the day when Thomas received that order, and by then he showed signs of a renewed hesitancy to follow Buell's sometimes unrealistic instructions. He thus ordered only one brigade, William B. Hazen's from Smith's division, to cross the river and occupy Danville. Accompanied by the 1st Kentucky Cavalry as well as their nominal corps commander's senator-father, Hazen's column easily pushed aside a token cavalry force Wheeler had left behind at the fairgrounds and entered the town to the cheers of its largely Unionist population. Like Harker to the north, Hazen would hold a captured town alone. The rest of Thomas's force remained west of the river as Buell wished.[19]

Hazen's arrival, small as it was, at least cheered Danville's citizens, for like Harrodsburg's population, Danville's had been on edge since news of the battle at Perryville first arrived. On the eighth, Confederate cavalrymen warned the wife of Centre College faculty member Robert Patterson that if the enemy compelled Bragg's army to retreat, "shells would be thrown and might strike our house, destroying it and all its inmates." Not surprisingly, many, notably Unionists, fled their homes. Those who stayed at home faced a long night. Confederate deserters fleeing the field began passing through that evening, heightening Danville's alarm even more. One, reeking of alcohol, banged on the Patterson door at 9 P.M. and demanded a meal and a place to sleep. As the soldier launched into a drunken defense of secession, another man arrived seeking shelter. The first rebel, eyeing the newcomer, remarked, "in order to please me I presume—'I declare to you, on my honor, I did not kill a single "Yank" to-day. I fired every time up into the air—but my friend there . . . I do think he must have shot ten or twelve at least.'" Unaffected, the newcomer, identified by Mrs. Patterson as a Georgian, ate his meal quietly and then led the first soldier away.

For the next two days, Danville's Unionists waited anxiously for some reliable word of their fate. Buffeted by rumors of a Federal defeat, and over-come by four hundred Confederate wounded, citizens exploded with joy at Hazen's appearance. When a soldier planted an American flag near the col-lege, "it was greeted with shouts and cheers by the Union men, and with tears of joy by the women." A young girl taunted the Confederate wounded with smaller flags until Mrs. Patterson told her that her behavior was not ladylike, and one of her slaves cried out "T'ank de Lo'd! T'ank de Lo'd! De Yanks is comin.'"[20]

The Yanks indeed were coming, but ever so slowly. So far, Buell had pursued Bragg cautiously, wary of stepping accidentally on the tiger's tail. Bragg had given him enough trouble in Perryville, and now Kirby Smith's command augmented the enemy force. The following day, a cold but thank-fully dry Sunday, saw little change in plan as Buell and Sill followed the bulk of the army into Harrodsburg. Ahead of them, Harker's brigade swung south on the Harrodsburg-Danville road, again cautiously advancing in line of battle, and rejoined its division. That afternoon, III Corps as well as Starkweather's brigade passed through town and halted on the connecting pike. Events farther south along the Danville front proved only slightly more active. Supported by Wood's division, Smith mounted a small reconnais-sance, marching to within four miles of Camp Dick Robinson before falling back after skirmishing with the gray-clad cavalry, Thomas, acting on orders from Buell, again held the bulk of II Corps west of town until evening. Gath-ering information from local Unionists and reconnoitering the neighboring road network, Thomas satisfied himself that Bragg had fallen back on his depot. The Confederates were said to be straggling and demoralized. On the other hand, all was not well, for Camp Dick Robinson reportedly brimmed with supplies. With renewed aggressiveness, Thomas begged Buell for or-ders.[21] Thomas's men also yearned for some decisive action that would bring the enemy to bay. "Marched up hill and down dale all day to no purpose," complained Nicholas Longworth Anderson of the 6th Ohio. "Nonsense. Am tired and mad."[22]

As he had for weeks, Buell disappointed them all. With Harrodsburg occupied and the enemy now conclusively located at Camp Dick Robinson, Buell determined to first unite his army in Bragg's front at Danville. He thus ordered Thomas to move but only a few miles into town, while the other corps converged in his rear at his previous camps. Buell would not allow Bragg to catch him again with only a fraction of his army in place.[23]

Buell's dilatory pursuit, careful and sluggish as it was, nonetheless severely limited Bragg's options. In retrospect, one can say that even more might have been done. A more spirited general might have pushed his men more vigorously along Bragg's left flank, cutting off the Confederates from their lifeline to the south and thus forcing a decisive battle that might well have altered the course of the war. The methodical Buell, however, habitually lacked such audacity on his best days, and clearly he still reeled from the Perryville surprise. He also knew he was the focus of attention in Washington, a fact which must have constrained him even more. Buell thus approached every troop movement like a chess player losing a championship match, using all the time allowed before shifting a pawn. So it was that Bragg's road out of Bryantsville, south to Lancaster, remained open. Lancaster in turn provided access to the Cumberland Gap road at the village of Crab Orchard. In pursuing his foe so slowly and carefully, Buell essentially offered Bragg the choice of either making a stand or slipping the developing noose and running for Tennessee. One surmises that Buell would not have minded the latter.

But if Buell hoped to avoid another battle, so did Bragg, who rapidly reached to grasp the second option his foe offered. Rumors began running through at least the officers' camps on the night of the eleventh that Bragg finally had concluded to abandon the campaign, especially after the general dispatched scouts to look for water along the road south. The night was, as a result, "one of the gloomiest of my life," according to Bragg aide Stoddard Johnston, for "it was clear to me that the campaign was over, and Kentucky lost." Whether his chief's mood accentuated the plain facts is unknown, but Johnston was right: there would be no second battle for possession of his native state.[24]

The following day, Bragg called a council of his generals to tell them what they already knew. In addition to Hardee and Polk, Kirby Smith, Humphrey Marshall, and Cheatham attended. The situation was dire, he told them. Bad news had arrived that Price and Van Dorn remained in Mississippi, defeated at Corinth by William Rosecrans a week earlier. No help could be counted on from that quarter. John C. Breckinridge's long-expected column remained in Tennessee as well. Meanwhile, Bragg said, there were rumors that Federal reinforcements were moving down from Cincinnati. The rumors were correct, for Gordon Granger's force, renamed the "Army of Kentucky," was en route to Lexington.

There was other news, equally bleak. Supplies accumulated at the depot turned out to be more meager than expected, providing enough rations for only four more days. With the surrounding countryside largely gleaned and the enemy destroying neighboring mills as fast as possible, they could not hold out much longer at Camp Dick Robinson. Buell's Federals in con-

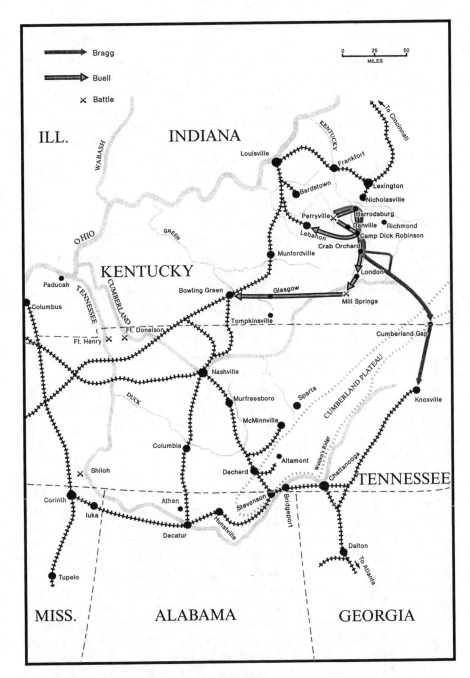

Map 15.1. Retreat to Tennessee, October 1862

trast drew supplies and reinforcements easily from Louisville. Finally, there were the Kentuckians. Instead of rising up en masse to help liberate their state, the men of the commonwealth remained aloof, content to allow others to do their fighting for them. With Buell about to cut the army's last path of escape and autumn's drenching rains approaching, there seemed no choice but to fall back into Tennessee and preserve the army. With the exception of the Kentuckian Marshall, who wanted to hold out north of the Kentucky River as long as possible before retreating eastward into Virginia, and according to some Kirby Smith as well, all agreed. Hardee later told one of Buckner's aides that he had advised retreat only because the men had lost all confidence in Bragg.

Bragg allowed Marshall to go back the way he came, and then announced preparations to otherwise begin the retreat at daybreak. The topography, shape of the roads, lack of forage, and need for haste all meant that the combined army could not expect to vacate Kentucky on the same road. Both remaining Confederate armies thus would march south to Lancaster, ten miles east of occupied Danville, and then divide. Bragg would lead his force south out of the Bluegrass via Crab Orchard and Mount Vernon, while Kirby Smith would strike east to Paint Lick and then move south along the same road he used to enter Kentucky in August. The two parallel armies would meet north of Barboursville at the roads' junction and pass through the gap. Taking command of all Confederate cavalry, Wheeler would provide rear and flank guards for both retreating columns but report directly to Kirby Smith. Withers, meanwhile, turned over command of his division and sped south to gather supplies for the approaching armies.[25]

The men rose well before sunrise the next morning, still unaware of their general's decision. Many assumed that another battle beckoned. Instead, disappointed soldiers prepared four days' rations, said their good-byes to those too sick to travel, formed ranks, and marched for Lancaster. Wheeled vehicles of every description, loaded down with supplies, formed the train. Behind them, like true Texas cowboys, Terry's Rangers herded droves of cattle. Back at the camp, flames rose as men set fire to all the stores they could not eat or carry with them, including barrels of pork soaked in commissary whiskey, which cruelly scented the air with the odor of bacon. The Alabamians of Lumsden's battery buried several captured cannon tubes in an apple orchard rather than let the enemy someday use them against them. As Bragg's army marched through Lancaster, the town's predominantly Unionist citizenry turned out to silently stare. Only a handful of pro-Confederates appeared, and they promptly fell into line with loaded wagons and slaves, eager to flee vengeful neighbors and Federal occupation. That night, after a tiring forced march of twenty miles, Bragg's army reached Crab Orchard, the end of the macadamized pike, and the still unblocked road south. Kirby Smith followed around midnight. They had slipped by Buell.[26] Exclaimed Polk, "God has opened the door for us!"[27]

For the next six days, the Army of the Mississippi trudged south toward the Cumberland Gap, averaging fifteen to twenty miles per day despite Federal skirmishers nipping at their heels and Unionist bushwhackers firing shots from seemingly everywhere. Encumbered by the longer train, loaded with captured small arms and ammunition, and assigned the more difficult road as well, Kirby Smith's worn-out column progressed more slowly and soon fell behind. Only the intervention of Cleburne, off-duty due to his wounds, saved the train at Big Hill when one of Kirby Smith's exasperated subordinates decided to burn it. Instead, Cleburne with typical ingenuity, organized parties that literally carried the train wagon by wagon up and over the steep eminence.

The topography grew more mountainous and difficult as both forces progressed, the roads becoming increasingly rocky and rough. As Bragg's army ascended Wildcat Mountain south of Crab Orchard, temperatures fell precipitously, making morning frosts and thick fogs commonplace. Frequent springs provided ample water, but the commissary would provide only a three-day allotment of half-rations at a time, consisting of biscuits, pickled pork or beef, and some parched corn until that ran out. Going through their rations quickly, they turned to foraging between dispersals, but the region's sparse and largely pro-Union population could supply little more to eat than occasional pumpkins and stray cattle. Many soldiers grew ill, and many more—hungry, lousy, ill clad, and barefoot—suffered immeasurably. Finally, despite a rash of broken down wagons and horses worked to death, the vanguard reached the fabled gap on October 18 and Morristown, Tennessee, two days later. There the men commenced entraining for Knoxville even as the column's rear and then Kirby Smith's slow-moving army passed through the gap. In Knoxville, ample food, new uniforms, and soap awaited their arrival, as did a new fallen snow.[28]

A weary, silent gloom enveloped the Confederates as they abandoned Kentucky after so much blood and effort. Sam Watkins remembered that "along the route it was nothing but tramp, tramp, tramp, and no sound or noise but the same inevitable, monotonous tramp, tramp, tramp." Not even a bird's song seemed to rent the stillness, he added, only the occasional "'close up'" or a briefly sung tune before weary silence returned. Men staggered along, often asleep.[29] Exhaustion and hunger no doubt were in part to blame for the men's languor. As historian Larry Daniel has noted, the retreat from Kentucky was the first sustained period of hunger for Bragg's troops. More was involved than physical discomfort, however. Beneath that quiet surface lurked frustration and rage. It occasionally surfaced, as at Cumberland Ford when Chalmers's Mississippians struck back at the hated bushwhackers, lynching sixteen of them in a single oak tree and leaving the bodies to swing in the breeze. On another occasion, Cheatham beat one of his own junior officers for some failure involving the train. Bragg's was an angry army.[30]

More often than not, however, the men expressed their resentment less violently. Watkins remembered his 1st Tennessee comrades openly cursing their generals. Hundreds of other worn-out men fell out every day and simply allowed themselves to be captured, so swamping the Federal pursuit with more hungry mouths that eventually all were paroled.[31] Following his regiment from Perryville, Levi Wagner of the 1st Ohio Infantry encountered a host of captured and paroled Confederates on their way to Louisville "where they expected transportation down the river. . . . They were quite jolly and had their pockets crammed with money." Wagner and his companions often banded together with their ostensible enemies for meals and lodging, paid for by the Federals with counterfeit greenbacks.[32]

Meanwhile, among those who would not straggle or desert, three principal targets of blame emerged around campfires and in bitter letters home. Retreat, privation, and the death of comrades caused a few men to give up on the Confederacy as a whole. Describing the cold and shoeless men around him, Georgia cavalryman John J. Hogg lamented that "the Confederate States of America I think will soon know its doom."[33] Others, agreeing with Bragg, incriminated Kentucky. The commonwealth's failure to support the campaign with men and material engendered a fearsome backlash. Confederates described most Kentuckians as base cowards who deserved the Federal occupation they had and would endure. Kirby Smith asserted that the commonwealth's men paled in comparison to its courageous women, while others defamed Kentuckians' masculinity in more bald terms. Augustus Cabarrus Kean of the 13th Tennessee complained that all the people of the state "acted a most pusillanimous part," deservedly earning the contempt of both warring factions.[34] Likewise, Tennessean George Winchester recorded in his diary that he had no respect for any Kentuckians except those already in gray. He conceded that the state was "hopelessly lost, her people now, prompted by an avaricious love of property higher than any consideration of patriotism . . . have bartered away in a position of neutrality the birthright descended from revolutionary ancestors."[35]

Edward N. Brown of the 45th Alabama said he left the state with few regrets: "As far as I am concerned, it may go to the Yankees." Brown, however, did not blame Kentuckians alone. Like many of Bragg's soldiers, he singled out his commander for special condemnation. He could not fathom why Bragg gave up a strong position like Camp Dick Robinson, he wrote his wife, but then "his whole tour through Tenn & Ky is a foggy affair to me."[36] Others were less generous. Going all the way back to his refusal to confront Buell at Munfordville, many soldiers censured Bragg as a blundering coward. The ultimate failure of the campaign, they vehemently maintained, was his. Hopeful rumors abounded that Richmond would replace Bragg, perhaps with Joseph E. Johnston.[37]

Regrettably for the future, many of Bragg's lieutenants, members of Congress, the Southern press, and, to an extent, even Bragg's wife essentially agreed. Complaining of his high-handed treatment and especially his usurpation of the better road, Kirby Smith led the chorus, grousing to anyone who would listen, but especially to his wife and a sympathetic Polk. Breckinridge, Buckner, Cleburne, Hardee, and Liddell all eagerly joined the anti-Bragg chorus, although other brigade commanders, men such as Adams, Anderson, Brown, Chalmers, Donelson, Smith, Stewart, Withers, and especially Wheeler, continued to offer him support. Bragg, meanwhile, eagerly sought to shift blame to his chief subordinates. Arriving in Knoxville ahead of the army, he found a summons from President Davis immediately ordering him to Richmond. Once in the capital, Bragg painted as rosy a picture as possible of the campaign and then convinced the president to approve his plan to shift the army into Middle Tennessee. He also apparently opened a war of words against Polk and Hardee that escalated in the months ahead. Bragg's narration of events in Kentucky concerned Davis enough to send for his friend Polk. In Richmond, the bishop responded to Bragg's allegations with denunciations of the army commander and pleas to replace him with Joe Johnston. A few days later, Davis heard the same and more from another favorite, Kirby Smith. Nonetheless, he stubbornly determined to leave Bragg in command, convinced that Bragg's administrative abilities and optimistic plans for Middle Tennessee mitigated any leadership deficiencies. Besides, Davis wrote Kirby Smith, no one else of appropriate rank except Lee could do any better, and he was otherwise engaged. Indeed, in many respects Bragg seemed to have outperformed Lee recently. Despite Perryville, he had driven the enemy from northern Alabama, much of Middle Tennessee, and the Cumberland Gap. In contrast, Lee, after his unsuccessful Maryland Campaign, was right back in northern Virginia.

In high spirits again after having triumphed over his critics, Bragg ordered his bedraggled army as well as Kirby Smith's west toward Nashville, to the town of Murfreesboro Within a month, Bragg would assume command of the combined armies, renamed the Army of Tennessee. He would now try to do what he had wanted to accomplish back in August before Kirby Smith dreamed his Kentucky dream: regain the rest of Tennessee for the Confederacy.[38]

Like Braxton Bragg, Don Carlos Buell's actions during the last days of the campaign also brought down upon his head a storm of condemnation. Arriving in Danville during the evening of October 13, Buell learned that Bragg and Kirby Smith had abandoned Camp Dick Robinson, marched through Lancaster, and were heading south toward Crab Orchard. While he correctly expected Kirby Smith to keep moving toward the Cumberland Gap on the Richmond road, Buell projected his own priorities upon Bragg and as a result once again misread him. Consumed as always with the Louisville-Nashville supply line, Buell repeated his error of August. Ignoring Bragg's logistical needs, he assumed that Bragg surely would strike directly for Nashville this time by moving southwest toward Somerset, on a road parallel to the one Bragg actually planned to take. From Somerset, Buell guessed Bragg would move into Middle Tennessee and threaten the capital. Accordingly, Buell ordered his divided army to converge at Crab Orchard within twenty-four hours, preliminary to a march to head off Bragg and save the city. Buell expressed confidence that Horatio Wright had enough troops to hold Kentucky in case Kirby Smith doubled back.[39]

The next day, marching toward the southeast from Danville, Thomas pushed II Corps toward Crab Orchard as Buell wished, getting as far as the town of Stanford before dark. McCook followed closely behind, while Gilbert passed through Danville and struck directly east for Lancaster to safeguard the flank. Federal cavalry skirmished all day with the Confederate rear guard in what was to become a common occurrence. More important, the horsemen discovered that, contrary to Buell's expectations, Bragg was headed south toward the Cumberland Gap. Reacting hurriedly, Buell issued new orders for II Corps to keep hard on the enemy's heels and pursue the retreating rebels as far as Mount Vernon. Because of crowded roads and a lack of forage, the other corps would hold up at Crab Orchard and await developments.[40]

Two days passed as Buell and II Corps followed Bragg south to Mount Vernon, their cavalry almost constantly involved with the Confederate rear guard. As he rode, Buell reconsidered his options. With Bragg's immediate destination now certainly Cumberland Gap and not Nashville, he could no longer see any good reason to keep up the chase into the barren hills of eastern Kentucky. Bragg surely would head west to Nashville once in Tennessee. Why not beat him to the punch? On October 16, he wired Halleck with a familiar litany of excuses for breaking off the pursuit. The region south of Crab Orchard was a "desert," he warned. There would be little food and forage for his army farther south, which would necessitate maintaining a longer and longer supply line over a single, bad mountain road. Bragg, in contrast, would draw ever closer to his base at the gap. The mountains also favored Bragg, providing ample opportunities for ambush and delay. "I deem it useless and inexpedient to continue the pursuit," he told Halleck bluntly, "but propose to direct the main force under my command rapidly upon Nashville." Bragg no doubt would strike the city at some point in the near future, Buell opined, so it only made sense to break off the pursuit and get there first.

Having ducked marching into the rugged mountains so many times before, a realistic Buell realized that Washington probably would reject his advice. Indeed, he suspected that letting Bragg slip by probably meant the end of his command. He plaintively conceded that "the present time is perhaps as convenient as any for making any changes that may be thought proper in the command of this army. It has not accomplished all that I had hoped or all that faction might demand." Buell nonetheless hoped to hold on to the army, and he went on to weakly argue his case. While he waited for Halleck's answer, Buell and II Corps pushed on after the Confederates the next day. Because of the lack of forage and felled trees blocking their path, progress was slow. That night, Buell sent Halleck a second telegram, again advocating giving up the pursuit and moving instead to Nashville. He frankly told Halleck the most he could hope to accomplish in eastern Kentucky was intercepting Kirby Smith's train, if even that.[41]

Halleck's reply to Buell's first message, written on October 18, demonstrated how tenuously Buell maintained command of his army. The general in chief had heard all of this from Buell before, and remained unimpressed. While offering faint praise for "your victory at Perryville," Halleck reiterated that "the great object to be attained is to drive the enemy from Kentucky and East Tennessee. If we cannot do it now we need never to hope for it." Detouring to Nashville would accomplish nothing except to leave East Tennessee in Confederate hands. Halleck therefore made it clear that he wanted Buell to follow Bragg all the way to Knoxville if not Chattanooga. Troops from other theaters could more than defend Nashville if Buell kept the pressure on Bragg.[42] Replying the next day to Buell's second telegram, Halleck restated his wishes and added ominously that President Lincoln fully concurred. Indeed, Lincoln now essentially ordered Buell to move into East Tennessee—and quickly, before winter made the roads impassable. Rejecting Buell's list of woes, both the president and the general in chief insisted that if Bragg could live off the country, so could he, "unless we admit the inferiority of our troops and our generals."[43]

Miffed by suggestions of incompetence as well as the rejection of his advice, Buell defiantly forged ahead with his Nashville plans. Encouraging Horatio Wright to advance to Frankfort both to protect Kentucky from guerrillas and to soothe Jere Boyle's ruffled nerves, Buell halted II Corps at London and ordered the rest of his army back to Danville, preparatory to shifting it to Nashville via Bowling Green in two columns. Hoping one last time to persuade Halleck and Lincoln of their error and preserve his command, Buell wired the former on October 22 from Danville while en route to Louisville to coordinate the campaign. Their plans, he lectured, were simply unrealistic. He maintained that it would take eighty thousand men to occupy East Tennessee, a force that could not be adequately fed without possession of Middle Tennessee's railroads, roads, and foodstuffs. Just as he had argued since taking command, Buell insisted that the Nashville region was the key to the rest of the state. The political necessity of liberating East Tennessee impressed Buell no more than it had a year before.

As for Lincoln's somewhat insulting suggestion that Buell march and fight under the same conditions as Bragg, Buell insisted that he could "give good reasons why we cannot do all that the enemy has attempted to do, such as operation without a base, &c., without ascribing the difference to the inferiority of our generals, though that may be true." Conditioned by "the spirit of the rebellion," and fearful of immediate execution for various offenses as well, Confederate troops simply exhibited better discipline. More to the point, Lincoln and Halleck seemed to miss the lesson of Bragg's campaign: that it had failed precisely because of poor logistics and the Rebels' desire to travel light and live off the countryside. They should not force him to make the same mistake.[44]

Buell's tortured refusal to comply with direct orders shocked Halleck, who did not immediately reveal the telegram to the president. Already under tremendous pressure from cabinet members Chase and Stanton, assorted influential Midwestern Republicans, and especially Governors Morton, Tod, and Yates to fire both Buell and McClellan, and in so doing regain public confidence before the November elections, Halleck made it clear that "to now withdraw your army to Nashville would have a most disastrous effect upon the country, already wearied with so many delays in our operations. . . . Neither the Government nor the country can endure these repeated delays." Once advised of Buell's position, Lincoln and Stanton not only agreed with Halleck's assessment but also decided that the time had come to replace him. On October 24, Stanton happily created the Department of the Cumberland and chose William Starke Rosecrans, the hero of Iuka and Corinth, to command it. The War Department immediately ordered Rosecrans to proceed to Louisville via Cincinnati, where he would take charge of the former Army of the Ohio, now designated the XIV Army Corps. Only after Stones River would it take on the more familiar name of Army of the Cumberland.[45]

Buell, in Louisville overseeing dispositions for his march on Nashville, first learned of his sacking from a newspaper article on October 29. While he waited for confirmation from Halleck, Buell informed Thomas, still with the army at Lebanon. "Under the circumstances," he told his second in command, "I am sure I do not grieve about it." The next day, an embarrassed Rosecrans sent Buell Halleck's orders and arranged a meeting. After conferring with the new commander, writing a last letter to Thomas, and penning an emotional farewell order full of praise for the men he had recently accused of being inferior to their enemies, Buell left Louisville for Indianapolis and new orders. Instead of a new command, however, those orders called for Buell to report to Cincinnati in November and appear before a commission being formed to investigate his conduct during the Kentucky campaign.[46]

Meanwhile, Buell's columns continued on toward Nashville without him, angry and disillusioned at both their treatment and the fact that their apparently cowardly or traitorous commander had yet again let Bragg slip away. Some despaired of ever defeating the Rebels, and hopeful rumors ran through their camps of a thirty-day truce followed by a negotiated peace. On the night of October 25, the nadir came when up to six inches of snow fell across eastern and central Kentucky. Noting their bloody footprints in the snow, some likened themselves to George Washington's suffering army at Valley Forge or Napoleon's army retreating from Moscow. Other veterans simply stole more blankets from dreaming comrades in the new regiments and went back to sleep, leading to angry confrontations in the morning. Some deserted and headed north. Such was the hungry, tentless, cold, angry, and exhausted army's morale when I Corps and III Corps first learned of Buell's dismissal at Lebanon on that snowy October 26. Over the next few days, the good news slowly wound its way to Crittenden's lead corps at Bowling Green.

Almost universally, the men reacted with cheers and joy. [47] P. V. Cox of the 1st Michigan Engineers and Mechanics wrote that "a new life seems to inspire all hearts, and joyous hope lights up every countenance." "You wanted to no how i like Bull," another soldier wrote a friend, "he is an old traitor but he is not over us now."[48] Mitchell's and Steedman's men expressed particular pleasure, having served under "Old Rosy" in either Mississippi or West Virginia. They sang his praises and assured their comrades that blunders and defeat were behind them forever.[49]

The men of Buell's old command also expressed joy because they assumed that they would now go into winter quarters. Instead, as soon as he joined his new command in the field, Rosecrans promptly adopted Buell's once-rejected general strategy and led the army back to Nashville to confront Bragg, who was now approaching the Nashville area just as his predecessor had warned he would. Thanks largely to Buell's unappreciated decision to initiate the Nashville march and continue it despite Washington's disapproval, McCook's lead elements arrived there on November 7, followed six days later by Rosecrans. After resting and reorganizing his army, he led it out of the city on the day after Christmas, intending to confront Bragg at Murfreesboro. At dawn on the morning of December 31, Bragg ordered Cheatham's division to follow McCown's against the Federal right flank. With bitter irony, Cheatham's men again effectively smashed into McCook's old corps and drove it to the rear. Only Phil Sheridan's dogged "stand in the cedars" delayed the Confederates long enough to permit Rosecrans to throw together an effective defensive line. Bragg had achieved a tactical victory, but he faltered when Rosecrans, like Buell, refused to retreat. After a nearly suicidal Confederate attack on January 2, one that many believed to be Bragg's attempt to punish Breckinridge and his Kentucky regiments for the recent sins of their brethren, Bragg again retreated. Unwilling to mount a quick pursuit, Rosecrans drew the ire of his superiors in Washington. The basic parameters and cast of characters along Stones River could come as no surprise to those who had fought at Perryville.[50]

THE WORLD HAS CHANGED

HOSPITALIZED IN NASHVILLE DURING EARLY NOVEMBER, CHARLES P. Carr of the battered 121st Ohio wrote sister-in-law Lib Rathburn a letter brimming with loss and despair. The cherished, happy days of their youth, the soldier lamented, were gone forever, much like their many friends who already had died in the war. "The world has changed," he sadly wrote, ". . . little did we think in our single days that . . . a cruel war would separate us from our dear ones but sutch is the case." He longed to see his wife, and he knew that Lib missed her husband. Would they all ever be together again? He hoped so, but after surviving the carnage at Perryville, "tis hard to tell and only him who rules the universe can answer whether we will be restored to our dear ones at home but Lib we must hope for the best and place our trust in God." If he or her husband fell in some future battle, he added, at least "we can die with the noble thought that we died in a just and good cause."[1]

Carr and Rathburn were far from alone in needing to come to grips with a world seemingly changed by the battle fought in the Chaplin Hills. While unscathed soldiers marched away to new battlefields, Perryville permanently redirected the lives of tens of thousands of Americans. According to long-accepted statistics, 4,211 Federals, approximately 7 percent of the Army of the Ohio's total strength at Perryville, became casualties: 845 killed in action, 2,851 wounded, and 515 missing. According to those same sources, an additional 3,396 Confederates, roughly 21 percent of the Army of the Mississippi's known effectives at the battle, fell: 510 killed, 2,635 wounded, and 251 missing. Based on incomplete records, the numbers are frustratingly inexact. One recent study suggests that the numbers are too low, for using a variety of printed sources and burial records at least 70 additional casualties have been identified.[2] Whatever the exact butcher bill, the total cost remained exorbitant. The wounded coped with scars both physical and psychological. Some never healed. Back home families dealt as best as they could with both the emotional and economic consequences of having a beloved father, son, or husband killed or wounded in action. In Perryville itself, residents struggled to rebuild their homes, farms, and lives. Above all, they and many others around the divided nation struggled just like Charles Carr to find meaning in Kentucky's great and terrible battle.

Long after the opposing armies marched off to Tennessee, Perryville remained an incredible panorama of destruction and loss. The Doctor's Creek neighborhood still bore all the marks of the recent fight. Returning to town on October 10, Dr. J.J. Polk, the Unionist physician and cleric, rode out to check on friends and look at the scene of the fighting. His subsequent memoirs describe one scene of devastation after another. The Federals had turned the Peters House into a hospital and used the orchard as a cemetery. Farther along at the Dixville Crossroads, the Russell House "was dotted over with hundreds of marks of musket and cannon balls. . . . The whole scene beggars description. The ground was strewn with soiled and torn clothes, muskets, blankets, and the various accouterments of the dead soldiers. Trees not more than one foot in diameter contained from twenty to thirty musket-balls and buck shot. . . . Farms all around were one unfenced common."[3]

The Russell farm was indeed in gory shambles. When Isaphena Russell May returned to her home after the battle, bringing with her a wounded Federal she had found in the woods, she discovered her home shot full of holes and without a chimney. Amputated limbs surrounded the dwelling, doctors having pitched them through windows during surgery. With apparently no help from occupying bluecoats, she and her relatives took up pitchforks and began loading the severed arms and legs into a wagon. They buried two or three wagonloads in a ditch on the edge of the property, covering the lifeless residue of battle with a plow. Later in life, John C. Russell compiled a more systematic account of his losses and applied to the Federal government for compensation. In seventeen days of occupation, he later testified, Federal troops took four of his horses, thirty cords of wood, forty barrels of corn, a hundred pounds of hay, and two thousand bundles of wheat, property losses totaling almost $900. Russell attributed much of his loss to Sill's men, who arrived after the battle. In the end, the government refused to pay the claim, maintaining that because Russell was not at home during the battle, he could not swear that Federal troops took the property. Russell did make some profit from the army, selling plowed-up minié balls for ten cents a piece.[4]

Sam Bottom's experience of Federal occupation resembled Russell's. Writing from Bottom's farm less than two weeks after the battle, one of Charles Carr's comrades, Harry Lewis of the 121st Ohio, surveyed the largely unchanged scene and concluded that "Kentucky has paid very dear, for her neutrality—the Country is completely cleared—wherever the armies have been—even the fences are used so much that thousand of acres are thrown into one field." The army already had used up Bottom's corn and fodder, Lewis explained, while his straw and harvested wheat lay strewn uselessly on the ground, trodden underfoot by the soldiers. At least as a Unionist like the

Russells, the Federals had spared Sam Bottom somewhat. Across the Mackville Road, Lewis maintained, Squire Henry Bottom's farm looked even worse, for the owner, a "rampant Secesh," had suffered accordingly.[5]

As Lewis's last comments suggest, while every resident within range of the guns suffered losses during the battle, the postbattle Federal garrison particularly targeted pro-Confederates once the shooting stopped. As the most prominent Confederate sympathizer on Doctor's Creek, the prosperous farmer and magistrate felt the heaviest blow. Squire Bottom's farm, the vortex of the fighting along Hardee's front, already resembled bedlam by nightfall on October 8. Bullet holes perforated many of his tenant cabins, wooden and stone fences lay broken, and his barn lay in charred ruins. Fire damage scorched earth plowed up by artillery. Hungry and angry Federals then exacted more tribute over the next several weeks. Years later, Bottom complained that after the battle the Federals deprived him of nearly $5,000 worth of property, including more than eight thousand pounds of pork, almost five thousand pounds of bacon, well over three thousand bushels of corn, fourteen tons of hay, and three hundred cords of wood. When coupled with the property destroyed during the battle, most notably his barn, as well as items taken by the Confederates, Bottom's losses amounted to a huge sum. For the first time in his life, he had to purchase food to feed his family. Replacing the barn alone cost at least $600, one neighbor testified. According to his neighbors, the squire, broken in spirit as well as financially by his losses, never recovered.[6]

In the short run, Bottom and his neighbors faced a more immediate problem: the hundreds of dead men and horses still scattered across their land. By the time Buell and his army pulled out, most of the Federal dead lay in long, neat, trenchlike graves, largely buried by their comrades but sometimes by impressed local slaves. Some regiments chose pastoral spots, shaded by cedars or oaks. Before they went after Bragg, many survivors also made wooden headstones that denoted units and in some cases expressed hope in Christian resurrection. Federals who remained in Perryville during the days that followed continued to promptly bury friends who died of their wounds. James Stewart of the 94th Ohio, for example, described how he and his friend Harrison Brecount stayed behind to care for his Brecount's brother Elmer. When Elmer finally expired, Stewart helped the dead man's brother bury him. "It was a pretty hard sight," Stewart confessed, "to see a man help lay his brother out and help dig his grave and help let him down in to his grave like a brave man."[7]

In contrast to the care lavished on the Federal dead, the blackened, bloated, and decomposing bodies of Confederates remained on the field unburied for a week after the fight. Still angry with the Rebels for robbing their dead, members of the Perryville garrison summarily refused to bury the fallen Confederates. If the enemy wanted their dead buried, one man asserted, they should have interred them themselves instead of wasting their time pillaging fallen Northerners. Nor did the Federal occupiers react immediately to more grisly problems. With so many dead men still above ground, feral hogs that usually occupied the woods swarmed the fields, devouring putrid body parts with aplomb until they too sickened and began to die from their gory repast. Squire Bottom valiantly attempted to drive the hogs off his scarred land, but the absence of fences permitted the hogs to return repeatedly. He had no more luck with his frightened neighbors, who refused to help him bury the dead Confederates strewn about his farm while the Federals remained nearby and were exacting retribution from perceived Confederate sympathizers.

Finally, with both the sight and smell of decomposing men growing "loathsome" to the soldiers remaining in the area, Col. William P. Reid of the 121st Ohio impressed Bottom, his slaves, and other local Secessionists to assist a hundred soldiers in accomplishing the grim task. Evidence suggests that the soldiers did little or nothing to help. Working with too few picks and shovels, burial parties also faced a difficult task breaking hard and rocky soil baked by the summer's drought. Eventually, they gave up and carved out shallow trenches, temporarily covering the dead with a thin blanket of earth in the vain hope of deterring the hogs. Not until two months later, after the 121st Ohio had departed, would Squire Bottom, other Perryville residents, and a group of students from Danville's Kentucky School for the Deaf exhume those Confederates and bury 347 of them in a compact mass grave located on Bottom's land. Bottom chose a spot above the swale where Federal artillery had decimated the 16th Tennessee. Using personal effects, he managed to identify a few, mostly Mississippians, but the identity of the others remains unknown.[8]

The living also demanded attention. More than eighteen hundred wounded soldiers from both armies remained in town, and hundreds more littered the path of Bragg's retreat. At least four unidentified town residents also lay wounded in hospitals. Scores of other men had fallen ill, primarily from typhoid fever thanks to Perryville's putrid water. Although the armies' remaining doctors, townspeople, and impressed African Americans associated with the Army of the Ohio did their best from the beginning to relieve suffering, conditions in Perryville's inadequate and overburdened hospitals remained, in the angry words of Dr. J. S. Newberry of the United States Sanitary Commission, "peculiarly distressing." Acting with the cooperation of military authorities in Louisville, Newberry moved quickly after the battle to alleviate the anguish of the wounded, dispatching A.W. Reed to the field as soon as news came of the fight. Obtaining three wagons and twenty-one ambulances from the army, Reed packed them with supplies and headed for the front. His first taste of what lay ahead came in Mackville, where he found 180 wounded or sick men crowded into a tavern. Twenty-five had cots, but the others lay on the floor. At least they had a resident doctor. Continuing on to Perryville, he encountered scores of ambulatory wounded determined to walk all the way to Louisville for assistance. He also discovered wounded men in nearly every house along the Mackville Road, all of them being tended with more or less skill by local women. None possessed proper medicine, and after the armies finished picking over the land, few had enough sustenance to feed their own families, much less their wounded houseguests. Reed hurriedly doled out medicine and moved on.

He reached Perryville after dark on October 11. "On our arrival," he reported, "we learned that we were the first to bring relief where help was needed more than tongue can tell." Although the army surgeons had done their best, they were simply overwhelmed by sheer numbers and by the lack of necessary food, supplies, and shelter. Many surgeons had operated for days without chloroform or even enough water to wash their hands. The next morning, Reed distributed medical supplies, clothing, and food and then inspected the makeshift hospitals. What he saw shocked him even more. The patients "were all very dirty, few had straw or other bedding, some were without blankets, others had no shirts, and even now . . . some were being brought in from temporary places of shelter, whose wounds had not yet been dressed." Conditions in Danville were, if anything, even worse. He found that many of the stricken men packed into the county courthouse had not eaten, there was no water due to dry wells, and basic needs such as pails and kettles were almost impossible to come by. Obtaining beef and water from a local butcher, Reed built a fire and boiled soup for the wounded until he collapsed from exhaustion.

Lacking enough medicines, Reed determined to obtain them from the closest possible source: Buell's army. Recovering somewhat, he rode off after Buell, finally catching up with Gilbert's column at Crab Orchard on October 15. He found the men poorly supplied and demoralized. Worse yet, the regimental surgeons had no medicines to spare. Reed turned back to Danville to find the situation there growing worse. More sick and wounded continued to arrive, and the newcomers had to remain outside because all the buildings were full. Reed finally persuaded the owner of a carriage shop to allow him to use it to at least provide a roof over the wounded's heads. Meanwhile, conditions had improved in Perryville, as he discovered upon his return. While Reed had been gone, Union surgeons had continued removing the wounded from field hospitals and relocating them to newly established hospitals located in churches, Perryville's public buildings, and nearly every private homes within a ten-mile radius. The two great exceptions were the Federal hospital at Antioch Church and the former Confederate hospital at the Goodknight House, both of which still held about three hundred patients each. The greatest problem now, he asserted, was overcrowding, for supplies were beginning to pour in from across the Midwest and the men at least were eating better.[9]

The army's surgeons later credited the Sanitary Commission's timely intervention with saving many lives. In turn, both Reed and Newberry defended the exhausted surgeons who tended the wounded from the usual charges of incompetence. The lack of preparation and callous indifference that now combined, in Newberry's words, to torture wounded Federal soldiers to death resulted in general from an antiquated War Department organization that zealously protected the Quartermaster and Commissary Departments from the perceived encroachments of doctors, and more directly from the singular apathy evinced by Buell throughout the campaign. Although logistics generally were his strength, Buell routinely had displayed a curious lack of interest in providing adequate medical care to his men. He had ordered his doctors to bring only one supply wagon per brigade when he initially went after Bragg in August in order to move more quickly. He opposed detailing soldiers to medical tasks, maintaining that the sick should care for the sick. Unlike Grant or McClellan, or for that matter Rosecrans after Buell's dismissal, Buell set up no ambulance corps or field hospitals, and never sought regular army surgeons for his command. Old army prejudices probably explain his attitude in part, but one also suspects that he was more comfortable with battle in the abstract than in reality. Perhaps the tactician did not want to contemplate the inevitable end result of war. At any rate, his men paid the price. Surgeons in the Army of the Ohio, Newberry complained, had been "prohibited, by a special order, from taking any medical supplies whatever. . . . Will it surprise you, then, if I tell you that . . . there was no adequate preparation for the wounded, and, as a consequence of this want of preparation, there was great suffering, and lives were lost?"[10]

Buell eventually did permit the establishment of new hospitals in Lebanon and nearby New Haven, which soon drained off some of the less injured men from Perryville's hospitals. Meanwhile, Federal authorities in Louisville had geared up to deal with the pressing needs of the wounded. They established more than a dozen hospitals in Louisville as well as in nearby New Albany, Indiana. Boyle dispatched ambulances to retrieve Union soldiers who could be moved from in and around Perryville. More ambulances began the longer trip from Lebanon with men who had already been moved once. Men who could walk to Louisville did so, saving room for more severely injured men in the wagons.[11] The transfer proved to be a painful ordeal for many of them. Wallace P. Benson of the 36th Illinois, who had been shot in the hip, wrote simply, "I thought it would kill me."[12]

Ormond Hupp of Simonson's battery also suffered greatly on the trip. Burned and severely wounded in the arm when an enemy shell ignited a limber, he thus far had managed to resist amputation of the injured limb. Transported in a bouncing supply wagon that left him exposed to heat and dust, Hupp's "sufferings were more than I can express, but I had made up my mind to reach [Louisville] if I lived." Along the way, food was scarce. He ate only twice, a friend securing some coffee, hardtack, and eventually a little meat. They also bought whiskey while passing through Bardstown. There, local women dressed his wound and those of others. Downing the whiskey to hold off the pain, Hupp arrived in the city only to be routed on across the river to New Albany.[13]

Most, however, thought Louisville worth the trip once they arrived. Unlike the makeshift affairs near the field, the city provided hospitals that were clean, neat, and adequately staffed. William T. Clark of the 79th Pennsylvania favorably compared his "new, clean & nice" Louisville establishment with the unheated, dilapidated, and rat-infested African-American church that had been his hospital in Lebanon. He added that his bed was the first he had slept in since joining the army.[14] Likewise, Charles W. Carr of the 21st Wisconsin informed his wife that "we have a comfortable place now. It is like going into Paradise compared with the places we have been at since the Battle. Have enough to eat and drink, plenty of good nurses, and a good place to sleep."[15] James H. McGregor of the 42nd Indiana wrote his wife that the four injured Perryville civilians had joined the soldiers in his hospital.[16]

There was, however, a problem. Before long, Louisville and New Albany contained so many wounded men that no more could be taken, especially after ambulatory men who had tried to remain with the army began to break down. Authorities accordingly established more hospitals in Frankfort and Lexington. Others died further south, such as Peter Schmitt of the 15th Kentucky who tried to remain with his regiment until he sickened and died in a Huntsville, Alabama, hospital. Nonetheless, the city continued to fill up with the wounded, unwounded friends, family members who traveled to Louisville to locate and care for their loved ones, and paroled Confederates.[17]

Meanwhile, the most severely injured remained in Perryville, Danville, and Harrodsburg. Wounded in the cornfield, David J. Ryan of the 21st Wisconsin remained on his back well into November, loudly cursing Buell for murdering his friends. Albert Waugh of the 1st Wisconsin, shot below the knee, wrote from there in December that he expected to still be in Perryville come spring. Most of the Confederate wounded lingered there as well, prisoners of war as well as wounded soldiers. Largely denied access to the better hospitals in Louisville and other cities, injured Confederates endured more difficult conditions. Two miles south of Perryville, hundreds lay outside, sheltered only by arbors or stacks of fodder[18] John Baker of the 96th Illinois wrote his father that five hundred wounded Confederates still lay in Harrodsburg hospitals in mid-November, and that three hundred more had died since the battle. "They are the hardest looking lot of men that I ever saw," Baker complained, ". . . nasty and ragged they was drest in all kinds of clothes and all holes. . . . the hospital is nasty as the devil and stinks worse than any hog pen."[19]

Conditions in Perryville hospitals indeed were "nasty," and certainly grim enough to worsen an already bad situation. One recent study reveals the results. Deaths occurred during certain peak moments for various reasons related to health care. By October 11, most of the mortally wounded had expired, largely from severe wounds and loss of blood. Incomplete hospital records reveal thirty deaths on October 9, but only fourteen two days later. Then, over the next four days, deaths among slightly less injured men peaked at thirty-nine on October 15. Poor hygiene, the lack of water, the prevailing lack of knowledge regarding bacterial infections, and loss of fluids led to sepsis, with its high fevers, fluid loss, cardiac arrhythmias, hypotension, or loss of renal function. The death rate again fell off after the fifteenth so that by October 19 the most severely affected were dead. Only nine men died in Perryville that day. Once again, however, the cycle repeated, as delayed infections, notably pneumonia and peritonitis, set in. Other men succumbed to blood clots or heart failure. Twenty-two men died on October 20. After another brief lull, the death rate rose again and peaked with twenty-three deaths on October 25, most likely due to organ failure, fluid loss, fevers, and organ damage due to a bout of sepsis. By month's end, "hospital gangrene" was setting in as well, killing many. Others simply starved to death, unable to eat or retain nourishment because of their wounds. Modern antibiotics, including those that have eliminated that strain of gangrene; advanced surgical techniques; soap and water; and hygiene would save most of those casualties today. Indeed, many men wounded later in the war would benefit from knowledge of wounds gained in army hospitals, notably the link between wound treatment and the occurrence of gangrene. Sadly, the relatively primitive state of medical science in 1862, coupled with worse than average conditions, doomed well over two hundred wounded soldiers to a slow and lingering demise.[20]

As wounded Confederates expired, townspeople buried them in area cemeteries. Federal authorities held those who recovered until they could be exchanged. While more seriously injured prisoners would journey in the coming months under guard as far as Delaware and Virginia for exchange, Boyle, acting under orders from Buell, transported the less injured as well as over thirteen hundred healthy Perryville prisoners and an undocumented number of pro-Confederate local civilians down the river to Vicksburg, where they exchanged the soldiers in December. Some rejoined their units quickly enough to fight at Murfreesboro. Others already had slipped away from lightly guarded hospitals and headed for home in hopes of rejoining their regiments. Federals wrote often of paroled and ill-clad Confederates, some heading to Louisville for transportation and exchange, others avoiding legal niceties and heading directly south toward their lines. Relations between the two groups, perhaps cemented by common sufferings, generally were positive and even sympathetic.[21]

Another commonality was that Confederates were not alone in disappearing from hospitals or camps. Some Federals took advantage of their wounds to desert as well. With home so close, Hoosiers in particular evaded authorities and walked away. Indiana authorities complained that it already was proving hard to recruit new men to replace the wounded. Desertion by healthy men thinned the ranks even more, as did the resignation of officers. Such men were wounded at least in spirit.[22]

The war moved on. Thirty additional months of campaigning and battle lay ahead before the divided nation would reunite under duress. Men who fought at Perryville, including many of the wounded and scarred, took part in much of that later fighting. In the years to come, Perryville would be only one of many battles that stirred their blood and elicited memories told and retold to comrades and families. For others, however, the Battle of Perryville remained the significant turning point in their lives. Some men never recovered physically, a sad fact that would forever affect their ability to compete economically. A survey of Perryville veterans from Tennessee who early in the twentieth century responded to the Tennessee Department of Archives and History's Civil War Veterans Questionnaires provides one glimpse of the results. George P. Alexander of the 9th Tennessee lost the use of both arms for four years after being wounded at Perryville. A farmer, he struggled even after regaining partial mobility. Raleigh P. Dodson of the 1st Tennessee, having suffered a similar wound, could never do physical labor again. He clerked for a while before becoming a horse trader. George W. Parks of the 16th Tennessee fared even better. Permanently disabled due to a leg wound, he nonetheless became a schoolteacher, a deputy sheriff, and eventually a justice of the peace.[23]

One may also systematically gauge veterans' lives after Perryville through pension records. An early list of casualties in the 41st Georgia named twenty-seven men killed outright, three mortally wounded, and forty-five "slightly wounded" or suffering slight injuries like "flesh wounds." The roll listed sixty-five other men with various wounds. Seventeen years after the battle, Georgia began awarding pensions to its Confederate veterans. Only "indigent" men qualified, however. Within those parameters, five Perryville veterans out of the list of sixty-five, all but one wounded seriously enough to never fight again, filed claims.

J.R. Marlow was one. Marlow lost his right leg in the battle. He made a living as best he could after the war, but by the end of the century required government assistance, as did George N. Lester, the former captain of Company B, who lost his right arm and became a Federal prisoner after the battle. Farmer J.W. Nations came home partially paralyzed with a shattered foot and ankle. Old and feeble by 1906, he listed some household goods and a cow as his only property. Wounded in the left hand and above the right hip, the latter ball never removed from his body, Joshua D. Tharp rejoined the regiment after being exchanged, but after the war weakened as he grew older. By age fifty he suffered constant pain and could no longer work due to his inoperable hand and partial paralysis. Like his comrade Nations, Tharp owned little or no property and struggled to survive as a farm laborer.[24]

James M. McElreath endured an ordeal worthy of the Book of Job. Hit twice in the leg during the battle, the bone shattered, the sixteen-year-old McElreath avoided amputation but had difficulty walking for the rest of his life. After the battle, Federal authorities took McElreath and several other captured rebels across the river to Indiana and abandoned them to their own devices. Somehow he got home to the Atlanta area, where in the summer of 1864 Sherman's invaders captured him in a hospital. In the years after the war, McElreath's condition worsened, to the point that he could neither work nor walk. To add insult to injury, Georgia authorities initially rejected his pension application because the records still listed him as a deserter.[25]

Severely wounded Federals also suffered, and some tragically embarked on a downhill path without end. William Woodward of the 79th Pennsylvania had been a plasterer before the war. Wounded four times during Starkweather's stand, he survived but could never again raise his left arm above his head, a condition that prevented him from resuming his old job. Worse, he also had trouble breathing, having taken two balls in the lungs. Although he eventually found work as a school janitor, Woodward seemed to many a broken man. He turned to drink for relief from constant pain and eventually succumbed to alcoholism. He and his family lived out a tragic existence.[26]

Woodward's later life suggests that Perryville veterans carried emotional scars as well as physical ailments. Eric Dean's recent comparative exploration of post-traumatic stress disorder during the Civil War and the Vietnam conflict confirms that the nineteenth century battle left men afflicted with conditions popularly associated with a more recent century. Focusing on Hoosier veterans confined to the Indiana Hospital for the Insane, Dean located at least three men whose mental illness seemed directly linked to service at the battle. Henry C. Carr of the 22nd Indiana lost a leg at Perryville. Although he more or less recovered physically, friends and neighbors testified that Carr returned to Indiana a changed man. Constantly frightened, he convinced himself that his life remained in danger. At night he steadfastly guarded his home from supposed intruders, sometimes firing his weapon into the darkness at imaginary attackers. Christian Fasig, in contrast, came home consumed with rage, constantly threatening to kill neighbors or burn down buildings until he was committed for the sake of the community. Veteran William Morris suffered a psychological collapse around the time of Perryville—it is not clear if he fought in the battle or not—and deserted. He spent the next thirty years in and out of the state mental hospital and the county farm. Observing through the experiences of a later war, a friend of Morris's widow provided a lay diagnosis of "shell shock." One wonders how many Perryville veterans came home with similar problems.[27]

Sad cases like those also remind one that former soldiers alone did not deal with the ramifications of Perryville. In the years following the battle, many wives, children, parents, siblings, and neighbors all had to cope with men broken in body or mind in the Chaplin Hills. Others dealt with the loss of loved ones who never came home. To be sure, antebellum culture had prepared them somewhat. Mid-nineteenth century Americans were more accustomed to death and more comfortable with it than modern Americans. They regarded it fatalistically, for death, especially among young children and the elderly, was common. Major disasters associated with the advent of industrialism, notably steamboat explosions, had more recently brought additional awareness of a new modern horror, death on a massive scale. With evangelical certainty, most antebellum Americans celebrated death as a passage that led to an individual Christian's heavenly reward and offered instruction on faith to those left behind. Death scenes fraught with pathos and faith, such as Little Eva's demise in *Uncle Tom's Cabin*, permeated middle-class literature and eventually gave rise to a distinct and popular subgenre called "consolation literature" or "necrophiliac drama," which offered lessons to middle-class women readers especially on how to mourn and die correctly. In the years before the war, experts further institutionalized death and took much of the care of the dead away from family and church. Americans slowly turned away from churchyard burials and instead memorialized the dead in pastoral, parklike cemeteries. Preparing the dead for burial, once a duty of loved ones, became a profession. Surveying the entire scene, historian Lewis O. Saum has gone so far as to argue that death "saturated" antebellum American culture.

The war, however, brought endless mourning on an unprecedented and staggering scale. Popular songs such as "All Quiet Along the Potomac" and "The Vacant Chair" signaled that death had become something more than commonplace. Instead of a family losing a child or two, a loss heavy enough to bear, some mothers lost all their sons, and many communities buried most of their young adult males. Farms like Squire Bottom's and towns like Perryville metamorphosed into grisly battlefields, hospital complexes, and burial grounds. War-related technological innovations in mortuary science and photography forced even those who technically escaped loss to face the ugly truth of omnipresent carnage. Amidst such bloodletting, Americans like hospitalized Buckeye Charles P. Carr still struggled to find reassurance and meaning. Some deaths, most concluded, were better than others. In the lexicon of the times, the men who fell in battle at Perryville had died a "good death," one effused with Christian meaning and martial glory. Their blood and that of all the others, some hoped, might redeem the nation just as the blood of Jesus had redeemed mankind.

Nonetheless, for those left behind, life went on despite the shadow of the war, the ceaseless casualty rolls, and ever-present black mourning clothes. Indeed, that shadow slowly wove its way into a community's social fabric, forever muting some of its brightest hues.[28] As historian Reid Mitchell points out, the Civil War dead never really disappeared from their homes and neighborhoods: "Americans thought of the nation as a community of the living and the dead. The American family extended in time. The dead remained part of the American nation; they still made claims upon the living."[29] Mitchell, of course, primarily meant the soldiers' ostensible demand that the war continue to victory, an obligation most forcefully argued by Lincoln at Gettysburg. After the war, the Southern "lost cause" and the North's "bloody shirt" would continue to call powerfully on the memories of those slain in battle in defining courses for the future.

Yet Mitchell's statement is true when one regards more mundane matters as well. Civil War soldiers killed in action remained inexorably linked in innumerable ways to their families and communities. Fields still had to be tilled, shops opened, bills paid, legal suits settled. Children who were raised without fathers developed psychological burdens and coping mechanisms that would dramatically shape the latter half of the century. The economic marginalization that often followed the loss of a breadwinner or valued hand would determine a family's future, and a community's if writ large. As much as the postwar generation might try to put the war behind it, the constant absence of the slain shaped the circumstances, responses, and perceptions of those who survived. They could not be forgotten because their absence remained tangible.[30]

So it was for those families who donned mourning clothes after Perryville. To better understand how the deaths of their loved ones affected them, one might consider the pension files of one sample regiment, in this case the hard-fighting 1st Wisconsin. In the brutal, hand-to-hand melee along the Federal left, the regiment lost fifty-four men killed and 198 total casualties, fully half of its strength. Empowered by a Congress that in 1862 awarded pensions to the dependents of Federal soldiers killed in service who could prove financial distress, and encouraged by increasingly generous subsequent acts, relatives of twenty-eight of the 1st Wisconsin soldiers who died during the battle or in Perryville's hospitals eventually filed for pensions citing economic need.[31]

Those survivors clearly had struggled to make ends meet in the wake of the war. Hardest hit were soldiers' parents. On mid-nineteenth century farms, adult sons remained important cogs in a family's economic machinery, as well as secondary caregivers and instructors for younger siblings. Traditionally, parents wanted their sons to remain at home until they were well into their twenties. As parents aged, they then expected their children to provide for them, or as scholar Joseph Kett puts it, to function as "a form of social security, unemployment insurance, and yearly support." Sons had increasingly disappointed their parents, however, leaving home for brighter prospects farther west, nonfarming jobs in the cities, or military service.[32]

The sons who composed the 1st Wisconsin proved no exception. His father disabled due to a bad back and crippling rheumatism, George W. Bowen was his mother's sole source of support before the war. Hit in the breast with a ball, Bowen died in Perryville on October 15. His death marked the escalation of the Bowen's Job-like sufferings. The following summer, a plague of insects destroyed the family's fifteen acres of crops, further plunging it into ruin. To survive, the Bowens began selling off their meager lands in Wisconsin and used the proceeds to buy cheaper property in first Iowa and then Kansas. When those funds ran out, and with the father a total invalid, Bowen's mother began to take in sewing and knitting in order to survive.[33]

Charles Lyons also supported his parents because of a father's disability. The Lyons men had worked together as carpenters until 1858, when a bout of typhoid fever and a rupture felled the elder man. Barely eking out an existence before the father's illness, the family experienced hard times. Charles moved to Milwaukee for better pay at a newspaper and then joined the army. He sent money home to his mother until he died on October 17 in a Perryville hospital. After that, Lyons's mother supported the family as a housekeeper and dressmaker.[34]

The evidence suggests that several Wisconsin men may have joined the army, at least in part, for the steady income and bounty money. Hale Cowles went to work at age thirteen as a farm laborer to support his widowed mother. After working the 1861 harvest, he gave her the money he had earned and joined the 1st Wisconsin. He sent part of his pay home each month until he died at Perryville. So did Charles Stephens, who died the day after the battle. John Ellis, born John Gustaf Jonsson, likewise went to work in a hotel at age fourteen to support his mother. His death left her in abject poverty. Americus Smith supported both his mother and a seriously retarded brother who, according to testimony, could barely dress himself, much less work. John Wineborn left a similar situation, except that his mother was blind.[35]

Few sons had more to bear than Daniel Hill, whose alcoholic father, derisively nicknamed "Whiskey" by his neighbors, worked only occasionally as a carpenter and day laborer, and even than drank up the proceeds. Daniel left home before the war to work on a neighboring farm and thereby became the sole source of support for his parents and four siblings. He later took a job in a mill, joined the army for the state bounty of $300, which he gave to his mother, and died at Perryville at age eighteen. Without her son, the mother was left to her own devices. She took in laundry, cleaned houses, and finally left her husband in 1874 to live with a just-married daughter. "It is true that I am not a widow woman," Ruth Hill testified, "but it is true that I am in a worse condition than widowhood."[36]

A number of men supported widower fathers. William M. Foster worked to feed his father and two younger brothers until he joined the army. William Trumbull completely supported his father before his enlistment and sent him his army pay afterward. So did former brick mason and mechanic Davis P. Buzzell, who continued to provide for an aged father and three brothers until he was shot through the head. With brother John's health ruined in the service as well, the father struggled to work until his health broke down completely. Disabled and nearly blind, Gilman Buzzell moved back to Vermont but eventually became a charity case and was placed in the care of a legal guardian chosen by the local court. The guardian filed the father's claim.[37]

One might wonder if a soldier's survivors inflated their distress to impress the Pension Bureau. Perhaps, but evidence otherwise suggests that parents often waited as long as possible to ask the government for assistance. Indeed, while some parents certainly filed claims as soon as possible, others such as Gilman Buzzell refused to do so until old age made a pension a necessity. George W. Wing's mother likewise applied only in 1892, over a decade after the death of her husband. Hit in the hip, DeWitt C. Spencer lingered for almost a month until he died at Perryville in November 1862. His father, a former laborer, waited until age eighty-five to file an application, and only then because he was exhausting the last of a small sum he had inherited years before. By 1888, the elder Spencer was unsound mentally as well as physically, maintaining that DeWitt died during the better-known battle at Gettysburg. He added that another son, Albert, died in the Wilderness in 1864, and that son Andrew came home physically unable to work.[38] Lois Smith, mother of Junius Smith, waited even longer, refusing to file a claim until 1908. "We verily believe," her daughter wrote, "that the reason she has delayed making application for pension has been the reason of pride. She is now destitute except for the support of her children."[39]

In contrast to fathers and mothers, few widows filed pension claims. The reason is simple: most of the twenty-eight soldiers in the sample had not married before they left for the front. Even when soldiers had spouses, the relatively young age of the couples and the economic necessity of a hasty remarriage created by women's narrowed opportunities certainly limited the number of claims, as did government regulations that limited a widow's opportunity to apply. Two striking features in widows' applications are that nearly all had married their husbands after the beginning of the war, a fact that may be related to the acceleration of romances spurred by the war, and that they almost always remarried before the war ended. Most of the widows who pursued pensions therefore did so for their young children, who remained eligible despite the presence of a stepfather until age sixteen.[40]

Less common, then, were cases like that of Zibiah Fox, who claimed to have married Frank N. Baker right before he left for the army, much to the displeasure of Baker's family. Baker died in one of Perryville's hospitals on October 13. Six months later, his widow remarried a man named Krake who had managed to avoid military service. Only after the death of her second husband did she file a pension application based on her marriage to Baker. After learning of her marriage to Krake, and amid allegations that Fox had never legally married either man, government authorities terminated her pension. Other second marriages, perhaps entered into much too hastily, proved unhappy. Orlando Wicks's widow Martha remarried in 1863, but her second husband deserted her and three children for another woman in 1888. She applied for Wicks's pension after divorcing the other man.[41]

In the end, pension records can reveal only so much. More than half of the 1st Wisconsin's Perryville dead left parents, widows, and orphans who never filed an application. Many no doubt were financially comfortable. Parents were established; widows remarried. Others, like Lois Smith, refused to ask the government for money out of pride. Nonetheless, the records do suggest that Perryville marked only the beginning of a long and painful struggle for many if not most of the bereaved. Like the soldiers who fought the battle, those left behind could never forget what happened on October 8, 1862, the day their lives began spiraling out of control.

Perryville could not forget either, although most of its residents tried to rebuild their shattered community and get on with life. Boyle County's war cruelly did not end with Bragg's retreat. Confederate raiders and partisans, including John Hunt Morgan, infamous guerrilla Sue Mundy, and the notorious Kansas raider William Clarke Quantrill, all periodically operated in the area until the end of the war. In January 1865, accompanied by several dozen followers including Jesse James's older brother Frank, Quantrill pillaged parts of Danville and fought a skirmish with Home Guards west of Harrodsburg on the Perryville road. Worried about such partisans as well as being suspicious of Kentucky's loyalties, Federal authorities maintained a heavy hand on the community and the commonwealth throughout the remainder of the conflict, particularly targeting suspected Confederate sympathizers. In reaction to that as well as to Lincoln's emancipation policies, 80 percent of Boyle County voters supported Democrat George McClellan's for president in 1864. Dr. J. J. Polk later remembered that only he and two others in his Perryville precinct voted Republican. The totals signaled a crucial shift of prewar Whigs toward the postwar Democratic Party, a redirection largely occasioned by Lincoln appointees' treatment of Kentucky as an almost-conquered province coupled with a desperate and increasingly forlorn hope of hanging onto their slaves. The sight of Black men in blue uniforms particularly galled local whites and stimulated a reaction. In the bitter years immediately following the war, Boyle County "Regulators" lynched three blacks and attempted to murder others. Some wags eventually opined that Kentucky had finally joined the Confederacy, only four years too late.[42]

In the face of such violence, Perryville's African Americans struggled to build a viable and self-sustaining community in the aftermath of emancipation and the Thirteenth Amendment. In 1865, a group of three extended families led by Preston Sleet, the former Boyle County slave who claimed to have taken up arms during the battle, occupied about 150 acres of battlefield land stretching from above Walker's Bend to the north side of the Mackville Road, property legally owned by Squire Bottom and John Dye. For several years, the male residents of Sleettown toiled as sharecroppers. They apparently worked hard and lived frugally, for in 1880 Preston and Henry Sleet purchased the property. During the years that followed, they added to it by buying additional, smaller tracts from the Bottoms. Sleettown survived well into the next century, its "'honky-tonk'" restaurant, general store, and taxi service providing a brief prosperity, while its church and one-room school otherwise enriched the lives of its populace. Only during the Great Depression of the 1930s did the town disappear, its residents selling the land and moving into Perryville.[43]

While Sleettown experienced its genesis, Federal soldiers returned to other parts of the field to supervise the reburial of their hastily buried dead in a national cemetery. Under orders from George Thomas, burial parties in 1865 exhumed 969 of the Union dead and moved the remains to a square, two-acre compound atop Peters Hill along the Springfield Pike. Workers carefully sifted through any extant evidence in an effort to identify as many of the dead as possible, but over two-third remained unknown. The cemetery, Doctor Polk later noted with pride, overlooked the entire battlefield. A handsome stone fence, five feet high, enclosed the cemetery, with two gates providing admittance to mourners. "In the center of the grounds," Polk added, "is a vacant space fifty-two feet square, on which it is intended to erect a suitable monument." Eight carriage roads, each ten feet wide, radiated from the monument site to a walkway bordering the stone wall, dividing the graveyard into eight distinct sections.[44]

The monument would never be erected, nor the grand design completed. Indeed, the ink had barely dried on Polk's 1867 autobiography when the government, unable to obtain legal title to the property due to the stipulations of a will, determined to close the new cemetery and transfer all of the Federal dead buried at Perryville and elsewhere in Kentucky to a larger, central facility at Camp Nelson, in Jessamine County. Aside from a few lost souls whose lonely graves remained unmarked and largely unknown, no Federal dead remained on the field after the summer of 1868. One cemetery still existed, however, that built by Squire Bottom as a final resting place for a sizable percentage of Confederates killed in the battle. In the years following the war, the Squire attempted to erect a stone wall around the plot, similar in design to that described by Polk around the Federal cemetery. One in a series of photographs taken in 1885 as models for engravings in *Century Magazine*'s *Battles and Leaders* series shows a wizened Bottom sitting on the incomplete wall, gazing wistfully into the distance.[45]

If Bottom seemed placid in the 1880s, others connected with the battle did not. To be sure, Perryville receded quickly from the American popular mind during the two decades following Appomattox. Many Americans were in the mood to forget the war entirely, and even those who still wanted to fight it out nonviolently increasingly focused on the Virginia campaigns. By 1884, Perryville veteran Marshall Thatcher could complain in his memoirs that no one remembered Perryville at all except as an unimportant skirmish, a situation that clearly galled him.[46] Just at that moment, however, the pub-

Figure 16.1. "Squire" Henry P. Bottom in 1885 at the Confederate cemetery he constructed. Photograph courtesy Massachusetts Commandery, Military Order of the Loyal Legion, and the U.S. Army Military History Institute.

lication of *Battles and Leaders*, as it did in so many other cases, reopened old wounds and brought new discord. Although both Wheeler and especially Gilbert seized the opportunity to put themselves in the best possible light by bending the truth, it was Buell's long narrative of the campaign and defense of his actions that created the greatest stir. Having settled in Kentucky after the war, the touchy and increasingly reclusive general emerged from his hermitage time and again to respond to any attempt to downgrade his accomplishments. His take on Shiloh, which played up his own contributions while downgrading those of Grant and Sherman, ruined his long friendship with the latter and instigated a long-running battle of words with both. Buell's pronouncements on Perryville, while not as factious in comparison, nonetheless further reinforced a growing image of Buell as defensive, petty, and too quick to blame others for his own failings. Many readers concluded that he really had been timid, a traitor, or both. Moreover, Buell did nothing to alter the opinions of the men who had once served under him, and who increasingly vented the bitterness they felt for their former commander in the dozens of memoirs and regimental histories cited here. Bragg's men would write scathingly of their commander as well, but his refusal to respond, coupled with his earlier demise, at least provided them with less ammunition than Buell gave his critics.[47]

Still, by focusing on Shiloh rather than Perryville, the Buell brouhaha nonetheless failed to change the growing popular perception of the battle as an affair of relatively minor importance, an interlude between Shiloh and Stones River. The birth of a new century, however, coupled with the approaching fortieth anniversary of the battle, spurred new interest in the battle. Aging veterans of a few units such as the 79th Pennsylvania began holding their annual regimental reunions on October 8, their most significant day. Alexander McCook's relatives surely were not alone in saving articles about the battle, such as Erasmus Wilson's vigorous recycling of John Beatty's angry attack on Buell at an 1886 reunion.[48]

Most importantly, the fortieth anniversary set off a growing movement intent upon revising the image of the battle by memorializing the battlefield. By the 1890s, battlefields had come to loom in the American mind both as sites made sacred by the blood of soldiers, and as outdoor classrooms superbly able to provide a tangible link to a more glorious past. To some they promised to play a role in sectional reconciliation as veterans of both armies returned for annual reunions. Others placed them within a revival of proclaiming the glories of the South. At the same time, a tug-of-war began nationally between battle survivors, who claimed dominion over the once bloody fields, and a growing host of artists, bureaucrats, and boosters who advocated giving control of battlefields to artists, landscape architects, government officials, and other Progressive Era "experts." Kentuckians, especially local citizens, took the lead in working to establish such a park at Perryville. Their task was by no means an easy one, for Perryville lagged behind other sites. Monuments already littered battlefields like Gettysburg, increasingly regarded as the nation's most important scene of combat as well as a tourist mecca. In contrast, by 1900 there was little left to suggest that a major battle had once taken place near Doctor's Creek. Only the Confederate cemetery marked the spot, and it stood in disrepair, its grounds and still incomplete wall overgrown with briars and weeds.

A stillborn attempt by Kentucky congressmen to have the area purchased for a National Military Park along the lines of the new facilities at Chickamauga and Gettysburg, opened in 1895, nonetheless served to refocus at least Kentucky's attention on Perryville. With much of the 1862 battlefield still in use as a working farm by the Bottom family, however, most of that interest automatically devolved on the Confederate cemetery and its immediate environs. While Southern state governments took the lead at the better-known sites, the Kentucky Division of the Daughters of the Confederacy spearheaded a drive to raise both public and private funds to erect an appropriate monument in the cemetery. The first decade of the twentieth century witnessed the peak of Civil War monument erection. That women led such a project is not surprising, since in the years between 1865 and 1885, elite women's groups and especially the Daughters had spearheaded most monument efforts. As in Perryville, more often than not they had erected the completed monuments in cemeteries, since it was presumed that Federal authorities would object less to commemoration confined to the dead. Although more town squares became home to monuments after 1885, Perryville's and Kentucky's peculiar situation empowered the earlier tradition, as did continuing Southern poverty that usually precluded state aid.

On October 8, 1902, forty years to the day after the battle, a crowd of at least five thousand celebrants gathered for the monument's unveiling. Among them were two Union veterans of the 10th Ohio, both carrying regimental flags and embodying the turn of the century's growing spirit of reconciliation, as evinced by the number of veterans from both sides attending "Blue-Gray reunions" and monument dedications. While Union veterans generally refused to participate in events that seemed to honor the Confederate cause, men like the veteran Ohioans had grown perfectly willing to salute the bravery of individual Johnny Rebs at places like Perryville. After prayer and a speech, the crowd followed the path of Donelson's brigade through the fateful ravine to the cemetery site. There, within the hastily completed stone wall, they found a granite shaft, twenty-eight feet high, and topped by the figure of an alert Confederate infantryman prepared to begin the manual of arms. The rather typical soldier atop the monument, of the sort increasingly mass produced commercially for Southern town squares, represented a new trend that had appeared after 1885. Earlier monuments tended to be simpler, funerary obelisks. Still, there was no mistaking the monument's essential purpose as a headstone. Inscribed with lines from Theodore O'Hara's already standard "Bivouac of the Dead," the shaft also provided the names of the roughly thirty men Squire Bottom had been able to identify.[49]

Despite the very public commemoration, the much desired acknowledgment of Perryville's first-rank importance did not follow, and the remainder of the field went back to the plow in the spring. Indeed, almost another thirty years would pass before Perryville's Federals received a similar honor. That is not surprising. Nationally, the 1930s marked a period of renewed interest in the Civil War, an upswing in interest created by both the widening Great Depression, which had Americans searching for hope in a simpler and more noble past, and the increased passing of many of the war's now elderly combatants. Battle anniversaries figured prominently. Perryville, like many other towns, participated fully in the wider trend. On October 8, 1931, the Perryville Women's Club and Perryville Battlefield Commission, the latter the latest incarnation of the town's booster spirit, unveiled a complementary Union monument near the cemetery. Symbolically smaller than the Confederate column, the Union obelisk drew its inspiration from the Washington Monument as well as the hundreds of memorial obelisks around the nation. Acknowledging the Federal dead's role in preserving the Union, the monument's creators also inscribed on it another verse from O'Hara. After the troubled unveiling—at first the shrouding veil refused to come off de-

Figure 16.2. Confederate monument. Photograph courtesy John Walsh Jr.

spite Herculean efforts—a tremendous downpour soaked the crowd and short-
ened the festivities. It was as if the pantheon of Confederate gods objected to
the monument's presence near the Southern dead.[50]

The Battlefield Commission already had bigger plans than merely erect-
ing an additional monument. Since the initial battlefield movement that three
decades earlier culminated in completing the Confederate cemetery,
Perryville's residents had continued hoping that they could persuade the federal government or the state to purchase the forty or fifty acres surrounding
the site, essentially the locale of the first clashes between Cheatham's and
Jackson's divisions, for a battlefield park. The new commission was no exception. Despite continued lobbying and anniversary celebrations, nothing
was done during the World War II years, a period when attendance at all
national battlefield parks plummeted. Indeed, by the early 1940s the battlefield once again bore signs of ongoing neglect and disrepair, an isolated spot
best suited for romantic assignations and other shadowy activities. A pond
largely filled in the ravine, while weeds and briars wound their way from its
banks up the hill toward the cemetery's stone wall. Vandals repeatedly defaced the monuments. Anniversary activities ceased during the war, and authorities finally hauled away the site's decorative cannons to melt down the
metal for scrap.[51]

With the end of the world war came a new, prosperous, and often nos-
talgic postwar era provided by the sacrifice of soldiers of another conflict

Figure 16.3. Union monument. Photograph courtesy John Walsh Jr.

and coupled with the fears and continuing nationalism stimulated by the Cold War. After 1945, the relatively new concept of "heritage" became an increasing preoccupation with many Americans, some of whom embraced it with missionary zeal. There emerged new hopes to memorialize the World War II soldiers' Civil War progenitors. In Perryville, the site's deterioration had grown so embarrassing to the community by 1952 that the Perryville Lions Club finally persuaded the State Conservation Commission to step in and create a state park, initially on eighteen acres surrounding the monuments. State workers rebuilt the stone wall around the cemetery, placed two cannons at its gate, sandblasted the older Confederate monument, erected a marker that described the battle, and instituted regular upkeep. Meanwhile, holding up their end of the bargain, the Lions raised funds to build a picnic pavilion with cooking amenities and rest rooms, and reshaped the pond. Later, a playground would be added, further cementing the park's role as a multiuse facility. Nearby farmers joined in, clearing the surrounding land and in so doing again subtly reshaped the battlefield landscape as other landowners had been doing since 1862.

On the ninety-second anniversary of the battle, October 8, 1954, Vice Pres. Alben W. Barkley officially opened the Perryville State Battlefield Site. The years that followed saw increased activity and continued small land acquisitions, the pace quickened by the impending centennial of the war. Working with the town Lions, the local Civil War Round Table created an hour-and-a-half bus tour of the battlefield that took visitors to major sites in and near town before dropping them off at the park. Boy Scouts and Girl Scouts, marching from Mackville and Harrodsburg, began annually retracing the steps of the armies, their leaders making sure that the young "soldiers" neither ate nor drank until arriving on park property and camping above the bluffs of Walker's Bend, where Donelson's men had dressed their lines and prepared to attack. The crowning achievement came on the hundredth anniversary, at the height of the Civil War Centennial, when the park curators opened a new museum and visitor's center near the cemetery. The new visitors' center meshed nicely with the commonwealth's myriad centennial observances, which in addition to essay contests and other educational activities emphasized developing the state's battlegrounds as potential tourist sites.

By the mid-1970s, Perryville as a state site existed beyond danger of further degeneration. It had grown over time to ninety-eight acres, largely encompassing the scene of action on the Confederate right from Donelson's initial charge, over the Open Knob and through the site of the cornfield, to the top of what had become known as "Starkweather's Ridge." More than seven thousand acres were recognized as a National Historic Landmark. The pond at the park disappeared. More changes were in the offing. Park management initiated a subtle shift that ultimately transformed the site from a multiuse park to a battlefield memorial. In response, despite Perryville's distance from the new interstate highways, the field attracted an increasing number of visitors—including the new breed of Civil War reenactors, the latter mounting an annual and still growing battle recreation every October. Perryville's increasing popularity was in part a function of national trends. After a brief downturn in the 1970s, Americans' interest in the Civil War again grew steadily through the next two decades, and attendance at parks like Perryville grew commensurately. It peaked in 1990 and 1991 after the initial broadcast of Ken and Ric Burns's blockbuster Public Broadcasting Service series *The Civil War.* By the late nineties, the Perryville battlefield still averaged a respectable hundred thousand visitors a year despite being closed during the winter months.[52]

More dramatic changes, however, were in the offing as the century drew to a close. The year 1990 saw not only the advent of Ken Burns, but also the creation of the Perryville Battlefield Protection Association (PBPA), a largely local group dedicated to preserving, enlarging, and interpreting the park through a combination of public and private monies. Like their spiritual predecessors throughout the century, PBPA members not only wanted to preserve and enlarge the field for its historical sake, but also hoped to increase local tourism and benefit the area economically. Working with the state government and several private conservation agencies, PBPA members drafted a battlefield management plan. In 1993, the same year that a congressional committee identified Perryville as a top priority site for preservation, Kentucky governor Brereton Jones provided an additional $2.5 million in federal funding and appointed a Perryville Battlefield Commission to oversee spending those and other public and private funds on implementing the finalized plan. Attorney and Civil War scholar Kent Masterson Brown, a native Kentuckian from nearby Danville and first president of the PBPA, agreed to chair the commission and spearhead the raising of the 20 percent of matching funds required by the state grant.

After appraising those privately held lands earmarked for battlefield expansion, the PBPA began purchasing property in the mid-nineties through the closely affiliated Perryville Enhancement Project (PEP). Among PEP's acquisitions were 149 acres from Melvin and Gladys Bottom, encompassing that part of the field north of the Mackville Road that witnessed Hardee's fierce series of attacks against Rousseau. That property alone, once donated to the state, more than doubled the size of the existing park to 251 acres and made possible a more or less complete tour of the entire battlefield. At the same time, other PBPA members purchased Squire Bottom's house, then in a sad state of disrepair; much of what had been Merchant's Row; and Bragg's headquarters at the Crawford House. At the dawn of a new millennium, with assistance from preservation groups and corporate sponsors, property acquisitions continue toward the eventual goal of an 800-acre park. The size of the park at this writing is 370 acres, and the PBPA has protected an additional 300 acres through protective easements. Hired consultants have developed a master interpretive plan, which probably will include the construction of representative cabins on appropriate sites after archaeological investigation, the simultaneous deconstruction of modern structures, restoration of the landscape to approximate the scene in 1862, the creation of a three-mile-long hiking trail to follow the Confederate march from town to the battlefield, creation of an audio driving tour, and the addition of nonobtrusive informational markers. A museum located in town in a period structure on the Harrodsburg Pike will replace the existing visitors' center.[53]

As the park expanded during the 1990s, those supporters interested in it further refined their goals. Battlefields nationally at the end of the century once again became contested ground between those who wanted to use them to teach important lessons, inculcate patriotism, right old wrongs, or preserve green space from rapacious developers. While some defended battlefields as sacred spots made holy by martyrs' blood, others chastised the keepers of battlefield parks for both idealizing war on beautiful pastoral grounds that misrepresent the horrible totality of what occurred there, and for ignoring troubling political, social, and ideological questions that belie the lingering benign spirit of blue-gray reconciliation. Still others asked if the parks had not already "wasted" enough space as they opposed expansion plans in favor of commercial development at places such as Manassas. In 1999, Illinois congressman Jesse Jackson Jr., inaugurated a particularly lively debate when he called on the National Park Service to move beyond strict battlefield interpretation and broaden coverage of slavery and other issues that caused the war.[54]

At Perryville, however, Clarence Wyatt, a professor at Centre College and the PBPA's second president, already had raised the issue two years earlier in the PBPA's member newsletter. "How do we preserve the past?" Wyatt wrote. "Whose past is preserved? Who chooses? By what standards? Those of us who support the Perryville project have a responsibility to examine our own answers to these questions." Admitting that many would focus solely on the battle, he continued: "are we really telling the full story of Perryville? What about the townspeople. . . . And can we speak of the residents as a monolithic group? What about women? African Americans, slave and free? And in the same way, what if we dismiss the military aspects of this story as old-fashioned or out of favor?"[55]

Noted Civil War scholar Gary Gallagher meanwhile has written eloquently of the expanding park's potential as a teaching tool. According to Gallagher, "Perryville will be a splendid place at which to help students and visiting adults make a connection to the past—to understand the motivations and aspirations of mid-19th century Americans and to explore the political and social issues of the time. . . . Such nearly pristine sites lend themselves most powerfully to a teacher's effort to summon the ghosts of the past and to encourage modern Americans to develop a grasp of our history."[56]

Today, many frequent visitors insist that summoned or not, ghosts indeed walk the field at Perryville. Living historians tell tales of mysterious soldiers who appear among reenacting companies in the vicinity of the Widow Gibson cabin site only to mysteriously vanish. Others speak of tortured souls that still lurk near the Bottom and Russell houses. On a moonlit night along the old Mackville Road, now called Hayes-Mayes Road, or a hot afternoon on top of the windy Open Knob, such stories are easy to accept. Still, one need not believe in the supernatural to understand that on the green rolling hills above the Chaplin River, where butterflies flutter in the spring and nearby cattle graze near scum-covered limestone ponds in late summer, havoc both grand and horrible once reigned. If ghosts do walk at Perryville, they must be consoled at least by the visible evidence that their sacrifice has not been forgotten, no matter how much the world has changed since they fell.

APPENDIX 1

ORDER OF BATTLE, OCTOBER 8, 1862[1]

a=approximate; s=strength; k=killed; w=wounded; m=missing; mw=mortally
wounded; %=casualty percentage

CONFEDERATE ARMY OF THE MISSISSIPPI

Gen. Braxton Bragg
(16,800as, 532k, 2,641w, 228m, 20.2%a)

ESCORT

3rd Tennessee Cavalry (4 companies), Capt. W. C. Bacot (?s, 1k, 0w, 0m, ?%)
13th Tennessee Cavalry Battalion (Company I) William W. Lilliard (?s, 0k, 0w, 0m, 0.0%)

RIGHT WING

Maj. Gen. Leonidas Polk
(7,349s, 306k, 1,142w, 79m, 20.8%)

CHEATHAM'S DIVISION

Maj. Gen. Benjamin Franklin Cheatham
(6,549s, 305k, 1,140w, 79m, 23.3%)

DONELSON'S BRIGADE

Brig. Gen. Daniel S. Donelson
(1,429s, 71k, 300w, 3m, 26.2%)
8th Tennessee Infantry, Col. William L. Moore (436s, 4k, 36w, 0m, 8.7%)
15th Tennessee Infantry, Col. Robert C. Tyler (?s, 7k, 27w, 0m, ?%)
16th Tennessee Infantry, Col. John H. Savage (w) (370s, 46k, 170w, 3m, 59.2%)
38th Tennessee Infantry, Col. John C. Carter (w) (?s, 5k, 38w, 0m, ?%)
51st Tennessee Infantry, Col. John Chester (?s, 8k, 26w, 0m, ?%)
Capt. William W. Carnes's Tennessee Battery (?s, 1k, 3w, 0m, ?%)

STEWART'S BRIGADE

Brig. Gen. Alexander P. Stewart
(1,466s, 62k, 336w, 25m, 28.8%)
4th Tennessee Infantry, Col. Otho F. Strahl (170s, 11k, 72w, 2m, 50.0%)
5th Tennessee Infantry, Col. Calvin D. Venable (w) (?s, 15k, 67w, 12m, ?%)
24th Tennessee Infantry, Lt. Col. Hugh L. W. Bratton (375s, 7k, 61w, 0m, 18.0%)
31st Tennessee Infantry, Col. Egbert E. Tansil (?s, 20k, 76w, 4m, ?%)
33rd Tennessee Infantry, Col. Warner P. Jones (?s, 8k, 58w, 7m, ?%)
Capt. T. J. Stanford's Mississippi Battery (112s, 1k, 2w, 0m, 3.0%)

MANEY'S BRIGADE

Brig. Gen. George Maney
(1,927s, 170k, 502w, 50m, 37.5%)
41st Georgia Infantry, Col. Charles A. McDaniel (mw) (520s, 42k, 106w, 3m, 29.0%)
1st Tennessee Infantry, Col. Hume R. Feild (400s, 56k, 122w, 1m, 45.0%)
6th Tennessee Infantry, Col. George C. Porter (314as, 15k, 66w, 10m, 29.0%a)
9th Tennessee Infantry, Lt. Col. John W. Buford (w) (378as, 37k, 127w, 25m, 50.0%a)
27th Tennessee Infantry, Lt. Col. William Frierson (210s, 20k, 77w, 11m, 51.4%)
Capt. Melanchon Smith's Mississippi Battery, Lt. William B. Turner (105s, 0k, 4w, om, 4.0%)

SMITH'S BRIGADE

Brig. Gen. Preston Smith
(1,727s, 2k, 2w, 1m, 0.2%)
12th Tennessee Infantry, Col. Tyree H. Bell (?s, 0k, 0w, 0m, 0.0%)
13th Tennessee Infantry, Col. Alfred J. Vaughan Jr. (?s, 1k, 2w, 1m, ?%)
47th Tennessee Infantry, Col. Munson R. Hill (?s, 0k, 0w, 0m, 0.0%)
154th Tennessee Senior Infantry, Col. Michael Magevney Jr. (?s, 0k, 0w, 0m, 0.0%)
9th Texas Infantry, Col. William H. Young (?s, 1k, 0w, 0m, ?%)
Capt. William L. Scott's Tennessee Battery (85s, 0k, 0w, 0m, 0.0%)

WHARTON'S CAVALRY BRIGADE

Col. John A. Wharton
(800s, 1k, ?w, ?m, ?%)
2nd Georgia Cavalry (5 companies), Lt. Col. Arthur Hood (?s, 1k, ?w, ?m, ?%)
1st Kentucky Cavalry (Companies C, D, I, K), Capt. Thomas A. Ireland (?s, 0k, ?w, ?m, ?%)
4th Tennessee Cavalry (5 companies), Maj. Baxter Smith (?s, 0k, 2w, 0m, ?%)
Davis's Tennessee Cavalry Battalion (4 companies), Maj. John Davis (?s, 0k, ?w, ?m, ?%)
8th Texas Cavalry, Lt. Col. Thomas Harrison (?s, 0k, ?w, ?m, ?%)

LEFT WING

Maj. Gen. William J. Hardee
(9,451s, 225k, 1,499w, 149m, 19.8%)

ANDERSON'S DIVISION

Brig. Gen. J. Patton Anderson
(?s, 110k, ?w, ?m, ?%)

BROWN'S BRIGADE

Brig. Gen. John C. Brown (?s, 47k, 190w, 2m, ?%)
1st Florida Infantry, Col. William Miller (?s, 13k, 19w, 2m, ?%)
3rd Florida Infantry, Col. Daniel B. Bird (247s, 12k, 90w, 0m, 41.3%)
41st Mississippi Infantry, Col. William F. Tucker (427s, 21k, 69w, 0m, 19.1%)
Battery A, 14th Battalion, Georgia Light Artillery, Capt. Joseph E. Palmer (125s, 1k, 12w, 0m, 10.4%)

ADAMS'S BRIGADE

Brig. Gen. Daniel W. Adams
(1,920s, 7k, 78w, 67m, 7.9%)
13th Louisiana Infantry, Col. Randall L. Gibson (328s, 1k, 15aw, 16am, 7.8%)
14th Battalion, Louisiana Sharpshooters, Maj. John E. Austin (150s, 1k, 11w, 2m, 9.3%)
16th Louisiana Infantry, Col. Daniel C. Gober (422s, 1k, 14w, 0m, 3.6%)
20th Louisiana Infantry, Col. August Reichard (360s, 1k, 15aw, 16m, 8.9%)
25th Louisiana Infantry, Col. Stewart W. Fisk (510as, 3k, 18aw, 20am, 8.0%a)
5th Company, Washington Artillery, Capt. Cuthbert H. Slocomb (150s, 0k, 5w, 13m, 12.0%)

POWELL'S BRIGADE

Col. Samuel Powell
(?s, 13k, ?w, ?m, ?%)
45th Alabama Infantry, Col. James G. Gilchrist (600s, 2k, ?w, ?m, ?%)
1st Arkansas Infantry, Col. John W. Colquitt (?s, 0k, 2w, 0m, ?%)
24th Mississippi Infantry, Col. William F. Dowd (?s, 10k, 11w, 0m, ?%)
29th Tennessee Infantry, Lt. Col. Horace Rice (?s, 1k, ?w, ?m, ?%)
Capt. Overton W. Barret's Missouri Battery, ?s, 0k, 0w, 0m, 0.0%)

JONES'S BRIGADE

Col. Thomas M. Jones
(?s, 42k, ?w, ?m, ?%)
27th Mississippi Infantry, Lt. Col. James L. Autry (350s, 15k, ?w, ?m, ?%)
30th Mississippi Infantry, Col. George G. F. Neill (?s, 2k, ?w, ?m, ?%)
34th Mississippi Infantry, Col. Samuel Benton (w) (300s, 24k, 125w, 1m, 50.0%)
Battery F, 2nd Alabama Light Artillery, Capt. Charles L. Lumsden (125s, 1k, ?w, ?m, ?%)

BUCKNER'S DIVISION

Maj. Gen. Simon Bolivar Buckner
(?s, 113k, ?w, ?m, ?%)

LIDDELL'S BRIGADE

Brig. Gen. St. John R. Liddell
(?s, 15k, 57w, 0m, ?%)
2nd Arkansas Infantry, Col. John Gratiot (?s, 1k, ?w, ?m, ?%)
5th Arkansas Infantry, Col. Lucius P. Featherston (?s, 4k, ?w, ?M, ?%)
6th Arkansas Infantry, Col. Alexander T. Hawthorn (?s, 2k, ?w, ?m, ?%)
7th Arkansas Infantry, Col. D. A. Gillespie (300s, 1k, ?w, ?m, ?%)
8th Arkansas Infantry, Col. John H. Kelly (?s, 6k, ?w, ?m, ?%)
Capt. Charles Swett's Mississippi Battery, Lt. Tom Havern (70s, 1k, 1w, 0m, 3.0%)

CLEBURNE'S BRIGADE

Brig. Gen. Patrick R. Cleburne
(900s, 26k, 325w, 0m, 38.9%)
13th/15th Arkansas Infantry, Col. Lucius E. Polk (w) (?s, 16k, ?w, ?m. ?%)
2nd Tennessee Infantry, Capt. C. P. Moore (188s, 2k, ?w, ?m. ?%)
35th Tennessee Infantry, Col. Benjamin J. Hill (270s, 4k, ?w, ?m, ?%)
48th Tennessee Infantry, Col. George H. Nixon (250s, 3k, ?w, ?m, ?%)
Lt. Thomas J. Key's Section, Calvert's Arkansas Battery, ?s, 1k, ?w, ?m, ?%)

JOHNSON'S BRIGADE

Brig. Gen. Bushrod R. Johnson
(1,540s, 32k, 164w, 9m, 13.3%)
5th Confederate Infantry, Col. James A. Smith (240s, 6k, 34w, 5m, 18.8%)
17th Tennessee Infantry, Col. Albert S. Marks (200s, 4k, 20w, 0m, 12.0%)
23rd Tennessee Infantry, Lt. Col. Richard H. Keeble (201s, 8k, 43w, 2m, 26.4%)
25th Tennessee Infantry, Col. John M. Hughes (375s, 0k, 8w, 1m, 2.1%)
37th Tennessee Infantry, Col. Moses White (230s, 0k, 28w, 1m, 12.6%)
44th Tennessee Infantry, Col. John S. Fulton (229s, 14k, 29w, 0m, 18.8%)
Capt. Putnam Darden's Mississippi Battery (65s, 0k, 2w, 0m, 3.0%)

WOOD'S BRIGADE

Brig. Gen. Sterling A. M. Wood (w)
(?s, 41k, ?w, ?m, ?%)
16th Alabama Infantry, Col. William B. Wood (600s, 0k, ?w, ?m, ?%)
33rd Alabama Infantry, Col. Samuel Adams (w) (380s, 14k, 153w, 0m, 44.0%)
3rd Confederate Infantry, Lt. Col. Henry V. Keep (?s, 0k, ?w, ?m, ?%)
3rd Georgia Cavalry (Companies G, F), Capt. Reuben L. Hill (?s, 0k, ?w, ?m, ?%)
15th Battalion Mississippi Sharpshooters, Maj. A. T. Hawkins (57s, 2k, 10w, 1m, 22.8%)
32nd Mississippi Infantry, Col. Mark. P. Lowrey (w) (?s, 7k, ?w, ?m, ?%)
45th Mississippi Infantry, Col. Aaron B. Hardcastle (?s, 17k, ?w, ?m, ?%)
Capt. Henry C. Semple's Alabama Battery (109s, 1k, ?w, ?m, ?%)

WHEELER'S CAVALRY BRIGADE

Col. Joseph Wheeler
(?s, 3k, ?w, ?m, ?%)
1st Alabama Cavalry, Col. William W. Allen (558s, 0k, ?w, ?m, ?%)

3rd Alabama Cavalry, Col. James Hagan (?s, 1k, ?w, ?m, ?%)
6th Confederate Cavalry, Lt. Col. James Pell (575s, 0k, ?w, ?m, ?%)
8th Confederate Cavalry, Col. W. B. Wade, (?s, 0k, ?w, ?m, ?%)
2nd Georgia Cavalry Battalion, Maj. C. A. Whaley (?s, 1k, ?w, ?m, ?%)
Smith's Georgia Cavalry Battalion, Col. John R. Hart (?s, 0k, ?w, ?m, ?%),
1st Kentucky Cavalry (Companies A, B, E, F, H), Maj. John W. Caldwell (?s, 0k, ?w, ?m, ?%)
6th Kentucky Cavalry (Companies A, B, D), J. Warren Grigsby (?s, 0k, ?w, ?m, ?%)
9th Tennessee Cavalry, James D. Bennett (?s, 1k, ?w, ?m, ?%)
12th Tennessee Cavalry Battalion (4 companies), Lt. Col. T.W. Adrian (?s, 0k, ?w, ?m, ?%)
Lt. S. G. Hanley's Section, Calvert's Arkansas Battery (?s, 0k, ?w, ?m. ?%)

UNION ARMY OF THE OHIO

Maj. Gen. Don Carlos Buell
Maj. Gen. George H. Thomas
(55,261s, 894k, 2,911w, 471m, 7.7%)

ESCORT

Anderson's Troop, Pennsylvania Cavalry, Lt. Thomas S. Maple (?s, ?k, ?w, 1m, ?%)
4th U.S. Cavalry (Companies B, C, D, G, I, K), Lt. Col. James Oakes (?s, ?k, ?m, ?%)

I CORPS

Maj. Gen. Alexander McDowell McCook
(13,121s, 700k, 2,235w, 384m, 25.3%)

3RD DIVISION

Brig. Gen. Lovell H. Rousseau
(7,544s, 498k, 1,535w, 181m, 29.3%)

9TH BRIGADE

Col. Leonard A. Harris
(2,250s, 142k, 4127w, 39m, 27.0%)
38th Indiana Infantry, Col. Benjamin F. Scribner (w) (436s, 38k, 132w, 0m, 39.0%)
2nd Ohio Infantry, Lt. Col. John Kell (460s, 31k, 77w, 2m, 23.9%)
33rd Ohio Infantry, Lt. Col. Oscar F. Moore (w) (388s, 26k, 78w, 5m, 28.1%)
94th Ohio Infantry, Col. Joseph W. Frizell (500s, 7k, 17w, 25m, 9.8%)
10th Wisconsin Infantry, Col. Alfred R. Chapin (376s, 38k, 109w, 2m, 40.0%)
5th Battery, Indiana Light Artillery, Capt. Peter Simonson (90s, 2k, 14w, 5m, 23.3%)

17TH BRIGADE

Col. William H. Lytle (w)
(2,580s, 187k, 614w, 35m, 32.4%)
42nd Indiana Infantry, Col. James G. Jones (490as, 20k, 133w, 21m, 35.5%a)
88th Indiana Infantry, Col. George Humphrey (434as, 2k, 20w, 0m, 5.0%)
15th Kentucky Infantry, Col. Curran Pope (w) (517s, 62k, 136w, 5m, 39.3%)

3rd Ohio Infantry, Col. John Beatty (500s, 42k, 148w, 0m, 38.0%)
10th Ohio Infantry, Lt. Col. Joseph Burke (528s, 60k, 169w, 8m, 44.9%)
1st Battery, Michigan Light Artillery, Capt. Cyrus O. Loomis (111s, 1k, 8w, 1m, 9.0%)

28TH BRIGADE

Col. John C. Starkweather
(2,514s, 169k, 476w, 103m, 30.0%)
24th Illinois Infantry, Capt. August Mauff (400s, 30k, 77w, 8m, 28.8%)
79th Pennsylvania Infantry, Col. Henry A. Hambright (420s, 40k, 146w, 30m, 51.4%)
1st Wisconsin Infantry, Lt. Col. George B. Bingham (407s, 54k, 132w, 12m, 49.0%)
21st Wisconsin Infantry, Col. Benjamin Sweet (w) (1,007as, 39k, 103w, 52m, 19.3%a)
4th Battery, Indiana Light Artillery, Capt. Asahel K. Bush (140as, 3k, 9w, 0m, 9.3%a)
Battery A, Kentucky Light Artillery, Capt. David C. Stone (140as, 3k, 9w, 1m, 9.3%a)

UNATTACHED

2nd Kentucky Cavalry (6 companies), Col. Buckner Board (?s, 0k, 4w, 1m, ?%)
1st Michigan Engineers and Mechanics (Companies A, C, K), Maj. Enos Hopkins (?s, 0k, 14w, 3m, ?%)

10TH DIVISION

Brig. Gen. James S. Jackson (k)
(5,577s, 202k, 700w, 203m, 19.8%)

33RD BRIGADE

Brig. Gen. William R. Terrill (k)
(2,406s, 112k, 335w, 59m, 21.9%)
Col. Theophilius T. Garrard's detachment (1 company, 7th Kentucky Infantry; 1 company 32nd Kentucky Infantry, 1 company 3rd Tennessee Infantry) (194s, 1k, 30w, 8m, 20.1%)
80th Illinois Infantry, Col. Thomas G. Allen (w) (659s, 15k, 41w, 0m, 8.5%)
123rd Illinois Infantry, Col. James Monroe (772s, 36k, 118w, 35m, 24.5%)
105th Ohio Infantry, Col. Albert S. Hall (645s, 50k, 147w, 6m, 31.5%)
Lt. Charles C. Parsons's (Improvised) Battery (136s, 10k, 19w, 10m, 28.7%)

34TH BRIGADE

Col. George Webster (k)
(3,171s, 90k, 345w, 144m, 18.3%)
80th Indiana Infantry, Col. Jonah R. Taylor (738s, 27k, 116w, 14m, 21.3%)
50th Ohio Infantry, Lt. Col. Silas Strickland (655s, 22k, 32w, 79m, 20.3%)
98th Ohio Infantry, Lt. Col. Christian Poorman (822s, 35k, 162w, 32m, 27.9%)
121st Ohio Infantry, Col. William P. Reid (814s, 3k, 23w, 16m, 5.2%)
19th Battery, Indiana Light Artillery, Capt. Samuel J. Harris (142s, 3k, 12w, 3m, 12.7%)

II CORPS

Maj. Gen. Thomas L. Crittenden
(20,000as, 2k, 4w, 6m, 0.1%)

4TH DIVISION

Brig. Gen. William Sooy Smith
(5,973s, 0k, 0w, 0m, 0.0%)

10TH BRIGADE

Col. William Grose
(2,152s, 0k, 0w, 0m, 0.0%)
84th Illinois Infantry, Col. Louis H. Waters (800s, 0k, 0w, 0m, 0.0%)
36th Indiana Infantry, Lt. Col. Oliver H. P. Carey (?s, 0k, 0w, 0m, 0.0%)
23rd Kentucky Infantry, Lt. Col. J. P. Jackson (?s, 0k, 0w, 0m, 0.0%)
6th Ohio Infantry, Col. N. L. Anderson (?s, 0k, 0w, 0m, 0.0%)
24th Ohio Infantry, Lt. Col. Frederick C. Jones (?s, 0k, 0w, 0m, 0.0%)
Battery H, 4th U.S. Artillery, Lt. S. Canby (?s, 0k, 0w, 0m, 0.0%)
Battery M, 4th U.S. Artillery (2 sections), Capt. John Mendenhall (?s, 0k, 0w, 0m, 0.0%)

19TH BRIGADE

Col. William B. Hazen
(2,350s, 0k, 0w, om, 0.0%)
110th Illinois Infantry, Col. Thomas S. Casey (?s, 0k, 0w, 0m, 0.0%)
9th Indiana Infantry, Col. William H. Blake (?s, 0k, 0w, 0m, 0.0%)
6th Kentucky Infantry, Col. Walter C. Whitaker (?s, 0k, 0w, 0m, 0.0%)
27th Kentucky Infantry, Col. Col. C. D. Pennebaker (?s, 0k, 0w, 0m, 0.0%)
41st Ohio Infantry, Lt. Col. George S. Mygatt (?s, 0k, 0w, 0m, 0.0%)
Battery F, 1st Ohio Light Artillery, Capt. Daniel T. Cockerill (?s, 0k, 0w, 0m, 0.0%)

22ND BRIGADE

Brig. Gen. Charles Cruft
(1,471s, 0k, 0w, 0m, 0.0%)
31st Indiana Infantry, Lt. Col. John Osborn (?s, 0k, 0w, 0m, 0.0%)
1st Kentucky Infantry, Lt. Col. David A. Enyart (?s, 0k, 0w, 0m, 0.0%)
2nd Kentucky Infantry, Col. Thomas D. Sedgewick (?s, 0k, 0w, 0m, 0.0%)
20th Kentucky Infantry, Lt. Col. Charles S. Hanson (?s, 0k, 0w, 0m, 0.0%)
90th Ohio Infantry, Col. Isaac N. Ross (?s, 0k, 0w, 0m, 0.0%)
Battery B, 1st Ohio Light Artillery, Capt. William E. Standart (?s, 0k, 0w, 0m, 0.0%)

CAVALRY

2nd Kentucky Cavalry (4 companies), Lt. Col. Thomas Cochran (?s, 0k, 0w, 0m, 0.0%)

5TH DIVISION

Brig. Gen. Horatio P. Van Cleve
(5,517s, 0k, 0w, 0m, 0.0%)

11TH BRIGADE

Col. Samuel Beatty
(1,815s, 0k, 0w, 0m, 0.0%)
79th Indiana Infantry, Col. Frederick Knefler (?s, 0k, 0w, 0m, 0.0%)
9th Kentucky Infantry, Lt. Col. George Cram (?s, 0k, 0w, 0m, 0.0%)
13th Kentucky Infantry, Lt. Col. J. B. Carlile (?s, 0k, 0w, 0m, 0.0%)
19th Ohio Infantry, Lt. Col. E. W. Hollingsworth (?s, 0k, 0w, 0m, 0.0%)
59th Ohio Infantry, Col. James P. Fyffe (?s, 0k, 0w, 0m, 0.0%)
7th Battery, Indiana Light Artillery, Capt. George Swallow (?s, 0k, 0w, 0m, 0.0%)

14TH BRIGADE

Col. Pierce B. Hawkins
(1,518s, 0k, 0w, 0m, 0.0%)
44th Indiana Infantry, Col. Hugh B. Reed (?s, 0k, 0w, 0m, 0.0%)
86th Indiana Infantry, Col. Orville S. Hamilton (?s, 0k. 0w, 0m, 0.0%)
11th Kentucky Infantry, Lt. Col. S. P. Love (?s, 0k, 0w, 0m, 0.0%)
26th Kentucky Infantry, Col. Cicero Maxwell (?s, 0k, 0w, 0m, 0.0%)
13th Ohio Infantry, Col. Joseph C. Hawkins (?s, 0k, 0w, 0m, 0.0%)
Battery B, 26th Pennsylvania Light Artillery, Lt. Alanson Stevens (?s, 0k, 0w, 0m, 0.0%)

23RD BRIGADE

Col. Stanley Matthews
(2,184s, 0k, 0w, 0m, 0.0%)
35th Indiana Infantry, Col. Bernard Mullen (?s, 0k, 0w, 0m, 0.0%)
8th Kentucky Infantry, Col. Sidney Barnes (?s, 0k, 0w, 0m, 0.0%)
21st Kentucky Infantry, Col. Samuel Woodson Price (?s, 0k, 0w, 0m, 0.0%)
51st Ohio Infantry, Lt. Col. Richard McClain (500s, 0k, 0w, 0m, 0.0%)
99th Ohio Infantry, Lt. Col. John E. Cummins (?s, 0k, 0w, 0m, 0.0%)
3rd Battery, Wisconsin Light Artillery, Capt. Lucius Drury (?s, 0k, 0w, 0m, 0.0%)

6TH DIVISION

Brig. Gen. Thomas J. Wood
(6,256s, 0k, 0w, 2m, 0.03%)

15TH BRIGADE

Brig. Gen. Milo S. Hascall
(2,399s, 0k, 0w, 0m, 0.0%)
100th Illinois Infantry, Col. Frederick Bartleson (298s, 0k, 0w, 0m, 0.0%)
17th Indiana Infantry, Lt. Col. George W. Gorman (?s, 0k, 0w, 0m, 0.0%)
58th Indiana Infantry, Col. George P. Buell (?s, 0k, 0w, 0m, 0.0%)
3rd Kentucky Infantry, Lt. Col. William Scott (?s, 0k, 0w, 0m, 0.0%)

26th Ohio Infantry, Maj. Chris Degenfeld (?s, 0k, 0w, 0m, 0.0%)
8th Battery, Indiana Light Artillery, Lt. George Estep (?s, 0k, 0w, 0m, 0.0%)

20TH BRIGADE

Col. Charles G. Harker
(1,883s, 0k, 0w, 0m, 0.0%)
51st Indiana Infantry, Col. Abel D. Streight (?s, 0k, 0w, 0m, 0.0%)
73rd Indiana Infantry, Col. Gilbert Hathaway (?s, 0k, 0w, 0m, 0.0%)
13th Michigan Infantry, Lt. Col. F. W. Gordon (?s, 0k, 0w, 0m, 0.0%)
64th Ohio Infantry, Col. John Ferguson (?s, 0k, 0w, 0m, 0.0%)
65th Ohio Infantry, Lt. Col. William Young (?s, 0k. 0w, 0m, 0.0%)
6th Battery, Ohio Light Artillery, Capt. Cullen Bradley (?s, 0k, 0w, 0m, 0.0%)

21ST BRIGADE

Col. George D. Wagner
(1,974s, 0k, 0w, 2m, 0.1%)
15th Indiana Infantry, Lt. Col. Gustavus Wood (?s, 0k, 0w, 0m, 0.0%)
40th Indiana Infantry, Col. John Blake (?s, 0k, 0w, 2m, ?%)
57th Indiana Infantry, Col. Cyrus Hines (?s, 0k, 0w, 0m, 0.0%)
24th Kentucky Infantry, Col. Lewis Braxton Grigsby (?s, 0k, 0w, 0m, 0.0%)
97th Ohio Infantry, Col. John Lane (?s, 0k, 0w, 0m, 0.0%)
10th Battery, Indiana Light Artillery, Capt. Jerome B. Cox (?s, 0k, 0w, 0m, 0.0%)

1ST CAVALRY BRIGADE

Col. Edward D. McCook
(2,000as, 2k, 4w, 4m, 0.5%a)
2nd Indiana Cavalry, Lt. Col. Robert Stewart (?s, 1k, 0w, 0m, ?%)
1st Kentucky Cavalry, Col. Frank Wolford (?s, 1k, 0w, 0m, ?%)
3rd Kentucky Cavalry, Col. Eli Murray (?s, 0k, 0w, 0m, 0.0%)
7th Pennsylvania Cavalry (1st Battalion), Maj. John E. Wynkoop (130s, 0k, 4w, 4m, 1.6%)
Battery M, 4th U.S. Light Artillery (1 section), Lt. Henry A. Huntington (?s, 0k, 0w, 0m, 0.0%)

UNATTACHED

1st Michigan Engineers and Mechanics (Companies B, E, I, K), Col. William Innes (?s, ?k, ?w, ?m, ?%)
1st Ohio Cavalry (4 companies), Maj. James Laughlin (?s, ?k, ?w, ?m, ?%)
3rd Ohio Cavalry (4 companies), Maj. John H. Foster (?s, ?k. ?w, ?m, ?%)

III CORPS

Brig. Gen. ("Acting Maj. Gen.") Charles C. Gilbert
(22,000s, 192k, 672w, 80m, 4.3%)

1ST DIVISION

Brig. Gen. Albin Schoepf
(7,760s, 4k, 14w, 7m, 0.3%)

1ST BRIGADE

Col. Moses B. Walker
(2,326s, 0k, 0w, 8m, 0.3%)
82nd Indiana Infantry, Col. Morton Hunter (?s, 0k, 0w, 0m, 0.0%)
12th Kentucky Infantry, Col. William Hoskins (?s, 0k, 0w, 0m, 0.0%)
17th Ohio Infantry, Col. John Connell (?s, 0k, 0w, 0m, 0.0%)
31st Ohio Infantry, Lt. Col. Frederick Lister (?s, 0k, 0w, 0m, 0.0%)
38th Ohio Infantry. Lt. Col. William Choate (?s, 0k, 0w, 0m, 0.0%)
Battery D, 1st Michigan Light Artillery, Capt. J. W. Church (?s, 0k, 0w, 0m, 0.0%)

2ND BRIGADE

Brig. Gen. Speed S. Fry
(2,391s, 4k, 7w, 0m, 0.5%)
10th Indiana Infantry, Col. William C. Kise (?s, 4k, 7w, 0m, ?%)
74th Indiana Infantry, Col. Charles W. Chapman (?s, 0k, 0w, 0m, 0.0%)
4th Kentucky Infantry, Col. John Croxton (?s, 0k, 0w, 0m,).0%)
10th Kentucky Infantry, Lt. Col. William Hayes (?s, 0k, 0w, 0m, 0.0%)
14th Ohio Infantry, Lt. Col. George Este (?s, 0k, 0w, 0m. 0.0%)
Battery C, 1st Ohio Light Artillery, Capt. D. K. Southwick (?s, 0k, 0w, 0m, 0.0%)

3RD BRIGADE

Brig. Gen. James B. Steedman
(3,043s, 0k, 7w, 7m, 0.5%)
87th Indiana Infantry, Col. Kline G. Shyrock (?s, 0k, 2w, 0m, ?%)
2nd Minnesota Infantry, Col. James George (?s, 0k, 0w, 1m, ?%)
9th Ohio Infantry, Lt. Col. Charles Joseph (?s, 0k, 1w, 2m, ?%)
35th Ohio Infantry, Col. Ferdinand Van Derveer (?s, 0k, 0w, 4m, ?%)
18th U.S. Infantry, Maj. Frederick Townsend (?s, 0k, 3w, 0m, ?%)
Battery I, 4th U.S. Light Artillery, Lt. Frank G. Smith (?s, 0k, 1w, 0m, ?%)

UNATTACHED

1st Ohio Cavalry (6 companies), Col. Minor Milliken (?s, ?k, ?w, ?m, ?%)

9TH DIVISION

Brig. Gen. Robert D. Mitchell
(?s, 133k, 344w, 58m, ?%)

13TH BRIGADE

Col. Michael Gooding (w)
(1,423s, 133k, 344w, 58m, 36.6%)
59th Illinois Infantry, Maj. Joshua C. Winters (325s, 29k, 55w, 29m, 34.7%)
74th Illinois Infantry, Col. James B. Kerr (?s, 0k, 0w, 0m, ?%)
75th Illinois Infantry, Lt. Col. John E. Bennett (730s, 44k, 169w, 12m, 30.1%)
22nd Indiana Infantry, Lt. Col. Squire I. Keith (k) (300s, 59k, 119w, 17m, 65.3%)
5th Battery, Wisconsin Light Artillery, Capt. Oscar F. Pinney (68s, 1k, 1w, 0m, 2.9%)

31ST BRIGADE

Col. William P. Carlin
(?s, 0k, 11w, 0m, ?%)
21st Illinois Infantry, Col. John Alexander (?s, 0k, 6w, 0m, ?%)
38th Illinois Infantry, Maj. Daniel Gilmer (?s, 0k, 0w, 0m, 0.0%)
101st Ohio Infantry, Col. Leander Stem (?s, 0k, 1w, 0m, ?%)
15th Wisconsin Infantry, Col. Hans Christian Heg (?s, 0k, 0w, 0m, 0.0%)
2nd Minnesota Battery (2 sections), Lt. Richard L. Dawley (?s, 0k, 4w, 0m, ?%)

32ND BRIGADE

Col. William W. Caldwell
(?s, 0k, 1w, 0m, ?%)
25th Illinois Infantry, Lt. Col. James McClelland (?s, 0k, 1w, 0m, ?%)
35th Illinois Infantry, Lt. Col. William Chandler (?s, 0k, 0w, 0m, 0.0%)
81st Indiana Infantry, Lt. Col. John Timberlake (?s, 0k, 0w, 0m, 0.0%)
8th Kansas Infantry Battalion, Lt. Col. John Martin (?s, 0k, 0w, 0m, 0.0%)
8th Battery, Wisconsin Light Artillery, Capt. Stephen J. Carpenter (?s, 0k, 0w, 0m, 0.0%)

CAVALRY

36th Illinois Cavalry (Company B), Capt. Samuel B. Sherer (?s, 0k, 0w, 0m, 0.0%)

11TH DIVISION

Brig. Gen. Philip H. Sheridan
(?s, 51k, 288w, 14m, ?%)

35TH BRIGADE

Lt. Col. Bernard Laiboldt
(?s, 22k, 102w, 1m, ?%)
44th Illinois Infantry, Capt. Wallace W. Barrett (290s, 1k, 11w, 0m, 4.1%)
73rd Illinois Infantry, Col. James F. Jaques (?s, 2k, 33w, 0m, ?%)
2nd Missouri Infantry, Capt. Walter Hoppe (?s, 18k, 51w, 1m, ?%)
15th Missouri Infantry, Maj. John Weber (?s, 1k, 7w, 0m, ?%)

36TH BRIGADE

Col. Daniel McCook
(?s, 8k, 62w, 9m, ?%)
85th Illinois Infantry, Col. Robert S. Moore (?s, 6k, 37w, 9m, ?%)
86th Illinois Infantry, Col. David D. Irons (460s, 1k, 14w, 0m, 3.3%)
125th Illinois Infantry, Col. Oscar Harmon (?s, 1k, 8w, 0m, ?%)
52nd Ohio Infantry, Lt. Col. Daniel D. T. Cowen (?s, 0k, 3w, 0m, ?%)

37TH BRIGADE

Col. Nicholas Greusel
(?s, 21k, 118w, 4m, ?%)

36th Illinois Infantry, Capt. Silas Miller (?s, 12k, 61w, 4m, ?%)
88th Illinois Infantry, Col. Francis T. Sherman (?s, 8k, 35w, 0m, ?%)
21st Michigan Infantry, Col. Ambrose Stevens (900s, 0k, 22w, 0m, 2.4%)
24th Wisconsin Infantry, Col. Charles H. Larrabee (1,024s, 1k, 0w, 0m, 0.1%)

ARTILLERY

Battery I, 2nd Illinois Light Artillery, Capt. Charles M. Barnett (?s, 0k, 3w, 0m, ?%)
Battery G, 1st Missouri Light Artillery, Capt. Henry Hescock (?s, 0k, 3w, 0m, ?%)

3RD CAVALRY BRIGADE

Capt. ("Acting Brig. Gen.") Ebenezer Gay
(1,700s, 4k, 13w, 0m, 1.0%)
9th Kentucky Cavalry (Companies A, B, D, F, H, I, K, M), Lt. Col. John Boyle (760as, 0k,
    1w, 1m, 0.2%)
2nd Michigan Cavalry, Lt. Col. Archibald Campbell (w) (300s, 4k, 14w, 1m, 5.7%)
9th Pennsylvania Cavalry, Lt. Col. Thomas James (600s, 0k, 0w, 0m, 0.0%)
2nd Battery, Minnesota Light Artillery (1 section), Capt. William A. Hotchkiss (40as, 0k,
    0w, 0m, 0.0%)

APPENDIX 2

ARTILLERY AT PERRYVILLE[1]

ARMY OF THE MISSISSIPPI

56 guns

RIGHT WING

16 guns

CHEATHAM'S DIVISION

16 guns

DONELSON'S BRIGADE

Carnes's Tennessee Battery (4), 6-pounders

STEWART'S BRIGADE

Stanford's Mississippi Battery (4), 3-inch rifled guns

MANEY'S BRIGADE

Smith's Mississippi Battery (4), 2 6-pounders, 2 12-pounders

SMITH'S BRIGADE

Scott's Tennessee Battery (4), 2 6-pounders, 2 12-pounders

LEFT WING

40 guns

ANDERSON'S DIVISION

18 guns

BROWN'S BRIGADE

Battery A, 14th Battalion Georgia Light Artillery (4), 2 6-pounders, 2 12-pounders

ADAMS'S BRIGADE

5th Company, Washington Artillery (6), 2 6-pounders, 2 12-pounders, 2 3.3-inch rifled guns

POWELL'S BRIGADE

Barret's Missouri Battery (4), 2 6-pounders, 2 12-pounders

JONES'S BRIGADE

Battery F, 2nd Alabama Light Artillery (4), 4 12-pounders

BUCKNER'S DIVISION

20 guns

LIDDELL'S BRIGADE

Swett's Mississippi Battery (8), 6 6-pounders, 2 12-pounders

CLEBURNE'S BRIGADE

Calvert's Arkansas Battery (1 section) (2), 2 12-pounders

JOHNSON'S BRIGADE

Darden's Mississippi Battery (4), 2 6-pounders, 2 12-pounders

WOOD'S BRIGADE

Semple's Alabama Battery (6), 4 12-pounders, 2 3.8-inch rifled guns

WHARTON'S CAVALRY BRIGADE

Calvert's Arkansas Battery (1 section) (2), 2 6-pounders

ARMY OF THE OHIO

147 guns

I Corps

38 guns

3rd Division

24 guns

9th Brigade

5th Battery, Indiana Light Artillery (6), 2 6-pounders, 2-12 pounders, 2 3.8-inch rifled guns

17th Brigade

Battery A, 1st Michigan Light Artillery (6), 6 Parrott rifles

28th Brigade

4th Battery, Indiana Light Artillery (6), 2 6-pounders, 2 12-pounders, 2 3.8-inch rifled guns
Battery A, 1st Kentucky Light Artillery (6), 2 6-pounders, 2 Parrott rifles, 2 3.8-inch rifled guns

10th Division

14 guns

33rd Brigade

Parsons's Improvised Battery (8), 7 12-pounders, 1 Parrott rifle

34th Brigade

19th Battery Indiana Light Artillery (6), 4 12-pounders, 2 3-inch rifles

II Corps

65 guns

4th Division

27 guns

10th Brigade

Battery H, 4th U.S. Light Artillery (6), 4 12-pounders, 2 Parrott rifles
Battery M, 4th U.S. Light Artillery (2 sections) (4), 2 12-pounders, 2 24-pounders

19th Brigade

Battery F, 1st Ohio Light Artillery (11), 6 12-pounders, 5 3.8-inch rifled guns

22ND BRIGADE

Battery B, 1st Ohio Light Artillery (6), 2 6-pounders, 4 3.8-inch rifles

5TH DIVISION

18 guns

11TH BRIGADE

7th Battery, Indiana Light Artillery (6), 2 12-pounders, 4 Parrott rifles

14TH BRIGADE

Battery B, 26th Pennsylvania Light Artillery (6), 6 6-pounders

23RD BRIGADE

3rd Battery, Wisconsin Light Artillery (6), 2 12-pounders, 4 Parrott rifles

6TH DIVISION

18 guns

15TH BRIGADE

8th Battery, Indiana Light Artillery (6), 4 6-pounders, 2 12-pounders

20TH BRIGADE

6th Battery, Ohio Light Artillery (6), 2 12-pounders, 4 Parrott rifles

21ST BRIGADE

10th Battery, Indiana Light Artillery (6), 2 12-pounders, 4 Parrott rifles

CAVALRY BRIGADE

Battery M, 4th U.S. Light Artillery (1 section) (2), 2 12-pounders

III CORPS

44 guns

1ST DIVISION

14 guns

1ST BRIGADE

Battery D, 1st Michigan Light Artillery (4), 2 12-pounders, 2 3.8-inch rifled guns

2ND BRIGADE

Battery C, 1st Ohio Light Artillery (6), 2 12-pounders, 4 3.8-inch rifled guns

3RD BRIGADE

Battery I, 4th U.S. Light Artillery (4), 4 12-pounders

9TH DIVISION

16 guns

30TH BRIGADE

5th Battery, Wisconsin Light Artillery (6), 4 12-pounders, 2 Parrott rifles

31ST BRIGADE

2nd Battery, Minnesota Light Artillery (2 sections) (4), 4 12-pounders

32ND BRIGADE

8th Battery, Indiana Light Artillery (6), 2 12-pounders, 4 3-inch rifled guns

11TH DIVISION

12 guns

Battery I, 2nd Illinois Light Artillery (6) 2 12-pounders, 2 Parrott rifles, 2 3.8-inch rifled guns
Battery G, 1st Missouri Light Artillery (6), 4 12-pounders, 2 Parrott Rifles

3RD CAVALRY BRIGADE

2nd Battery, Minnesota Light Artillery (1 section) (2), 2 12-pounders

NOTES

INTRODUCTION

1. "An Ex-Kentuckian" [pseud.], "Kentucky Invasion of 1862," 409. On the idea of historic memory, I am strongly influenced by Kammen, *Mystic Chords of Memory*.

2. *OR* 1, 16, pt. 1, 1055. *OR* citations are given by series number, volume number, part number if applicable, and page numbers.

3. Watkins, *"Co. Aytch,"* 61, 63.

4. Thatcher, *Hundred Battles*, 75.

5. Connolly, *Army of the Heartland*, x–xiv; and more especially *Marble Man*; Foster, *Ghosts of the Confederacy*, esp. 47–62, 91–95, 115–26, 180–91; Kammen, *Mystic Chords of Memory*, 9–10; McDonough, *War in Kentucky*, xii–xiii; 323–25; McMurry, *Two Great Rebel Armies*, 1–5; Piston, *Lee's Tarnished Lieutenant*, 95–188.

6. See, for example, Gallagher, *Confederate War.*

7. Notably, see Connolly, *Army of the Heartland*; Engle, *Don Carlos Buell*; Harrison, *Civil War in Kentucky*; Jones, *Confederate Strategy*; McMurry, *Two Great Rebel Armies*; McWhiney, *Braxton Bragg*; Woodworth, *Jefferson Davis.*

8. Hafendorfer, *Perryville*; Hess, *Banners to the Breeze*; McDonough, *War in Kentucky*. Hess's work appeared just as I completed this volume, but his account of the battle largely is derived from Hafendorfer and McDonough. Brief treatments include Grimsley, "A Wade in the High Tide," 18, 22, 24, 26; Harrison, "Perryville: Death on a Dry River," 4–6, 8–9, 44–47; Sanders, "'Every Mother's Son',"; and two treatments by Richard J. Reid, *Army That Buell Built* and *They Met at Perryville*. See also my initial Perryville foray, a paper given in 1997 and published three years later as Noe, "'Grand Havoc.'" Several of my interpretations have, to be sure, evolved since then.

9. Vinovskis, "Social Historians," 34–58.

10. Rable, "'Missing in Action,'" 134. In regard to the academic attitudes, I must point to a colleague who, told of my plans to write about a Civil War battle, responded, "But Ken, what about your career?"

11. McPherson, Foreword to Clinton and Silber, *Divided Houses*, esp. xiv–xvi. McPherson expanded upon the same ideas in *Drawn With the Sword*, 231–53.

12. A complete list would be vast, as proven in one earlier attempt, Noe and Wilson, eds., *Civil War in Appalachia*, xxix–xxx, n 6. Examples that particularly influenced me in writing about Perryville would include Daniel, *Soldiering*; Gramm, "Chances of War," 75–100; Grimsley, *Hard Hand of War*; Hess, *Union Soldier in Battle*; Linderman, *Embattled Courage*; Mitchell, *Civil War Soldiers*, and *Vacant Chair*; Power, *Lee's Miserables*; Priest, *Antietam*; Rable, "'It Is Well That War Is So Terrible,'" 48–79; Sutherland, *Seasons of War*; Wilkinson, *Never See the Sights*. I would also point to a book about the American Revolution, Babits, *Devil of a Whipping.*

13. Piston and Hatcher III, *Wilson's Creek*. Indeed, Piston influenced my Perryville research almost at the moment I began to conceive it with an unpublished paper, "'Beyond Drums and Trumpets,'" presented at the Southern Historical Association meeting in Louisville, Nov. 10, 1994. Another volume that went beyond the usual, although not strictly social history, is Shea and Hess, *Pea Ridge*. I would also point to two other books, more traditional yet model battle narratives that nonetheless shaped this volume: Hennessy, *Return to Bull Run;* and Rhea, *Battle of the Wilderness*.

14. Readers only vaguely familiar with terms such as "poststructuralism" and "postmodernism," both increasingly value laden in political discourse, will profit from Storey, *Introductory Guide*, esp. 69–96, 154–80. For more mainstream attempts to wrestle with the same problem, see Fussell, *Great War and Modern Memory*, 169–79, 310–15; Hess, *Union Soldier in Battle*, esp. 158–90; and Linderman, *Embattled Courage*, 3, 266–97.

15. Marshall. Foreword to Sword, *Shiloh*, ix.

16. In quoting soldiers, I do not change spelling or punctuation except when vitally necessary, and then I use brackets to indicate such changes. All emphasized words appeared as such in the original texts. With regard to letters, for the sake of brevity I cite only the closest town rather than leave the long descriptions soldiers sometimes used, such as "at Camp Jones 4 mi. North of Smith, Kentucky."

17. Whitman, *Works of Walt Whitman*, vol. 2, 76, 31.

CHAPTER 1

1. Trollope, *North America*, vol. 2, 71, 78; Glendinning, *Anthony Trollope*, 26–31, 306–19.

2. Trollope, *North America*, vol. 2, 72.

3. Ibid., 75–78, 108 (first quotation, 108; second quotation 77, third quotation, 74); Glendinning, *Trollope*, 318–19.

4. Trollope, *North America*, 109–13 (quotation, 111).

5. Ibid., 113.

6. Miller and Smith, eds., *Dictionary of Afro-American Slavery*, 383.

7. Lambert, *Ripe Pears*, xv–xvii, 1–2; Peck, *Berea's First Century*, 1–19; Kleber, ed., *Kentucky Encyclopedia*, 828.

8. The standard source remains Coulter's dated *Civil War and Readjustment*, see esp. 1–18. It should be supplemented with Harrison, *Civil War in Kentucky*, 1–4, as well as Harrison's "Civil War in Kentucky," 2; Davis, *Orphan Brigade*, 1–6; and McMurry, "Union and Confederate Grand Strategy."

9. *B&L*, vol. 2, 373–74; Coulter, *Civil War and Readjustment*, 19–25; Davis, *Breckinridge*, 222–47; Harrison, *Civil War in Kentucky*, 3–4.

10. Johnston, "Kentucky," 19.

11. *OR* 1, 2, 678; *OR* 1, 4, 546. See also Cheek, ed., "Mrs. E. B. Patterson," 349–50; *B&L*, vol. 2, 374; Coulter, *Civil War and Readjustment*, 25–56, 82–84, 87; Harrison, "Civil War in Kentucky," 3–4; Harrison, *Civil War in Kentucky*, 6–10 (quotation, 9); Johnston, "Kentucky," 20–23, 25–27, 33–35; Davis, *Orphan Brigade*, 6–11; Stickles, *Simon Bolivar Buckner*, 5–69.

12. *OR* 1, 4, 367, 373–74, 376, 378; *B&L*, vol. 2, 377.

13. Johnston, "Kentucky," 22–23.

14. Harrison, *Civil War in Kentucky*, 9.

15. *B&L*, vol. 2, 374. See also *OR* 1, 4, 396–97, 399–400; Jacobs, "Campaigning with Buell," 3; Davis, *Breckinridge*, 266–67.

16. See McDonough, *War in Kentucky*, 61.

17. Abraham Lincoln to Orville H. Browning, Sept. 22, 1861, in Basler, ed., *Abraham Lincoln*, vol. 4, 532.

18. Coulter, *Civil War and Readjustment*, 9; McDonough, *War in Kentucky*, 61–63; McPherson, *Battle Cry of Freedom*, 284.

19. *OR* 1, 4, 251, 254, 257, 378, 450–51; *B&L*, vol. 2, 375–78; Farrelly, "John Marshall Harlan," 8, 14–15; Coulter, *Civil War and Readjustment*, 57–80, 94–110; Harrison, *Civil War in Kentucky*, 10–14; Jenkins, "Shooting at the Galt House," 103; Johnston, "Kentucky," 25, 30–31; McDowell, *City of Conflict*, 2–3; Roland, *Albert Sidney Johnston*, 262; Stickles, *Simon Bolivar Buckner*, 84–85.

20. *OR* 1, 3, 478, 619, 685–87, 699, 733; *OR* 1, 4, 176–89, 190, 196–99, 287–89, 363–64, 402, 403, 451; *B&L*, vol. 2, 378–79; Davis, *Jefferson Davis*, 28–29, 376–77; Connelly, *Army of the Heartland*, 46–55; Coulter, *Civil War and Readjustment*, 106–10, 114–20; Davis, *Breckinridge*, 285; Harrison, *Civil War in Kentucky*, 12; Simon, "Holding Kentucky for the Union, 1861."

21. *OR* 1, 4: 288; Jacobs, "Campaigning with Buell," 3; Coulter, *Civil War and Readjustment*, 125–31; McDowell, *City of Conflict*, 1.

22. *OR* 1, 4, 193–94, 205–14, 284–85, 291, 310–11, 321, 368–69, 402–6, 420–21, 439, 444, 448, 455, 462–63, 483; Connelly, *Army of the Heartland*, 4, 14–25, 63–72, 74–77, 78–85; Davis, *Jefferson Davis*, 377–78, 380; Hughes, *General William J. Hardee*, 81–82; Stickles, *Simon Bolivar Buckner*, 86–87, 93–98.

23. Harrison, *Civil War in Kentucky*, 20–23.

24. Marszalek, *Sherman*, 154–64.

25. Engle's *Don Carlos Buell* thankfully appeared just as this work was completed. See esp. xi–98 for Buell's early career. See also *OR* 1, 4: 342, 349, 358; Chumney, "Don Carlos Buell," 1–7; *B&L*, vol. 2, 385; Reid, *They Met at Perryville*, 4.

26. This sketch of Buell is based on *OR* 1, 7, 443–44, 447, 450, 457–58, 468, 473–74, 480, 526, 530–31, 532–33, 926, 927, 928–29, 931–33; *OR* 1, 16, pt. 1, 24; *B&L*, vol. 2, 385–86; Engle, *Don Carlos Buell*, 16–18, 35, 42, 45–49, 54, 66, 77–78, 68–69, 95, 98–113, 116–20; Chumney, "Don Carlos Buell," 7–9, 27–50; Engle, "Don Carlos Buell," 89–98; Cooling, *Fort Donelson's Legacy*, 18; Frank and Reaves, "*Seeing the Elephant*," 61, 73–74; Grimsley, *Hard Hand of War*, 63–64. For the railroad, see Brown, "Battle of Munfordville," 137–39.

27. Transcript, *New York Times*, Aug. 7, 1864, McCook Family Papers, LC.

28. *OR* 1, 7, 443–44. See also Engle, "Don Carlos Buell," 96–97; Engle, *Don Carlos Buell*, 51–52.

29. *OR* 1, 3, 570; *OR* 1, 4, 278–79, 295, 297, 299, 300, 306–8, 314, 324–25, 327, 333, 341, 350, 357–58; *OR* 1, 7, 75–116, 459, 475, 492, 753, 773; *B&L*, vol. 2, 387–97; Connelly, *Army of the Heartland*, 86–99, 103–39; Coulter, *Civil War and Readjustment*, 133–36; Engle, "Don Carlos Buell," 98–100; Engle, *Don Carlos Buell*, 89–90, 152–55; Harrison, *Civil War in Kentucky*, 23–32; Johnston, "Kentucky," 53–65. Harrison, in "Civil War in Kentucky," 5–10, maintains that Johnston never really had a chance to hold Kentucky, but worsened his odds even more by spreading out his forces too much.

30. For the Confederate retreat from Nashville and the concentration at Corinth, see Connelly, *Army of the Heartland*, 3–10, 126–42; Cooling, *Fort Donelson's Legacy*, 26–28, 47–49; Daniel, *Shiloh*; Frank and Reaves, "*Seeing the Elephant*," 12–13, 70–71; Hughes, *General William J. Hardee*, 90–98; and Sword, *Shiloh*, 49–84.

31. The preceding paragraphs are drawn from McWhiney's definitive biography, *Braxton Bragg*, 1–227. See also *OR* 1, 1, 448; "Gen. and Mrs. Braxton Bragg," 103; Davis, *Jefferson Davis*, 158, 160, 311, 331–33, 400; Jones, *Confederate Strategy*, 55; McDonough, *War in Kentucky*, 2; and Sword, *Shiloh*, 75–83.

32. Hallock, *Braxton Bragg*, 4–5, 269–73.

33. Goodwin and Jamison, *Manic-Depressive Illness*, esp. 3–11, 22–29, 36–44, 55–70, 128–29, 142–46, 356–60; Jackson, *Melancholia and Depression*, esp. 3, 188–95, 217, 243, 249–310, 386.

34. Johnson, *Character Styles*, 41–47, 155–91. I am grateful to psychologist Tobin Hart for both suggesting this source and narcissistic personality disorder in general.

35. *OR* 1, 7, 595; *OR* 1, 10, pt. 2, 28–29, 613; Connelly, *Army of the Heartland*, 139–42; Daniel, *Shiloh*, 69–70, 112–14; Engle, "Don Carlos Buell," 103; Engle, *Don Carlos Buell*, 171–72, 215–16; Frank and Reaves, "*Seeing the Elephant*," 12; Sword, *Shiloh*, 82–86, 90–1, 115–16.

36. For the battle itself, see Daniel, *Shiloh*, 143–303; McDonough, *Shiloh*, 86–213; and Sword, *Shiloh*, 141–422.

37. Frank and Reeves, "*Seeing the Elephant*," 129, 134–41, 152, 161–63, 168.

38. *OR* 1, 16, pt. 1, 88; Daniel, *Shiloh*, 252–56, 265–66, 293–94, 305, 306–7; Engle, "Don Carlos Buell," 103; Frank and Reaves, "*Seeing the Elephant*," 142–44; Sword, *Shiloh*, 439. The controversy over who won at Shiloh dragged on for decades, eventually pitting Buell against Grants and Sherman. See Engle, *Don Carlos Buell*, 235–6, 239, 353–58.

39. McWhiney, *Braxton Bragg*, 228–60; Frank and Reaves, "*Seeing the Elephant*," 143–45; Connelly, *Army of the Heartland*, 166–67.

40. McPherson, *Battle Cry of Freedom*, 416. See also Trask Journal, 28, W. L. Trask Papers no. 380, EU (hereafter Trask Journal).

41. Connelly, *Army of the Heartland*, 177–83; Cozzens, *Darkest Days*, 40.

42. *OR* 1, 17, pt. 2, 601, 614.

CHAPTER 2

1. Braxton Bragg telegram, book 32, no. 54, Lewis Leigh Jr. Collection, USAMHI.

2. *OR* 1, 17, pt. 2, 626.

3. *OR* 1, 16, pt. 1, 83; *OR* 1, 17, pt. 2, 618; Bragg telegram, Leigh Collection, USAMHI; Ezekiel John Ellis War Recollections, 47, Civil War Miscellaneous Collection—New Material, USAMHI (hereafter Ellis War Recollections); John Forman to Sarah Newell, July 28, 1862, Robert A. Newell Papers, LSU; Trask Journal, 29; *B&L*, vol. 3, 2; Kundahl, *Confederate Engineer*, 154; McWhiney, *Braxton Bragg*, 274–77; McWhiney, "Controversy in Kentucky," 6–9. Manic-depression would not preclude such successes; see Goodwin and Jamison, *Manic-Depressive Illness*, 356–60.

4. *OR* 1, 17, pt. 2, 626; Hattaway and Jones, *How the North Won*, 217.

5. E. John Ellis Diary, 24, LSU (hereafter Ellis Diary).

6. Watkins, "*Co, Aytch*," 56.

7. Trask Journal, 29.

8. Buie to his father, Sept. 30, 1862, John Buie Papers, Duke.

9. Ellis War Recollections, 41, 46. See also Dr. S.H. Stout's comments in "Tributes to Gen. Braxton Bragg," 132. Stout claimed that instead of a chicken, the soldier actually shot "a negro child."

10. *OR* 1, 16, pt. 2, 8, 62–63; *OR* 1, 17, pt. 2, 618. Halleck's decision to divide the army was criticized by, among others, Bruce Catton and Allan Nevins. More recently, Halleck has been defended more or less by Herman Hattaway and Archer Jones, Earl J. Hess, Nathaniel Cheairs Hughes Jr., James Lee McDonough, and James M. McPherson. See Catton, *Grant Moves South*, 278–80; Hattaway and Jones, *How the North Won*, 205–8, 214–17; Hess, *Banners to the Breeze*, 3–6; Hughes, *General William J. Hardee*, 117–18; McDonough, *War in Kentucky*, 32–42; McPherson, *Battle Cry of Freedom*, 511–13; and

Nevins, *War for the Union*, vol. 2, 112. Cozzens, in *Darkest Days*, notes that by June 35 percent of the men in the force occupying Corinth were sick anyway.

11. *OR* 1, 10, pt. 1, 641–43; *OR* 1, 10, pt. 2, 280; *OR* 1, 16, pt. 1, 30–31; *OR* 1, 16, pt. 2: 8, 62–63; *B&L*, vol. 3, 31–35; *B&L*, vol. 3, 1; Engle, "Don Carlos Buell," 104–5; Engle, *Don Carlos Buell*, 202–4, 212, 243, 245–47; Gates, *Agriculture and the Civil War*, 86, 116; Lambert, *Ripe Pears*, 2; McPherson, *Battle Cry of Freedom*, 511–13.

12. *B&L*, vol. 3, 35–38; Noe, ed., *Southern Boy in Blue*, 77–83; Patterson, ed., *Campaigns of the 38th Illinois*, 10–11; Shaw, *Tenth Regiment*, 168; Engle, "Don Carlos Buell," 105–9; *OR* 1, 16, pt. 2, 104, 360–61; McDonough, *War in Kentucky*, 42–60.

13. *B&L*, vol. 3, 35.

14. McDonough, *War in Kentucky*, 71–74; McWhiney, *Braxton Bragg*, 261–68; Woodworth, *Jefferson Davis*, 129–31; Jackson, *Melancholia and Depression*, 201. Even Halleck's leading modern defenders, Herman Hattaway and Archer Jones, criticize Halleck's strategy regarding Buell, although they blame it ultimately on Old Brains's "optimism and inadequate information" (*How the North Won*, 214–15). In fact, Halleck had all the information he needed had he taken Buell's reports seriously.

15. *B&L*, vol. 3, 1–2; McWhiney, *Braxton Bragg*, 266–68. McWhiney suggests the possibility of a fifth factor, namely Elise Bragg, who urged her husband to advance into Tennessee. McWhiney wisely points out, however, that there is no way to be sure whether Elise was telling Bragg what he wanted to hear or truly expressing her strategic ideas.

16. *B&L*, vol. 3, 600.

17. Harrison, "George W. Johnson," Harrison, *Civil War in Kentucky*, 80–83; Connelly and Jones, *The Politics of Command*, 52–76; Davis, *Jefferson Davis*, 379–80, 465; Donaldson, "'Into Africa'," 448, 450; McMurry, *Two Great Rebel Armies*, 10–13, 169; Coulter, *Civil War and Readjustment*, 147–60.

18. Historians variously refer to the general as "Smith" or "Kirby Smith." He himself used Smith until 1861, when he began to sign his name E. Kirby Smith to set him apart from other Smiths in the army. After his death, the family changed the name to Kirby-Smith. His biographer uses Smith when discussing the prewar years and Kirby Smith thereafter. That precedent is followed here. See Parks, *General Edmund Kirby Smith*, 117–19.

19. Parks, *General Edmund Kirby Smith*, 6–155; Davis, *Battle at Bull Run*, 224–26, 23–31; Davis, *Jefferson Davis*, 314, 400, 449, 462.

20. *B&L*, vol. 3, 62–64; Woodworth, *Jefferson Davis*, 125–28; Parks, *General Edmund Kirby Smith*, 155–74; Groce, "Social Origins," in *Civil War in Appalachia*, ed. Noe and Wilson, 30–48; Wallenstein, "'Helping to Save the Union,'" in *Civil War in Appalachia*, ed. Noe and Wilson, 1–18.

21. *OR* 1, 16, pt. 2, 727, 729, 730; Cozzens, *Darkest Days*, 39; McWhiney, "Controversy in Kentucky," 9–10; Parks, *General Edmund Kirby Smith*, 195–99.

22. *OR* 1, 16, pt. 2, 734–35.

23. McDonough, *War in Kentucky*, 70. Hess, in *Banners to the Breeze*, 20–21, is more sympathetic to Bragg's inaction, linking it at least in part to the paucity of wagons in his army.

24. *OR* 1, 52, pt. 2, 330; Woodworth, *Jefferson Davis*, 134–35; Goodwin and Jamison, *Manic-Depressive Illness*, 356–57.

25. *OR* 1, 52, pt. 2, 331–32. Beauregard completely agreed with Bragg. Connelly and Jones, in *Politics of Command*, 104–5, note the emergence of the salient ideas of the so-called western concentration bloc in the plan.

26. Ellis War Recollections, 48; Forman to Newell, July 28, 1862, Newel Papers, LSU; Cross, *Camp and Field*, 35–36; Little and Maxwell, *History of Lumsden's Battery*, 9–

10; Sutherland, ed., *Reminiscences*, 87; Connelly, *Army of the Heartland*, 202–4; Hattaway and Jones, *How the North Won*, 218; Jones, *Confederate Strategy*, 73; Parks, *General Edmund Kirby Smith*, 199.

27. "William P. Rogers," 64–65.

28. Semmes to his wife, Aug. 8, 1862, Benedict J. Semmes Papers, SHC-UNC.

29. Patrick to his sister, Apr. 1, 1862, Robert D. Patrick Letters, LSU.

30. *OR* 1, 16, pt. 1, 731–84; Harrison, *Civil War in Kentucky*, 35–40.

31. Cheek, ed., "Mrs. E. B. Patterson," 351–69, describes the panic Morgan could create from a local perspective. For the wider reaction, see Basler, *Abraham Lincoln*, vol. 5, 322; Harrison, *Civil War in Kentucky*, 38.

32. *OR* 1, 16, pt. 2, 733–34. See also *OR* 1, 16, pt. 1, 768–70.

33. Parks, *General Edmund Kirby Smith*, 201–2.

34. Kirby Smith to his wife, Aug. 1, 1862, Edmund Kirby Smith Papers, SHC-UNC.

35. *OR* 1, 16, pt. 2, 741.

36. Connelly, *Army of the Heartland*, 207. McDonough, in *War in Kentucky*, 78, is more favorable in his assessment.

37. Crist, ed., *Papers of Jefferson Davis*, vol. 8, 322; Davis, *Jefferson Davis*, 465–66.

38. *OR* 1, 16, pt. 2, 745–46; *OR* 1, 17, pt. 2, 619, 627; Connelly, *Army of the Heartland*, 206–7; Connelly and Jones, *Politics of Command*, 106–7; Davis, *Jefferson Davis*, 406; McWhiney, *Braxton Bragg*, 273; Woodworth, *Jefferson Davis*, 135–37.

39. Lambert, *Ripe Pears*, 7; Warner, *Generals in Gray*, 283.

40. Symonds, *Stonewall of the West*, 10–87.

41. *OR* 1, 16, pt. 2, 748; Lambert, *Ripe Pears*, 7.

42. *OR* 1, 16, pt. 2, 748–49.

43. McWhiney, *Braxton Bragg*, 274; Woodworth, *Jefferson Davis*, 137.

44. Woodworth, *Jefferson Davis*, 137–38. After reviewing this passage, psychologist Tobin Hart suggested that Kirby Smith, like Bragg, may have been a narcissistic personality. If so, their relationship was a recipe for disaster from the beginning.

45. *OR* 1, 16, pt. 2, 751.

46. Ibid., 752–53; Davis, *Jefferson Davis*, 314, 400, 441.

47. *OR* 1, 16, pt. 2, 754–55; *OR* 1, 17, pt. 1, 119–21, 376–77; *OR* 1, 17, pt. 2, 675–76, 677, 682, 683, 685, 687, 688, 690, 691–93, 694, 695–96. By the far the best account of Van Dorn, Price, and the Iuka-Corinth campaign is Cozzens, *Darkest Days*.

48. *OR* 1, 16, pt. 2, 754–55, 755–56.

49. "Life of Augustus Cabarrus Kean," 11–13, Cabarrus and Slade Family Papers, SHC-UNC; "William P. Rogers," 66; *OR* 1, 16, pt. 2, 775–76, 780; Brown, "On the Firing Line," 331; Connelly, *Army of the Heartland*, 212. Hess, in *Banners to the Breeze*, 32, also stresses Kirby Smith's knowledge of terrain.

50. "William P. Rogers," 66–67. See also "Fighting Forty-eighth Tennessee," 247.

51. *OR* 1, 16, pt. 2, 766–67; 768–69, 771, 780; Donaldson, "'Into Africa'," 453.

52. Connelly, *Army of the Heartland*, 212–13. See also Woodworth, *Jefferson Davis*, 138.

53. The definitive account of the battle and its aftermath is Lambert, *Ripe Pears*. See also Frierson, "Campaign in Kentucky," 295; Ryan, "Kentucky Campaign," 158–60; "Fighting Forty-eighth Tennessee," 247–48; *B&L*, vol. 3, 5.

54. Lindsley, ed., *Military Annals*, vol. 1, 148; Ryan, "Kentucky Campaign," 160; Symonds, *Stonewall of the West*, 89–92; Semmes to his wife, Oct. 1, 1862, Benedict J. Semmes Papers, SHC-UNC.

55. "William P. Rogers," 69.

56. "Fighting Forty-eighth Tennessee," 248.

57. "Life of Augustus Cabarrus Kean," 14–15, Cabarrus and Slade Family Papers, SHC-UNC (hereafter "Augustus Cabarrus Kean"); William French to Chalaron, Sept. 6, 1862, J. A. Chalaron Papers, TU; Donaldson, "'Into Africa'," 459.

58. Kirby Smith to his wife, Sept. 4, 6, and 20, 1862, Smith Papers, SHC-UNC.

59. *OR* 1, 16, pt. 2, 796, 797, 799, 804–807, 811–12, 814–15, 821, 830, 831; Hammond, "Kirby Smith's Campaign," 70; Connelly, *Army of the Heartland*, 217–20; McDonough, *War in Kentucky*, 153–54.

60. *OR* 1, 16, pt. 2, 846.

61. Ibid., 830.

62. Ibid., 830.

CHAPTER 3

1. Millard, "Battle of Perryville," 1. See also Engle, *Don Carlos Buell*, 264.

2. Warner, *Generals in Blue*, 100.

3. Wright, "West Point," 18; Warner, *Generals in Blue*, 294; McDonough, *War in Kentucky*, 206.

4. K. McCook Knox, trans., "Recollections of Hettie Beatty McCook," McCook Family Papers, LC.

5. George Landrum to Mrs. Obed J. Wilson, Aug. 11, 1862, George W. Landrum Letters, OHS. See also Landrum's letter of Aug. 19, 1862 as well as *OR* 1, 16, pt. 1, 517–18; and Hess, *Banners to the Breeze*, 9–10.

6. *OR* 1, 16, pt. 1, 106, 164, 247, 250, 473–76, 602–7; *OR* 1, 16, pt. 2, 32–35; *B&L*, vol. 3, 35–39; General Orders no. 56, 63, Hazen Letter Book, USAMHI; Landrum to Mrs. Obed J. Wilson, Aug. 11 and 19, 1862, Landrum Letters, OHS; Putnam, *Journalistic History*, vol. 1, 112–13; Wright, "Glimpse of Perryville," 149; *Cincinnati Daily Commercial*, Oct. 1, 1862; Engle, "Don Carlos Buell," 105–13, Engle, *Don Carlos Buell*, 246. Occasionally, Federals also acquired food from Confederate pickets through trade. Benjamin Scribner of the 38th Indiana Infantry described a brisk trade at Battle Creek with the 3rd Florida Infantry. See Scribner, Camp Solomon, Battle Creek, to Ned, July 24, 1862, Scribner Letters, InHS.

7. Putnam, *Journalistic History*, 112.

8. *OR* 1, 10, pt. 2, 213, 294, 295; *OR* 1, 16, pt. 1, 347–49, 350, 354–55, 477–79, 637, 640, 642–44; *OR* 1, 16, pt. 2, 71, 80, 92, 99, 273–78; McCook to his aunt, Aug. 8, 1862, McCook Family Papers, LC; *Louisville Daily Journal*, Sept. 12, 1862; Engle, *Don Carlos Buell*, 264, 267–69; Grimsley, *Hard Hand of War*, 78–85; Warner, *Generals in Blue*, 511.

9. Putnam, *Journalistic History*, 113. See also Grebner, *"We Were the Ninth,"* 109–11; Mills, *My Story*, 84–85.

10. *OR* 1, 16, pt. 1, 607; *OR* 1, 16, pt. 2, 35–36; *B&L*, vol. 3, 37–38; Engle, *Don Carlos Buell*, 275–76; Hess, *Banners to the Breeze*, 11–12.

11. *OR* 1, 16, pt. 1, 14–15, 36–40, 41, 87, 109, 131, 147, 150, 153; *OR* 1, 16, pt. 2, 381, 383, 387–88, 389, 406–7, 416–17; *B&L*, vol. 3, 37–40; Hess, *Banners to the Breeze*, 12.

12. *OR* 1, 16, pt. 1, 107; *OR* 1, 16, pt. 2, 37–38; *B&L*, vol. 3, 40–41.

13. *B&L*, vol. 3, 40.

14. *OR* 1, 16, pt. 2, 376.

15. *OR* 1, 16, pt. 1, 102; 109–10; *OR* 1, 16, pt. 2, 377, 381, 418, 429, 438; Grose, *Story of the Marches*, 127–28; Keil, *Thirty-fifth Ohio*, 90; *B&L*, vol. 3, 40.

16. *OR* 1, 16, pt. 1, 39; *OR* 1, 16, pt. 2, 376; F. J. Jones to Lt. Col. Burke, Aug. 22, 1862, Jones to Col. W. H. Lytle, Aug. 22 and 23, 1862, Jones to Dr. Parks, Aug. 24, 1862, telegrams to Maj. Gen. Buell, Aug. 22, 1862, and W. P. McDowell to Capt. J. R. Paul,

Aug. 29, 1862, all in Army of the Ohio and 14th Army Corps, Letters and Circulars Sent, vol. 16, RG 393, NARA; Phelps to friends, Aug. 28, 1862, Frank M. Phelps Letters, Lewis Leigh Jr. Collection, USAMHI; Scribner, *How Soldiers Were Made*, 53.

17. *OR* 1, 16, pt. 1, 605. Most of Buell's witnesses touched on the matter, but see especially ibid., 279, 328, 519, 474–76, 627–30, 634–36.

18. *OR* 1, 16, pt. 1, 157, 218, 228; Phelps to friends, Aug. 28, 1862, Phelps Letters, USAMHI; Sturges to his family, Aug. 29, 1862, Eden P. Sturges Correspondence, *Civil War Times Illustrated* Collection, USAMHI; Butler, *My Story*, 162–63, 166–73; Grebner, *"We Were the Ninth,"* 111; Hinman, *Sherman Brigade*, 248–58; *History of the Services*, 12; Inskeep Diary, Aug. 27, 28, 1862, OHS (hereafter Inskeep Diary); Shaw, *Tenth Regiment*, 168; Thomas to his sister, Sept. 8, 1862, James S. Thomas Letters, InHS; Levi Wagner Memoirs, 40, *Civil War Times Illustrated* Collection, USAMHI (hereafter Wagner Memoirs); Winn Diary, Aug. 26, 1862, OHS (hereafter Winn Diary); *Cincinnati Daily Commercial*, Oct. 1, 1862.

19. Keil, *Thirty-fifth Ohio*, 90.

20. Butler, *My Story*, 172; Grebner, *"We Were the Ninth,"* 110.

21. Hinman, *Sherman Brigade*, 254.

22. Keil, *Thirty-fifth Ohio*, 91.

23. Trask Journal, 37–38.

24. Winn Diary, Aug. 27, 29, and 31, 1862.

25. Stuckey to Helen Stuckey, Aug. 25, 1862, William Roberts Stuckey Letters, InHS.

26. Keil, *Thirty-fifth Ohio*, 91; *OR* 1, 16, pt. 1, 350, 354; *OR* 1, 16, pt. 2, 451.

27. Noe, ed., *Southern Boy in Blue*, 89.

28. *OR* 1, 16, pt. 1, 39; *B&L*, vol. 3, 40; Rerick, *Forty-fourth Indiana*, 67–68.

29. Hinman, *Sherman Brigade*, 250.

30. *OR* 1, 16, pt. 1, 41, 139–40, 154, 155, 156, 182–83, 188, 189, 191, 202–3, 552; *OR* 1, 16, pt. 2, 391–93; *B&L*, vol. 3, 7; Grose, *Story of the Marches*, 128.

31. *OR* 1, 16, pt. 2, 399–400. See also *OR* 1, 16, pt. 1, 361, 362, 364, 387–88, 398.

32. *OR* 1, 16, pt. 2, 410, 420–21.

33. *OR* 1, 16, pt. 2, 419. See also Jacobs, "Campaigning with Buell," 3.

34. *OR* 1, 16, pt. 2, 406–7; *OR* 1, 16, pt. 2, 40–42.

35. Trask Journal, 31–33.

36. Noe, ed., *Southern Boy in Blue*, 84. B. F. Scribner remembered that "much chaff and bandinage passed to and fro between the men, for the river was low and the distance short (*How Soldiers Were Made*, 52).

37. Hartpence, *Fifty-first Indiana*, 76–77.

38. Grose, *Story of the Marches*, 128.

39. Noe, ed., *Southern Boy in Blue*, 88.

40. Landrum to Mrs. Wilson, Aug. 19, 1862, Landrum Letters, OHS. See also Anderson, ed., *Nicholas Longworth Anderson*, 158; George W. Botkin to Baker, Aug. 22, 1862, Sidney C. Baker Letters, OHS.

41. McCook later admitted that his "spies had misinformed me" (*OR* 1, 16, pt. 1, 105). In 1903, on the occasion of McCook's death, former staff officer Horace Fisher claimed that neither McCook nor Buell had been fooled. Far from it, according to Fisher, for Federal troopers of the 2nd Indiana Cavalry discovered at Battle Creek a letter from Isham Harris that fully detailed Bragg's plans to march on and seize Louisville. For reasons unexplained, the three men and three other unnamed officers took an oath not to reveal the existence of the letter for six months. Buell then outlined his entire subsequent campaign to the others. Such a story ignores not only the evidence, but also the simple

fact that only later did Bragg consider seizing Louisville. See clipping, *Boston Transcript*, June 13, 1903, McCook Family Papers, LC.

42. Gold Questionnaire Data, Confederate Collection, TSLA; Hess, *Banners to the Breeze*, 57.

43. *OR* 1, 16, pt. 2, 775; J. M. Withers to Captain [?], Aug. 19, 1862, and Cheatham to Polk, Aug. 27, 1862, both letters in Leonidas Polk Papers, Papers of Various Confederate Notables, RG 109, NARA (hereafter Polk Papers). For a response from one of the officers so blamed, see Claiborne, "The Campaign of 1862 into Kentucky of Gen'l Braxton Bragg," 1–4, Thomas Claiborne Reminiscences, SHC-UNC. Fired from a staff position by Bragg after the latter replaced Beauregard, Claiborne despised Bragg and blamed the general himself for the delay and almost everything else that subsequently went wrong. Claiborne entered Kentucky as a member of Buckner's staff. "Bragg was not ready to move when the trains rolled into Chattanooga," Claiborne asserted (quotation, 3).

44. Little and Maxwell, *History of Lumsden's Battery*, 10–11.

45. Henry C. Semple to his wife, Aug. 19, 1862, Confederate Artillery Batteries: Lumsden's Battery-Waters' Battery, ADAH.

46. *OR* 1, 16, pt. 2, 759; Hughes, *General William J. Hardee*, is the definitive biography. See also Connelly, *Army of the Heartland*, 223; and McWhiney, "Controversy in Kentucky," 13.

47. James Patton Anderson Autobiography, 1–7, SHC-UNC; McWhiney, "Controversy in Kentucky," 14; Sword, *Shiloh*, 293; *OR* 1, 16, pt. 2, 761.

48. Cooling, *Forts Henry and Donelson*, 200–13, 221, 222, 259, 263; Stickles, *Simon Bolivar Buckner*, 124–95; *OR* 1, 16, pt. 2, 759, 766, 767, 772.

49. Taylor, *Destruction and Reconstruction*, 100.

50. Parks's *General Leonidas Polk* remains the major biography of Polk. See also Connelly, *Army of the Heartland*, 223; McWhiney, "Controversy in Kentucky," 13,

51. Losson, *Tennessee's Forgotten Warriors*, 1–57.

52. Warner, *Generals in Gray*, 342–43; Connelly, *Army of the Heartland*, 223.

53. Semple to his wife, Aug. 19, 1862, Semple Papers, ADAH.

54. *OR* 1, 16, pt. 2, 779.

55. Ibid., 782–83.

56. John Ellis to E. P. Ellis, Aug. 21, 1862, E. P. Ellis and Family Papers, LSU.

57. *OR* 1, 16, pt. 1, 14–16; *OR* 1, 16, pt. 2, 781–2, 783, 785, 787; Cheatham to Polk, Aug. 27, 1862, Polk Papers; "Thirty-third Regiment Ohio Volunteer Infantry," Nelson Purdum Papers, OHS; *B&L*, vol. 3, 7; Connelly, *Army of the Heartland*, 221; McDonough, *War in Kentucky*, 111–12.

58. *OR* 1, 16, pt. 1, 88, 111, 429, 438, 439, 443–44, 451, 893; *B&L*, vol. 3, 8; Wagner Memoirs, 40.

59. *OR* 1, 16, pt. 1, 40, 44–45, *OR* 1, 16, pt. 2, 416–17, 425–26, 429, 432–34, 441–42, 451, 452–53, 461–62; Hupp, *My Diary*, 16; *B&L*, vol. 3, 41; Carter, ed., *For Honor, Glory & Union*, 138–39. The Buell Commission concluded that Buell erred seriously in retreating without a fight, and more recent commentators agree. See for example *OR* 1, 16, pt. 1, 9, 16; McDonough, *War in Kentucky*, 110–13.

60. *OR* 1, 16, pt. 1, 150–51, 224; *OR* 1, 16, pt. 2, 471. The defendant asserted before the Buell Commission, that he did not learn of Thomas's plan until the hearings. See *OR* 1, 16, pt. 1, 41, 45.

61. Duncan Diary, 8, *Civil War Times Illustrated* Collection, USAMHI (hereafter Duncan Diary).

62. Ball to Brother Quig, Sept. 2, 1862, William H. Ball Collection, USAMHI.

63. Stuckey to Helen Stuckey, Sept. 2, 1862, William Roberts Stuckey Letters, InHS; Lars Olsen Dokken to his family, Sept. 5, 1862, Lars and Knudt Dokken Papers,

SHSW; Inskeep Diary, Sept. 5, 1862; Parkinson to his brother, Oct. 27, 1862, William M. Parkinson Correspondence, OHS; Horrall, *Forty-second Indiana*, 138; Keil, *Thirty-fifth Ohio*, 92–93; Kerwood, *Fifty-seventh Regiment*, 107.

64. Hinman, *Sherman Brigade*, 258–59.

65. *OR* 1, 16, pt. 1, 328–29, 333; Calkins Memoirs, 9, *Civil War Times Illustrated* Collection, USAMHI (hereafter Calkins Memoirs). See also Ball to Brother Quig, Sept. 2, 1862, Ball Collection, USAMHI; Householder Diary, Aug. 31, 1862, Civil War Miscellaneous Collection, USAMHI; Quiner Scrapbooks, "Correspondence of the Wisconsin Volunteers, 1861–1865," vol. 5, 192–93, SHSW.

66. *OR* 1, 16, pt. 2, 470–71, 490.

67. *OR* 1, 16, pt. 2, 495, 496, 497.

68. *OR* 1, 16, pt. 2, 500.

69. Jones to his wife, Sept. 8, 12, 1862, Lewis H. Jones Diary and Letters, USAMHI; James A. Price Diaries, 24–25, Civil War Miscellaneous Collection, USAMHI (hereafter Price Diaries).

70. John Eicker Memoir, 5, 12, Harrisburg Civil War Round Table Collection, USAMHI (hereafter Eicker Memoir).

71. *OR* 1, 16, pt. 1, 15–16; *OR* 1, 16, pt. 2, 515.

72. *OR* 1, 16, pt. 1, 697–98; *OR* 1, 16, pt. 2, 461, 490; Ball to Brother Smith, Sept. 18, 1862, Ball Collection, USAMHI; Cozzens, ed., "Ambition Carries the Day," 139. Although his interpretation differs somewhat from mine, see also Cooling's excellent discussion in *Fort Donelson's Legacy*, 126–28.

73. *OR* 1, 16, pt. 1, 88, 166, 171, 192, 664, 698; *OR* 1, 16, pt. 2, 493, 515; *B&L*, vol. 3, 42; Cooling, *Fort Donelson's Legacy*, 128–29.

CHAPTER 4

1. Edward Brown, Sparta, Tenn., to Fannie Brown, Sept. 4, 1862, Brown Letters, ADAH; Cheatham to Polk Aug. 27, 1862, Polk Papers; Rufus W. Daniel Diary, 16, Civil War Miscellaneous Collection, USAMHI (hereafter Daniel Diary); Ellis to his mother, Oct. 2, 1862, Ellis and Family Papers, LSU; Ellis Diary, 25; Ellis War Recollections, 49; Gold Questionnaire Data, Confederate Collection, TSLA; Hall Diary, 53–54, James Iredell Hall Papers, SHC-UNC (hereafter Hall Diary); Talley Autobiography, 22–23, Civil War Miscellany Files, GDAH (hereafter Talley Autobiography); Trask Journal, 33–35, 38; Coles, "Ancient City Defenders," 83; Nichols, ed., "Reminiscing from 1861 to 1865," 9.

2. "Short Record of Thomas Benton Ellis, Sr.," 2, FSH (hereafter Ellis Record). For the poor condition of the army's horses and mules at the outset of the campaign, see Semple to his wife, Aug. 22, 1862, Henry C. Semple Papers, ADAH.

3. Trask Journal, 36, 41.

4. *OR* 1, 16, pt. 1, 307; Daniel Diary, 17; John T. Irien, "Fifth Tennessee Infantry," 3, Confederate Collection, TSLA (hereafter "Fifth Tennesse Infantry); W. E. Mathews Preston, "33rd Alabama," ed. L. B. Williams, 22–23, 28, ADAH (hereafter "33rd Alabama"). Rumors of Bragg's harsh discipline extended even into Buell's army, where Federal officers yearned for the same powers, especially the right to enact the death penalty in the field. See Lovell Rousseau's comments in *OR* 1, 16, pt. 1, 348–49, 354–55.

5. Taylor Beatty Diary, Aug. 30 and Sept. 1, 1862, SHC-UNC (hereafter Beatty Diary); Ellis Record, 2; Talley Autobiography, 23; A. Oswald McDonnell Diary, Sept. 14, 1862, UF (hereafter McDonnell Diary); Trask Journal 40, 42; Head, *Campaigns and Battles*, 91–92; James R. Thompson, "Hear the Wax Fry: Memoirs of James R. Thompson," 8, PSHS; Womack, *Diary of Capt. J. J. Womack*, 58; Coles, "Ancient City Defenders," 83; Connelly, *Army of the Heartland*, 224.

6. Trask Journal, 37.

7. Johnston, "Bragg's Campaign in Kentucky, by a Staff Officer. No. 1—From Chattanooga to Munfordville," J. Stoddard Johnston Papers, Filson (hereafter "Campaign in Kentucky, No. 1"). See also Spence, "Campaigning in Kentucky," 22.

8. "Campaign in Kentucky, No. 1"; Ellis Diary, 25; Tapp, "Battle of Perryville," 161; Hess, *Banners to the Breeze*, 62; Hughes, ed., *Liddell's Record*, 82; Connelly, *Army of the Heartland*, 224.

9. *OR* 1, 16, pt. 2, 799–800, 804; Connelly, *Army of the Heartland*, 226.

10. Claiborne, "Campaign of 1862," 5–7; *OR* 1, 16, pt. 2, 805, 806, 808, 811, 818; Connelly, *Army of the Heartland*, 226.

11. *OR* 1, 16, pt. 2, 806. For additional expectations of a battle at Cave City, see ibid., 811–12.

12. *OR* 1, 16, pt. 2, 815, 816, 817–18, 820; Daniel Diary, 17; Trask Journal, 41–49; Thompson, "Hear the Wax Fry," 8; "Campaign in Kentucky, No. 1"; Connelly, *Army of the Heartland*, 227; Sutherland, ed., *Reminiscences*, 89–91; Hughes, *General William J. Hardee*, 122; Kundahl, *Confederate Engineer*, 164–65.

13. *OR* 1, 16, pt. 2, 822–23.

14. Ibid., 809. See also ibid., 815

15. Kundahl, *Confederate Engineer*, 165.

16. George Winchester Diary, 53, James Winchester Papers, TSLA (hereafter Winchester Diary).

17. Cross, *Camp and Field*, 52.

18. W. L. Trask reported a "pale woman" crying out a most similar welcome to Louisianans on September 15 (Trask Journal, 49).

19. *OR* 1, 16, pt. 2, 815; *OR* 1, 16, pt. 1, 968.

20. Trask Journal, 45; Graber, *Life Record*, 156. According to Graber, "half of them deserted us before we passed through Cumberland Gap and soon after they found that we were unable to hold Kentucky." See also "Campaign in Kentucky, No. 1."

21. *OR* 1, 16, pt. 1, 968; *OR* 1, 16, pt. 2, 815; Harris to Bragg, Sept. 15, 1862, David Bullock Harris Papers, Duke; Connelly, *Army of the Heartland*, 227–28.

22. *OR* 1, 16, pt. 1, 16.

23. Ibid., 205, 208, 213, 959, 963; *OR* 1, 16, pt. 2, 818–19; Sykes, "Cursory Sketch," 466–67; Stickles, *Simon Bolivar Buckner*, 197–98. McDonough, *War in Kentucky*, 158–82, examines the Munfordville affair in considerable depth, as does Kent Masterson Brown in "Munfordville," in *Civil War in Kentucky*, ed. K. M. Brown, 137–73.

24. *OR* 1, 16, pt. 1, 974, 978, 959; Parks, *General Edmund Kirby Smith*, 221; James, "Perryville," 136; Sykes, "Cursory Sketch," 467.

25. *OR* 1, 16, pt. 1, 208, 213, 315, 354, 386, 959–64, 974–78; Sykes, "Cursory Sketch," 467–68. Several civilians later testified that they delivered urgent requests for help from Wilder to Buell, but the general and other officers denied receiving them.

26. *OR* 1, 16, pt. 1, 207, 978. See also Sykes, "Cursory Sketch," 468.

27. Hall Diary; Trask Journal, 47–48.

28. *OR* 1, 16, pt. 1, 980, 968, 978; *OR* 1, 16, pt. 2, 825, 825–28; *B&L*, vol. 3, 9.

29. "Campaign in Kentucky, No. 1."

30. Ellis to his wife, Oct. 2, 1862, Ellis and Family Papers, LSU; Hall Diary; John Inglis Diary, Sept. 15–17, 1862, FSU (hereafter Inglis Diary); Trask Journal, 47–51; Cross, *Camp and Field*, 54–55; Malone, *Memoir*, 126–27; *OR* 1, 16, pt. 1, 209–10, 962, 966, 968–71; Connelly, *Army of the Heartland*, 229; Stickles, *Simon Bolivar Buckner*, 200–4.

31. *OR* 1, 16, pt. 1, 962, 968; Lindsley, ed., *Military Annals*, vol. 1, 352.

32. *OR* 1, 16, pt. 2, 968.

33. *OR* 1, 16, pt. 1, 208, 216; *B&L*, vol. 3, 10; Connelly, *Army of the Heartland*, 230.

34. Ellis Diary, 26.

35. Inglis Diary, Sept. 17, 1862.

36. Trask Journal, 51. In later years, a few ex-Confederates still heaped praise on Bragg for his capture of the garrison. See Dyer and Moore, *Tennessee Civil War Veterans*, vol. 5, 1846-47.

37. Ellis Diary, 26; Inglis Diary, Sept. 17, 1862; James Searcy letter transcription, undated, Semple's Alabama Battery File, PSHS; *OR* 1, 16, pt. 1, 894; Johnston, "Bragg's Campaign in Kentucky, by a Staff Officer. No. 3—From Munfordville to Frankfort," Johnston Papers, Filson (hereafter "Campaign in Kentucky, No. 3"); Connelly, *Army of the Heartland*, 231.

38. *OR* 1, 16, pt. 1, 290. Buell had urged Breckinridge to bring his troops north to join him once permitted by Van Dorn, Breckinridge's commander. Van Dorn, however, had dawdled. Once they arrived in Chattanooga, Samuel Jones then pulled rank to keep the units in Tennessee. See Connelly, *Army of the Heartland*, 270-71, 272.

39. "Campaign in Kentucky, No. 3."

40. *OR* 1, 16, pt. 1, 894-95; *OR* 1, 16, pt. 2, 848-49; *B&L*, vol. 3, 601.

41. *B&L*, vol. 3, 10. Wheeler incorrectly gives the date of the meeting as September 18, but details such as Buckner's orders clearly show that it must have occurred the next day.

42. *OR* 1, 16, pt. 1, 894-95; *OR* 1, 16, pt. 2, 848-49, 855, 856, 859, 861, 864.

43. *B&L*, vol. 3, 601.

44. Ellis Diary, 26; Inglis Diary, Sept. 22-23, 1862; "33rd Alabama," 12; Trask Journal, 54, 57; Head, *Campaigns and Battles*, 93-94; Little and Maxwell, *History of Lumsden's Battery*, 11; Spradlin, ed., "Diary of George W. Jones," 8; Sutherland, ed., *Reminiscences*, 93-94; Brown, "Munfordville," 167. M. A. Rapier, a Unionist Kentucky legislator, testified to the Buell Commission that he saw Bragg's column "in a very great hurry," moving north of Munfordville at the double-quick, "some of them . . . walking very fast and some running." Even if such a thing were possible, accounts from Confederate soldiers contradict Rapier's testimony. Moreover, Rapier made so many other extravagant claims, notably that Bragg had seventy thousand men, that even the commission doubted his veracity. See *OR* 1, 16, pt. 1, 15, 320-22.

45. "33rd Alabama," 24.

46. Hall Diary, 56.

47. *OR* 1, 16, pt. 1, 991-96; *OR*, 16, pt. 2, 849-51, 859, 860, 864-65; Kirby Smith to Johnston, Oct. 31, 1866, J. Stoddard Johnston Papers, Filson; "Campaign in Kentucky, No. 3." For criticisms of Bragg's decision not to fight at Munfordville, see *B&L*, vol. 3, 10, 20, 22, 27; Hammond, "Kirby Smith's Campaign," 159-60; Quisenberry, "Confederate Campaign in Kentucky," 32-33; Brown, "Munfordville," 160-68; Horn, *Army of Tennessee*, 163-72; McMurry, *Two Great Rebel Armies*, 152-53. Hess, in *Banners to the Breeze*, 69-71, 76, admits that Bragg took the safest course but suggests that the possible results would have been worth the risk. For opposing views, see Connelly, *Army of the Heartland*, 231-34; Hafendorfer, *Perryville*, 53-55; McDonough, *War in Kentucky*, 183-87; McWhiney, *Braxton Bragg*, 286-92; and Woodworth, *Jefferson Davis*, 146-47.

48. Hughes, ed., *Liddell's Record*, 83.

49. For an argument that Bragg's decision to reduce Munfordville was the correct one, see Brown, "Munfordville," 139-40, 160.

50. *OR* 1, 16, pt. 1, 218, 224, 354, 365, 366, 554, 640, 893-94; Ball to Brother Quig, Sept. 15, 1862, Ball Collection, USAMHI; H. Borchsenius, "Mem. In relation to movements of 15th Reg't," Adjutant General, Records of Civil War Regiments, 1861-

1900, 15th Wisconsin Infantry, SHSW; George W. Botkin to Baker, Sept. 11, 1862, Sidney C. Baker Letters, OHS; Chandler, "History of the 5th Ind. Battery," 13–16, Daniel H. Chandler Collection, InSL (hereafter "5th Ind. Battery"); William T. Clark Diary, vol. 2, 29–38, USAMHI (hereafter Clark Diary); A. T. Coburn to his father, Sept. 15, 1862, Charles L. Coburn Letters, OHS; Jesse B. Connelly Diary, Sept. 27, 1862, InSL (hereafter Connelly Diary); Robert Foster Diary, Sept. 16, 20, 1862, OHS; Galpin to his parents, Sept. 9, 1862, Alfred Galpin Family Papers, SHSW; Parkinson to his brother, Oct. 27, 1982, Parkinson Correspondence, OHS; Price Diaries, 26; Stuckey to Helen Stuckey, Sept. 4, 11, and 13, 1862, Stuckey Letters, InHS; Duncan Thompson to his father, Sept. 29, 1862, Timothy Brookes Collection, USAMHI; Webster Diary, 24–25, Civil War Miscellaneous Collection, USAMHI (hereafter Webster Diary); Wagner Memoirs, 41–43; *Louisville Daily Journal,* Oct. 1, 1862; *Cincinnati Daily Commercial,* Oct. 1, 1862; *Princeton Clarion,* Oct. 4, 1862; Anderson, ed., *Nicholas Longworth Anderson,* 159–60; Beatty, *Citizen-Soldier,* 175; Bisbee, *Through Four American Wars,* 118–19; Bishop, *Story of a Regiment,* 68; Cozzens, ed., "Ambition Carries the Day," 140; Duff, *Terrors and Horrors of Prison Life,* 1–2; Herr, *Nine Campaigns,* 106–8; Kirkpatrick, *Experiences,* 12; Knight and Cowden, eds., "Two Immigrants," 124–25; Mosgrove, "Two Mighty Armies," 7; Noe, ed., *Southern Boy in Blue,* 93–97; Patterson, ed., *38th Regiment,* 12–15; Butler, *My Story,* 176–78; Cutter, *Our Battery,* 70–71; Grebner, *"We Were the Ninth,"* 112–13; Grose, *Story of the Marches,* 132–33; Hartpence, *Fifty-first Indiana,* 77–79; Hinman, *Sherman Brigade,* 260–78; *History of the Services,* 12–13; Horrall, *Forty-second Indiana,* 138–39, 145; Keil, *Thirty-fifth Ohio,* 93; Rerick, *Forty-fourth Indiana,* 67–70; Scribner, *How Soldiers Were Made,* 54–56; Shaw, *History of the Tenth Indiana,* 169–70. Hinman's is the fullest account from a common soldier's perspective.

51. *OR* 1, 16, pt. 1, 77–81, 133–34, 148; Ball, undated letter fragment, Ball Collection, USAMHI; Parkinson to his brother, Oct. 27, 1862, Parkinson Correspondence, OHS; Price Diaries, 28–29; Stuckey to Helen Stuckey, Sept. 4, 1862, Stuckey Letters, InHS; John W. Tuttle Diary Transcript, Sept. 16, 1862, UK (hereafter Tuttle Diary); *Cincinnati Daily Commercial,* Oct. 1, 1862; Butler, *My Story,* 214; Hartpence, *Fifty-first Indiana,* 77–79; Hinman, *Sherman Brigade,* 260; Hupp, *My Diary,* 17; Martin, *Eighth Kansas,* 16; Noe, ed., *Southern Boy in Blue,* 96–98; *Report of the Adjutant General,* vol. 1, 106; Scribner, *How Soldiers Were Made,* 54–55. The Buell Commission later exonerated Buell for "the failure to relieve Munfordville," the second charge against him, and placed the blame on Department of the Ohio commander Horatio Wright, who ordered Wilder not to retreat from his post. See *OR* 1, 16, pt. 1, 9–10.

52. Hinman, *Sherman Brigade,* 275.

53. *B&L,* vol. 3, 41–42. See also *OR* 1, 16, pt. 1, 48–49, 101, 112, 162, 208; *OR* 1, 16, pt. 2, 526, 527, 530, 531–32; Chumney, "Don Carlos Buell," 158–60.

54. Cozzens, ed., "Ambition Carries the Day," 140.

55. *B&L,* vol. 3, 41–42. See also *OR* 1, 16, pt. 1, 48–49, 101, 112, 162, 208; *OR* 1, 16, pt. 2, 526, 527, 530, 531–32; Chumney, "Don Carlos Buell," 158–60.

56. *OR* 1, 16, pt. 1, 18–19, 48–49; *OR* 1, 16, pt. 2, 534, 536–37.

57. *OR* 1, 16, pt. 2, 534, 546; Ball, undated letter fragment; *Cincinnati Daily Commercial,* Oct. 1, 1862; Duncan Diary, 8; Inskeep Diary, Sept. 19, 20, 24, 25, 1862; Tuttle Diary, Sept. 22, 23, 24, 25, 1862; Anderson, ed., *Nicholas Longworth Anderson,* 159–60; Bircher, *Drummer-Boy's Diary,* 44; Bishop, *Story of a Regiment,* 68–69; Butler, *My Story,* 214–17; DeVelling, *Seventeenth Regiment,* 70; Grebner, *"We Were the Ninth,"* 113–14; Hinman, *Sherman Brigade,* 277–80; Hupp, *My Diary,* 17–19; Keil, *Thirty-fifth Ohio,* 94; Kimberly and Holloway, *Forty-first Ohio,* 32–33; Kirkpatrick, *Experiences,* 13; Patterson, ed., *38th Regiment,* 13–15; Price Diaries, 29–33; Rerick, *Forty-fourth Indiana,* 70; John

Sipe to Sallie, Sept. 28, 1862, Civil War Regimental History—38th Indiana, InSL; Webster Diary, 26–27; *OR* 1,16, pt. 2, 530.

58. Scribner, *How Soldiers Were Made*, 56. See also Hinman, *Sherman Brigade*, 280; Shaw, *Tenth Regiment*, 169.

59. Alverson to his father, Sept. 26, 1862, George H. Alverson Letters, Civil War Miscellaneous Collection, USAMHI.

60. T. J. Stephenson to Gullion, Sept. 28, 1862, Joseph Gullion Letters, InHS. See also Phelps to friends, Sept. 28, 1862, Phelps Letters, USAMHI.

61. Thomas M. Small Diary, Sept. 22, 1862, InHS (hereafter Small Diary). See also Albertson, ed., *Letters Home*, letter 57, 1–2; "5th Ind. Battery"; *Cincinnati Daily Commercial*, Sept. 30, 1862; Galpin to his father, Sept. 26, 1862, Galpin Family Papers, SHSW; Herr, *Nine Campaigns*, 106–8; Lathrop, *Fifty-ninth Regiment*, 154–55; Osborn Diary, Sept. 7, 20, 1862, OHS.

62. Tuttle Diary, Sept. 25, 1862.

63. Calkins Diary, 40–41, Emerson Rood Calkins Papers, SHSW (hereafter Calkins Diary). See also Duncan Diary, 8. The brothers-in-law myth had a long life. As late as 1908, one writer could assert it as fact. See clipping, Pittsburgh *Gazette Times*, Oct. 12, 1908, McCook Family Papers, LC.

64. *Cincinnati Daily Commercial*, Oct. 1, 1862. See also Patterson, ed., *38th Regiment*, 15.

CHAPTER 5

1. Dicey, *Spectator of America*, 175–81 (quotations, 175, 176, 181, 177). For confirmation, see McDowell, *City of Conflict*, 13–16, 44–51, 56.

2. John Jefferson Diary, June 1–Oct. 1, 1862, Filson (hereafter Jefferson Diary).

3. *OR* 1, 16, pt. 2, 336, 337, 344, 348, 351, 352–53, 355, 357, 359–60, 365–66, 373; Daviess, *Mercer and Boyle Counties*, 133.

4. *OR* 1, 16, pt. 2, 360.

5. Tourgée, *Story of a Thousand*, 69–70.

6. *OR* 1, 16, pt. 2, 374–75, 385; Boatner, *Civil War Dictionary*, 730, 949; Warner, *Generals in Blue*, 575.

7. *OR* 1, 16, pt. 2, 404–5, 421. Halleck referred to James Guthrie, at age seventy-one a leader of Kentucky's conservative Unionists, and James Speed, perhaps Kentucky's leading Radical Republican and in 1864 Lincoln's attorney general. John Speed, Lincoln's close friend from Illinois, was a lesser member of the Speed faction. See Kleber, ed., *Kentucky Encyclopedia*, 369, 840–41.

8. *OR* 1, 16, pt. 2, 385–86, 393, 404–4, 405, 406, 411, 415–16, 421, 434–35, 436–37, 446, 447–48, 455; Paddock to Hattie, Aug. 14, 1862, Byron D. Paddock Letters, Civil War Miscellaneous Collection, USAMHI; Tourgée. *Story of a Thousand*, 71.

9. *OR* 1, 16, pt. 2, 448, 449, 456, 457–59, 464–65; Glauser, trans., *Private Josiah Ayre*, 3; Tourgée, *Story of a Thousand*, 58–81; Julius B. Work Diary, 2, OHS (hereafter Work Diary, OHS).

10. *OR* 1, 16, pt. 1, 372, 375, 376, 693; Julius Birney Work Diary, 2–3, Civil War Miscellaneous Collection, USAMHI (hereafter Work Diary, USAMHI); Warner, *Generals in Blue*, 173–74.

11. *OR* 1, 16, pt. 2, 510. See also 513.

12. Warner, *Generals in Blue*, 174.

13. Barnard Diary, 1–4, InSL; Lester Dewitt Taylor Diary, 2, Civil War Miscellaneous Collection—New Material, USAMHI (hereafter Taylor Diary, USAMHI); Bow-

ers, "Memories of a Retreat," 3; Ford, "That Famous Retreat," 3; Glauser, trans., *Private Josiah Ayre*, 3; *History of the Seventy-third Indiana*, 104–5; Mitchell Memoir, 8–10, OHS; Tourgée, *Story of a Thousand*, 81–95.

14. Tourgée, *Story of a Thousand*, 83, 87–92, 94 (quotation, 83). See also J. H. Tilford Diary, Sept. 5, 1862, Filson (hereafter Tilford Diary); and Work, "A Famous Retreat," 3.

15. *OR* 1, 16, pt. 2, 474, 477, 491; Phillips, ed., *Civil War Diary*, 1.

16. Ibid., 465.

17. *OR* 1, 16, pt. 1, 296–97, 426; *OR* 1, 16, pt. 2, 466, 471–72.

18. *OR* 1, 16, pt. 1, 6.

19. Ibid., 430; Comstock to his mother and sister, Sept. 20, 1862, and to his father, Sept. 23, 1862, Eugene E. Comstock Letters, SHSW; Frank McKenzie to Nettlehorst, Sept. 13, 1862, Louis Nettlehorst Letters, InHS; "Life of L. A. Ross," 41, Levi Adolphus Ross Papers, IlSHL (hereafter "Life of L. A. Ross"); Shelly to his sister, Sept. 19, 1862, Oliver Shelly Letters, InHS; Taylor Diary, 2, USAMHI; Tilford Diary, Aug. 27–Sept. 20, 1862; Work Diary, 2, OHS; Althouse and Hughes, eds., *John A. Boon*, 5–8; Aten, *Eighty-fifth Regiment*, 25–26; Francis, *Narrative*, 46–49; Glauser, trans., *Diary of Josiah Ayre*, 4–6; *History of the Seventy-ninth Indiana*, 47–49; Kinnear, *Eighty-sixth Regiment*, 10–11; Reid, *Ohio in the War*, vol. 2, 523; Tourgée, *Story of a Thousand*, 101–2. As a gauge of rawness, one might note that only in January 1863 did the 32nd Kentucky Infantry request a copy of army regulations as well as four copies of infantry tactics manuals. See Special Requisition, Jan. 15, 1863, 32nd Kentucky Volunteer Infantry Quartermaster Records, KDMA.

20. Frazee to [?], Aug. 31, 1862, Thomas J. Frazee Letters, IlSHL; Weissert to his wife and children, [Sept.] 16, 1862, and Rothfuss, "A German Michigander in the Civil War," both in the John Weissert Papers, UMBHL; Butler, ed., *Letters Home*, 3. For another expression of confidence, see Henry F. Jackson Diary, Sept, 20, 1862, Civil War Miscellaneous Collection, USAMHI.

21. "Life of L. A Ross," 42; Althouse and Hughes, eds., *John A. Boon*, 7.

22. *OR* 1, 16, pt. 2, 475–76, 478–79, 480–82, 486–87, 487–88, 492, 499–500, 503.

23. James, "Perryville," 137–38; *OR* 1, 16, pt. 1, 296–97; *OR* 1, 16, pt. 2, 492–93, 499–500, 502, 504–6, 507.

24. *Louisville Daily Journal*, Sept. 16, 1862.

25. *OR* 1, 16, pt. 2, 505–6, 507–9, 518.

26. *OR* 1, 16, pt. 1, 426, 429–30, 693; *OR* 1, 16, pt. 2, 518, 523–24, 526, 527, 528, 540; Nelson to Buell, Sept. 24, 1862, General's Papers and Books, Papers of Don Carlos Buell, RG 94, NARA (hereafter Buell Papers); Watson to Jennie, Sept. 20, 1862, Richard H. Watson Letters, Civil War Miscellaneous Collection, USAMHI; Glauser, trans., *Private Josiah Ayre*, 4–5, 9–11; Kinnear, *Eighty-sixth Regiment*, 11; Larew, ed., *Garret Larew*, 148–49; Marcoot, *Five Years*, 15–16; Phillips, ed., *Civil War Diary*, 1; Winters, *In the 50th Ohio*, 9–14.

27. *Louisville Daily Journal*, Sept. 24, 1862.

28. *OR* 1, 16, pt. 1, 663–64; Conkey to Mollie Sheets, Sept. 25, 1862, J. Lincoln Conkey Letters, Filson; Larew, ed, *Garret Larew*, 149.

29. Morse to his mother, Sept. 22, 1862, Bliss Morse Papers, OHS; Barnard Diary, 9; Jefferson Diary, Sept. 22–24, 1862. See also *OR* 1, 16, pt. 1, 308, 427, 430; Cuthbert Bullet to S. P. Chase, Sept. 22, 1862, Salmon P. Chase Papers, LC; Conkey to Sheets, Sept. 25, 1862, Conkey Letters, Filson; Johnson W. Culp Diary, 43–48, Civil War Miscellaneous Collection, USAMHI; Tilford Diary, Sept. 23–25, 1862; Frazee to [?], Sept. 24, 1862, and Frazee to his brother, Sept. 25, 1862, Frazee Letters, IlSHL; Rothrock to his sister, Sept. 24, 1862, Joseph Rothrock Letters, InSL; Alva C. Griest Memoir, 11–12, Harrisburg Civil War Round Table Collection, USAMHI; Morse to his mother, Sept.

25, 1862, Morse Papers, OHS; "Life of L. A. Ross," 43; William Spencer to his father, Sept. 22, 1862, and to [?], n.d. [fragment], William and Joseph Spencer Letters, OHS; Taylor Diary, 3, USAMHI; Walker Diary, vol. 2, 1, John S. Walker Diary and Letters, Harrisburg Civil War Round Table Collection, USAMHI (hereafter Walker Diary); *Louisville Daily Journal*, Sept. 17, 1862; Aten, *Eighty-fifth Regiment*, 27–30; Glauser, trans., *Private Josiah Ayre*, 9–11; "His Mother," *Young Chaplain*, 96–97; McDowell, *City of Conflict*, 83–86.

30. James, "Perryville," 138; *OR* 1, 16, pt. 2, 540, 542.

31. Wright, *Eighth Regiment*, 96.

32. *OR* 1, 16, pt. 1, 372–73, 524–25, 640–41, 664; Ball, undated letter fragment, and Ball to his family, Sept. 27, 1862, Ball Collection, USAMHI; G. W. Brown to Rev. G. Chandler, Oct. 17, 1862, U.S. Army Letters, Duke; Calkins Memoirs, 10–11; Calkins Diary, 38–39; Heg to his wife, Sept. 26, 1862, Hans Christian Heg Letters, SHSW; Inskeep Diary, Sept. 26–30, 1862; Isaac Longenecker to J. F. Lenz, Fulton-Lenz Correspondence, *Civil War Times Illustrated* Collection, USAMHI; Pinney to Eliza, Sept. 27, 1862, Oscar F. Pinney Papers, SHSW; Edward B. Quiner Scrapbooks, "Correspondence of the Wisconsin Volunteers, 1861–1865," vol. 5, 192, SHSW (hereafter Quiner Scrapbooks); Tuttle Diary, Sept. 26, 1862; Samuel C. Vance to W. H. H. Terrell, June 27, 1867, Regimental Correspondence of the Adjutant General of Indiana, 10th Indiana Infantry, InSA; Wagner Memoirs, 44; Webster Diary, Sept. 27–28, 1862; Albertson, ed., *Letters Home*, letter 57, 3; Anderson, ed., *Nicholas Longworth Anderson*, 160; Bircher, *Drummer-Boy's Diary*, 44; Cutter, *Our Battery*, 75–76; Hinman, *Sherman Brigade*, 280–87; Hupp, *My Diary*, 19; Martin, *Eighth Kansas*, 17–18; Olson, trans., *Rollin Olson*, letter, Sept. 29, 1862; Patterson, ed., *38th Regiment*, 15; Perry, *Thirty-eighth Regiment*, 24–26; Waddle, *Three Years*, 28.

33. *OR* 1, 16, pt. 1, 664–65; Benton to his father, Nov. 22, 1862, Aaron J. Benton Letters, *Civil War Times Illustrated* Collection, USAMHI; Gardner, "Perryville," 3.

34. Winn Diary, Sept. 27–30, 1862; Noe, ed., *Southern Boy in Blue*, 100.

35. Edgar R. Kellogg Recollections, 22, Civil War Miscellaneous Collection, USAMHI.

36. Davis to his wife, Oct. 7, 1862, Davis Papers, Iowa.

37. Duncan Diary, 8.

38. Jefferson Diary, Sept. 26, 1862; Drake to his brother, Sept. 26, 1862, Henry T. Drake Letters, SHSW; Harry Lewis to his family, Sept. 26, 1862, Lewis Family Letters, OHS; Sheridan, *Personal Memoirs*, vol. 1, 181.

39. Holmes, *Soldier*, 87; Jones, *Private of the Cumberland*, 9–10.

40. Hartpence, *Fifty-first Indiana*, 84.

41. Stuckey to Helen Stuckey, Sept. 13, 1862, Stuckey Letters, InHS. See also Eicker Memoir, 9; and Price Diaries, 35.

42. Shaw, *Tenth Regiment*, 170.

43. Connelly Diary, 57; Sipe to Sallie, Sept. 28, 1862, Civil War Regimental History—38th Indiana, InSL; Francis, *Narrative*, 50.

44. Frederick Schumacher to Col. B. J. Sweet, Oct. 1, 1862, Army of the Ohio and 14th Army Corps, Letters and Reports Received, 1862–65, RG 393, NARA; Fitch, *Echoes*, 41–42.

45. Tuttle Diary, Sept. 26 [*sic*], 1862.

46. *OR* 1, 16, pt. 2, 546, 549–51; telegram, Wright to Buell, Oct. 1, 1862, and telegrams, Morton to Buell, Sept. 26, 1862, Buell Papers; Hartpence, *Fifty-first Indiana*, 86–87; Kirkpatrick, *Experiences*, 13; Horrall, *Forty-second Indiana*, 147.

47. Horrall, *Forty-second Indiana*, 147.

48. This account is based on the most recent discussion of the murder, Jenkins,

"Shooting at the Galt House," esp. 105–10. For Hazen, see his *Narrative*, 59–60. See also "Life of L. A. Ross," 44; Tourgée, *Story of a Thousand*, 104–5.

49. Milo Blanchard to Harry Lewis, Sept. 27, 1862, Lewis Family Letters, OHS; Barnes, Carnahan, and McCain, *Eighty-sixth Indiana*, 52; Bennett and Haigh, *Thirty-sixth Regiment*, 237–38; Crary, *Crary Memoirs*, 70; Francis, *Narrative*, 51–52; Hinman, *Sherman Brigade*, 286; Kimberly and Holloway, *Forty-first Ohio*, 33; Marshall, *Historical Sketch*, 23; Tourgée, *Story of a Thousand*, 104–5; Wright, *Eighth Regiment*, 96; Jenkins, "Shooting at the Galt House," 110. A pro-Nelson exception is Waddle, *Three Years*, 28–29. Lathrop, *Fifty-ninth Regiment*, 156–61, contains a particularly fanciful account of Davis's confrontations with Nelson, which depicts a meek Davis versus a "sneering," swearing Nelson.

50. A. T. Coburn to his father, Sept. 30, 1862, Coburn Letters, OHS.

51. *OR* 1, 16, pt. 1, 232–33; *OR* 1, 16, pt. 2, 360, 421, 530, 538–39, 554, 555, 557–58. For party pressure to fire Buell, see B. P. A to Chase, Sept. 17, 1862; D. H. Allen to B. Morris, Oct. 20, 1862; W. D. Bickham to Chase, Sept. 8 and 19, 1862; David Chambers to Dear Sir, Oct. 25, 1862; S. S. Coy to Dear Sir, Oct. 20, 1862; O. Follett to Chase, Oct. 6, 1862; Thomas Heaton to Chase, Oct. 21, 1862; Simeon Nash to Chase, Sept. 5, 1862; R. S. Newton to Chase, Oct. 20, 1862; Kingsley Roy to Chase, Oct. 24, 1862; William Stoms to Chase, Oct. 19, 1862; and the Salmon P. Chase Diary, Oct. 5, 1862; all in the Salmon P. Chase Papers, LC.

52. *OR* 1, 16, pt. 1, 49, 89, 99, 107, 126, 134, 184–85, 188–89; Boatner, *Civil War Dictionary*, 431; Tourgée, *Story of a Thousand*, 86–87, 89–91, 101–2; Warner, *Generals in Blue*, 448–49; Barnard Diary, Sept. 29, 1862.

53. *Louisville Daily Journal*, Sept. 12, 1862; Boatner, *Civil War Dictionary*, 710; *OR* 1, 16, pt. 1, 348–49; McDowell, *City of Conflict*, 36–37.

54. Bachelor, "Soldiers' Ancedotes," 19.

55. Warner, *Generals in Blue*, 464, 521.

56. Ibid., 569; *OR* 1, 16, pt. 1, 173.

57. *OR* 1, 16, pt. 1, 134–35, 138, 234, 285, 376, 377, 382, 542–45, 576–77, 594–95, 598–99; *OR* 1, 16, pt. 2, 558–59, 560; Warner, *Generals in Blue*, 329, 424–25.

58. *OR* 1, 16, pt. 1, 92, 372, 384; Sheridan, *Personal Memoirs*, vol. 1, 189–90.

59. Keil, *Thirty-fifth Ohio*, 96; Shaw, *Tenth Regiment*, 171. Such incidents apparently were not out of the ordinary. See Grebner, *"We Were the Ninth,"* 114–15.

60. General Order no. 3, 3rd Corps, Army of Louisville, Sept. 30, 1862, Gilbert File, PSHS.

61. *B&L*, vol. 3, 47. See also *OR* 1, 16, pt. 1, 184; *OR* 1, 16, pt. 2, 56—61, 566; John Richardson to [?], Sept. 25, 1862, and Wright to Buell, Sept. 29, 1862, Buell Papers.

62. *OR* 1, 16, pt. 2, 876.

63. Inglis Diary, Sept. 24, 1862; Coles, "Ancient City Defenders,"84. For a similar description, see Watkins, *"Co. Aytch,"* 59–60.

64. Trask Journal, 60. See also Daniel Diary, 18; and Ellis War Recollections, 51.

65. Little and Maxwell, *History of Lumsden's Battery*, 11.

66. Claiborne, "Campaign of 1862," 9–10; Ellis to his mother, Oct. 2, 1862, Ellis and Family Papers, LSU; Inglis Diary, Sept. 24, 1862; Hall Diary, 56; McDonnell Diary, Sept. 26, 1862; Nichols, ed., "Reminiscing from 1861 to 1865," 7; Street to his wife, Sept. 26, 1862, John K. Street and Melinda East (Pace) Correspondence, SHC-UNC; Thompson, "Hear the Wax Fry," 8; Trask Journal 58–63; Winchester Diary, 67–68; Wood to his wife, Sept. 26, 1862, Wood Papers, ADAH; *Atlanta Southern Confederacy*, Oct. 9, 1862; Little and Maxwell, *History of Lumsden's Battery*, 11.

67. Joel Campbell Dubose, "Third Alabama Cavalry, Confederate Army," Confederate Alabama Cavalry Files: 3rd and 4th Cavalry, ADAH.

68. Trask Journal, 62.

69. *OR* 1, 16, pt. 1, 991; *OR*, 1, 16, pt. 2, 887; *Louisville Daily Journal*, Oct. 2, 1862; Bragg to Buckner, Sept. 27, 1862, Bragg Papers, WRHS.

70. Crist, ed., *Papers of Jefferson Davis*, 417; Ellis to his mother, Oct. 2, 1862, Ellis and Family Papers, LSU.

71. Wood to his wife, Sept. 26, 1862, Wood Papers, ADAH.

72. *Atlanta Southern Confederacy*, Oct. 2, 1862.

73. Trask Journal, 59.

74. Ellis Diary, 27.

75. Hughes, ed., *Liddell's Record*, 84.

76. *OR* 1, 16, pt. 2, 876. See also Bragg to Kirby Smith, Oct. 23, 1862, Bragg Papers, WRHS, for a similar letter. For a modern scholar who echoes Bragg's condemnation of Price and especially Van Dorn, see Cozzens, *Darkest Days*, 317–18.

77. For Bragg's zeal to conduct courts-martial, see H. W. Walter to Polk, Sept. 28, 1862, Polk Papers. McWhiney, "Controversy in Kentucky," 23, stresses an additional factor, exhaustion.

78. Kirby Smith to Bragg, Sept. 24, 1862, Bragg Papers, WRHS; George Brent to [?], Sept. 25, 1862, Bragg Papers, WRHS; Harris to Bragg, Sept. 24 and 25, 1862, Harris Papers, Duke; "Campaign in Kentucky, No. 3"; McWhiney, "Controversy in Kentucky," 22–23; Kundahl, *Confederate Engineer*, 168–69, 251.

79. *OR* 1, 16, pt. 2, 892; *OR* 1, 52, pt. 2, 340; Davis, *Orphan Brigade*, 123–33.

80. Crist, ed., *Papers of Jefferson Davis*, vol. 8, 416–17.

81. Bragg to Buckner, Sept. 27, 1862, Bragg Papers, WRHS; Connelly, *Army of the Heartland*, 235.

82. *OR* 1, 16, pt. 2, 892–93.

83. Ibid., 891; Crist, ed., *Papers of Jefferson Davis*, vol. 8, 417.

84. Cheek, ed., "Mrs. E. B. Patterson," 369–71.

85. *OR* 1, 16, pt. 2, 886, 891.

86. "Memorandum of Water on 4 roads from Bardstown to Danville," Sept. 24, 1862, Bragg Papers, WRHS; D. R. Harris to Captain [?], Sept. 25, 1862, Bragg Papers, WRHS; "Campaign in Kentucky, No. 3."

87. Cross, *Camp and Field*, 59–60. For the controversial Presbyterian cleric and antislavery activist Breckinridge, who taught at Danville Theological Seminary from 1853 until 1869, see Kleber, ed., *Kentucky Encyclopedia*, 120.

88. Crist, *Papers of Jefferson Davis*, vol. 8, 417; OR 1, 16, pt. 2, 891–92, 1016–17; Brent to Colonel, Sept. 25, 1862; Goodwin and Jamison, *Manic-Depressive Illness*, 357.

89. *OR* 1, 16, pt. 2, 895; Kirby Smith to his wife, Oct. 5, 1862, Smith Papers, SHC-UNC. See also Kirby Smith's Oct. 22, 1862, letter from Knoxville.

CHAPTER 6

1. This sketch is based on the Manuscript Census, Kentucky, Boyle County, Schedule I, 1860, NARA; Brown, *History of Danville*, esp. 2–4, 7, 10–11, 16–35, 42, and "Underground Railroad"; Daviess, *Mercer and Boyle Counties*, 96–101, 109–11, 136; Edwards, "Kentucky's First Settlement," 2; Harmon, *Chaplin Hills*, 2–6, 9, 15, 16–17, 19, 27–30, 37, 59, 61; "History of Perryville, Kentucky"; Polk, *Dr. J. J. Polk*, 68–71, 80–81; Kleber, ed., *Kentucky Encyclopedia*, 110. The spring and cave remain, and may be seen behind the Karrick-Parks House on modern Buell Street.

2. Polk, *Dr. J. J. Polk*, 92.

3. Ruger and Kilp, "Map of the Battlefield of Perryville, Ky."; *OR* 1, 16, pt. 1, 114,

1024, 1120; *B&L*, vol. 3, 52; Clark Memoirs, Confederate Collection, TSLA (hereafter Clark Memoirs); Toney, *Privations*, 42.

4. Head, *Campaigns and Battles*, 95.

5. *OR* 1, 16, pt. 1, 89, 525, 665; *OR* 1, 16, pt. 2, 560–61; Althouse and Hughes, eds., *John A. Boon*, 15.

6. Herr, *Nine Campaigns*, 110. Not every soldier marched with eagerness, however. Thomas Small of the near mutinous 10th Indiana noted "some swearing quite a time to get the boys to march but Pap. Thomas final command and we went 15 miles." Small Diary, Oct. 1, 1862.

7. *OR* 1, 16, pt. 1, 640–41; John G. Cavis Diary, Oct. 1, 1862, IlSHL (hereafter Cavis Diary); Galpin Diary, Oct. 1, 1862, Alfred Galpin Family Papers, SHSW (hereafter Galpin Diary); Joseph P. Glezen Diary, Oct. 1, 1862, InSL (hereafter Glezen Diary); W. E. Patterson Memoir, 34, UMWHMC (hereafter Patterson Memoir); John Henry Otto Memoirs, 79–81, SHSW (hereafter Otto Memoirs); "Life of L. A. Ross," 45; Robert B. Taylor Diary, 3–4, KHS (hereafter Taylor Diary, KHS); Benson, *Soldier's Diary*, 29; Butler, *Letters Home*, 10; Cutter, *Our Battery*, 76–77; Francis, *Narrative*, 53; Hazen, *Narrative*, 60–61; *History of the Seventy-third Regiment*, 96; Hupp, *My Diary*, 20; Marcoot, *Five Years*, 16; Martin, *Eighth Kansas*, 18; Morris, *Eighty-first Regiment*, 13; Olson, trans., *Rollin Olson*, letter, Sept. 30, 1862; Perry, *Thirty-eighth Regiment*, 26; Tourgée, *Story of a Thousand*, 113–15.

8. Hinman, *Sherman Brigade*, 288–90.

9. *OR* 1, 16, pt. 2, 876–77, 883–84, 897–98; Davis to his wife, Oct. 7, 1862, Davis Papers, Iowa; Grose, *Story of the Marches*, 136; Noe, ed., *Southern Boy in Blue*, 101; Simmons, *84th Reg't*, 14. Bragg sent Forrest back to Tennessee to raise six new regiments, which he was to use to harass the Federals around Nashville. Wharton is vividly described in Johnson, "Some Generals I Have Known," 120.

10. *OR* 1, 16, pt. 2, 565.

11. Otto Memoirs, Oct. 2, 1862; Fitch, *Echoes*, 65–73; Holmes, *Soldier*, 91–92.

12. *OR* 1, 16, pt. 2, 565, 898, 900–3; *OR* 1, 16, pt. 1, 89; Clark Diary, vol. 2, 41; Galpin Diary, Oct. 2 and 3, 1862; Morse Diary, Oct. 2 and 3, 1862, Bliss Morse Papers, OHS (hereafter Morse Diary); Otto Memoirs, Oct. 2, 1862; Webster Diary, 27; Winn Diary, Oct. 2, 1862; Angle, ed., *Three Years in the Army*, 18–20; Beatty, *Citizen-Soldier*, 176; Fitch, *Echoes*, 55; Graber, *Life Record*, 158; Glauser, trans., *Private Josiah Ayre*, 15–16; Holmes, *Soldier*, 91–92; Hupp, *My Diary*, 21; Perry, *Thirty-eighth Regiment*, 26–27; *Record of the Ninety-fourth Regiment*, 18.

13. Hupp, *My Diary*, 21; Kaiser, ed., "Civil War Letters," 267; Angle, ed., *Three Years in the Army*, 19.

14. Otto Memoirs, Oct. 3 and 4, 1862. For briefer accounts that differ slightly, see Carr to Sarah, Oct. 10, 1862, Charles Carr Collection, CHS; and Fitch, *Echoes*, 55–56.

15. *OR* 1, 16, pt. 2, 570–71; Winn Diary, Oct. 4 and 5, 1862.

16. Clark Diary, vol. 2, 42; Galpin Diary, Oct. 4 and 5, 1862. See also Otto Memoirs, Oct. 4, 1862; Taylor Diary, Oct. 5, 1862, KHS.

17. "From the Twenty-first Regiment," Oct. 5, 1862, in Quiner Scrapbooks, vol. 6, 142.

18. *OR* 1, 16, pt. 1, 89; *OR* 1, 16, pt. 2, 575; A. McD. McCook to Fry, Oct. 5, 1864, Buell Papers.

19. Taylor Diary, Oct. 5 and 7, 1862, KHS. See also unidentified clipping, Washington newspaper, 1881, McCook Family Papers, LC.

20. *OR* 1, 16, pt. 2, 575, 578–79 (quotation, 575); *OR* 1, 16, pt. 1, 89. Clark Diary, vol. 2, 42; Galpin Diary, Oct. 5 and 6, 1862; Morse Diary, Oct. 6, 1862; Otto Memoirs,

Oct. 6, 1862; Taylor Diary, Oct. 6, 1862, KHS; Sill to A. McD. McCook, Oct. 4, 1862, Buell Papers; Webster Diary, 28; Glauser, trans., *Private Josiah Ayre*, 17–18.

21. Hupp, *My Diary*, 21.

22. *OR* 1, 16, pt. 2, 566, 568–69, 572–73, 897–98; *B&L*, vol. 3, 47; Norman W. Calkins Note Book, Oct. 2, 1862, Civil War Miscellaneous Collection, USAMHI (hereafter Calkins Notebook); Walker Diary, vol. 2, 2; Anderson, ed., *Nicholas Longworth Anderson*, 161; Butler, *My Story*, 220–21; *Cincinnati Daily Commercial*, Oct. 6 and 10, 1862; Cutter, *Our Battery*, 77–78; Grose, *Story of the Marches*, 136; Hight and Stormont, *Fifty-eighth Indiana*, 98; "His Mother," *Young Chaplain*, 99; Noe, ed., *Southern Boy in Blue*, 101–2.

23. *History of the Seventy-third Regiment*, 96–97; Rerick, *Forty-fourth Indiana*, 71; Woodruff, *Fifteen Years Ago*, 231–32.

24. *Cincinnati Daily Commercial*, Oct. 10, 1862.

25. *OR* 1, 16, pt. 1, 525, 896, 1019. See also *Cincinnati Daily Commercial*, Oct. 10, Oct. 11, 1862; Grose, *Story of the Marches*, 136; "His Mother," *Young Chaplain*, 99–100; *History of the Seventy-third Indiana*, 108; Woodruff, *Fifteen Years Ago*, 232–33.

26. Noe, ed., *Southern Boy in Blue*, 102. See also Anderson, ed., *Nicholas Longworth Anderson*, 161.

27. *OR* 1, 16, pt. 1, 526, 555.

28. "His Mother," *Young Chaplain*, 100. See also *OR* 1, 16, pt. 2, 576, 577; Calkins Note Book, Oct. 5, 1862, USAMHI.

29. "His Mother," *Young Chaplain*, 100–1. See also Hight and Stormont, *Fifty-eighth Indiana*, 100.

30. Barnes, Carnahan, and McCain, *Eighty-sixth Regiment*, 56; Hinman, *Sherman Brigade*, 291.

31. Anderson, ed., *Nicholas Longworth Anderson*, 161.

32. *OR* 1, 16, pt. 1, 896; Calkins Note Book, Oct. 6, 1862, USAMHI; Anderson, ed., *Nicholas Longworth Anderson*, 161; Hinman, *Sherman Brigade*, 292–93; *History of the Seventy-ninth Indiana*, 50; *History of the Seventy-third Indiana*, 109; Noe, ed., *Southern Boy in Blue*, 102; Phillips, ed., *Civil War Diary*, Oct. 6. Springfield merchant E. L. Davison, owner of the whiskey, left a vivid description of drunken Federals pillaging his property; see Davison, *Autobiography*, 41–44.

33. Barnes, Carnahan, and McCain, *Eighty-sixth Regiment*, 56–58.

34. *OR* 1, 16, pt. 1, 1018–19; *OR* 1, 16, pt. 2, 566; Mitchell to Thomas Blackman, Oct. 18, 1862, Elijah R. Mitchell Letter, InHS; Patterson Memoir, Oct. 3, 1862; Blegen, ed., *Civil War Letters*, 142; Butler, ed., *Letters Home*, 10.

35. Thatcher, *Hundred Battles*, 73–74. See also Work Diary, 3, USAMHI.

36. Ulery to his uncle and aunt, Oct. 3, 1862, Abraham Ulery Letter, Filson; "Life of L. A. Ross," 45–46.

37. Crary, *Crary Memoirs*, 71–72. See also Benson, *Soldier's Diary*, 29.

38. Lathrop, *Fifty-ninth Regiment*, 163.

39. Althouse and Hughes, *John A. Boon*, 15.

40. "Life of L. A. Ross," 45.

41. *OR* 1, 16, pt. 2, 576; Inskeep Diary, Oct. 4, 1862; Mitchell to Blackman, Oct. 18, 1862, Mitchell Letter, InHS; Patterson Memoir, Oct. 4, 1862; Gilbert, "Bragg's Invasion of Kentucky," 341; Shaw, *Tenth Regiment*, 171.

42. Francis, *Narrative*, 54.

43. Culp Diary, 54; Inskeep Diary, Oct. 5, 6, 1862; Patterson Memoir, Oct. 5, 1862; "Life of L. A. Ross," 45–47; Small Diary, Oct. 6, 1862; *Aurora (Ill.) Weekly Beacon*, Nov. 6, 1862; Bishop, *Story of a Regiment*, 71; Butler, ed., *Letters Home*, 11; Keil, *Thirty-fifth Ohio*, 97; Shaw, *Tenth Regiment*, 171.

44. Morris, *Eighty-first Regiment*, 14.

45. Culp Diary, Oct. 6, 1862; Allen L. Fahnestock Diary, Oct. 6, 1862, Peoria Public Library, Peoria, Ill. (hereafter Fahnestock Diary); Ball, "At Perryville," 2.

46. Butler, ed., *Letters Home*, 11–12.

47. Gilbert to Sheridan, Oct. 5, 1862, Army of the Ohio and 14th Army Corps, Letters and Reports Received, 1862–1865, RG 393, NARA.

48. Bennett and Haigh, *Thirty-sixth Regiment*, 240–41. See also "Life of L. A. Ross," 46.

49. Shaw, *Tenth Regiment*, 171–72.

CHAPTER 7

1. *OR* 1, 16, pt. 2, 896–97; Cleburne to Polk, Oct. 1, 1862, Bragg Papers, WRHS; Garrett, trans, *Robert D. Smith*, Oct. 1 and 2, 1862.

2. Kirby Smith to Johnston, Oct. 31, 1866, Johnston Papers, Filson.

3. Connelly, *Army of the Heartland*, 247.

4. *OR* 1, 16, pt. 2, 898.

5. Polk to Bragg, Oct. 2, 1862, Bragg Papers, Duke; Hardee to Bragg, Oct. 2, 1862, Bragg Papers, WRHS.

6. J. Stoddard Johnston Diary, Oct. 3, 1862, Bragg Papers, WRHS (hereafter Johnston Diary); *OR* 1, 16, pt. 2, 903–4.

7. *OR* 1, 16, pt. 1, 1091; *OR* 1, 16, pt. 2, 900–3; Daniel Diary, 19; McWhiney, "Controversy in Kentucky," 26–27; Parks, *General Leonidas Polk*, 264–65.

8. Street to his wife, Oct. 10, 1862, Street and East (Pace) Correspondence, SHC-UNC. Street began this letter on Oct. 3 and continued it over several days.

9. Inglis Diary, Oct. 4, 5, and 6, 1862. See also John Euclid Magee Diary, Oct. 4, 1862, Duke (hereafter Magee Diary).

10. Beatty Diary, Oct. 4, 1862; Gipson, "About the Battle," 163; "33rd Alabama," 25.

11. Sutherland, ed., *Reminiscences*, 95.

12. *OR* 1, 16, pt. 2, 900, 901; Connelly, *Army of the Heartland*, 248; Hattaway and Jones, *How the North Won*, 257; Horn, *Army of Tennessee*, 179; McWhiney, *Braxton Bragg*, 303; Woodworth, *Jefferson Davis*, 156–57. A contemporary who supported Polk was Mosgrove, "Battle of Perryville," 3.

13. *OR* 1, 16, pt. 1, 1091.

14. Johnston Diary, Oct. 4, 1862; *OR* 1, 16, pt. 2, 901, 904–5.

15. Johnston Diary, Oct. 4, 1862; Johnston, "Bragg's Campaign in Kentucky, by a Staff Officer. No. 4—From Frankfort to Perryville," Johnston Papers, Filson (hereafter "Campaign in Kentucky, No. 4"); Connelly, *Army of the Heartland*, 251; Harrison, "George W. Johnson," 28–35; Woodworth, *Jefferson Davis*, 157. Much confusion exists as to the exact sequence of events, no doubt reflecting the chaos that followed. Marshall speaks before or after Bragg and Hawes in various accounts. The shelling begins during or after Hawes's speech. Couriers appear during the speech or afterward. In attempting to reconstruct what happened, I have relied wherever possible upon eyewitnesses' contemporary accounts. Even they may not be accurate, however. Kentuckian Stoddard Johnston, for example, remained mortified about the day's events, and his anger must have shaped his recollections.

16. *OR* 1, 16, pt. 2, 905; Harrison, "George W. Johnson," 35.

17. "Campaign in Kentucky, No. 4." See also Claiborne, "Campaign of 1862," 13; Harrison, "George W. Johnson," 35.

18. Hughes, ed., *Liddell's Record*, 85.

19. Johnston Diary, Oct. 4 and 5, 1862; "Campaign in Kentucky, No. 4"; *OR* 1, 16, pt. 2, 905–6, 911–12. Hess, *Banners to the Breeze*, 84, notes that in hindsight it was "a fortunate move" that brought Hardee and Polk together.

20. *OR* 1, 16, pt. 2, 915; "Campaign in Kentucky, No. 4."

21. Dumont to Buell, Oct. 5, 1862, and Sill to McCook, Oct. 5, 1862, Buell Papers.

22. Hall Diary, 58.

23. Daviess, *Mercer and Boyle Counties*, 105.

24. Street to his wife, Oct. 10, 1862, Street and East (Pace) Correspondence, SHC-UNC; Magee Diary, Oct. 5, 1862.

25. Hughes, ed., *Liddell's Record*, 86.

26. Watkins, *"Co. Aytch,"* 60.

27. *OR* 1, 16, pt. 1, 1091–92, 1095 (quotation), 1109, 1119; *OR* 1, 16, pt. 2, 917; Claiborne, "Campaign of 1862," 13–14; Ellis Diary, 27; Johnston Diary, Oct. 5 and 6, 1862; Hardee to George Williamson, Dec. 1, 1862, Bragg Papers, WRHS; Johnston Diary, Oct. 5 and 6, 1862; Garrett, trans., *Robert D. Smith*, Oct. 6, 1862; Connelly, *Army of the Heartland*, 254–55.

28. Polk to his wife, Oct. 7, 1862, Polk Papers, SHC-UNC; Parks, *General Leonidas Polk*, 267–68.

29. *OR* 1, 16, pt. 1, 1092–93; *OR* 1, 16, pt. 2, 918.

30. Johnston Diary, Oct. 6, 1862.

31. During a 1909 interview with a reporter from the *Nashville Banner*, Buckner claimed that he knew through a spy that much of Buell's army was at Mackville, not north of the river, and that he personally had tried to convince Bragg to concentrate and strike the southern Federal force. Unable to change the general's mind, Buckner then claimed to have gone to Polk, who proceeded to make the same unsuccessful entreaty to Bragg. See Stickles, *Simon Bolivar Buckner*, 207–8.

32. *OR* 1, 16, pt. 1, 1092–93, 1095–96; Connelly, *Army of the Heartland*, 257.

33. *OR* 1, 16, pt. 1, 1120; Patton Anderson to Henry C. Semple, June 10, 1863, Confederate Artillery Batteries, Lumsden's Battery-Waters' Battery, ADAH; Daniel Diary, 19; Semple to Hardee, Nov. 28, 1862, Confederate Artillery Batteries, Lumsden's Battery-Waters' Battery, ADAH; "33rd Alabama." 25.

34. *OR* 1, 16, pt. 1, 1120–21, 1157; Daniel Diary, 19; Searcy letter transcription, Semple's Alabama Battery File, PSHS; Hughes, ed., *Liddell's Record*, 86–88; "33rd Alabama," 25. In the *OR*, Liddell writes that he placed his men in position on "the morning of the 7th instant" (1157). In his memoir, however, he states that it was "later in the evening" on Oct. 6 (87). Other sources support the former statement. He also refers to the owner of the home incorrectly as the "Widow Paddock." See the Manuscript Census, Kentucky, Boyle County, Schedule I, NARA.

The Sam Bottom House burned in 1859, after which its owner rebuilt it. Rubble from the ruin remains on the site. Darrell Young Interview, July 16, 1999, Author's Perryville Tour Notes, PSHS.

35. *OR* 1, 16, pt. 1, 1157–58; Barnhill, *Fighting Fifth*, 44–45; Collier, *First In–Last Out*, 47; Daniel, *Shiloh*, 151, 184; Sword, *Shiloh*, 141, 151–54, 163, 203, 204, 293–94.

36. *OR* 1, 16, pt. 1, 89; Galpin Diary, Oct. 7, 1862; Landrum to Mrs. Obed J. Wilson, Oct. 12, 1862, Landrum Letters, OHS; Otto Memoirs, 96; Slack to his parents, Oct. 7, 1862, Albert L. Slack Correspondence no. 459, EU; Taylor Diary, 34, KHS; Glauser, trans., *Private Josiah Ayre*, 18; Hupp, *My Diary*, 22; Kendall, "Battle of Perryville," 6; *Record of the Ninety-fourth Regiment*, 18.

37. *OR* 1, 16, pt. 1, 525–27; *OR* 1, 16, pt. 2, 580; Tilford Diary, Oct. 7, 1862; Tuttle Diary, Oct. 7, 1862; Anderson, ed., *Nicholas Longworth Anderson*, 161; Cutter, *Our Battery*,

80–81; Davison, *Autobiography*, 44; Grose, *Story of the Marches*, 136–37; Hight and Stormont, *Fifty-eighth Indiana*, 100–1; Hinman, *Sherman Brigade*, 292; "His Mother," *Young Chaplain*, 102; *History of the Seventy-ninth Indiana*, 50; Kerwood, *Fifty-seventh Regiment*, 127; Noe, ed., *Southern Boy in Blue*, 102–3; Woodruff, *Fifteen Years Ago*, 233. Some exhausted soldiers indicated that Rolling Fork was four or five miles from the Lebanon road; it surely must have seemed that way.

38. Kerwood, *Fifty-seventh Regiment*, 128.

39. Barnes, Carnahan, and McCain, *Eighty-sixth Regiment*, 60.

40. Fahnestock Diary, Oct. 7, 1862; "Life of L. A. Ross," 48; Aten, *Eighty-fifth Regiment*, 33; Martin, *Eighth Kansas*, 19.

41. Butler, *Letters Home*, 12.

42. *OR* 1, 16, pt. 1, 1037; *OR* 1, 16, pt. 2, 661–62, 896–97; Wheeler to Major [?], Oct. 7, 1862, Bragg Papers, WRHS; Ford, "That Famous Retreat," 3; Kurt Holman to author, Nov. 5 and 6, 1998, and May 26, 2000, Author's Miscellaneous Letters, PSHS. The exact location of the ambush remains hard to pin down, but local sources most often identify the hill behind the modern Beech Grove Baptist Church, just west of the Boyle County line in Washington County, as the position Wheeler first occupied. Projectiles from small arms and artillery have been found west of that site along the road from the church toward Pottsville (Author's Perryville Tour Notes, July 18, 1999, PSHS).

43. Gay to Major [?], Sept. 28, 1862, Buell Papers; Ford, "That Famous Retreat," 3; Thatcher, *Hundred Battles*, 74. Thatcher erroneously refers to the Kentucky regiment as the Seventh.

44. *OR* 1, 16, pt. 1, 896–97; Wheeler to Major [?], Oct. 7, 1862, Bragg Papers, WRHS; Thatcher, *Hundred Battles*, 74–75 (quotation 74–75); Barnhill, *Fighting Fifth*, 45; Clay, *Introduction to the Archaeology*, 34–35; Holman to author, Nov. 5 and 6, 1998, and May 26, 2000.

45. Hardee to Major [?], Dec. 1, 1862, Bragg Papers, WRHS; George Brent Diary, Oct. 7, 1862, Bragg Papers, WRHS (hereafter Brent Diary); Ford, "That Famous Retreat," 3; Connelly, *Army of the Heartland*, 256.

46. *OR* 1, 16, pt. 1, 897; *OR* 1, 16, pt. 2, 581; *B&L*, vol. 3, 15, 52; Joel Campbell DuBose, "First Alabama Cavalry, Confederate Army," Confederate Alabama Cavalry Files: 1st and 2nd Cavalry, ADAH; R. R. Gaines, "Reminiscences of the 3d. Ala. Cavalry," Confederate Alabama Cavalry Files: 3rd and 4th Cavalry, ADAH; James Hagan, "History and Organization of Third Regiment Alabama Cavalry," Confederate Alabama Cavalry Files: 3rd and 4th Cavalry, ADAH; *Milwaukee Sentinel*, Oct. 17, 1862, Ulmer to his mother, Nov. 9, 1862, Isaac Barton Ulmer Papers, SHC-UNC; Dodge, *Waif of the War*, 33; Gilbert, "Bragg's Invasion of Kentucky," 431; Hughes, ed. *Liddell's Record*, 88; Martin, *Eighth Kansas*, 19; Morris, *Eighty-first Regiment*, 15; Straw, "Battle of Perryville"; Thatcher, *Hundred Battles*, 75–76; Barnhill, *Fighting Fifth*, 45.

47. Sheaffer, "Battle of Perryville," 4; Chumney, "Don Carlos Buell," 168–69.

48. Hardee to Bragg, Oct. 7, 1862, 3:20 P.M., Bragg Papers, WRHS.

49. Hardee to Major [?], Dec. 1, 1862, Bragg Papers, WRHS.

50. *OR* 1, 16, pt. 1, 1096.

51. Hardee to Bragg, Oct. 7, 1862, 7:30 P.M., Bragg Papers, WRHS.

52. Brown to Fannie Brown, Oct. 24, 1862, Edward N. Brown Letters, ADAH; William F. Dowd Recollections, William H. McCardle Papers, MDAH (hereafter Dowd Recollections); Talley Autobiography, 24; Finley, "Battle of Perryville," 242; Garrett, trans., *Robert D. Smith*, Oct. 7, 1862; Headley, *Confederate Operations*, 55–56; Little and Maxwell, *History of Lumsden's Battery*, 12; Hafendorfer, ed., "Simon B. Buckner's," 55.

53. Winchester Diary, 73–74. See also Hall Diary, 58–59; Thomas R. Hooper Di-

ary, Oct. 7, 1862, Stones River National Battlefield Library, Murfreesboro, Tenn. (hereafter Hooper Diary); Trask Journal, 63; Malone, *Memoir*, 127; "William P. Rogers," 72.

54. Here my interpretation differs from Hafendorfer's (*Perryville*, 113, 127–28), who has the division cross the Chaplin River to form a second line of battle in front of Hardee's wing. To be sure, all the sources do not agree on exactly what happened. Marcus Toney of the 1st Tennessee Infantry writes powerfully of sleeping in a cemetery, presumably the town cemetery west of the river (*Privations*, 42); Hafendorfer's account is based largely on Toney. Sam Watkins of the same regiment also mentions sleeping in the cemetery ("*Co. Aytch*," 61). Thomas Head of the 16th Tennessee Infantry, however, writes that "Hardee's Corps was placed in front of Perryville, and Polk's corps was placed upon an elevation behind the town, and held as a reserve." Only if Head somehow mixed up the corps would his account agree with Toney's and Watson's (*Campaigns and Battles*, 94). That Head was so confused seems unlikely. Moreover, other sources, certainly most of the contemporary ones, indicate that Cheatham's division formed up east of the river on the left and slightly to the rear of one continuous Confederate line (*Atlanta Southern Confederacy*, Oct. 21, 1862; *Confederate Veteran* 33 (1925): 141; Daniel S. Donelson, to Marcus J. Wright, Oct. 26, 1862, Bragg Papers, WRHS; Magee Diary, Oct. 7, 1862; Winchester Diary, 74; Womack, *Diary of J. J. Womack*, 61–62. Current Perryville resident and archeologist Darrell Young adds that archeological evidence, other than that linked to Liddell and Wheeler, suggests that no Confederate campsites existed west of the river (Kurt Holman to author, Nov. 5, 1998, Author's Miscellaneous Letters, PSHS). Most importantly, Cheatham himself later wrote, "I reported to General Hardee, who placed me in line of battle on the extreme left of his corps, to the left and beyond Perryville from the direction of Harrodsburg" (Cheatham, "Battle of Perryville," 704). Exhausted as they were, one suspects that Toney, Watkins, and others must have stumbled away from the main line in the darkness.

55. Watkins, "*Co. Aytch*," 61.

56. *B&L*, vol. 3, 52.

57. Bennett and Haigh, *Thirty-sixth Regiment*, 247.

58. *Cleveland Plain Dealer*, Oct. 14, 1862.

59. *OR* 1, 16, pt. 1, 124–25, 134–36, 221–22.

60. Ibid., 49–50, 89; *OR* 1, 16, pt. 2, 580–81; Manuscript Census, Kentucky, Boyle County, Schedule I, 1850, NARA.

CHAPTER 8

1. Watkins, "*Co. Aytch*," 61–62. Watkins also claimed that his companion was a Federal soldier. That seems most unlikely unless the man was a deserter or prisoner. No other source indicates the presence of any Federals in town. See also Crawford, "Battle of Perryville," 263.

2. Tarrant, *Wild Riders*, 118. See also Crawford, "Battle of Perryville," 262; Author's Perryville Tour Notes, July 17, 1999, PSHS.

3. Betty Ann Keiser to author, Dec. 16, 1997, and Kurt Holman to author, Jan. 28, 1999, Author's Collection, PSHS.

4. "Diary of Lora Parks," Civilians File, PSHS; Harmon, *Chaplin Hills*, 35–36; "General's Tour," 43. A historical marker in front of the home, now called the Karrick-Parks House, relates the same story.

5. Clipping, Confederate Regimental History Files, 45th Alabama Infantry Regiment, ADAH; Harmon, *Chaplin Hills*, 54, 55.

6. *OR* 1, 16, pt. 1, 219, 233; Gilbert, "Bragg's Invasion of Kentucky," 433.

7. Brown, Murphy, and Putney, *Behind the Guns*, 35. See also Dr. J. G. Hatchitt's report in *Medical and Surgical History*, vol. 2, 254.

8. *B&L*, vol. 3, 52; Thomas G. Wan to Mrs. M. Hagins, Nov. 1, 1862, Wan Letter, ArHC; Grimshaw, "Battle of Perryville," 3; James, "Perryville," 143.

9. *OR* 1, 16, pt. 1, 219, 1074, 1158.

10. Ibid., 1158; Hughes, ed., *Liddell's Record*, 88.

11. *OR* 1, 16, pt. 1, 238, 1081, 1083.

12. "Memories of Mrs. Anson G. McCook," and unidentified clipping from a Washington, D.C., newspaper, 1881 (quotation), both in McCook Family Papers, LC; Boatner, *Civil War Dictionary*, 527; Reid, *Ohio in the War*, vol. 2, 314–16; Morris, *Sheridan*, 89; Stewart, *Dan McCook's Regiment*, 11–14.

13. *OR* 1, 16, pt. 1, 219, 238, 1083; Althouse and Hughes, eds., *John A. Boon*, 17; Brown, Murphy, and Putney, *Behind the Guns*, 28, 29, 35.

14. Fahnestock Diary, Oct. 8, 1862.

15. *OR* 1, 16, pt. 1, 219, 238, 1083; Althouse and Hughes, eds., *John A. Boon*, 17; Fahnestock Diary, Oct. 8, 1862; Work Diary, Oct. 8, 1862, OHS; Aten, *Eighty-fifth Regiment*, 34.

16. *OR* 1, 16, pt. 1, 1083.

17. Ibid., 219, 238–39, 1074, 1083, 1085; Althouse and Hughes, eds., *John A. Boon*, 17; Brown to Chandler, Oct. 17, 1862, U.S. Army Letters, Duke; Fahnestock Diary, Oct. 8, 1862; Grimshaw, "Battle of Perryville," 3; Price Diaries, 40; Work Diary, Oct. 8, 1862, OHS; Aten, *Eighty-fifth Regiment*, 34; Brown, Murphy, and Putney, *Behind the Guns*, 29, 36; Kinnear, *Eighty-sixth Regiment*, 12; Shaw, *Tenth Regiment*, 173.

Hafendorfer, *Perryville*, 132–35, 140–41, has neither the 10th Indiana nor the 86th Illinois take part in the initial capture of the hill. However, according to Captain Fahnestock: "At 4 o'clock in the morning I saw the rebles fire the first shots, then a volley, then the firing became general on our right. Our regiment was up and in line of battle, the 10 Indiana regiment on the right. General Frey rose up and commanded both regiments, we moved forward a half mile where our skirmishers engaged the enemy." G. W. Brown of the 86th Illinois also suggests that the two left regiments moved quickly in conjunction with McCook's main body, writing that "the battle was commenced a little before day light by the pickets of the 125, and 85, Ill., and very soon carried on by the pickets of the 86 Ill. and the 10 Ind." Finally, L. A. Ross of the 86th Illinois asserts bluntly: "Sharp skirmishing ensued in which the 86th took an active part. A little after daylight the rebel pickets fell back" ("Life of L. A. Ross," 48). The confusion seems to derive from Shaw's account. He states that his regiment encountered the *5th* Arkansas, as it would subsequently. Perhaps Shaw confused his Arkansans; he clearly is describing the capture of Peters Hill rather than Bottom Hill, for he later has Sheridan taking a hill to the front, which could only be Bottom Hill.

18. Shaw, *Tenth Regiment*, 173. Two secondary sources, Barnhill, *Fighting Fifth*, 47, and Collier, *First In–Last Out*, 48, depict the 7th Arkansas in a more favorable light than Shaw or Federal accounts in the *OR* suggest. Collier has the regiment retreat at 8 A.M. "with steady calm," while Barnhill maintains that the 7th Arkansas held Peters Hill for an hour before retreating. Unfortunately, both undocumented accounts are suspect. The times are off in both, and Collier notably has Cheatham's 2 P.M. attack occurring at the same time as the fall of Peters Hill. A better indication is to be found in Liddell's report (*OR* 1, 16, pt. 1, 1158), in which he states, "the enemy began a brisk fire upon my advanced line of skirmishers, and with superior numbers drove them from the woods." Nor does McCook's low casualty total, thirty-three men in all, suggest a dogged, hour-long resistance. As outnumbered skirmishers, the men of the 7th Arkansas seem to have acted

412 Notes to pages 151-156

exactly as they were supposed to by falling back upon the main body when heavily pressed. Lieutenant Colonel Daniel D. T. Cowen of the 52nd Ohio reported that his men "drove the pickets over the crest of the hill and through the field and wood beyond." (*OR* 1, 16, pt. 1, 1085).

19. *OR* 1, 16, pt. 1, 239, 1083, 1158; Althouse and Hughes, eds., *John A. Boon*, 17; Clay, *Introduction to the Archaeology*, 24, 49; Kurt Holman to author, Mar. 23, 2000, Author's Collection, PSHS.

20. *OR* 1, 16, pt. 1, 239, 1083; "Life of L. A. Ross, " 48–49; Althouse and Hughes, eds., *John A. Boon*, 17; Brown, Murphy and Putney, *Behind the Guns*, 29, 36.

21. Brown, Murphy, and Putney, *Behind the Guns*, 29.

22. *OR* 1, 16, pt. 1, 1158.

23. Ibid., 239, 1081, 1083; Brown, Murphy, and Putney, *Behind the Guns*, 29.

24. *OR* 1, 16, pt. 1, 239, 1083; Francis, *Narrative*, 56–57.

25. *OR* 1, 16, pt. 1, 1037; Thomas McCahan Diary, Oct. 8, 1862, 9th Pennsylvania Cavalry File, PSHS (hereafter McCahan Diary); Straw, "Battle of Perryville"; Thatcher, *Hundred Battles*, 77.

26. Thatcher, *Hundred Battles*, 77.

27. *OR* 1, 16, pt. 1, 1037, 1158; McCahan Diary, Oct. 8, 1862; Bowers, "Memories of a Retreat," 3 (quotation, 3); Hughes, ed., *Liddell's Record*, 88; Straw, "Battle of Perryville." For the Pennsylvanians' armament, see "Yankee Horse Soldiers—The 9th. Pennsylvania Cavalry."

28. *OR* 1, 16, pt. 1, 239.

29. Ibid., 1037.

30. Thatcher, *Hundred Battles*, 77–78.

31. Hughes, ed., *Liddell's Record*, 88–89.

32. Cavis Diary, Oct. 8, 1862.

33. Trauernicht, "McCook's Corps," 3.

34. James, "Perryville," 144.

35. *OR* 1, 16, pt. 1, 239, 1081, 1083–84; Brown to Chandler, Oct. 17, 1862, U.S. Army Letters, Duke; Straw, "Battle of Perryville"; Hughes, ed., *Liddell's Record*, 89; Straw, "Battle of Perryville"; Hafendorfer, *Perryville*, 147–48; McDonough, *War in Kentucky*, 222; and Morris, *Sheridan*, 91 all indicate that the 2nd and 15th Missouri led the assault followed by the two Illinois regiments. While Brown, Murphy, and Putney (*Behind the Guns*, 36, 37) agree, John Cavis of the 36th Illinois (Cavis Diary, Oct. 8, 1862), McCook (*OR* 1, 16, pt. 1, 239, 1083) and Thatcher (*Hundred Battles*, 78) all indicate that the 44th Illinois and not the 15th Missouri joined the 2nd Missouri in forming Laiboldt's line. Moreover, none of the three mention the other two regiments taking part in the assault at all. Nor does Thomas J. Frazee of the 73rd Illinois in a letter to his parents written Oct. 13, 1862 (Thomas J. Frazee Letters, IISHL). Frazee adds that one member of his regiment was killed and thirty-five were wounded during the artillery bombardment. Henry Trauernicht, a member of the 2nd Missouri who lost a leg in the assault, says only that "the 44th Ill. and 15th Mo. came to our assistance" (*National Tribune*, Sept. 30, 1886, 3). Certainly all the contemporary accounts support the interpretation provided here.

In the decades following the war, a controversy erupted over the 2nd Missouri's role in the battle. See Allinger, "Battle of Perryville," 3; Allinger, "2nd Mo. at Perryville," 3; Starkweather, "Perryville," 2.

36. Thatcher, *Hundred Battles*, 78.

37. *OR* 1, 16, pt. 1, 239, 1081; Aten, *Eighty-fifth Regiment*, 35; Hughes, ed., *Liddell's Record*, 89.

38. Brown to Chandler, Oct. 17, 1862, U.S. Army Letters, Duke.

39. Hughes, ed., *Liddell's Record*, 89.

40. *OR* 1, 16, pt. 1, 1158; Work Diary, Oct. 8, 1862, OHS; Hafendorfer, ed., "Simon B. Buckner's," 55; Hughes, ed., *Liddell's Record*, 89–90; Straw, "Battle of Perryville"; Trauernicht, "McCook's Corps," 3.

41. *OR* 1, 16, pt. 1, 1092, 1096.

42. Davis, "Recollections of Perryville," 554.

43. *OR* 1, 16, pt. 1, 1110, 1102; Connelly, *Army of the Heartland*, 259. Thomas Claiborne, a member of Buckner's staff, later claimed in "Battle of Perryville," 225, that Polk actually planned to retreat, and would have done so had not Bragg later arrived.

44. *B&L*, vol. 3, 15.

45. Connelly, *Army of the Heartland*, 260–61; McDonough, *War in Kentucky*, 228–32; McWhiney, *Braxton Bragg*, 306–7, and "Controversy in Kentucky," 30–32; Woodworth, *Jefferson Davis*, 156–59. Horn and Parks, both generally favorable to Polk, note the incident without comment (Horn, *Army of Tennessee*, 183; Parks, *General Leonidas Polk*, 269–70).

46. Cummings, "Sheridan at Perryville," 10.

47. *B&L*, vol. 3, 53.

48. *OR* 1, 16, pt. 1, 239, 1084; Aten, *Eighty-fifth Regiment*, 35; Hughes, ed., *Liddell's Record*, 89; Sheridan, *Personal Memoirs*, 195; Stewart, *Dan McCook's Regiment*, 26–27. No modern evidence of the much-discussed rifle pits remains.

49. *Cincinnati Daily Enquirer*, Oct. 14, 1862.

50. Davison, *Autobiography*, 45; James, "Perryville," 144 (quotation, 144); Appendix 1.

CHAPTER 9

1. *OR* 1, 16, pt. 1, 50, 89–90, 293–94, 1022, 1038; Landrum to Mrs. Wilson, Oct. 12, 1862, Landrum Letters, OHS; Winn Diary, Oct. 8, 1862; Otto Memoirs, 98; *Record of the Ninety-fourth Regiment*, 18; Scribner, *How Soldiers Were Made*, 57–58; Waddle, *Three Years*, 29.

2. *OR* 1, 16, pt. 1, 343; Duncan Diary, 8; Waddle to his sister, Oct. 11, 1862, Ellen Waddle McCoy Papers, MHS; Landrum to Mrs. Wilson, Oct. 12, 1862, Landrum Letters, OHS; *Cleveland Plain Dealer*, Oct. 17, 1862; *New Albany (Ind.) Daily Ledger*, Oct. 14, 1862; *Princeton (Ind.) Clarion*, Oct. 25, 1862; Beatty, *Citizen-Soldier*, 176–77; Horrall, *Forty-second Indiana*, 150; Hupp, *My Diary*, 22; Kirkpatrick, *Experiences*, 14; Perry, *Thirty-eighth Regiment*, 27.

3. Waddle, *Three Years*, 29.

4. *OR* 1, 16, pt. 1, 69, 90, 343, 1038, 1044; Landrum to Mrs. Wilson, Oct. 12, 1862, Landrum Letters, OHS; Manuscript Census, Kentucky, Boyle County, Schedules I, II, III, 1860, NARA; *Cincinnati Daily Commercial*, Oct. 24, 1862; *New Albany (Ind.) Daily Ledger*, Oct. 14, 1862; "Real War," 3; Charles Kays, interview with Morland Russell, Indianapolis, Ind., Aug. 23, 1992, Author's Collection, PSHS.

5. *OR* 1, 16, pt. 1, 69, 343–44, 1038, 1044; *B&L*, vol. 3, 54; Duncan Diary, 8; Landrum to Mrs. Wilson, Oct. 12, 1862, Landrum Letters, OHS; McDowell Reminiscence, Filson; *Cincinnati Daily Enquirer*, Oct. 14, 1862; Cheatham, "Battle of Perryville," 705; Reid, *Ohio in the War*, vol. 2, 78–79; Switlik, "Loomis' Battery," 2–5, 15–21, 26, 32.

6. McDowell Reminiscence.

7. Landrum to Mrs. Wilson, Oct. 12, 1862, Landrum Letters, OHS; Beatty, *Citizen-Soldier*, 177; *Cincinnati Daily Commercial*, Oct. 24, 1862. In the last quotation, I substitute the correct name of the road, "Mackville," for "Harrodsburg," for the sake of clarity. See also *New Albany (Ind.) Daily Ledger*, Oct. 16, 1862.

8. Thatcher, *Hundred Battles*, 79–80. For Loomis, see Switlik, "Loomis' Battery," 5.

9. *OR* 1, 16, pt. 1, 69, 90, 343, 356, 1044–45, 1056; McDowell Reminiscence;

Daily Evansville Journal, Oct. 21, 1862; *Princeton (Ind.) Clarion*, Oct. 17, 1862; Horrall, *Forty-second Indiana*, 150–51; Kirkpatrick, *Experiences*, 14; Author's Perryville Tour Notes, July 17, 1999, PSHS.

10. Hoover, "Battle of Perryville," 3.

11. Knowles, "Battle of Perryville," 3.

12. *OR* 1, 16, pt. 1, 293–94, 344, 1045; Glezen Diary, Oct. 8, 1862; Otto Memoirs, 98; A. D. Cleaver to his wife, Oct. 11, 1862, 123rd Illinois File, PSHS; Silas Emerson to Nancy Ann Emerson, Oct. 14, 1862, Nancy Ann Emerson Letters, OHS; Winters, *In the 50th Ohio*, 19.

13. *OR* 1, 16, pt. 1, 186, 526–27, 555–56, 561; Calkins Note Book, USAMHI, Oct. 7–8, 1862; Phillips, ed., *Civil War Diary*, Oct. 8, 1862; Sturges letter fragment, Eden P. Sturges Correspondence, *Civil War Times Illustrated* Collection, USAMHI; Tarrant, *Wild Riders*, 117.

14. *OR* 1, 16, pt. 1, 897–98 (quotation, 897); Joseph Wheeler's report (typescript), Confederate Alabama Cavalry Files, 1st and 2nd Cavalry, ADAH; Ulmer to his mother, Nov. 8, 1862, Isaac Barton Ulmer Papers, SHC-UNC; Tarrant, *Wild Riders*, 118–19; Author's Perryville Tour Notes, July 17–18, 1999, PSHS.

15. *OR* 1, 16, pt. 1, 526, 527, 555–56, 1070; *B&L*, vol. 3, 16; Sturges letter fragment, Sturges Correspondence, USAMHI; Barnes, Carnahan, and McCain, *Eighty-sixth Regiment*, 62–63; Butler, *My Story*, 222; Cutter, *Our Battery*, 80–81; Grose, *Story of the Marches*, 137; James, "Perryville," 144–45; Kimberly and Holloway, *Forty-first Ohio*, 34; Noe, ed., *Southern Boy in Blue*, 103; Simmons, *84th Reg't*, 14–15; Tarrant, *Wild Riders*, 117–18.

16. *OR* 1, 16, pt. 1, 526; Wright, "Glimpse of Perryville," 150.

17. McDonough, *War in Kentucky*, 226.

18. "Campaign in Kentucky, No. 4"; Connelly, *Army of the Heartland*, 259; McWhiney, "Controversy in Kentucky," 31.

19. Bragg to Jefferson Davis, May 22, 1863, Bragg Papers, Duke.

20. *OR* 1, 16, pt. 1, 1092; Brent Diary, Oct. 7 and 8, 1862; Johnston Diary, Oct. 8, 1862.

21. *OR* 1, 16, Pt. 1, 1087; Brent Diary, Oct. 8, 1862; Claiborne, "Campaign of 1862," 15; Johnston Diary, Oct. 8, 1862; Manuscript Census, Kentucky, Boyle County, Schedule I, 1850, NARA; Claiborne, "Battle of Perryville," 225; Hughes, ed., *Liddell's Record*, 90.

22. Brent Diary, Oct. 8, 1862.

23. Johnston, "Bragg's Campaign in Kentucky, by a Staff Officer. No. 5—Battle of Perryville," Johnston Papers, Filson (hereafter "Campaign in Kentucky, No. 5").

24. *OR* 1, 16, pt. 1, 897; *B&L*, vol. 3, 16.

25. W. W. Carnes to Bishop Quintard, Feb. 13, 1895, Charles Todd Quintard Papers, Duke; Ellis Diary, 27; Hall Diary, 59; Inglis Diary, Oct. 8, 1862; Magee Diary, Oct. 8, 1862; Talley Autobiography, 24; Head, *Campaigns and Battles*, 94; Thompson, "Hear the Wax Fry," 9; Womack, *Diary of J. J. Womack*, 62.

26. Cross, *Camp and Field*, 61.

27. *OR* 1, 16, pt. 1, 1122–23. Archeological evidence places Semple's rifled guns farther north near the Dye House, suggesting that the section remained with Wood. See Kurt Holman to author, May 25, 2000, Author's Collection, PSHS.

28. *OR* 1, 16, pt. 1, 1122–23; Trask Journal, 30, 66–67; Headley, *Confederate Operations*, 56; Boatner, *Civil War Dictionary*, 3, 885; Author's Perryville Tour Notes, July 16, 1999, PSHS. Both Hafendorfer, *Perryville*, 192–93, 228; and McDonough, *War in Kentucky*, 267–70, assume that Adams stopped at Bottom Hill and then crossed Sheridan's

Peters Hill position toward the Squire Bottom House later in the day, and in full view of Sheridan as well. That assumption leads both authors to discuss at some length the reasons why Sheridan might have acted (or not acted) so inexplicably, and why he covered up his strange inaction in his report and later memoirs. However, W. L. Trask strongly suggests that Adams never stopped on Bottom Hill, but instead turned off the road and moved almost a mile to the northeast (Trask Journal, 66–67). The terrain in the sector is such that a brigade in column could easily pass behind Bottom Hill and largely escape notice from Sheridan. Such a movement simply makes more sense. I am grateful to John Walsh for his thoughts on Adams's march.

29. *OR* 1, 16, pt. 1, 1122.

30. Ibid., 1122–23; Dowd Recollections; Sutherland, ed., *Reminiscences*, 97. Hafendorfer, *Perryville*, 192, 258; Author's Perryville Tour Notes, July 16, 1999.

31. *OR* 1, 16, pt. 1, 1124–25.

32. Ibid., 1131–32, 1133.

33. Garrett, trans., *Robert D. Smith*, 33. See also Dowd Recollections; Buck, *Cleburne*, 66–67.

34. "33rd Alabama," 26.

35. *OR* 1, 16, pt. 1, 69, 1121; "Campaign in Kentucky, No. 5"; "33rd Alabama Infantry, Company 'B'," 33rd Alabama Infantry File, PSHS, 25; *Macon Daily Telegraph*, Nov. 18, 1862; Hafendorfer, ed., "Simon B. Buckner's," 56. See also note 78.

36. A. S. Hamilton to Wood, Mar. 25, 1863, Sterling A. M. Wood Papers. ADAH. See also *Macon Daily Telegraph*, Nov. 18, 1862; Hafendorfer, ed., "Simon B. Buckner's," 56.

37. Kennedy, "Fighting Preacher," 34.

38. Carnes, "Artillery," 8; Losson, *Tennessee's Forgotten Warriors*, 66; *Bradenton (Fla.) Herald*, May 26, 1933, copied in Thomas Potter to Kurt Holman, Oct. 31, 1999, Author's Collection, PSHS.

39. *OR* 1, 16, pt. 1, 69; Landrum to Amanda, Oct. 12, 1862, Landrum Letters, OHS. For the alcohol, see Samuel M. Starling to his daughters, Nov. 16, 1862, Lewis-Starling Collection, Western Kentucky University Library, Bowling Green, Ky.

40. Millard, "Battle of Perryville," 1.

41. Landrum to Amanda, Oct. 12, 1862, Landrum Letters, OHS. For the regiment see Reid, *Ohio in the War*. vol. 2, 23–24. See also Scribner, *How Soldiers Were Made*, 58.

42. This account is drawn from *OR* 1, 16, pt. 1, 343, 1037–38, 1045; Landrum, to Amanda, Oct. 12, 1862; and *Cleveland Plain Dealer*, Oct. 17, 1862. For a slightly different account, see Hartman, "Battle of Perryville," 3.

43. Landrum to Amanda, Oct. 12, 1862, Landrum Letters, OHS.

44. Horrall, *Forty-second Indiana*, 150–51.

45. *Daily Evansville Journal*, Oct. 21, 1862.

46. *OR* 1, 16, pt. 1, 343. See also McDowell Reminiscence; Beatty, *Citizen-Soldier*, 177; Reid, *Ohio in the War*, vol. 2, 79.

47. *Cincinnati Daily Enquirer*, Oct. 14, 1862.

48. Carnes to Quintard, Feb. 13, 1895, Quintard Papers, Duke. For a slightly different account, see Carnes, "Artillery," 8. The accuracy of Loomis's pieces, determined by a recent examination of shell fragments found in the vicinity of Carnes's position, is noted in Author's Perryville Tour Notes, July 17, 1999, PSHS. The lack of smoothbore hits there suggests that Hotchkiss did not reach the target, if indeed he even tried. For the sound of the cannon, see Cheek, ed., "Mrs. E. B. Patterson," 372. For civilians, see Kays interview, Author's Collection, PSHS.

49. Spradlin, ed., "Diary of George W. Jones," 8. John Euclid Magee identified the men killed as "Raycraft" and "Calvin McCale" (Magee Diary, 40).

50. Magee Diary, 40. Archeological evidence supports Stanford's southerly movement, see Kurt Holman to author, Mar. 28, 2000, Author's Collection, PSHS.

51. "33rd Alabama Infantry, Company 'B'," 1; "33rd Alabama," 25–26; Sumrall, *Light on the Hill*, 4, 7; Sword, *Shiloh*, 202.

52. Carter, ed., *For Honor, Glory & Union*, 1–30, 137–46; Boatner, *Civil War Dictionary*, 498.

53. *OR* 1, 16, pt. 1, 1038, 1056–57; McDowell Reminiscence; *Daily Evansville Journal*, Oct. 22, 1862; *Louisville Daily Journal*, Oct. 21, 1862; *Princeton (Ind.) Clarion*, Oct. 25, 1862; Beatty, *Citizen-Soldier*, 177–78; Reid, *Ohio in the War*, vol. 2, 30, 79; Holman, "Henry P. 'Squire' Bottom's War Claim."

54. *OR* 1, 16, pt. 1, 69, 1045; Waddle to his sister, Oct. 11, 1862, McCoy Papers, MHS; "5th Ind. Battery"; *Cincinnati Daily Enquirer*, Oct. 14, 1862; *New Albany (Ind.) Daily Ledger*, Oct. 16, 24, 1862; Hupp, *My Diary*, 23; Scribner, *How Soldiers Were Made*, 58–59; Perry, *Thirty-eighth Regiment*, 28–29.

55. Phelps to friends, Oct. 16, 1862, Phelps Letters, USAMHI.

56. Reprinted in the *Cleveland Plain Dealer*, Oct. 14, 1862.

57. *Cincinnati Daily Enquirer*, Oct. 14, 1862.

58. Landrum to Amanda, Oct. 12, 1862, Landrum Letters, OHS.

59. *OR* 1, 16, pt. 1, 1056, 1057.

60. *Cleveland Plain Dealer*, Oct. 14, 1862.

61. *OR*, 1, 16, pt. 1, 70–71, 343, 1055, 1057; "5th Ind. Battery"; *Cincinnati Daily Commercial*, Oct. 24, 1862; Phelps to friends, Oct. 16, 1862, Phelps Letters, USAMHI; Beatty, *Citizen-Soldier*, 178; Hupp, *My Diary*, 23; Reid, *Ohio in the War*, vol. 2, 79; Switlik, "Loomis' Battery," 37.

62. Landrum to Amanda, Oct. 12, 1862, Landrum Letters, OHS.

63. Shanklin, "*Dear Lizzie*," 226–27. See also *Princeton (Ind.) Clarion*, Oct. 25, 1862.

CHAPTER 10

1. This account is based on *OR* 1, 16, pt. 1, 1110, 1114, 1116, 1118; Clark Memoirs, 25; Donelson to Wright, Oct. 26, 1862, Bragg Papers, WRHS; Hooper Diary, Oct. 8, 1862; "Campaign in Kentucky, No. 5"; Magee Diary, 39; [George E. Maney] to Marcus J. Wright, Oct. 24, 1862, and Alexander P. Stewart to Marcus J. Wright, Oct. 28, 1862, Bragg Papers, WRHS; Milledgeville [Ga.] *Confederate Union*, Oct. 28, 1862; Carnes, "Artillery," 8; Cheatham. "Battle of Perryville," 704; Cross, *Camp and Field*, 61; Malone, *Memoir*, 128; Savage, *Life of John H. Savage*, 118; Womack, *Diary of J. J. Womack*, 62; Crawford, "Battle of Perryville," 263; "General's Tour," 41, 43, Losson, *Tennessee's Forgotten Warriors*, 65–66. Hafendorfer, *Perryville*, 165, identifies the road Cheatham followed from the Crawford house by its modern name, the Old Chaplin River Road. There is no evidence that the road had any name at the time of the battle, however. Indeed, Kurt Holman indicates that the name came into general usage among Perryville residents only after the publication of Hafendorfer's book. See Kurt Holman to author, Feb. 19, 1999, Author's Collection, PSHS.

2. *OR* 1, 16, pt. 1, 1110; Graber, *Life Record*, 171; Tapp, "Battle of Perryville," 171.

3. *OR* 1, 16, pt. 1, 1110.

4. "Campaign in Kentucky, No. 5."

5. *OR* 1, 16, pt. 1, 1110, 1113, 1114, 1116; Clark Memoirs, 25; Stewart to Wright, Oct. 28, 1862, Bragg Papers, WRHS; *Atlanta Southern Confederacy*, Oct. 21, 1862; Reynolds, *Henry County Commands*, 45; Head, *Campaigns and Battles*, 95; Savage, *Life of John H. Savage*, 119; Thompson, "Hear the Wax Fry," 9; Womack, *Diary of J. J. Womack*,

62; Connelly, *Army of the Heartland*, 263. Contrary to modern myth (repeated most recently in Hafendorfer, *Perryville*, 240 and Hess, *Banners to the Breeze*, 89) there is no contemporary evidence that the Dug Road received its name just after the battle because the Confederate artillerymen of Lt. William B. Turner's Mississippi Battery had to widen it as they went to get their gun carriages to the top of the bluff. The path clearly existed long before the battle, and none of the sources above mentions widening it that day. Indeed, I will maintain that Turner did not even use it that day. Most likely no one "dug" the road until 1912 when the Hankla family, still owners of the old Goodknight farm, improved it. An early use of the name is found in Crawford, "Battle of Perryville," 263. See also Kurt Holman to author, Apr. 10, 1999, Author's Collection, PSHS.

6. *OR* 1, 16, pt. 1, 1110–11; Giles, *Terry's Texas Rangers*, 45–46; Jeffries, *Terry's Rangers*, 59; Williams and Wooster, eds., "With Terry's Texas Rangers," 310; Holman to author, Feb. 19, 1999. The bed of the old, now-abandoned County Road (sometimes called the Dixville road, not to be confused with the Benton "Dixville" road), Wharton's route, still exists and can be seen at several places. Indeed, thanks to Darrell Young I have walked some of it. See Author's Perryville Tour Notes, July 17, 1999.

7. *OR* 1, 16, pt. 1, 90, 104, 1039.

8. Ibid., 90.

9. Ibid., 1040, 1059–60; Glezen Diary, Oct. 8, 1862; *Cincinnati Daily Commercial*, Nov. 8, 1862; Brooks, *Battle of Perryville* pamphlet, IlSHL; Winters, *In the 50th Ohio*, 19.

10. *OR* 1, 16, pt. 1, 1066; S. J. Harris, to S. Noble, Nov. 29, 1862 (quotation), and Harris, to S. Noble, Jan. 19, 1864, Regimental Correspondence of the Adjutant General of Indiana, 19th Indiana Battery, InSA.

11. *OR* 1, 16, pt. 1, 1066–67; Glezen Diary, Oct. 8, 1862; *Cincinnati Daily Commercial*, Oct. 24, 1862; Manuscript Census, Kentucky, Boyle County, Schedule I, 1860; Brooks, *Battle of Perryville* pamphlet, IlSHL; Milner, "'A Human Document,'" 6; Kurt Holman to author, Dec. 23, 1998, and Mar. 11, 1999, Author's Collection, PSHS.

12. *Cincinnati Daily Commercial*, Nov. 8, 1862.

13. Glezen Diary, Oct. 8, 1862. A slightly different account, part of a photocopy entitled "Abstract from the Diary of Private Glezen" can be found in the 80th Indiana Infantry File, PSHS.

14. *OR* 1, 16, pt. 1, 90, 1039; Finley, "Battle of Perryville," 243.

15. *OR* 1, 16, pt. 1, 90.

16. Hilliard, "You Are Strangely Deluded," 13–15; Hess, *Banners to the Breeze*, 43; Sword, *Shiloh*, 392–94.

17. Morse to his mother, Sept. 28, 1862, Morse Papers, OHS. See also Glauser, trans., *Private Josiah Ayre*, 5.

18. Hilliard, "You Are Strangely Deluded," 15–18.

19. *OR* 1, 16, pt. 1, 1062, 1064; Glauser, trans., *Private Josiah Ayre*, 3; Tourgée, *Story of a Thousand*, 116–17, 137–39.

20. Tourgée, *Story of a Thousand*, 138–39.

21. Ibid., 116.

22. *OR* 1, 16, pt. 1, 1062; Cleaver to his wife, Oct. 11, 1862, 123rd Illinois File; Taylor Diary, 2, KHS; Tourgée, *Story of a Thousand*, 116–18.

23. *OR* 1, 16, pt. 1, 90.

24. Ibid., 1040–1.

25. Johnston, *Soldier Boy's Diary*, 22. See also Kurt Holman to author, Mar. 24, 2000, Author's Collection, PSHS.

26. Otto Memoirs, 98.

27. Carr to Sarah, Oct. 10, 1862, Carr Collection, CHS; *Oshkosh (Wisc.) Courier*,

Oct. 24, 1862; Holmes, *Soldier*, 93; Hoover, "Battle of Perryville," 3; Johnston, *Soldier Boy's Diary*, 22; Knowles, "Battle of Perryville," 3; Starkweather, "Perryville," 2.

28. Otto Memoirs, 98–102. For a similar account, see Fitch, *Echoes*, 57–58.

29. *OR* 1, 16, pt. 1, 1045, 1155.

30. Ibid., 1045. See also Otto Memoirs, 74–75.

31. *OR* 1, 16, pt. 1, 1041, 1045, 1060; D. C. Stone to Sir, Oct. 17, 1862, Stone to Sir, Feb. 28, 1863, "Commonwealth of Kentucky, Court-Martial of D. C. Stone," and J. Holt to Edward R. S. Canby, May 26, 1863, all in Battery A, Kentucky Artillery Collection, Union Artillery-Primary Sources, KDMA; Holmes, *Soldier*, 98; Hoover, "Battle of Perryville," 3. Documentary evidence suggests that only Stone fired on Wharton, but the presence of a single twelve-pound solid shot, found on private property near a ten-pound Schenkl obviously fired from a James rifle, suggests that both batteries engaged. See Kurt Holman to author, June 19, 2000, Author's Collection, PSHS.

32. Millard, "Battle of Perryville," 1.

33. *OR* 1, 16, pt. 1, 344, 1041, 1045, 1060. See also Eicker Memoir, 10; Otto Memoirs, 105; Quiner Scrapbooks, vol. 6, 142, 148; Hoover, "Battle of Perryville," 3; Knowles, "Battle of Perryville," 3; Fitch, *Echoes*, 58–59.

34. Babits, *Devil of a Whipping*, 119–20, 155–59. Babits is concerned with the collapse of the elite 71st Regiment of Foot, Fraser's Highlanders, at the American Revolution's Battle of Cowpens.

35. Kurt Holman originated the "X" analogy in describing the battle to visitors at the PSHS. I use it here with his permission. See Holman to author, Mar. 11, 1999.

36. *OR* 1, 16, pt. 1, 1040, 1045; Waddle to his sister, Oct. 11, 1862, McCoy Papers, MHS; Burnett, *Humorous*, 38–39; Giles, *Terry's Texas Rangers*, 46; Graber, *Life Record*, 172–73; Waddle, *Three Years*, 29–30; *New Albany Daily Ledger*, Oct. 16, 1862; Clay, *Introduction to the Archaeology*, 39–42, 46–47; Jeffries, *Terry's Rangers*, 59.

37. Waddle to his sister, Oct. 11, 1862, McCoy Papers, MHS; Waddle, *Three Years*, 30. The quotation is from Waddle's book.

38. *OR* 1, 16, pt. 1, 1110.

39. Author's Perryville Tour Notes, July 17–18, 1999, PSHS. I am grateful to Kurt Holman for first pointing out the optical illusion of the two hills.

40. Donelson to Wright, Oct. 26, 1862, Bragg Papers, WRHS; *Atlanta Southern Confederacy*, Nov. 13, 1862; Cheatham, "Battle of Perryville," 704; Head, *Campaigns and Battles*, 95; Savage, *Life of John H. Savage*, 118–19; Thompson, "Hear the Wax Fry," 9; Womack, *Diary of J. J. Womack*, 62; Losson, *Tennessee's Forgotten Warriors*, 66.

41. Landrum to Amanda, Oct. 12, 1862, Landrum Letters, OHS.

42. Savage, *Life of John H. Savage*, 115, 119, 130–33 (quotations, 119). See also Cross, *Camp and Field*, 64–65; Warner, *Generals in Gray*, 74–75; and Author's Perryville Tour Notes, July 17, 1999, PSHS.

43. Clark Memoirs, 27; Donelson to Wright, Oct. 26, 1862, Bragg Papers, WRHS; Biggs, "Incidents," 141–42; Savage, *Life of John H. Savage*, 122, 126.

44. Hooper Diary, Oct. 8, 1862.

45. "Biographical Sketch of B. F. Cheatham," Quintard Papers, Duke.

46. Head, *Campaigns and Battles*, 95.

47. Womack, *Diary of J. J. Womack*, 62. See also Thompson, "Hear the Wax Fry," 9.

48. "Campaign in Kentucky, No. 5."

49. *Atlanta Southern Confederacy*, Nov. 13, 1862. Using a secondary reprinting of the article, Hafendorfer (*Perryville*, 242–43) identifies the brigade in question as Stewart's rather than Donelson's.

50. *OR* 1, 16, pt. 1, 1049, 1053; Biggs, "Incidents," 142; *Cincinnati Daily Commer-*

cial, Oct. 24, 1862; Brooks, *Battle of Perryville* pamphlet, IlSHL; Head, *Campaigns and Battles*, 95–96; Savage, *Life of John H. Savage*, 119. Writing in the *Princeton (Ind.) Clarion*, Oct. 25, 1862, "Simonson" claimed that Donelson's column "was in our own uniform and carrying the Stars and Stripes, this I saw."

51. Clark Memoirs, 27. See also Head, *Campaigns and Battles*, 95.

52. Clark Memoirs, 27; Hooper Diary, Oct. 8, 1862; Womack, *Diary of J. J. Womack*, 62–63.

53. Landrum to Amanda, Oct. 12, 1862, Landrum Letters, OHS.

54. Hupp, *My Diary*, 23; Clay, *Introduction to the Archaeology*, 45, 49.

55. Hupp, *My Diary*, 23.

56. *OR* 1, 16, pt. 1, 1060, Savage, *Life of John H. Savage*, 119. See also Donelson to Wright, Oct. 26, 1862, Bragg Papers, WRHS; *Princeton (Ind.) Clarion*, Oct. 25, 1862; Clay, *Introduction to the Archaeology*, 42, 50; Author's Perryville Tour Notes, July 18, 1999, PSHS.

57. Clark Memoirs, 27.

58. Head, untitled article, 435.

59. Savage, *Life of John H. Savage*, 120–21.

60. Donelson to Wright, Oct. 26, 1862, Bragg Papers, WRHS; Head, *Campaigns and Battles*, 96.

61. *OR* 1, 16, pt. 1, 1064; *Atlanta Southern Confederacy*, Nov. 13, 1862; Womack, *Diary of J. J. Womack*, 63.

62. Waddle to his sister, Oct. 11, 1862, McCoy Papers, MHS.

63. Thompson, "Hear the Wax Fry," 9. See also Hooper Diary, 74.

64. Glezen Diary, Oct. 8, 1862.

65. Waddle to his sister, Oct. 11, 1862, McCoy Papers, MHS. Head, *Campaigns and Battles*, 96; Savage, *Life of John H. Savage*, 115, 120–21, Thompson, "Hear the Wax Fry," 9; Waddle, *Three Years*, 37.

66. Savage, *Life of John H. Savage*, 120–21. The exact nature of the buildings remains unknown, but both Hafendorfer and Kurt Holman believe that they were outbuildings on the Gibson farm. Ongoing archaeological investigations at the site should reveal more in the years to come. See Hafendorfer, *Perryville*, 207; Holman to author, Mar. 11, 1999; and Richard Stallings to author, Mar. 12, 1999, Author's Collection, PSHS.

67. *OR* 1, 16, pt. 1, 1045, 1051, 1053; Chandler Diary, 20–22, Daniel H. Chandler Collection, InSL; Duncan C. Milner to his friends, Oct. 10, 1862, U.S. History, Civil War Biography, CHS; Otto Memoirs, 105; Waddle to his sister, Oct. 11, 1862, McCoy Papers, MHS; *Cincinnati Daily Commercial*, Oct. 23, 24, Nov. 8, 1862; Brooks, *Battle of Perryville* pamphlet, IlSHL; Kendall, "Battle of Perryville," 8; *Record of the Ninety-fourth Infantry*, 18, 20; Scribner, *How Soldiers Were Made*, 58–59; Starkweather, "Perryville," 2; Waddle, *Three Years*, 30; Winters, *In the 50th Ohio*, 20–22.

68. Glezen Diary, Oct. 8, 1862. See also *Cincinnati Daily Commercial*, Nov. 8, 1862.

69. Clark Memoirs, 26–28; Donelson to Wright, Oct. 26, 1862, Bragg Papers, WRHS; Hooper Diary, 75; Biggs, "Incidents," 142; Hupp, *My Diary*, 23; Savage, *Life of John H. Savage*, 115, 121; Thompson, "Hear the Wax Fry," 9; Womack, *Diary of J. J. Womack*, 63; Holman to author, Mar 11, 1999.

70. [Maney] to Wright, Oct. 24, 1862, Bragg Papers, WRHS.

71. Warner, *Generals in Gray*, 210.

72. *OR* 1, 16, pt. 1, 1113–15; [Maney] to Wright, Oct. 24, 1862, Bragg Papers, WRHS; Toney, *Privations*, 42; Warner, *Generals in Gray*, 210.

73. [Maney] to Wright, Oct. 24, 1862, Bragg Papers, WRHS. For Parson's firing at Wharton, see Tourgée, *Story of a Thousand*, 117.

74. *Cleveland Plain Dealer*, Oct. 17, 1862.

75. *OR* 1, 16, pt. 1, 1060, 1062–64; Hall Diary, 59; [Maney] to Wright, Oct. 24, 1862, Bragg Papers, WRHS; Starling to his daughters, Nov. 16, 1862, Lewis-Starling Collection, WKUL; Tourgée, *Story of a Thousand*, 119, 132, 138–39.

76. "Skirmish Line," 567. For Buford's wound, see Hall Diary, 59.

77. *OR* 1, 16, pt. 1, 1060, 1062–64; [Maney] to Wright, Oct. 24, 1862, Bragg Papers, WRHS; Tourgée, *Story of a Thousand*, 119, 138–39.

78. [Maney] to Wright, Oct. 24, 1862, Bragg Papers, WRHS.

79. Unidentified newspaper clipping, 41st Georgia Infantry File, PSHS.

80. *OR* 1, 16, pt. 1, 1115.

81. Angle, ed., *Three Years in the Army*, 21.

82. *OR* 1, 16, pt. 1, 1118.

83. Tourgée, *Story of a Thousand*, 117–19 (quotation, 119). See also Taylor Diary, 3, USAMHI. Taylor maintained that Parson's Battery was already "deserted" by the time the regiment arrived.

84. *OR* 1, 16, pt. 1, 1060, 1062–64; Starling to his daughters, Nov. 16, 1862, Lewis-Starling Collection, WKUL; Tourgée, *Story of a Thousand*, 120–21, 133.

85. Tourgée, *Story of a Thousand*, 133–34.

86. Starling to his daughters, Nov. 16, 1862, Lewis-Starling Collection, WKUL. See also *OR* 1, 16, pt. 1, 1063; Angle, ed., *Three Years in the Army*, 21; *New Albany Daily Ledger*, Oct. 14, 1862; Kurt Holman, "Revised Location of Parson's Battery," n.d., 2.

87. Again, as noted earlier, Turner did not use the "Dug Road," much less did his gunners give it the name by digging it out with picks and shovels to make it wide enough for their gun carriages and limbers. No sources exist to confirm such a story, although it is often repeated. The route described, rather, is the shortest and most obvious. For Turner's iron six-pounders, see Holman to author, Mar. 24, 2000.

88. *OR* 1, 16, pt. 1, 1063, 1065; Taylor Diary, 3, USAMHI; Taylor Diary, 52, KHS; Bascom, ed., *"Dear Lizzie,"* 31; Cheatham, "Battle of Perryville," 705; Federico and Wright, eds. *Civil War*, 63–64; Radcliffe, "Terrill's Brigade," 3; Tourgée, *Story of a Thousand*, 121, 141; Reid, *Ohio in the War*, vol. 2, 566; Holman to author, Apr. 10, 1999.

89. Tourgée, *Story of a Thousand*, 121.

90. Morse to his mother, Oct. 15, 1862, Morse Papers, OHS.

91. *OR* 1, 16, pt. 1, 1113.

92. Malone, *Memoir*, 129.

93. *OR* 1, 16, pt. 1, 1113, 1115.

94. Ibid., 1115.

95. Ibid., 1063; Hall Diary, 59–60; [Maney] to Wright, Oct. 24, 1862, Bragg Papers, WRHS; Tourgée, *Story of a Thousand*, 121.

96. Tourgée, *Story of a Thousand*, 121.

97. *OR* 1, 16, pt. 1, 1063; Hall Diary, 59–60; [Maney] to Wright, Oct. 24, 1862, Bragg Papers, WRHS; Tourgée, *Story of a Thousand*, 121–23.

98. Malone, *Memoir*, 130; *Atlanta Southern Confederacy*, Mar. 22, 1862.

99. [Maney] to Wright, Oct. 24, 1862, Bragg Papers, WRHS. See also *OR* 1, 16, pt. 1, 1113; Cheatham, "Battle of Perryville," 705.

100. Hall Diary, 59–60. See also Glauser, trans., *Private Josiah Ayre*, 20; Malone, *Memoir*, 131.

101. Radcliffe, "Terrill's Brigade," 3.

102. Glauser, trans., *Private Josiah Ayre*, 20.

103. *OR* 1, 16, pt. 1, 1060, 1063, 1116, 1118; Morse to his mother, Oct. 14, 1862, Morse Papers, OHS; Taylor Diary, 3, USAMHI; Taylor Diary, 52, KHS; Federico and

Wright, eds., *Civil War*, 63–64; Glauser, trans., *Private Josiah Ayre*, 20; Radcliffe, "Terrill's Brigade," 3; Tourgée, *Story of a Thousand*, 121–23.

104. *OR* 1, 16, pt. 1, 1065; Radcliffe, "Terrill's Brigade," 3.

105. *OR* 1, 16, pt. 1, 1063, 1118; *B&L*, vol. 3, 61; Hall Diary, 59–60; Malone, *Memoir*, 131. Quintard, *Doctor Quintard*, 57–59; Tourgée, *Story of a Thousand*, 139–40; Wright, "Glimpse of Perryville," 152–53.

106. *OR* 1, 16, pt. 1, 1113.

107. Ibid., 1034, 1108; Tourgée, *Story of a Thousand*, 131–35; Fradenburgh, *In Memoriam*, 43–44, 47.

108. *OR* 1, 16, pt. 1, 1113–14, 1115–17; Cleaver to his wife, Oct. 11, 1862, 123rd Illinois File. One document accentuating the rawness of Terrill's men is a special requisition dated Jan. 15, 1863, found in the 32nd Kentucky Volunteer Infantry File, Kentucky Quartermaster Records, KDMA. Regimental officers did not request any copies of tactical manuals and army regulations, the basic texts for new officers learning how to lead men in battle, before that date.

CHAPTER 11

1. "Campaign in Kentucky, No. 5."

2. Wheeler says nothing about reporting to his superiors in either *OR* 1, 16, pt. 1, 897–98, or *B&L*, vol. 3, 16–17. See also *OR* 1, 16, pt. 1, 1016.

3. *OR* 1, 16, pt. 1, 284, 245–46; Chumney, "Don Carlos Buell," 171–72, 175–76. For a succinct layman's guide to the science of acoustic shadow, see Ross, "ssh! Battle in Progress!" 56–62. Ross does err in describing the weather at Perryville as "cool."

4. *OR* 1, 16, pt. 1, 50–51; *B&L*, vol. 3, 48.

5. *OR* 1, 16, pt. 1, 247.

6. Gilbert, "Bragg's Invasion of Kentucky," 467. Acoustic shadow still occurs in the Chaplin Hills. Several years ago, Darrell Young, planning to attend a reenactment of the battle, noticed that the wind was blowing just as it had on the day of the battle. Driving to the Dorsey House instead of the battlefield park, he heard nothing of the mock battle occurring three miles to the east. Author's Perryville Tour Notes, July 18, 1999, PSHS.

7. Hafendorfer, ed., "Simon B. Buckner's," 58.

8. Ibid. Cheatham, unfortunately, says nothing about Jones and states only that "Anderson's division was on the left" ("Battle of Perryville," 705).

9. *OR* 1, 16, pt. 1, 1121; Boatner, *Civil War Dictionary*, 444, 888. For the implication that Jones simply moved according to orders, see, for example, McDonough, *War in Kentucky*, 258–59; and Hafendorfer, *Perryville*, 215, 217, 221.

10. *Memphis Daily Appeal*, Nov. 8, 1862. See also *OR* 1, 16, pt. 1, 1121; Berkley, trans., *In Defense of This Flag*, 165–66; Robert A. Jarman Manuscript, MDAH (hereafter Jarman Manuscript); *New Albany (Ind.) Daily Ledger*, Oct. 14, 1862.

11. *OR* 1, 16, pt. 1, 1054–56; Chandler Diary, 20–22; Catherine Anne Hiemer, ed., Untitled excerpts from J. Robert Kohlsdorf's letters, 10th Wisconsin Infantry File, PSHS; Jarman Manuscript; Hupp, *My Diary*, 23; Perry, *Thirty-eighth Regiment*, 28; Scribner, *How Soldiers Were Made*, 58–59; Berkley, trans., *In Defense of This Flag*, 165–66; Author's Perryville Tour Notes, July 18, 1999, PSHS.

12. Phelps to friends, Oct. 16, 1862, Phelps Letters, USAMHI. Phelps noted that his regiment wore the dress blue uniforms of regulars.

13. *OR* 1, 16, pt. 1, 1054–56; Chandler Diary, 20–22; Phelps to friends, Oct. 16, 1862, Phelps Letters, USAMHI; Hiemer, ed., Untitled excerpts; Jarman Manuscript;

Hupp, *My Diary*, 23; Scribner, *How Soldiers Were Made*, 58–59; Berkley, trans., *In Defense of This Flag*, 165–66; Hafendorfer, *Perryville*, 238; Holman, "Casualty Percentages of Individual Units," "Confederate Comments," and "Known Strengths and Casualties at the Battle of Perryville," Kurt Holman to author, Dec. 8, 1999, Author's Collection, PSHS. The wounded figure is an estimate based on eight of thirty companies' known casualties as detailed in "Confederate Comments," and assumes a fairly consistent rate of fire across Jones's front. Holman indicated that the 34th Mississippi suffered 50 percent casualties.

14. *OR* 1, 16, pt. 1, 1049, 1055–56; Chandler Diary, 22; *New Albany (Ind.) Daily Ledger*, Oct. 16, 1862; Berkley, ed., *In the Defense of This Flag*, 167.

15. This paragraph is distilled from Cummings's insightful *Yankee Quaker, Confederate General*.

16. Hafendorfer, ed., "Simon B. Buckner's," 56, 58 (quotation 58).

17. *OR* 1, 16, pt. 1, 1056–58, 1126, 1130–33; Gipson, "About the Battle," 163.

18. Headley, *Confederate Operations*, 57. My subsequent discussion of Adams's brigade owes much to a close student of the organization, John Walsh. See Walsh, "Summary for Adams, Johnson, and Cleburne."

19. Trask Journal, 66. See also *OR* 1, 16, pt. 1, 1122, 1123; Headley, *Confederate Operations*, 56–57.

20. Trask Journal, 66. See also Headley, *Confederate Operations*, 56–57.

21. *New Orleans Bee*, Nov. 1, 1862.

22. Trask Journal, 66; H. Slocomb, "Historical Notes on 5th Co., 1862–1865," Books, Battalion Washington Artillery Collection, Civil War Papers, Louisiana Historical Collection, TU (hereafter "Historical Notes").

23. *OR* 1, 16, pt. 1, 1121, 1125–26; "Historical Notes"; Horrall, *Forty-second Indiana*, 151; Shanklin, "*Dear Lizzie*," 224, 227, 228–31; *Daily Evansville Journal*, Oct. 21, 1862 *Daily Evansville Journal*, Oct. 21, 1862; *Princeton (Ind.) Clarion*, Oct. 25, 1862. Although canister largely replaced traditional grapeshot in Civil War armies, rendering "grapeshot" almost a generic term, archaeological digging at the site has indeed uncovered two-inch grapeshot. See Kurt Holman to author, Apr. 20, 1999, Author's Collection, PSHS.

24. Stuckey to Helen Stuckey, Oct. 19, 1862, Stuckey Letters, InHS; Holman to author, Apr. 20, 1999.

25. *OR* 1, 16, pt. 1, 1126, 1130, 1133; Bartlett, *Military Record*, 9.

26. *OR* 1, 16, pt. 1, 1056–58, 1126, 1132–33; Gipson, "About the Battle," 163. No direct evidence exists as to the identity of the Federal skirmishers. Some authorities suggest that they came from the 10th Ohio. See *Cleveland Plain Dealer*, Oct. 17, 1862; Hafendorfer, *Perryville*, 221. See also Kurt Holman to author, Apr. 26, 2000, Author's Collection, PSHS.

27. *OR* 1, 16, pt. 1, 1126, 1131, 1130, 1133.

28. Ibid., 1126, 1130, 1133; Bennett and Haigh, *History of the 36th Regiment*, 262–64.

29. *OR* 1, 16, pt. 1, 1126, 1128–26; Hafendorfer, ed., "Simon B. Buckner's," 56.

30. *OR* 1, 16, pt. 1, 1126, 1132–33; *Princeton (Ind.) Clarion*, Oct. 25, 1862.

31. *OR* 1, 16, pt. 1, 70, 1038, 1056, 1057, 1126, 1128, 1132; Duncan Diary, 8; Beatty, *Citizen Soldier*, 178; *Cleveland Plain Dealer*, Oct. 17, 1862; *Daily Evansville Journal*, Oct. 18, 1862; Gipson, "About the Battle," 163; Lindsley, ed., *Military Annals*, vol. 1, 148, 353; Hafendorfer, ed., "Simon B. Buckner's," 58; Switlik, "Loomis' Battery," 35.

32. Lindsley, ed., *Military Annals*, vol. 1, 148.

33. *OR* 1, 16, pt. 1, 70.

34. Beatty, *Citizen Soldier*, 178. For the men's dislike of Beatty, see Duncan Diary, 10.

35. *OR* 1, 16, pt. 1, 1058. Duncan Diary, 8.

36. "Campaign in Kentucky, No. 5"; Gipson, "About the Battle," 163; Lindsley, ed., *Military Annals*, vol. 1, 148, 353, 502.

37. *OR* 1, 16, pt. 1, 1056–58, 1128–29, 1132; Duncan Diary, 10; Gipson, "About the Battle," 163.

38. Lindsley, ed., *Military Annals*, vol. 1, 148.

39. Trask Journal, 67–68.

40. *OR* 1, 16, pt. 1, 1126; Hafendorfer, ed., "Simon B. Buckner's," 58. Claiborne later claimed that Buckner knew about Adams's presence earlier, and indeed that was Buckner who halted the friendly fire incident by sending Claiborne to Adams ("Battle of Perryville," 226). Buckner's report, however, does not support such a contention. Moreover, other passages of Claiborne's twentieth century article, such as Polk retreating from Perryville when Bragg arrived, are suspect.

41. "Historical Notes"; "Reminiscences of the Fifth Company," 8, Battalion of Washington Artillery Collection, pt. 2, Civil War Papers, Louisiana Historical Collection, TU (hereafter "Reminiscences of the Fifth Company"; Trask Journal, 32–33; *Daily Evansville Journal*, Oct. 16, 1862; *New Orleans Bee*, Nov. 1, 1862; Herald, "Terrible Sight," 10; Headley, *Confederate Operations*, 57 (quotation); Horrall, *Forty-second Indiana*, 152–53; Nichols, ed., "Reminiscing from 1861 to 1865," 9–10; Bishop, "Civil War Field Artillery," 49; Wooster, "Confederate Success at Perryville," 318–23. See also Appendix 2.

42. Headley, *Confederate Operations*, 57. See also *OR* 1, 16, pt. 1, 1056.

43. *OR* 1, 16, pt. 1, 70, 1056–58; Duncan Diary, 10; Beatty, *Citizen Soldier*, 178l Lindsley, ed., *Military Annals*, vol. 1, 148; *Daily Evansville Journal*, Oct. 18, 1862; Holman, "Henry P. 'Squire' Bottom's War Claim."

44. *OR* 1, 16, pt. 1, 1058, 1123, 1132; Trask Journal, 67; *Cincinnati Daily Enquirer*, Oct. 14, 1862; *Daily Evansville Journal*, Oct. 18, 1862; *Louisville Daily Journal*, Oct. 21, 1862; Beatty, *Citizen-Soldier*, 179; Headley, *Confederate Operations*, 57; McDowell, "Fifteenth Kentucky," 248.

45. *Cincinnati Daily Enquirer*, Oct. 14, 1862. The author, identified only by the initials "Y. S.," may have been Uriah Shook of Company D, see Kurt Holman to author, Mar. 29, 2000, Author's Collection, PSHS.

46. T. S. Bell to Gov. James H. Robinson, Oct. 15, 1862, 15th Kentucky Infantry Collection, Union Infantry-Primary Sources, KDMA; McDowell Reminiscence; *Cincinnati Daily Enquirer*, Oct. 14, 1862; *Louisville Daily Journal*, Oct. 11, 1862; Beatty, *Citizen-Soldier*, 179.

47. *Louisville Daily Journal*, Oct. 11, 21, 1862. See also McDowell Reminiscence.

48. Headley, *Confederate Operations*, 57.

49. *OR* 1, 16, pt. 1, 1058; *Louisville Daily Journal*, Oct. 21, 1862; Beatty, *Citizen-Soldier*, 179; Headley, *Confederate Operations*, 57–58; Tapp, "Battle of Perryville," 174.

50. Ball to Brother Smith, Sept. 8, 1862, Ball Collection, USAMHI; John Ellis to his sister, Oct. 29, 1862, Ellis and Family Papers, LSU; Sturges letter fragment, Sturges Correspondence, USAMHI; Trask Journal, 69. For Blacks in Kentucky regiments, see Noe, ed., *Southern Boy in Blue*, 95–146–48, 149, 297, 301; Darrell Young interview, July 17, 1999, notes in Author's Perryville Tour Notes, PSHS. According to Young, Sleet later claimed that he fought in the battle. Unfortunately, the only documentary evidence is in the Squire Bottom claim, when Sleet identifies himself as camping after the battle with the 89th Illinois Infantry of Sill's command. He later left town with that regiment. See RG 56, General Records of the Department of the Treasury, Records of the Division of Captured Property, Claims, and Lands, Case nos. 9877 and 2514 consolidated, NARA. Bottom's war claim is summarized in Holman, "Henry P. 'Squire' Bottom's War Claim."

51. *OR* 1, 16, pt. 1, 70; *B&L*, vol. 3, 16; *New Albany (Ind.) Daily Ledger*, Oct. 14, 1862; Hafendorfer, *Perryville*, 219–20; McDonough, *War in Kentucky*, 287.

52. For accounts of Gilbert's men watching the fighting in frustration, see Mitchell to Blackman, Oct. 18, 1862, Mitchell Letter, InHS; "Letter from Lt. Col. McKee, Fifteenth Regt," Quiner Scrapbooks, vol. 5, 193; Stewart, *Dan McCook's Regiment*, 27.

53. *OR* 1, 16, pt. 1, 239–40, 1038, 1082.

54. Bennett and Haigh, *History of the 36th Regiment*, 261–62.

55. *OR* 1, 16, pt. 1, 284, 1040, 1082 (quotation, 1040); Mosgrove, "Battle of Perryville," 3; Sheridan, *Personal Memoirs*, vol. 1, 195–96; "Historical Notes"; Aten, *Eighty-fifth Regiment*, 35–36; Brown, Murphy, and Putney, *Behind the Guns*, 37; Bennett and Haigh, *History of the 36th Regiment*, 262–63.

56. See Hafendorfer, *Perryville*, 228, as well as the more critical account in McDonough, *War in Kentucky*, 267–69.

57. Sheridan, *Personal Memoirs*, vol. 1, 196–97.

58. *OR* 1, 16, pt. 1, 284, 1038, 1082; *Cincinnati Daily Enquirer*, Oct. 14, 1862; Gilbert, "Bragg's Invasion of Kentucky," 466; Sheridan, *Personal Memoirs*, vol. 1, 196–97; Thatcher, *Hundred Battles*, 81–82.

59. *OR* 1, 16, pt. 1, 1082, 1121; clipping, Confederate Regimental Infantry Files: 45th Alabama Infantry, ADAH; Brown to Fannie Brown, Oct. 24, 1862, Brown Letters, ADAH; Dowd Recollections; Sutherland, ed., *Reminiscences*, 98–99; Aten, *Eighty-fifth Regiment*, 35–36.

60. *OR* 1, 16, pt. 1, 91, 100, 104, 1040; *B&L*, vol. 3, 57–58; *Chicago Times*, Oct. 21, 23, 1862; Gilbert, "Bragg's Invasion of Kentucky," 466–67; James, "Perryville," 155; Noe, ed., *Southern Boy in Blue*, 103–4; Chumney, "Don Carlos Buell," 175–76; Hafendorfer, *Perryville*, 280–81. At least one man later claimed that McCook did attempt to inform Buell promptly of the attack. Byron A. Dunn, author of a turn-of-the-century novel about a member of Thomas's staff, claimed in a footnote that signal officer Capt. Julius R. Fitch sent a message from McCook to Buell at 2:10 p.m. stating "The enemy has attacked me in force with infantry and artillery." Fitch further maintained that through his glass he saw Buell read the message. There is of course no corroborating evidence, and events suggest that the Fitch account was fictional as well, but see Dunn's *On General Thomas's Staff*, 142.

61. *OR* 1, 16, pt. 1, 187, 275–76, 278 (quotation, 278).

62. Ibid., 187–88, 241, 278, 535; Davis to his wife, Oct. 16, 1862, Davis Papers, Iowa; Sturges letter fragment, Sturges Correspondence, USAMHI; *Daily Evansville Journal*, Nov. 14, 1862; Goodspeed, *Fifteen Years Ago*, 233; Joyce, *Checkered Life*, 73; Noe, ed., *Southern Boy in Blue*, 103; Rerick, *Forty-fourth Indiana*, 72.

63. Barnes, Carnahan, and McCain, *Eighty-sixth Regiment*, 64.

64. Sturges letter fragment, Sturges Correspondence, USAMHI.

65. *OR* 1, 16, pt. 1, 897–98; Sturges letter fragment, Sturges Correspondence, USAMHI; Anderson, ed., *Nicholas Longworth Anderson*, 161; Simmons, *84th Reg't*, 14–15.

66. Tarrant, *Wild Riders*, 119.

67. *B&L*, vol. 3, 16; Hafendorfer, *Perryville*, 219–20; McDonough, *War in Kentucky*, 287.

68. Hafendorfer, *Perryville*, 259.

69. *OR* 1, 16, pt. 1, 1123, 1126–27.

70. Ellis Record, 1–2; Inglis Diary, Oct. 8, 1862; General William Miller Report, 3, FSA (hereafter Miller Report); Talley Autobiography, 20–22; *Atlanta Southern Confederacy*, Nov. 15, 1862; Boatner, *Civil War Dictionary*, 91; Coles, "Ancient City Defenders," 81.

71. Inglis Diary, Oct. 8, 1862. See also William A. Bryant to his mother, Oct. 11, 1862, 3rd Florida Infantry File, PSHS; *Macon Daily Telegraph*, Nov. 18, 1862; For the initial experience of battle in general, see Hess, *Union Soldier in Battle*, 9–29.

72. Talley Autobiography, 24.

73. Inglis Diary, Oct. 8, 1862. See also Miller Report, 3, 5; Talley Autobiography, 24; *Macon Daily Telegraph*, Nov. 18, 1862. For the mystery of who sent the brigade into action, see *OR* 1, 16, pt. 1, 1121; and Hafendorfer, ed., "Simon B. Buckner's." Hafendorfer, in *Perryville*, 251, surmises that the 3rd Florida formed a second line, an assertion not borne out by the Inglis account.

74. *OR* 1, 16, pt. 1, 1056; Miller Report, 3; Talley Autobiography, 24; *Macon Daily Telegraph*, Nov. 18, 1862.

75. *OR* 1, 16, pt. 1, 1050; *New Albany (Ind.) Daily Ledger*, Oct. 16, 1862; "Tale From the 41st Mississippi," 2.

76. Bryant to his mother, Oct. 11, 1862, 3rd Florida Infantry File, PSHS; Thomas Benton Ellis Diary, 3, FHS (hereafter T. B. Ellis Diary); Inglis Diary, Oct. 8, 1862; Phelps to friends, Oct. 16, 1862, Phelps Letters, USAMHI; Talley Autobiography, 24; *Atlanta Southern Confederacy*, Nov. 15, 1862; "Tale From the 41st Mississippi," 2.

77. Inglis Diary, Oct. 8, 1862.

78. *OR* 1, 16, pt. 1, 1046, 1050; Robert Kohlsdorf to the Home League Newspapers, Oct. 13, 1862, 10th Wisconsin File, PSHS; Phelps to friends, Oct. 16, 1862, Phelps Letters, USAMHI; John Sipe to Sallie, Oct. 16, 1862, Civil War Regimental History—38th Indiana, InSL; Webster Diary, 28; *New Albany (Ind.) Daily Ledger*, Oct. 31, 1862; Scribner, *How Soldiers Were Made*, 59.

79. Sipe to Sallie, Oct. 16, 1862, Civil War Regimental History—38th Indiana, InSL.

80. Miller Report, 3–4.

81. *OR* 1, 16, pt. 1, 1127, 1128, 1129–30, 1132. While Johnson stated that he went to Cleburne around 5 P.M., evidence suggests that it happened closer to four.

CHAPTER 12

1. Boatner, *Civil War Dictionary*, 798; Elliott, *Soldier of Tennessee*, 38–45; Sword, *Shiloh*, 179, 201–2, 413.

2. Stewart to Wright, Oct. 28, 1862, Bragg Papers, WRHS; Cheatham, "Battle of Perryville," 704–5.

3. Reynolds, *Henry County Commands*, 45.

4. Stewart to Wright, Oct. 28, 1862, Bragg Papers, WRHS; Magee Diary, 39–40; Milledgeville [Ga.] *Confederate Union*, Oct. 28, 1862; Cheatham, "Battle of Perryville," 704–5; Head, *Campaigns and Battles*, 96; Losson, *Tennessee's Forgotten Warriors*, 69–70.

5. Clark Memoirs, 25–26; Donelson to Wright, Oct. 26, 1862, Bragg Papers, WRHS; Glezen Diary, Oct. 8, 1862; Hooper Diary, Oct. 8, 1862; Landrum to Mrs. Wilson, Oct. 12, 1862, Landrum Letters, OHS; Moore to his parents, Oct. 16, 1862, Thomas D. Moore Papers, USAMHI; *Cincinnati Daily Commercial*, Oct. 24, 1862; Milledgeville [Ga.] *Confederate Union*, Oct. 28, 1862; Burnett, *Humorous*, 39; Reynolds, *Henry County Commands*, 46; Savage, *Life of John H. Savage*, 122, 123, 126; Thompson, "Hear the Wax Fry," 9–10; Winters, *In the 50th Ohio*, 19–20; Womack, *Civil War Diary*, 63. The 24th Illinois's nickname can be found in Dahlmer to a friend, May 5, 1862, Charles Dahlmer Letter, IlSHL.

6. Burnett, *Humorous*, 39. Burnett identifies the unit only as "an Illinois regiment," but as the 123rd Illinois fell back with Terrill toward Starkweather's lines (Angle, ed., *Three Years in the Army*, 21–22), the regiment had to be the 80th Illinois from Terrill's right. See also Hartman, "Battle of Perryville," 3.

7. *Indianapolis Daily Journal*, Oct. 24, 1862 (first quotation); *New Albany (Ind.) Daily Ledger*, Oct. 14, 1862 (second quotation). See also Hartman, "Battle of Perryville," 3.

8. *Cincinnati Daily Commercial,* Oct. 24, 1862. See also Waddle, *Three Years,* 30.

9. *Indianapolis Daily Journal,* Oct. 24, 1862.

10. Burnett, *Humorous,* 39. For the distance between the lines, see Waddle to his sister, Oct. 11, 1862, McCoy Papers, MHS.

11. Womack, *Diary of J. J. Womack,* 63. See also *Indianapolis Daily Journal,* Oct. 29, 1862.

12. Donelson to Wright, Oct. 26, 1862, Bragg Papers, WRHS.

13. *OR* 1, 16, pt. 1, 1115; Donelson to Wright, Oct. 26, 1862 (quotation), and Stewart to Wright, Oct. 28, 1862, Bragg Papers, WRHS; "Fifth Tennessee Infantry," 4; Burnett, *Humorous,* 39; Head, *Campaigns and Battles,* 96–97; Reynolds, *Henry County Commands,* 45–47; Thompson, "Hear the Wax Fry," 9.

Hafendorfer, *Perryville,* 242, has Stewart's brigade approach in two lines: the 24th, 5th, and 4th Tennessee in the first, and the 31st and 33rd Tennessee in the second. Moreover, they angle between Donelson and Maney in his telling. Elliott, *Soldier of Tennessee,* 54–59, follows that account, but most sources do not seem to support such a contention. Hafendorfer bases much of his account on an interview conducted with Joseph E. Riley in 1911, included in Dyer and Moore, *Tennessee Civil War Veterans,* vol. 5, 1847. Unfortunately, Riley's account, transcribed forty-nine years after the fact but only a few days before his death, is muddled and untrustworthy. For example, he has "Donaldson," not Maney, capturing Parsons's guns. He also implies that the 5th Tennessee from Stewart's brigade was part of "Donaldson's" assault wave. Perhaps he meant the 15th Tennessee. While useful for the sorts of memories that do not fade—notably his wound—Riley's biography nonetheless is too suspect to use as a definitive source and must be approached with caution. In contrast, Stewart himself reported that he brought his brigade forward, in the order I relate, "without holding any in reserve." Head also is adamant that Stewart's men—some of them at least—came up to the left of Donelson's brigade, not the right.

14. Starkweather, "Perryville," 2.

15. *OR* 1, 16, pt. 1, 1049; Mitchell Reminiscences, OHS; *Record of the Ninety-fourth Regiment,* 20; Scribner, *How Soldiers Were Made,* 59.

16. *Record of the Ninety-Fourth Regiment,* 20–21.

17. Donelson to Wright, Oct. 26, 1862, Bragg Papers, WRHS. See also Glezen Diary, Oct. 6, 1862; Burnett, *Humorous,* 40–41; Head, *Campaigns and Battles,* 96; *Record of the Ninety-Fourth Regiment,* 20–21; Thompson, "Hear the Wax Fry," 9; Womack, *Diary of J. J. Womack,* 63.

18. Gold Questionnaire Data, Confederate Collection, TSLA.

19. *OR* 1, 16, pt. 1, 1053; Landrum to Amanda Wilson, Oct. 12, 1862, Landrum Letters, OHS; Burnett, *Humorous,* 40–41.

20. [Maney] to Wright, Oct. 24, 1862, Bragg Papers, WRHS. See also *OR* 1, 16, pt. 1, 1113, 1115, 1118–19; Hall Diary, 61; Cheatham, "Battle of Perryville," 705; Malone, *Memoir,* 130–32; McFarland, "Maney's Brigade," 469; Reynolds, *Henry County Commands,* 46–47; Sword, *Shiloh,* 180.

21. *OR* 1, 16, pt. 1, 1065; Taylor Diary, 3, USAMHI; Glauser, trans., *Private Josiah Ayre,* 20; Tourgée, *Story of a Thousand,* 123–24; Clay, *Introduction to the Archaeology,* 53.

22. Tourgée, *Story of a Thousand,* 124. See also Morse to his mother, Oct. 14, 1862, Morse Papers, OHS; Radcliffe, "Terrill's Brigade," 3.

23. Taylor Diary, 3, USAMHI.

24. Tourgée, *Story of a Thousand,* 124. See also Glauser, trans., *Private Josiah Ayre,* 21; *New Albany (Ind.) Daily Ledger,* Oct. 14, 1862.

25. *OR* 1, 16, pt. 1, 1046, 1113, 1115, 1116–17, 1118; Clark Diary, vol. 2, 43; Hall Diary, 61; Martin Hoffmann to Jacob Weinman, Jan. 6, 1863, Civil War Miscellaneous

Collection—New Material, USAMHI; "Fifth Tennessee Infantry," 4; Kaiser, ed. "Civil War Letters," 268–69; [Maney] to Wright, Oct. 24, 1862, Bragg Papers, WRHS; Otto Memoirs, 104–5; Charles Paine to his father, Oct. 11, 1862, Edward L. Paine Papers, SHSW; Quiner Scrapbooks, vol. 6, 142, 143, 146, 148; John C. Starkweather, "Perryville," 2; B. J. Sweet to Gov. Edward Saloman, Oct. 20, 1862, and Untitled History of the 21st Wisconsin, 1–3, both in Adjutant General, Records of Civil War Regiments, 1861–1865, SHSW; Fitch, *Echoes*, 58–60; Holmes, *Soldier*, 93–94.

26. Quotations are from Otto Memoirs, 105–7. See also *OR* 1, 16, pt. 1, 1046, 1113, 1115, 1116–17, 1118; Clark Diary, vol. 2, 43; Hall Diary, 61; Hoffmann to Weinman, Jan. 6, 1863, Civil War Miscellaneous Collection—New Material, USAMHI; "Fifth Tennessee Infantry," 4; Kaiser, ed."Civil War Letters," 268–69; [Maney] to Wright, Oct. 24, 1862, Bragg Papers, WRHS; Paine to his father, Oct. 11, 1862, Paine Papers, SHSW; Quiner Scrapbooks, vol. 6, 142, 143, 146, 148; Starkweather, "Perryville," 2; Sweet to Saloman, Oct. 20, 1862, and Untitled History of the 21st Wisconsin, 1–3, both in Adjutant General, Records of Civil War Regiments, 1861–1865, SHSW; Dyer and Moore, *Tennessee Civil War Veterans*, vol. 3, 983; Fitch, *Echoes*, 60–61; Holmes, *Soldier*, 93–94.

27. Clark Diary, vol. 2, 43.

28. Evan Davis Speech, University of Wisconsin-Oskosh (hereafter Davis Speech). See also *OR* 1, 16, pt. 1, 1046; Clinton Letter, Oct. 9, 1862, SHSW; Paine to his father, Oct. 11, 1862, Paine Papers, SHSW; Quiner Scrapbooks, vol. 6, 143; Taylor Diary, 56, KHS; *Oshkosh (Wisc.) Courier*, Oct. 24, 1862; Radcliffe, "Terrill's Brigade," 8; Angle, ed., *Three Years in the Army*, 21. That Parsons was working his own gun is conjecture, but see Kurt Holman to author, July 26, 1999, Author's Collection, PSHS.

29. *OR* 1, 16, pt. 1, 1115, 1116–17, 1118; Otto Memoirs, 107; Reynolds, *Henry County Commands*, 48–49. Stone was exonerated of cowardice by a court-martial in March 1863 but found guilty of three others offenses, including being absent without leave and behaving in an abusive manner toward Lt. Thomas S. Thomasson, the officer who brought the charges. Enlisting the aid of old friends who could testify to his loyalties, Stone later managed to have the convictions overturned. See Holt to Canby, May 26, 1863, and General Orders no. 49, Murfreesboro, Tenn., May 15, 1863, both in Battery A, Kentucky Artillery Collection, Union Artillery—Primary Sources, KDMA. In his official report, Stone claimed credit for the canister fire that stopped the Confederate attack. See Stone to Sir, Oct. 17, 1862, Battery A, Kentucky Artillery Collection, Union Artillery-Primary Sources, KDMA.

30. Otto Memoirs, 107.

31. Otto Memoirs, 107–8, SHSW. See also Eicker Memoir, 11; Reynolds, *Henry County Commands*, 49.

32. Carnes to Quintard, Feb. 13, 1895 (quotations), Quintard Papers, Duke; Carnes, "Artillery," 8; "Campaign in Kentucky, No. 5."

33. *OR* 1, 16, pt. 1, 1113; Clark Diary, vol. 2, 43–44; Eicker Memoir, 11; [Maney] to Wright, Oct. 24, 1862, Bragg Papers, WRHS; Paine to his father, Oct. 11, 1862, Paine Papers, SHSW; Quiner Scrapbooks, vol. 6, 143; Starkweather, "Battle of Perryville," 2; Quiner Scrapbooks, vol. 6, 143; *Oshkosh (Wisc.) Courier*, Oct. 24, 1862; Fitch, *Echoes*, 61–62; Toney, *Privations*, 43.

34. Watkins, "*Co. Aytch*," 63, 62.

35. "Historical Sketch of the 4th Indiana Battery," 16–17, Haddock Collection, InHS; Quiner Scrapbooks, vol. 6, 147 (quotation); Hoover, "Battle of Perryville," 3; Knowles, "Battle of Perryville," 3; Noll, ed., *Doctor Quintard*, 61; Starkweather, "Battle of Perryville," 2; Toney, *Privations*, 43; Watkins, "*Co. Aytch*," 63.

36. Watkins, "*Co. Aytch*," 63.

37. *OR* 1, 16, pt. 1, 1113 (quotation, 1113); [Maney] to Wright, Oct. 24, 1862, Bragg Papers, WRHS; Quiner Scrapbooks, vol. 6, 143; Cheatham, "Battle of Perryville," 705; Malone, *Memoir*, 132.

38. Davis Speech; Otto Memoirs, 108–9; Tourgée, *Story of a Thousand*, 126, 146.

39. *OR* 1, 16, pt. 1, 1113 (quotation, 1113); Carnes to Quintard, Feb. 13, 1895, Quintard Papers, Duke; Davis Speech; [Maney] to Wright, Oct. 24, 1862, Bragg Papers, WRHS; Stone to Sir, Oct. 17, 1862, Battery A, Kentucky Artillery Collection, Union Artillery-Primary Sources, KDMA; Knowles, "Battle of Perryville," 3; Starkweather, "Perryville," 2; *Valparaiso (Ind.) Republic*, Nov. 13, 1862.

40. *OR* 1, 16, pt. 1, 1065; Taylor Diary, 53, 56, 62 (quotation 53), KHS; Tourgée, *Story of a Thousand*, 126.

41. Angle, ed., *Three Years in the Army*, 21. See also Radcliffe, "Terrill's Brigade," 3; Hafendorfer, *Perryville*, 271; McDonough, *War in Kentucky*, 279

42. Taylor Diary, 56, 58, KHS.

43. Carnes to Quintard, Feb. 13, 1895, Quintard Papers, Duke. Kurt Holman suspects that Carnes meant Sam Harris's battery, not Loomis's. See Holman to author, Apr. 7, 2000, Author's Collection, PSHS.

44. "Campaign in Kentucky, No. 5." Filing a widow's pension application decades after the war, Georgian A. C. Brown's widow Rachel affirmed that according to witnesses her husband died when first hit by artillery and then bayoneted in the chest. Such wounds suggest the brutal fight for Starkweather's guns. See Rachel Brown application (Microfilm 274/16), Confederate Pension Applications, GDAH.

45. *OR* 1, 16, pt. 1, 1113. See also [Maney] to Wright, Oct. 24, 1862 (quotation), Bragg Papers, WRHS; Taylor Diary, 56, 58, KHS; *Valparaiso (Ind.) Republic*, Nov. 13, 1862; Malone, *Memoir*, 132.

46. [Maney] to Wright, Oct. 24, 1862, Bragg Papers, WRHS. See also Clark Diary, vol. 2, 44; *Valparaiso (Ind.) Republic*, Nov. 13, 1862. Few items have been more controversial in the twentieth century than the 1st Tennessee's captured flag. In the years that followed the war, many 1st Tennessee veterans denied that the 1st Wisconsin had taken their flag, indicating instead that the captured banner belonged to the 41st Georgia. That assertion instigated a controversy with survivors of the Georgia regiment. See Marcus Toney's comments in the *Atlanta Constitution*, Oct. 30, 1905, as well as J. D. H.'s reply published early in November. Those and related clippings are held in the Turner Collection, Troup County Archives, LaGrange, Ga., as is Weaver's "My War Record." Turner claimed to be the man who carried the 41st Georgia's flag safely from the field. More recently, a brouhaha erupted in Wisconsin when the Wisconsin Veteran Museum's announced its plan to return the flag to Tennessee. That state's governor subsequently blocked the plan.

47. [Steele], "Charge of the First Tennessee," 69.

48. *OR* 1, 16, pt. 1, 1115, 1117 (quotation 1117); Eicker Memoir, 11; Stewart to Wright, Oct. 28, 1862, Bragg Papers, WRHS; Starkweather, "Perryville," 2; Malone, *Memoir*, 132, 135.

49. *OR*, 1, 16, pt. 1, 1115, 1117; Clark Diary, vol. 2, 44; Stone to Sir, Oct. 17, 1862, Battery A, Kentucky Artillery Collection, Union Artillery-Primary Sources, KDMA; Quiner Scrapbooks, vol. 6, 143; Untitled history of the 21st Wisconsin, Adjutant General, Records of Civil War Regiments, 1861–1900, SHSW; Hoover, "Battle of Perryville," 3; Knowles, "Battle of Perryville," 3; Starkweather, "Perryville," 2; Holmes, *Soldier*, 94; *Valparaiso (Ind.) Republic*, Nov. 13, 1862; Williams, "Regimental History," 27–28.

50. Davis Speech.

51. *OR* 1, 16, pt. 1, 1115, 1117; Eicker Memoir, 11; Stewart to Wright, Oct. 28,

1862, Bragg Papers, WRHS; Starkweather, "Perryville," 2; Malone, *Memoir,* 132, 135; Reynolds, *Henry County Commands,* 47–49. Archaeological evidence based on generations of relic hunting also supports this account. See Author's Perryville Tour Notes, July 17, 1999, PSHS.

52. *OR* 1, 16, pt. 1, 1113; Pollard Diary, 4, Confederate Collection, TSLA; "Fatalities in One Company," 210; Holman, "Casualty Percentages of Individual Units," "Known Strengths and Casualties, and "Units Stats," all in Author's Collection, PSHS.

53. *OR* 1, 16, pt. 1, 1040.

54. Hafendorfer, *Perryville,* 307; Kurt Holman to author, Apr. 19, 2000, and John Walsh Jr. to author, Apr. 19, 2000, both letters in Author's Collection, PSHS.

55. Yeatman Memoirs, Confederate Collection, TSLA (hereafter Yeatman Memoirs); Daniel, *Shiloh,* 93.

56. Lindsley, ed., *Military Annals,* vol. 1, 148.

57. *OR* 1, 16, pt. 1, 1127; *OR* 1, 52, pt. 1, 51–52; Yeatman Memoirs; Gipson, "About the Battle," 163; [Sam Watkins], *Southern Bivouac,* 223; Buck, *Cleburne,* 68; Garrett, trans., *Robert D. Smith,* 33.

58. *OR* 1, 16, pt. 1, 70, 1058, 1123; *OR* 1, 52, pt. 1, 52, 53; "Historical Notes"; Trask Journal, 69, Trask Papers, EU; 95; Yeatman Memoirs; *Cincinnati Daily Enquirer,* Oct. 17, 1862; *Louisville Daily Journal,* Oct. 21, 1862; Beatty, *Citizen-Soldier,* 179–82; Buck, *Cleburne,* 68–69; Headley, *Confederate Operations,* 58–59; Symonds, *Stonewall of the West.*

59. *OR* 1, 16, pt. 1, 1058; *OR* 1, 52, pt. 1, 52, 53; "Historical Notes"; Trask Journal, 69; *Cincinnati Daily Enquirer,* Oct. 17, 1862; Beatty, *Citizen-Soldier,* 179; Buck, *Cleburne,* 68–69; Symonds, *Stonewall of the West,* 95.

60. *OR* 1, 16, pt. 1, 1127; *OR* 1, 52, pt. 1, 52; Buck, *Cleburne,* 68–69.

61. *OR* 1, 16, pt. 1, 70, 1058, 1123; *OR* 1, 52, pt. 1, 52; Yeatman Memoirs; Herald, "Terrible Sight," 10; Beatty, *Citizen-Soldier,* 181–82; Dyer and Moore, *Tennessee Civil War Veterans,* vol. 4, 1659; Headley, *Confederate Operations,* 58–59; Garrett, trans., *Robert D. Smith,* 33; Buck, *Cleburne,* 69–70.

62. Miller Report, 4.

63. Hafendorfer, ed. "Simon B. Buckner's," 59.

64. *OR* 1, 16, pt. 1, 1121; W. F. Hall to Baldwin, Jan. 18, 1863, E. E. Baldwin Letters, MDAH; Unidentified diary, 22, 33rd Alabama Infantry File, PSHS; "33rd Alabama," 26 (quotation, 26); Williams, "33rd Alabama," 14, ADAH; Crowson and Brogden, eds., *Bloody Banners,* 13; Dyer and Moore, *Tennessee Civil War Veterans,* vol. 2, 439–40; Kurt Holman to author, Aug. 15, 1997, Author's Collection, PSHS. A Federal staff officer, writing nearly three years after the battle in the *Monongahela Daily Republican* (Jan. 12, 1865, clipping in Woodward Collection, PEP), indicated the capture of a wounded woman who had fought with Wood's brigade. According to the writer, the twenty-year-old woman, having joined the army in Tupelo to be with her husband, E. L. Stone, had been wounded in the left side. He surmised that she had passed as a youth, for "she would have appeared large among her own sex." Covered with a blanket by order of Rousseau, she later was sent to the hospital at the Russell House. The author's recollection unfortunately is problematic. He lists Mrs. Stone as a member of the 15th Alabama, a regiment that was not at the Battle of Perryville. A check of all of Wood's former or present regiments with extant compiled service records—the 45th Mississippi's are unavailable—lists no Stone. Several Stones are listed among the 15th Alabama, but not E. L. Stone. As a result, the woman's presence cannot be confirmed. See Compiled Service Records, 16th Alabama Infantry, 33rd Alabama Infantry, 15th Battalion Mississippi Sharpshooters, 32nd Mississippi Infantry, 33rd Mississippi Infantry, 44th Tennessee Infantry, M-269, RG 94, NARA.

65. *Corinth (Miss.) Herald*, Mar. 27, 1902, reprinted in "Corinth Information Database," paper copy in 32nd Mississippi Infantry file, PSHS.

66. *OR* 1, 16, pt. 1, 1121; Hall to Baldwin, Jan. 18, 1863, Baldwin Letters, MDAH; Unidentified diary, 22, 33rd Alabama Infantry File, PSHS; "33rd Alabama," 26 (quotation); Williams, *Sketch of the 33rd Alabama*, 14; Crowson and Brogden, eds., *Bloody Banners*, 13; Dyer and Moore, *Tennessee Civil War Veterans*, vol. 2, 439–40; Kurt Holman to author, Aug. 15, 1997, Author's Collection, PSHS. Company Return-Record of Events, 15th Battalion Mississippi Sharpshooters, Compiled Service Records, M-269, RG 94, NARA, notes that the battalion participated in the battle but took only a handful of casualties. I surmise that they were not in the front rank. See also Holman to author, Apr. 19, 2000.

67. Unidentified diary, 22, 33rd Alabama Infantry File, PSHS; "33rd Alabama," 26–28; Crowson and Brogden, eds. *Bloody Banners*, 14.

68. Donelson to Wright, Oct. 26, 1862, Bragg Papers, WRHS; Glezen Diary, Oct. 8, 1862; Phelps to friends, Oct. 16, 1862, Phelps Letters, USAMHI; *Cincinnati Daily Commercial*, Oct. 24, 1862; *Fayetteville (Tenn.) Observer*, Nov. 13, 1862, *Indianapolis Daily Journal*, Oct. 26, 29, 1862; Brooks, *Battle of Perryville* pamphlet, IlSHL; Milner, "'Human Document,'" 6; Elliott, *Soldier of Tennessee*, 58.

69. *OR* 1, 16, pt. 1, 1050, 1056; Chandler Diary, 22–23; Unidentified diary, 22, 33rd Alabama Infantry File, PSHS; Hupp, *My Diary*, 23–25; *Corinth (Miss.) Herald*, Mar. 27, 1902, "Corinth Information Database," 32nd Mississippi File, PSHS; *Daily Evansville Journal*, Oct. 16, 1862; Reid, *Ohio in the War*, vol. 2, 79; " Tale From the 41st Mississippi" 2.

70. "33rd Alabama," 26–28.

71. *Daily Evansville Journal*, Oct. 16, 1862.

72. *OR* 1, 16, pt. 1, 1050, 1056; Chandler Diary, 22–23; Hupp, *My Diary*, 23–25; Reid, *Ohio in the War*, vol. 2, 79.

73. *OR* 1, 16, pt. 1, 1050, 1052; Inglis Diary, Oct. 8, 1862; Scribner, *How Soldiers Were Made*, 59–60; Daniel, *Soldiering*, 5. Largely because of the Inglis Diary and the Miller Report, this account of Brown's brigade differs markedly from that found in Hafendorfer's *Perryville*, 250–56, 278. Hafendorfer contends that Harris successfully defended the ridge against Brown's attack, driving it back as he had Jones earlier, and only pulled back later in the calm that followed the storm due to casualties and a lack of ammunition.

74. *OR* 1, 16, pt. 1, 70, 1058, 1123; *OR* 1, 52, pt. 1, 52; Yeatman Memoirs; Herald, "Terrible Sight," 10; Beatty, *Citizen-Soldier*, 181–82; Dyer and Moore, *Tennessee Civil War Veterans*, vol. 4, 1659; Headley, *Confederate Operations*, 58–59; Garrett, trans., *Robert D. Smith*, 33; Buck, *Cleburne*, 69–70. The Black man, according to Yeatman, claimed to be the cook for "Genl. Woolfolk." No such general fought at Perryville. He may have meant Col. Frank Wolford of the 1st Kentucky Cavalry. Then again, the man may have hoped that identifying himself as a cook rather than a combatant would save his life. There is no indication of whether or not it worked.

75. Trask Journal, 69.

76. *OR* 1, 16, pt. 1, 1127; *OR* 1, 52, pt. 1, 52; Trask Journal, 69; *Daily Evansville Journal*, Oct. 16, 1862 (quotation); Bartlett, *Military Record*, 9–10; Buck, *Cleburne*, 69–70; Dyer and Moore, *Tennessee Civil War Veterans*, vol. 4, 1659; Headley, *Confederate Operations*, 58–59.

77. *OR* 1, 16, pt. 1, 1056–57, 1127; Trask Journal, 69; Headley, *Confederate Operations*, 58; Horrall, *Forty-second Indiana*, 151; Kirkpatrick, *Experiences*, 14; *Cincinnati Daily Enquirer*, Oct. 17, 1862; *Princeton (Ind.) Clarion*, Oct. 26, 1862; "General's Tour," 37.

78. *Daily Evansville Journal*, Oct. 18, 1862.

79. Shanklin, *"Dear Lizzie,"* 230. See also *OR* 1, 16, pt. 1, 1127; *OR* 1, 52, pt. 1, 54; "Historical Notes"; Hafendorfer, ed., "Simon B. Buckner's," 58; Lindsley, ed., *Military Annals*, vol. 1, 353.

80. Patrick to his sister, Apr. 1, 1862, Patrick Letters, LSU. For the 13th Louisiana's dress that day, see Daniel, *Shiloh*, 93; and J. P. Walsh to Kurt Holman, Apr. 29, 1999, Author's Collection, PSHS.

81. Sword, *Shiloh*, 185, 221, 245, 247–55, 440.

82. Horrall, *Forty-second Indiana*, 152.

83. *OR* 1, 16, pt. 1, 1127; Hafendorfer, ed., "Simon B. Buckner's," 59.

84. Shanklin, *"Dear Lizzie,"* 230–31.

85. Kirkpatrick, *Experiences*, 14.

86. Headley, *Confederate Operations*, 59.

87. *OR* 1, 52, pt. 1, 52; Trask Journal, 69; Horrall, *Forty-second Indiana*, 151–53; Kirkpatrick, *Experiences*, 14–15; *Princeton (Ind.) Clarion*, Oct. 25, 1862; Shanklin, *"Dear Lizzie,"* 231–32.

88. *OR* 1, 52, pt. 1, 52; Trask Journal, 69; Horrall, *Forty-second Indiana*, 151–53. See also *Princeton (Ind.) Clarion*, Oct. 25, 1862; Kirkpatrick, *Experiences*, 14–15; and Shanklin, *"Dear Lizzie,"* 231–32. Hafendorfer, *Perryville*, 242–43, 298, 457, identifies Carlton's group as "Carlton's Texas Sharpshooters." Cleburne's biographer, Craig Symonds, maintains that no such unit ever existed. The sharpshooters, he suspects, were drawn from existing regiments under Cleburne's command, possibly through shooting contests. See Craig Symonds to author, June 25, 1998, Kurt Holman to author, July 20, 1999; and Mauriel Phillips Johnson to Kurt Holman, July 26, 1999, all in Author's Collection, PSHS.

89. *OR* 1, 16, pt. 1, 1040, 1047, 1056–57, 1058.

90. Ibid., 1040–41; Glezen Diary, Oct. 8, 1862; Moore to his parents, Oct. 16, 1862, Moore Papers, USAMHI; Al E. Reeder to his parents, Oct. 11, 1862, Ursula M. Scott Collection, UMWHMC; *Cincinnati Daily Commercial*, Oct. 24, Nov. 8, 12, 1862; Milner, "'Human Document,'" 6; Brooks, *Battle of Perryville* pamphlet, IlSHL.

91. Milner, "'Human Document,'" 6. See also Duncan Chambers Milner Letter, U.S. History, Civil War Biography, Chicago Historical Society.

92. McCormick and DuBro, eds., "'If I Live to Get Home'," 23–24.

93. *OR* 1, 16, pt. 1, 1040, 1047, 1056–57, 1058; *Louisville Daily Journal*, Oct. 21, 1862 (quotation); Beatty, *Citizen-Soldier*, 180.

94. *OR* 1, 16, pt. 1, 1040–41, 1047; James M. Sligh to his father, Oct. 17, 1862, and George D. Walker to J. M. Sligh, Oct. 18, 1862, both in Sligh Family Papers; UMBHL; *Cleveland Plain Dealer*, Oct. 17, 1862; *New Albany (Ind.) Daily Ledger*, Oct. 14, 1862; Bachelor, "Soldiers' Anecdotes," 19; Sligh, *First Regiment Michigan Engineers*, 7, 12.

95. *OR* 1, 16, pt. 1, 1041, 1047.

96. Ibid., 1047; *OR* 1, 52, pt. 1, 52; *Princeton (Ind.) Clarion*, Oct. 25, 1862. See also Shanklin, *"Dear Lizzie,"* 231–32; Garrett, trans. *Robert D. Smith*, 33; Symonds, *Stonewall of the West*, 96–97.

97. Yeatman Memoirs.

98. Hartman, "Battle of Perryville," 3.

CHAPTER 13

1. Bennett and Haigh, *Thirty-sixth Regiment*, 258–61. The authors overestimate the effect that Hescock's fire had on the Confederate assault, essentially arguing that their battery alone blunted the attack.

2. *OR* 1, 16, pt. 1, 1084; Anderson to Semple, June 10, 1863, Confederate Artil-

lery Batteries, Lumsden's Battery-Waters' Battery, ADAH; Dowd Recollections; Drake to his brother, Oct. 13, 1862, Drake Letters, SHSW; Ellis Diary, 25; clipping, *Montgomery Daily Advertiser,* Nov. 26, 1864, and typescript, "Perry and Smith's Montgomery Directory, 1866," 97–98, both in the Confederate Regimental History Files: 45th Alabama Infantry Regiment, ADAH; Semple to his wife, Aug. 2, 1862, Henry C. Semple Papers, SHC-UNC; Althouse and Hughes, eds., *John A. Boon,* 17; Sutherland, ed., *Reminiscences,* 99.

   3. *OR* 1, 16, pt. 1, 1082; Dowd Recollections; Ellis Diary, 25; clipping, *Montgomery Daily Adverstiser,* Nov. 26, 1864, and typescript, "Perry and Smith's Montgomery Directory, 1866," 97–98; Bennett and Haigh, *History of the 36th Regiment,* 259; Sutherland, ed., *Reminiscences,* 99; Draper, "Sketch of Hon. Charles H. Larrabee," 381.

   4. *OR* 1, 16, pt. 1, 1082, 1084; Cavis Diary, Oct. 8, 1862; Dowd Recollections; *Aurora (Ill.) Weekly Beacon,* Nov. 16, 1862; Aten, *Eighty-fifth Regiment,* 36; Bennett and Haigh, *Thirty-sixth Regiment,* 263–64; Brown, Murphy, and Putney, *Behind the Guns,* 37; Sutherland, ed., *Reminiscences,* 99.

   5. *OR* 1, 16, pt. 1, 1084; Drake to his brother, Oct. 13, 1862, Drake Letters, SHSW; Quiner Scrapbooks, vol. 6, 247; Bennett and Haigh, *Thirty-sixth Regiment,* 254–55; Ford, *Rank and File,* 7; Francis, *Narrative,* 56–57; *Milwaukee Sentinel,* Oct. 17, 1862; Draper, "Sketch of Hon. Charles H. Larrabee," 381.

   6. *History of the Seventy-third Regiment,* 99–100.

   7. Work Diary, Oct. 8, 1862, OHS; Aten, *Eighty-fifth Regiment,* 36; Bennett and Haigh, *Thirty-sixth Regiment,* 262–63; Brown, Murphy and Putney, *Behind the Guns,* 37; Stewart, *Dan McCook's Regiment,* 27.

   8. Bennett and Haigh, *Thirty-sixth Regiment,* 264.

   9. *OR* 1, 16, pt. 1, 1084; Cavis Diary, Oct. 8, 1862; Dowd Recollections; Drake to his brother, Oct. 13, 1862, Drake Letters, SHSW; Bennett and Haigh, *Thirty-sixth Regiment,* 265; Benson, *Soldier's Diary,* 29; Brown, Murphy and Putney, *Behind the Guns,* 37–38; Draper, "Sketch of Hon. Charles H. Larrabee," 381. There is no exact account of the composition of Powell's lines. For a different interpretation, see Hafendorfer, *Perryville,* 290–91.

   10. Dowd Recollections. Bennett and Haigh also mention the Confederates taking careful aim against the Federal line (*Thirty-sixth Regiment,* 265).

   11. Cavis Diary, Oct. 8, 1862; Comstock to his mother, Oct. 10, 1862, Comstock Letters, SHSW; Cummins Diary, undated entry, George A. Cummins Papers, IISHL (hereafter Cummins Diary); Drake to his brother, Oct. 13, 1862, Drake Letters, SHSW; Frazee to his parents, Oct. 13 and 16, 1862, Frazee Letters, IISHL; *Milwaukee Sentinel,* Oct. 17, 1862; Benson, *Soldier's Diary,* 30; Ford, *Rank and File,* 7–8; Work, "Perryville," 3.

   12. *Milwaukee Sentinel,* Oct. 17, 1862; Comstock to his mother, Oct. 10, 1862, Comstock Letters, SHSW.

   13. Cavis Diary, Oct. 8, 1862; Comstock to his mother, Oct. 10, 1862, Comstock Letters, SHSW; Diary, undated entry; Lars Olsen Dokken to his parents, Oct. 10, 1862, Dokken Papers, SHSW; Drake to his brother, Oct. 13, 1862, Drake Letters, SHSW; *Milwaukee Sentinel,* Oct. 17, 1862; Althouse and Hughes, eds., *John A. Boon,* 17; Benson, *Soldier's Diary,* 30; Ford, *Rank and File,* 7–8; Francis, *Narrative,* 57; *History of the Seventy-third Regiment,* 100–1; Newlin, *Cherished Memories,* 2; Work, "Perryville," 3.

   14. "Missouri Soldier," 21.

   15. *Louisville Daily Journal,* Oct. 22, 1862; Kerwood, *Fifty-seventh Regiment,* 131–32.

   16. Kerwood, *Fifty-seventh Regiment,* 132.

   17. Davis to his wife, Oct. 16, 1862, Davis Papers, Iowa; James Sears to Father, Oct. 21, 1862, Sears Letters, Civil War Miscellaneous Collection—New Material, USAMHI; Joyce, *Checkered Life,* 73; Kerwood, *Fifty-seventh Regiment,* 132; Osburn, "Gen. George D. Wagner," 3.

18. Osburn, "Gen. George D. Wagner," 3.

19. Althouse and Hughes, eds., *John A. Boon*, 17.

20. *OR* 1, 16, pt. 1, 94, 1073, 1077.

21. Work, "Perryville," 3.

22. *OR* 1, 16, pt. 1, 1086; Cummins Diary, undated entry; *Aurora (Ill.) Weekly Beacon*, Nov. 16, 1862 (quotation); *Milwaukee Sentinel*, Oct. 17, 1862; Bennett and Haigh, *Thirty-sixth Regiment*, 266–68; Brown, Murphy and Putney, *Behind the Guns*, 38; Draper, "Sketch of Charles H. Larrabee," 382.

23. *OR* 1, 16, pt. 1, 1086; Brown, Murphy and Putney, *Behind the Guns*, 38. See also Dowd Recollections; Bennett and Haigh, *Thirty-sixth Regiment*, 268.

24. *Louisville Daily Journal*, Oct. 22, 1862; Althouse and Hughes, eds., *John A. Boon*, 17; Bennett and Haigh, *Thirty-sixth Regiment*, 268–69; Draper, "Sketch of Charles Larrabee," 382.

25. Comstock to his mother, Oct. 10, 1862, Comstock Letters, SHSW.

26. Bennett and Haigh, *Thirty-sixth Regiment*, 268–69.

27. Brown to Fannie Brown, Oct. 24, 1862, Brown Letters, ADAH; Cummins Diary, undated entry; Comstock to his mother, Oct. 10, 1862, Comstock Letters, SHSW; Dowd Recollections; Life of L. A. Ross," 48; *Aurora [Ill.] Weekly Beacon*, Nov. 16, 1862; *Milwaukee Sentinel*, Oct. 17, 1862; Francis. *Narrative*, 51–52; *History of the Seventy-third Regiment*, 100–1; Stewart, *Dan McCook's Regiment*, 271; Draper, "Sketch of Charles Larrabee," 382.

28. Bennett and Haigh, *Thirty-sixth Regiment*, 259–60. See also *OR* 1, 16, pt. 1, 1082; Brown, Murphy and Putney, *Behind the Guns*, 38; Sheridan, *Personal Memoirs*, vol. 1, 197; Work, "Perryville," 3.

29. *OR* 1, 16, pt. 1, 240.

30. Ibid., 94, 96, 1076–77; Boatner, *Civil War Dictionary*, 557.

31. *OR* 1, 16, pt. 1, 94, 96, 98 (quotations, 96, 98).

32. Ibid., 94, 1076–77; Cozzens, ed., "Ambition Carries the Day," 144.

33. Blegen, ed., *Letters of Hans Christian Heg*, 145. See also Dokken to his parents, Oct. 10, 1862, Dokken Papers, SHSW; Klement, *Wisconsin in the Civil War*, 88.

34. *OR* 1, 16, pt. 1, 94; Aten, *Eighty-fifth Regiment*, 36; Bennett and Haigh, *Thirty-sixth Regiment*, 269–72; Cleven, translation of Buslett, *Femtende Wisconsin*, 30, WVM; Sheridan, *Personal Memoirs*, 197.

35. *OR* 1, 16, pt. 1, 94; Dowd Recollections; Patterson Memoir, Oct. 8, 1862; Ole Thostenson Reminiscence, SHSW (hereafter Thostenson Reminiscence); Aten, *Eighty-fifth Regiment*, 36; Bennett and Haigh, *Thirty-sixth Regiment*, 269–72; Cozzens, ed., "Ambition Carries the Day," 142, 145; Fleming, ed., "Letters From a Canadian Recruit," 163; Sheridan, *Personal Memoirs*, 197; Boatner, *Civil War Dictionary*, 123.

36. *OR* 1, 16, pt. 1, 94; Patterson Memoir, Oct. 8, 1862; Quiner Scrapbooks, vol. 5, 194; Blegen, ed., *Letters of Hans Christian Heg*, 145 (quotation, 145).

37. Cleven, translation of Buslett, *Femtende Wisconsin*, 31, WVM. See also Patterson Memoir, Oct. 8, 1862; Blegen, ed., *Letters of Hans Christian Heg*, 145.

38. *OR* 1, 16, pt. 1, 94; Dokken to his parents, Oct. 10, 1862, Dokken Papers, SHSW; Quiner Scrapbooks, vol. 5, 193; Fleming, ed., "Letters From a Canadian Recruit," 163.

39. Anderson to Semple, June 10, 1863, Confederate Artillery Batteries, Lumsden's Battery-Waters' Battery, ADAH; Brown to Fannie Brown, Oct. 24, 1862, Brown Letters, ADAH; Ellis Diary, 27–28; Semple to his wife, Aug. 2, 1862, Semple Papers, SHC-UNC; "Historical Notes"; Street to his wife, Oct. 10, 1862, Street and East (Pace) Correspondence, SHC-UNC; Thostenson Reminiscence; Sutherland, ed., *Reminiscences*, 99.

40. Dokken to his parents, Oct. 10, 1862, Dokken Papers, SHSW; Ole C. Johnson

to his brother, Oct. 10, 1862, Albert O. Barton Papers, SHSW; Patterson Memoir, Oct. 8, 1862; Quiner Scrapbooks, vol. 5, 193; Thostenson Reminiscence; *Cincinnati Daily Enquirer,* Oct. 29. 1862; Blegen, ed., *Letters of Hans Christian Heg,* 145; Butler, *Letters Home,* 14–16; Cozzens, ed., "Ambition Carries the Day," 145 (quotation).

41. Ellis Diary, 28.

42. *OR* 1, 16, pt. 1, 94, 1078, 1123; Anderson to Semple, June 10, 1863, Confederate Artillery Batteries, Lumsden's Battery-Waters' Battery, ADAH; Brown to Fannie Brown, Oct. 24, 1862, Brown Letters, ADAH; Dokken to his parents, Oct. 10, 1862, Dokken Papers, SHSW; Ellis Diary, 27–28; Johnson to his brother, Oct. 10, 1862, Barton Papers, SHSW; "Augustus Cabarrus Kean," 16; Patterson Memoir, Oct. 8, 1862; Quiner Scrapbooks, vol. 5, 193; "Reminiscences of the Fifth Company"; "Historical Notes"; Thostenson Reminiscence; Blegen, ed., *Letters of Hans Christian Heg,* 145; Butler, *Letters Home,* 14–16; Mitchell identified the 38th Illinois as the unit that captured the Confederate train, but several of the sources listed above indicate that it was indeed the 15th Wisconsin.

43. *OR* 1, 16, pt. 1, 1071; Davis to his wife, Oct. 16, 1862, Davis Papers, Iowa; Joyce, *Checkered Life,* 73; Kerwood, *Fifty-seventh Regiment,* 133.

44. Mavity, "Condensed Letters," 3.

45. *B&L,* vol. 3, 57–58. Gilbert told the same story in "Bragg's Invasion of Kentucky," 467.

46. *OR* 1, 16, pt. 1, 277, 1072 (quotation, 277).

47. Ibid., 187.

48. Ibid., 557.

49. Gilbert, "Bragg's Invasion of Kentucky," 468.

50. *B&L,* vol. 3, 57–58 (quotation, 58); *OR* 1, 16, pt. 1, 1072–73; Gilbert, "Bragg's Invasion of Kentucky," 467–68.

51. *B&L,* vol. 3, 58.

52. Ibid.; DeVelling, *Seventeenth Regiment,* 70; Gilbert, "Bragg's Invasion of Kentucky," 468–69; Hunter, *Eighty-second Indiana,* 24.

53. *B&L,* vol. 3, 48. See also *OR* 1, 16, pt. 1, 50–51, 277, 1025, 1073; Davison, *Autobiography,* 48.

54. *OR* 1, 16, pt. 1, 1025. See also *B&L,* vol. 3, 48.

55. Hafendorfer, *Perryville,* 289–90.

56. *OR* 1, 16, pt. 1, 655, 1075; Keil, *Thirty-fifth Ohio,* 99; Wright, "Glimpse of Perryville," 151. A Buell loyalist after the war, Wright disputed the story that he found Schoepf "weeping in rage because he was not permitted to carry his division to the rescue. He was not weeping when I saw him; he seemed to be in a placid frame of mind and he made no comment on the fact that he was not ordered to go with his two brigades" (151).

57. *OR* 1, 16, pt. 1, 94, 95, 97.

58. Ibid., 94, 97; Dokken to his parents, Oct. 10, 1862, Dokken Papers, SHSW; Patterson Memoir, Oct. 8, 1862.

59. *OR* 1, 16, pt. 1, 1040–41; *New Albany (Ind.) Daily Ledger,* Oct. 16, 1862; *Princeton (Ind.) Clarion,* Oct. 25, 1862; *OR-Supp,* 1, 3, 277.

60. Wright, "Glimpse of Perryville," 151.

61. *OR* 1, 16, pt. 1, 1041, 1123; "Historical Notes"; Trask Journal, 69; Gipson, "About the Battle," 163; Brown, Murphy and Putney, *Behind the Guns,* 38; Morris, *Sheridan,* 95 (quotation, 95).

62. *OR* 1, 16, pt. 1, 1127.

63. Bennett and Haigh, *Thirty-sixth Regiment,* 260.

64. *OR* 1, 16, pt. 1, 1123.

65. Bennett and Haigh, *Thirty-sixth Regiment,* 260.

66. *OR* 1, 16, pt. 1, 1123; "Historical Notes"; Trask Journal, 69–70.

67. Trask Journal, 70.

68. *OR* 1, 16, pt. 1, 1123; Hess, *Union Soldier in Battle*, 82–83. Might Adams have done more? Kenneth Hafendorfer also thinks so, but for different reasons. See his *Perryville*, 332–33.

69. M. P. Lowrey Autobiography, 3, USM; Crowson and Brogden, eds. *Bloody Banners*, 14.

70. Crowson and Brogden, eds. *Bloody Banners*, 14.

71. *OR* 1, 16, pt. 1, 1038, 1080; Ball, "At Perryville," 2; Gardner, "Perryville," 3; Wright, "Glimpse of Perryville," 152; *Indianapolis Daily Journal*, Oct. 21, 1862; Dodge, *Waif of the War*, 45; Lathrop, *Fifty-ninth Regiment*, 164; Marshall, *Historical Sketch*, 23; Newton, "Fight at Perryville," 3; Scribner, *How Soldiers Were Made*, 60–61. My description of the original line is at variance with accepted wisdom as well as Gooding's report. It is instead based on the report of the 22nd Indiana's Col. Thomas B. Tanner, published in the *Indianapolis Daily Journal*, Oct. 21, 1862, as well as Ball's article.

72. *OR* 1, 16, pt. 1, 1047.

73. Wright, "Glimpse of Perryville," 152.

74. *OR* 1, 16, pt. 1, 1080; Ball to Lib, Oct. 18, 1862, Ball Collection, USAMHI; Duncan Diary, 9; *Louisville Daily Journal*, Oct. 11, 1862; Ball, "At Perryville," 2 (quotation, 2); Gardner, "Perryville," 3; Lathrop, *Fifty-ninth Regiment*, 164; Marshall, *Historical Sketch*, 23; Newton, "Fight at Perryville," 3; "General's Tour," 40.

75. Pinney to [?], Oct. 10, 1862, and "Capt. Oscar F. Pinney," Pinney Papers, SHSW; Gardner, "Perryville," 2 (quotation, 2).

76. *OR* 1, 16, pt. 1, 1080.

77. Hall to Baldwin, Jan. 18, 1863, Baldwin Letters, MDAH; "33rd Alabama," 26; Crowson and Brogden, eds., *Bloody Banners*, 14; Dodge, *Waif of the War*, 44. Riding along his line, Gooding faced similar problems. Much to his indignation, he later complained, he encountered Capt. Elijah Stapleton of the 22nd Indiana's Company F hiding in a small ravine behind his company's line, frozen with fear. Stapleton's men would however later defend their captain, charging that Gooding was the coward. See M. Gooding to O. P. Morton, Nov. 13, 1862, and William F. Riggs et al. to [?], Dec. 6, 1862, both in Regimental Correspondence of the Adjutant General of Indiana, 22nd Indiana Infantry, ISA.

78. Wright, "Glimpse of Perryville," 153.

79. Crary, *Crary Memoirs*, 76.

80. Williams, "33rd Alabama," 26–27, ADAH.

81. *OR* 1, 16, pt. 1, 1080; "33rd Alabama," 27.

82. Johnston Diary, Oct. 8, 1862.

83. Hughes, ed., *Liddell's Record*, 90–91. See also *OR* 1, 16, pt. 1, 1159; *Knoxville Daily Register*, Oct. 29, 1862.

84. Hughes, ed., *Liddell's Record*, 91.

85. Ibid., 91–92. See also *OR* 1, 16, pt. 1, 1159; *Knoxville Daily Register*, Oct. 29, 1862.

86. "33rd Alabama," 27.

87. Crowson and Brogden, eds., *Bloody Banners*, 14; Hughes, ed., *Liddell's Record*, 92.

88. Hafendorfer, "Major General Simon B. Buckner's," 59; *OR—Supp*, 1, 3, 276–77.

89. Hughes, ed., *Liddell's Record*, 92. See also *OR* 1, 16, pt. 1, 1159; *Knoxville Daily Register*, Oct. 29, 1862.

90. *OR* 1, 16, pt. 1, 1080; *Indianapolis Daily Journal*, Oct. 21, 1862; *Knoxville Daily Register*, Oct. 29, 1862.

91. Hughes, ed., *Liddell's Record*, 92–93. See also *OR* 1, 16, pt. 1, 1080; *Knoxville Daily Register*, Oct. 29, 1862.

92. This account is based on slightly differing versions found in the *Knoxville Daily Register*, Oct. 29, 1862; "Co. Aytch: An Adventure of General Leonidas Polk," 403–4; Hughes, ed., *Liddell's Record*, 92–93; Parks, *General Leonidas Polk*, 271–72; and "Quick Witted Bishop Polk," 270. See also Sanders, "'Every Mother's Son'," 52–59.

93. Hughes, ed., *Liddell's Record*, 93.

94. *Knoxville Daily Register*, Oct. 29, 1862.

95. *OR* 1, 16, pt. 1, 1159; Daniel Diary, 19; Sipe to Sallie, Oct. 16, 1862, Civil War Regimental History—38th Indiana, InSL; *Indianapolis Daily Journal*, Oct. 21, 1862; Ball, "At Perryville," 2; Barnhart, ed., "Hoosier Invades the Confederacy," 149–50; Berry, "Reminiscences From Missouri," 73; Gardner, "Perryville," 3; Herr, *Nine Campaigns*, 113–15; Hughes, ed., *Liddell's Record*, 93; Marshall, *Historical Sketch*, 23–24; McCouley, "Who Was That Officer?" 406; Gates, ed., *The Rough Side of War*, 30 Collier, *First In–Last Out*, 50–51; Holman, "Casualty Percentages of Individual Units."

96. "Capt. Oscar F. Pinney"; Ball, "At Perryville," 2; Dodge, *Waif of the War*, 44–47; Herr, *Nine Campaigns*, 115; Lathrop, *Fifty-ninth Regiment*, 165–66; Gates, ed., *The Rough Side of War*, 30. I have followed Ball's directions rather than his indication of units, for I believe he had them mixed up in his account.

97. *OR* 1, 16, pt. 1, 1159; Hughes, ed., *Liddell's Record*, 93.

98. Hughes, ed., *Liddell's Record*, 93.

99. *OR* 1, 16, pt. 1, 137, 656, 1075 (quotations, 656, 137). See also Keil, *Thirty-fifth Ohio*, 99.

100. *OR* 1, 16, pt. 1, 137.

101. Keil, *Thirty-fifth Ohio*, 99.

102. *OR* 1, 16, pt. 1, 137, 1075; Daniel E. Bruce Memorandum, 5, InHS; Albertson, ed. *Letters Home*, letter 58, p. 1; " Bircher, *Drummer-Boy's Diary*, 45–46; Bishop, *Story of a Regiment*, 72; Grebner, *"We Were the Ninth,"* 115; Keil, *Thirty-fifth Ohio*, 99–100.

103. Albertson, ed., *Letters Home*, letter 58, 1.

104. Grebner, *"We Were the Ninth,"* 115; Keil, *Thirty-fifth Ohio*, 100.

105. Bishop, *Story of a Regiment*, 72–73.

106. Hughes, ed., *Liddell's Record*, 94. See also *OR* 1, 16, pt. 1, 1159; Daniel Diary, 19.

107. Gardner, ""Perryville," 3. See also Pinney to [?], Oct. 10, 1862; "Capt. Oscar F. Pinney," Pinney Papers, SHSW.

CHAPTER 14

1. Ellis Record, 3; F. B. Kendrick Memoirs, 20–21, TSLA; Otto Memoirs, 110–14; Talley Autobiography, 25; Trask Journal, 70–73; Searcy letter transcription, Semple's Alabama Battery File, PSHS; *Cincinnati Daily Enquirer*, Oct. 17, 1862; Barnhart, ed., "Hoosier Invades the Confederacy," 150; Davis, "Recollections of Perryville," 554; Hinman, *Sherman Brigade*, 295; Kirkpatrick, *Experiences*, 17; Thatcher, *Hundred Battles*, 83; Tourgée, *Story of a Thousand*, 127; Womack, *Diary of J. J. Womack*, 64; Dyer and Moore, *Tennessee Civil War Veterans*, vol. 3, 983.

2. Watkins, "Co. Aytch," 63. See also Manzy Diary, Oct. 8, 1862, Confederate Collection, TSLA; Cheatham, "Battle of Perryville," 705; Dyer and Moore, *Tennessee Civil War Veterans*, vol. 2, 701–2.

3. Toney, *Privations*, 45.

4. Malone, *Memoir*, 133.

5. Carnes to Quintard, Feb. 13, 1895, Quintard Papers, Duke.

6. "33rd Alabama," 27.

7. Davis, "Recollections of Perryville," 554.

8. "Reminiscences of the Fifth Company."

9. Beatty, *Citizen-Soldier*, 180–81. See also Fitch, *Echoes*, 62–63; Tourgée, *Story of a Thousand*, 150; Winters, *In the 50th Ohio*, 21.

10. Eicker Memoir, 11; Christian Mattern to Mrs. Lewis Jones, n.d., Lewis H. Jones Diary and Letters, Civil War Miscellaneous Collection, USAMHI; Reid, *Ohio in the War*, vol. 2, 620.

11. Holmes, *Soldier*, 94–95.

12. Calkins Diary, 42.

13. Morris, *Eighty-first Regiment*, 17.

14. Bennet and Haigh, *Thirty-sixth Regiment*, 273, 274.

15. Jarman Manuscript; Potts to his mother, Dec. 14, 1862, Samuel J. Potts Letters, OHS; *Cincinnati Daily Enquirer*, Oct. 17, 1862; Head, *Campaigns and Battles*, 98.

16. Otto Memoirs, 110.

17. Crawford, "Battle of Perryville," 4. Crawford described the fleeing slaves with undisguised amusement. See also Adams, *Doctors in Blue*, 62, 83.

18. Crawford, "Rear of Perryville," 3.

19. Cross, *Camp and Field*, 61–63.

20. Winchester Diary, 79–80. See also Toney, *Privations*, 45.

21. Hall Diary, 62–63.

22. Noll, ed., *Doctor Quintard*, 60.

23. Herald, "Terrible Sight," 10; Margaret Woodward Forsyth, "Story of the Old Canteen," and Jeff Vaughan to Mary C. Breeding, Aug. 16, 1995, both in William Woodward Collection, PEP. The Woodward heirs still own the canteen as of this writing. See also Morse to his mother, Oct. 14, 1862, Morse Papers, OHS.

24. Trask Journal, 70–72. See also Hughes, ed., *Liddell's Record*, 94. Kurt Holman tentatively identifies the boy as James M. Bowling of Company C, 15th Kentucky, which would have made him older than twelve. See Kurt Holman to author, Feb. 3, 2000, Author's Collection, PSHS.

25. Morris, *Eighty-first Regiment*, 17.

26. Waddle, *Three Years*, 37.

27. *Cincinnati Daily Enquirer*, Oct. 17, 1862. See also Otto Memoirs, 113–16; Kendall, *Battle of Perryville*, 10; *New Albany (Ind.) Daily Ledger*, Oct. 16, 1862; Shanklin, "*Dear Lizzie*," 232; *Valparaiso (Ind.) Republic*, Nov. 13, 1862.

28. Ben Logan to his sister, Oct. 14, 1862, 98th Ohio Infantry File, PSHS; Biggs, "Incidents," 142; Waddle, *Three Years*, 37–38.

29. Hughes, ed., *Liddell's Record*, 94–96; One suspect is the 7th Arkansas's C. M. McCouley. See his "Who Was that Officer?" 406, for a very different description of an encounter with a Federal officer.

30. Phelps to friends, Oct. 16, 1862, Phelps Letters, USAMHI; Street to his wife, Oct. 10, 1862, Street and East (Pace) Correspondence, SHC-UNC; Stuckey to Helen Stuckey, Oct. 19, 1862, Stuckey Letters, InHS; Winn Diary, Oct. 9, 1862; *Princeton (Ind.) Clarion*, Oct. 25, 1862; *Valparaiso (Ind.) Republic*, Nov. 13, 1862; Cheatham, "Battle of Perryville," 705; Crowson and Brogden, ed., *Bloody Banners*, 14–15; Hughes, ed., *Liddell's Record*, 94; Kendall, *Battle of Perryville*, 10; Kirkpatrick, *Experiences*, 17; Malone, *Memoir*, 133; Watkins, "*Co. Aytch*," 63.

31. Hooper Diary, Oct. 8, 1862; Phelps to friends, Oct. 16, 1862, Phelps Letters, USAMHI; Hughes, ed., *Liddell's Record*, 94, 96; Little and Maxwell, *History of Lumsden's Battery*, 12–13;

32. Malone, *Memoir*, 133. See also Starling to his daughters, Nov. 16, 1862, Lewis-Starling Collection, WKUL.

33. "33rd Alabama," 27; Moore to his brother, Nov. 1, 1862, Moore Papers, USAMHI.

34. *OR* 1, 16, pt. 1, 1088, 1093; *B&L*, vol. 3, 17; "Campaign in Kentucky, No. 5"; Johnston Diary, Oct. 8 and 9, 1862; Claiborne, "Battle of Perryville," 226; Connelly, *Army of the Heartland*, 266–67; Hughes, *General William J. Hardee*, 131.

35. *OR* 1, 16, pt. 1, 898, 1093; *OR* 1, 16, pt. 2, 925, 926–27; *B&L*, vol. 3, 17; Brent Diary, Oct. 8, 1862; Brown to Fannie Brown, Oct. 24, 1862, Brown Letters, ADAH; "Campaign in Kentucky, No. 5"; Johnston Diary, Oct. 8 and 9, 1862; Claiborne, "Battle of Perryville," 226; Hughes, *General William J. Hardee*, 131.

36. Donelson to Wright, Oct. 26, 1862, Bragg Papers, WRHS; Magee Diary, Oct. 9, 1862; Trask Journal, 73; Headley, *Confederate Operations*, 59; Steely and Taylor, eds., "Bragg's Kentucky Campaign," 52.

37. Bryant to his mother, Oct. 11, 1862, 3rd Florida Infantry File, PSHS; Inglis Diary, 84–87; Miller Report, 5–6.

38. Clark Diary, vol. 2, 45; Toney, *Privations*, 45–46; Rieger, annotator, *Through One Man's Eyes*, 14; *Daily Evansville Journal*, Oct. 16, 1862; Losson, *Tennessee's Forgotten Warriors*, 74; Dyer and Moore, *Tennessee Civil War Veterans*, vol. 1, 184–85, 400–2, 701–2; vol. 2, 543–44; vol. 4, 1688–89; Perry, *Thirty-eighth Regiment*, 37; Daniel, *Soldiering*, 71.

39. "Campaign in Kentucky, No. 5." See also Trask Journal, 75; Garrett, trans., *Robert D. Smith*, Oct. 9, 1862; "William P. Rogers," 72; Losson, *Tennessee's Forgotten Warriors*, 74.

40. Hughes, ed., *Liddell's Record*, 97. See also Dyer and Moore, *Tennessee Civil War Veterans*, vol. 3, 963–64.

41. Sheridan, *Personal Memoirs*, vol. 1, 199; Morris, *Sheridan*, 96.

42. Sheridan, *Personal Memoirs*, vol. 1, 199.

43. *OR* 1, 16, pt. 1, 345.

44. Ibid., 99, 345.

45. Ibid., 94, 99, 187, 188 (quotation, 94).

46. Ibid., 94, 99, 102–3, 115, 193 (quotation, 102); *B&L*, vol. 3, 48–49. Gilbert later claimed to be there as well, but the recollections of others firmly dismiss that assertion. Thomas notably remembered the conversation differently (see *OR* 1, 16, pt. 1, 193).

47. *OR* 1, 16, pt. 1, 102.

48. Ibid., 115–17, 187, 193, 510, 657; *OR* 1, 16, pt. 2, 598; *B&L*, vol. 3, 48–49; Gilbert, "Bragg's Invasion of Kentucky," 470–71, 472; *Cincinnati Daily Commercial*, Oct. 17, 1862.

49. *OR* 1, 16, pt. 1, 181–82, 193, 510.

50. Ibid., 235–36, 241–42; Davis to his wife, Oct. 16, 1862, Davis Papers, Iowa; Dokken to his parents, Oct. 10, 1862, Dokken Papers, SHSW; Day, *One Hundred and First Ohio*, 55; Hinman, *Sherman Brigade*, 295–96.

51. *OR* 1, 16, pt. 1, 235–36, 238, 242; Davis to his wife, Oct. 16, 1862, Davis Papers, Iowa; Hartpence, *Fifty-first Indiana*, 88. Hinman, *Sherman Brigade*, 295–96.

52. *OR* 1, 16, pt. 1, 181–82. Before the Buell Commission, Wood attempted to shift the blame to his brigade commanders, maintaining that he never strayed more than a hundred yards from his main body, and could have been easily found.

53. Ibid., 98; Simmons, *84th Reg't*, 15.

54. Simmons, *84th Reg't*, 15. See also Barnes, Carnahan, and McCain, *Eighty-sixth Regiment*, 65.

55. *OR* 1, 16, pt. 1, 193–94, 510, 536; *B&L*, vol. 3, 49; Joseph K. Marshall Diary, Oct. 9, 1862, 90th Ohio Infantry File, PSHS; Anderson, ed., *Nicholas Longworth Anderson*, 162; Noe, ed., *Southern Boy in Blue*, 104; Smith, *Thirty-first Regiment*, 33.

56. *OR* 1, 16, pt. 1, 98, 1079; Cozzens, ed., "Ambition Carries the Day," 146; Dokken to his parents, Oct. 10, 1862, Dokken Papers, SHSW; Patterson Memoir, 39, Oct. 9, 1862; Bennett and Haigh, *Thirty-sixth Regiment*, 274–75; Day, *One Hundred and First Ohio*, 55; Lathrop, *Fifty-ninth Regiment*, 170; *Report of the Adjutant General*, vol. 1, 109.

57. *OR* 1, 16, pt. 1, 657, 665.

58. Federico and Wright, eds., *Civil War*, 64.

59. *OR* 1, 16, pt. 1, 509–10; *OR* 1, 16, pt. 2, 597, 598.

60. *OR* 1, 16, pt. 1, 510–12; *OR* 1, 16, pt. 2, 597–98.

61. *OR* 1, 16, pt. 2, 599; Cozzens, ed., "Ambition Carries the Day," 146; Dokken to his parents, Oct. 10, 1862, Dokken Papers, SHSW; Patterson Memoir, 39, Oct. 9, 1862; Tuttle Diary, Oct. 9, 1862; *Cincinnati Daily Commercial*, Oct. 17, 1862; Aten, *Eighty-fifth Regiment*, 41–42; Barnes, Carnahan, and McCain, *Eighty-sixth Regiment*, 65; Bennett and Haigh, *Thirty-sixth Regiment*, 274–75; Brown, Murphy, and Putney, *Behind the Guns*, 40; Butler, *My Story*, 226; Day, *One Hundred and First Ohio*, 55; *History of the Seventy-ninth Indiana*, 50–51; Kinnear, *Eighty-sixth Regiment*, 13; Morris, *Eighty-first Regiment*, 17; Perry, *Thirty-eighth Regiment*, 38–39; *Report of the Adjutant General*, vol. 1, 109; Simmons, *84th Reg't*, 15.

62. Noe, ed., *Southern Boy in Blue*, 104–5. See also Brown to Chandler, Oct. 17, 1862, U.S. Army Letters, Duke; Clark Diary, vol. 2, 44; Blegen, ed., *Civil War Letters*, 147; "His Mother," *Young Chaplain*, 103.

63. *New Albany (Ind.) Daily Ledger*, Oct. 21, 1862. See also Frazee to his parents, Oct. 13 and 16, 1862, Frazee Letters, IlSHL.

64. Johnson to his brother, Oct. 10, 1862, Barton Papers, SHSW.

65. Sipe to Sallie, Oct. 16, 1862, Civil War Regimental History—38th Indiana, InSL.

66. For Confederates swollen black (or green), see William Spencer to his sister, Oct. 10, 1862, Spencer Letters, OHS; *Valparaiso (Ind.) Republic*, Nov. 13, 1862; Francis, *Narrative*, 59; Morris, *Eighty-first Regiment*, 17. For an opposing view, see Robinson, "Perryville," 3.

67. Landrum to Amanda, Oct. 12, 1862, Landrum Letters, OHS.

68. Johnson to his brother, Oct. 10, 1862, Barton Papers, SHSW. See also *Monongahela Daily Republican*, Jan. 12, 1865, clipping in Woodward Collection, PEP.

69. Drake to his brother, Oct. 13, 1862, Drake Letters, SHSW; Map, 38th Indiana Burials, Regimental Correspondence of the Adjutant General of Indiana—38th Indiana, ISA; Otto Memoirs, 116–17, 118–19; Bennett and Haigh, *Thirty-sixth Regiment*, 277; Crary, *Crary Memoirs*, 77–79; Holmes, *Soldier*, 95; Lathrop, *Fifty-ninth Regiment*, 170; Marshall, *Historical Sketch*, 24.

70. Calkins Diary, 42. See also Truex to his wife, Oct. 11, 1862, John Truex Letters, InSL.

71. Comstock to Eliza Comstock, Oct. 16, 1862, Comstock Letters, SHSW; Drake to his brother, Oct. 13, 1862, Drake Letters, SHSW; McCahan Diary, Oct. 9, 1862; Work Diary, 4, USAMHI; *Monongahela Daily Republican*, Jan. 12, 1865, Woodward Collection, PEP; Aten, *Eighty-fifth Regiment*, 42; Francis, *Narrative*, 59; Holmes, *Soldier*, 96.

72. McCahan Diary, Oct. 9, 1862.

73. Morris, *Eighty-first Regiment*, 17.

74. *Monongahela Daily Republican*, Jan. 12, 1865, Woodward Collection, PEP.

75. *New Albany (Ind.) Daily Ledger*, Oct. 21, 1862. See also Brown to Chandler, Oct. 17, 1862, U.S. Army Letters, Duke; "Life of L. A. Ross," 50; Albertson, ed., *Letters Home*, letter 58, 1–2; Hinman, *Sherman Brigade*, 296; Stewart, *Dan McCook's Regiment*, 29; Brown, *History of Danville*, 36–37.

76. Morris, *Eighty-first Regiment*, 17.

77. Day, *One Hundred and First Ohio*, 55.

78. Hinman, *Sherman Brigade*, 296. For a similar account, see Kimberly and Holloway, *Forty-first Ohio*, 35.

79. Quiner Scrapbooks, vol. 6, 148–49, SHSW.

80. Johnston, *Soldier Boy's Diary*, 24.

81. Potts to his mother, Dec. 14, 1862, Potts Letters, OHS.

82. Comstock to Eliza Comstock, Oct. 16, 1862; Johnson to his brother, Oct. 10, 1862, Barton Papers, SHSW; Curran Pope to Hon. James Robinson, Oct. 9, 1862, 15th Kentucky Infantry Collection, Union Infantry-Primary Sources, KDMA; Spencer to his sister, Oct. 11, 1862, Spencer Letters, OHS; Genco, ed., *Sound of Musketry*, 57; Winters, *In the 50th Ohio*, 21.

83. Noe, ed., *Southern Boy in Blue*, 105.

84. Connelly Diary, 58; Jacobs, "Campaigning with Buell," 3; Francis, *Narrative*, 58; Hazen, *Narrative*, 62; Perry, *Thirty-eighth Regiment*, 38; Trautman, ed., *"We Were the Ninth,"* 116.

85. Barnes, Carnahan, and McCain, *Eighty-sixth Regiment*, 65.

86. "Life of L. A. Ross," 50–51. See also Winters, *In the 50th Ohio*, 22.

CHAPTER 15

1. "Campaign in Kentucky, No. 5"; Trask Journal, 75; Dyer and Moore, *Tennessee Civil War Veterans*, vol. 1, 335–36; vol. 3, 913–15; vol. 4, 1448–49; Headley, *Confederate Operations*, 58; Hughes, ed., *Liddell's Record*, 97; Steely and Taylor, eds., "Bragg's Kentucky Campaign," 52.

2. Daviess, *Mercer and Boyle Counties*, 106. See also Inglis Diary, Oct. 9, 1862; Afflick, "Southern Aid Society," 30; Garrett, trans., *Robert D. Smith*, 34.

3. Thomas to Fry, Oct. 9, 1862, Buell Papers. See also Brent Diary, Oct. 9, 1862; Ellis Diary, 28.

4. Daviess, *Mercer and Boyle Counties*, 106. See also Sutherland, ed., *Reminiscences*, 99.

5. Davis to his wife, Oct. 16, 1862, Davis Papers, Iowa.

6. OR 1, 16, pt. 1, 1093. Bushrod R. Johnson Diary, Oct. 9, 1862, Papers of Various Confederate Notables, RG 109, NARA; Johnston Diary, Oct. 9, 1862; Trask Journal, 75; Connelly, *Army of the Heartland*, 266–68. Connelly's interpretation is different from the one given here, for he rejects the notion of an indecisive Bragg.

7. OR 1, 16, pt. 2, 930; Inglis Diary, 86–87; Johnston Diary, Oct. 9 and 10, 1862; Magee Diary, Oct. 10, 1862; Trask Journal, 75; Garrett, trans., *Robert D. Smith*, 34; Steely and Taylor, eds., "Bragg's Kentucky Campaign," 52; Womack, *Diary of J. J. Womack*, 64.

8. OR 1, 16, pt. 1, 1093; Bryant to his mother, Oct. 11, 1862, 3rd Florida Infantry File, PSHS; Daniel Diary, 19; Ellis Diary, 28; Hooper Diary, Oct. 9 and 10, 1862; Magee Diary, Oct. 9, 10, and 12, 1862; Trask Journal, 75; Cross, *Camp and Field*, 64; Garrett, trans., *Robert D. Smith*," 34; Steely and Taylor, eds., "Bragg's Kentucky Campaign," 52; Womack, *Diary of J. J. Womack*, 64. .

9. Claiborne, "Campaign of 1862," 15–16; Inglis Diary, Oct. 9, 1862; "An Ex-Kentuckian," "Kentucky Invasion of 1862," 409.

10. OR 1, 16, pt. 1, 1134; OR 1, 16, pt. 2, 925–26; Johnston Diary, Oct. 10, 1862; "Campaign in Kentucky, No. 5"; Hammond, "Kirby Smith's Campaign," 70–71; Parks, *General Edmund Kirby Smith*, 234–35.

11. OR 1, 16, pt. 1, 1134, 1135–36; OR 1, 16, pt. 2, 927–28; Johnston Diary, Oct. 10, 1862; Hammond, "Kirby Smith's Campaign," 70–71.

12. Kirby Smith to Johnston, Oct. 31, 1866, Johnston Papers, Filson; Johnston Diary, Oct. 10, 1862; Street to his wife, Oct. 28, 1862, Street and East (Pace) Collection, SHC-UNC; Fowler, ed., "Johnny Reb's Impressions," 208; Hammond, "Kirby Smith's Campaign," 71–73; Noll, ed., *Doctor Quintard*, 61–62; "William P. Rogers," 72; Connelly, *Army of the Heartland*, 268–69; Daniel, *Soldiering*, 71; Parks, *General Edmund Kirby Smith*, 237. After the war, a myth that Bragg commanded a concentrated Confederate force at Harrodsburg yet declined battle and fled in panic, propagated by Kirby Smith and amplified by supporters such as the Kentucky cavalryman Basil Duke and former staff officer Paul F. Hammond, developed into gospel. Like the Munfordville myth, the Harrodsburg myth has no substance. There was no concentration in Harrodsburg to begin with. Moreover, as Thomas Connolly has effectively maintained, to have fought there no doubt would have been disastrous. Cut off from both his base and his line of retreat, his back to the river, the army might well have ceased to exist, and with it Confederate hopes in the west. Retreat from Harrodsburg was the proper decision. See Connelly, *Army of the Heartland*, 267–70. For criticism of Bragg at Harrodsburg, see Hammond, "Kirby Smith's Campaign," 73–74; Hughes, *General William J. Hardee*, 133; and Parks, *General Edmund Kirby Smith*, 237–39.

Citing a secondary source, Hafendorfer (*Perryville*, 412), dates Polk's celebrated visit to the church on October 9. Quintard himself states that the incident occurred three days after the battle.

13. *OR* 1, 16, pt. 2, 597–99, 602, 604; Hartpence, *Fifty-first Indiana*, 89; *History of the Seventy-third Regiment*, 103; *History of the Seventy-third Indiana*, 110; Martin, *Eighth Kansas*, 21; Morris, *Eighty-first Regiment*, 18; Tarrant, *Wild Riders*, 121–22.

14. *OR* 1, 16, pt. 1, 1137; *OR* 1, 16, pt. 2, 600–1; Tuttle Diary, Oct. 10, 1862; Anderson, ed., *Nicholas Longworth Anderson*, 162; Barnes, Carnahan, and McCain, *Eighty-sixth Regiment*, 66–67; Cutter, *Our Battery*, 83; Dillman, *Henry F. Dillman*, 5; Hight and Stormont, *Fifty-eighth Indiana*, 102–3; Hinman, *Sherman Brigade*, 296–97; Smith, *Thirty-first Regiment*, 33.

15. Dokken to his family, Oct. 19, 1862, Dokken Papers, SHSW; Patterson Memoir, 39–40, Oct. 10, 1862; *Milwaukee Sentinel*, Oct. 17, 1862; Bircher, *Drummer Boy's Diary*, 46; Lathrop, *Fifty-ninth Regiment*, 170–71; Martin, *Eighth Kansas*, 21; Morris, *Eighty-first Regiment*, 18. Using Martin alone, Hafendorfer, *Perryville*. 413, implies that III Corps marched early, spearheaded by Mitchell's division. However, Martin states that his brigade did not move out until "the night of the 10th, about 10 o'clock" (21). Bircher in contrast describes a morning march. Dokken, Lathrop, and Patterson, also members of Mitchell's division, clearly state that they did not leave Perryville until the following morning.

16. *OR* 1, 16, pt. 2, 605–6; Hartpence, *Fifty-first Indiana*, 89; *History of the Seventy-third Indiana*, 110.

17. *OR* 1, 16, pt. 2, 601–2, 606; Harry Lewis to his family, Oct. 19, 1862, Lewis Family Letters, OHS; "5th Ind. Battery"; Aten, *Eighty-fifth Regiment*, 44–45; Beatty, *Citizen-Soldier*, 182; Holmes, *Soldier*, 96–97; Kinnear, *Eighty-sixth Regiment*, 13.

18. Stewart, *Dan McCook's Regiment*, 30.

19. *OR* 1, 16, pt. 1, 1137; *OR* 1, 16, pt. 2, 604–5, 605–6, 611; Dokken to his family, Oct. 19, 1862, Dokken Papers, SHSW; Patterson Memoir, 39–40, Oct. 11, 1862; Tuttle Diary, Oct. 11, 1862; Anderson, ed., *Nicholas Longworth Anderson*, 162; Barnes, Carnahan, and McCain, *Eighty-sixth Regiment*, 66–67; Butler, *My Story*, 228; Hazen, *Narrative*, 63; Hinman, *Sherman Brigade*, 297–98; Kerwood, *Fifty-seventh Regiment*, 134–35; Kimberly and Holloway, *Forty-first Ohio*, 35; Lathrop, *Fifty-ninth Regiment*, 171.

20. Cheek, ed., "Mrs. E. B. Patterson," 332–79 (quotations, 377–78, 379). See also Daniel, *Soldiering*, 71.

21. *OR* 1, 16, pt. 1, 1137; *OR* 1, 16, pt. 2, 607–8, 611; Tuttle Diary, Oct. 12, 1862; John Henry Otto Memoirs, 124; Aten, *Eighty-fifth Regiment*, 44–45; Barnes, Carnahan, and McCain, *Eighty-sixth Regiment*, 68–69; Brown, Murphy, and Putney, *Behind the Guns*, 40; Cutter, *Our Battery*, 84–85; Dillman, *Henry F. Dillman*, 5; Hartpence, *Fifty-first Indiana*, 89; *History of the Seventy-ninth Indiana*, 51; *History of the Seventy-third Indiana*, 110; Kimberly and Holloway, *Forty-first Ohio*, 35; Lathrop, *Fifty-ninth Regiment*, 171; Gates, *Rough Side of War*, 30; Phillips, ed., *Civil War Diary*, Oct. 12, 1862; Engle, *Don Carlos Buell*, 311–12.

22. Anderson, ed., *Nicholas Longworth Anderson*, 162. For similar sentiments, see Keil, *Thirty-fifth Ohio*, 102.

23. *OR* 1, 16, pt. 2, 607.

24. "Campaign in Kentucky, No. 5." See also Claiborne, "Campaign of 1862," 17; Walter P. Morris to W. B. Harris, Oct. 12, 1862, Harris Papers, Duke; Connelly, *Army of the Heartland*, 270–80.

25. *OR* 1, 16, pt. 1, 898, 1088, 1093; *OR* 1, 16, pt. 2, 938–9, 940–41; Claiborne, "Campaign of 1862," 17; "Campaign in Kentucky, No. 5"; Kirby Smith to Johnston, Oct. 31, 1866, Johnston Papers, Filson; Brent Diary, Oct. 12, 1862; Johnston Diary, Oct. 12, 1862; Fowler, ed., "Johnny Reb's Impressions," 208–9; *Atlanta Southern Confederacy*, Nov. 13, 1862; Bearss, "General Bragg Abandons Kentucky," 217–19; Connelly, *Army of the Heartland*, 270–80; Kundahl, *Confederate Engineer*, 178–80; McWhiney, "Controversy in Kentucky," 35–36.

26. Inglis Diary, Oct. 13, 1862; Trask Journal, 77–78; Cross, *Camp and Field*, 66–67; "An Ex-Kentuckian," "The Kentucky Invasion of 1861," 409; Fowler, ed., "Johnny Reb's Impressions," 209; Little and Maxwell, *History of Lumsden's Battery*, 13; "William P. Rogers," 73; Womack, *Diary of J. J. Womack*, 65; Bearss, "General Bragg Abandons Kentucky," 219–21; Kundahl, *Confederate Engineer*, 179; Parks, *General Edmund Kirby Smith*, 239; Woodworth, *Jefferson Davis*, 159.

27. *Atlanta Southern Confederacy*, Nov. 13, 1862.

28. Ellis Diary, 28; Inglis Diary, Oct. 14–18, 1862; "Augustus Cabarrus Kean," 17–18; "Fifth Tennessee Infantry," 4–5; Magee Diary, Oct. 14–22, 1862; Semple to Hardee, Nov. 26 and 28, 1862, Confederate Artillery Batteries: Lumsden's Battery-Waters' Battery, ADAH; Talley Autobiography, 25; Trask Journal, 78–79; Wan to Mrs. Hagins, Nov. 1, 1862; Berry, "Reminiscences from Missouri," 73; Buck, *Cleburne*, 73–74; Cutrer, ed., "'We Are Stern and Resolved,'" 206–7; Garrett, trans., *Robert D. Smith*, 34; Guild, *Fourth Tennessee Cavalry*, 236–37; Hammond, "Kirby Smith's Campaign," 74–76; Little and Maxwell, *History of Lumsden's Battery*, 13; Reynolds, *Henry County Commands*, 50; Steely and Taylor, "Bragg's Kentucky Campaign," 52–53; Sutherland, ed., *Reminiscences*, 101; Vaughan, *Thirteenth Regiment*, 23; Watkins, "*Co. Aytch*," 66–67; "William J. Rogers Memorandum Book," 73; "33rd Alabama," 29; Williams and Wooster, eds., "With Terry's Texas Rangers," 310–11; Womack, *Diary of J. J. Womack*, 65–66; Daniel, *Soldiering*, 17, 43, 54; Symonds, *Stonewall of the West*, 97–98. Bearss expertly describes the retreat in great detail in "General Bragg Abandons Kentucky," 221–44.

29. Watkins, "*Co. Aytch*," 66–70 (quotation, 67).

30. Magee Diary, Oct. 18 and 20, 1862; "Augustus Cabarrus Kean," 17–18; Headley, *Confederate Operations*, 60; Reynolds, *Henry County Commands*, 50; Vaughan, *Thirteenth Regiment*, 23; Daniel, *Soldiering*, 54; Losson, *Tennessee's Forgotten Warriors*, 75.

31. Comstock to his father, Oct. 18, 1862, Eugene E. Comstock Letters, SHSW; Dokken to his family, Oct. 19, 1862, Dokken Papers, SHSW; Drake to his brother, Oct. 16, 1862, Drake Letters, SHSW; Morse to his mother, Oct. 15, 1862, Morse Papers, OHS; [Philip Sheridan] to Capt. Stacy, Oct. 15, 1862, Army of the Ohio and 14th Army

Corps, Letters and Reports Received, 1862–65, RG 393, NARA; Hartpence, *Fifty-first Indiana*, 89; Watkins, *"Co. Aytch,"* 69.

32. Wagner Memoirs, 47, 49, 53–54.

33. Hogg to Susan, Oct. 22, 1862, John J. Hogg Letters, GHS. See also Hogg's letter of Oct. 19.

34. "Augustus Cabarrus Kean," 17. See also Kirby Smith to his wife, Oct. 22, 1862, Smith Papers, SHC-UNC; *Knoxville Daily Register*, Nov. 11, 1862.

35. Winchester Diary, 80.

36. Brown to Fannie Brown, Oct. 24, 1862, Brown Letters, ADAH.

37. "Life of Augustus Cabarrus Kean," 17, Cabarrus and Slade Papers, SHC-UNC; Magee Diary, Oct. 16 and 25, 1862; Street to his wife, Nov. 3, 1862, Street and East (Pace) Correspondence, SHC-UNC.

38. *OR* 1, 16, pt. 1, 1093; Bragg to Davis, May 22, 1863, Bragg Papers, WRHS; Claiborne, "Campaign of 1862," 17; Smith to his wife, Oct. 20 and 22, 1862, Edmund Kirby Smith Papers, UNC-SHC; New Orleans *Daily Picayune*, Oct. 11, 1862; *Richmond Whig*, Oct. 20, 1862; "Bragg and His Generals," *Southern Bivouac* 1 (Oct. 1885): 289–90; Crist, ed., *Papers of Jefferson Davis*, vol. 8, 468–70; Cozzens, *No Better Place to Die*, 7–11, 29–30; Hughes, *General William J. Hardee*, 133–35; Hughes, ed., *Liddell's Record*, 97–101; McDonough, *Stones River*, 30–34; McWhiney, *Braxton Bragg*, 323–36; Parks, *General Edmund Kirby Smith*, 240–41; Parks, *General Leonidas Polk*, 279–80; Woodworth, *Jefferson Davis*, 159–61; Boatner, *Civil War Dictionary*, 828.

39. *OR* 1, 16, pt. 2, 611.

40. Ibid., 612, 618.

41. Ibid., 619, 621–22.

42. Ibid., 623.

43. Ibid., 626–27.

44. Ibid., 630–1, 634, 636–38 (quotation 637). See also Boyle to Capt. Darr, Oct. 11, 1862, Buell Papers.

45. *OR* 1, 16, pt. 2, 634, 638, 640–42, 650, 652 (quotation, 639); Engle, *Don Carlos Buell*, 314–18. For Republican pressure to fire Buell, see William Stoms to Chase, Oct. 19, 1862; D. H. Allen to B. Morris, Oct. 20, 1862; S. S. Coy to Dear Sir, Oct. 20, 1862; R. S. Newton to Chase, Oct. 20, 1862; Thomas Heaton to Chase, Oct. 21, 1862; C. Kingsley to Chase, Oct. 22, 1862; Kingsley Roy to Chase, Oct. 24, 1862; and David Chambers to Dear Sir, Oct. 25, 1862, all in the Chase Papers, LC. Democrats, in contrast, supported Buell and blamed McCook, Rousseau, and Governor Morton for the defeat. See *Chicago Times*, Oct. 21, 23, 27, 1862; *New Albany (Ind.) Daily Ledger*, Oct. 23, 24, 29, Nov. 3, 1862.

46. *OR* 1, 16, pt. 2, 651, 652, 653, 654 (quotation, 652); Engle, *Don Carlos Buell*, 318, 322–24.

47. Ball to Lib, Oct. 18, 1862, Ball Collection, USAMHI; Calkins Note Book, Oct. 13, 14, 16, 26, and 30, 1862, USAMHI; Chandler Diary, 27; Comstock to his father, Oct. 18, 1862, Comstock Letters, SHSW; Davis to his wife, Oct. 27, 1862, Davis Papers, Iowa; Heg to Gnuild, Oct. 26, 1862, Heg Letters, SHSW; Rhoads to his sister, Nov. 5, 1862, William Rhoads Letters, OHS; Shields to his mother, Oct. 31, 1862, Alfred Shields Letters, InHS; Thomas to his sister, Oct. 23, 1862, Thomas Letters, InHS; Price Diaries, Oct. 25, 1862; *Aurora (Ill.) Weekly Beacon*, Nov. 16, 1862; Anderson, ed., *Nicholas Longworth Anderson*, 163; Angle, ed., *Three Years in the Army*, 27; Cutter, *Our Battery*, 90–91; Grose, *Story of the Marches*, 140; Hartpence, *Fifty-first Indiana*, 89; Hunter, *Eighty-second Indiana*, 26–27; Kimberly and Holloway, *Forty-first Ohio*, 36–37; Lathrop, *Fifty-ninth Regiment*, 171; Smith, *Thirty-first Regiment*, 34. For a rosy exception, see Shouldise to his mother, Oct. 19, 1862, Henry Shouldise Letters, Civil War Miscellaneous Collection, USAMHI.

Shouldise assured his mother that he was eating well, had enough warm clothing, got enough healthy exercise, and avoided all un-Christian temptations.

48. Cox to Ida, Nov. 2, 1862, P. V. Cox Letters, Civil War Miscellaneous Collection—New Material, USAMHI; Frank McKenzie to Louis Nettelhorst, Nov. 25, 1862, Nettelhorst Papers, InHS.

49. Heg to Gnuild, Oct. 26, 1862, Heg Letters, SHSW; Martin, *Eighth Kansas*, 23–24; Patterson, ed., *38th Regiment*, 18; Trautman, ed., *"We Were the Ninth,"* 116–17.

50. The major narratives of the battle are Cozzens, *No Better Place to Die;* and McDonough, *Stones River.* For the hope of winter quarters, see Rieger, annotator, *Through One Man's Eyes*, 15.

CHAPTER 16

1. Charles P. Carr to his sister-in-law, Nov. 8, [1862], Rathburn Papers, USAMHI.

2. Boatner, *Civil War Dictionary*, 644; Fox, *Regimental Losses*, 544; Hafendorfer, *Perryville*, 444–59; Holman, "Known Strengths and Casualties," and "Perryville Order of Battle." Holman's latest figures are given in appendix 1.

3. Polk, *Dr. J. J. Polk*, 96–97.

4. Kays interview, Author's Collection, PSHS; John C. Russell Claim, File 217/1019, RG 92, NARA.

5. Lewis to his family, Oct. 19, 1862, Lewis Family Letters, OHS.

6. Case nos. 9877 and 2514 consolidated, RG 56, NARA. Bottom's war claim is summarized in Holman, "Henry P. 'Squire' Bottom's War Claim."

7. Stewart to his wife, Nov. 8, 1862, James Stewart Letter, Filson. See also *Cincinnati Daily Commercial*, Nov. 12, 1862; Polk, *Dr. J. J. Polk*, 96–98, Thoburn, ed., *My Experiences*, Oct. 13, 1862.

8. Lewis to his family, Oct. 19 and Nov. 8, 1862, Lewis Family Letters, OHS; Morse to his mother, Oct. 14,15, 1862, Morse Papers, OHS; *United States Sanitary Commission*, vol. 1, doc. no. 55, 9; *Cincinnati Daily Commercial*, Nov. 12, 1862 (quotation); "Graves of Our Dead at Perryville," 385; Head, *Campaigns and Battles*, 98–99; Polk, *Dr. J. J. Polk*, 96–98; Thoburn, ed., *My Experiences*, Oct. 13, 1862; Brown, *History of Danville*, 36–37; Harmon, *Chaplin Hills;* Tapp, "Battle of Perryville," 180–81.

9. *United States Sanitary Commission*, vol. 1, doc. no. 55, 6, 8–10. See also E. Gay to Buell, Oct. 11, 1862, Buell Papers; J. M. Wright, Orders, Oct. 9, 1862, Army of the Ohio and 14th Army Corps, Letters and Reports Received, 1862–65, RG 393, NARA; James H. McGregor to Elisabeth McGregor, Oct. 15, 1862, Andrew J. McGarrah Letters, InHS; Johnston, *Soldier Boy's Diary*, 24; *Medical and Surgical History*, vol. 2, 253, 254–55; Polk, *Dr. J. J. Polk*, 98.

10. *United States Sanitary Commission*, vol. 1, doc. no. 55, 4–5; *Medical and Surgical History*, vol. 2, 252. See also Adams, *Doctors in Blue*, 62, 83.

11. J. A. Campbell to Sheridan, Oct. 26, 1862, Army of the Ohio and 14th Army Corps, Letters and Reports Received, 1862–65, RG 393, NARA; Clark Diary, vol. 2, 46–54; Quiner Scrapbooks, vol. 6, 150; Johnston, *Soldier Boy's Diary*, 24–25; Kaiser, ed., "Civil War Letters," 269.

12. Benson, *Soldier's Diary*, 30.

13. Hupp, *My Diary*, 24–28 (quotation, 27).

14. Clark Diary, vol. 2, 47–54.

15. Kaiser, ed., "Civil War Letters," 269. See also Quiner Scrapbooks, vol. 6, 150.

16. McGregor to Elisabeth McGregor, Oct. 15, 1862, McGarrah Letters, InHS.

17. Edward Mead to Kentucky adjutant general, June 7, 1866, and James L. Mor-

row to John W. Finnel, Oct. 30, 1862, both in 15th Kentucky Infantry Collection, Union Infantry—Primary Sources, KDMA; Jonathan Wood Memoir, 2, Civil War Miscellaneous Collection, USAMHI; *Cincinnati Daily Commercial*, Oct. 16, 1862.

18. Alfred Galpin to [?], Oct. 30, 1862, Galpin Family Papers, SHSW; Confederate Pension Applications, James M. McElreath (Microfilm 272/61), GDAH; Quiner Scrapbooks, vol. 6, 148; Waugh to Ernst, Dec. 19, 1862, Albert F. Waugh Letters, SHSW; *Medical and Surgical History*, vol. 2, 255. See also Toney, *Privations*, 47–48.

19. John Baker to his father, Nov. 16, 1862, Baker Family Letters, Filson.

20. Baas, "Preliminary Analysis," 3. Baas based his analysis on data collected by Kurt and Dawn Holman. See their chart in Holman, "Post Battle Death Rates," as well as Holman to author, Sept. 4, 1997, Author's Collection, PSHS.

21. T. B. Ellis Diary, 3–4; Joseph Hodgson to Thomas M. Owen, Feb. 14, 1911, Confederate Alabama Cavalry Files: 1st and 2nd Cavalry, ADAH; Morse to his mother, Oct. 15, 1862, Morse Papers, OHS; Wagner Memoirs, 45–54; *Chicago Times*, Oct. 14, 1862; *Cincinnati Daily Enquirer*, Oct. 30, 1862; Dyer and Moore, *Tennessee Civil War Veterans*, vol. 1, 184–85, 400–2, vol. 2, 543–44, 701–2, vol. 3, 899–90, 938–39, vol. 4, 1322–23, 1492, 1508, 1645–46, vol. 5, 1896; Head, *Campaigns and Battles*, 99.

22. W. W. Caldwell to O. P. Morton, Dec. 3, 1862, 81st Indiana Infantry; James Jones to Oliver Morton, Nov. 24, 1862, 42nd Indiana Infantry; A. Morrison to S. W. Davis, Feb. 20, 1863, 5th Indiana Battery; and "Report for Desertion, Co. A," 82nd Indiana Infantry, all in Regimental Correspondence of the Adjutant General of Indiana, InSA; Shelly to his brother, Oct. 24, 1862, Shelly Letters, InHS.

23. Dyer and Moore, *Tennessee Civil War Veterans*, vol. 1, 184–85, vol. 2, 701–2, vol. 4, 1688–89.

24. To create the sample, I began with a particularly descriptive casualty roll of the regiment in the Oct. 21, 1862 issue of the *Atlanta Southern Confederacy*. I then cross-referenced the names of men listed as killed, mortally wounded, or wounded more than slightly with White, trans., *Confederate Pension Files*. For the men mentioned, see George N. Lester (Microfilm 272/14), J. R. Marlow (Microfilm 271/58, 272/30), J. W. Nations (Microfilm 272/80), and Joshua D. Tharp (Microfilm 276/45), Confederate Pension Applications, GDAH.

25. James M. McElreath (Microfilm 272/61), Confederate Pension Applications, GDAH.

26. Photocopies of pension applications and files; Obituary, *Monongahela Daily Republican*, Mar. 27, 1916; and Jeff Vaughan to Mary C. Breeding, Aug. 3 and 16, 1995, all in Woodward Collection, PEP.

27. Dean, *Shook Over Hell*, 73, 101, 124, 127, 273, 282.

28. Buck, *Road to Reunion*, 3–25; Douglas, *Feminization of American Culture*, 240–72, and Douglas, "Heaven Our Home," 496–515; Farrell, *American Way of Death*, esp. 35–43, 74–82, 99–115, 146–47; Foster, *Ghosts of the Confederacy*, 31–33, 36–46; Mitchell, *Vacant Chair*, 135–50; Mitford, *American Way of Death Revisited*, 81–82, 144–48; Paludan, *"People's Contest,"* 364–74; Saum, "Death in the Mind," 477–95. This passage and the one that follows are taken from my "'Coming to Us Dead,'" 289–304.

29. Mitchell, *Vacant Chair*, 144.

30. Kett, *Rites of Passage*, 168–71; Marten, *Children's Civil War*, 99–100, 116, 188–90, 204–42; Mitchell, *Vacant Chair*, 19–37, 144–47.

31. I first identified names of members of the regiment killed by using "List of Killed and Wounded, 1st Wis Vols Inf, Battle Chaplin Hills, Oct. 8 1862," Starkweather Papers, SHSW. I then searched for pension applications using NARA microfilm publication T-289, "Index to Pension Files of Veterans Who Served Between 1861 & 1900," 1st

Wisconsin Infantry, Rolls 608, 609. That directed me to files found in RG 15, Records of the Veterans Administration, Pensions Application Files Based Upon Service in the Civil War and Spanish-American War. NARA personnel were unable to locate application nos. 224,356, 239,699; and certificate nos. 33,167, 221,785, 243,542, or 1,054,684. Pension files used hereafter are cited only by record group and certificate number. For pensions in general, see McConnell, *Glorious Contentment*, 143–53.

I also located ten applications filed by widows of 41st Georgia soldiers killed in combat. Unfortunately, Georgia pension files required nothing more of them than evidence of their marriage to their husbands and proof of widowhood without remarriage. Their secondhand descriptions of their husbands' deaths at least speak to the emotional toll of war. See Ann E. Benson (Microfilm 272/10), Rachel Brown (Microfilm 274/16), Mary Curtright (Microfilm 276/42), Eliza Freeman (Microfilm 274/21), Nancy A. Gurley (Microfilm 271/56), Dicy Howell (Microfilm 272/14), V. V. Lundy (Microfilm 272/11), E. T. Nutt (Microfilm 274/32), Martha J. Reddin (Microfilm 276/44), and Mary Williams (Microfilm 271/62), all in Confederate Pension Applications, GDAH.

32. Kett, *Rites of Passage*, 23–31, 111–13, 168–71. See also Chudacoff, *How Old Are You?* 9–127; Graff, *Conflicting Paths*, 97–70; Noe, "'Coming to Us Dead,'" 303; Rose, *Victorian America*, 163, 166, 173–74, 188.

33. Certificate no. 262,252, RG 15, NARA.

34. Certificate no. 208,396, ibid.

35. Certificate nos. 45,851, 244,712, 406,507, 14,333, 167,234, ibid.

36. Certificate no. 11,158, ibid.

37. Certificate nos. 172,679, 216, 220, 1,016,100, ibid.

38. Certificate nos. 359,131, 358,048, ibid.

39. Certificate no. 673,827, ibid.

40. Certificate nos. 11,471, 45,657, 153,516, 163,468, ibid. Only one application came directly from children through their guardians. Their mother already dead, the daughters of Charles McKenzie, ages nine and seven, became orphans after Perryville. They seem to have moved from relative to relative before ending up with older siblings. See Certificate no. 17,877, ibid. See also McConnell, *Glorious Contentment*, 143–44.

41. Certificate nos. 651,503, 22,210, RG 15, NARA.

42. Polk, *Dr. J. J. Polk*, 46; Brown, *History of Danville*, 38–47.

43. Edwards, "Sleettown Was Booming Community, Town Had Store, Taxi and Cafe," Danville (Ky.) *Advocate-Messenger*, www.amnews.com/hist_htm/hist10_5a.html, paper copy in Author's Collection, PSHS.

44. Polk, *Dr. J. J. Polk*, 98–101; "Account of the Re-interment of Soldiers Buried on the Battlefield," in *Roll of Honor*. In terms of identifying the dead, things have not improved very much. Kurt Holman, who has spent more than a decade attempting to identify every known grave of men killed or mortally wounded at Perryville, indicates that as of this writing, only 626 Perryville casualties lay identified in marked graves, roughly a quarter of the battle's casualties. See Kurt Holman to author, May 26, 2000, Author's Collection, PSHS.

45. Danville *Kentucky Advocate*, Apr. 2, 1900, clipping in Woodward Collection, PEP; "Account of the Re-interment;" Kleber, ed., *Kentucky Encyclopedia*, 158.

46. Thatcher, *Hundred Battles*, 75.

47. *B&L*, vol. 3, 1–61; Engle, *Don Carlos Buell*, 346–39. For criticism of Buell from his soldiers, it is not an overstatement to suggest almost any Federal source cited in this volume.

48. Danville *Kentucky Advocate*, Apr. 2, 1900, and *Monongahela Daily Republican*, Oct. 1912, clippings in Woodward Collection, PEP; *Pittsburgh Gazette Times*, Oct. 12, 1908, clipping in McCook Family Papers, LC.

49. Danville [Ky.] *Kentucky Advocate*, Apr. 2, 1900, and *Monongahela Daily Republican*, Oct. 1912, clippings in Woodward Collection, PEP; Harmon, *Chaplin Hills*, chap. 11; Buck, *Road to Reunion*, 257–62; Foster, *Ghosts of the Confederacy*, 40–42, 44, 129–30, 158, 167–68; Kinsel, "Turning Point to Peace Memorial," 205–22; Kammen, *Mystic Chords of Memory*, 106–18; McConnell, *Glorious Contentment*, 189–93; Patterson, "Battle Ground to Pleasure Ground," 128–40. Perryville's experience is similar in many ways to another largely forgotten battle, Pea Ridge. See Shea and Hess, *Pea Ridge*, 327–30.

50. Harmon, *Chaplin Hills*, chap. 11; Kammen, *Mystic Chords of Memory*, 456; Kinsel, "Turning Point to Peace Memorial," 218–19.

51. Harmon, *Chaplin Hills*, chap.11; Patterson, "Battle Ground to Pleasure Ground," 142.

52. Harmon, *Chaplin Hills*, chap. 11; "Information Sheet," Perryville Enhancement Project, n.d.; Kammen, *Mystic Chords of Memory*, 533, 538–39, 572, 590–605; Patterson, "Battle Ground to Pleasure Ground," 142–43; Kurt Holman to author, Mar. 3, 2000, Author's Collection, PSHS.

53. See especially the following issues of PBPA's newsletter, *Action Front:* July 1993, 1–3; Oct. 1994, 1–4; July 1995, 1–3; Apr. 1996, 1–4; Aug. 1996, 2; Oct. 1996, 1–3; Jan. 1997, 1; Apr. 1997, 1–3; July 1997, 1; Jan. 1998, 1; Apr. 1998, 1; Oct. 1998, 1, 4; July 1999, 1, 2. Up-to-date information is provided on the PBPA website: www.perryville.net.

54. Linenthal, *Sacred Ground*, 1–6, 89–118; Kinsel, "Turning Point to Peace Memorial," 221–22; Masur, "Changes in the Offing," *Perspectives Online*, Mar. 2000, www.theaha.org/perspectives, paper copy in Author's Collection, PSHS; Miller, "Capitol Commentary," 11. Jackson's call led to a long debate on H-CIVWAR, an electronic "list server" maintained by Michigan State University.

55. *Action Front*, Oct. 1997, 1.

56. *Action Front*, Oct. 1998, 3.

APPENDIX 1

1. *OR* 1, 16, pt. 1, 1033–36, 1108, 1112; *B&L*, vol. 3, 29–30; Hafendorfer, *Perryville*, 444–59; Holman, "Perryville Order of Battle." Kurt Holman kindly loaned me a summary of his several years' of research into numbers and losses at Perryville. Using a variety of sources, Holman has constructed a computerized database of casualty figures.

APPENDIX 2

1. Holman, "Perryville Order of Battle."

WORKS CONSULTED

Readers should note that in the interest of stimulating further research on the Battle of Perryville and the Kentucky Campaign, I have deposited my research notes at the Perryville State Historic Site, Perryville, Kentucky.

PRIMARY SOURCES

MANUSCRIPT COLLECTIONS

Alabama Department of Archives and History, Montgomery
  Edward Norphlet Brown Letters
  Confederate Alabama Cavalry Files: 1st and 2nd Cavalry
  Confederate Alabama Cavalry Files: 3rd and 4th Cavalry
  Confederate Batteries: Lumsden's Battery-Waters' Battery
  Confederate Regimental History Files: 45th Alabama Infantry Regiment
  W. E. Mathews Preston, "The 33rd Alabama Regiment in the Civil War." Ed. L. B. Williams
  Henry C. Semple Papers
  Sterling A. M. Wood Papers
Arkansas Historical Commission, Little Rock
  Thomas G. Wan Letter
Chicago Historical Society
  Charles Carr Collection
  U.S. History, Civil War Biography
      Duncan Chambers Milner Letter
Duke University Library, Rare Book, Manuscript, and Special Collections Library, Durham, N.C.
  Braxton Bragg Papers
  John Buie Papers
  David Bullock Harris Papers
  John Euclid Magee Diary
  Charles Todd Quintard Papers
  Unites States Army, U.S. Army Officers, and Miscellaneous Letters
Emory University, Special Collections, Robert W. Woodruff Library, Atlanta, Ga.
  Albert L. Slack Correspondence no. 459
  W. L. Trask Papers no. 380
Filson Club Historical Society, Louisville, Ky.
  Baker Family Letters

J. Lincoln Conkey Letters
Johnson W. Culp Diary
John Jefferson Diary
William P. McDowell Reminiscence
James Stewart Letter
J. Stoddard Johnston Papers
J. H. Tilford Diary
Abraham Ulery Letter
Florida Historical Society, Tebeau-Field Library, Cocoa
    Thomas Benton Ellis Diary
Florida State Archives, Tallahassee
    General William Miller Report
Florida State University, Robert Manning Strozier Library, Tallahassee
    John Inglis Diary
Georgia Department of Archives and History, Atlanta
    Civil War Miscellany Files
        William Ralston Talley Autobiography
    Confederate Pension Applications
Georgia Historical Society, Savannah
    John J. Hogg Letters (MS no. 389)
Illinois State Historical Library, Springfield
    Lewis Brooks, *Battle of Perryville, Oct. 8, 1862. Report of Col. Lewis Brooks, 80th
        Indiana Vol.* (pamphlet)
    John G. Cavis Diary
    George A. Cummins Papers
    Charles Dahlmer Letter
    Thomas J. Frazee Letters
    Hamilton Family Papers
    Levi Adolphus Ross Papers
Indiana Historical Society, Indianapolis
    Joseph Gullion Letters, SC662
    Joseph C. Haddock Collection, SC664
    Andrew J. McGarrah Letters, SC1023
    Elijah R. Mitchell Letter, SC1097
    Louis Nettlehorst Letters, SC1136
    Benjamin Franklin Scribner Letters, SC1322
    Oliver Shelly Letters, SC1332
    Alfred Shields Letters, SC1337
    Thomas M. Small Diary, SC1355
    William Roberts Stuckey Letters, M269
    James S. Thomas Letters, SC1448
Indiana State Archives, Indianapolis
    Regimental Correspondence, Records of the Adjutant General of Indiana
Indiana State Library, Indianapolis
    Job Barnard Diary
    Daniel E. Bruce Memorandum
    Daniel H. Chandler Collection
    Civil War Regimental History—38th Indiana
    Jesse B. Connelly Diary
    Joseph P. Glezen Diary (microfilm)

Joseph Rothrock Letters
John Truex Letters
Kentucky Department of Military Affairs, Military Records and Research Bureau, Frankfort
Battery A, Kentucky Artillery Collection, Union Artillery-Primary Sources
15th Kentucky Infantry Collection, Union Infantry-Primary Sources
32nd Kentucky Volunteer Infantry Quartermaster Records
Kentucky Historical Society, Special Collections and Archives, Frankfort
Robert B. Taylor Diary 92SC82 (microfilm 1146)
Library of Congress, Washington, D.C.
Salmon P. Chase Papers
McCook Family Papers
Louisiana State University Libraries, Special Collections, Baton Rouge
E. John Ellis Diary Transcription, MSS 2795
E. P. Ellis and Family Papers, MSS 663
Robert A. Newell Papers, MSS 653
Robert D. Patrick Letters, MSS 893
Mississippi Department of Archives and History, Jackson
E. E. Baldwin Letters (microfilm)
Robert A. Jarman Manuscript
William H. McCardle Papers
Missouri Historical Society, St. Louis
Ellen Waddle McCoy Papers
National Archives and Records Administration, Washington, D.C.
Index to Pension Files of Veterans Who Served Between 1861 and 1900, 1st Wisconsin Infantry, Microfilm T-289
Manuscript Census, Kentucky, Boyle County, Schedule I, 1860
Record Group 15, Records of the Veterans Administration
Pension Applications Files Based Upon Service in the Civil War and Spanish-American War
Record Group 56, General Records of the Department of the Treasury
Records of the Division of Captured Property, Claims, and Lands
Record Group 92, Records of the Quartermaster General
Record Group 94, Records of the Adjutant General's Office, 1780s–1917
Compiled Service Records, 15th Alabama Infantry, 16th Alabama Infantry, 33rd Alabama Infantry, 15th Battalion Mississippi Sharpshooters, 32nd Mississippi Infantry, 33rd Mississippi Infantry, 44th Tennessee Infantry, M-269
General's Papers and Books, Papers of Don Carlos Buell
Record Group 109, War Department Collection of Confederate Records, General Records of the Government of the Confederate States of America
Letters Sent, 1861–62, Generals Polk, Hardee, Johnston, Beauregard, Bragg
Papers of Various Confederate Notables
Record Group 393, Records of U.S. Army Continental Commands
Army of the Ohio and 14th Army Corps, Letters and Circulars Sent, vol. 16
Army of the Ohio and 14th Army Corps, Letters and Reports Received, 1862–1865
Ohio Historical Society, Columbus
Sidney C. Baker Letters, VFM 1727
Charles L. Coburn Letters, VFM 2516
Nancy Ann Emerson Letters, VFM 805
Robert Foster Diary, VFM 4835
John D. Inskeep Diary, VOL 323–329, VFM 3187

George W. Landrum Letters, VFM 4704
Lewis Family Letters, VFM 2590
James Mitchell Memoir, VFM 1605
James Mitchell Memior, VFM 1605
Bliss Morse Papers, MSS 1035
Henry M. Osborn Diary, VOL 194
William M. Parkinson Correspondence, VFM 1170
Samuel J. Potts Letters, VFM 3326
Nelson Purdum Papers, VFM 2107
William Rhoads Letters, VFM 1428
William and Joseph Spencer Letters, VFM 2459
Robert J. Winn Diary, MSS 1135
Julius B. Work Diary, VOL 1162

Peoria Public Library, Peoria, Ill.
Allen L. Fahnestock Diary

Perryville Enhancement Project, Perryville, Ky.
William Woodward Collection

Perryville State Historic Site, Perryville, Ky.
"Abstract of the Diary of Private Glezen," 80th Indiana Infantry File
Author's Collection
Author's Perryville Tour Notes
Civilians File
41st Georgia Infantry File
General Orders, Charles C. Gilbert File
9th Pennsylvania Cavalry File
90th Ohio Infantry File
123rd Illinois Infantry File
James Searcy Letter, Semple's Alabama Battery File
James R. Thompson, "Hear the Wax Fry: Memoirs of James R. Thompson," 16th
     Tennessee Infantry File
10th Wisconsin Infantry File
3rd Florida Infantry File
32nd Mississippi Infantry File
33rd Alabama Infantry File

State Historical Society of Wisconsin, Madison
Adjutant General, Records of Civil War Regiments, 1861–1900
Albert O. Barton Papers
Emerson Rood Calkins Family Papers (microfilm)
Orson P. Clinton Letter (microfilm)
Eugene E. Comstock Letters
Lars and Knudt Dokken Papers
Henry T. Drake Letters
Alfred Galpin Family Papers
Hans Christian Heg Letters
John Henry Otto Memoirs
Edward L. Paine Family Papers (microfilm)
Oscar F. Pinney Papers
Edward B. Quiner Scrapbooks, "Correspondence of the Wisconsin Volunteers"
Ole Thostenson Reminiscence
Albert F. Waugh Letters

Stones River National Battlefield Library, Murfreesboro, Tenn.
    Thomas R. Hooper Diary
Tennessee State Library and Archives, Nashville
    Confederate Collection
            Carroll Henderson Clark Memoirs
            John Ephriam Gold Questionnaire Data
            John T. Irien, "Fifth Tennessee Infantry"
            Michael Manzy Diary
            William Mebane Pollard Diary
            W. E. Yeatman Memoirs
    F. B. Kendrick Memoirs
    James Winchester Papers
Troup County Archives, LaGrange, Ga.
    William Weaver Turner Collection, MS 058
Tulane University, Louisiana Historical Collection, New Orleans
    J. A. Chalaron Papers
    Louisiana Historical Collections
            Civil War Papers
U.S. Army Military History Institute Archives, Carlisle Barracks, Pa.
    William H. Ball Collection
    Timothy Brookes Collection
    Civil War Miscellaneous Collection
            George H. Alverson Letters
            Norman W. Calkins Note Book
            Rufus W. Daniel Diary
            John M. Householder Diary
            Henry F. Jackson Diary
            Lewis H. Jones Diary and Letters
            Edgar R. Kellogg Recollections
            Byron D. Paddock Letters
            James A. Price Diaries
            Henry Shouldise Letters
            Richard H. Watson Letters
            Jackson E. Webster Diary
            Jonathan Wood Memoir
            Julius Birney Work Diary
    Civil War Miscellaneous Collection—New Material
            P. V. Cox Letters
            Ezekiel John Ellis War Recollection
            Sears Family Letters
            Lester Dewitt Taylor Diary
    Civil War Times Illustrated Collection
            Aaron J. Benton Letters
            Emerson Calkins Memoirs
            John A. Duncan Diary
            Fulton-Lenz Correspondence
            Eden P. Sturges Correspondence
            Levi Wagner Memoirs
    William T. Clark Diary
    Harrisburg Civil War Round Table Collection

John Eicker Memoir
Alva C. Griest Memoir
John S. Walker Diary and Letters
William B. Hazen Letter Book
Lewis Leigh Jr., Collection
Braxton Bragg Telegram, Book 32, no. 54
Frank M. Phelps Letters, Book 14
Thomas D. Moore Papers
John N. Rathburn Papers
Univ. of Florida, P. K. Yonge Library of Florida History, Gainesville
A. Oswald McDonnell Diary
Univ. of Iowa Libraries, Iowa City
Andrew Foster Davis Papers
Univ. of Kentucky, Special Collections and Archives, Lexington
John W. Tuttle Diary Transcript (69M40)
Univ. of Michigan, Bentley Historical Library, Ann Arbor
Sligh Family Papers
John Weissert Papers
Univ. of Missouri-Columbia, Western Historical Manuscript Collection
W. E. Patterson Memoir, n.d.
Ursula M. Scott Collection, c. 1841–1936
Univ. of North Carolina, Southern Historical Collection, Wilson Library, Chapel Hill
James Patton Anderson Autobiography, Coll. #1480
Taylor Beatty Diaries, Coll. no. 54
Cabarrus and Slade Family Papers, Coll. no. 1886
Thomas Claiborne Reminiscence, no. 152
Edmund Kirby Smith Papers, Coll. no. 404
James Iredell Hall Diary, Coll. no. 302
Leonidas Polk Papers, Coll. no. M-2965
Benedict J. Semmes Papers, Coll. no. 2333
Henry C. Semple Papers, Coll. no. 655
John K. Street and Melinda East (Pace) Correspondence, Coll. no. 4180
Isaac Barton Ulmer Papers, Coll. no. 1834
Univ. of Southern Mississippi, William D. McCain Library and Archives, Hattiesburg
M. P. Lowrey Autobiography
Univ. of Wisconsin-Oshkosh
Evan Davis Speech, SC 85
Western Kentucky University, Department of Library Special Collections, Manuscripts, Bowling Green
Lewis-Starling Collection
Western Reserve Historical Society, Cleveland, Ohio
Braxton Bragg Papers
Wisconsin Veterans Museum, Madison
Harry T. Cleven, translation of O. A. Buslett, *Femtende Wisconsin*

BOOKS

Albertson, Joan W., ed. *Letters Home to Minnesota: 2nd Minnesota Volunteers*. Spokane, Wash.: P. D. Enterprises, 1992.

Althouse, Jerry A., and Ruth Lauer Hughes, eds. *The Civil War Letters of John A. Boon.* Lincoln, Neb.: Richard C. Ludden, n.d.

Anderson, Isabel, ed. *The Letters and Journals of General Nicholas Longworth Anderson: Harvard, Civil War, Washington, 1854–1892.* New York: Fleming H. Revell, 1942.

Angle, Paul M., ed. *Three Years in the Army of the Cumberland: The Letters and Diary of Major James A. Connolly.* Bloomington: Indiana Univ. Press, 1959.

Aten, Henry J. *History of the Eighty-Fifth Regiment, Illinois Volunteer Infantry.* Hiawatha, Kans.: Regimental Association, 1901.

Barnes, James A., James R. Carnahan, and Thomas H. B. McCain. *The Eighty-sixth Regiment, Indiana Volunteer Infantry. A Narrative of Its Services in the Civil War of 1861–1865.* Crawfordsville, Ind.: Journal, 1895.

Bartlett, Napier. *Military Record of Louisiana: Including Biographical and Historical Papers Relating to the Military Organizations of the State.* New Orleans: L. Graham, 1875; reprint, Baton Rouge: Louisiana State Univ. Press, 1996.

Bascom, Elizabeth Ethel Parker, ed. *"Dear Lizzie": Letters Written by James "Jimmy" Garvin Crawford to his Sweetheart Martha Elizabeth "Lizzie" Wilson While He Was in the Federal Army during the War Between the States, 1862–1865.* Ridgewood, N.Y.: Bascom, 1978.

Basler, Roy P., ed. *The Collected Works of Abraham Lincoln.* 9 vols. New Brunswick, N.J.: Rutgers Univ. Press, 1953–55.

Beatty, John. *The Citizen-Soldier; or, Memoirs of a Volunteer.* Cincinnati: Wilstach, Baldwin, 1879.

Bennett, L. G., and William M. Haigh. *History of the Thirty-sixth Regiment Illinois Volunteers, During the War of the Rebellion.* Aurora, Ill.: Knickerbocker and Hodder, 1876.

Benson, Wallace P. *A Soldier's Diary: Diary of Wallace P. Benson of Company H 36th Illinois Volunteers.* N.p.: F. Raymond Benson and Ernest L. Benson, 1919.

Berkley, John Lee, trans. *In Defense of This Flag: The Civil War Diary of Pvt. Ormond Hupp, 5th Indiana Light Artillery.* Bradenton, Fla.: McGuinn and McGuire, 1994.

Bircher, William. *A Drummer-Boy's Diary: Comprising Four Years of Service with the Second Regiment Minnesota Veteran Volunteers, 1861–1865.* St. Paul: St. Paul Book and Stationery Co., 1889.

Bisbee, William Henry. *Through Four American Wars: The Impressions and Experiences of Brigadier General William Henry Bisbee as Told to His Grandson William Haymond Bisbee.* Boston: Meador, 1931.

Bishop, Judson W. *The Story of a Regiment, Being a Narrative of the Service of the Second Regiment, Minnesota Veteran Volunteer Infantry, in the Civil War of 1861–1865.* St. Paul: n.p., 1890.

Blegen, Theodore C., ed. *The Civil War Letters of Colonel Hans Christian Heg.* Northfield, Minn.: Norwegian-American Historical Association, 1936.

Brown, Thaddeus C. S., Samuel J. Murphy, and William G. Putney. *Behind the Guns: The History of Battery I, 2nd Regiment, Illinois Light Artillery.* Ed. Clyde C. Walton. Preface by W. G. Putney. Carbondale and Edwardsville: Southern Illinois Univ. Press, 1965.

Buck, Irving A. *Cleburne and His Command.* New York: Neale, 1908.

Burnett, Alf. *Humorous, Pathetic, and Descriptive Incidents of the War.* Cincinnati: R. W. Carroll, 1864.

Butler, M. B. *My Story of the Civil War and the Underground Railroad.* Huntington, Ind.: United Brethren, 1914.

Butler, Watson Hubbard, ed. *Letters Home: Jay Caldwell Butler, Captain, 101st Ohio Volunteer Infantry.* N.p.: n.p., 1930.

Carter, Ruth C., ed. *For Honor, Glory & Union: The Mexican and Civil War Letters of Brig. Gen. William Haines Lytle.* Lexington: Univ. Press of Kentucky, 1999.

Crary, A. M. *The A. M. Crary Memoirs and Memoranda*. Herington, Kans.: Herington Times, 1915.

Crist, Lynda Lasswell, ed. *The Papers of Jefferson Davis*. Vol. 8. Baton Rouge: Louisiana State Univ. Press, 1995.

Cross, Joseph. *Camp and Field: Papers from the Portfolio of an Army Chaplain*. Macon, Ga.: Burke, Boykin, 1864.

Crowson, Noel, and John V. Brogden, eds. *Bloody Banners and Barefoot Boys: A History of the 27th Regiment Alabama Infantry CSA: The Civil War Memoirs and Diary Entries of J. P. Cannon, M.D.* Shippensburg, Pa.: Burd Street Press, 1997.

Cutter, O. P. *Our Battery; or the Journal of Company B, 1st O.V.A.* Cleveland: Nevins, 1864.

Davison, E. L. *Autobiography of E. L. Davison*. N.p.: n.p., 1901.

Day, L. W. *Story of the One Hundred and First Ohio Infantry*. Cleveland: W. M. Bayne, 1894.

DeVelling, C. T. *History of the Seventeenth Regiment, First Brigade, Third Division, Fourteenth Corps, Army of the Cumberland, War of the Rebellion*. Zanesville, Ohio: E. R. Sullivan, 1889.

Dicey, Edward. *Spectator of America*. Ed. Herbert Mitgang. Chicago: Quadrangle, 1971; reprint, Athens: Univ. of Georgia Press, 1989.

Dillman, Henry F. *A Diary Written by Henry F. Dillman During the Civil War*. Bloomington, Ind.: Monroe County Historical Society and Monroe County Civil War Centennial Commission, 1982.

Documents of the United States Sanitary Commission. 3 vols. New York: n.p., 1866–71.

Dodge, William Sumner. *A Waif of the War; or, The History of the Seventy-fifth Illinois Infantry, Embracing the Entire Campaigns of the Army of the Cumberland*. Chicago: Church and Goodman, 1866.

Dyer, Gustavus W., and John Trotwood Moore, comps. *The Tennessee Civil War Veterans Questionnaires*. 5 vols. Ed. Colleen Morse Elliott and Louise Armstrong Moxley. Easley, S.C.: Southern Historical, 1985.

Duff, W. H. *Terrors and Horrors of Prison Life, or Six Months a Prisoner at Camp Chase, Ohio*. N.p.: n.p., 1927.

Federico, Bianca Morse, and Betty Louise Wright, eds. *Civil War: The Letters of John Holbrook Morse 1861–1865*. Washington, D.C.: Federico, 1975.

Fitch, Michael H. *Echoes of the Civil War As I Hear Them*. New York: R. F. Fenno, 1905.

Ford, Thomas J. *With the Rank and File: Incidents and Anecdotes During the War of the Rebellion, As Remembered by One of the Non-Commissioned Officers*. Milwaukee: Evening Wisconsin, 1898.

Francis, Charles Lewis. *Narrative of a Private Soldier in the Volunteer Army of the United States, During a Portion of the Period Covered by the Great War of the Rebellion of 1861*. Brooklyn: William Jenkins, 1879.

Garrett, Jill K., trans. *Confederate Diary of Robert D. Smith*. Columbia, Tenn.: Capt. James Madison Sparkman Chapter, United Daughters of the Confederacy, 1975.

Gates, Arnold, ed. *The Rough Side of War: The Civil War Journal of Chesley A. Mosman, 1st Lieutenant, Company D, 59th Illinois Volunteer Infantry Regiment*. Garden City, N.Y.: Basin, 1987.

Genco, James G., ed. *To the Sound of Musketry and Tap of the Drum: A History of Michigan's Battery D Through the Letters of Artificer Harold J. Bartlett, 1861–1864*. Rochester, Mich.: Ray Russell Books, 1883.

Giles, L. B. *Terry's Texas Rangers*. Austin: Van Boeckman-Jones, 1911; reprint, Austin: Pemberton, 1967.

Glauser, James, trans. *The Civil War Diary of Private Josiah Ayre*. N.p.: n.p., n.d.

Graber, H. W. *The Life Record of H. W. Graber: A Terry Texas Ranger, 1861–1865, Sixty-two Years in Texas.* A.p.: n.p., 1916.

Grebner, Constantin. *"We Were the Ninth": A History of the Ninth Regiment, Ohio Volunteer Infantry April 17, 1861, to June 7, 1864.* Trans. and ed. Frederic Trautmann. Kent, Ohio: Kent State Univ. Press, 1987.

Grose, William. *The Story of the Marches, Battles and Incidents of the 36th Regiment Indiana Volunteer Infantry.* New Castle, Ind.: Courier, 1891.

Guild, George B. *A Brief Narrative of the Fourth Tennessee Cavalry Regiment, Wheeler's Corps, Army of Tennessee.* Nashville: n.p., 1913.

Hartpence, William R. *History of the Fifty-first Indiana Veteran Volunteer Infantry. A Narrative of Its Organizations, Marches, Battles and Other Experiences in Camp and Prison; From 1861 to 1866.* Cincinnati: Robert Clarke, 1894.

Hazen, W. B. *A Narrative of Military Service.* Boston: Ticknor, 1885.

Head, Thomas A. *Campaigns and Battles of the Sixteenth Regiment, Tennessee Volunteers, in the War Between the States, With Incidental Sketches of the Part Performed by Other Tennessee Troops in the Same War. 1861–1865.* Nashville: Cumberland Presbyterian, 1885.

Headley, John W. *Confederate Operations in Canada and New York.* New York: Neale, 1906.

Heard, Jessie Burke, compiler. *Letters of Pvt. Benjamin F. Burke Written while in the Terry's Texas Rangers, 1861–1864.* N.p.: n.p., 1965.

Herr, George W. *Nine Campaigns in Nine States: Fremont in Missouri—Curtis in Missouri and Arkansas—Halleck's Siege of Corinth—Buell in Kentucky—Rosecrans in Kentucky and Tennessee—Grant at the Battle of Chattanooga—Sherman's from Chattanooga to Atlanta—Thomas in Tennessee and North Carolina—Stanley in Texas. In Which is Comprised the History of the Fifty-ninth Regiment Illinois Veteran Volunteer Infantry—Together with Special Mention of the Various Regiments with which it was Brigaded from 1861 to 1865.* San Francisco: Bancroft, 1890.

Hewett, Janet B., et al. *Supplement to the Official Records of the Union and Confederate Armies.* 95 vols. Wilmington, N.C.: Broadfoot, 1994–.

Hight, John J., and Gilbert R. Stormont. *History of the Fifty-eighth Indiana: Its Organization, Campaigns and Battles From 1861 to 1865.* Princeton, Ind.: Clarion, 1895.

Hinman, Wilbur F. *The Story of the Sherman Brigade: The Camp, the March, the Bivouac, the Battle, and How "The Boys" Lived and Died During Four Years of Active Service.* Alliance, Ohio: Daily Review, 1897.

"His Mother." *The Young Chaplain.* New York: N. Tibbals and Sons, 1876.

History of the Services of the Third Battery Wisconsin Light Artillery in the Civil War of the United States, 1861–65. Berlin, Wisc.: Courant, 1902.

History of the Seventy-ninth Regiment Indiana Volunteer Infantry in the Civil War of Eighteen Sixty-one. Indianapolis: Hollenbeck, 1899.

History of the Seventy-third Indiana Volunteers in the War of 1861–65. Washington, D.C.: Carnahan, 1909.

History of the Seventy-third Regiment of Illinois Infantry Volunteers: Its Services and Experiences in Camp, On the March, On the Picket and Skirmish Lines, and In many Battles of the War 1861–65. Including a Sketch in Full of the Valuable and Indispensable Services Rendered by Opdyck's First Brigade, Second Division, Fourth Army Corps, In the Campaign in Tennessee in the Fall of 1864, Embracing an Account of the Movement From Columbia to Nashville, and The Battles of Spring Hill and Franklin. Also, Including Many Other Interesting, Miscellaneous Sketches, The latter being Made Up of Recitals of Individual Experiences of Capture, Imprisonment, and Escape; And an Account of the Visit of James F. Jaquess, Colonel of the Seventy-third, To Richmond, Virginia, In The

Summer of 1864. N.p.: Regimental Reunion Association of Survivors of the 73rd Illinois Infantry Volunteers, 1890.

Holmes, Mead. *Soldier of the Cumberland: Memoir of Mead Holes, Jr., Sergeant of Company K, 21st Regiment Wisconsin Volunteers.* Boston: American Tract Society, 1864.

Horrall, S. F. *History of the Forty-second Indiana Volunteer Infantry.* Chicago: Donohue and Henneberry, 1892.

Hughes, Nathaniel Cheairs Jr., ed. *Liddell's Record: St. John Richardson Liddell.* Dayton, Ohio: Morningside, 1985.

Hunter, Alf G. *History of the Eighty-second Indiana Volunteer Infantry, Its Organization, Campaigns and Battles.* Indianapolis: William B. Burford, 1893.

Hupp, Ormond. *My Diary.* Np: n.p., n.d.

James, F. B. "Perryville and the Kentucky Campaign of 1862." In *Sketches of War History 1861–1865: Papers Prepared for the Commandery of the State of Ohio, Military Order of the Loyal Legion of the United States, 1896–1903,* ed. W. H. Chamberlin et al. Cincinnati: Robert Clarke, 1903.

Johnson, Robert Underwood, and Clarence Clough Buel, eds. *Battles and Leaders of the Civil War.* 4 vols. New York: Century, 1887–88; reprint, New York: Thomas Yoseloff, 1956.

Johnston, Adam S. *The Soldier Boy's Diary Book; or, Memorandums of the Alphabetical First Lessons of Military Trade.* Pittsburgh: n.p., 1866.

Johnston, J. Stoddard. "Kentucky." In *Confederate Military History: A Library of Confederate States History, Written by Distinguished Men of the South, and Edited by Gen. Clement A. Evans of Georgia.* Vol. 9. Atlanta: Confederate, 1899.

Jones, A. J. *A Private of the Cumberland: Memoirs and Reminiscences of the Civil War.* N.p.: n.p., n.d.

Joyce, John A. *A Checkered Life.* Chicago: S. F. Rounds Jr., 1883.

Keil, F. W. *Thirty-fifth Ohio: A Narrative of Service from August, 1861 to 1864.* Fort Wayne, Ind.: Archer, Housh, 1894.

Kerwood, Asbury L. *Annals of the Fifty-seventh Regiment Indiana Volunteers. Marches, Battles, and Incidents of Army Life.* Dayton: W. J. Shuey, 1868.

Kimberly, Robert L., and Ephraim S. Holloway. *The Forty-first Ohio Veteran Volunteer Infantry in the War of the Rebellion, 1861–1865.* Cleveland: W. R. Smellie, 1897.

Kinnear, J. R. *History of the Eighty-sixth Regiment Illinois Volunteer Infantry, During its Term of Service.* Chicago: Tribune, 1866.

Kirkpatrick, George Morgan. *The Experiences of a Private Soldier of the Civil War.* Chicago: Elite, 1924; reprint, Indianapolis: Hoosier Bookshop, 1973.

Larew, Karl G., ed. *Garrett Larew, Civil War Soldier: With an Account of His Ancestors and of His Descendants.* Baltimore: Gateway, 1975.

Lathrop, D. *The History of the Fifty-ninth Regiment Illinois Volunteers, or A Three Years' Campaign Through Missouri, Arkansas, Mississippi, Tennessee and Kentucky, With a Description of the Country, Towns, Skirmishes and Battles—Incidents, Casualties and Anecdotes Met With On the Way; and Embellished With Twenty-four Lithographed Portraits of the Officers of the Regiment.* Indianapolis: Hall and Hutchinson, 1865.

Little, George, and James R. Maxwell. *A History of Lumsden's Battery C.S.A.* Tuscaloosa, Ala.: R. E. Rodes Chapter, United Daughters of the Confederacy, 1905.

Lindsley, John Berrien, ed. *The Military Annals of Tennessee. Confederate. First Series: Embracing a Review of Military Operations, With Regimental Histories and Memorial Rolls, Compiled from Original and Official Sources.* Vol. 1. Nashville: J. M. Lindsley, 1886; reprint, Wilmington, N.C.: Broadfoot, 1995.

Malone, Thomas H. *Memoir of Thomas H. Malone: An Autobiography Written For His Children.* Introduction by J. M. Dickinson. Nashville: Baird-Ward, 1928.

Marcoot, Maurice. *Five Years in the Sunny South: Reminiscences of Maurice Marcoot, Late of Co. "B," 15th Reg. Missouri Veteran Volunteer Infantry from 1861 to 1865.* N.p.: n.p., n.d.

Marshall, R. V. *An Historical Sketch of the Twenty-second Regiment Indiana Volunteers, From Its Organization to the Close of the War, Its Battles, Its Marches, and Its Hardships, Its Brave Officers and Its Honored Dead.* Madison, Ind.: Courier, 1884.

Martin, John A. *Military History of the Eighth Kansas Veteran Volunteer Infantry.* Leavenworth: Daily Bulletin, 1896.

Medical and Surgical History of the Civil War. 15 vols. Wilmington, Del.: Broadfoot, 1990–92.

Mills, Anson. *My Story.* Ed. C. H. Claudy. Washington, D.C.: Byron S. Adams, 1918.

Morris, George W. *History of the Eighty-first Regiment of Indiana Volunteer Infantry In the Great War of the Rebellion, 1861–1865: Telling of Its Origin and Organization; A Description of the Material of Which It Was Composed; Its Rapid and Severe Marches; Hard Service and Fierce Conflicts on Many Bloody Fields. Pathetic Scenes, Amusing Incidents and Thrilling Episodes. A Regimental Roster. Prison Life, Adventures, Etc.* Louisville: Franklin, 1901.

Newlin, W. H. *Cherished Memories: Illinois Leadership in War and Peace.* N.p.: n.p., 1902.

Noe, Kenneth W., ed. *A Southern Boy in Blue: The Memoir of Marcus Woodcock, 9th Kentucky Infantry (U.S.A.).* Knoxville: Univ. of Tennessee Press, 1996.

Olson, Morgan A., trans. *Rollin Olson, 15th Regiment, Wisconsin Volunteer Infantry: Civil War Letters.* Minneapolis: n.p., 1981.

Patterson, Lowell Wayne, ed. *Campaigns of the 38th Regiment of the Illinois Volunteer Infantry Company K, 1861–1863: The Diary of William Elwood Patterson.* Bowie, Md.: Heritage, 1992.

Perry, Henry Fales. *History of the Thirty-eighth Regiment Indiana Volunteer Infantry: One of the Three Hundred Fighting Regiments of the Union Army, In the War of the Rebellion 1861–1865.* Palo Alto, Calif.: F. A. Stuart, 1906.

Phillips, W. Louis, ed. *Civil War Diary of Joseph K. Marshall.* Columbus, Ohio: The Editor, 1982.

Polk, Jefferson J. *Autobiography of Dr. J. J. Polk: To Which is Added His Occasional Writings and Biographies of Worthy Men and Women of Boyle County, Ky.* Louisville: John P. Morton, 1867.

Putnam, J. H. *A Journalistic History of the Thirty-first Regiment, Ohio Volunteer Infantry, With its Lights and Shadows.* Vol. 1. Louisville: John P. Morton, 1862.

Quintard, Charles T. *Doctor Quintard: Chaplain C.S.A. and Second Bishop of Tennessee, Being His Story of the War (1861–1865).* Edited and extended by Arthur Howard Noll. Sewanee, Tenn.: University Press, 1905.

Record of the Ninety-fourth Regiment Ohio Volunteer Infantry in the War of the Rebellion. Cincinnati: Ohio Valley Press, 1890.

Report of the Adjutant General of the State of Kansas, 1861–65. Vol. 1. Topeka: Kansas State Printing, 1896.

Rerick, John H. *The Forty-fourth Indiana Volunteer Infantry: History of its Services in the War of the Rebellion and a Personal Record of its Members.* Lagrange, Ind.: The Author, 1880.

Reynolds, Edwin H. *A History of the Henry County Commands Which Served in the Confederate States Army, Including Rosters of the Various Companies Enlisted in Henry County, Tenn.* Jacksonville, Fla.: Sun, 1904; reprint, Kennesaw, Ga.: Continental, 1961.

Rieger, Paul E., annotator. *Through One Man's Eyes: The Civil War Experiences of a Belmont County Volunteer. Letters of James G. Theaker.* Mount Vernon, Ohio: Print Arts, 1974.

Roll of Honor: Names of Soldiers Who Died in Defence of the American Union, Interred in the

National and Public Cemeteries in Kentucky, and at New Albany, Jeffersonville, and Madison, Indiana, Lawton (Millen), and Andersonville, Georgia (supplementary). Washington, D.C.: Government Printing Office, 1868.

Savage, John H. *The Life of John H. Savage: Citizen, Soldier, Lawyer, Congressman, Written by Himself.* Nashville: The Author, 1903.

Scribner, B. F. *How Soldiers Were Made; or The War as I Saw It, Under Buell, Rosecrans, Thomas, Grant and Sherman.* New Albany, Ind.: Chicago, Donohue, and Henneberry, 1887.

Shaw, James Birney. *History of the Tenth Regiment Indiana Volunteer Infantry, Three Months and Three Years Organizations.* Lafayette: Burt-Haywood, 1912.

Sheridan, Philip H. *Personal Memoirs of P.H. Sheridan. General United States Army.* 2 vols. New York: Charles L. Webster, 1888.

Simmons, L. A. *The History of the 84th Reg't Ill. Vols.* Macomb, Ill.: Hampton Brothers, 1866.

Sligh, Charles R. *History of the Services of the First Regiment Michigan Engineers and Mechanics During the Civil War, 1861–1865.* Grand Rapids, Mich.: White, 1921.

Smith, John Thomas. *A History of the Thirty-first Regiment of Indiana Volunteer Infantry in the War of the Rebellion.* Cincinnati: Western Methodist Book Concern, 1900.

Stewart, Nixon B. *Dan. McCook's Regiment, 52nd O. V. I.: A History of the Regiment, Its Campaigns and Battles. From 1862 to 1865.* N.p.: The Author, 1900.

Sutherland, Daniel E., ed. *Reminiscences of a Private: William E. Bevens of the First Arkansas Infantry, C.S.A.* Fayetteville: Univ. of Arkansas Press, 1992.

Tarrant. E. *The Wild Riders of the First Kentucky Cavalry: A History of the Regiment, In the Great War of the Rebellion 1861–1865, Telling of Its Origin and Organization; A Description of the Material of Which It was Composed; Its Rapid and Severe Marches, Hard Service, and Fierce Conflicts on Many a Bloody Field. Pathetic Scenes, Amusing Incidents, and Thrilling Episodes. A Regimental Roster. Prison Life, Adventures and Escapes.* N.p.: A Committee of the Regiment, 1894.

Taylor, Richard. *Destruction and Reconstruction.* New York: D. Appleton, 1879.

Thatcher, Marshall P. *A Hundred Battles in the West. St Louis to Atlanta, 1861–65. The Second Michigan Cavalry With the Armies of the Mississippi, Ohio, Kentucky and Cumberland, Under Generals Halleck, Sherman, Pope, Rosecrans, Thomas and Others; With mention of a Few of the Famous Regiments and Brigades of the West.* Detroit: The Author, 1884.

Thoburn, Lyle, ed. *My Experiences During the Civil War.* Cleveland: n.p., 1963.

Toney, Marcus B. *The Privations of a Private. The Campaign Under Gen. R. E. Lee; The Campaign Under Gen. Stonewall Jackson; Bragg's Invasion of Kentucky; The Chickamauga Campaign; The Wilderness Campaign; Prison Life in the North; The Privations of a Citizen; The Ku-Klux Klan; A United Citizenship.* Nashville: The Author, 1905.

Tourgée, Albion W. *The Story of a Thousand. Being a History of the Service of the 105th Ohio Volunteer Infantry, in the War for the Union from August 21, 1862 to June 6, 1865.* Buffalo: S. McGerald and Son, 1896.

Trollope, Anthony. *North America.* 2 vols. London: Chapman and Hall, 1862; reprint, New York: St. Martin's, 1986.

U.S. War Department. *The War of the Rebellion: A Compilation of the Official Records of the Union and Confederate Armies.* 129 vols. Washington, D.C.: 1880–1901.

Vaughan, A. J. *Personal Record of the Thirteenth Regiment, Tennessee Infantry, By Its Old Commander.* Memphis: S. C. Toof, 1897.

Waddle, Angus L. *Three Years With the Armies of the Ohio and the Cumberland.* Chillicothe, Ohio: Scioto Gazette, 1889.

Watkins, Sam R. *"Co. Aytch," Maury Grays, First Tennessee Regiment; or, A Side Show of the Big Show.* Chattanooga: Times, 1900; reprint, New York: Collier, 1962.

Whitman, Walt. *The Works of Walt Whitman, in Two Volumes, as Prepared by Him for the Deathbed Edition.* 2 vols. New York: Funk and Wagnalls, 1968.

Winters, Erastus. *In the 50th Ohio Serving Uncle Sam: Memoirs of One Who Wore the Blue—Battle of Perryville—Camp Scenes in Old Kentucky and Tennessee—The Atlanta Campaign—Back in Tennessee—Battle of Franklin—Captured by the Enemy—A Hot Place Between the Firing Lines—Prison Experience—The Destruction of the Steamer "Sultana"—Frightful Loss of Life—Horrible and Heartrending Scenes—Writer's Escape, and Arrival at Home—Enjoys the Warm Hospitality of Relatives and Friends—End of the War—Prosperity of the Country Under "Old Glory."* East Walnut Hills, Ohio: n.p., 1895.

Womack, J. J. *The Civil War Diary of Capt. J. J. Womack, Co. E, Sixteenth Regiment, Tennessee Volunteers.* McMinnville, Tenn.: Womack, 1961.

Woodruff, George H. *Fifteen Years Ago; or The Patriotism of Will County, Designed to Preserve the Names and Memory of Will County Soldiers, Both Officers and Privates—Both Living and Dead: To Tell Something of What They Did, And of What They Suffered, In The Great Struggle to Preserve Our Nationality.* Joliet, Ill.: Joliet Republican Book and Job Steam Printing House, 1876.

Wright, T. J. *History of the Eighth Regiment Kentucky Vol. Inf. during Its three Years Campaigns Embracing Organization, Marches, Skirmishes, and Battles of the Command, with Much of the History of the Old Reliable Third Brigade, Commanded by Hon. Stanley Matthews, and Containing Many Interesting and Amusing Incidents of Army Life.* St. Joseph, Mo.: St. Joseph Steam Printing, 1880.

ARTICLES

Afflick, Mary Hunt. "Southern Aid Society, Harrodsburg, 1861–65." *Confederate Veteran* 21 (1913): 30.

Allinger, Charles. "The Battle of Perryville." *National Tribune*, Aug. 26, 1886, 3.

———. "The 2nd Mo. At Perryville." *National Tribune*, Dec. 2, 1886, 3.

Bachelor, G. N. "Soldiers' Anecdotes." *National Tribune*, Mar. 1879, 19.

Ball, William H. "At Perryville." *National Tribune*, Dec. 15, 1887, 1–2.

Barnhart, John D., ed. "A Hoosier Invades the Confederacy: Letters and Diaries of Leroy S. Mayfield." *Indiana Magazine of History* 39 (1943): 144–91.

Berry, John M. "Reminiscences From Missouri." *Confederate Veteran* 8 (1900): 73.

Biggs, Davis. "Incidents in the Battle of Perryville, Ky." *Confederate Veteran* 33 (1925): 141–42.

Bowers, George W. "Memories of a Retreat." *National Tribune*, June 11, 1896, 3.

"Bragg and His Generals." *Southern Bivouac* 1 (Oct. 1885): 286–91.

Brown, A. H. "On the Firing Line With Bragg." *Confederate Veteran* 17 (1909): 331.

Carnes, W. W. "Artillery at the Battle of Perryville, Ky." *Confederate Veteran* 33 (1925): 8–9.

Cheatham, B. F. "The Battle of Perryville." *Southern Bivouac*, n.s., 1 (Apr. 1886): 704–5.

Cheek, Christen Ashby, ed. "Memoirs of Mrs. E. B. Patterson: A Perspective on Danville during the Civil War." *Register of the Kentucky Historical Society* 92 (Autumn 1994): 347–99.

Claiborne, Thomas. "Battle of Perryville, Ky." *Confederate Veteran* 16 (May 1908): 225–27.

"Co. Aytch" [Watkins, Sam]. "An Adventure of General Leonidas Polk at the Battle of Perryville." *Southern Bivouac* 2 (May 1884): 403–4.

———. Untitled, signed paragraph. *Southern Bivouac* 1 (Jan. 1883): 223–24.

Cozzens, Peter, ed. "Ambition Carries the Day: William Passmore Carlin Recalls the Battle of Perryville, Kentucky." *Columbiad* 1 (Spring 1997): 138–48.

Crawford, S.K. "Battle of Perryville." *National Tribune*, Apr. 2, 1893, 4.

————. "Rear of Perryville." *National Tribune*, June 8, 1893, 3.

Cummings, James. "Sheridan at Perryville." *National Tribune*, Apr. 28, 1904, 10.

Cutrer, Thomas W. "'We Are Stern and Resolved': The Civil War Letters of John Wesley Rabb, Terry's Texas Rangers." *Southwestern Historical Quarterly* 91 (1987): 185–226.

Davis, W. H. "Recollections of Perryville." *Confederate Veteran* 24 (1916): 554.

"An Ex-Kentuckian" [pseud.]. "The Kentucky Invasion of 1862." *Confederate Veteran* 23 (1915): 408–10.

"Fatalities in One Company at Perryville, Ky." *Confederate Veteran* 20 (1912): 210.

"The 'Fighting' Forty-eighth Tennessee Regiment." *Southern Bivouac* 2 (Feb. 1884): 246–51.

Finley, Luke W. "The Battle of Perryville." *Southern Historical Society Papers* 30 (1902): 242.

Fleming, Doris, ed. "Letters From a Canadian Recruit in the Union Army." *Tennessee Historical Quarterly* 16 (June 1957): 159–66.

Frierson, Robert M. "Gen. E. Kirby Smith's Campaign in Kentucky." *Confederate Veteran* 1 (1893): 295.

Ford, H. M. "That Famous Retreat." *National Tribune*, July 9, 1896, 3.

Fowler, Nolan, ed. "Johnny Reb's Impressions of Kentucky in the Fall of 1862." *Register of the Kentucky Historical Society* 48 (July 1950): 205–11.

Gardner, George Q. "Perryville." *National Tribune*, Apr. 23, 1885, 3.

"Gen. and Mrs. Braxton Bragg." *Confederate Veteran* 4 (1896): 102–3.

Gilbert, C.C. "Bragg's Invasion of Kentucky." *Southern Bivouac*, n.s., 1 (Aug. 1885): 217–22; (Sept. 1885): 296–301; (Nov. 1885): 336–42; (Dec. 1885): 430–36; (Jan. 1886): 465–77: (Feb. 1886): 550–56.

Gipson, W. C. "About the Battle of Perryville." *Confederate Veteran* 9 (1901): 163.

"Graves of Our Dead at Perryville." *Confederate Veteran* 3 (1895): 385.

Grimshaw, Samuel. "The Battle of Perryville." *National Tribune*, Sept. 17, 1903, 3.

Hafendorfer, Kenneth A., ed. "Major General Simon B. Buckner's Unpublished After-Action Report on the Battle of Perryville." *Civil War Regiments* 4 (1995): 50–64.

Hammond, Paul F. "General Kirby Smith's Campaign in Kentucky." *Southern Historical Society Papers* 10 (1882): 70–76.

————. "The Kentucky Campaign." *Southern Historical Society Papers* 10 (1882): 158–61.

Hartman, Samuel L. "Battle of Perryville." *National Tribune*, Aug. 13, 1903, 3.

Head, T. A. Untitled Article. *Confederate Veteran* 5 (1987): 435.

Herald, A. J. "Terrible Sight at Perryville." *National Tribune*, Apr. 28, 1904, 10.

Hoover, Elias H. "Battle of Perryville." *National Tribune*, June 20, 1889, 3.

Jacobs, W. W. "Campaigning with Buell." *National Tribune*, Oct. 23, 1902, 3.

Johnson, E. Polk. "Some Generals I Have Known." *Southern Bivouac* 1 (July 1885): 120–22.

Kaiser, Leo M., ed. "Civil War Letters of Charles W. Carr of the 21st Wisconsin Volunteers." *Wisconsin Magazine of History* 43 (Summer 1960): 264–72.

Kendall, Henry M. "The Battle of Perryville." *Military Order of the Loyal Legion of the United States, Commandery of the District of Columbia, War Papers* 43 (1902): 3–13.

Knight, Carol Lynn H., and Gerald S. Cowden, eds. "Two Immigrants for the Union: Their Civil War Letters." Trans. Della Kittleson Catuna. *Norwegian-American Studies* 28 (1979): 109–37.

Knowles, L. E. "Battle of Perryville." *National Tribune*, May 9, 1889, 3.

Mavity, J. S. "Condensed Letters." *National Tribune*, Dec. 9, 1886, 3.

McCormick, Edgar L., and Gary DuBro, eds. "'If I Live to Get Home. . . .': The Civil War Letters of Private Jonathan McElderry." *Serif* 3 (Mar. 1966): 21–30.

McCouley, C. M. "Who Was That Officer?" *Confederate Veteran* 7 (1899): 406.

McDowell, William P. "The Fifteenth Kentucky." *Southern Bivouac* 5 (1886): 246–53.

McFarland, L. B. "Maney's Brigade at the Battle of Perryville." *Confederate Veteran* 30 (1922): 467–69.

Millard, Harrison. "Battle of Perryville." *National Tribune*, Aug. 8, 1889, 1–2.

Milner, Duncan C. "'A Human Document.'" *National Tribune*, Sept. 27, 1906, 6.

"A Missouri Soldier: August Reimers." *Military Images*, May-June, 1992, 18–23.

Mosgrove, George Dallas. "The Battle of Perryville." *National Tribune*, Feb. 5, 1903, 3.

————."Two Mighty Armies Racing." *National Tribune*, Jan. 15, 1903, 7.

Newton, J. L. "The Fight at Perryville." *National Tribune*, Nov. 18, 1886, 3.

Nichols, James L., ed. "Reminiscing from 1861 to 1865: An 'Ex Confed,' H. P. Morrow." *East Texas Historical Journal* 9 (Mar. 1971): 5–19.

Osburn, D. M. "Gen. George D. Wagner." *National Tribune*, Jan. 20, 1887, 3.

Radcliffe, Charles K. "Terrill's Brigade at Perryville." *National Tribune*, June 14, 1906, 3.

Robinson, John. "Perryville." *National Tribune*, July 15, 1886, 3.

Ryan, Frank T. "The Kentucky Campaign and Battle of Richmond." *Confederate Veteran* 26 (1918): 158–60.

Sheaffer, J. W. "Battle of Perryville." *National Tribune*, Apr. 24, 1890, 4.

"The Skirmish Line." *Southern Bivouac* 2 (Aug. 1884): 567.

Spence, Philip B. "Campaigning in Kentucky." *Confederate Veteran* 9 (1901): 22–23.

Spradlin, Mike, ed. "The Diary of George W. Jones: A Partial History of Stanford's Mississippi Battery." *Camp Chase Gazette* (April 1981): 6–11.

Starkweather, John. "Perryville." *National Tribune*, Nov. 4, 1886, 2.

[Steele, B. P.]. "Charge of the First Tennessee at Perryville." *Southern Bivouac* 3 (Oct. 1884): 67–69.

Steely, Will Frank, and Orville W. Taylor, eds. "Bragg's Kentucky Campaign: A Confederate Soldier's Account." *Register of the Kentucky Historical Society* 57 (Jan. 1959): 49–55.

Straw, A. B. "Battle of Perryville." *National Tribune*, Mar. 10, 1904, 3.

Sykes, E. T. "A Cursory Sketch of General Bragg's Campaigns." *Southern Historical Society Papers* 11 (1883): 466–74, 490–97.

Trauernicht, Henry. "McCook's Corps at Perryville." *National Tribune*, Sept. 30, 1886, 3.

"Tributes to Gen. Braxton Bragg." *Confederate Veteran* 3 (1895): 132.

"William P. Rogers' Memorandum Book." *West Tennessee Historical Society Papers* 9 (1955): 59–92.

Williams, Robert W. Jr., and Ralph A. Wooster, eds. "With Terry's Texas Rangers: The Letters of Dunbar Affleck." *Civil War History* 9 (Mar. 1963): 299–319.

Work, J. B. "A Famous Retreat." *National Tribune*, July 16, 1896, 3.

————. "Perryville." *National Tribune*, Dec. 21, 1893, 3.

Wright, J. M. "A Glimpse of Perryville." *Southern Bivouac* 1 (Aug. 1885): 149–54.

————. "West Point before the War." *Southern Bivouac* 1 (June 1885): 13–21.

NEWSPAPERS

Atlanta Southern Confederacy
Aurora (Ill.) Weekly Beacon
Chicago Times
Cincinnati Daily Commercial
Cincinnati Daily Enquirer
Cleveland Plain Dealer

Daily Evansville Journal
Fayetteville (Tenn.) Observer
Indianapolis Daily Journal
Knoxville Daily Register
Louisville Daily Journal
Macon Daily Telegraph
Memphis Daily Appeal
Milledgeville (Ga.) Confederate Union
Milwaukee Sentinel
New Albany (Ind.) Daily Ledger
New Orleans Bee
New Orleans Daily Picayune
Oshkosh (Wisc.) Courier
Princeton (Ind.) Clarion
Richmond Whig
Valparaiso (Ind.) Republic

MAPS

Ruger, Edward, and Anton Kilp, surveyors and comps. "Map of the Battle of Perryville, Ky." Washington, D.C.: War Department, 1877; reprint, Lexington: Univ. of Kentucky Press, 1979.

SECONDARY SOURCES

BOOKS

Adams, George Worthington. *Doctors in Blue: The Medical History of the Union Army in the Civil War.* New York: Henry Schuman, 1952.

Babits, Lawrence E. *A Devil of a Whipping: The Battle of Cowpens.* Chapel Hill: Univ. of North Carolina Press, 1998.

Barnhill, Floyd R. *The Fighting Fifth: Pat Cleburne's Cutting Edge: The Fifth Arkansas Infantry Regiment, C.S.A.* Jonesboro, Ark.: The Author, 1990.

Boatner, Mark M. *The Civil War Dictionary.* Revised ed. New York: Vintage, 1988.

Brown, Kent Masterson. "Munfordville: The Campaign and Battle Along Kentucky's Strategic Axis." In *The Civil War in Kentucky: Battle for the Bluegrass State*, ed. Kent Masterson Brown, 137–73. Mason City, Iowa: Savas, 2000.

Brown, Richard C. *A History of Danville and Boyle County, Kentucky, 1774–1992.* Danville, Ky.: Bicentennial Books, 1992.

Buck, Paul H. *The Road to Reunion, 1865–1900.* Boston: Little, Brown, 1937.

Catton, Bruce. *Grant Moves South.* Boston: Little, Brown, 1960.

Chudacoff, Howard P. *How Old Are You? Age Consciousness in American Culture.* Princeton: Princeton Univ. Press, 1989.

Clay, R. Berle. *An Introduction to the Archaeology of Civil War Battles in Kentucky: Battlefield Survey and Planning: Perryville Battlefield.* Lexington: Office of State Archaeology, Univ. of Kentucky, 1994.

Collier, Calvin L. *First In–Last Out: The Capitol Guards, Ark. Brigade.* Little Rock: Pioneer Press, 1961.

Connelly, Thomas Lawrence. *Army of the Heartland: the Army of Tennessee, 1861–1862.* Baton Rouge: Louisiana State Univ. Press, 1967.

————. *The Marble Man: Robert E. Lee and His Image in American Society.* Baton Rouge: Louisiana State Univ. Press, 1977.

————, and Archer Jones. *The Politics of Command: Factions and Ideas in Confederate Strategy.* Baton Rouge: Louisiana State Univ. Press, 1973.

Cooling, Benjamin Franklin. *Fort Donelson's Legacy: War and Society in Kentucky and Tennessee, 1862–1863.* Knoxville: Univ. of Tennessee Press, 1997.

————. *Forts Henry and Donelson: the Key to the Confederate Heartland.* Knoxville: Univ. of Tennessee Press, 1987.

Coulter, E. Merton. *The Civil War and Readjustment in Kentucky.* Chapel Hill: Univ. of North Carolina Press, 1926; reprint, Gloucester, Mass.: Peter Smith, 1966.

Cozzens, Peter. *The Darkest Days of the War: The Battles of Iuka and Corinth.* Chapel Hill: Univ. of North Carolina Press, 1997.

————. *No Better Place to Die: The Battle of Stones River.* Urbana: Univ. of Illinois Press, 1990.

Cummings, Charles M. *Yankee Quaker, Confederate General: The Curious Career of Bushrod Rust Johnson.* Rutherford, N.J.: Fairleigh Dickinson Univ. Press, 1971.

Daniel, Larry J. *Shiloh: The Battle That Changed the Civil War.* New York: Simon and Schuster, 1997.

————. *Soldiering in the Army of Tennessee: A Portrait of Life in a Confederate Army.* Chapel Hill: Univ. of North Carolina Press, 1991.

Daviess, Maria T. *History of Mercer and Boyle Counties.* Harrodsburg, Ky.: Harrodsburg Herald, 1924.

Davis, William C. *Breckinridge: Statesman, Soldier, Symbol.* Baton Rouge: Louisiana State Univ. Press, 1974.

————. *Battle at Bull Run: A History of the First Major Campaign of the Civil War.* Garden City, N.Y.: Doubleday, 1977

————. *The Orphan Brigade: The Kentucky Confederates Who Couldn't Go Home.* Baton Rouge: Louisiana State Univ. Press, 1980.

————. *Jefferson Davis: The Man and His Hour.* New York: HarperCollins, 1991.

Dean, Eric T. Jr. *Shook Over Hell: Post-Traumatic Stress, Vietnam, and the Civil War.* Cambridge, Mass.: Harvard Univ. Press, 1997.

Douglas, Ann. *The Feminization of American Culture.* New York: Knopf, 1977.

Dunn, Byron A. *On General Thomas's Staff.* Chicago: A. C. McClurg, 1899.

Elliott, Sam Davis. *Soldier of Tennessee: General Alexander P. Stewart and the Civil War in the West.* Baton Rouge: Louisiana State Univ. Press, 1999.

Engle, Stephen D. *Don Carlos Buell: Most Promising of All.* Chapel Hill: Univ. of North Carolina Press, 1999.

Farrell, James J. *Inventing the American Way of Death, 1830–1920.* Philadelphia: Temple Univ. Press, 1980.

Foster, Gaines M. *Ghosts of the Confederacy: Defeat, the Lost Cause, and the Emergence of the New South, 1865 to 1913.* New York: Oxford Univ. Press, 1987.

Fox, William F. *Regimental Losses in the American Civil War, 1861–1865: A Treatise on the Extent and Nature of the Mortuary Losses in the Union Regiments, With Full and Exhaustive Statistics Compiled From the Official records On File in the State Military Bureaus and At Washington.* Albany, N.Y.: Albany Publishing, 1889.

Fradenburgh, J. N. *In Memoriam: Henry Harrison Cummings, Charlotte J. Cummings.* Oil City, Pa.: Derrick, 1913.

Frank, Joseph Allan, and George A. Reaves. *"Seeing the Elephant": Raw Recruits at the Battle of Shiloh.* New York: Greenwood, 1989.

Fussell, Paul. *The Great War and Modern Memory.* New York: Oxford Univ. Press, 1975.

Gallagher, Gary W. *The Confederate War.* Cambridge: Harvard Univ. Press, 1997.

Gates, Paul W. *Agriculture and the Civil War*. New York: Alfred A. Knopf, 1965.

Glendinning, Victoria. *Anthony Trollope*. Paperback ed., New York: Penguin, 1994.

Goodwin, Frederick K., and Kay Redfield Jamison. *Manic-Depressive Illness*. New York: Oxford Univ. Press, 1990.

Graff, Harvey J. *Conflicting Paths: Growing Up in America*. Cambridge: Harvard Univ. Press, 1992.

Gramm, Kent. "The Chances of War: Lee, Longstreet, Sickles, and the First Minnesota Volunteers." In *The Gettysburg Nobody Knows*, ed. Gabor S. Borritt, 75–100. New York Oxford Univ. Press, 1997.

Grimsley, Mark. *The Hard Hand of War: Union Military Policy Toward Southern Civilians, 1861–1865*. New York: Cambridge Univ. Press, 1995.

Groce, W. Todd. "The Social Origins of East Tennessee's Confederate Leadership." In *The Civil War in Appalachia: Collected Essays*, eds. Kenneth W. Noe and Shannon H. Wilson, 30–54. Knoxville: Univ. of Tennessee Press, 1997.

Hafendorfer, Kenneth A. *Perryville: Battle for Kentucky*. 2nd ed. Louisville: KH Press, 1991.

Hallock, Judith Lee. *Braxton Bragg and Confederate Defeat*. Vol. 2. Tuscaloosa: Univ. of Alabama Press, 1991.

Harmon, Geraldine Crain. *Chaplin Hills: History of Perryville, Kentucky, Boyle County*. Danville, Ky.: Bluegrass, 1971.

Harrison, Lowell H. *The Civil War in Kentucky*. Lexington: Univ. Press of Kentucky, 1975.

Hattaway, Herman, and Archer Jones. *How the North Won: A Military History of the Civil War*. Urbana: Univ. of Illinois Press, 1983.

Hennessy, John J. *Return to Bull Run: The Campaign and Battle of Second Manassas*. New York: Simon and Schuster, 1993.

Hess, Earl J. *Banners to the Breeze: The Kentucky Campaign, Corinth, and Stones River*. Lincoln: Univ. of Nebraska Press, 2000.

———. *The Union Soldier in Battle: Enduring the Ordeal of Combat*. Lawrence: Univ. of Kansas Press, 1997.

Horn, Stanley F. *The Army of Tennessee*. Indianapolis: Bobbs-Merrill, 1941.

Hughes, Nathaniel Cheairs Jr. *General William J. Hardee: Old Reliable*. Baton Rouge: Louisiana State Univ. Press, 1965.

Jackson, Stanley W. *Melancholia and Depression: From Hippocratic Times to Modern Times*. New Haven, Conn.: Yale Univ. Press, 1986.

Jeffries, C. C. *Terry's Rangers*. New York: Vantage, 1962.

Johnson, Stephen M. *Character Styles*. New York: W. W. Norton, 1994.

Jones, Archer. *Confederate Strategy from Shiloh to Vicksburg*. Baton Rouge: Louisiana State Univ. Press, 1961.

Kammen, Michael. *Mystic Chords of Memory: The Transformation of Tradition in American Culture*. New York: Alfred A. Knopf, 1991.

Kett, Joseph F. *Rites of Passage: Adolescence in America, 1790 to the Present*. New York: Basic Books, 1977.

Kinsel, Amy J. "From Turning Point to Peace Memorial: A Cultural Legacy." In *The Gettysburg Nobody Knows*, ed. Gabor S. Boritt. New York: Oxford Univ. Press, 1997.

Kleber, John E., ed. *The Kentucky Encyclopedia*. Lexington: Univ. Press of Kentucky, 1992.

Klement, Frank L. *Wisconsin in the Civil War: The Home Front and the Battle Front, 1861–1865*. Madison: State Historical Society of Wisconsin, 1997.

Kundahl, George G. *Confederate Engineer: Training and Campaigning With John Morris Wampler*. Knoxville: Univ. of Tennessee Press, 2000.

Lambert, D. Warren. *When the Ripe Pears Fell: The Battle of Richmond, Kentucky*. Richmond: Madison County Historical Society, 1995.

Linderman, Gerald. *Embattled Courage: The Experience of Combat in the American Civil War*. New York: Free Press, 1987.

Linenthal, Edward Tabor. *Sacred Ground: Americans and Their Battlefields*. Urbana: Univ. of Illinois Press, 1991.

Losson, Christopher. *Tennessee's Forgotten Warriors: Frank Cheatham and His Confederate Division*. Knoxville: Univ. of Tennessee Press, 1989.

Marszalek, John F. *Sherman: A Soldier's Passion for Order*. New York: Free Press, 1993.

Marten, James. *The Children's Civil War*. Chapel Hill: Univ. of North Carolina Press, 1998.

McConnell, Stuart. *Glorious Contentment: The Grand Army of the Republic, 1865–1900*. Chapel Hill: Univ. of North Carolina Press, 1992.

McDonough, James Lee. *Shiloh—in Hell before Night*. Knoxville: Univ. of Tennessee Press, 1977.

———. *Stones River—Bloody Winter in Tennessee*. Knoxville: Univ. of Tennessee Press, 1980.

———. *War in Kentucky: From Shiloh to Perryville*. Knoxville: Univ. of Tennessee Press, 1994.

McDowell, Robert Emmett. *City of Conflict: Louisville in the Civil War, 1861–1865*. Louisville: Louisville Civil War Round Table, 1962.

McMurry, Richard M. *Two Great Rebel Armies: An Essay in Confederate Military History*. Chapel Hill: Univ. of North Carolina Press, 1989.

McPherson, James M. *Battle Cry of Freedom: The Civil War Era*. New York: Oxford Univ. Press, 1988.

———. *Drawn With the Sword: Reflections on the American Civil War*. New York: Oxford Univ. Press, 1996.

———. Foreword to Catherine Clinton and Nina Silber, eds., *Divided Houses: Gender and the Civil War*, xii–xvii. New York: Oxford Univ. Press, 1992.

McWhiney, Grady. *Braxton Bragg and Confederate Defeat*. Vol. 1, *Field Command*. New York: Columbia Univ. Press, 1969.

Miller, Randall M., and John Davis Smith. *Dictionary of Afro-American Slavery*. Updated with a new introduction. Westport, Conn.: Praeger, 1997.

Mitchell, Reid. *Civil War Soldiers*. New York: Viking, 1988.

———. *The Vacant Chair: The Northern Soldier Leaves Home*. New York: Oxford Univ. Press, 1993.

Mitford, Jessica. *The American Way of Death Revisited*. New York: Knopf, 1998.

Morris, Roy Jr. *Sheridan: The Life and Wars of General Phil Sheridan*. New York: Crown, 1992.

Nevins, Allan. *The War for the Union*. 4 vols. New York: Charles Scribner's Sons, 1960.

Noe, Kenneth W. "'Grand Havoc': The Climactic Battle of Perryville." In *The Civil War in Kentucky: Battle for the Bluegrass State*, ed. Kent Masterson Brown. Mason City, Iowa: Savas, 2000.

Paludan, Philip Shaw. *"A People's Contest": The Union and the Civil War, 1861–1865*. New York: Harper, 1988.

Parks, Joseph H. *General Edmund Kirby Smith C. S. A.* Baton Rouge: Louisiana State Univ. Press, 1954.

———. *General Leonidas Polk C.S.A.: The Fighting Bishop*. Baton Rouge: Louisiana State Univ. Press, 1962.

Patterson, John S. "From Battle Ground to Pleasure Ground: Gettysburg as a Historic Site." In *History Museums in the United States: A Critical Assessment*, ed. Warren Leon and Roy Rosenweig. Urbana: Univ. of Illinois Press, 1989.

Peck, Elisabeth S. *Berea's First Century, 1855–1955*. Lexington: Univ. of Kentucky Press, 1955.

Piston, William Garrett. *Lee's Tarnished Lieutenant: James Longstreet and His Place in Southern History.* Athens: Univ. of Georgia Press, 1987.

————, and Richard W. Hatcher III. *Wilson's Creek: The Second Battle of the Civil War and the Men Who Fought It.* Chapel Hill: Univ. of North Carolina Press, 2000.

Power, J. Tracy. *Lee's Miserables: Life in the Army of Northern Virginia from the Wilderness to Appomattox.* Chapel Hill: Univ. of North Carolina Press, 1998.

Priest, John Michael. *Antietam: The Soldier's Battle.* Shippensburg, Pa.: White Mane, 1989.

Rable, George. "It is Well That War is So Terrible: The Carnage at Fredericksburg." In *The Fredericksburg Campaign: Decision on the Rappahannock,* ed. Gary W. Gallagher, 48–79. Chapel Hill: Univ. of North Carolina Press, 1995.

————."'Missing in Action': Women of the Confederacy." In *Divided Houses: Gender and the Civil War,* ed. Catherine Clinton and Nina Silber, 134–46. New York: Oxford Univ. Press, 1992.

Reid, Richard J. *The Army That Buell Built.* Fordsville, Ky.: Wendell Sandefur, 1994.

————. *They Met at Perryville.* Owensboro, Ky.: Commercial Printing, 1987.

Reid, Whitelaw. *Ohio in the War: Her Statesmen, Generals and Soldiers.* 2 vols. Cincinnati: Robert Clarke, 1895.

Rhea, Gordon C. *The Battle of the Wilderness, May 5–6, 1864.* Baton Rouge: Louisiana State Univ. Press, 1994.

Roland, Charles P. *Albert Sidney Johnston: Soldier of Three Republics.* Austin: Univ. Of Texas Press, 1964.

Rose, Anne C. *Victorian America and the Civil War.* New York: Cambridge Univ. Press, 1992.

Sears, Stephen W. *To the Gates of Richmond: The Peninsula Campaign.* New York: Ticknor and Fields, 1992.

Shea, William L., and Earl J. Hess. *Pea Ridge: Civil War Campaign in the West.* Chapel Hill: Univ. of North Carolina Press, 1992.

Stickles, Arndt M. *Simon Bolivar Buckner: Borderland Knight.* Chapel Hill: Univ. of North Carolina Press, 1940.

Storey, John. *An Introductory Guide to Cultural Theory and Popular Culture.* Athens: Univ. of Georgia Press, 1993.

Sumrall, Robbie Neal. *A Light on the Hill: A History of Blue Mountain College.* Nashville, Benson: n.d.

Sutherland, Daniel. *Seasons of War: The Ordeal of a Confederate Community, 1861–1865.* New York: Free Press, 1995.

Sword, Wiley. *Shiloh: Bloody April.* New York: William Morrow, 1974.

Symonds, Craig L. *Stonewall of the West: Patrick Cleburne and the Civil War.* Lawrence: Univ. Press of Kansas, 1997.

Wallenstein, Peter. "'Helping to Save the Union': The Social Origins, Wartime Experiences, and Military Impact of White Union Troops from East Tennessee." In *The Civil War in Appalachia: Collected Essays,* eds. Kenneth W. Noe and Shannon H. Wilson, 1–29. Knoxville: Univ. of Tennessee Press, 1997.

Warner, Ezra J. *Generals in Blue: Lives of the Union Commanders.* Baton Rouge: Louisiana State Univ. Press, 1964.

————. *Generals in Gray: Lives of the Confederate Commanders.* Baton Rouge: Louisiana State Univ. Press, 1959.

White, Virgil D., comp. *Index to Georgia Civil War Confederate Pension Files.* Waynesboro, Tenn.: National Historical Publishing, 1996.

Wilkinson, Warren. *Mother, May You Never See the Sights I have Seen: The Fifty-seventh Massachusetts Veteran Volunteers in the Last Year of the Civil War.* New York: Quill, 1990.

Williams, L. B. *A Sketch of the 33rd Alabama Volunteer Infantry Regiment And its Role in*

Cleburne's Elite Division of The Army of Tennessee 1862–1865. Auburn, Ala.: The Author, 1990.

Woodworth, Steven E. *Jefferson Davis and His Generals: The Failure of Confederate Command in the West.* Lawrence: Univ. Press of Kansas, 1990.

ARTICLES

Baas, William P., M.D. "Preliminary Analysis of Post-battle Deaths at Perryville." *Action Front,* Oct. 1997, 3.

Bearss, Edwin C. "General Bragg Abandons Kentucky." *Register of the Kentucky Historical Society* 59 (July 1861): 217–44.

Coles, David J. "Ancient City Defenders: The St. Augustine Blues." *El Escibano* 23 (1986): 65–89.

Crawford, Thomas C. "The Battle of Perryville." *Confederate Veteran* 40 (1932): 262–64.

Donaldson, Gary. "'Into Africa': Kirby Smith and Braxton Bragg's Invasion of Kentucky," *Filson Club History Quarterly* 61 (1987): 444–65.

Douglas, Ann. "Heaven Our Home: Consolation Literature in the Northern United States, 1830–1880." *American Quarterly* 26 (1974): 496–515.

Draper, Lyman C. "Sketch of Hon. Charles H. Larrabee." *Collections of the State Historical Society of Wisconsin* 9 (1882): 366–88.

Edwards, Brenda S. "Kentucky's First Settlers." *Action Front,* Jan. 1998, 2.

Engle, Stephen D. "Don Carlos Buell: Military Philosophy and Command Problems in the West." *Civil War History* 41 (1995): 89–115.

Farrelly, David G. "John Marshall Harlan and the Union Cause in Kentucky, 1861." *Filson Club History Quarterly* (Jan. 1963): 5–23.

"The General's Tour: The Battle of Perryville." *Blue & Grey Magazine* (Oct.-Nov. 1983), 21–39.

Grimsley, Mark. "A Wade in the High Tide at Perryville." *Civil War Times Illustrated* 31 (Nov.-Dec. 1991): 18, 22, 24, 26.

Harrison, Lowell H. "The Civil War in Kentucky: Some Persistent Questions." *Register of the Kentucky Historical Society* 76 (Jan. 1978): 1–21.

———. "George W. Johnson and Richard Hawes: the Governors of Confederate Kentucky." *Register of the Kentucky Historical Society* 79 (Winter 1981): 3–39.

———. "Perryville: Death on a Dry River." *Civil War Times Illustrated,* May 1979, 4–6, 8–9, 44–47.

Hilliard, James M. "You Are Strangely Deluded." *Civil War Times Illustrated,* Feb. 1975, 12–18.

"The History of Perryville, Kentucky." Brochure, Perryville Enhancement Project, n.d.

Jenkins, Kirk C. "A Shooting at the Galt House: The Death of General William Nelson." *Civil War History* 43 (June 1997): 101–18.

McWhiney, Grady. "Controversy in Kentucky: Braxton Bragg's Campaign of 1862." *Civil War History* 6 (1960): 5–42.

Miller, Page Putnam. "Capitol Commentary." *OAH Newsletter,* Feb. 2000, 9, 11.

Musick, Michael P. "Honorable Reports: Battles, Campaigns, and Skirmishes—Civil War Records and Research." *Prologue* 27 (Fall 1995): 259–77.

Noe, Kenneth W. "'Coming to Us Dead': A Civil War Casualty and His Estate." *Journal of Illinois History* 2 (1999): 289–304.

Quisenberry, A. C. "The Confederate Campaign in Kentucky, 1862: The Battle of Perryville." *Register of the Kentucky State Historical Society* 17 (Jan. 1919): 30–38.

"Real War: The H. P. Bottom House." *Action Front,* Oct. 1997, 3–4.

Ross, Charles. "ssh! Battle in Progress!" *Civil War Times Illustrated*, Dec. 1996, 56–62.

Sanders, Stuart W. "'Every Mother's Son of Them Are Yankees!'" *Civil War Times Illustrated*, Oct. 1999, 52–59.

Saum, Lewis O. "Death in the Mind of Pre-Civil War America." *American Quarterly* 26 (1974): 477–95.

"A Tale From the 41st Mississippi." *Action Front* (Oct. 1998), 2.

Tapp, Hambleton. "The Battle of Perryville, 1862." *Filson Club History Quarterly* 9 (1935): 158–81.

Vinovskis, Maris A. "Have Social Historians Lost the Civil War? Some Preliminary Demographic Speculations." *Journal of American History* 76 (June 1989): 34–58.

Williams, Harrison C. "Regimental History of the 79th Pennsylvania Volunteers of the Civil War: The Lancaster County Regiment." *Journal of the Lancaster County Historical Society* 84 (1980): 17–36.

Wooster, Ralph A. "Confederate Success at Perryville." *Register of the Kentucky Historical Society* 59 (Oct. 1961): 318–23.

DISSERTATIONS, THESES, UNPUBLISHED PAPERS

Adams, Roger C. "Bibliography of the Battle of Perryville and the Kentucky Campaign, 1862." Unpublished paper, n.d. In possession of the author, Manhattan, Kansas.

Bishop, Charles W. F. "Civil War Field Artillery in the West, 1862–1863." Master's thesis, Univ. of British Columbia, 1967.

Chumney, James Robert Jr. "Don Carlos Buell, Gentleman General." Ph.D. diss., Rice University, 1964.

Holman, Kurt. "Casualty Percentages of Individual Units." Unpublished paper, n.d. In possession of the author, Perryville, Ky.

———. "Confederate Comments: Comments Fields from Confederate Units Database." Unpublished paper, n.d. In possession of the author, Perryville, Ky.

———. "Henry P. 'Squire' Bottom's War Claim." Unpublished paper, n.d. In possession of the author, Perryville, Ky.

———. "Known Strengths and Casualties at the Battle of Perryville." Unpublished paper, n.d. In possession of the author, Perryville, Ky.

———. "Post Battle Death Rates." Unpublished paper, n.d. In possession of the author, Perryville, Ky.

———. "Revised Location of Parson's Battery." Unpublished paper, n.d. In possession of the author, Perryville, Ky.

———. "Unit Stats." Unpublished paper, n.d. In possession of the author, Perryville, Ky.

———. Untitled Order of Battle, n.d. In possession of the author, Perryville, Ky.

———, and Dawn Holman. "Post Battle Death Rates, Oct. 9–Oct. 31, 1862, Perryville, Ky." Unpublished chart, n.p., 1997. In possession of the author, Perryville, Ky.

Kennedy, Larry Wells. "The Fighting Preacher of the Army of Tennessee: General Mark Perrin Lowrey." Ph.D. diss., Mississippi State University, 1976.

McMurry, Richard. "Union and Confederate Grand Strategy to Hold Kentucky." Paper Presented to the American Civil War Institute Summer Symposium, Campbellsville, Ky., July 30, 1997.

Piston, William Garrett. "Beyond Drums and Trumpets: The Battle of Wilson's Creek and the 'New Military History.'" Paper presented at the Southern Historical Association meeting, Louisville, Nov. 10, 1994.

Simon, John Y. "Holding Kentucky for the Union, 1861." Paper Presented to the American Civil War Institute Summer Symposium, Campbellsville, Ky., July 30, 1997.

Switlik, Matthew C. "Loomis' Battery: First Michigan Light Artillery, 1859–1865."
    Master's thesis, Wayne State University, 1975.
Walsh, John P. Jr. "Summary for Adams, Johnson, and Cleburne." Unpublished paper,
    2000. In possession of the author, Arlington Heights, Ill.

ELECTRONIC SOURCES

The Civil War CD-ROM. Version 1.0. Carmel, Ind.: Guild, 1997.
"Corinth Information Database. Version 1.3." http://www2.tsixroads.com/
    Corinth_MLSANDY/histcw1.html.
[Danville, Ky.] Advocate-Messenger. http://www.amnews.com.
Masur, Kate. "Changes in the Offing for Civil War Sites." Perspectives Online.
    www.theaha.org/perspectives.
"Yankee Horse Soldiers—The 9th. Pennsylvania Cavalry." http://home.att.net/~sy13.

INDEX

Page references to illustrations are in italics

abolition, 1, 58

acoustic shadow, xiii, 215, 421 n 6

Adams, Brig. Gen. Daniel W., 172, 23, 241, 277, 298, 371; advances brigade, 172–73, 220–21, 226; arrives in Perryville, 140; attacked by Sheridan's artillery, 284; background, 172; brigade in action, 228–30, 231, 264, 266, 270–71, 277, 292–94, 303, 414–15 n 28; and Buckner, 432 n 40; supports Bragg, 339

Adams, Col. Samuel, 372

Adrian, Lt. Col. T.W., 373

African Americans: and Civil War historiography, xvi; as Confederate soldiers, 230, 270; employed by Federals, 42, 85, 86, 88, 347; follow Federal columns, 59, 85; join Union troops in battle, 230–31, 430 n 74; killed by Confederates, 390 n 9; and lynching, 358; and Nelson, 93; in Perryville, 108–9, 145; postwar community on battlefield, 358–59; and support for Union, 333

Alabama troops: Lumsden's artillery, 54, 55, 99, 312, 336, 382; Semple's artillery, 133, 172, 174, 175, 177, 217, 264, 266, 286, 372, 382; 1st cavalry, 138, 167, 372; 3rd cavalry, 138, 167, 373; 15th infantry, 429 n 64; 16th infantry, 267; 27th infantry, 267, 372; 33rd infantry, 267, 296, *297*, 307, 313, 372; 45th infantry, 277, 280, 283, 338, 371

Alabama University, 147

Albany, Ky., 59, 64

Alexander, George P., 352

Alexander, Col. John, 379

Allen, Col. Thomas G., 374

Allen, Col. William W., 371

"All Quiet Along the Potomac" (song), 354

Altamont, Tenn., 48, 51, 53, 59

Alverson, George H., 78

Anderson, Col. Nicholas Longworth, 333, 375

Anderson, Brig. Gen. J. Patton, 99, 157, 158, 238, 239, 286, 291, 292, 303, 315, 371, 421 n 8; advances division, 172–73; arrives in Perryville, 140; background, 55–56; and Jones's attack, 216; march to Perryville, 132; supports Bragg, 127

Anderson, Brig. Gen. Robert, 8

Antietam, Battle of, xv, 78, 158

anti-semitism, 90

Appomattox, Va., 359

Arkansas troops: Calvert's artillery, 137, 177, 264, 372, 373, 382; 1st infantry, 34, 127, 278, 285, 327, 371; 2nd infantry, 134, 298, 302, 372; 5th infantry, 134, 149, 151, 159, 372, 411 n 17; 6th infantry, 302, 305, 372; 7th infantry, 134, 135, 143, 145, 147, 149, 151, 159, 302, 372, 411–12 n 18; 8th infantry, 134, 301, 302, 312, 372; 13th infantry, 242, 263, 264, 265, 372; 15th infantry, 34, 242, 263, 264, 265, 272, 372

Army of Kentucky (CS), 86, 103, 113, 128, 329

Army of Kentucky (US), 334

Army of Tennessee. *See* Army of the Mississippi (CS)